all my efforts. to convert
Roosevelt votes for Hoover, I'm
glad my efforts were defeated;
and hereafter I will vote
and work for any party
that has at it's head a
man of your ability and
sincerity as a leader.
More power to you, and
may your efforts be suc-
cessful far beyond your
expecttations. They can't
help but be with a
nation of people behind
you.

     May God bless
you and give you strength
to carry on.

          Very humbly Yours
          Lena Englman

THE PEOPLE AND THE PRESIDENT

THE PEOPLE AND THE PRESIDENT

America's Conversation with FDR

LAWRENCE W. LEVINE

and

CORNELIA R. LEVINE

Beacon Press

BOSTON

Beacon Press
25 Beacon Street
Boston, Massachusetts 02108-2892
www.beacon.org

Beacon Press books are published under the auspices
of the Unitarian Universalist Association of Congregations.

Grateful acknowledgment is made to the following for permission to reprint selections from the following volumes: Maxine Kumin, "Remembering Pearl Harbor at the Tutankhamen Exhibit" from *Our Ground Time Here Will Be Brief* by Maxine Kumin, first published at Viking Press © 1982, reprinted by permission of the author, Maxine Kumin, and her agent, Giles Anderson; Carl Carmer, "April 14, 1945" from *Franklin Delano Roosevelt: A Memorial* edited by Donald P. Geddes, first published at Pocket Books © 1945, reprinted by permission of the four Carmer heirs, Elizabeth Cary Black Smith, Kingsley Black Moore, Willis Carmer Bailey, and Herbert Gibbs; Ruth Albert Cook, "Blackout" from *Opportunity: Journal of Negro Life*, first published by The National Urban League, Inc., © 1942, reprinted by permission of Lee Daniels, Director of Publications, at The National Urban League. Photograph page 160 courtesy of the National Archives; photograph page 410 courtesy Library of Congress; all others courtesy FDR Library.

This book is printed on acid-free paper that meets the uncoated paper
ANSI/NISO specifications for permanence as revised in 1992.

Text design by Dean Bornstein
Composition by Wilsted & Taylor Publishing Services

Library of Congress Cataloging-in-Publication Data
Levine, Lawrence W.
The people and the President : America's conversation with FDR /
Lawrence W. Levine and Cornelia R. Levine.
p. cm.
Includes bibliographical references and index.
ISBN 0-8070-5510-7 (alk. paper)
1. United States—Politics and government—1933–1945—Sources.
2. United States—Social conditions—1933–1945—Sources. 3. Roosevelt, Franklin D.
(Franklin Delano), 1882–1945—Correspondence. 4. Presidents—United States—
Correspondence. 5. American letters. I. Levine, Cornelia R. II. Title.
E806.L485 2002
2002002263

For Our Grandchildren

STEPHANIE

BENJAMIN

and

JONAH

Who Continue Our Education

CONTENTS

CONTENTS

PREFACE

I never saw him —
But I *knew* him. Can you have forgotten
How, with his voice, he came into our house,
The President of these United States,
Calling us friends. . . .

Carl Carmer, "April 14, 1945"

You have spoken to me in your fireside chats about matters which are too important to leave settled by a one way conversation; hence I am now addressing you in the only way I have of replying.

Nelson Handsalter, St. Paul, Minnesota,
to FDR, May 29, 1941

IN 1934 THE HUMORIST James Thurber attempted to convince his readers that Walt Disney was the person to make Homer's *Odyssey* popular. "I'm sure Mr. Disney will do the 'Odyssey' if we all ask him please. . . . Let's all write to him about it, or to Roosevelt."[1] Thurber may have had his tongue partly — though only partly — in his cheek when he suggested Walt Disney as the modern interpreter of Homer's epic poem. But he was doubtless serious in his suggestion that one way to achieve that end — or *any* end — was to write to Franklin D. Roosevelt. Millions of Americans had already hit upon this strategy and millions more would follow them throughout FDR's presidency.

During the twelve years and five weeks he served as President of the United States, Franklin Roosevelt received an unprecedented number of letters from the American people, some fifteen million of which were preserved in the Franklin D. Roosevelt Library and millions more in the National Archives.[2] The American people wrote these letters to the President during years of extraordinary national and international trauma. Franklin

Roosevelt's presidency — the longest one in American history — opened in the depths of the nation's gravest economic crisis and closed during the final days of its most prolonged and widespread foreign war. The years of FDR's tenure proved to be a watershed in American economic, social, and political history. Before 1929 it might have been possible for large numbers of Americans to close their eyes to the realities of an increasingly organized and bureaucratic society and cling to long-standing American myths of autonomous individuals pursuing their independent destinies, but the sixteen years of depression and war that followed the stock market crash of 1929 profoundly eroded those certainties. Though millions of Americans — then and since — were to remain deeply ambivalent about their dependence upon institutions, Franklin Roosevelt accustomed them to look to Washington, D.C., and the federal government both as a protector from forces they could not control, and often could not even identify, and as a provider in moments of dire need.

Believing that it was the government's responsibility to assure the well-being of its citizens, Roosevelt proclaimed "a New Deal for the American people" and moved the national government decisively into area after area: insuring people's bank deposits; reforming the stock market; providing relief and jobs for the unemployed; building dams that controlled floods and electrified rural areas; establishing minimum wages and maximum hours for workers and assuring their right to organize; enabling both businesspeople and farmers to organize to control their output and their prices; providing unemployment and old age insurance; enabling marginal farmers to move to more productive land; helping home owners refinance their mortgages and save their homes; organizing and regulating the wartime economy on a scale so massive it created the production "miracle" that helped to win the war; aiding the fifteen million war veterans to find jobs, go to college, and buy homes.

In moving into these and many other areas between 1933 and 1945, FDR transformed the role of the federal government and the nature of the presidency. He was more exposed to and better known by the American people than any of his predecessors. As this book will demonstrate, among the many profound changes he presided over was what constituted a revolution in the pattern of communication between Americans and their Chief Executive. He and his staff not only understood what was taking place, they profoundly appreciated and encouraged it, as was manifest in the ways in which they treated the vast correspondence FDR received. "I have often

heard it said," a Chicagoan wrote Eleanor Roosevelt, "that if a common citizen writes a letter to the President it is read by his secretary and then
thrown in the waste basket."[3] Happily, she was wrong; the millions upon
millions of letters from "common" citizens were opened and read, and
while they were not always answered or heeded, it is one of the distinctions
of the Roosevelt Administration that they were decidedly not "thrown in
the waste basket."

Although an indeterminate number of these letters have been lost or destroyed, the bulk remain and constitute our only direct, unmediated contemporary record of the consciousness of substantial numbers of people
who lived through the crises of depression and war. They are an invaluable
source for understanding the American people during these trying years —
keys to the lives of millions of men and women who, until very recently,
have been ignored and thus have been simply excised from our history.[4]

While historians gradually have come to comprehend the significance of
the letters FDR received during his tenure, their very number renders them
a formidable source to use. It is obviously impossible to read the vast
archive of testimony from somewhere between fifteen and thirty million
Americans. Our concern in this volume was to find a way of exploring as
wide a range of these letters as possible without becoming overwhelmed by
their sheer bulk. We decided that one approach would be to read the letters
people wrote in response to a discrete body of FDR's speeches. We chose
the Fireside Chats he delivered over the radio because they were broadcast
throughout his presidency (the first Chat was delivered eight days after he
assumed office, and the last Chat was given three months and six days before his death); they dealt with almost every major domestic and international issue; they attempted to address the *entire* population; and they were
widely accessible to a nation in which 62 percent of all households owned
radios at the beginning of FDR's presidency and almost 90 percent owned
radios at its close. Not only were they accessible, they were accessed and attracted huge radio audiences, such as the 79 percent of all American households that tuned in to his Fireside Chat of December 9, 1941, and the 80
percent of all adult Americans who either heard or read his Fireside Chat
of February 23, 1942.[5]

We have read the letters FDR received after each one of these thirty-one
radio addresses and have selected examples that will convey a sense of
American attitudes during two of the major events of the twentieth century.
But these letters do more: they help to re-create the conversation between

FDR and the American people from 1933 to 1945 and demonstrate the ways in which radio functioned as a primary medium of communication.

Unless otherwise noted, all of the letters in this volume are housed in the Franklin Delano Roosevelt Library in Hyde Park, New York, and can be found in the President's Personal File 200 (PPF 200), Public Response. Those lacking a specific date are headed by asterisks. In order to present as many and as wide a variety of letters as possible, we have made editorial cuts — indicated by ellipses — of excessively long, detailed, or redundant portions of the letters. In all other respects, we are printing these letters as we found them in terms of their spelling, punctuation, and style and in terms too of their spirit, tone, and contents. Their principles and prejudices, their strengths and foibles, their manner of referring to people in the center and on the margins of the society are those of the 1930s and 1940s and not of our own day, which is precisely their value to us.

INTRODUCTION

> You have no fireplace? How do you listen to the President's speeches?
>
> Groucho Marx, *Room Service* (1935)

> Radio sets were not then very powerful, and there was always static. Families had to sit near the set, with someone always fiddling with the knobs. It was like sitting around a hearth, with someone poking the fire; and to that hearth came the crackling voices of Winston Churchill, or George Burns and Gracie Allen, and of FDR. The fireside chats . . . It was not FDR who was at his fireside . . . it was we who were at our firesides.
>
> Henry Fairlie, *New Republic,* January 27, 1982

THE ADVENT OF RADIO in the 1920s and especially the 1930s changed things indelibly. It was what the novelist Margaret Atwood has called one of those "definitive moments, moments we use as references, because they break our sense of continuity, they change the direction of time. We can look at these events and we can say that after them things were never the same again."[1] Radio, of course, was the first form of mass media that had the quality of simultaneity, creating what Hadley Cantril called "the largest grouping of people ever known."[2] In a series of articles she wrote on radio for the *New York Times Magazine* in the spring of 1932, the political correspondent Anne O'Hare McCormick spoke of "this incredible audience," "millions of ears contracted into one ear and cocked at the same moment to the same sound."[3] In their 1935 book, *The Psychology of Radio,* Hadley Cantril and Gordon Allport estimated that "our countrymen spend approximately 150,000,000 hours a week before the [movie] screen, but nearly 1,000,000,000 hours before the [radio] loud-speaker." Radio, they maintained, is "the greatest single democratizing agent since the invention of printing."[4] Lew Sarett and William Trufant Foster compared radio to the ancient Greek Acropolis: "a place from which the Elders might speak to all the citizens at once."[5]

Contemporaries grasped the force and significance of radio very early. Though they often made the mistake of equating the populist potential of radio with democracy — a parallel the career of Adolf Hitler alone should have disabused them of — they nevertheless comprehended radio's enormous capacity to reach and affect people in numbers and ways formerly inconceivable. The memories of those who experienced the Great Depression and the war that followed it were commonly and often inextricably bound to the radio. Thus the poet Maxine Kumin remembering Pearl Harbor:

> The Day
> of Infamy, Roosevelt called it. I was
> a young girl listening to the radio
> on a Sunday of hard weather . . .[6]

Though listening to radio quickly became a common experience, for many it remained somehow magical. V. T. Chastain recalled that his father had the first radio in Holly Springs, South Carolina: "Neighbors from all around congregated at our house to see and hear the amazing radio! One man I remember in particular really enjoyed a certain musical rendition, and he told Dad, 'Make 'em play that one again, Wade.' Nothing Dad could say would convince him that the musicians were in Greenville and not somewhere, somehow, inside that box!" Evelyn Tomason remembered her grandfather in the early 1930s listening to local election returns and suddenly holding his hand up high, asking the radio: "Repeat that please!" In 1934 Gus Wentz looked "into the back of the radio to try to see the 'little people' in there," and Trina Nochisaki couldn't remember "how many times I tried to sneak up on the real little people I just *knew* lived in the radio — if only I could catch them unawares."[7]

The millions of Americans who heard the first Fireside Chat on March 12, 1933, certainly didn't think FDR was one of those tiny people nestled within their radios, but radio was still such a new force that they did feel his presence in a manner so novel and extraordinary to them that we — to whom the wonders of radio, television, and the computer have become so familiar — have to make a leap of empathy to appreciate what they experienced. Myra King Whitson of Houston, who described herself as a mother "with young mouths to feed, young minds to educate, young fears to quiet," who had been living through what she called a "long nightmare," thanked FDR for "your talk last night, when our radio seemed to bring you to us in person — there is a deep happiness — a feeling that we have a real share in our government, and that our government is making our welfare its chief concern."[8] The mayor of Richland Center, Wisconsin, informed Roosevelt, "An old friend said to me this morning 'I almost wept during the President's talk last night, it seemed he was sitting by my side talking in plain simple words to me.' "[9]

The mystique of the Chats lasted far beyond the initial one. "Listening to you," Nathan Weldon wrote in 1935, "I could feel the prescence of your honest sincerity in the room. I found myself answering you, nodding to you, chatting to you, and agreeing with you."[10] Five years later, Florence Gunnar Nelson wrote: "With only the lighted dial of our radio for illumination, a feeling of deep gratitude came over me. With no lites to disclose my surroundings I might imagine myself in the same room — at the same fireside as our great President Roosevelt, listening to his stirring words."[11]

FDR received these letters from a wide spectrum of the American people — farmers, businessmen, salesmen, housewives, doctors, nurses, teachers, entertainers, ministers, priests, and rabbis, retired people, the unemployed, students, lawyers, workers, union leaders and members, local and state government officials of all kinds, members of a wide variety of ethnic organizations and clubs, residents of large urban centers, small towns, and villages, Democrats as well as large numbers of Republicans, and not a few Socialists and Communists, people from all sections of the country — responding to their President in a period of deep domestic, and ultimately international, crisis.*

They jotted their thoughts down on every imaginable kind of paper, from formal stationery to lined notebook pages, from three-by-five-inch filing cards to the backs of business cards, from scraps of paper to gaudy greeting cards. They enclosed editorials, articles, cartoons, and pamphlets

---

*Studies of radio in the 1930s indicated that while the wealthy owned disproportionately more radios, middle- and lower-income groups listened more frequently and wrote more mail to radio stations and personalities than higher-income groups. A study of the mail Roosevelt received during a five-day period in March 1934 confirms these findings: 46 percent of his letters were from laborers, 17 percent from businessmen, 15 percent from farmers, 14 percent from clerical workers, 3 percent from professionals, 1 percent from government officials, 1 percent from students, 1 percent from children, and 2 percent from organizations (Leila Sussmann, *Dear FDR: A Study of Political Letter Writing* [Totowa, N.J.: Bedminster Press, 1963], 141).

they thought the President should see, as well as poems, drawings, photos, stories, jokes, and recipes they wanted to share with him. Their letters allow us to approach FDR and the New Deal through the eyes of contemporaries who viewed what was transpiring in Washington from outside the centers of power, to be sure, but who felt its effects at first hand and who responded to their President with gratitude and censure, criticism and advice. Here is the *other*, less known and less understood side of radio: the audience.

Radio inspired and encouraged this correspondence; it was one of the prime modern forces that helped to circumvent the structural barriers the Founders had erected to insulate the federal government from direct popular influence. By the Great Depression, and especially during the Great Depression, communication between the public and its national leaders had become a much more immediate process. As a number of scholars have observed, the written word was increasingly replaced by the spoken word. Radio certainly stimulated the rise of what has been called the "rhetorical presidency," in which FDR used his speeches as "events" in and of themselves in an attempt to communicate with the public over the heads of the legislature and the newspapers.[12]

But while radio undeniably elevated the centrality of the spoken word, it also greatly stimulated the importance of the written word in the form of the growing stream of letters from listeners. "The mail room in a big broadcasting station is the most amazing exhibit in the whole radio show," Anne O'Hare McCormick observed. "It is a human document in endless volumes, an orgy of the kind of old-fashioned letter writing the social historian saw vanish with the horse and the darning egg."[13] Radio stations, which in their formative years had no other means to measure the size and attitudes of their audiences, literally trained their listeners to write letters by constantly urging them to send in their opinions and responses to programs. In the early 1930s, about two-thirds of NBC programs requested listeners to write in. The success of these appeals is clear. NBC received 383,000 letters in 1926; 775,000 in 1928; 1 million in 1929; 2 million in 1930; 7 million in 1931. CBS was even more successful, receiving 12.6 million letters from its listeners in 1931 alone.[14] When, in January 1931, the Catholic priest Father Coughlin, who was to build his extremely popular Sunday radio talks into a national dissident movement, asked his listeners to endorse his speeches by writing to the broadcasting stations, there was a deluge of

485,252 letters.[15] "Listening-in for a decade," a *Times* reporter observed in 1932, "has created a habit of letter-writing."[16]

FDR was a central part of this process. Roosevelt's radio speeches helped make participants — even activists — out of his audience. When in the midst of one address Roosevelt invited his audience to "tell me your troubles," Ira Smith, the White House Chief of Mails, testified that large numbers of people "believed that he was speaking to them personally and immediately wrote him a letter. It was months before we managed to swim out of *that* flood of mail." The letters came in so fast, Smith remembered, that "within a week I had some 450,000 letters stacked all over the office."[17] Precisely the same happened after FDR's Fireside Chat of July 24, 1933, in which he asked employers — "the big fellows and the little fellows" — who intended to participate in the National Recovery Administration "to write or telegraph to me personally at the White House." "The response to that was immediate and perfectly overwhelming," according to Hugh Johnson, the head of the NRA. "Telegrams and letters by the tens of thousands poured into Washington for days. No such volume of mail had ever been received by the government."[18] The flood of letters delighted Roosevelt. He told reporters that the great volume of mail demonstrated "an increasing and wholesome reawakening of public interest in the affairs of government" — a statement that could only encourage people to continue writing to him.[19] Whenever the influx of letters decreased, Ira Smith recalled, "we could expect to hear from him or one of his secretaries, who wanted to know what was the matter — was the President losing his grip on the public?"[20]

FDR especially valued these letters because, as he informed his adviser Louis Howe, who supervised the President's correspondence both before and directly after he became President, personal mail from everyday folks, who tended to express their convictions honestly, constituted the "most perfect index to the state of mind of the people."[21] Thus FDR insisted that the letters he received be read and answered. Personal letters from the President's family and friends were sent unopened to his office. The bulk of the correspondence was opened and read by clerks, who forwarded the substantial number of specific queries and requests to appropriate departmental and agency offices, such as the Federal Emergency Relief Administration (FERA), the Works Progress Administration (WPA), and the Department of Agriculture, which were directed to read and respond to them.[22] The remainder were read and answered by presidential secretaries and assistants within the White House itself, and FDR seems to have stayed very much within the loop.

The President, Ira Smith noted, "does see a good many letters, and the summaries and other data that are supplied him make it possible for him to keep a close tab on public opinion and on the problems that are uppermost in the minds of ordinary people."[23] FDR, Howe recorded, "likes to see a cross section of the daily mail, and not infrequently answers, himself, some of the letters contained in this batch. . . . I have seen him spend precious moments poring over letters scribbled on butcher paper or ruled pages torn from a cheap pad, often directing special attention or replies to the writers of such letters."[24] During such particularly trying moments as the struggle over the Supreme Court, the 1937 recession, American intervention in the European war, the question of whether to run for a third term, FDR relied on what were known as "mail briefs" — analyses of his mail by his staff that gave him a pro and con breakdown with excerpts from each group — to help him grasp public feeling. Lela Stiles, who chose the excerpts FDR would see, maintained that she did not spare the President's feelings even when the opposing letters grew bitter.[25]

Eleanor Roosevelt also received a considerable mail — over three hundred thousand letters in 1933 alone — which, she wrote, "often kept me busy far into the night." She insisted that all the letters be answered by her staff or herself since "the times were too serious and the requests too desperate" to send mere form replies. She made a practice of sharing her more interesting letters with her husband: "I always prepared small piles of my letters for him." These she often placed on the table next to his bed: "I learned to save anything I wanted to tell him till he was in bed, for that was likely to be the only quiet time in the whole day."[26] Some of her correspondents counted on just such behavior on her part. As one woman wrote: "Centuries back Catholics prayed to the Virgin Mary because they thought she might intercede with a diety who could not take time to hear every petitioner. In some such spirit we turn to you."[27] Albert Moreau's letter to FDR was addressed to Eleanor Roosevelt "because I know our dear President is to busy to read these letters but I hope you will tell him how we stand with him."[28]

If Eleanor Roosevelt tried her best to avoid form replies to her correspondents, her husband, whose volume of mail was much larger, didn't have that luxury. The names of those presidential assistants and secretaries who signed the replies — Louis McHenry Howe, Marguerite (Missy) LeHand, Stephen Early, Marvin McIntyre, Grace Tully, Major General Edwin M. (Pa) Watson, and for a time FDR's son James — were generally known to the public, which doubtless pleased his correspondents and reassured them that their letters were not being ignored. "I have written to you twice before and got a repley at once," Margie DeBett informed FDR with obvious pleasure in 1934.[29] The replies, however, were often formulaic. In 1941 C. V. Easterwood began his letter to FDR by congratulating him "on your speech last night" and then went on to demand that workers who went on strike be drafted into the army or sent to a concentration camp. He was answered by Edwin Watson, who skipped the substance of the letter and wrote simply: "Thank you very much in the President's behalf for your kind message of congratulations in reference to his recent radio address."[30]

Within this formulaic structure there could be varying touches of a personal answer. When Charles Fisher wrote FDR in December of 1940: "Altho I am colored & am out of the conscription age at present, you will find me ready to serve anytime men of my age are needed, either in peace or in war," Stephen Early responded with the usual: "Your letter of December twenty-ninth has been received and will be brought to the President's attention," and then added, "Meanwhile, I know he would want me to thank you for this evidence of your loyalty and good will."[31] On another occasion, Edwin Watson wrote Mary Jester, "What you say concerning your son who is a member of the armed forces has been noted with appreciative understanding and the President wants you to know how profoundly conscious he is of your pride in your boy and his service to our country's cause."[32] Ten-year-old Velma Hess's letter inviting FDR to visit her family in Martinsburg, West Virginia, was answered by Grace Tully, who thanked her for her "nice little letter," and added "the President's grateful thanks to your mother for remembrance in prayer," but ignored the invitation to visit.[33]

While his correspondents had little chance of hearing from FDR directly, some came close. Robert Woolley's opening comment in his letter to FDR, "This note may never reach you personally. Just the same I am deriving a world of satisfaction from writing it," received this response from Stephen Early: "Permit me first to assure you that the President did read your letter of May twenty-eighth and derived as much satisfaction from reading it as you did in writing it."[34] Some writers addressed their letters directly to one of the President's secretaries and occasionally obtained the results they were aiming at. Marvin McIntyre responded to one such letter from Detroit: "Your expressions of faith were such that I took the liberty of showing it to the President. He found it extremely interesting and asked me to express his thanks."[35] Although all the letters were read, only the positive ones received replies, as J. T. Cannon of Philadelphia discovered when he tried a little experiment: he sent a number of positive letters to the President and received prompt acknowledgments. "On the other hand, not once did I get a reply from a letter of criticism, nor do I know of anyone else that ever did."[36]*

The attempts of Franklin and Eleanor Roosevelt to respond to their millions of correspondents were often imperfect and perfunctory, but they nevertheless intensified the profound feelings of connection Americans felt toward them. This was affirmed by Lorena Hickock, who traveled through the nation during the early years of the New Deal describing the conditions she found to FDR's relief administrator, Harry Hopkins. Reporting on Alabama in the spring of 1934, she commented on "the number of letters you see around over the President's and Mrs. Roosevelt's signatures. They are seldom anything more than the briefest and most formal acknowledgment of a letter. . . . But I doubt if any other President — or his wife — has ever been so punctilious about acknowledging letters. And these people take them all very seriously, as establishing a personal relation."[37]

In letter after letter, the President's correspondents informed him — often with enclosed copies — of the letters they sent to their Representatives and Senators demanding that they support New Deal policies. FDR directly encouraged this development. According to the *New York Times,* by the beginning of 1934 members of Congress were receiving fifty thousand letters a day, forty thousand addressed to Representatives and ten thousand to Senators.[38] A year later the *Times* described the "stooped shoulders" of the twenty-four postmen who handled the "bulging mail-

---

*Our own research in the responses to the Fireside Chats confirmed Mr. Cannon's impressions. The letters replying to the Fireside Chats are organized in the FDR Library by the date of the Chat to which they are responding, the names of the respondents in alphabetical order, and whether they are pro or con. The latter, of course, could have been ascertained only if the letters were read. Other signs that they were read include underlinings and other markings by FDR's staff directly on the letters as well as a notation of the date of the acknowledgment, if any. The negative letters went unacknowledged, though they were neither uncounted nor destroyed, as at least one of FDR's correspondents feared (Mrs. Walter S. Cooke, Worcester, Massachusetts, to FDR, March 10, 1937).

sacks" containing eighty-five thousand letters a day — forty thousand incoming and forty-five thousand outgoing — that made their way through the post office of the U.S. Senate alone.[39] In 1934 Senator Simeon Fess, Republican of Ohio, demonstrated what he called this "enormous" volume of mail by bringing to the Senate floor the letters and telegrams he had received during the past twelve hours, the bulk of which urged him to support the President's monetary policies. "Some of the letters," he informed his colleagues, "even ask us totally to abdicate all responsibility of expressing judgment and vote as rubber stamps."[40] Fess's experience was typical. "The name that appears in the letters more often than any other," a press report concluded, "is that of President Roosevelt. Senators and Representatives, regardless of party affiliation, are urged to 'stand by the President,' and are threatened with defeat at the polls if they fail to support his recovery program."[41]

As the first year of the New Deal wound down, the journalist Stanley High marveled at the ways in which it had made "the average, garden-variety American voter Washington-conscious," brought the government and its people closer to each other than ever before, and turned the entire nation into something resembling a New England town meeting. "It is probable," he observed, "that in the last twelve months more hitherto inarticulate American citizens have 'taken their pens in hand' for political purposes than during any such period in our whole history." For this he credited the President: "The spirit, even more than the content, of his 'My Friends' speeches was something new in the annals of our democracy. There is a latch-string-is-always-out quality about them. They invite familiarity." The country, High concluded, "sends its orders to its Congressmen. But it talks things over with its President."[42] If the extraordinary number of letters arriving at the White House were any indication, another journalist noted, "more Americans are awakened to their public duty and quickened with the sense of social responsibility than at any other time in recent history. The whole land appears to be thinking, [and] wanting to help the President to think."[43]

At the very least, FDR helped to school people in the significance and legitimacy of writing freely to the head of their government and other elected officials, an activity that really began in a significant way during the Great Depression and continues vigorously to this day. "When I first went to work at the White House," Ira Smith has testified, "President McKinley was getting an average of perhaps 100 letters a day, and there were frequent complaints that something would have to be done about such an avalanche of mail. . . . In President Hoover's time, the mail averaged about 800 a day, and during the New Deal it averaged about 8000 a day, with peak days on which we would go down under a count of 150,000 letters and parcels. . . . The mere physical handling of the mail required a staff that grew from one man — myself — to twenty-two regularly employed persons and in emergencies to seventy persons."[44] Leila Sussmann calculated that during the Civil War Lincoln received 44 letters annually for every 10,000 literate adults in the nation, during World War One Wilson received 47, and during the Great Depression FDR received 160.[45] On December 16, 1933, the White House announced that it would institute a night shift for the first time in its history in order to handle the unprecedented volume of mail.[46]

Louis Howe told the readers of a national magazine that his recurrent nightmare "finds me in an airplane, high up, so that the whole map of the United States lies spread out beneath me. . . . It appears to be covered with a white blanket flowing toward one point. As the airplane descends, I find to my horror that the white blanket consists of letters — letters from every part of the country — and their ultimate destination is the White House."[47] As with most dreams, Howe's embodied elements of barely disguised reality. Franklin Roosevelt, with the indispensable aid of radio, was presiding over a revolution in mass political letter writing.

FDR not only stimulated an enormous increase in the number of letters sent to the President, but he used this correspondence innovatively to pressure his opponents inside and outside the Congress and to justify his actions. "All we have to do," he told his advisers during one legislative battle, "is to let the flood of mail settle on Congress . . . and the opposition will be beating a path to the White House door."[48] Above all, he employed his enormous correspondence to fathom the attitudes of the American people and to free himself of the dependency previous Presidents had upon members of Congress to learn what their constituents were thinking. FDR was convinced that he possessed an independent pipeline to the public far more extensive than anyone in Congress, and he used it to help shape and implement his program. Nor did Roosevelt feel, as many of his predecessors had, dependent on newspaper reporters to help him keep his finger on the pulse of the people. "I am more closely in touch with public opinion in the United States than any individual in this room," he told a group of newspaper editors. "I get a better cross section of opinion."[49] There was, Eleanor Roosevelt recalled after the President's death, "a real dialogue between

Franklin and the people. He would read samplings of his mail. . . . He always knew what the reaction was to what he was doing, and he could respond to that reaction."[50]

Sam Rosenman, one of the President's principal speechwriters, gives a number of instances of the impact of mail upon FDR. After a Chicago speech in 1937 in which the President stated that an "epidemic of world lawlessness" was spreading and made an analogy with epidemics of physical disease, which were dealt with by quarantine "in order to protect the health of the community," he received such a negative flood of antiwar telegrams opposing what became known as his "quarantine the aggressors" speech that he was forced to back down at his press conference the very next day.[51] "It's a terrible thing," he remarked to Rosenman, "to look over your shoulder when you are trying to lead — and to find no one there." Conversely, Rosenman cites the President's May 26, 1940, Fireside Chat calling for enhanced American military preparedness as receiving such a positive response that it emboldened FDR to go to Congress just five days later requesting additional appropriations for national defense.[52] During the first six months of 1940, FDR asked for daily mail briefs on what his correspondents thought about his seeking a third term and discovered, according to Leila Sussmann, that "the letter-writers were overwhelmingly in favor of his running again and that among them, the objection to breaking the two-term tradition carried little weight."[53] In the final year of the war, FDR received many letters revealing the public's fear of renewed economic depression and hardship when peace returned. He sent such letters on to Rosenman as "speech suggestions" and did in fact include these matters both in his speeches and in his plans for peacetime reconstruction.[54]

One of the most common requests in his letters was that FDR deliver his Fireside Chats more frequently: monthly or even weekly. Charles Flaig of Richmond, Indiana, was typical: "I hope you will come before the people oftener. Since 80% of the press, magazines and their other loud speakers are daily vomiting out their hate and criticism against you, it is confusing many people and clouding the real facts and issues. Our only salvation is the radio, we must use it often."[55]

FDR certainly agreed that radio had become essential to American democracy. In an address he gave as governor of New York at the beginning of 1929, he estimated that "whereas five years ago ninety-nine out of one hundred people took their arguments from the editorials and the news columns of the daily press, today at least half of the voters sitting at their own firesides listen to the actual words of the political leaders on both sides and make their decision on what they hear rather than what they read."[56] Accordingly, he supported the efforts of those within his administration who wanted to produce public service and educational radio shows for the networks. By 1939 there were forty-two different New Deal agencies, bureaus, and departments engaging in radio programming, ranging from the Department of Agriculture's "Farm and Home Hour," the Public Health Service's "Help Yourself to Health," and the Children's Bureau's "Your Child" to dramatizations by the Social Security Board and the Federal Housing Administration explaining their services. The Department of the Interior had its own weekly drama series, "What Price America," highlighting the nation's battle to control and conserve its natural resources, and the Office of Education series "Americans All — Immigrants All" explored the roles played by different religions, races, and nationalities in America's cultural and economic life. Then there were the Federal Theatre Project's radio productions of famous plays, including a series of Shakespearean dramas. The public responded to many of these programs exactly as it responded to the Fireside Chats: with a barrage of letters. The Office of Education — the federal agency producing the largest number of radio programs until Congress cut its budget in 1940 — received four hundred thousand letters in 1937, eight hundred thousand in 1939, and almost a million in 1940.[57]

The President, of course, was the undisputed star of the New Deal's broadcasting endeavors. Nevertheless, he resolutely refused to heed pleas that he himself use radio more often. After his election in 1932 but before he had taken office, the president of NBC offered him airtime and urged him to speak to the people fifteen to twenty minutes once a week. FDR responded: "I fully expect to give personal talks from time to time on all kinds of subjects of national interest, but I do not believe that it would be advisable to make one each week."[58] It was a position from which he never deviated. "Sometimes I wish I could carry out your thought of more frequent talking on the air on my part," he wrote Russell Leffingwell in March of 1942, "but the one thing I dread is that my talks should be so frequent as to lose their effectiveness."[59] A week later he wrote Mary Norton: "For the sake of not becoming a platitude to the public, I ought not to appear oftener. . . . I am inclined to think that in England Churchill, for a while, talked too much, and I don't want to do that."[60]

Thus, in spite of his striking radio successes, he continued to use the radio format sparingly: only thirty-one Fireside Chats from March 1933 to

January 1945, and these were not evenly spread out but tended to come in clusters during periods of crisis. Accordingly, the Chats became significant and widely anticipated events. Belle Conwell of Birmingham, Alabama, assured FDR: "I must tell you that when it is announced that the President is to speak, we fore-go any engagements to be at home. It is akin to a visit with a good friend."[61] "I would not have missed hearing it for anything," B.J. Campbell of Memphis wrote. "Mrs. Campbell and me were invited to an egg nog party so in order to hear it I phoned our host and he said go ahead. I have postponed the party until after the President's message."[62]

The Administration created suspense by refusing to divulge the subjects the President would include and only gradually and grudgingly giving out any details of the coming broadcast, thus making the contents of his Chats national news before and not merely after he gave them. On May 13, 1941, for example, the *New York Times* announced that FDR would deliver a Fireside Chat on May 27 and noted, "The Executive seldom makes fireside chats except upon important matters." On May 23 it announced: "The President spent four hours today working on his speech." The next day it gave the list of those who would constitute FDR's small — and very silent — live audience and specified the local stations that would carry the Chat. On May 25 a *Times* headline, referring to press secretary Stephen Early, proclaimed: "ROOSEVELT SPEECH WON'T PLEASE FOES OF DEMOCRACY, SAYS EARLY," and the paper spent considerable space speculating on what the President would say. On the morning of the speech, the *Times* reported that FDR "was devoting more time to preparation of this speech than to any previous address he had made to the American people" and that according to White House sources "the President's speech would be one of the most important he ever made."[63] Radio stations treated the Chats as important events by giving the President free airtime and by rebroadcasting them the next day "for the benefit of those unable to hear it at the regular time."[64] Similarly, newspapers all over the country summarized and often printed the Chats in full or part.[65]

Those who did not own radios wrote him of their sense of deprivation. "I wish I had a small Radio in my lonely Furnish Room," Elizabeth Berg wrote from New York City, "so I could hear your Talk. I Receive so little Money for Rent and Food. so I cant Buy any."[66] Walter Edison of Oakland, California, was one of the many who wrote for a transcript of a Fireside Chat, explaining, "I can't afford a radio or well afford buying a newspaper with it published in as I'm on un-employables inadequate relief."[67]

For Roosevelt, the radio turned out to be very much a two-edged sword. While many letters were characterized by adulation and compared Roosevelt to biblical figures (Moses, Gideon, Solomon, Jesus, even God) or famous secular leaders (Caesar, Washington, Wilson, and especially Abraham Lincoln), there was also a frankness and a willingness to push FDR in directions he didn't seem to be embracing with enough will or decisiveness, or to urge him to move with more deliberateness and caution. He was besieged with advice concerning his economic and social programs, alerting him to defects, counseling him to alter or supplement his approaches, warning him of conditions his advisers were ignoring, or simply praising his efforts. There was no dearth of voluntary advisers anxious to have the President peruse their solutions for the crisis. "Plans, plans, and plans," Louis Howe exclaimed in 1934. "Some two pages long, some thick manuscripts handsomely bound and carefully indexed; every day brings a flood of them to the White House door."[68]

When FDR took a serious misstep, as many felt he did when he tried to "pack" the Supreme Court or involve the United States in the European conflict, numerous supporters wrote him anguished letters of reproach, pleading with him to adhere to his own principles and the historic American system. On the Court issue, for example, Paul Barrett of Philadelphia informed FDR: "Your remarks filled me with a deep sense of sorrow and chagrin," and a group of stenographers implored him: "Don't throw over our love and loyalty for a stubborn idea. . . . Don't sell us out in order to personally triumph over a few political enemies."[69] And of course there were those who never pretended to be his admirers and kept up a drumbeat of rancorous opposition in their responses to his Fireside Chats: "PLEASE GET OFF THE AIR WE WANT TO HEAR OUR FAVORITE PROGRAM," A. M. Tebbetts of St. Louis, Missouri, telegraphed in 1941.[70] A New Jersey resident felt it necessary to inform the President: "I wouldn't urinate on you if you were burning at the stake."[71]

It has been said of Father Coughlin that he "built an electronic neighborhood."[72] This describes precisely what FDR did as well, and unlike Coughlin, whose reign as the "radio priest" was relatively brief, the President was able to maintain his neighborhood through the long years of depression and war. FDR's creation of a new form of public discourse flowered in the years of his presidency but had its origins during his governorship of New York from 1928 to 1932, when, as he wrote in 1938, "it was often necessary for me to appeal for public support over the heads of the Legislature and sometimes over the almost united opposition of the newspapers of the State. . . . The use of the radio by me in those days not only to appeal directly to the people, but also to describe fully the facts about the legislation which were not always given by many press reports, was the beginning of similar use of the radio by me as President in what have come to be known as 'Fireside Chats.' The radio has proved to be a direct contact with the people which was available to only two presidents before me. It has been invaluable as a means of public approach."[73] The day before his initial Fireside Chat, FDR explained its purpose in a statement issued from the White House: "The Constitution has laid upon me the duty of conveying the condition of the country to the Congress assembled at Washington. I believe I have a like duty to convey to the people themselves a clear picture of the situation at Washington itself whenever there is danger of any confusion as to what the Government is undertaking."[74]

The aims and purposes of the Fireside Chats remained the same as the gubernatorial chats. What changes there were emanated primarily from Roosevelt's increasingly sophisticated use of radio. He simply got better and better at it. What has not been stressed sufficiently is how much FDR *needed* radio. Radio began to develop as a major genre of communication in the 1920s, during the very years when Roosevelt suffered the devastating effects of polio. Radio offered enormous compensation for that illness since it allowed Roosevelt to reach the American people with his *voice*. This is not to minimize the extent to which FDR continued to travel as President — by railroad alone he made 399 trips logging over half a million miles, and he put in many more miles by air, sea, and auto — speaking in person with aggregations of people large and small, something he loved to do and did with superb skill.[75] But polio prevented him from moving among and mingling with people. Radio allowed him to enter people's homes, their neighborhoods, their lives. Without radio, he undoubtedly would have had a markedly different political career than the one he did have.

Many of FDR's political and official speeches, such as his four Inaugural Addresses and many of his Annual Messages, were carried on the radio, but each one of the Fireside Chats was designed from the beginning as a *radio* address. FDR and his speechwriters worked diligently to make these speeches accessible and comprehensible to as large an audience as possible. Indeed, FDR adopted so basic a vocabulary that 70 percent of his words were among the five hundred most commonly used words in the English vocabulary and 80 percent were among the one thousand most commonly used words.[76] The Fireside Chats were relatively brief, ranging from fifteen to forty-five minutes and averaging twenty-six minutes in length. They emanated from the White House or, in two instances, from FDR's home in Hyde Park, New York. They were broadcast on all the national networks, most often on Sundays, Mondays, and Tuesdays at around ten in the evening, Eastern Time — when Easterners were still awake and people in other parts of the country were already home from their day's activities — in order to attract a peak national audience. Each Chat was generally devoted to a single subject or to a small cluster of related subjects. Roosevelt's purpose in these Chats was not to make ringing statements for posterity but to speak in a face-to-face style.

In his initial Chat, it was FDR's intention to demystify a banking system shrouded in enigma to a people enveloped by anxiety.[77] Thus his first Fireside Chat, delivered in the midst of a momentous crisis that could have altered the American political system fundamentally, began conversationally with FDR speaking "for a few minutes" about banking to "the comparatively few who understand the mechanics of banking, but more particularly with the overwhelming majority of you who use banks for the making of deposits and the drawing of checks. I want to tell you what has been done in the last few days, and why it was done, and what the next steps are going to be." This patient, gentle tone prevailed throughout and turned to mild exhortation only at the conclusion: "You people must have faith; you must not be stampeded by rumors or guesses. Let us unite in banishing fear."[78]

FDR's delivery fit seamlessly with the simplicity and accessibility of his words. He spoke calmly, slowly, usually not much more than 100 to 120 words per minute, some 30 percent less than was common in radio broadcasts — at the other end of the spectrum the news commentator Walter Winchell spoke 200 words per minute — and when the situation was particularly grave, as in his Fireside Chat following the attack on Pearl Harbor, he dropped the pace to 88 words per minute. This unusually deliberate pace allowed FDR to pay attention to his phrasing, his pauses, and his vocal pacing, all of which he became a master at — elongating and prolonging his vowels and consonants, using silences effectively, varying his emphases and the modulation of his tenor voice. How deeply Roosevelt cared about these matters was made evident both before and after he delivered a Chat. He would read a draft out loud, Robert Sherwood reported, "to see how it sounded and to detect any tongue-twisting phrases that would be difficult on the radio." At the close of his Fireside Chats he would eagerly query the radio announcers and technicians in the room: "Was I all right?" "Did I go too fast?" "Did I put too much emphasis on this point?" "Did I slur over that word?"[79] He displayed precisely the same attitude toward the cameramen who shot portions of the Chats for the movie newsreels, asking them: "How did that go? Need another take?" and using professional terms like "take," "cut," "footage," "fadeout."[80]

"I am not an expert on radio technique," Felix Ury wrote FDR in 1937, "but . . . I can honestly say from my own point of view that your delivery last night over the radio was your 'Masterpiece'. You were just right — not too fast or not too slow and your tone was one of genuine sincerity . . . from the heart."[81] "The thing which impressed me, and inspired me to send this letter," W. M. Holmberg wrote during the war, "was the calm confidence and strength of your voice which carried a real message of assurance of ultimate victory for the United Nations."[82] Glowing reviews of FDR's voice were not confined to his radio audiences. John Carlile, who worked as a voice expert for CBS, characterized the President's voice as revealing "sincerity, good-will and kindliness, determination, conviction, strength, courage and abounding happiness."[83] "Like his picture," Professor Jane Zimmerman of Columbia University's Teachers College asserted, "his voice gives the impression of a genial smile."[84] "His tone and manner were as near perfection as any one can come over the radio," the *New York Times* proclaimed on its editorial page after FDR's Chat in April 1935.[85] "His voice lent itself remarkably to the radio," Eleanor Roosevelt later wrote. "It was a natural gift, for in his whole life he never had a lesson in diction or public speaking. His voice unquestionably helped him to make the people of the country feel that they were an intelligent and understanding part of every government undertaking during his administration."[86]

What is more difficult to describe about his delivery was its spirit and tone. This patrician from the Hudson River Valley had mastered the art of conversational speaking over the radio to a diverse audience of tens of millions of people — as many as 83 percent of those who owned radios tuned in to his Chats on at least two occasions.[87] Harry Butcher, the CBS official who coined the term "Fireside Chats," was told by the President "that he thought of his radio talks as himself sitting in the White House and talking to one person in his own home. To make this picture more simple for himself, the President said he picked some object on the mantel and imagined, while dictating or working on a draft of his 'chat,' that object to be the person to whom he was speaking."[88] FDR was obviously able to bring that conception into the actual broadcast of the Chats. Even someone as conditioned to political oratory as the radio correspondent Richard Strout testified: "You felt he was there talking to you, not to 50 million others, but to you personally."[89]

FDR also knew precisely how to set the right informal tone in the makeshift White House studio from which the Fireside Chats were broadcast and which was filled with presidential aides, secret servicemen, invited guests, radio technicians, newspaper reporters, photographers, and newsreel cameramen. Two minutes before he went on the air with his second Chat, he looked up from his text, which he had been perusing one last time, observed the silent, tense gathering and broke the nervous pall that enveloped the room by announcing with a broad smile: "If anybody has to sneeze, he'd better do it now!"[90]

The open but restrained quality of FDR's initial Chat, which Raymond Moley, his close adviser during his first term, called "as simple and moving as any presidential utterance in the history of this country,"[91] belied the intense preparation that went into it and all of his subsequent Fireside Chats. The Fireside Chats, Eleanor Roosevelt testified, "entailed a great deal of work on Franklin's part. . . . I have known . . . Franklin to take a speech that had almost reached the final stages and tear it up and dictate it from the beginning, because he felt the others had not made it clear enough for the layman to understand. Franklin had a gift for simplification."[92] Robert Sherwood, the playwright who worked on Roosevelt's speeches, observed that FDR "knew that all of those words would constitute the bulk of the estate that he would leave to posterity," and thus "utmost importance was attached to his public utterances and utmost care exercised in their preparation."[93]

FDR himself made it clear how hard he worked on his Fireside Chats to make them sound like simple conversation. In a letter to one of those urging him to give more Fireside Chats, FDR wrote: "I suppose you know that every time I talk over the air it means four or five days of long, overtime work in the preparation of what I say."[94] He explained on another occasion: "I usually take the various drafts and suggestions which have been submitted to me and also the material which has been accumulated in the speech file on various subjects, read them carefully, lay them aside, and then dictate my own draft. . . . On some of my speeches I have prepared as many as five or six successive drafts myself after reading drafts and suggestions submitted by other people." He acknowledged the help he received in creating his speeches but wrote that those who claimed authorship of his speeches "are not accurate" — a conclusion with which every one of his major speechwriters agreed.[95]

The journalist Charles Michelson, who worked on some of FDR's early speeches, remembered an occasion when he, Hugh Johnson, and Raymond Moley each prepared a draft of a speech. Roosevelt went over the three drafts, "stretched himself on a couch and with his eyes on the ceiling dictated his own version, occasionally using one of our phrases but generally culling the best ideas that had been submitted and putting them in his own way." His experiences led Michelson to conclude that "Franklin Roosevelt is a better phrase maker than anybody he ever had around him."[96] Frances Perkins recalled what happened when FDR asked her to contribute to an address on social security: "I summed up one section by saying, 'We are trying to construct a more inclusive society.' I heard that speech over the radio some weeks later, and this is how he, with his instinct for simplicity, wound up that section: 'We are going to make a country in which no one is left out.' "[97] "The speeches were always Roosevelt's," Sam Rosenman testified. "He had gone over every point, every word, time and again. He had studied, reviewed, and read aloud each draft, and had changed it again and again, . . . by the time he delivered a speech he knew it almost by heart." Even when the draft was finished the President was not, and he altered it as he spoke, a habit that drove his speechwriters to form the "Society for Prevention of Ad-Libbing," but to no avail. "Poppa just thought of it at the last minute," he would explain when they complained about his departures from the text. "It was remarkable how little trouble he got into," Rosenman wrote, "considering how much ad-libbing he did."[98]

If studying the Fireside Chats and the responses to them teaches us about how FDR used the radio, it also helps us to learn about an equally important and even more neglected subject: how the American people used the radio. Radio was still new enough that people commented on the quality of the reception. E. D. Warren from Jackson, Michigan, wrote after the second Fireside Chat: "Both my sister and I heard it very clearly for the most part, altho there was a great deal of static."[99] "We heard your splendid speech over our radio last night," Harry Nelson of Ithaca, Nebraska, wrote, "it came in as clear as if you were right in the room with us."[100] Calling radio "a modern miracle," Frank Mercato reported from San Francisco that he had his radio "adjusted so finely, I could hear your Excellency, every time you took a breath. I really had a very front seat in your audience."[101]

We know that FDR had a large and constant audience. Almost two-thirds of those questioned by a 1939 *Fortune* Survey responded that they "usually" or "sometimes" listened to the Fireside Chats, and as we've seen, his audience frequently rose far above that percentage.[102] Aside from its size, we know little concerning the ways in which that audience approached the Chats and what effects — immediate and long-term — the Chats had on listeners. Answers to these questions are contained in the letters themselves. Americans filled their letters to FDR with details describing how they listened to his Fireside Chats: where and with whom they listened, what they were doing and saying as they listened, and what they did after they listened.

Radio listening "was by no means antithetical to a sense of folk or community . . . before, during, and after the Great Depression, people enjoyed popular culture not as atomized beings vulnerable to an overpowering external force but as part of social groups in which they experienced the performance or with which they shared it after the fact."[103] The Fireside Chats bear this out: the majority of their listeners heard the Fireside Chats not in isolation but as part of groups, large and small. They listened with families and friends at home; in churches and synagogues; in offices, hotel lobbies, and movie theaters; in barracks and camps; in the streets and in parks; at celebrations, conventions, and business meetings. It was not uncommon for FDR to receive telegrams informing him: "TWENTY BUSINESS AND PROFESSIONAL MEN ASSEMBLED IN MY HOME TO HEAR YOUR MESSAGE."[104] "THE COLORADO CHIROPRACTORS . . . LISTENED TO YOUR ADDRESS TONIGHT EN MASSE."[105] "NEGRO FRATERNAL COUNCIL OF CHURCHES IN SESSION AT CLEVELAND . . . STOPPED OUR PROGRAM LAST NIGHT TO HEAR YOUR MESSAGE TO THE NATION."[106] "OVER THREE THOUSAND PEOPLE LISTENED TONIGHT IN RAPT ATTENTION TO YOUR BRILLIANT AND INSPIRING SPEECH WHICH WAS REBROADCAST TO THE BALLROOM OF THE PENN ATHLETIC CLUB RITTENHOUSE SQUARE PHILADELPHIA."[107]

The Reverend James W. Henley of the Centenary Methodist Episcopal Church, South, in Chattanooga, assured the President that even church services were not allowed to interfere: "A loud speaker was placed in the church auditorium and the service was arranged so as to make way for your radio address at the scheduled moment."[108] In Chicago a synagogue brought in a radio and made FDR "our principal speaker and guest of honor (in voice and spirit — although not in person.)"[109] Members of the Portuguese Workers Music Club in New York City "met in this club to hear your radio talk tonight."[110] Sidney Rothschild wrote following the Chat of April 14, 1938, that his daughter was in downtown Manhattan, "and she said that people were clustered around Taxi Cabs with Radios listening to your talk, and she went into a Childs resturant, There the waitress and customers were all listening."[111] Six years later, in another place called Manhattan — this one in Kansas — the room clerk at the Wareham Hotel wrote: "Tonight when you came on the air the lobby filled with people of all walks of life, they all listened to every word you said."[112]

Even when people listened alone, their experience could be a communal one. The novelist Saul Bellow, then a college student, recalled walking along Chicago's Midway past a row of parked cars whose drivers had pulled over "and turned on their radios to hear Roosevelt. They had rolled down the windows and opened the car doors. Everywhere the same voice, its odd Eastern accent, which in anyone else would have irritated Midwesterners. You could follow without missing a single word as you strolled by. You felt joined to these unknown drivers, men and women smoking their cigarettes in silence, not so much considering the President's words as affirming the rightness of his tone and taking assurance from it. You had some sense of the weight of troubles that made them so attentive, and of the ponderable fact, the one common element (Roosevelt), on which so many unknowns could agree."[113]

People not only listened, but reacted, together. Patrick H. O'Dea of Washington, D.C., wrote FDR that after listening to his Fireside Chat on banking, "the Banquet Committee of the Ancient Order of Hibernians and Ladies' Auxiliary, then in session, by a sort of spontaneous intuition began to sing 'Happy Days are Here Again.' "[114] The director of publicity for a movie chain wrote that his "fifteen (15) theatres in Philadelphia carried the entire Presidents address of Sunday Evening to their audiences thru a special hook-up from the radio to the regular theatre loud speakers." He reported that "the majority of the audiences kept their seats and only a few of the younger people left during the address. . . . After the address the majority of all the audiences applauded most generously."[115] Generally, after broadcasting his Chat, FDR repeated portions of it before newsreel cameras. "I was at a movie last night where there was a packed house, at least 4,000 people," Samuel Traum wrote in 1941. "When the reading of your speech was shown on the screen, there was a loud and vigorous applause."[116]

Other gatherings were smaller but no less revealing: In Brooklyn Ruth Lieberman gathered with her parents to hear FDR's first Chat: "My father, who is a determined pessimist, was airing his views on the banking situation. He was sure that the banks would never open — — that he would never regain his savings. Then you spoke. For fifteen minutes Dad was silent, his brow wrinkled in thought. Then, when you had concluded your talk, he grinned sheepishly and said, 'Oh well, I wasn't really afraid of losing my money anyhow.'"[117]

Listening to FDR on the radio was often a prelude to action. Following his Fireside Chats, many listeners functioned as FDR's eyes and ears and his self-appointed pollsters. A New Yorker named Hutchinson wrote on New York Athletic Club stationery: "I made it my business to circulate among clubs and hotel lobbies, after your last night's speech, for several hours. I do wish you could have been present and could have heard what I heard said about you. Men were slapping each other on their backs and enthusiastically shaking hands in self congratulation that, at last, the public has a BUDDY in the White House."[118] Roosevelt's 1937 Chat on his controversial plan to add Justices to the Supreme Court prompted a number of impromptu polls. F. P. McMahon strolled through his Omaha, Nebraska, neighborhood and reported: "I have checked carefully the people who live on my street of average 5 room homes, and find that at least 7 out of 10 voters are in favor of your plan."[119] A. J. Hamilton, "a travling man working on trains between Atlanta and New Orleans," wrote: "I have interviewed 3812 passengers relative to your Court reform proposal and here is the result — 2759 for and 1052 against." While he made no record of "non committals," he was sensitive to the nuances of class: "To my supprise a greater percent of Pullman passengers was for your proposal."[120] A resident of Galesburg, Illinois, also checking the reactions on railroads, telegraphed: "TEN PASSENGERS ON TRAIN HAVE JUST HEARD YOUR FIRESIDE CHAT. EIGHT OF US ARE STILL AGAINST YOUR PLAN. ONE IS FOR YOU. ONE SLEPT THRU YOUR TALK AND IS UNDECIDED."[121]

To judge from the letters FDR received, the radio was not an instrument inducing intellectual and political passivity in its audiences. On the contrary, the Fireside Chats — and we know this was also true of the radio addresses of Father Coughlin and Huey Long and of many other genres of radio as well — tended to *counter* passivity, to stimulate audiences to thought and action, and to give them a sense of participation and inclusion — often for the first time in their political lives. Throughout the Great Depression and World War Two, the radio presented the American people with an alternative and increasingly necessary means of learning about and understanding what was happening to them and others like and unlike them. The radio quickly eclipsed the newspaper as the chief means of disseminating national and international news. Seventy-one percent of radio owners queried by the Office of Radio Research in 1939 regularly listened to news broadcasts. In the fall of 1938, the American Institute of Public Opinion found that in all economic classes in both urban and rural areas decisive majorities of those interviewed expressed greater interest in radio than in newspaper accounts of the European crisis. In November 1945, a poll asked which medium — magazines, newspapers, moving pictures, or radio — best served the public during the war: 67 percent listed radio first, with newspapers a distant second at 17 percent.[122]

Perhaps even more indicative of the growing ubiquity and popularity of radio were the results of a 1939 *Fortune* Survey that asked: "If you had to give up either going to the movies or listening to the radio, which one would you give up?" More than 79 percent were willing to give up movies, while less than 14 percent were willing to abandon the radio. The survey concluded "that not a single group of people by class or occupation, or age or sex, votes less than 70 per cent for giving up the movies rather than the radio." Six years later a national survey repeated the question and found that the number willing to give up movies rather than radio had grown to 84 percent, while only 11 percent expressed willingness to forgo their radios.[123]

The letters Roosevelt received reinforce the findings of these polls and clearly demonstrate that the American people understood the revolutionary changes radio inaugurated. They appreciated, just as early and as explicitly as the many commentators and theorists, the democratizing potential of radio, and they made it their most popular form of leisure activity with bewildering rapidity. By the end of World War Two, some 90 percent of the population owned radios, 36 percent owned more than one, and almost a quarter of those surveyed had a radio in their cars.[124] Because so much of what was broadcast on radio fell into what by the 1920s and 1930s was classified as "lowbrow" culture — vaudeville, melodrama, adventure stories, comedy, children's shows, breakfast chatter, country and dance music — intellectuals and scholars have tended to ignore a medium that has had an incalculable impact on American politics, culture, and society. Happily, there are a number of hopeful signs that we are at long last ready to give radio its due in comprehending and recounting our history. There are equally encouraging signs that we are prepared, finally, to listen to the voices of all the American people.

PART ONE

THE NADIR: 1933–1936

Never can there have been a closer, a more intense union of leader and led . . . his mastery of radio was something never before known. His stature increased. He glowed and gave out light. The people responded.

Rexford Guy Tugwell, *The Democratic Roosevelt*

You are the first President to come into our homes; to make us feel you are working for us; to let us know what you are doing. Until last night, to me, the President of the United States was merely a legend. A picture to look at. A newspaper item. But you are real. I know your voice; what you are trying to do. Give radio credit. But to you goes the greater credit for your courage to use it as you have.

Mildred I. Goldstein, Joliet, Illinois,
to FDR, March 13, 1933

CLOSING THE BANKS:
MARCH 12, 1933

"MY FRIENDS, I WANT TO TALK for a few minutes with the people of the United States about banking. . . ."[1] With these unassuming words, Franklin D. Roosevelt began his first radio address to the American people following his decision on March 6, two days after his inauguration, to close the doors of all of the banks in the United States, an action euphemistically termed a "bank holiday." It was the first of those national radio addresses, broadcast directly from the White House at prime time and delivered slowly, in simple language devoid of rhetorical flourishes, that were soon to be called his "Fireside Chats."

But if Roosevelt's approach was relatively low-key, the moment was one of the most dangerous and disheartening in American history. Although Roosevelt's Inaugural Address eight days earlier was widely noted — both then and since — for his assertion that "the only thing we have to fear is fear itself," the new President used the occasion of his inauguration to give voice to the monumental problems that beset the nation and gave rise to what were, in fact, very legitimate fears:

> Values have shrunken to fantastic levels; taxes have risen; our ability to pay has fallen; government of all kinds is faced by serious curtailment of income; the means of exchange are frozen in the currents of trade; the withered leaves of industrial enterprise lie on every side; farmers find no markets for their produce; the savings of many years in thousands of families are gone.
>
> More important, a host of unemployed citizens face the grim problem of existence, and an equally great number toil with little return. Only a foolish optimist can deny the dark realities of the moment.[2]

It is customary and convenient to depict the nation's plight statistically: a gross national product that had fallen by 1933 to somewhere between half and two-thirds of what it had been in 1929; corporate net profits and farm income figures that were well under half of what they had been only four years earlier; construction expenditures that had dropped by more than 70 percent; investment rates that were 98 percent below 1929 rates; unemployment figures that, according to Roosevelt's Secretary of Labor, Frances Perkins, ranged from 13.3 million to 17.9 million in 1933 and embraced at least one out of every four American workers, only about one quarter of whom were getting any sort of relief, most of it grossly inadequate. No one could estimate how many *under*employed Americans there were by 1933, as hard-pressed employers converted their employees into part-time workers. United States Steel, which employed 224,980 full-time workers in 1929, had not a single full-time worker on April 1, 1933. The Governor of Pennsylvania reported in early 1933 that only two out of five employable persons in his state had full-time jobs with full pay.[3]

Figures like these are crucial to our understanding of the Great Depression but give us only a partial picture of the American people during the nadir of their great crisis. If ever a people were unprepared for prolonged economic disaster Americans in 1929 were that people. Their culture had not only taught them to believe in continuing progress but had equated that progress with material growth and expansion. Thus, in one cruel blow, events from 1929 to 1933 stripped away a substantial part of their expectations and certainties. Their country had been transformed from a golden land of promise and opportunity to a place characterized by cruel incongruities: Everywhere there was want and everywhere there was plenty. People were undernourished while crops rotted in the fields. Children went without adequate clothes and shoes while clothing and shoe factories closed down for want of markets. As FDR frequently observed, the American people displayed remarkable patience as the calamities multiplied, but it was a patience accompanied by a pervasive bewilderment and a sense of impotent anger as they were beset by malevolent forces they could neither identify nor comprehend. Rational purpose had given way to confusion and inaction well symbolized by the more than one million men and women drifting through the country on foot and in freight cars in a massive display of movement without direction.[4]

Franklin Roosevelt understood the spiritual and psychic costs of the Depression far more clearly than his predecessor had. Shortly before taking his oath of office, he had written to Felix Frankfurter, a law professor at Harvard whom he would later appoint to the Supreme Court, of "the mood of depression, of dire and weary depression" when "the hand of discour-

agement has fallen upon us, when it seems that things are in a rut, fixed, settled, that the world has grown old and tired and very much out of joint."[5]
During his campaign for a fourth term in 1944, FDR would look back on
the early years of the Great Depression as "a time in which the spiritual
strength of our people was put to the test."

> Our people in those days, might have turned to alien ideologies
> — like communism or fascism.
> But — our democratic faith was too sturdy. What the Ameri-
> can people demanded in 1933 was not less democracy but more
> democracy, and that's what they got.[6]

FDR's Fireside Chats proved to be an important element in this democratic thrust. One of the most salient of the "dark realities" facing the nation — and the one that became a symbol of the entire crisis — was the destruction of the banking system marked by the failing of thousands of banks
in the years after the onset of the Depression in 1929. Without a system
of federal deposit insurance — which was not to be implemented until late
in FDR's first hundred days — the closing of banks imperiled and often
wiped out the savings of millions of Americans. Roosevelt well understood
that this blow to the hopes of middle- and working-class Americans endan-
gered not only the country's finances but the political and social fabric
of the nation. Thus banking became the focus of his first informal radio
address to the American people. In replying to an inquiry from one of his
Hyde Park neighbors in the autumn of 1933, he revealed that he had aimed
his first Chat at "the type of individual whom I thought of as the 'average
depositor.' " He described how he had sat at his desk and tried "to visualize
the types representative of the overwhelming majority. I tried to picture a
mason, at work on a new building, a girl behind a counter and a farmer in
his field. Perhaps my thoughts went back to this kind of individual citizen
whom I have known so well in Dutchess County all my life."[7]

FDR had three goals in that initial Fireside Chat. The most immediate
was to explain the banking system in extremely basic terms to those who
used it primarily for modest savings and checking accounts.

> First of all, let me state the simple fact that when you deposit
> money in a bank the bank does not put the money into a safe de-
> posit vault. It invests your money in many different forms of
> credit. . . . In other words, the bank puts your money to work

to keep the wheels of industry and of agriculture turning round. A comparatively small part of the money that you put into the bank is kept in currency — an amount which in normal times is wholly sufficient to cover the cash needs of the average citizen.

Since these were not "normal times," his second goal was to illuminate the present crisis — to try to put a face on the forces behind the emergency — and to explain why "it became the government's job to straighten out this situation and to do it as quickly as possible." "We have had a bad banking situation," he told the American people, but at no point did he blame the system itself; the culprits were those who had misused it. "Some of our bankers had shown themselves either incompetent or dishonest" by using the funds entrusted to them "in speculations and unwise loans." This, he assured his listeners, was "not true in the vast majority of our banks, but it was true in enough of them to shock the people of the United States for a time into a sense of insecurity" so that they no longer could differentiate between sound and unsound banks.

> What, then, happened during the last few days of February and the first few days of March? Because of undermined confidence on the part of the public, there was a general rush by a large portion of our population to turn bank deposits into currency or gold — a rush so great that the soundest banks couldn't get enough currency to meet the demand. . . .
>
> By the afternoon of March 3, a week ago last Friday, scarcely a bank in the country was open to do business. Proclamations closing them in whole or in part had been issued by the governors in almost all of the states.
>
> It was then that I issued the proclamation providing for the national bank holiday, and this was the first step in the government's reconstruction of our financial and economic fabric.

His third goal was to subordinate platitude to detail and to take the American people into his confidence regarding the staggered system of bank reopenings so that they could comprehend what was about to happen:

> We start tomorrow, Monday, with the opening of banks in the twelve federal reserve bank cities — those banks which on first

examination by the Treasury have already been found to be all right. That will be followed on Tuesday by the resumption of all other functions by banks already found to be sound in cities where there are recognized clearing houses. That means about 250 cities of the United States. . . .

On Wednesday and succeeding days banks in smaller places all through the country will resume business. . . . It is necessary that the reopening of banks be extended over a period in order to permit the banks to . . . obtain currency needed to meet their requirements, and to enable the government to make commonsense checkups.

Please let me make it clear to you that if your bank does not open the first day, you are by no means justified in believing that it will not open. A bank that opens on one of the subsequent days is in exactly the same status as the bank that opens tomorrow.

The point of this involved plan was to ensure that the history of the past few years would not be repeated. "We do not want and will not have another epidemic of bank failures." The banks that reopened, he pledged, "will be able to meet every legitimate call."

I do not promise you that every bank will be reopened or that individual losses will not be suffered, but there will be no losses that possibly could be avoided; and there would have been more and greater losses had we continued to drift. I can even promise you salvation for some at least of the sorely pressed banks. We shall be engaged not merely in reopening sound banks but in the creation of more sound banks through reorganization.

Inevitably, he predicted, some "who have not recovered from their fear" would resume their panicky withdrawals once the banks reopened, but he was convinced they constituted a distinct minority.

It needs no prophet to tell you that when the people find that they can get their money — that they can get it when they want it for all legitimate purposes — the phantom of fear will soon be laid. People will again be glad to have their money where it will be safely taken care of and where they can use it conveniently at

any time. I can assure you, my friends, that it is safer to keep
your money in a reopened bank than it is to keep it under the
mattress.

FDR's overarching purpose in this and in most of his subsequent Fireside Chats was to engage the American people, give them a sense of direction, and fortify their morale, or as he explained some years later, "to ban-
ish, so far as possible, the fear of the present and of the future which held
the American people and the American spirit in its grasp."[8] If the President
placed part of the blame for the banking crisis upon an insecure people who
flooded banks with demands for their savings, he also placed the means of
deliverance in their hands. It was on this note that he brought his first Fireside Chat to a close:

> There is an element in the readjustment of our financial system
> more important than currency, more important than gold, and
> that is the confidence of the people themselves. Confidence
> and courage are the essentials of success in carrying out our
> plan. . . . We have provided the machinery to restore our fi-
> nancial system; and it is up to you to support and make it
> work.
>
> It is your problem, my friends, your problem no less than it
> is mine. Together we cannot fail.

"Our President took such a dry subject as banking," the comedian Will
Rogers commented the next day, "and made everybody understand it, even
the bankers."[9] Raymond Moley, at the time one of Roosevelt's principal advisers, viewed the Chat of March 12 as the capstone of the events that began
with Roosevelt's inaugural on March 4. "Capitalism," Moley proclaimed in
his account of these events, "was saved in eight days."[10] It is certainly true
that there were a number of courses FDR could have followed concerning
the moribund banking system he inherited when he took office, particularly nationalization advocated by several Congressmen. Senator Bronson
Cutting of New Mexico argued that the government could have taken over
the bankrupt banks "without a word of protest."[11] The path FDR chose
was the conservative one of reviving rather than drastically altering the
banking system, and his first Fireside Chat proved to be a crucial step toward that end.

"My bank opened today," Will Rogers noted on March 15. "Instead of
being there to draw my little dab out, I didn't even go to town. Shows you I

heard Roosevelt on the radio."[12] Rogers had a lot of company; the American people seemed to have taken Roosevelt at his word. As the nation's banks reopened, deposits so far exceeded withdrawals that the hundreds of millions of dollars worth of new federal reserve banknotes on hand to ensure that the reopened banks had sufficient funds for the expected demand were scarcely used. As Roosevelt promised, no new run on the banks ensued. By the end of March, more than $1.2 billion had been restored to the banks by their depositors, and by April 12, roughly five weeks after FDR closed the banks, 12,817 of them had fully reopened.[13]

The *New York Times* marveled at the "wonderful power of appeal to the people" that radio had given the President. When, during the fight over the League of Nations in 1919, Woodrow Wilson decided to appeal to the people directly, "it meant wearisome travel and many speeches to different audiences. Now President Roosevelt can sit at ease in his own study and be sure of a multitude of hearers beyond the dreams of the old-style campaigner."[14] That Roosevelt's first Fireside Chat, to an audience one newspaper correspondent estimated — probably too conservatively — at some forty million people, helped to stem the panic and to restore confidence in the banking system is amply demonstrated by the remarkable flood of letters and telegrams that began to pour in upon FDR almost as soon as he left the microphone.[15] It was the beginning of a conversation that was to characterize FDR's presidency through all the days of depression and war.

MARCH 13, 1933

The President of the greatest Nation on earth honored every home with a personal visit last night. He came into our living-room in a kindly neighborly way and in simple words explained the great things he had done so that all of us unfamiliar with the technicalities might understand. When his voice died away we realized our "friend" had gone home again but left us his courage, his faith and absolute confidence.

As long as you talk to your people there is not one thing you cannot accomplish. From the lips of neighbors, acquaintances and strangers we hear this sentiment. Congress and other law-makers will find themselves puny interference when you have but to turn to the Radio and enter our home a welcome and revered guest. If you could only hear our response — but, I'm sure you sense the great hope and reliance of your people, We believe in you!

Of all precedents you have shattered is the theory that a man must come from the lowly to understand the needs of the common people. We love you for that perception that could only come from a great unselfish heart.

We are just a modest middle-class people having lost what little we had, but, since March 4th, . . . we knew we were not fighting alone. We have a LEADER at last.

If this should ever reach your eyes — don't take anyone's valuable time for acknowledgement when there is so much to be done. I hope that when the major things have been disposed of you will not forget a national old-age bill such as you fostered in New York. It will alleviate so much suffering and humiliation.

Since you addressed us as "friends" we have written our letter in this spirit and to express our faith.

Respectfully,

F. B. Graham
Mrs. F. B. Graham
Dubuque, Iowa

MARCH 14, 1933

My dear Mr. President:

Several neighbors (Republican and Democrat) happened to be spending Sunday evening with Mrs. Cregg and myself when it was announced over the radio that you were to talk on the banking situation in the United States at ten o'clock.

There was silence for a moment and then the discussion began. There seemed to be a wide divergence of opinion as to whether or not you were going to make good and whether or not you had the confidence of the people. They were unanimous, however, in agreeing that your Inaugural Address was a masterpiece, and that your message to Congress shot straight from the shoulder. Yet some were frantic and expressed the hope that your message would be such as to allow them to withdraw their life savings from some of the local banks.

When your radio talk began everyone seemed to become hypnotized, because there wasn't a word spoken by anyone until you had finished and then as if one voice were speaking all spoke in unison "We are saved." The frantic individuals of a few moments before declared that they would leave their money in the banks and that they were not afraid of the future. This little episode convinces me more than ever that you have the confidence of the people, that you are the man of the hour, and that with the united support of all its people, you are going to rehabilitate this great nation.

May God bless you.

Sincerely,

Frank J. Cregg
(Justice of the New York Supreme Court)
Syracuse, N.Y.

MARCH 13, 1933

Dear Sir.

While listening to your broadcast Sunday night, our little home seemed a church, our radio the pulpit — and you the preacher.

Thank you for the courage and faith you have given us.

May God bless and keep you to carry on the fight and we, the American people, will help you win.

Respectfully yours,

(Mrs.) Louise Hill
Chicago, Illinois

MARCH 15, 1933

Dear Mr. President:

You cannot hear yourself talk over the radio, so you must accept the testimony of others. You have a marvelous radio voice, distinct and clear. It almost seemed the other night, sitting in my easy chair in the library, that you were across the room from me. A great many of my friends have said the same thing. I suppose hundreds have told you this, but I thought you would like to know how perfectly your message reached us. As for the message itself, it was clear, forcible and direct — a wonderful thing for the President of the United States to talk to the people as you talked to them.

With regards, I am,

Respectfully,

James A. Green
Cincinnati, Ohio

MARCH 13, 1933

Dear Mr. President:

Your talk, last night, over the air, on our Banking Problems, was most inspiring. . . .

Most people, have very little money, and saving, a little for that "Rainy Day," is continual pinching, planning, scraping, and self-denial. And then it does not amount to very much. But at least, one has the feeling that in case of sickness, or unemployment, there is something in the Bank, to help out during a bad time. Then, out of a clear sky, one awakes to find oneself, out of work, and the bank holding the small savings, closed. And though worry does not help at all, one cannot do anything else but worry.

But you, Mr. President have instilled a new Courage, into the hearts of the American People. Even though, I have not worked for almost a year, and my savings are tied up, in a closed bank, I, and millions of others like me, feel, that at last, we can hope for the lifting of that terrible depression, that had almost broken the spirit of a good many of us.

To tell you that we are thankful to you, for the new lease on life that you have given us, would not describe how we feel. So instead we'll pray that God speed you in your good work.

With all Good Wishes for your success, I am,

Gratefully yours

Jane Covant
Fair Haven, N.J.

SUNDAY, MARCH 12

My dear Mr. President:

I thought it would interest you — and perhaps enhearten you —to know just how your radio address on the re-opening of the banks was received in one place tonight. Although the entire contents of your message was known to all of us many minutes before you began to talk (the A.P. sent it out about 9:30), the loudspeaker's audience consisted of the following:

. . . The Herald's editor . . . managing editor . . . financial editor, the night city-editor, five desk men, six reporters, four sports writers, two office-boys, and a couple of bums who had wandered in off the streets. Not one person spoke during your talk, hardly a word was said after you had finished, and everybody (except the two bums) went quietly back to work.

Our office radio is a pretty good barometer of public interest, and never before has it had such a large audience, except on broadcasts of big fights and Al Smith's speeches! Never, I can truthfully say, has it had a more serious and appreciative audience. Somehow you have captured the confidence and devotion of the people in a way that no public man has in our generation. Please, Mr. President, don't be careless with it.

Sincerely yours,

Leonard Ware, Jr.
Boston, Massachusetts

MARCH 14, 1933

AT A MEETING TODAY OF THE DIRECTORS OF OUR COMPANY I WAS RE-
QUESTED TO EXPRESS TO YOU OUR ADMIRATION OF THE MANNER IN
WHICH YOU HAVE HANDLED THE BANKING SITUATION AND PARTICULARLY
YOUR ABLE AND CONVINCING ADDRESS OVER THE RADIO LAST EVENING
WHICH HAS HAD A FAR REACHING EFFECT IN ALLAYING FEAR. ALSO TO EX-
PRESS OUR CONFIDENCE THAT THROUGH YOUR CONTINUED FIRM LEADER-
SHIP THIS COUNTRY WILL BE RETURNED TO PROSPERITY.

> STANDARD OIL COMPANY OF CALIFORNIA
> BY K. R. KINGSBURY, PRESIDENT
> SAN FRANCISCO, CALIF.

MARCH 14, 1933

Dear Mr. President:

I have never yet written a "mail-fan" letter, but I cannot let your radio talk of last Sunday go by, without writing how I feel about your splendid talk of that evening.

Like all other business men, I have been going about in a daze for the past several months. Your talk, as well as your executive actions since you have taken office, has been a tonic to me as it probably has been to millions of others. I am glad that at last we have a man in the White house instead of a commission. If you could talk to the people every week for just fifteen minutes as you did last Sunday, I think that confidence would again be the order of the day.

I pray, that you retain your phenomenal vitality, so that under your leadership, we will emerge triumphant from this depression. I beg to remain,

> Most humbly and sincerely,

> Mark L. Rothman
> Philadelphia, Pa.

MARCH 12, 1933

Dear President;

I would like to tell you that I enjoyed the speech which you have just finished giving. I have regained faith in the banks due to your earnest beliefs. I had decided that, as soon as the banks in Minneapolis reopened, I would withdraw my money. When you said that people's money would be safer in the banks than under their mattresses I decided I'd leave my money just where it is.

Although I'm only a high school student I take a great interest in the country's problems. I firmly believe that the country is on the upward grade and I believe that if people will remain calm and composed that the government will pull the United States out of this terrible depression.

. . . "God be with you and bless you," dear President.

Very respectfully Yours,

Viola Hazelberger
Minneapolis, Minnesota

MARCH 12, 1933

My dear Mr. President —

It is 9:30 pm. Central Standard Time and we have just had the great pleasure of listening to your talk over the air. Its effect on our little group was just short of being miraculous. Our group was a son & wife entertaining father and mother, who are of foreign descent with little education, not accustomed to listening to radio talks and all Staunch, hard shelled Republicans. No sooner had your voice died on the air when Mother, 70 years of age, jumped from her chair saying, "Isn't he a fine man" and father with tears in his eyes said "I feel 100% better already." He had been worrying about his small savings of a lifetime.

This, I am certain is the effect your talk must have had on all who heard you tonight. Couched in such simple language that all could understand, it could only serve to instill the deepest affection for and confidence in you and your undertakings.

Prayers and good wishes are going out to you for your continued success. We are strongly behind you and believe in you —

Sincerely yours

(Mrs H. C.) Bertha M. Lindquist
Minneapolis, Minn.

MARCH 13, 1933

Dear Mr. Roosevelt: —

The loop is packed with people, business is being transacted and their is a happy and cheerful feeling.

The high spot in your radio talk was its directness and also the 100% American language you used. Please keep it up.

I think our country is again united — all except a few people who would still ride in horse cars.

I talked to lawyers, brokers elevator men doctors janitors and the comment is the same in all quarters concerning your talk on the banks. All say — fine, just fine.

One old janitor said "I know everything he talks about, even my boy could understand, no foolish words but all good plain talk, and our president is already helping the people."

We are all catching the spirit of your courage and optomism — as we cannot have one quality without the other.

Very truly yours

Chester E. Bruns — One of the average citizens.
Chicago, Ill.

MARCH 20, 1933

My dear President Roosevelt,

I just want to tell you personally how much your recent radio speech impressed me — particularly our Jewish people, who are all with you. Every word you uttered came straight from the heart and struck a responsive cord in our hearts as well.

The next morning early, at the nearby synagogues our people offered up fervent prayers to God to guard and keep you in good health and happiness for many, many years to come. . . .

WITH SINCERE AND FRIENDLY WISHES FOR YOUR GOOD-HEALTH AND WELL-BEING

I am

(Mrs.) Betty Seigel
Roxbury, Mass.

* * *

Dear Mr. President,

Never having written to a President before even though I am a public school teacher, I am a little bit shaky as to correct address, etc. but after listening to your simple, concise address tonight, I just felt I had to write to you.

I am forty-three years old and during the past week is really the first time that I have felt that I am an active part of the U.S.A. — Your humane leadership has brought out all my latent patriotism and, Mr. President, I'm for you one hundred percent. . . .

One of your grateful people,

Mabel L. Morrissey
Brooklyn, N.Y.

MARCH 15, 1933

Dear Mr. President:

On Sunday evening . . . I went to my home and had as my guests about sixteen young people . . . from Harvard, Radcliffe, Technology, and Simmons College. At ten o'clock they requested that we turn on the radio and listen to the new president. As we stood together, or sat, some on the couch, some on the floor, we heard your voice.

May I assure you it was an inspiration to those youngsters. Washington has seemed a long way off to them and to many of us of the older generation, too. Some how, last night, we were made too feel that we are a part of the government and that we have some responsibility. That sense has been lacking on part of many of us who would have it otherwise. There was an intimacy and a summons about those fifteen minutes that had a tremendously wholesome effect on us all. . . .

Very respectfully,

Newton C. Fetter
(Minister to Students for the Baptists of Greater Boston)
Cambridge, Mass.

MARCH 14, 1933

Honorable Sir:

Believing that a humble citizen of the United States now has entry to the President, I beg leave to congratulate you upon the course you are following, but in particular to tell you how myself and other millions of your countrymen accepted your speech of March 12th.

To Washington it was given to insure the freedom of this country but at the cost of a bloody war with the country which was still "Home" to a large percentage of his countrymen.

To Lincoln it was given to preserve the Union of the States, but again at the cost of a bloody war — in many cases friend against friend, relative against relative.

But to you, Franklin D. Roosevelt, it has been given to preserve the existence of the United States, as a nation of happy contented workers, of healthy happy children, the land of opportunity. And this by the simple means of convincing the people of your sincerity, your capability, and your humanness by a speech which will go down in history as the greatest ever made.

Not sufficient is it to merely reopen the banks of this country, you have assured the only thing which can keep them open, the confidence of the people.

God Bless you Franklin Roosevelt. The need has again brought forth the man.

Ferris D. Gaskill
Chicago, Ill.

*   *   *

Dear Presedent — our Presedent

    after listening to your wonderful talk Sunday a week ago — we all felt the magnetism, of the tone of your Voice — that you were sent for our delivery. When in times of deep distress God took pity on His people. He sent Moses to deliver the oppressed. Then He sent Jesus Christ — to show His people how to live — to redeem them — Then you a Comforter to put confidence in this so great a people. And you will do it — for God is at the helm. Our City needed help, so many idle, my son making every effort for a support after lost business. This is from no office seeker. I need my son here — for daily needs. I know that when the country at large is helped, we will be helped. An ardent, admirer and supporter

Mrs. J. R. Adams
Birmingham, Ala.

I am a widow, still clinging to my husband's name.

MARCH 13, 1933

Dear Mr. President: —

    I want to thank you from the bottom of my heart for your splendid explanation of the Bank situation on last evening's broadcast over the National hookup. Out here on the Coast, we doubly appreciated this extra effort on your part to enlighten us, when our hearts are heavy and saddened by Friday's Quake, and our nerves still "on edge" by the continual tremors which we are still having; quite a severe one this morning at 5:00.

    The broadcast brought you so close to us, and you spoke in such clear concise terms, our confidence in the Bank Holiday was greatly strengthened. . . .

    May I suggest that whenever it is possible, you speak from 1 to 5 minutes on any outstanding Governmental move at the beginning of a week day Coast to Coast program such as the Tuesday's Lucky Strike, Rudy Vallee or the Chicago Mert & Marge program, when the whole country is tuned in for their program. . . .

    Mr. President, you have an unusually fine radio voice, and undoubtedly your campaign radio speeches is what piled up your tremendous majority of votes. Your voice radiates so much human sympathy and tenderness, and Oh, how the public does love that, on the radio especially. I realize it takes time to prepare radio talks; that is why I suggest short ones, but it is surely the best way to get things over to the public the way you want it done, and not the way the Press decides on. . . .

Please pardon my presumption, but I see by this mornings Los Angeles Times, that you have been eating most of your meals on a tray in your office the past week. In the name of "All that Holy", please, Oh please give your body the rest and care it needs. As you well know, there's a limit to human indurance. We all need you so very much, and no one can take your place at this time. It would be a terrible calamity if you should break under the heavy strain, so do TAKE the required rest you should have, even if you have to keep Kings or Queens waiting outside your door.

Why not have an easy reclining chair with a head rest in your office and receive your interviewers in an easy resting position? Your strength will hold out much better. I know — have tried it and it works. One can think quicker and better when the head is resting on a pillow and the spine is relieved of all strain and weight. . . .

Gratefully yours, for your supreme efforts and quick action in our Country's behalf,

Virginia Miller
Sierra Madre, California

*   *   *

Dear Presedent

It gave me pleasure to hear your over the radio a Sunday night for what you have accomplished since you have taken office was never done by no other man that was ever in the white house for it was a God send for the way the people suffered this winter when you have to sit in your house and cannot get coal I am for one I could not buy a bit of coal in two months and I am not the only one there are thousands of others but thank God the time has come at last when we have got a man like you to save us from any more suffering for as God had sent Moses to deliver his chosen people out of the land of bondage so also I think he send you to free us from the hands of a

◆§ 46 §◆

lot of robbers like wall st. . . . I do also admire the courage of your wife for the part she is taking to relieve this present distress the day that you had the bank bill passed around nine OClock we had an extra paper and when my wife heard the boys with it she worried she thought that they shot you I had to get one to make sure of it for every night when she says her prayers she says a prayer that nothing will happen to you I am wishing you a long and prosperous life to yourself and family from a friend

Thomas Kennedy
Troy, N.Y.

P.S. Please excuse this letter for I am not a very good hand at writing letters also please excuse mistakes

MARCH 15, 1933

His Excellency;
The President,

Don't cut any fire for a long, long, time.

Think of having the President talk to us in our parlor. Thats great!!! good voice too.

If you have the responsibility, Congress must positively give you the authority. This Dictator talk gives me the wearies. Anyhow, I'd rather have an honest man tell me what to do, and what not to do, than be up in the air all the time. . . .

Yes, drive out the money changers, as our Dear Lord did of old. Approach the throne of grace, often, often, often. the supply of power from thence, is inexhaustible. Our Dear Lord keep you.

Sincerely Yours

John Watson
Reiffton, Pa.

MARCH 15, 1933

Dear President Roosevelt:

. . . In your ten minute radio talk Sunday Night you said more than Mr. Hoover did in four years, and although you have culture, aristocratic breeding and wealth you have one priceless gift, that of reaching out to the "common people" with a deep sympathy and understanding, that goes into their hearts and you can talk their language and when you talked banking you talked banking so all could understand.

Even hide bound Republicans are saying "Roosevelt will be one of the greatest presidents this nation has ever known". So you will be if you do not over work. We framed your picture that was used for the cover of a recent Literary Digest. It hangs on the wall in our very humble home and we are very proud of it. . . .

Some fault finders say "America has a King". Well if America has a King we must have needed one, and thank heaven we have a good one in our Franklin Roosevelt. You are too burdened with duties, do not think I expect you to answer this. I only wished to write you some things that are over flowing the heart and mind of one of the common people.

With sincere wishes for your success in your wonderful plans for the good of this whole nation and hoping you will keep quite well and fit for all the strenous duties you are facing I am

Sincerely yours,

Mrs. Paul H. Russell
Haskell, Okla.

MARCH 13, 1933

Dear Mr. Roosevelt:

In all fairness, I must tell you that politically I was on the opposite side of the fence, but even in this rock-ribbed Republican community, we are back of you to the last ditch.

I listened to your inaugural address, and I never heard a public utterance to equal it. Your talk over the radio last night was a good follow-up. Won't you please keep on talking to us in one-syllable words, and take us into your confidence? That is what the garden variety of us need so much.

I have written to our Senator Reed, and told him how we feel, and have asked him to please stand by you. Suppose you do make mistakes — isn't it all trial and error, anyway? And you have wrought miracles this week —you put some backbone in the people. Aren't you proud of your friends? (I love that "My friends — " it warms my heart.) . . .

Faithfully,

(Mrs. A. L.) Mary L. Woodruff
Glenolden, Pennsylvania

MARCH 13, 1933

My dear Sir:

After hearing your radio address last evening, March 12th, in regard to banking, in which address you used words of one and two syllables and showed such a tremendous underlying sincerity in what you were saying that I felt heartily ashamed that I did not vote for you last November and I sincerely hope that your acts will be successful in relieving our country of at least some of it's present depressing influences so that I will feel even more ashamed of myself.

With my best possible wishes for success in your various undertakings in your not to be envied position, I am

Yours very truly,

G. J. Hansen
Milwaukee, Wis.

MARCH 18, 1933

Dear Friend;

And I address you thus in all sincerity, as I feel you are the peoples friend.

I am a dentist and am coming in contact with people all day long, and because of the nature of my work have quite an exceptionally good opportunity to talk to my patients on various subjects. I have been talking to them for two weeks now principaly about you, and I want to tell you Mr President, that you have Mr Average Citizen behind you almost 100%. They are all hoping that you will keep up just as you have started.

I a good Republican, am delighted with you, and sort of feel like one of my patients did, who said he felt like kicking himself because he did not vote for you. I am absolutely in favor of everything that you have done so far, including the beer bill, and I am a Dry. . . .

Mr President, go right to it, for the vast majority of us are right behind you, in fact the Republicans that I come in contact with are behind you just as much as the Democrats are.

Sincerely yours

W. H. Daniels
Paterson, N.J.
A good Republican or used to be.

MARCH 13, 1933

My dear Mr. Roosevelt:

The fact that I voted for the Socialist candidate in the last election should make this note all the more of a tribute. Your speech on the radio, Sunday night, March 12 made me feel, first, that the main reason you wanted the job of our chief executive in this most trying period of the world's history was because you wished the opportunity to help; second, that one should be thankful to be an American; third, that at the end of four years, in the same breath with the name of Abraham Lincoln, we shall mention that of Franklin D. Roosevelt.

Sincerely,

Carolyn Harrow
New York, N.Y.

MARCH 14, 1933

Dear Sir: —

I want to thank you for that splendid talk you gave us last Sunday night. We do appreciate the way in which you have literally taken "time by the forelocks" in this big banking problem of our's, and we know much will be accomplished — when confidence is restored.

We are not soon forgetting the folly of the last Congress, how those leaders spent time and money, when such vital issues were at stake, parleying over legalized beer.

To we, who were on the outer circles trying to inspire confidence and faith in our government — Well this was nauseating. Many poor souls threadbare in heart and soul, bowed down with want and debts — They do not want beer, to add to their misery and degradation, they want a chance to live, once more, honestly, and soberly; that is the desire of your American citizens. And we the christian citizens of U.S.A. will stand right back of you with our prayers, and this battle will be gloriously won; but please remember, Christ and beer will not mix, confidence will never be restored by legalized alcohol in any form, Do not make a "Pontious Pilate" of your self, for those clamoring for greed and money. Please do not seek to balance the budget by sacrificing the lives of our youth.

Humbly Submitted

(Mrs) Harvey K. Garrison
Bridgeton, N.J.

MARCH 22, 1933

Esteemed Mr. President: —

. . . On all sides, Mr. President, there are assurances that the nation supports you. These assurances may be gathered from the remarks of public speakers, from the pages of newspapers and magazines, and, above all, from the conversations of the great, common people assembled in groups and knots at every fireside and street corner. . . .

The final victory reserved for you, Mr. President, is to secure legislation compelling industry to divide profits equitably. Both capital and labor produce finished goods: both must share equitably in the fruits of production. A just profit to the factory or plant owner, a just "living wage" to the workingman! . . .

Your grateful fellow-citizen,

B. A. Bonte
Bellevue, Kentucky

MARCH 16, 1933

Dear Mr. President:

. . . Mr. President, so many people that I know, including many dyed-in-the-wool Republicans have become your enthusiastic supporters since listening to your radio talks, that I think it lies within your power to "turn the tide", as regards public spending. As you are aware, many persons well able to afford purchases have with held them due to the fear instilled in them during the last few years. The time has come to dispel this fear, and you, probably you alone, can end it.

Now this, Mr. President is my plan. If you, in your next radio talk, would tell the public, that you, having done, and continuing to do, together with your administration, everything possible to bring conditions to normal, now put it up to the American people to do their share, and request those among us who are able, every man, woman and child, to cast aside our fears, and spend for those things that we would legitimately spend if conditions had never deviated from normal. And, very important, to spend, not on "bargains", but wisely and well, not on the products of "coolie" or sweatshop labor, ground out by unscrupulous employers. Such "cheap" purchasing, for the consideration of price alone, is not consistent with the American tradition and should be condemned.

Mr. President, if you would do the above, I believe American business would receive the stimulus it so badly needs at the present time. Verily you will become a second Moses, leading your people out of the wilderness.

Most respectfully,

Theodore Abrams
New York, New York

MARCH 15, 1933

MY DEAR MR. PRESIDENT. AS AN INDIANA BUSINESS MAN I WANT TO EX-
PRESS MY PERSONAL APPRECIATION OF THE SUCCESS OF YOUR STAND IN
THE RECENT BANK SITUATION AND THE CONSTRUCTIVE POLICIES YOU ARE
CARRYING THROUGH. I FEEL POSITIVE YOUR RADIO MESSAGE TO THE
AMERICAN PUBLIC LAST SUNDAY NIGHT DID MORE TO BUILD CONFIDENCE
AND ELIMINATE FEAR WHICH HAS BEEN THE PRIMARY CAUSE OF OUR DIFFI-
CULTIES THAN ANY OTHER EXECUTIVE ACTION IN YEARS. IN MY HUMBLE
WAY PERMIT ME TO SUGGEST THAT YOU BROADCAST TO YOUR CITIZENS
NEXT SUNDAY EVENING THE THOUGHT THAT THE WEEK OF MARCH TWENTY
FIRST BE DEDICATED BY EVERY PATRIOTIC CITIZEN TO THE PAYMENT OF
EVERY JUST DEBT THAT IT IS POSSIBLE FOR HIM TO PERFORM. YOU COULD
EASILY CONVINCE THE PUBLIC AND EVERY BUSINESS MAN THAT THE END-
LESS CHAIN OF BENEFIT ACCRUING FROM THIS PROGRAM WOULD RESULT
IN A WONDERFULLY IMPROVED BUSINESS SITUATION THAT WOULD REACT
TO THE BENEFIT OF EVERY AMERICAN CITIZEN.

J. E. FEHSENFELD
INDIANAPOLIS, IND.

MARCH 12, 1933

Dear Sir,

Your wonderfully clear exposition (on the radio, just finished) of the
bank and banking situation will do a great deal toward restoring confidence
in our banking institutions, and I am sure has done much toward giving
you the fullest support of the country. May I suggest an additional thought
to you, viz: — that you announce to the people that bankers who have betrayed trusts imposed in them shall be brought to trial and punished. That
easy escape shall be impossible and sentences not be light.

Your assurance to the public along these lines is all that is now needed
to restore their fullest confidence.

Very truly yours,

H. A. Plusch
Philadelphia

MARCH 22, 1933

Sir:

May I say that I feel your batting average to date is perfect? Also that your radio address on the banking situation, in its simplicity and clearness, in its sympathetic presentation, and in its potency could not be excelled? When you need to enlist the masses, for you the radio is a perfect organ.

My visits to our national parks, from McKinley in Alaska to the Grand Canyon, have shown me that they all need more and better roads, as well as guard rails and walls, for the comfort of the people. May I suggest that I believe from 5,000 to 10,000 men could well be employed in this way?

May I express the opinion, based on a visit to Russia last summer, that your recognition of the Soviet Republics would within a comparatively few months be completely approved by practically all Americans?

Very truly yours,

Thos. C. Blaisdell
Slippery Rock, Pennsylvania

MARCH 16, 1933

My dear President:

I wish to congratulate you sincerely on your militant leadership, and to tell you that I was particularly pleased with your radio talk of last Sunday evening.

May I suggest, not in a critical, but in a helpful, spirit, that "status" is pronounced with a long "a", not a short one. Men in high positions often are feared by others who dare not make suggestions such as I have made, but I know you are the type of person who wishes to do things right and will welcome this information. . . .

Sincerely yours,

Carl Wheaton
St. Louis, Mo.

MARCH 13, 1933

My President Roosevelt: —

While not a member of your party, I wish to congratulate you upon the splendid work that you have done since March 4th. . . .

May I, with all due respect, suggest that when concluding a radio address to the people, such as the one you gave last night, that you close by saying, "Good-night" or "Good-bye"?

When an address is concluded so abruptly as the one was last night, it leaves one with a peculiar feeling that something has been left out. . . .

Yours very respectfully,

J. J. Quinn
Rahway, N.J.

MARCH 13, 1933

Our dear President Roosevelt.

We live in eastern Colo. on our homestead of 18 yrs. ago. I've been wondering if a letter, written by an insignificant little farmers wife, would ever reach you. So curiosity has persuaded me to try it. After hearing of your wonderful address, last nite, we felt you must be, for the benefit of we poor, harding working people. We sincerely hope so. For we done all we could for you. We are having a struggle during these perilous times but feel confident you are going to get us out. We have two boys. We are trying to put the oldest one thru high school, he is 16, a senior, hardly see how we are going to graduate him, but we're hoping for better prices soon. We have a little grain & if we can raise $25. or $50. we will be Sitting on Top of the World. Hoping you are going to do all possible, I am Sincerely

Mrs Frank Owens
Lycan, Colo.

MARCH 12, 1933

Dear President.

I am writing you this letter from my little farm home, which I bought two years ago, and for which my Dad put up the dough. I am an American born citizen, and so are my parents. . . . I have been a steam engineer for 27 years. I lost my left hand at the wrist that long ago, and have followed up the steam work until about two years ago, and since that time find it impossible to get work in that line, or any other. I am on the unemployed list, work, get a food order, only the work is about one day in three weeks. I am not starving or anything like that, as I raised most of the eats, but others I know are in bad shape. We help them out as we can, with clothes etc. My Nephew gave us a Radio about a month ago, and we heard your March 4 Inaguration Speech, and tonight Your Speech on Banking Situation, on our Radio. I think you are the man for the job. I feel you have the courage to go ahead and do things, and I say to you that all people in my section have wonderful faith in you. I hope you get my letter. I would love to have you please send a line or two direct from you to my Dear old Democrat Dad, who is also crippled. . . .

Adolph F. Brior
Rohrsburg, Pa.

Please read my letter, and let me know you got it.

MARCH 13, 1933

Dear President Roosevelt: —

I am writing in the name of the Citizens of Chicago to express our joy in our new President, we have suffered for 4 years and now we hope everything will be alright.

I heard you on the radio and I started to cry, for 3 years I have no work and have 4 children for 2 years we pay no rent, we lived in very bad conditions. For 28 years I have been a citizen and have never remember suffering before like this, when I heard your wonderful speech on the radio my heart felt good, I know we are going to have better times now.

I hope you'll not only be President for 4 years but for many, many years and the Best of Everything for Mrs. Roosevelt & Family. My name is Josie D'Natale. . . .

Don't forget you're the "Father of the United States" and Mrs. Roosevelt the "Mother" and we will look to you like a Child looks to its Mother and Father, to lead us in the right way. . . .

Best regards to you and your family.

yours truly,

Josie D'Natale
Chicago, Ill.

MARCH 12, 1933

Dear Preisdent Roosevelt

Please except this letter of thanks for your very very fine speech over the Raido this evening. it sure put the hearts back in the farmers around here and we are putting the old Grays in the plows in the morning and turn over the sod of prosperity again and feel like working, . . .

Yours very truly

Fred J. Mohrbacher and Family
New Brighton, Pa.

Please talk some more over the Raido when you get in shape and rested up. But do not over due your self,
We are all glad to hear you speak anytime
Thanks
Good Luck & health
God Bless you
I do not know how to write a letter to a Preidesent. But we are trying to tell you from our hearts.

MARCH 21, 1933

Dear Mr. President:

. . . I am only one of many thousands of citizens who have carried a burden that has been at the breaking point for some time. Our incomes, sav-

ings, homes, everything taken from us and we were helpless to defend ourselves against the forces that seemed bent on our destruction. But now our
heads are up again, and our backs will stiffen, too, because you have given
us a new hope — the hope that we can once again find ourselves and also
recover the pride in our country which we have been taught from the
cradle.

You will have plenty of opposition, Mr. President, and no doubt there
will be many bitter struggles for you, but one thing you may be sure of —
every honest man and woman in this great country is with you. If you have
any doubt of that you have only to talk to us as you did a week ago Sunday
night, telling us in the same simple, straightforward way what you want to
do, and we will see that Congress backs you up. Your greatest and surest
aid will be the radio.

May God bless you and keep you, Mr. President. We are a sorely tried
people and we need you very much, so please take care of yourself that you
may go on with the fine work you are doing. You will probably never fully
realize what you mean to so many of us.

Very sincerely yours,

Frances I. Hundley
Brooklyn, New York

MARCH 12, 1933

Hon. Sir,

I listened gratifiedly to your radio address anent the banking situation
this evening. From this humble quarter is reflected your own confidence of
the future stability of the banking system. However, Mr. President, I beg to
ask, "Then what?" . . .

In a brief note, Mr. President, I can only write in generalities, but permit
me to express this much; having stabilized the banks, and established the
soundness of America's financial "structure," you have made an impression
in your Herculean tasks by comparison as the vacancy created in a huge
granary by the removal of one grain by the toiling ant.

You must be well aware of what yet lies before you. Let us be warned,
then, not to indulge in previous exultation, lest we relax our efforts ere we
have attained the ultimate consummation of our aims.

I have presumed to address you thus, Mr. President, because I am imbued with the idea that you would welcome expressions of this character from humble citizens.

Respectfully,

Eugene V. Krell
St. Louis, Mo.

A NEW DEAL:
MAY 7, 1933

EUGENE KRELL, the author of the last letter printed in the previous section, was correct: banking reform was not enough. Thus eight weeks after FDR's first Fireside Chat — just past the middle point of the special session of the Seventy-Third Congress, which lasted from March 9 to June 16 — he took to the air to inform the American people how well he was performing what Krell called "Herculean tasks." He reminded his listeners that when he assumed office "the country was dying by inches." The crisis that beset the nation in March of 1933 "did not call for any complicated consideration of economic panaceas or fancy plans. We were faced by a condition and not a theory."[16]

As these words indicate, FDR was at pains throughout his second Chat to demonstrate that he had not been seduced by the Sirens of radical ideology — as most American radicals would have readily agreed. There had been only two alternatives open to him when he took office, he insisted. The first was to allow the process of deflation to continue until the entire economy was recapitalized at a lower level. The result would have been "extraordinary hardships on all property owners and all bank depositors, and . . . all persons working for wages through an increase in unemployment and a further reduction of the wage scale." He had concluded even before becoming President that such a policy "was too much to ask the American people to bear. It involved not only a further loss of homes and farms and savings and wages, but also a loss of spiritual values — the loss of that sense of security for the present and the future that is so necessary to the peace and contentment of the individual and of his family." The second alternative was to adopt a "prompt program applied as quickly as possible." Accordingly, he turned to members of both parties in Congress who agreed with him that "the methods of normal times had to be replaced in the emergency by measures that were suited to the serious and pressing requirements of the moment." Congress had not surrendered power, he declared; it had merely designated the President "as the agency to carry out certain of the purposes of the Congress. This was constitutional and is constitutional, and it is in keeping with the past American tradition."

Doubtless many listeners to FDR's second Fireside Chat — and certainly most members of Congress — recalled the military metaphors the President had used in his Inaugural Address two months earlier when he called for "a unity of duty hitherto evoked only in time of armed strife" and for the need to "move as a trained and loyal army willing to sacrifice for the good of a common discipline." He hoped that the normal balance of executive and legislative authority would be "wholly adequate to meet the unprecedented task before us." Should it not be, he would ask for the "broad Executive power that would be given to me if we were in fact invaded by a foreign foe." The people of the United States, he concluded, "have asked for discipline and direction under leadership. They have made me the present instrument of their wishes. In the spirit of the gift I take it."[17]

Eleanor Roosevelt found it "a little terrifying" that when her husband warned those gathered at his inauguration that he would assume wartime powers if necessary, "he received his biggest demonstration."[18] She was likely discomfited as well by the blasé reaction of the nation's newspapers, which reported his address in a matter-of-fact manner under such headlines as "FOR DICTATORSHIP IF NECESSARY," and were filled with statements like that of Representative Loring Black of New York praising Roosevelt's courageous willingness "to assume the entire burden of the complex problem himself."[19] "The iron hand of a national dictator," Governor Alfred M. Landon of Kansas remarked, "is in preference to a paralytic stroke."[20] Several weeks before Roosevelt's inauguration, the business magazine *Barron's* confessed that "we have been longing to see the superman emerge," and suggested to the incoming President that "a genial and light-hearted dictator might be a relief from the pompous futility of such a congress as we have recently had. . . . Only, let our semi-dictator smile upon us as he semi-dictates."[21]

Comparisons between Roosevelt and Mussolini and between the New Deal and fascism were common, but as the Socialist Party leader Norman Thomas understood, and as FDR demonstrated over and over, the new President had neither the temperament nor the inclination to be a dictator, even a genial one.[22] Indeed, Rexford Guy Tugwell, who as an economic adviser to FDR observed the New Deal closely from within, concluded that if not for Roosevelt, "we might have succumbed to a dictatorship. For that was the alternative, much in the air, when he took charge."[23] In many ways, FDR was an ideological innocent who accepted the politics — as he accepted the religion — he had been brought up with. Secretary of Labor

Frances Perkins — the first female Cabinet member in American history — was present during the following colloquy between Roosevelt and a young reporter:

> "Mr. President, are you a Communist?"
> "No."
> "Are you a capitalist?"
> "No."
> "Are you a Socialist?"
> "No," he said, with a look of surprise as if he were wondering what he was being cross examined about.
> The young man said, "Well, what is your philosophy then?"
> "Philosophy?" asked the President, puzzled.
> "Philosophy? I am a Christian and a Democrat — that's all."[24]

"He never talked about his religion or his beliefs," Eleanor Roosevelt observed, "and never seemed to have any intellectual difficulties about what he believed."[25]

Roosevelt lacked the strain of strong ideology that had prevented Herbert Hoover from reacting more freely and decisively to the economic and social crises wreaking havoc around him, or that prompted others to believe that the Depression afforded the country the opportunity to set off on a new course entirely. But that is not to say that he lacked a set of beliefs that guided him and set very real constraints around what he was able and willing to do. If there was a consistency in the many complex and often confusing turns the New Deal took, it was Roosevelt's threefold determination to end the suffering, to restore the confidence and spirit of the American people, and to save capitalism from itself through a program of reform. His characteristic openness allowed him to pursue these goals in an innovative manner. "The rules and remedies of the past probably do not form an answer to the restoration of the machine," he had declared as Governor of New York in 1930, "it is therefore only logical and not radical to insist that through experimentation . . . we must solve the social and economic difficulties of the present." A year later, Governor Roosevelt declared that it was the government's "definite obligation to prevent the starvation or the dire want of any of its fellow men or women who try to maintain themselves but cannot."[26]

FDR's willingness to search for and experiment with new remedies and his strong sense of the responsibility of the state to its people made him in his own words, "a little to the left of center," but he always carried with him a strongly traditional sense of the way things should be.[27] Roosevelt has often been treated as the complete political pragmatist — his adviser Raymond Moley grumbled about the President's "pragmatic oversoul"[28] — who could say along with Ralph Waldo Emerson: "no facts are to me sacred, none are profane. I simply experiment, an endless seeker, with no past at my back." To a much greater extent than he himself sometimes recognized, FDR did have a past at this back, a past that influenced him profoundly. He would open the presidential campaign of 1936 by declaring that liberalism was the best protection for farsighted conservatives: "Wise and prudent men — intelligent conservatives — have long known that in a changing world worthy institutions can be conserved only by adjusting them to the changing time. In the words of the great essayist, 'The voice of great events is proclaiming to us. Reform if you would preserve.' I am that kind of conservative because I am that kind of liberal."[29] The "so-called New Deal," Eleanor Roosevelt has written, "was, of course, nothing more than an effort to preserve our economic system."[30]

In his Fireside Chat of May 7, Roosevelt may have spoken of himself as the instrument designated to carry out the purposes of Congress, but his tone was that of a democratic leader trying to convince the American people that the "well-grounded, well-rounded plan" he proposed — much of which was still before Congress — was necessary if the nation was to be rescued from its calamity. Indeed, at the time of his second Chat, Congress had passed only three major pieces of reform or relief legislation: the Emergency Banking Act, which established the ground rules for the reopening of the banks; an act authorizing states to raise tax revenue and create jobs by allowing the sale of beer, which presaged the ratification of the Twenty-First Amendment ending Prohibition on December 5, 1933; and the act creating the Civilian Conservation Corps (CCC), which enlisted a quarter of a million unemployed young men — five hundred thousand at its peak in 1935 and more than three million overall by 1942 — to work in reforestation, flood prevention, and other conservation-oriented endeavors.

It was now necessary, FDR told his millions of listeners, for Congress to pass the rest of the legislation he had requested or was about to request. He mentioned specifically the Tennessee Valley Authority (TVA) to provide public coordination and development of the resources of a large and troubled area of the nation; the Farm Credit Administration (FCA) and the

Home Owners Loan Corporation (HOLC) to "ease the mortgage distress among the farmers and among the homeowners of the nation," and help them save their homes and farms; the Federal Emergency Relief Administration (FERA) to grant half a billion dollars to help states, counties, and municipalities "care for those who at this time need direct and immediate relief," and to create jobs through work relief for the employable needy; the Agricultural Adjustment Administration (AAA) to increase farm income and stem agricultural overproduction; the National Recovery Administration (NRA) "to give to the industrial workers of the country a more fair wage return, to prevent cutthroat competition, to prevent unduly long hours for labor, and at the same time to encourage each industry to prevent overproduction," by adopting codes governing their industry; the Public Works Administration (PWA) to provide more than three billion dollars to "enable the government to undertake public works, thus stimulating directly and indirectly the employment of many . . . in well-considered projects"; the Railroad Coordination Act to stimulate railroads, with government assistance, to create a more rational transportation system with less duplication and waste.

These measures of reform and relief, along with a number of acts not mentioned by FDR, made the first three months of his Administration — which newspaper reporters came to call the "Hundred Days" — one of the most productive and creative in the nation's history. It would be "wholly wrong" to call what he was proposing government control, Roosevelt insisted:

> It is rather a partnership — a partnership between Government and farming, a partnership between Government and industry, and a partnership between Government and transportation. Not a partnership in profits, because the profits will still go to the private citizen, but rather a partnership in planning, and a partnership to see that the plans are carried out.

Raymond Moley, who helped to write the second Fireside Chat, did not let this statement go without prolonged discussion. "You realize, then, that you're taking an enormous step away from the philosophy of equalitarianism and laissez-faire?" he asked the President as they worked on the Chat. "F.D.R. looked graver than he had been at any moment since the night before his inauguration," Moley recalled. After long moments of silence, Roosevelt replied: "If that philosophy hadn't proved to be bankrupt,

Herbert Hoover would be sitting here right now. I never felt surer of anything in my life than I do of the soundness of this passage."[31]

While he did not ignore completely the problem of the maldistribu-
tion of wealth that made it impossible for millions of Americans to buy the
goods being produced, Roosevelt's propensity to view the nation's problems as the result of aberrations rather than fundamental flaws in the system
made him more comfortable focusing on the problem of overproduction,
which, in a nation where there was so much want and outright hunger,
seemed to many to be no problem at all: "The people of this country have
been erroneously encouraged to believe that they could keep on increasing
the output of farm and of factory indefinitely and that some magician would
find ways and means for that increased output to be consumed with reasonable profit to the producer." "We cannot," he emphasized, "ballyhoo ourselves back to prosperity." Mere optimism was not enough: coordination
and planning were essential in industry, in agriculture, and in the world of
finance. He demonstrated his point with the cotton-goods industry. Ninety
percent of cotton manufacturers would agree tomorrow to eliminate starvation wages, child labor, long hours of employment, and overproduction,
he asserted.

> But, my friends, what good is such an agreement of the 90 per-
> cent if the other 10 percent of the cotton manufacturers pay star-
> vation wages and require long hours and employ children in
> their mills and turn out burdensome surpluses? The unfair 10
> percent could produce goods so cheaply that the fair 90 percent
> would be compelled to meet the unfair conditions. And that is
> where government comes in. Government ought to have the
> right and will have the right, after surveying and planning for
> an industry, to prevent, with the assistance of the overwhelm-
> ing majority of that industry, all unfair practices and to enforce
> that agreement by the authority of government. . . .
>
> And, my friends, the same principle that is illustrated by that
> example applies to farm products and to transportation and to
> every other field of organized private industry.

"Our policies are wholly within the purposes for which our American
constitutional government was established 150 years ago," he reiterated. "I
do not deny that we may make some mistakes of procedure as we carry out
this policy," he admitted, and then turned to familiar cultural metaphors, a

device he used frequently in his Fireside Chats: "I have no expectation of making a hit every time I come to bat. What I seek is the highest possible batting average, not only for myself but for the team."

He closed his second Fireside Chat by thanking the American people:

> Throughout the depression you have been patient. You have granted us wide powers; you have encouraged us with a widespread approval of our purposes. Every ounce of strength, every resource at our command, we have devoted and we are devoting to the end of justifying your confidence. We are encouraged to believe that a wise and sensible beginning has been made. In the present spirit of mutual confidence, in the present spirit of mutual encouragement we go forward.

MAY 8, 1933

My dear Mr. President: —

I have just listened to your broadcast over the radio and feel that I have to write to you. I must tell you what effect your address to the people has had on me.

I am a member of the graduating class of the Abraham Lincoln High School of Brooklyn, New York and am not eighteen yet. Things aren't as nice at home as they might be. Bills keep coming in and Dad has to scrape up every cent he can get hold of to pay up. I see the way the world is treating him. With this staring me in the face I was a bit gloomy about my future. However, after listening to your speech, I feel as if there is a silver lining to every cloud. I feel inspired. I feel that if I go to college for more education I will not lose any opportunity that I might find during the four years to go to work. . . .

I am now going to go to bed with a fervent prayer in my heart for you, our country and God.

May God bless you!

Yours sincerely,

Jack Hamovitz
Brooklyn, N.Y.

MAY 8, 1933

My Dear President: —

For 25 years, I have been an ardent Socialist. the soap box, the lecture platform, the class-room are the means that I have used to further the Cause. I have been in jail for it at times.

Since your inauguration, I have withheld judgement — for once in my life I have not used the expression "He is only a Henchman of the Capitlast classes" I have faith in you and the people I meet every day in the business world have faith in you. I hardly think that you realize the power that you really have over the American people. You don't half realize what faith they have in you and they are willing to follow you blindly. If I a Socialist trust you, I can see why they worship you.

Your speech to-night was magnificent — and remember when a soap-boxer admits the other fellow speech is good — thats something

Mr. President, this ecomic distress that we are suffering from is getting too much for us all to stand. If you will help alleviate some of the suffering I see every day well let the historians of the future draw the conclusion

Well its a pleasure to listen to you — and Mr. President — I have a suspicion that you know your Karl Marx pretty well.

Good Luck to you and my best wishes to your family — who knows I am liable to call up my friend & comrade Norman Thomas three years from now & tell him I am out working for Franklin D. and I am going to vote for him and the party can throw me out if they want to.

As a former officer of the U.S.A. I salute the Greatest President since Lincoln.

Sincerely yours,

Harry N. Perlmutter
Brooklyn, N.Y.

MAY 16, 1933

My dear Mr. President: —

It is with genuine pleasure that I refer to your radio talk of Sunday night of May 7th.

Dictators dictate, Mr. President, Democrats discuss. The important difference is not so much in what they do, as the spirit in which they do it.

The dictatorship myth, woven so industriously about your excellency, was knocked over the fence on Sunday night. And it was all so simple. You took advantage of the radio and the great American Sunday evening at home, and for the second time talked over the problems of the day as a family matter with the families of the nation. You talked as easily and as informally as a neighbor who had just dropped in to visit the folks.

There was no more authority, mystery or pose about your talk than in the old time political arguments around the stove and cracker barrel of a country store or in the old fashioned wooden Indian city cigar store. Truly Mr. Roosevelt you revived the modes and manners of the primitive forums of American democracy. The old town meeting is now a nation's meeting.

The simplicity of your language was matched by the clearness of the thought. The democracy of your good self was reflected in your use of a baseball term to make it plain to everybody. The value of the great American game in teaching men and women how to visualize social, economic and political set ups and conditions was forcefully demonstrated when you said "I have no expectations of making a hit every time I come to bat — what I seek is the highest possible batting average, not only for myself but for the team".

Every man, woman and child over six knows exactly what it means. How could you say it so well and so plainly, if there was no game like baseball that everybody from president to street sweeper understands. . . .

Finally the clear statement of what you and the people want in the way of control of business. The dictionaries are crammed with long words which describe all the variations and shadings of the possible relations of government and private business. You used none of them. But you told your whole story in one word "partnership" — a word that is almost primer English, and has meant more in America than anywhere else. . . .

Partnership and dictatorship are at the two opposite poles of political thought and feeling — and never the twain shall meet. The grumpy men who insist on looking for gloom and who do not realize that America is not chained in slavery to worn-out ideas can sit in the dark corner and mumble the word "dictator" to themselves as long as they please. This country, under your great leadership, is going ahead without them.

It is the writer's intention to visit Washington at some future date and it will be his pleasure to make the necessary arrangements to meet you.

Very respectfully yours,

James J. Dunn
Chicago, Ill.

MAY 10, 1933

Dear President Rosevelt

You will no dout think I am a good one to write this as I am a woman with very little Education as you can see by my letter. but we can know Jesus just the same. I listened to you talk on the Radio and enjoyed it so mutch. people did not need a high school Education to understand it eather. what

I want is to ask you if you would not like to set one hour for the whole United states to pray that the Lord would hold fast to you and our Congres guiding you in all that is said & done that his power will sweep our country as a christian nation making our government one led by him for the word says with out him we will fall. it seams to me one hour the 30 day of May would be a nice time as that day we shoe our respect to the old soldiers. In Jesus God the Father & our government means all in all to us. God bless & help you to trust all with him

Mrs. Nellie Spunaugler
Salina, Kans.

MAY 8, 1933

Dear President Roosevelt

What could have been more wonderful I cannot find words too high to praise you your speech, was not a speech, but, a heart to heart talk, like a Brother talking to Brothers and Sisters. . . .

Your voice was as clear as a Bell and as steady as a rock —

When you coughed a little, I wanted to run and get you some water, yes we all love you, and pray for your good health and also that of your whole family

Yours very Sincerely

Mrs Anna Koulevard
Pawtucket, R.I.

MAY 10, 1933

Dear Mr. Roosevelt: —

I listened to your speech over the radio Sunday and want to say that I surely enjoyed it very much.

I am sure every right thinking American would say that what you have done so far has been for the benefit of mankind and not for the profiteers alone.

If you can in some way start the factories running again I think that will be one of the greatest blessings that could come to the American people.

In this connection I wish to suggest or ask about the employment of women in industry. It is my understanding that millions of women who do not have to work for a living are now employed I have spent most of my life in Detroit, Mich and from my own experience in trying to secure a position as an accountant I find most all positions are held by girls and women and also in applying for any kind of factory work conditions are the same.

I have always beleived and think it is true that the home is the heart of the nation, if the home is destroyed the nation surely will be.

Could not something be done to prohibit employers from hiring any woman that does not of necessity have to work. If possible I am sure millions more heads of families would be put back to work at better wages than are paid women and many homes saved as well as many made happier.

Considering the Christian spirit of all your undertakings I do hope you may find some remedy for what I think is one of the greatest evils of the country.

Anticipating a favorable reply at your convenience I will close wishing Gods richest blessing on you. Very truly yours

Norman Best
Greenville, Ohio

MAY 8, 1933

Dear Sir:

I heard your radio address last night and regarded it as encouraging.

I classify myself as a conservative but realize that present conditions required measures that might not be justified under other circumstances. I sincerely hope that an effort will be made to keep the government out of business as much as possible and that we will not have such inflation as to make money and security values doubtful.

I have always been a Republican but desire to say that I am very pleased with your official acts and likewise am pleased to express to you that the general sentiment is ninety per cent in your favor. This is considerably more than the seventy-five per cent that you referred to in your address last night. . . .

You have the commendation of the people of this country and will continue to have it unless your measures become too extreme. At present you are "ace high".

With best wishes for your continued success, I am,

Sincerely,

George Livesey
Bellingham, Washington

MAY 9, 1933

Dear Mr. President —

I have listened with great interest to your two broadcasts over the radio and I sincerely hope that somehow this short letter may reach you. I am a proprietor of a drug store in an industrial neighborhood and am familiar in a small way with the condition and hardships of the workingman. Within the last two months, in our neighborhood I have heard on good authority that several aeroplane factories have been hiring technical school boys for sheet metal and other work at very meagre wages while former employees are still waiting for their jobs. A number of these places are working on contracts for the government — General Aviation Corp. and Glen Martin — aeroplane manufacturer.

It seems to me that such action is contrary to the principles brought out in your talks. . . .

We — small insignificant citizens are following as never before in history — the action of our president and we are all behind him in his fight for prosperity. The influential citizen, however too often preaches one thing and practices something entirely different.

Very Truly,

John Donnet
Baltimore, Md.

MAY 8, 1933

Dear Sir

I listened to your speech last night and read it again this morning. Thank you!

There is hope that the measures you are taking may be effective. When you took office we were rapidly drifting toward a bloody revolution. Thanks to you there is now some light ahead.

Sincerely yours

L. L. Brande
Chicago, Ill.

MAY 8, 1933

Dear President:

Listened to your Radio address last night telling about what the National Legislature had done for the "Forgotten Man" Nothing has been done to help him according to my way of thinking.

Everything that has been done is constitutional you said in your address maybe so, but I demand you read the Declaration of Independence as you seem to have Forgotten that there is anything like equality for all the people of this land as all men are created equal. . . .

The Democratic party has had a great opportunity to do something for the people but does not seem to care to take advantage of the chance to go down in history as fighting the battle of the Forgotten man.

The Forgotten man will have to fight his own battle alone and without any help from the National Government. . . .

It is ridiculous for the Mortgage holders of this Nation to demand payment of interest when there is not enough money in circulation to even carry on the exchange of commodities necessary for the welfare of the people. I would write more a lot more but I feel that it is useless as it does not seem to have any effect whatever.

Hawkin Anderson
Clayton, Wisconsin

MAY 10, 1933

The Honorable President Of This Great Country. Please Except my Sincere Congratulations on your Wonderful, Sincere from the Heart, Radio Speech, of the Past Sabbath Day. My Object in Writing is many fold. Having been out of Employment the Past Three years, I am unable to send A Telegram of Congratulations, Is One Reason, another Reason is because I want to Apologize for not Having Voted for you. I am Sure, Had I known, That you realy were with the forgotten Man, I would Have Voted More Intelligently, and lastly I want to make a Suggestion, which might meet with your Approval. It is your Desire, to put as Many Men as Possible to Work, to the best Interest of this Great Country. As you Drive along the Highways you Notice many Pedestrians walking along on the Auto Right of way, Endangering their Own lives, and the lives of the occupants of the cars. Why not put Thousands of men to work Building about 14 or 18 Inch cement walks along the Roadways and Prevent Many Serious Axidents, to School Children, and Pedestrians. In General, Thank you, I am with Greatest Trust and Respect, yours very truly,

H. H. Greenberg
Cleveland, Ohio

MAY 10, 1933

Dear Friend

I have to Congratulate you that address you give us over the air last Sunday night and I know you don the whole Country good I heard so many People talk about that Address you maid over the Radio last Sunday night . . . there is one thing that I will ask you if you could do something about them Banks that Closed in 1930 and 1931 where we Poor working People lost nearly all our little savings that we had I'm one of them Mr Roosevelt I had a few $100 in the United Security Trust Company Phila Pa they Close there Doors Oct 1931 and got a small amount of it in three different Payments But the remainder is still over $500 the 27th day of November 1932 was the last that I heard of them which I'm very much in need of now I'm about 19 months out of work now Carpenter by trade for 31 years and was Raised on a Farm Schwenksville Pa My age is 52 Healthy and able to do any kind of work when ask for a Job they ask me if I have a Family I say no I ask a Man here some time ago weather a man like me is suppose to starve he said No, My Wife died in 1919 and had two Babies to Raise which are 2 Boys yong gentelman now 16 and 18 years of age and I'm very Proud of them But all most ashamed to look in there face now because I was never before out of a Job and had Money to Pay for there good training But I hope there is a better day coming again it looks so. . . .

> I remain
> Sincere Yours
>
> Benj B Tyson
> Lansdale, Pa.

P.S. Hope to here From you Some time

MAY 8, 1933

Dear Sir

I have heard your wonderful speech over the Radio and it was wonderful.

I am comming to you for help in the line of labor as all my money is now in the Bldg & loan Assn of which was taken over by the State for Liquidation of which i can not get nothing to live on so i ask you to give me a job so i can support my family

Thanking you for your help and also see that i get my money out of this Bldg & loan assn. for if Ever i knead my money it now

> You Trully
>
> John Harmon
> Toledo, Ohio

MAY 9, 1933

Dear Mr. Roosevelt,

I heard your message on the air last night, and think you are the most wonderful president we have ever had, you are a life saver to the whole world same as the States. But all your bills you have put before the Houses you have not given the widows that is left with children a thought. I have four small ones oldest 12 youngest 6, been a widow over 4 years, up to over a year ago had a job that paid where I saved some. But now I've used it all up so what is to become off the widows, and men, and women of to-morrow. if some way is not provided for the mothers to support them. I do not want help from the county, as they have more now than they can pay, as no one is able hardly to pay taxes and that is what the county depends on. All I ask for is a job that I can make an honest living with. Will close as every second of you time is very valuable to the whole U.S.A.

A Worried Widow
Leesburg, Fla.

P.S. My husband is dead.

MAY 15, 1933

Dear Friend,

I have heard your wonderfull talk over the Radio and I know you are sincere in your help for the farmer. I have my garden all planted we have had splendid rains here this spring but a drought for two years before could I ask you just where I could borrow $52 for baby chicks and the feed to start them out. the 50 for the chicks and two for chick mash. I have only 25 hens and they are Leghorns and of course they do not sit. I have been waiting for the New Deal. but it is getting late for baby chicks. I should get them by the 22th of May — so they will lay for us this winter. I would be glad too pay this back out of the chickens this fall. I want too can the garden surplus and raise chickens and help out my Husband in any way I can. our bank in Canby is just cashing cream checks. Could you find time to ans my letter I would be more than pleased.

Respectfully

Mrs. George Plack
Canby, Minn.

MAY 7, 1933

Dear Mr. Roosvelt:

I have just heard that splendid talk over the radio. It sure did come in good and clear. "We are for you."

My Father and Mother died some years ago leaving me to care for myself. I was reared on the farm I am now finishing School by my own efforts. It has been a tough battle.

What would you sugjest for me to do now? I am past twenty years old but like advice.

Very sincerely yours,

Walter C. Tabor
Oklahoma City, Okla.

*   *   *

Sir:

Please accept the enclosed poem as my means of congratulating you on your splendid work.

Your successful speech Sunday night gave me the inspiration.

I hope it pleases you.

Sincerely,

Laura E. Park
Greenville, Illinois

OUR PRESIDENT

The Hero of our hopeless hour,
   Alone to fight the foe —
Into the battle front he rides
   To fight Depression's Woe . . .

We are saved from grave disaster,
   We are free from selfish scorn.
Our President has faced the Night;
   And a new day is born.

THE FIRST HUNDRED DAYS:
JULY 24 AND OCTOBER 22, 1933

FDR'S NEXT TWO FIRESIDE CHATS — the last ones he was to deliver during his first year in office — were devoted to explaining and defending the accomplishments of the first hundred days, which he insisted were "not just a collection of haphazard schemes but rather the orderly component parts of a connected and logical whole."[32]

In the first of these addresses, on July 24, Roosevelt took obvious pride in the success of his banking policy — "Today only about 5 per cent of the deposits in national banks are still tied up" — and the various acts designed to help Americans pay off their mortgages and save their homes and farms. He described how the Civilian Conservation Corps had not only given employment to three hundred thousand young men in "practical and useful work" but also used their wages to help support "the nearly one million people who constitute their families."* He explained how the more than three billion dollars in public works would provide jobs in "thousands of self-sustaining state and municipal improvements." These he described as "the foundation stones" — the measures necessary to reestablish credit and provide "as much work as possible through governmental agencies."

He then turned to what he called "the links which will build us a more lasting prosperity." Although overproduction remained high on Roosevelt's list of the prime evils crippling the nation, he finally focused on the problem of distribution of income as well. Paraphrasing Lincoln's famous pronouncement that a nation cannot exist half slave and half free, Roosevelt decreed that "lasting prosperity" cannot be attained "in a nation half boom and half broke."

> If all our people have work and fair wages and fair profits, they
> can buy the products of their neighbors and business is good.
> But if you take away the wages and the profits of half of them,

---

*The CCC provided room and board for its enrollees and paid them thirty dollars a month, twenty-five dollars of which was sent directly to their families.

business is only half as good. It doesn't help much if the fortunate half is very prosperous — the best way is for everybody to be reasonably prosperous.

FDR singled out the National Recovery Administration — to which he devoted the substantial portion of this Chat — as the instrument best designed to assure this "reasonable" national prosperity. What he termed the "economic hell of the past four years" had been created by the lack of coordination and cooperation in industry. The NRA was based upon the model of industrial self-government and cooperation experimented with during World War One and continued in the private trade associations of the 1920s. The New Deal added to this voluntary program the guiding hand of the government, which authorized industries, in consultation with representatives of labor and the general public, to establish codes regulating wages, competition, and labor practices. These would be submitted to the government and when approved would be binding on all members of the industry. Labor's right to organize and bargain collectively was guaranteed. This "democratic self-discipline in industry," carried out "in the big industries, in the little shops, in the great cities and in the small villages" would make possible "general increases in wages and shortening of hours sufficient to enable industry to pay its own workers enough to let those workers buy and use the things that their labor produces." It was an old principle, FDR insisted, "that people acting in a group can accomplish things which no individual acting alone could even hope to bring about."

As in his Inaugural Address, Roosevelt utilized the metaphors of war to rally the American people "in this great summer offensive against unemployment." He asked that all businesses that adopted NRA codes display on their premises as "a badge of honor" an emblem with the NRA's official blue eagle and the legend "We do our part." He asked the American people to favor those employers. While "the shirking employer may undersell his competitor," Roosevelt charged, "the saving he thus makes is made at the expense of his country's welfare." He requested all businesses — "the big fellows and the little fellows" — to "write or telegraph to me personally at the White House, expressing their intention of going through with the plan. And it is my purpose to keep posted in the post office of every town, a Roll of Honor of all those who join with me." As Roosevelt hoped, the NRA with its symbolic Blue Eagle, its parades, and its ebullient director,

General Hugh Johnson, whose bearing matched his title, became for a time the very symbol of national unity and recovery. The ubiquitous eagle became a familiar part of American popular and folk culture. It wasn't long before the Mississippi bluesman Walter Vinson was singing:

> Now, the Government said right from the start,
> Do as he say do: "We will do our part." . . .
>
> It's on windows and doors in the shape of a bird,
> You don't have to wonder or neither say you heard.
> Lord, the Government's before me, oh, and I can't go wrong,
> Oh, the reason I'm singing this old lonesome song.[33]

FDR ended his July Chat by turning to the deeply ingrained American notion of will. He related the question asked after Andrew Jackson's death: "Will he go to Heaven?" and the reply: "He will if he wants to."

> If I am asked whether the American people will pull themselves out of this depression, I answer, "They will if they want to." . . . I have no faith in "cure-alls" but I believe that we can greatly influence economic forces. I have no sympathy with the professional economists who insist that things must run their course and that human agencies can have no influence on economic ills . . . but I do have faith, and retain faith, in the strength of common purpose, and in the strength of unified action taken by the American people.

It was in the midst of this third Fireside Chat that FDR reminded his audience that they were not only listening to the President of the United States but to a fellow human being. He paused, asked for a glass of water, took an audible sip, and explained: "My friends, it's very hot here in Washington tonight."[34] He then assured the people that they had weathered the worst:

> We are not going through another Winter like the last. I doubt if ever any people so bravely and cheerfully endured a season half so bitter. We cannot ask America to continue to face such needless hardships.

Within the first hour after the Chat FDR received five thousand telegrams and enough phone calls to swamp the White House lines. "AF-

TER LISTENING TO THE PRESIDENT'S APPEAL," a woman telegraphed from Long Island, "I AM RAISING MY MAID'S WAGES 10 PER CENT." The following day, as the telegrams multiplied, the firm of Farrar & Rinehart followed suit, informing the President: "EMPLOY-EES' SALARIES INCREASED 10 PER CENT."[35] Hugh Johnson, the head of the NRA, called this "deluge of telegrams of approval and agreement . . . the most inspiring thing that has happened in this country since the war — the men and women of a great nation, who for more than four years have been stunned and helpless under one of the worst blights that ever plagued a people, suddenly stirring to one man's voice, and rising together like a vast army from a dismal bivouac at a clear bugle call at day-break."[36]

It was on a considerably cooler night in October that FDR delivered his fourth and final Fireside Chat of 1933. He took up where he had left off in July, examining the state of the nation. Although some economic indices — especially production — were lower than they had been when he last ad-dressed his fellow citizens, Roosevelt remained upbeat in a Chat which Rexford Guy Tugwell characterized as "a masterpiece." Looking back on the address more than four decades later, Tugwell wrote: "As I read it through now, so many years afterward, and recall the troubled situation of that fall, I am still amazed at its confidence and its appeal. It did certainly put a better face on the situation than was warranted; but it had almost the same calming effect as the Inaugural."[37]

Roosevelt contrasted what his administration had inherited — "In the early spring of this year there were actually and proportionately more peo-ple out of work in this country than in any other nation in the world" — with "the edifice of recovery" the New Deal was endeavoring to construct: "the temple which, when completed, will no longer be a temple of money-changers or of beggars, but rather a temple dedicated to and maintained for a greater social justice, a greater welfare for America." Once more he spoke of the millions of jobs being created, of the humanitarian relief being extended, of the public works projects being constructed. Once more he made it clear how directly involved the New Deal was in the lives of the American people by asking all creditors to refrain from foreclosing on farms and homes "until every mortgagor in the country shall have had full opportunity to take advantage of Federal credit," and by urging "any family in the United States about to lose its home" to telegraph "at once either to the Farm Credit Administration or the Home Owners Loan Corporation in Washington requesting their help." In the face of often well founded criticisms that the billions of dollars of public works projects were being implemented too slowly and deliberately out of a determination not to create scandals by spending the funds too loosely, FDR appealed to states and municipalities to create "proper projects" and apply to Washington for public works money as quickly as they could. Once more he dwelt on the NRA: "It has abolished child labor. It has eliminated the sweat shop. It has ended sixty cents a week paid in some mills and eighty cents a week paid in some mines."

Finally, he revealed the newly adopted and, as it turned out, relatively short-lived policy of restoring prices from their deflated state by manipulating the currency through the government purchases of gold at prices above the world market. Though this policy may not have worked as he hoped it would, and though there were complaints that it was one of the few proposals he set forth that was unclear,[38] the purposes FDR articulated — "the permanent welfare and security of every class of our people" — registered with his audience:

> The object has been the attainment of such a [price] level as will enable agriculture and industry once more to give work to the unemployed. It has been to make possible the payment of public and private debts more nearly at the price level at which they were incurred. It has been gradually to restore a balance in the price structure so that farmers may exchange their products for the products of industry on a fairer exchange basis.

"I have told you tonight the story of our steady but sure work in building our common recovery," Roosevelt concluded:

> In my promises to you both before and after March 4th, I made two things plain: First, that I pledged no miracles and, second, that I would do my best.
>
> I thank you for your patience and your faith. Our troubles will not be over tomorrow, but we are on our way and we are headed in the right direction.

JULY 24, 1933

Dear Mr. Roosevelt: —

I just listened to your talk on the radio.

May I say that it gave me the thrill of a life time.

It made me feel as though you were really one of us — in other words, a man that you could say to, "Come on, here's a can of worms, let's go fishing." Trudge down a dusty road, arm in arm, your poles over the shoulders and be close to — well, a regular guy.

With every best wish for your success and health, I am,

Sincerely yours,

Frank W. Hadley
Oakland, Calif.

P.S. Of course I realize that the chances of Mr. Roosevelt ever seeing this letter is very remote but at least a good thought can hurt nobody.

JULY 26, 1933

[Addressed to Marvin H. McIntyre, Secretary to the President]

Dear Sir:

My reason for addressing this communication to you is that I realize full well the absurdity of my hoping to reach President Roosevelt himself by letter.

In this morning's Washington Post I read that shortly after his broadcast of monday evening the President asked Mr. Butcher of Columbia Broadcasting Company: "Was it all right for me to have said that about the glass of water?"

I want to tell you what my own reaction was to that spontaneous insertion: I was already inspired by the challenging manner in which the Chief was making his appeal to the country, but I was inspired by words coming from the height of a great man in a great office — down to me. When the speaker uttered the parenthesis about the glass of water, however, the human element of the speech was immeasurably reinforced. I was reminded that it was a man of flesh and blood who was talking to the country and to me, and my own attitude of comradeship and loyalty was correspondingly strengthened.

Among the group of my family and friends who listened to the speech there was a general laugh, a laugh of friendship and understanding, and from the later comments of others I am certain that the unpremeditated remark was received in the most favorable way.

If there is an opportunity, and you happen to think of it, would you be so kind as to mention this letter to the President? My identity is of no importance. I would just like for him to know what I know about his listeners' reaction to the remark which he is reported to have questioned.

Respectfully yours,

J. Harvey Edmonston
Washington, D.C.

P.S. TO MR. MCINTYRE's SECRETARY: Please show this letter to Mr. McIntyre.

JULY 25, 1933

Dear Mr. President;

Doubtless the men who necessarily supervise your mail, and who do not know what the "little man" is, will not let you ever see this letter, but you ought to see it. . . .

The forgotten man has been forgotten, if he was ever really remembered. I happen to be an approved attorney for the Federal Land Bank, and on publication of the information about the new loan legislation, the little man came to see me vainly hoping that at last he had been remembered. He is representative of thousands of farmers in North Carolina, owning maybe 50 acres of land and doing all of his own work, and about to lose his farm under a mortgage. But to get the loan he is obliged to pay $20 in advance for appraisals, and another $10 for a survey, and he no more has that much cash than he has the moon. I have written to everyone from Mr. Morgenthau on down about this, and no one is interested. The prevailing idea seems to be that if a man is that poor, he should stay poor.

Before any of this loan and public works legislation was enacted, I wrote you that you ought to put at least one human being in each supervising body, and by that I meant a man who actually knows there is a "little man" in this nation and that he never has had a fair chance, and that he deserves one. I hope yet that somehow you may remember this forgotten little man, who has no one in high places to befriend him.

Respectfully yours,

Bruce Craven
Trinity, North Carolina

JULY 25, 1933

Dear Mr. President:

As I telegraphed you, I went purposely last night to the New York Athletic Club to hear your magnificent speech, and also to get the reaction of men, none of whom I knew or knew me.

There were between three or four hundred men in the room listening to what you had to say. During your speech there were bursts of applause several times and when it was ending I wandered from group to group exchanging a few words here and there to get their reaction. There was not a man present who did not, in every way, back up everything you said and they were especially pleased at the way you handled the Child Labor situation throughout this nation. You told the truth when you said that we could not go through another winter like the last one. The situation is drastic, but I feel convinced, more than ever, that the outcome will be a great success, and that at least five or six million men will be back to work by Christmas through the moves you are making. As I see it it also comes to the front door, at this moment, of every good citizen in this country to back you up to the full, and I want you to know that as far as I am concerned, I will be only too delighted to drop all business and other things that I am doing and fulfill any small job, naturally without any compensation, from now until as long as you want me, to try and help this matter out, if you should desire my services. I also feel that I can, should you wish it, round up many other men who feel exactly the way I do. I have seen enough of the unemployed when I was connected with them on Long Island to know that we must find work for them at once. It is impossible, as you know to raise money any more from those who would be only too delighted to give, but are not in a position to do so.

Again wishing you all the success in the world in this undertaking, which you are so fearlessly going into, and in which I know the entire nation is behind.

Yours as ever,

Aymar Johnson
New York

JULY 25, 1933

My dear President:

Your radio talk last night was the brightest ray of hope for the future of the American Nation that I have seen in many a year. . . .

At present I have $.22 in my pocket but we have a home and other real estate free from encumbrance except $12,000.00 on a 200 acre farm in Logan Co. I was with my brother in the architect business until the slump nearly closed us up. He is still keeping the chair warm in the office in the hope that the New Deal will finally bring results although he has not been able to pay expenses for several years. I have been out since 1929 and have used up all my savings. Our bank has been closed since March 4th which has tied up my wife's and son's small savings. We are living on what my son gets working three days a week for $9.00. I am registered at the local labor bureau but being 62 years old there is little chance of results from there unless my technical training gives me a chance upon the Farm Relief or some other Federal project. I will starve before I will pauperize myself as required by the new Illinois relief law by applying for relief. There are thousands of others of the same mind.

. . . The Republican Party has been controlled by the exploiters and I hope now that the American people are convinced that it is not a good business proposition to turn all their savings over to private individuals to use as they see fit for private profit. The control of the money was given Congress by the Constitution and it should be taken from private control and returned to the Government. The time is again ripe for driving the money changers from the temple.

Like Frankenstine they have created an immortal monster in human form with all the human selfishness in concentrated form but without the redeeming features of a soul, conscience, love and the Divine human qualities that separate man from the beasts. If we do not wake up to the danger and realize what we have done this corporate monster is going to utterly destroy us and own and control all branches of profitable business and all humanity will be again abject slaves. . . .

You have already eliminated child slavery from industry are you going to be able to free us all from wage slavery and the domination of wealth and material possessions? . . .

Yours truly,

Ralph W. Braucher
Chicago, Ill.

JULY 24, 1933

My Dear Mr. President.

Have just heard your wonderful broadcast and it so filled me with new hope that I find it difficult to restrain from writing you to express my feelings toward you.

Your outstanding achievement is the abolition of child labor (of which I have been a victim) a blot on the American nation that was perpetuated till now. . . .

And your statement regards the workingman and his rights made me feel as if we the workers are about to enter a new world.

If I may, I have elevated you in my mind on an equal with Abraham Lincoln.

Abraham Lincoln freed the chattel slaves and now Mr. President you are about to free the child and wage slaves.

May you have strength and health to continue the great work in the emancipation of the workers.

Yours Respectfully,

Rocco Verri
Dania, Fla.

JULY 31, 1933

Dear Mr. President,

Your radio address of July 25th, dealing with business and industrial problems, was highly stimulating and inspiring to the entire nation. However, there is another group of activities in gripping need of the same kind of encouragement from the head of the nation — namely the cultural arts.

At this particular time orchestras, opera companies, civic theatres and other similar organizations are engaged in the difficult task of raising sufficient funds for their continued existence in the autumn. This means a desperate struggle, not only to save valuable and important art organizations, but also to prevent a large increase of unemployed among the already huge number of musicians, actors, etc. without means of subsistence or prospect of work.

If you, Mr. President, were willing to state that the arts should not be neglected in the general plan for industrial and commercial recovery, the uplifting and practical result would be incalculably great and far-reaching.

The successful maintenance of our musical and art institutions means the employment of many thousands, and an important contribution to the higher culture of our country.

A few words from you at this critical moment would inspire many to acts of courage and generosity.

Sincerely yours,

Ossip Gabrilowitsch
Detroit, Michigan

OCTOBER 23, 1933

Dear Mr. President:

A recent New York Times Magazine says you get several thousand letters a day, mostly encouraging and approving but some of a different tone. You could hardly expect the confidence and approval to be unanimous. But around here it is nearly so. Even most of the farmers are not yet afflicted with the heart sickness which is said to come from hope deferred. They believe in you and trust you and I am sure that trust and confidence will be greatly enhanced by your radio address of last night. I have listened with profound interest to all of your radio addresses. May I say that they are gems, — models of lucidity, simplicity, clarity, and vastly effective. They ring true, with no adulteration of demagogic sophistry. To illustrate:

A twelve-year-old boy was deeply immersed in a tale of stirring adventure last night when your address came on (8 P.M., M.S.T.). He was asked to lay aside his book and listen to the address of the President.

"Aw, Ma, what's the use? The president's talk is not for me. I won't understand it."

"Well, listen awhile, anyway. You may get something out of it that will help you in school."

So he did. After two minutes the interest and understanding were apparent in his face. He moved over close where no word would escape him in what seems to be the inevitable "fading" in all radios. At your conclusion his Mother asked him if he liked it.

"Sure I liked it. Anybody could understand that."

I have been making public addresses of a sort for a good many years and would welcome a compliment like that. But I doubt if I shall ever get or deserve it. You get it, and what is more, merit it. That opinion seems unanimous around here even among those few who are inclined to question the contour, strength and efficacy of some of the pillars of the economic structure you are earnestly trying to build for your country. You are listened to not only with the respect your office commands, but with interest and understanding because you have the gift of simple words well and effectively chosen and spoken. The people like you. Even though they may not agree with you in all things you have their faith and trust. Your voice sounds friendly and sincere. The money changers may squirm under your scourge, but they have no rightful place in your temple any more than they had in that at ancient Jerusalem. The "forgotten man" feels that you remember him and it warms his heart toward you.

With all good wishes.

Respectfully and sincerely, yours,

Walter Aitken
Bozeman, Montana

OCTOBER 23, 1933

Dear Mr. President:

Please accept my heartiest congratulations upon your splendid radio talk last night. Not only did your voice come through clearly, (and may I say you have a splendid radio voice), but what you had to say thrilled Mrs. Howell and myself as we haven't been thrilled since the time of your in-augeral address, which came over the radio perfectly. It would seem to me that no patriotic American could listen to that explanation of what your administration is doing, and be not only thrilled, but filled with a burning desire to co-operate in every way possible. . . .

I want to assure you also that I am wonderfully pleased with your decision to recognize Soviet Russia. I have been a follower of the Socialist philosophy for a long time, and have fought the battles of Soviet Russia in this part of the country when it was almost heretical to mention the names of Lenin and Trosky.

This letter is already too long for a busy man, but I want also to say that while I didn't vote for you, being a Socialist, I am convinced that what you are doing at Muscle Shoals, and with the NRA is giving us the substance of Socialism without the name, which is just as satisfactory to me.

I am a busy physician, and in writing this I want you to know I am not seeking any political appointment. However, if there is any non-remunerative work I can do in this part of the country, please feel at liberty to call on me at any time.

With sincerest wishes for the continued success of your administration, and kindest personal regards, I am

Very truly yours,

J. C. Howell
Orlando, Florida

OCTOBER 24, 1933

Dear Mr. President,

Last Sunday evening six of our friends came in for dinner and contract. The men were not so much depressed as thoroughly frightened — their wives were wonderful — pretending to make light of the situation with such remarks as "You know, John, always worries about the things that never happen," etc. but in my dressing room after dinner they spoke differently — i.e. "I wonder if the President means to make a Soviet Russia of this country," "Why the new tie-up?" "I don't pretend to follow politics, but I hope things ar'n't a tenth as bad as John imagines" —

At ten o'clock all playing ceased, while each and everyone strained forward to catch the least inflection of your magnetic, inspiring voice. As you finished, the effect was a combustion of gaiety — taut nerves let loose. The men fairly jumped up and down like happy children, the women were inwardly thanking God, and one dear soul let loose the flood gates of tears of relief —

Mr. President, I'm sure that scene was duplicated in thousands of homes the length and breadth of the land, and I can't help writing you to thank you. You said you couldn't preform miracles — but you have!

I haven't been in Washington since the time my father and I were guests of President and Mrs. Wilson, but if Fate or Chance bring me there during your administration I hope I may have the privilege of thanking you personally.

With the assurance of my highest regard,

(Mrs. H. Howard Harper) Marguerite Harper
New York

OCTOBER 24, 1933

Dear Mr. President:

. . . I am of Scottish birth and humble origin, coming to America nearly half a century ago, to follow my trade of granite cutting, and with pride let me say it, that my skill such as it was, entered in to the construction of a few of the finest of our public buildings in Washington, namely the Congressional Library Building, the old Washington Post Office, and the National Museum. I mention these things that you may get a mental picture of the writer.

I am prouder of my adopted country since you were inducted in-to the Presidency than ever I have been before, because of the courageous leadership you are giving to millions of your fellow citizens, in all walks of life, and especially to those that may be described as under priveleged.

When you made your speech at the Chicago Democratic convention, I was listening on the radio with my wife and we have been following you ever since, I and many others did not have any idea what kind of a deal you were going to give us, but you established your-self in the confidence of a great majority of your people that it would not only be a new deal, but a good deal. . . .

You are bringing to reality dreams that I have had nearly all my life about social reform, brought about in an orderly and lawful manner, such reformation as you are inaugurating would in some countries have only been possible of attainment after violent revolution and much blood shed. . . .

I am,

Your loyal and obedient fellow citizen

Jas. H. Paterson
Charlotte, N.C.

OCTOBER 22, 1933

FROM EVERY PORTION OF THIS LAND
DELIGHTED PEOPLE GRASP YOUR HAND
RIGHT WELL WE KNOW YOU STILL COMMAND
NEW COURAGE GRIPS OUR HEARTS TONIGHT
RESPONSIVE TO YOUR SPEECH FORTHRIGHT
AND GIVES US STRENGTH TO PRESS THE FIGHT
AMERICA IS STRONG AGAIN
AROUSED OUR RED BLOODED MEN
AND ALL OUR CHILDREN SAY AMEN

FRANK M. PADDEN
CHICAGO, ILL.

"RELIEF, RECOVERY, REFORM
AND RECONSTRUCTION":
JUNE 28, 1934

DURING THE EIGHT MONTHS of his presidency in 1933, FDR delivered a Fireside Chat every two or three months. Always fearful of overdoing this direct approach in spite of the many letters he received pleading with him to go on the air even more frequently, Roosevelt allowed eight months to elapse between his final Chat in 1933 and the first Chat of 1934. "I am purposely avoiding the use of the air," he wrote Colonel House, who had been one of Woodrow Wilson's principal advisers, in the beginning of May, "because to use it at the controversial stage of a controversial legislative body spells more controversy!" He would speak to the people as soon as Congress adjourned in June, he told House and assured him that his radio silence indicated no slackening of reform: "there will be many new manifestations of the New Deal, even though the orthodox protest and the heathen roar! Do you not think I am right?"[39]

He asked the very same question of the American people when he finally did take to the air on June 28, with Congress adjourned until 1935. He thanked Congress for its cooperation and praised it for displaying "a greater freedom from mere partisanship than any other peacetime Congress since the administration of President Washington himself."[40] He outlined three related steps his administration had taken "toward the saving and safeguarding of our national life." The first was relief "because the primary concern of any government dominated by the humane ideals of democracy is the simple principle that in a land of vast resources no one should be permitted to starve." Relief would be administered on two principles: "First, that direct giving shall, wherever possible, be supplemented by provision for useful and remunerative work and, second, that where families in their existing surroundings will in all human probability never find an opportunity for full self-maintenance, happiness, and enjoyment, we will try to give them a new chance in new surroundings."

The second step was recovery, which economic data confirmed was well under way. FDR supplemented that data with a more immediate test of recovery that allowed him to reach out and make his audience participants:

> Are you better off than you were last year? Are your debts less
> burdensome? Is your bank account more secure? Are your
> working conditions better? Is your faith in your own individual
> future more firmly grounded?

Had the American people paid too high a price for these gains? Citing
those "plausible self-seekers and theoretical diehards" who lamented the
loss of individual liberty, the President again asked his listeners to judge
these claims by the realities of their own lives:

> Have you lost any of your rights or liberty or constitutional free-
> dom of action and choice? Turn to the Bill of Rights of the Con-
> stitution, which I have solemnly sworn to maintain and under
> which your freedom rests secure. Read each provision of that
> Bill of Rights and ask yourself whether you personally have
> suffered the impairment of a single jot of these great assurances.
> I have no question in my mind as to what your answer will be.

Those denying "the substantial gains of the past year" were not the
"overwhelming majority of the farmers or manufacturers or workers" but
rather the seekers after special political or financial privilege. In the imple-
mentation of "a great national program which seeks the primary good of
the greater number" the only toes stepped on were those of "the comparative few who seek to retain or to gain position or riches or both by some
shortcut which is harmful to the greater good."

Intimately connected to these considerations was his third and final
step, reform and reconstruction: "reform because much of our trouble . . .
has been due to a lack of understanding of the elementary principles of justice and fairness by those in whom leadership in business and finance was
placed; reconstruction because new conditions in our economic life as well
as old but neglected conditions had to be corrected." The nation was in the
process of making gains in eliminating child labor, establishing fair minimum wages and shorter hours, and creating conditions that protected consumers from skyrocketing retail prices. The goal of all of this activity was
"the security of the men, women, and children of the nation."

> That security involves added means of providing better
> homes for the people of the nation. That is the first principle of
> our future program.

The second is to plan the use of land and water resources of this country to the end that the means of livelihood of our citizens may be more adequate to meet their daily needs.

And, finally, the third principle is to use the agencies of government to assist in the establishment of means to provide sound and adequate protection against the vicissitudes of modern life — in other words, social insurance.

Those who fear progress, Roosevelt warned, "will try to give you new and strange names for what we are doing. Sometimes they will call it 'Fascism,' sometimes 'Communism,' sometimes 'regimentation,' sometimes 'Socialism.'" In truth, he assured his listeners, "what we are doing today is a necessary fulfillment of . . . old and tested American ideals." Characteristically reaching for familiar, simple metaphors to drive his point home, FDR spoke of the renovation of the White House office building that would begin during that summer. The additions would include modern electrical wiring, plumbing, and air cooling, but the structural lines of the old building would remain.

> The artistic lines of the White House buildings were the creation of master builders when our republic was young. The simplicity and the strength of the structure remain in the face of every modern test. But within this magnificent pattern, the necessities of modern government business require constant reorganization and rebuilding. . . . It is this combination of the old and the new that marks orderly peaceful progress — not only in building buildings but in building government itself.
>
> Our new structure is a part of and a fulfillment of the old.
>
> All that we do seeks to fulfill the historic traditions of the American people.

FDR concluded by speaking, as he frequently did, of his immediate plans and shared with his audience the excitement with which he was embarking on a ten-thousand-mile trip beginning on the first of July. He would board the USS *Houston* at Annapolis, sail to the Caribbean, Colombia, Panama, Hawaii; then to the Pacific Northwest, from which he would embark on an inspection of projects on the Colombia, Missouri, and Mississippi Rivers, visit several national parks, and "learn much of actual conditions during the trip across the continent back to Washington." He ended on a note of patriotism and destiny:

> While I was in France during the war our boys used to call the United States "God's country." Let us make and keep it "God's country."

*   *   *

Dear Mr. President,

For the first time in my life I am writing to a public official. For the first time in my life I feel that I have a President. I read what you write, I listen to what you say. I believe in you. I talk to you.

You asked us tonight to take stock of our own particular affairs. Yes, I am better off. My brother, who was out of work for over three years got a job last January and I no longer have to contribute to his support. I do not earn more money but have a feeling of greater security in my position. But better than the economic side is my feeling of pride and satisfaction in you as my President. I — together with millions of other Americans — have become 'President conscious'. For the first time I feel that the leader of my country has some interest in me — that those in my walk of life are not altogether forgotten.

I hope you have a pleasant vacation and that you will continue to enjoy the confidence of your followers. And you will because I am convinced that your program is grounded in sincerity and we Americans fundamentally recognize and 'lay up to' this rare trait. It's what we want. Not perfection, nor miracles but a square deal.

Sincerely,

Alice Timoney
New York, New York

JULY 1, 1934

Dear Sir,

You asked in your radio address of June 28, 'Are you better off than you were last year?' I believe that there are thousands who would answer in the negative. I know many that would. Professional men, teachers and others who have been provident and thrifty, who have lost their positions or have had salary cuts, and who have seen their savings and investments adversely affected by measures of your administration, which seems to assume that all debtors are good, all creditors, bad. But unfortunately for them, fortunately for you, they are not organized. They are 'those exceptions in professional pursuits whose economic improvement, of necessity (Why 'of necessity'?) will be delayed'.

And is it good sportsmanship or even good politics to admit no errors on the part of your administration and to brand all criticism or opposite views as due to partisanship, ignorance or some evil motive?

You were elected by a bipartisan vote; your sole aim should be to work for the welfare of all. It should not be divided between this and the welfare of your party and securing a second term for yourself.

Very truly yours,

George Ellas Wisewell
Rochester, New York

JUNE 28, 1934

Dear President,

Tonight is the first time I heard you speak. I was listening to your speech as a child does when he listens to grandmother tell a Mickey Mouse Story or The Three Bears. I sat close to the Radio so I would be sure, I would get every word you spoke. And I did too. . . .

My father is a farmer. He lives with his wife and us seven children in his ranch 8½ miles from the nearest town. He does not understand that the English very well, but he understood your speech just the same. You speak to the stand where every one understands you.

I am a graduate from La Joya High School . . . and wish to continue my education, so some day I will earn the sufficient money and go to visit the White House. . . .

Wishing you success in your summer trip.

Your friend,

Miss Micaela Chapa
Mission, Texas

JULY 14, 1934

Honorable Roosevelt;

. . . You seem to be anxious to help the people who are in debt. But you fail to remember that those debts were incurred with the intention of making a profit. If the debtor made a profit, I am sure he would not divide it with the rest of us. But because he failed to make a profit, you want to help him, and make the rest of us suffer thru devaluation of the dollar, experiments, and inflationary measures. I have a little life insurance, together with two hundred dollars in the bank, left. I hope you will not take it away from me thru further devaluation, purchases of gold, and silver. I am anxious concerning the security you are promising to us thru your radio address.

Another matter, I, together with you am anxious that nobody starve here in this abundant land of ours. The needy must be fed. But, I do not think that the savers and the thrifty should suffer, because of the errors of others who squandered their money. Further-more, I do not see why people who have farms, buildings, lands, and other capital goods, in fact more than they can handle, receive aid from our government in various forms.

I am sending you this letter in answer to your radio address, and for the common good of the people of the U.S. I hope you will accept this letter in that friendly spirit. I do not wish to compete with the Brain-Trusters of Washington, D.C., but if you should need further plans, ideas, reforms, and programs concerning recovery, I will be glad to furnish them upon request.

Yours respectfully,

Michael Cornwall
Garfield, N.J.

JUNE 29, 1934

Dear Sir:

I heard your message to the people last night over the radio and was very much empressed with it. You asked in your Message are you better off than you were last year? My answer I am sorry to say is, I am not. I have not had very much work in the past year. Another one of your questions was, Is your faith in your own individual future more firmly grounded? To that I am glad to say It most certainly is. If I did not have more faith in the future than I have had in the past three years I don't know what in the world I would do. Although I havent got a job and havent had one lately. I have eight (8) in family encluding my wife's father which is 81 years old. Her Mother having died some three months ago. But I am hoping and praying that through Gods help that you will pull us through this crisis. Which you are doing at a rapid rate. You are doing wonderful work just keep it up I think the N.R.A. is grand although I think I lost my job on account of talking for it. The Co. got turned in for working us mechanic from 60 to 70 hours per wk. and they suspect me of writing them up. I am an auto mechanic by trade and I have been working with Cooke Chev. Co. Wadesboro, N.C. This year up until the 19th of May the first work I have had in over a year. I hope you will pardon me for writing you, but I wanted to thank you for what you have done for us and to endorce your new deal whole heartedly. Well hears hoping you will have a grand time and the best of health on your vacation. Also hoping I will get a job soon or get me a little place on my own which I am trying to do. Hope to be of service to my country some time.

Remain as loyal as ever,

John W. Meeks
Wadesboro, N.C.

JUNE 29, 1934

My dear Mr. President:

In your radio address last night you asked a number of questions of the individual and I assume from this that I may answer individually and collectively for Leas & McVitty, Inc., because I am the head of this company that has been in operation since 1812. We are in the tanning business and employ 525 people.

You ask:

Question: Are you better off than you were last year?

This is answered by comparing this week with the week that you took office sixteen months ago.

We are securing only 4.7% more for our leather now.

We are paying 122% more for our hides.

We have had the dollar contracted to 59% of it's former value.

Question: Are your debts less burdensome?

Answer: Our debts are 150% increased.

Question: Is your bank account more secure?

Answer: We think it is, but what it is securing seems more doubtful.

Question: Are your working conditions better?

Answer: Judging from a committee representing our men, we would say "no." These men reported that they were entirely satisfied with the increase in hourly rate of wages, but they are dissatisfied with the limitation of hours and their liberty of choice.

Question: Is your faith in your own individual future more firmly grounded?

Answer: It is utterly shaken.

Question: Have you as an individual paid too high a price for these gains?

Answer: The above are not gains. Your policies have added to our confusion by taking away our former standards of stability and giving us no future guide.

Respectfully yours,

S. H. McVitty
Salem, Va.

JUNE 30, 1934

Dear President; I listened with profound interest to your Broadcast, the other night, and want to assure you, that your diagnosis was absolutely true.

I have since 1880, owned and operated a small department store at Ashville, Ohio. A comparison of the figures, as shown by my books, for the first six months of 1934, compared with the first six months of 1933, show a gain of 64$\frac{1}{10}$% am past 70 yrs. of age, Am confident by the end of the first 6 months of 1935, we'll be showing parallels of 1928 business.

Yours truly

G. A. Hook
Ashville, Ohio

JUNE 29, 1934

Dear President: —

I read in the Memphis Commercial Appeal your radio address of last night about the New Deal. I believe all that you have done is very profitable to all masses of the people and will result in great improvement of business conditions.

I am a Jewish merchant in a small town and during the years of the depression it was hard sailing for me and for all the people. Since you have been in office my business is better and all the business in my community is better. You have inspired faith and courage and helped the poor and oppressed. I think you are the best President since George Washington and greater than Moses for it took him 40 years to bring the Jewish people out of the wilderness and you have accomplished wonders in such a short time. I am a good Democrat and in my opinion it would be unnecessary to have an election for next term as it should be the unanimous consent of the people for you to remain in office for life. I am not fishing for a job but only good-will.

Your admirer,

Victor Zieff
Newbern, Tenn.

JUNE 29, 1934

Honorable President Roosevelt:

In answer to your radio address of last evening, I wish to state that I would answer NO to all of your questions. . . .

If Labor and Capitol do not go hand in hand, we will not get out of this depression, and as long as your General Johnson sees fit to antagonize Capitol, all the Public Work money that you can print and give away will not help because as soon as it is all used up we will be right where we started. It has to be perment and must come with the help of Capitol, and Capitol is not going to help as long as it is soaked upon every turn.

I respectfully ask you to forgive this frank message, but now that it is out of my system I feel better.

Yours sincerely,

Alvin Icke
San Antonio, Texas

JULY 3, 1934

My dear Mr. President: —

Thank you many times for your cheerful message over the Radio. My family and I answered each of your questions as they were asked, in the afirmative, some in the negative. "Are you better of than last year" Yes, decidedly. "Are your debts less burdensome" Yes, Yes, thanks to your H.O.L.C. [Home Owners Loan Corporation] — Heretofor only the wealthy could hope to receive favors from our Goverment, but now even the "forgotten man" is remembered. "Is your bank account more secure?" Absolutely! "Is your faith in your future more firmly grounded?" Yes.

And now the negatives.

"Have you lost any rights of freedom of action or choice" None whatever, but I have gained some sense of greater freedom under the New Deal — But let the Goverment continue to appoint and manage The [New] Dealers, and not listen to the clammering of the Old Crowd, the "Malfactors of great wealth."

Sincerely

John Pauer
Sacramento, Calif.

JULY 12, 1934

Dear Mr. Roosevelt:

Several weeks ago in a radio address, shortly before you sailed on your vacation, you asked the public to answer two questions. My answer, in both cases, is emphatically "yes", but if I am not too impertinent, I would like to ask you a few questions and shall earnestly hope for some explanation of the questions that have been troubling me.

First — why do you consider it necessary and wise to extend Government control and regulation to business through the actions and activities of the tremendous number of new bureaus that have been established in Washington?

Second — don't you think it was a horrible mistake to devalue the American Dollar and repudiate the promises of the United States Government to pay off it's obligations in Gold coin or money of a certain stated gold value?

Third — Isn't it a stupid thing to do, to kill so many pigs and to plow up so many crops when people are both hungry and unclothed, and isn't it still more stupid to pay a farmer more for failing to produce something, than he would receive for creating something that could be used?

Fourth — Isn't it silly to artificially raise the price of American Cotton, which is one of our largest export commodities, first, by reducing the acreage, and second, by debasing the dollar when such actions must, inevitably, act to stimulate production in foreign countries?

Fifth — Isn't it absurd to suppose that anyone, regardless of whether they are Government, industry or individual, can continue to consume more than they produce?

Sixth — Just what is the theory back of the thought, that people can work less, produce less and earn more? Is it true that the Government is prepared to accept full responsibility for each and every one of us, and that it is no longer necessary to teach our children self-denial, self-discipline, self-reliance, and some sort of a plan for saving for their old age?

These are some of the things that have been troubling me and your answers to these troubling problems will be very much appreciated.

Yours very truly,

H. W. Spencer
Louisville, Ky.

JUNE 29, 1934

Dear Sir,

I listened to your address last night with a great deal of interest. I would enjoy your radio talks even if you were not President.

I want to tell you how my family was situated a year ago as compared with today.

In 1932, we lost everything we had, even cashed in our insurances. My daughter could not get a job, my husband was selling furniture on commission for a store on the verge of bankruptcy. We were desperate, we felt the end of the world had come.

The store decided to join the N.R.A. In reorganizing, they decided to make my husband manager. The same week my daughter got a job secretary to an insurance executive. Today both my husband and daughter are making a fine salary and the store has paid off its obligations and is paying the same dividends it paid when prosperity was at its peak.

That is our story.

A year can make unbelievable changes, especially when the people have confidence in their President.

Yours very truly,

Mrs. L. H. Thompson
Atlanta, Ga.

JUNE 28, 1934

Dear Mr. President: —

Permit me the liberty of congratulating you, on the clear and lucid address delivered to-night to the people of the U.S.A. It was forceful and convincing beyond words to express; and the pleasing and captivating voice, was vibrant with utter sincerity.

You invited your listeners to test "Recovery" in the light of their own circumstances. May I offer mine?

My parish is in the great metropolitan area. Mostly industrial. My church membership is over a thousand. In addition I conduct a "Men's Bible Class" of about 300. A "Women's Bible Class" of 150. I have struggled through the "depression" and done many unusual things to help my needy folk. I have greatly alleviated their distresses and lack of employment.

To-day the complexion of the situation is completely changed.

Since your administration began, there is such improvement, that my humble efforts are really no longer necessary. My long list of unemployed men and women, is no longer in evidence. The N.R.A. did it.

This is the acid test, and I regard my own as no mean one.

May I be further permitted, to wish you the pleasure you so much deserve, in your approaching holiday, and that your wish to make America, "God's Country" may be fully realized, and may the Grace of Christ, support you.

Respectfully,
Your humble servant,

John M. Macmillan
Kearny, New Jersey

JUNE 28, 1934

Dear Sir: —

Your words of tonight have touched me, so that I appreciate, as never before, the gigantic efforts you are making in behalf of your fellow human beings.

I am an alien. For over ten years I have remained deliberately so, having felt all along that there could be no security in this country, with so much corruption and selfishness. Now, before the week is over, I shall apply for citizenship, determined to be amoung the millions of proud and priviliged people you address as "fellow citizens and friends;" determined to help, if only spiritually, to ease the gigantic burden you so gamely and ably struggle with in order to make America truly "God's Country." For, like millions of others, I now feel secure. There is no longer that fear for the immediate future, as looming up from behind the black clouds of doubt. . . .

Yours Humbly,

Robert E. Reid
Corona, New York

JUNE 29, 1934

My Dear beloved President.

I heard your talk on the radio last night and it was grate But in the same time when I heard you that you are going on your vacation for a few weeks, so I am very much afraid of about your safty my heart tells me same thing I don't know what so for good protection pleas dear beloved President be very carffuly whit your every step.

> A good Cityzen.
>
> Sam Zelmanowitz
> New York, New York

ORDER OUT OF CHAOS:
SEPTEMBER 30, 1934

FDR REMARKED more than once that he found going out among the American people a tonic; he much preferred it to working in his White House office. "I regain strength by just meeting the American people," he enthused. His extensive trip West in the summer of 1934 was no exception. After his return, he told his Emergency Council that the faces of those who crowded around him wherever he went were different than they had been when he had traveled the country during the campaign of 1932. "You could tell what the difference was by standing on the end of the car and looking at the crowd. They were a hopeful people. They had courage written all over their faces. They looked cheerful. They knew they were 'up against it,' but they were going to see the thing through."[41]

While he praised the everyday folk for their courage and persistence, he had different emotions for those in his own party, including the former presidential candidates John W. Davis and Al Smith, who — along with such business magnates as the du Ponts, Alfred P. Sloan, Jr., of General Motors, J. Howard Pew of Sun Oil, Nathan Miller of U.S. Steel, and Sewell L. Avery of Montgomery Ward — formed the American Liberty League in August 1934 to oppose the New Deal and its leader with an unrelenting vehemence that led the journalist Marquis Childs to brand them "the Roosevelt Haters." The President's ultimate desire, the League charged over and over again in the coming months and years, was to destroy liberty: "Louis XIV never went so far. Neither Mussolini nor Hitler, nor Stalin of Russia, have gone so far."[42]

But Roosevelt's troubles were not confined to those he dubbed the "I CAN'T TAKE IT CLUB." He also found himself at odds with close advisers like his Budget Director Lewis Douglas, who in April of 1933 had called Roosevelt's abandonment of the gold standard "the end of Western civilization" and in August of 1934 resigned in disagreement with his chief's policies of public works and deficit spending, which he denounced as the road to socialism. During the summer of 1934, FDR also resisted the counsel of another principal adviser, Raymond Moley, who urged him to declare that with the addition of a social security program, the New Deal's legislative program was complete. FDR believed, as he confided to Colonel House in May, "We must keep the sheer momentum from slacking up too much and I have no intention of relinquishing the offensive in favor of defensive tactics. I think we can keep the tide on the flood for a good long time to come."[43]

During these months, the Book of the Month Club offered as a selection Herbert Hoover's *The Challenge to Liberty,* in which the former President characterized the New Deal as a system of national regimentation bordering on fascism and called it "the most stupendous invasion of the whole spirit of Liberty that the nation has witnessed since the days of Colonial America."[44] The nature of the conservative attacks on FDR throughout most of his tenure bring to mind the remark of Rexford Guy Tugwell that Roosevelt's reputation as a "political wonder-worker" was in part due to his political genius and in part "due to the extremely bad judgment and to the incredible ineptness of the conservative opposition." At one point, after committing what he considered to be an egregious political blunder, FDR himself commented: "Oh well, I always have one comfort. The opposition will come up with a worse boner tomorrow or next day — soon enough to blanket mine."[45]

In this heated atmosphere, FDR delivered his second and final Fireside Chat of 1934 just a little more than a month before the November midterm elections.[46] In the face of his myriad attackers, he reminded the nation of the New Deal's accomplishments thus far: "after years of uncertainty, . . . we are bringing order out of the old chaos." He adroitly quoted the words of Elihu Root, the elderly Republican corporate lawyer who had served as Theodore Roosevelt's Secretary of State, in order to let a respected member of the Republican establishment articulate the realities of the context in which the New Deal was operating: "Instead of the give and take of free individual contract," Root had written,

> the tremendous power of organization has combined great aggregations of capital in enormous industrial establishments . . . so great in the mass that each individual concerned in them is quite helpless by himself. The relations between the employer and the employed, . . . between the small producer, the small trader, the consumer, and the great transporting and manufacturing and distributing agencies, all present new questions for the solution of which the old reliance upon the free action of in-

dividual wills appears quite inadequate. And in many directions, the intervention of that organized control which we call government seems necessary to produce the same result of just and right conduct which obtained through the attrition of individuals before the new conditions arose.

FDR dwelled on his Administration's successful efforts to heal the sickness prevailing in banking and investment and then turned to the National Recovery Administration's efforts to halt child labor, raise wages, create jobs, and produce standards of fair competition. He admitted that much remained to be done: "There is no magic formula, no economic panacea, which could simply revive over-night for example the heavy industries and the trades that are dependent upon them. Nevertheless, my friends, the gains of trade and industry, as a whole, have been substantial and everybody knows it."

FDR then launched into a surprisingly detailed technical assessment of the NRA, which had been under intense criticism for favoring those business groups that were already entrenched and powerful and thus in the best position to utilize the powers of setting prices and allocating production quotas. Some have interpreted Roosevelt's remarks as a warning to businessmen that if they didn't acknowledge the benefits bestowed on them by the New Deal and continued to carp and criticize, those benefits could be reviewed and withdrawn, while others have seen in them evidence that FDR was hardening his attitudes toward big business and moving to the left. The President's statements doubtless manifested a bit of both. He admitted that some of the codes adopted for various businesses and industries might be too complicated or too prone to price fixing and limitation of production but stressed that this is what businessmen had wanted since "the representatives of trade and industry were permitted to write their own ideas into the codes."

> It is now time to review these actions as a whole to determine
> . . . the wisdom of many of those devices to control production,
> or to prevent destructive price cutting which many business organizations have insisted were necessary, or whether their effect
> may have been to prevent . . . lower prices and increased employment. Another question arises as to whether in fixing minimum wages on the basis of an hourly or a weekly wage we have
> reached into the heart of the problem which is to provide such

annual earnings, earnings throughout the year, for the lowest paid worker — such earnings as will meet his minimum needs. And we question also the wisdom of extending code requirements suited to the great industrial centers and suited to large employers, to . . . the great number of small employers in the smaller communities.

While reiterating his support for Section 7(a) of the National Industrial Recovery Act (NIRA) guaranteeing labor's right to organize and bargain collectively, Roosevelt noted that during the past twelve months "our industrial recovery has been to some extent retarded by strikes" and asked both labor and industry to "lay aside the weapons common to industrial war" at least for the duration of the economic crisis and "civilize our industrial civilization" by availing themselves of the vehicles of mediation and arbitration established just a few months earlier by the National Labor Relations Board (NLRB). He then turned to the public works provisions of the NIRA, which were "designed to put more men back to work, both directly on the public works themselves, and indirectly in the industries supplying the materials for these public works." He answered those critics who maintained that public works were a wasteful and unaffordable indulgence by declaring that "no country, however rich, can afford the waste of its human resources. Demoralization caused by vast unemployment is our greatest extravagance. Morally, it is the greatest menace to our social order."

> Some people try to tell me that we must make up our minds that for the future we shall permanently have millions of unemployed . . . I stand or fall by my refusal to accept as a necessary condition of our future a permanent army of unemployed. On the contrary, we must make it a national principle that we will not tolerate a large army of the unemployed, that we will arrange our national economy to end our present unemployment as soon as we can and then to take wise measures against its return. I do not want to think that it is the destiny of any American to remain permanently on relief rolls.

The President turned with scorn to those "who are frightened by boldness, who are cowed by the necessity for making decisions, [who] complain that all we have done is unnecessary and that all we have done is subject to great risks." He was especially irate at those in the business community who had urgently sought his aid in the deeply troubled early months of 1933 and then with the onset of recovery began to oppose the very measures that had saved them. "Now that these people are coming out of their storm cellars, they forget that there ever was a storm." But FDR affirmed his faith in the "sensible and calm" American people. "We do not get greatly excited nor is our peace of mind disturbed, whether we be business men or workers or farmers, by awesome pronouncements concerning the unconstitutionality of some of our measures of recovery and relief and reform. We are not frightened by reactionary lawyers or by political editors. All of these cries have been heard before." He joined with former Chief Justice Edward Douglas White who in the days of Theodore Roosevelt and Woodrow Wilson decried those "creating the general impression that the Constitution is but a barrier to progress instead of being the broad highway through which alone true progress may be enjoyed."

In his program of reform, FDR argued, "we have avoided . . . the theory that business should and must be taken over into an all-embracing Government . . . [and] the equally untenable theory that it is an interference with Liberty to offer reasonable help when private enterprise is in need of help." The course the New Deal was taking "fits the American practice of Government — a practice of taking action step by step, of regulating only to meet concrete needs — a practice of courageous recognition of change." There was no more potent political icon during the Depression than Abraham Lincoln, and FDR eagerly aligned himself with Lincoln's definition of the legitimate object of government: "to do for a community of people whatever they need to have done but cannot do at all or cannot do so well for themselves in their separate and in their individual capacities." "My friends," Roosevelt concluded:

> I still believe in ideals. I am not for a return to that definition of Liberty under which for many years a free people were being gradually regimented into the service of the privileged few. I prefer and I am sure you prefer that broader definition of Liberty under which we are moving forward to greater freedom, to greater security for the average man than he has ever known before in the history of America.

OCTOBER 3, 1934

Dear Mr. President:

One hundred and twenty millions of Americans ought to go down on their knees daily to thank the Almighty God that a man of your caliber is at the head of this Nation.

Of the remaining few, some are to be pitied, while others deserve the hospitality of Alcatraz Island —

Your stirring address to the Nation last Sunday night was a master piece of statemanship, honesty, frankness and knowledge.

Mr. President I have a wife and a child —, I love them but I do worship you —

Someday I hope to have the pleasure to see you — this is one of my ambition in life.

With best wishes for your health and success, I am

Devoted yours

Joe Frigo
Keystone, W.Va.

OCTOBER 1, 1934

Dear Mr. President:

Everybody who has any sense and was able to get to a radio heard your speech last night. I desire to add my firm approval to every utterance which came from your lips.

Surely under the guidance of your great constructive genius the country is gaining. It is well that you take us into your confidence and tell us Mr. President; your address reveals what we had not heard. There is such a welter of publicity about the alphabetized programmes that much wisdom is lost in confusion, but when you speak everybody understands.

You know what your government is doing. You know how to explain it. You know where you are heading and you are on your way.

God bless and keep you strong for the battle Mr. President is the sincere wish of a red-hot, jet-black Democrat.

Melvin J. Chisum
(Field Secretary of the National Negro Press Association)
Philadelphia, Pa.

SEPTEMBER 30, 1934

My dear Mr. Roosevelt:

In my little apartment here about as far away from you as I could be I have listened with great interest to your talk tonight and when you were through, I wished that you were here or I were there because there were many things that I wanted to hear more about. I detected a bit more of the fighting spirit than in previous speeches and I heartily endorse your unwillingness to believe in the necessity of continued unemployment and its subsequent human waste: also regimentation of free people to work for the privileged few.

From childhood one of my greatest anxieties has been concerning the material inequalities of our 'land of the free', the mental and moral inequalities can never be regulated so satisfactorily as can the material, but they too will be lessened when, under the guidance of men with ideals similar to yours, the material needs of every human being are permantly and irrevocably provided for. I'm confident it can be done and I wish, impatiently, that I could do something tangible toward advancing the day. Isn't there anything I could do to help?

Congratulations on your success so far and best wishes for satisfactory future developments.

Sincerely your friend,

Beth Fisher
Long Beach, Calif.

OCTOBER 1, 1934

Sir:

I wish to express my appreciation of your very reassuring message over the radio last evening. As the wife of one of the many millions of men still unemployed, I believe I was especially grateful for your statement to the effect that it was not the destiny of any American to be continuously unemployed. Such a statement must do much towards restoring the confidence and self-respect of those worthy men who are forced to be supported by either the relief agencies or relatives.

During this trying period, we have been very fortunate in that I have been able to maintain the home for the past three years, but such a condition, grateful as we are, does not engender a spirit of happiness in a man, and it is difficult for him to maintain his self-respect. We have a boy of six and I certainly would hate to see him grow up to join the army of unemployed that we have been told lately would have to be supported in the United States.

Our prayers are with you, Mr. President, and we know that with right motives you can and must succeed in your efforts to lift the country out of its present state.

Yours very respectfully,

(Mrs. George S. Hardy) Madge B. Hardy
Chicago, Illinois

OCTOBER 2, 1934

Dear President of the United States of America

Listened to your talk Sunday evening. All things considered, needed no adding to, and could not have been rendered in a more friendly or determined spirit. . . .

I am at present working as a laborer on one of the many FERA [Federal Emergency Relief Administration] projects. Commencing only last week, and although I am 54 years of age, these few days, mark the greatest days of my life. Picture me with a pick and a shovel, right out on the end of Point Loma near the old Spanish light house, helping make things ready for a little park, working under overseers, who seem able and considerate, for all concerned. . . .

Now as I work on the project mentioned, the days I labor, hark me back twenty years or more, when as individuals and in bodies we were trying for the programs of today. And at that time we said, there is a class who cannot or will not see, and because of selfishness and lust, the life blood of labor is dripping from their house tops. . . .

These are great days, because the dreams we dispared of in our life, surely are closing in on us, through the timely efforts of a Great President and his able assistants. . . .

George W. Ball
San Diego, Calif.

OCTOBER 1, 1934

Honored Sir:

With thousands of other citizens of the United States I listened to your talk over the radio last night. I am wondering if there are not many others who have the same questions to ask which came to me as you finished your talk.

Your concern seems to be over two classes of people or possibly I may say three groups, the employer, the wage earner or employee and the farmer.

What percentage of our people form the employer, the union wage earner and the farmer? Is there not a large class who are not included in either of the above groups, such as the salesman, agent, professional man or woman, clerk, etc who have no connection with any union, chamber of commerce, society etc. These people of whom I am one are struggling to keep going with rising prices and dropping off of business.

Uncomplainingly we have paid the mounting taxes which have been increased from time to time to care for the unemployed, the cotton grower and the western farmer. Now we are militantly demanding something should be done indirectly to step up prosperity for us.

Your administration has never mentioned that there are thousands of law abiding citizens who have reached the age where their services are not wanted by an employer. No union cares whether these people exist or not.

As one of this group I with the members of my family are too proud to beg, too proud to look to relief agencies who would probably refuse any assistance, no matter how urgent the need because we have in the days gone by accumulated some property, life insurance, a car and by frugal effort built up what looks like a well to do existence.

As a member of this group I ask that you use your good office to institute some new course of action which will bring to us some hope of something better than being the underlings, forever ground between the millstones of excessive wealth and poverty.

Sincerely yours,

F. W. Allen
Erie, Penna.

OCTOBER 3, 1934

My dear President Roosevelt:

Your fireside talk was very fine, and I am one of your admirers. Next time I hope you will include some conclusion on the thoughtless increase in population of those dependent on relief, or with very small earning capacity.

It is unfair to children to bring them into the world doomed to misery, nor should the more far sighted be taxed to support them. . . .

Sterilization of the unfit should follow, and our crime record would not be so shocking. There are 40,000 persons in New Jersey who should be segregated. 10,000 only can be accommodated in our excellent institutions.

These people cannot help being a burden to the normal, but should never have come into the world.

With best wishes for continued success,

Sincerely,

Florence K. Amos
Princeton, New Jersey

SEPTEMBER 30, 1934

Dear Sir: —

Recently I read an article by Stuart Chase (econimist) which said you must soon take a leftward (liberal) course or a rightward (reactionary) one. Your speech with its emphasis on protection of the billions in American industry seemed to be pandering to the money of the country and not the people. Till now I have had the utmost faith in you. I feel a little sick now. Hope I have misunderstood or am wrong.

Very truly,

Richard Martin
San Francisco, Calif.

OCTOBER 1, 1934

My dear Mr. President:

I listened to your radio talk last night. It occurs to me that you would be interested in knowing the reaction of the average man.

In order that you may get the proper background, I will tell you something of my past history — as a boy, I had nothing. I worked hard, was economical, sacrificed many of the pleasures that the average young man endulged in, married a girl who was no better off than I was, and together we suffered many sacrifices. We finally managed to save enough money to get into business, our business grew and flourished. . . .

I have a program of expansion that has been in the balance for many months because of the uncertainty of the political situation. This expansion program would give employment to quite a number of people, but because of uncertainties, we do not want to go ahead.

I was in hopes in your talk last night you would say something that would encourage the average businessman, but from what I can gather, you propose to go thru with the New Deal as is.

The thing that worries me is the class of people that you have surrounded yourself with — I refer to . . . the bunch of college professors that are nothing more than theorists, and very impractical to say the least, in addition to having Socialistic and Communistic tendencies that scare the average good citizen. . . .

What we need in the White House, is a man who is courageous enough to put into effect a program to balance the budget, reduce our taxes and quit spending the peoples' money wrecklessly.

I have gone along with you up to the present time, but if matters do not get better and if business does not have a fair shake, then I will take my little 30 cents, put it away in a tin can and live off of it for my few remaining years — that is what many people are doing and being driven to by these Brain Truster ideas.

This letter is not intended in any way to be disrespectful, and I hope that you will agree that my contentions have some merit.

Yours very truly,

R. R. Englehart
Davenport, Iowa

* * *

My dear President:

Your speech last night should go down in history, along with many of your previous acts, as a display of mental incompetancy. A small time politician could really have done better. However, the poor people of our glorious country are governed by their emotions and prejudices and you know it, so we can expect you to continue the way you have been going. But as "Eddie" Leonard used to say "You can fool some of the people some of the time, but you can't fool all of the people all of the time."

Hugh F. Colliton Jr.
Wayland, Mass.

OCTOBER 1, 1934

YOU STUTTER TERRIBLY IN YOUR SPEECHES I DONT THINK YOU HAVE THE CONFIDENCE I DONT REALLY BELIEVE YOU ARE SOLD ON YOUR OWN IDEAS ANSWER ME WHO WROTE YOUR SPEECH AGAINST PUBLIC SENTIMENT I NEED AN ANSWER.

E. B. SCARSDALE
DAYTON, OHIO

OCTOBER 1, 1934

RESPECTFULLY ALWAYS MY DEAR FRANK . . . DONT LET THEM KID YOU TO-NIGHTS TALK WAS AS UNCONVINCING AS A CREAM PUFF ASSAULT ON THE GREAT WALL OF CHINA. DO STOP THIS SHADOW BOXING WITH REALITIES. DONT LET ANYONE TELL YOU THAT INDUSTRY WONT COOPERATE. THE TRAGEDY IS THAT INDUSTRYS ATTITUDE HAS BEEN DISTORTED THERE IS MORE GUT AND ROMANCE IN INDUSTRY THAN THERE EVER HAS BEEN IN POLITICS. LET US CUT OUT THIS SLIDE RULE AND STRATOSPHERE THEO-RIZING AND IF I CAN BE OF ANY SERVICE IN THIS EMERGENCY YOU HAVE ONLY TO COMMAND ME. DO TAKE THIS COMMUNICATION IN THE SPIRIT IN WHICH IT IS SENT FOR I HAVE NO AXE TO GRIND BUT I DO BELIEVE IN IN-

DUSTRY AND THE MEN WHO ARE STILL ON A SIXTEEN HOUR DAY TRYING TO
KEEP THEIR MEN EMPLOYED.

FRANK C. REILLY
DETROIT, MICHIGAN

SEPTEMBER 30, 1934

DEAR MR PRESIDENT ALTHOUGH I AM A REPUBLICAN AND A FRIEND OF
THOSE OTHER GREAT PRESIDENTS THEODORE ROOSEVELT THE LATE PRES-
IDENT TAFT AND FORMER PRESIDENT HOOVER I DESIRE TO AVAIL MYSELF
OF THIS OPPORTUNITY TO CONGRATULATE YOU ON YOUR SOUND SPEECH
OF TONIGHT WHICH HAS JUST COME OVER THE RADIO IN MAGNIFICENT
MANNER. YOU ARE DOING A GRAND JOB UNDER THE MOST DIFFICULT CIR-
CUMSTANCES AND JUSTLY DESERVE THE INDIVIDUAL AND COLLECTIVE
SUPPORT AND SYMPATHY OF EVERY TRUE AMERICAN WHO PUTS HIS COUN-
TRYS NEEDS ABOVE PARTY POLITICS OR PERSONAL INTERESTS. I CONGRAT-
ULATE YOU AND WISH YOU SUCCESS.

ELMER R. JONES
(PRESIDENT WELLS FARGO & CO.)
NEW YORK, N.Y.

OCTOBER 1, 1934

BUSINESS MEN OF THIS TOWN ENDORSE YOUR PROGRAM AS OUTLINED IN
YOUR RADIO ADDRESS OF SUNDAY NIGHT. THE NEW DEAL HAS BROUGHT
PROSPERITY TO THE FARMERS OF THIS SECTION AND THAT MEANS PROS-
PERITY FOR OUR TOWN OF KENBRIDGE. IT WOULD DO YOUR HEART GOOD
TO SEE THE HAPPY FLUE CURED TOBACCO GROWERS OF THIS GOLDEN TO-
BACCO BELT UNDER THE AAA WHO WERE POVERTY STRIKEN UNDER THE
OLD RAW DEAL OF OTHER DAYS.

CHARLES M. ALLEN
(PRESIDENT KENBRIGE CHAMBER OF COMMERCE)
KENBRIDGE, VIR.

OCTOBER 1, 1934

Dear Mr. President: —

Please, not that it matters, but as an encouragement, please, keep it up. Your speech last night was one of your BEST. Now you talking turkey thats the language they will understand and will right back they go, in the storm cellar with the rats.

Please, fear NOTHING the people are WITH YOU!

Get that full dictatorship, you will never get them to do things otherwise. Get them with the coming Congress, they will be yours you MUST ACT NOW or later it will be too late, people will be out of bounds, even you will not be able to control them.

God bless you and more power to you!

HAIL ROOSEVELT!

Very respectfully yours.

Oliver Kovacs
Perth Amboy, N.J.

OCTOBER 2, 1934

Dear Sir,

Heard your radio talk on Sunday . . . big business is not playing cricket. The small wage earner, the farmer and small business are for you. Big business has legal and financial aid to try and thwart your efforts. If you abolish the Federal Reserve and establish National Bank I don't think you would have the trouble with the bankers that you spoke of Sunday. I think any profits to be made from the distribution of money should go to the government.

If labor gets out of hand troops are called out to put them in order. With the government bank in effect if big business got out of hand, call in their money to put them in order. In either case after a settlement is reached the cancellation of privelages is lifted. I think this would shorten strikes considerably. In any event it would put labor and big business on an even footing if they were not willing to arbitrate. Hope you dont think I am a crank or nit-wit.

Here's hoping for your continued Success.

W. S. Wilson
Philadelphia, Pa.

occupation — auto-mechanic
age 31
color white
Employed at $.50 an hr.
13 years experience

OCTOBER 3, 1934

Dear Mr. President,

Following your radio address of Sunday evening I felt much as one would who, having been invited to a dinner, goes away hungry — Or as a child, having asked for milk — is given water. Not one word about balancing our Government budget. Not a bit of assurance about this monetary policy. No help promised investors in large corporations or small business men. . . .

The Administration has invited strikes when it assured strikers that it would care for them with relief when unemployed. Better have announced that any one receiving fair wage & in decent working condition — who enticed a strike would be ineligible to Federal Relief & considered an obstructionist to Recovery. Labor has become insolent and violent. . . .

HOLC [Home Owners Loan Corporation] in Philadelphia is in many instances inefficient and most unbusiness like — to put it mildly.

House wives in Pennsylvania know full well how much more it costs to fill the market basket — and what few incomes have increased. In fact, some of us wonder how we can keep our homes and carry on the education of our children with securities, even Government bonds — below what we paid for them. . . .

We've tried to follow our leader, Mr. President, but the past six months — we wonder where we may be led. Too many experiments — too much corn-hog money just before elections — too much radical thought — too little good common sense on cost-balance and private initiative.

Respectfully — but earnestly,

Mrs H. H. Smith
Ardmore, Penna.

OCTOBER 1, 1934

Mr. President:

Thank you for your profoundly impressive radio address of last evening. I was particularly pleased with its leftward leanings. The rebukes which you gave your reactionary adversaries struck me as being polite, forceful, and unbeatable in their logic.

I am convinced that more and more Maine people are coming to believe that the interests of those called "middle class" are more closely tied up with the interests of the workers than with the interests of the owners. This trend accounts to some extent for the outcome of the Maine elections. . . .

Respectfully yours,

Robert F. Skillings
Portland, Maine

SEPTEMBER 27, 1934

My dear President:

Your radio address this evening was as usual very pleasing to hear, I never miss your friendly talks when it is possible for me to listen.

. . . We judge the new deal by the opposition it receives from the bankers, if they are against it surely it must be all right for the majority.

Many of us think this administration is headed in the right direction, but is to easy, has made to many threats and no action. I have heard even Republicans say that the NRA is O.K. if it was enforced.

Why delay action any longer? If this new deal is for the little fellow as most of us think, then lets fight the big fellow now and not allow him to hinder progress or to tear down that which has been rebuilt. They are fighting us, lets fight back. If the money changers refuse to loosen up, take it away from them, confiscate their property, declare their money null & void. Step all over them, show them who is boss.

The constitution. Who started all this talk about preserving the constitution? It seems as though the opposing side has taken quite a liking to that document all of a sudden, if they want it let them have it, it is only a scrap of paper, and so far out of date that it has become useless. When G. Washington and his companions drew up that document little did they ever dream that this great land of ours was some day to have three nation wreckers in a row as Presidents. Harding, Coolidge and Hoover. If it is constitutional for a few to gobble up all the money, then it is constitutional to take it away from them. Who thought about the constitution when millions of us were out of work, and still are. I tasted unemployment for 3 long years and yet never mentioned the constitution. . . .

A 30 hour week and 75 cents per hour as a minimum wage will do more than all the NRA's to bring a return of prosperity providing the manufacturers are prevented from reducing their payrolls by the use of labor saving devices. Companys should be compelled to add more men instead of laying them off. In the plant I work 4 men could be added nicely if the employers were not so set on making one man do two mens work.

Your success is my daily prayer and I hope God will bless you in every way.

Faithfully Yours

O. D. Armstrong
Dishman, Wash.

P.S. I hope this letter gets past the examiners, If the President does'nt personally receive one of my letters soon I shall quit writing.

SEPTEMBER 30, 1934

Dear Mr. President:

I am writing at the close of your Sunday night address before I see or hear comments by other persons. . . .

The policy you uphold is the best under the circumstances. The outcome will be very largely a success.

But — permanent security and prosperity can rest only on a much more extensive socialization of the larger enterprises in production and distribution. I hope this Larger Deal will come in your lifetime so that you may see the fruitage of the New Deal which has in it the promise of an ultimate economic revolution on the basis of human brotherhood.

Very respectfully yours,

H. L. Latham
Chicago, Illinois

OCTOBER 6, 1934

Dear Sir: —

I want to congratulate you upon your recent radio address, during which you outlined so courageously the stand of the New Deal in it's relation to human liberty. . . .

I have been following your efforts, since you took office, with the keenest interest and I am fully aware of the appalling problems, which confront you. Of these problems, I think, none is harder than to convince our big business leaders of their responsibility towards the citizens of this country and towards the common good. While life and nature seem to point to an everlasting struggle among the forces of the cosmos, there is no reason, why human beings endowed with reasoning power should not be taught, by force if necessary, to hold a helpful attitude towards each other. That attitude can be brought about through the education of the young or it must, as in our present case, be brought about through government regulation. . . .

All this means reforms of a most drastic manner, but reforms, which in their final effect will free us from the fear of an old age in poverty or from the humiliating spectacle of the soup kitchen or other forms of a hit and miss existence, which had been the order of the day until you became President. If all this be loss of Liberty to the money changers, but freedom from serfdom to the average wholesome American family, then I feel that the gain outweighs the loss and my wish is, that I shall be able in some way to contribute my own efforts towards the building of that better life for all of us, which you are trying so hard to give to this generation and it's future descendants. . . .

Sincerely yours,

H. W. Arth
San Fransisco, Cal.

OCTOBER 2, 1934

Dear Mr. President:

Sunday evening I spent with a friend in the country, a man who runs a small chicken ranch. About six thirty oclock, as we sat there talking, neighbors who had no radios began to drop in to listen to your talk which came to us at seven oclock.

As your voice began to come to us, the room became very quiet. If you could have seen the faces of those folks, hanging on your every word; their expressions when your talk was finished, you would have new strength to go ahead. During the following Monday, friends called at the studio to pass the time of day. All sorts of people; a newspaper representative, a writer of action stories, a house-to-house solicitor, the postman, express man, and grocery man. The first word of all was, "Did you hear Roosevelt's talk?"

In the evening, the Ritchfield Newsflashes told us the bankers were not satisfied, you had not made the promises they had hoped for; that business was dissatisfied; that the Socialists were distrustful.

Looks like nobody was satisfied but old John Public.

But the ordinary people with whom I came in contact showed new faith and courage after listening to your words. To them, your talk promised one thing, you would not turn back, and they were satisfied with that. That, in fact, was all they wished to know. They are willing to follow as long as you face forward.

Sincerely

C. H. Van Scoy
Seattle, Washington

OCTOBER 2, 1934

Dear Mr. Presidents;

We want you to know that we appreciate your Broadcasts over the Radio. In the past 3 years that I have searched for work and so far have not had to go on relief rolls. Your radio talks have did a great deal to give me encourgement to keep on trying. A great many more of my friends feel the same way and we are looking forward to more of your interesting chats soon. Being a

Boilermaker and Ship Yard worker, I like your efforts in trying new things. Many thanks Mr. President.

Very Truly Yours,

M. J. Lane
Chicago, Illinois

OCTOBER 1, 1934

Mr. Secretary to the President,

Dear Sir: Do you happen to have in your files a picture of President Roosevelt taken a short time ago when at West Point reviewing the Cadets? I saw him in the "Movie" at that time and as he opened his mouth to speak I noticed the absence of a lower tooth and immediately felt a "bond of sympathy" as I too have lost a lower tooth at the same point and at once said "I wish I had a picture of him in that pose — something unusual.* I listened eagerly last night to see if I could detect a lisp as mine has caused me, but I could not and imagine he has had his replaced and not deferring from the same reason I have — he is young — I am seventy this month — so it is hardly worth while. . . .

Very Truly Yours,

(Mrs) Florence D. Price
Dania, Florida

---

*FDR did in fact have a false tooth that he kept in a small silver box when he was not using it. More than once, just before he began a Fireside Chat, he discovered he had left the box on a table near his bed and a Secret Service man had to be sent to retrieve it. It was, then, quite possible he had left the tooth behind when he made his trip to West Point. See Grace Tully, *F.D.R. My Boss* (New York: Charles Scribner's Sons, 1949), 100.

PROTECTING THE WEAK:
APRIL 28, 1935

LESS THAN FIVE WEEKS after the September 30 Fireside Chat, the American people went to the polls for the midterm elections of 1934. Rather than reducing the congressional margins of the party in power — which they normally did in midterm elections — voters strengthened the Democratic hold on the national government, increasing their numbers in the House from 313 to 322 and in the Senate from 59 to 69, more than two-thirds majorities in both houses. The Republicans had only 103 seats in the House and 25 in the Senate — their slimmest representation in Congress since before the Civil War.

The historian Charles Beard viewed the victory as "thunder on the left." Many members of the Seventy-fifth Congress were now clearly to the left of the President, while as the *New York Times* observed, the election had "literally destroyed the right wing of the Republican Party." It was, the *Times* proclaimed, "the most overwhelming victory in the history of American politics." FDR could not have been completely surprised. After his August trip across the country, he had remarked: "The reception was grand and I am more than ever convinced that, so far as having the people with us goes, we are just as strong — perhaps stronger — than ever before."[47]

But even Roosevelt could not have predicted how broad his mandate would be. Now, as in the early months of his presidency, FDR may have had a potential opportunity to alter the system in directions many of his opponents ceaselessly claimed he desired to. He could have attempted a permanent realignment of parties, endeavored to inject the government more powerfully and permanently into the fundamental matrix of the economy, experimented with alternate and more vigorous forms of central planning and collective action. Though he did speak from time to time of reshuffling the parties so that by the end of the eight years he hoped to serve there might or might not be a Democratic party but would be a Progressive one — a goal he never implemented — he had neither the plans nor the intentions to initiate radical change. Secretary of Labor Frances Perkins surely was correct when she observed that FDR had no central unified plan: "he had, I am sure, no thought or desire to impose any overall economic or political change on the United States."[48]

It was this lack of planning that led to Rexford Guy Tugwell's famous complaint that 1933 had been "a lost year of opportunities passed over." Instead of leading a weary nation down new and better paths, Roosevelt fell back on restoring confidence and bolstering faith in the very institutions that had created the disaster. On March 4, 1933, "Americans would have followed him anywhere," Tugwell asserted, but FDR "had no place much to take them." It is certainly true that Roosevelt had no new ideas or destination that would have structurally reconstituted the American system. His goal was to make that system work more efficiently and justly by creating greater balance between its parts and extending greater security and equity to its people. Tugwell, a Columbia University economics professor who was serving as Assistant Secretary of Agriculture, was a loyal New Dealer who supported and worked for these ends until he resigned after the election of 1936, but from the beginning he feared that the New Deal's patchwork of reforms would ultimately leave the old economic establishment "more solidly planted than ever," its functions not nationalized, its elite not disciplined. FDR, Tugwell concluded in retrospect, had erred "on the minimal side. He could have emerged from the orthodox progressive chrysalis and led us into a new world. He chose rather rickety repairs for an old one."[49]

Tugwell's was a distinctly minority voice among New Dealers, most of whom found themselves enthused by the "repairs" being implemented. After the elections of 1934, FDR's relief administrator, Harry Hopkins, turned to his staff and proclaimed: "Boys — this is our hour. We've got to get everything we want — a works program, social security, wages and hours, everything — now or never. Get your minds to work on developing a complete ticket to provide security for all the folks of this country up and down and across the board."[50]

Though a substantial number of those responding to the Fireside Chats continued to urge the President to deliver them as often as possible, FDR created his own deliberate pace. He tended to give the Chats more frequently in periods of crisis and reduce the number when events seemed under control, as they certainly did following the November elections. In the face of FDR's long radio silence after his September 1934 Chat, the old Wilsonian Democrat Ray Stannard Baker wrote in March 1935 pleading with him to keep before the country a vision of high moral purpose. FDR respectfully reminded Baker that "the public psychology and, for that matter, individual psychology, cannot, because of human weakness, be attuned for long periods of time to a constant repetition of the highest note in the scale. . . . People tire of seeing the same name day after day in the important headlines of the papers, and the same voice night after night over the radio." Nevertheless, he did agree that "the time is soon at hand for a new stimulation of united American action. I am proposing that very thing before the year is out."[51]

Whatever FDR's own inclination might have been — and there were those like *Time* magazine who predicted that he would reconcile with business and end reform — the nation itself seemed to be moving to the left. Not only the midterm elections attested to that, but the rise of voices demanding more intensified reform appeared to be everywhere. In Wisconsin, Senator Robert La Follette and his brother, Governor Philip La Follette, created the Wisconsin Progressive Party to work for the more equal distribution of wealth. In Minnesota, the Farmer-Labor Party under Governor Floyd Olson called not for a New Deal but for a New Deck. In California, the novelist Upton Sinclair established the End Poverty in California movement (EPIC) to create a production-for-use economy in which the state would take over idle farms and factories and allow the unemployed to use them to produce for their own needs. Sinclair won the Democratic gubernatorial primary and almost won the election in spite of FDR's refusal to support him. Demands for radical change were hardly confined to these states. Father Charles E. Coughlin's immensely popular radio programs, along with his National Union for Social Justice, demanded an end to an exploitative economic system ruled by the greedy few; Huey Long's Share Our Wealth movement advocated redistributing wealth by limiting personal fortunes and providing a five thousand dollars estate for every American family; Dr. Francis Townsend articulated a widely acclaimed plan to give two hundred dollars a month to every American over the age of sixty if they pledged to spend it within thirty days. Such movements enlisted millions of supporters and spread the ferment of left-leaning "thunder" throughout the nation.

It was in the midst of this agitation that Roosevelt finally returned to the airwaves on April 28, 1935, almost seven months after his last Fireside

Chat.[52] He began with still another defense against those — on the left and the right — who accused him of having no definite course of action. He assured the nation that the New Deal's programs were not haphazard: "Each of our steps has a definite relationship to every other step." He documented his assertion not with details but with a homey metaphor comparing the creation of a program for the nation's welfare to the building of a great sea-going ship. When such a ship was under construction it was difficult to tell what it would finally look like when sailing the high seas. "It may seem confused to some, but out of the multitude of detailed parts that go into the making of the structure, the creation of a useful instrument for man ultimately comes. It is that way with the making of a national policy."

The objective of the nation had changed greatly in the past three years, he assured his audience. Where "individual self-interest and group self-ishness" had been paramount, where the "general good was at a discount," now people "are considering the whole rather than a mere part, a part relating to one section, or to one crop, or to one industry, or to one individual private occupation. That is a tremendous gain for the principles of democracy." He defended himself also against the charge that he was moving too slowly. The overwhelming majority of the people, he asserted, "know that the process of the constructive rebuilding of America cannot be done in a day or a year, but that it is being done in spite of the few who seek to confuse them and to profit by their confusion. Americans as a whole are feeling a lot better — a lot more cheerful than for many, many years."

To maintain and further this mood, it was crucial to make plans to eliminate unemployment in the future and to deal with the immediate necessities of the unemployed in the present. The first objective would be aided by the Social Security Act pending before Congress (it would be passed by the House on August 8, by the Senate a day later, and signed into law on August 14):

> It proposes, by means of old age pensions, to help those who have reached the age of retirement to give up their jobs and thus give to the younger generation greater opportunities for work and to give to all, old and young alike, a feeling of security as they look toward old age.
>
> The unemployment insurance part of the legislation will not only help to guard the individual in future periods of lay-

off against dependence upon relief, but it will, by sustaining the purchasing power of the nation, cushion the shock of economic distress.

The second objective — to meet the current needs of those still unemployed — would be met by the Emergency Relief Appropriation Act, which Congress had passed earlier that month, under which FDR established the Works Progress Administration (WPA) a week later. More than 80 percent of the WPA's funds went directly as wages to its workers, some 90 percent of whom were classified as needy. The WPA would employ as many as 3.3 million jobless Americans at one time, and before it was phased out in 1943, its workers had repaired 85,000 public buildings and 572,000 miles of roads, built 78,000 new bridges and viaducts, laid 67,000 miles of city streets and 24,000 miles of sidewalks, created 8,000 parks, built 350 airports and 40,000 buildings, improved flood control on rivers and water and sewage systems in cities and towns, produced books in braille for the blind, decorated uncounted public buildings with the works of unemployed artists in the Federal Arts Project, sent out unemployed actors in the Federal Theatre Project to bring theater to Americans throughout the nation, hired unemployed photographers to save the nation's images for posterity and unemployed writers in the Federal Writers' Project to record the oral histories of its people, including two thousand former slaves. It was, in short, enormously creative and useful in the ways in which it injected more than ten billion dollars into a stagnating economy, although it never had the funds necessary to employ more than one-third of the people in need of jobs.[53]

His Fireside Chat reflects the fact that FDR understood that the opponents of a project of this magnitude would distort it by claims of corruption and by painting images of indolent men leaning on shovels, and thus he patiently explained the fundamental principles for his work relief program: projects should be useful; most of the money spent should go directly into wages; funds should be spent promptly; employment should be given first to those on the relief rolls; projects would be allocated to localities in relation to the number of workers on the relief rolls in those areas. Through the WPA, Roosevelt converted the dole into work relief on a scale the United States has never known before or since. It was in some ways his most radical act, and politicians after him, for all their excoriation of the dole — giving relief payments without demanding work in return — have never exhibited

FDR's courage or determination in creating programs of work relief that conservatives envision as competing with capitalism but that Roosevelt saw as saving his people body and soul from the failures of capitalism. "This is a great national crusade," he told his listeners, "a crusade to destroy enforced idleness which is an enemy of the human spirit generated by this depression." Once again he endeavored to turn his constituents into participants:

> I call upon my fellow citizens everywhere to cooperate with me in making this the most efficient and the cleanest example of public enterprise the world has ever seen. It is time to provide a smashing answer for those cynical men who say that a democracy cannot be honest, cannot be efficient. If you will help, this can be done. I therefore hope that you will watch the work in every corner of the nation. Feel free to criticize. Tell me of instances where work can be done better, or where improper practices prevail. Neither you nor I want criticism conceived in a purely fault-finding or partisan spirit, but I am jealous of the right of every citizen to call to the attention of his or her government examples of how the public money can be more effectively spent for the benefit of the American people.

He devoted the remainder of his Chat to legislation pending before Congress. He called for the renewal of the NRA (the Supreme Court would declare it unconstitutional on May 27); passage of the Public Utility Holding Company Act, which provided for "the elimination of unnecessary holding companies in the public utility field" (a weaker law than he requested was signed into law on August 28); the strengthening of the Interstate Commerce Commission (signed into law on August 3); and most important, passage of the Banking Act of 1935, which made central banking more feasible by concentrating power in the Federal Reserve Board (signed into law on August 23).

All of these measures, he insisted, were "wise provisions for the protection of the weak against the strong."

> Never since my inauguration in March, 1933, have I felt so unmistakably the atmosphere of American recovery. But it is more than the recovery of the material basis of our individual lives. It is the recovery of confidence in our democratic processes, our republican institutions. We have survived all of the

arduous burdens and the threatening dangers of a great economic calamity. We have in the darkest moments of our national trials retained our faith in our own ability to master our own destiny. Fear is vanishing. Confidence is growing on every side, renewed faith in the vast possibilities of human beings to improve their material and spiritual status through the instrumentality of the democratic form of government. That faith is receiving its just reward. For that we can be thankful to the God who watches over America.

APRIL 29, 1935

My Dear Mr. President: —

Your inspiring talk to the Nation over the Radio of last evening prompts me to set an example in patriotism by offering my service gratis to you in whatever capacity I can be the most helpful.

I have the honor to remain

Your most obedient servant,

Walter R. Dodson
Richmond, Va.

The following poem suggested itself to me while listening to your Radio talk:

> What builds a Nation great and strong,
> What makes it mighty to defy,
> The foes that 'round it throng?
> Not gold, but only men can make
> A Nation great and strong;
> Men, who for truth and honor's sake,
> Hold fast and suffer long;
> Men who work while others sleep,
> Who dare when others sigh —
> They make a Nation great and strong,
> And lift it to the sky.

APRIL 28, 1935

PLEASE STOP TALKING WE WANT TO HEAR SOME MUSIC.

[UNSIGNED]
LYNCHBURG, VIR.

APRIL 28, 1935

Honorable and Respected Sir: —

I have just heard what I consider a speech from you which will stand out in bold relief as one, if not the most note-worthy, of the many speeches which you have made since you assumed your present exalted office.

As a humble textile weaver, unemployed for the greater part of the past four years, at the present time in temporary employment, I beg to tender to you my thanks as a rank and file worker and citizen for the greater consideration you have given, and evident from your speech of this evening, is continuing to give, to alleviating the burden carried by those willing to work but can get no job.

A firm believer that an Almighty Creator has in the past given leaders of this nation inspiration and strength to grapple with the critical times and crises, so I believe that "thou art the man" chosen to lead us out of this slough of despondency through which we have been wallowing these many years past.

May God grant to you health, inspiration and wisdom in continuance of your good work for the welfare of the people of our country.

Yours very humbly and respectfully

William G. Ingham
Philadelphia, Penna.

APRIL 30, 1935

Dear Mr. President:

. . . The socialization of this Government worries no right thinking man and I personally feel that the only criticism which I can make is that it is not rapid enough. Drastic times demand drastic measures and in a free Government like this often drastic measures cannot be taken on account of the many ramifications of the Government in its initial set up and that created by the construction of the Courts. I do wish that the Courts were more ready to see the handwriting on the wall and join whole-heartedly with you in these efforts. . . .

Believe me to be,

Sincerely and respectfully yours,

C. T. Graydon
Columbia, S.C.

APRIL 30, 1935

Sir:

Your latest piece of glorified propaganda — miscalled fireside chats — was disheartening and sickening. I must confess, I am ashamed that I once had some faith in you and your New Deal.

Prosperity? How you mock us. There can never be any true prosperity under your administration. Nothing but a vast destruction of wealth and hope, — a degrading and demoralizing of our national character.

Why not be perfectly frank with your people just once, and admit that you are engaged in a subtle and gigantic effort to ruin the investing classes, big and little. Why not come out in the open, and declare your unalterable and all too evident purpose to usher in government ownership of all important businesses and a Socialist state.

For the hypocricy of the New Deal is revolting.

Raymond E. Click
Prospect, Ohio

*   *   *

Dear Sir

I listened to your speech tonight and heard all your fine words about justice.

As a Utility stockholder your sense of justice sounded rather flat. You evidently dont care one single dam about justice to the Utility stockholders as long as you can gratify your inbred hatred to the industry. It is as evident that stubborn dutch streak in your being wont be satisfied until you ruin hundreds of thousand of us. . . .

I voted for you in 1932. Ordinary I take little interest in polotics but I have a hatred for you now that exceeds any you have for the heads of the Utility industry. I swear by every fiber of my being to preach and do every thing in my power to influence people against you and there will be a million others like me.

If I cant influence 50 people I will be ashamed of myself.

Fred S. Willard
Rockville Centre, New York

MAY 3, 1935

Dear Mr. President:

Your talk last Sunday night, in my opinion, was wonderful and inspirational. It created a further feeling of confidence and I don't know what more you could have said.

This letter is prompted by the resolutions of criticism that are being adopted at Washington at the present time by the National Chamber of Commerce. When one reads them and knows the selfishness and the small caliber minds that are behind some of them, they lose weight. In reading them, I could not help but think where these giant intellectualists and captains of industry were during March and April of 1933 when the banks were popping all over the country. They were willing enough then to pass the buck to the new President. Where were they when the public utility holding companies stock dropped in some cases from $250.00 to less than $5.00 per share?

The wonderful banking fraternity did not have any solution for preventing the captains of finance from using the mails for exploiting stocks and bonds and unloading them on the public at high prices, an enormous percentage of which were absolutely worthless. And then they have the audacity to criticise an administration that is interfering with business. My dear

Mr. President, you are not interfering with business, you are interfering with road agents and bandits and every thinking man in this country knows it. . . .

Yours truly,

Thos. J. Vernia
Chicago, Illinois

P.S. Don't you think Mr. President that it would be a good idea to have your heart to heart talk to the people oftener? I attended four or five conventions of the Chamber — and know.

APRIL 29, 1935

Dear Mr. President:

In your radio address Sunday night you invited comment and criticism. Therefore I would first like to make the statement that I was not particularly impressed, nor did I find any word of encouragement to the average American citizen.

You likened the present Administration to the building of a ship, wherein no one but the builders know what the ship would look like until it was completed. This is not true. Anyone who would be sufficiently interested in the construction of an ordinary vessel, would have no difficulty in being shown the draftsman's completed work. Take the new French liner the "Normandie" as an example. Long before she was launched, the papers published photographs of the artist's conception.

Why, therefore, is it not possible for the American citizen to have your conception of the ultimate finished work in which you ask us now to place so much confidence?

Yours very truly,

F. C. Elkins
Philadelphia, Pa.

APRIL 29, 1935

My dear Mr. President:

I had great pleasure in listening to your radio talk last night and, at your suggestion, I am taking this opportunity of writing.

In the discussion of this great public works' appropriation, no one, so far as I know, has stressed the very important point that the people of the United States will be wealthier by the tangible increases in the real wealth of the Federal government, as a result of the proposed expenditures.

This great fund will not be used simply to give men work. It will give to us, the people, more highways, more Boulder Dams, more civic improvements, more bridges, more tunnels, better harbors, etc., etc.

The balance sheet of the United States of America, if such a thing could be prepared, would reflect a tremendous increase on the asset side, and the proprietary interest of each citizen (for that, after all, is what the bonds represent), will increase enormously. . . .

So few people see this. Our New England reactionaries, particularly, can not realize that as long as men are willing to work, we should put them to work. We should have brains enough to arrange our affairs so that we, the people, can have and enjoy the countless things that these very people are anxious and willing to produce.

I consider it a great privilege to be able to write to you, and I can assure you of my small but wholehearted cooperation in this great endeavor of yours. I am

Very respectfully yours,

F. W. Beinecke
Boston

APRIL 28, 1935

President Roosevelt;

I was very much disappointed in your talk over the Radio Sunday night and I believe so were thousands of other people. To begin with you said there was not much graft or red tape in the U.S. Government. If you think that I'm pretty sure you're the only educated person in the U.S. who believes that. Everyone knows there is more dirty work carried on in the government today then in any other business or profession. Men who are not statesmen but politicians that get huge salaries, do nothing but argue and call each other names, and who pays, the poor American citizen. Things may be picking up in the East but as far as the Middle West is concerned things are worse than ever and there is no use kidding ourselfves that things are improving when they're not.

Millions of dollars being spent now for temporary work for men. The minute the work is completed they are as bad off as they were before they started. It looks as if those politicians, who are being paid such immense salaries (for doing nothing) and are suppose to be such intelligent, educated men could think up something that would be permanent, without taxing the citizen to the limit and doing nothing else.

If something isn't soon done this country will reach its end and there is no use in kidding ourselves about that either.

Just an Unemployed College Girl,

Hope Adams
Tulsa, Okla.

APRIL 28, 1935

Dear Mr. President,

. . . several weeks ago I had an opportunity to visit at Washington on a week-end excursion. I spent all of Sunday, April 28th, just browsing about the federal buildings there. When I passed through several of the buildings, I became impressed with the magnitude of our government. . . .

Of course, the government is of people not buildings but anyway the structures seem to cast some kind of awe upon the average citizen. We often wonder whether all of the work that goes on in these buildings really means much or what it should to the individual American. It seems so aloof and one cannot imagine himself as a part of the government. When I looked at the physical structure of our government, I thought of the poor and downtrodden coal miners and workers back home. I recalled their plight and squalor and their loss of hope and I thought of their attitude toward their government. I couldn't help but think of what dependence they place upon their government to bolster their lives — to help them to have new hope and to gain decent livings. The hopelessness of the people during the past years is, no doubt, gradually being allayed but everything seems to be so slow.

Mr. President, I am a student at West Virginia University and my main purpose in writing to convey to you the appreciation of the many students here, who like myself have only been able to remain in school by working their way through. I refer to the F.E.R.A. work that has been carried on in our University and in other schools of the nation. Many of the students are really deserving and to many of them this work has been a godsend. True it has only been enough to pay our tuition and a little extra but it has meant very much to us. . . .

Very truly yours

William Nels
Pursglove, West Virginia

APRIL 29, 1935

Dear President: —

We listened to your chat with all of us over the air last evening and enjoyed it, you are very sincere and as you say there are many chiselers and grafters.

Just a word or two of comment.

The government has been more than generous in taking care of the unemployed and there are many of the lower class of people also some of the colored ones, who think they should have more. Dear Sir they have more than any working man who works every day but does not get enough only to pay his bills and nothing left to buy things we need so badly.

My husband is in a place to see these things they are paid so much a month, given clothes bedding food, coal etc and then they take the money for entertainment and I used to worry about it but those out of work are cared for better than we. Until the wages of the common man is raised so he can purchase the many things we need business will never be any better, we dont have it to buy with, and I'll go with out sooner than have collectors hounding the door all the time. One house dress in 3 yrs, mend, patch, and fix it sure gets tiresome. We need new mattresses clothes floor coverings bedding. . . .

Employers just want to pocket the money and make one work for a pittance.

Excuse my long letter but you are so sincere in your talk I just wanted to tell you where one trouble is. Best wishes and much good health be yours and I hope you can live to fulfill all your hopes —

Yours truly,

Mrs. H. A. Thompson
Cedar Rapids, Iowa

APRIL 27, 1935

Sir

Your talk over the radio Sunday night, plainly shows your complete ignorance as to present conditions, in other words, you say that you are dealing out that enormous sum of money, borrowed to finance the Work Relief Bill, to the most irresponsible, lazy, dishonest and shiftless group of people in the U.S.A.

The people who have the decency and pride to get along without relief, even though they have had to go far in debt and even loose the roof over their head, will get no help or consideration. I refer to the taxpayers, principly, and to the old people, who will never be able to regain their great loss, while the lowest, possibly the least deserving element among our people get help.

For God's sake, I beg of you, consider what you do.

Very Truly Yours,

(Mrs.) Laura Manning
Pleasantville, N.J.

APRIL 29, 1935

Dear Sir,

After I had listened to you talk over the Raido, I had to just relax and rejoice in how wounderful you have brought the present conditions about, at the beginning of your work I did not think it was possible, but thank God and our President we have learned that all things are possible. . . . I have ben living on Relief my self for nearly a year now, and do not know what I would have done if it had not ben for the Relief. I was a merchant here for years, But went down to the Bottom in the depression just finishing up a year ago. I am not to good to work and am very grateful to think I am going to have a chance to earn my living in an honist way and by the swet of my Brow, in my last days, I was just about at the point to become discouraged as living on Relief and too old to get a job in Factorys or other industries any more, I had begun to think I was doomed. But God will Bless you Mr. Roosevelt for what you are trying to do, and that all things will work out for the best, and myself a small mind, doing things in a small way, you have my support heart and sole as one American citizen.

from

Mr. Archie Tickner
Waukegan, Ill.

APRIL 30, 1935

My dear Mr. President:

. . . Your Social Security program seems a most important step for a great betterment and spiritual advancement of our citizens. In this connection, may I mention for your consideration that, whatever old age pensions are given it be done in the spirit and on conditions that the recipients are ENTITLED to it and not given to them as mendicants. Why entitled, you may ask. Because, at the age reached, the average person has contributed a life work to the sum total of labor and wealth of the country. . . . Age gathers wisdom that the country needs disseminated among its people, tho it could not be if smothered under the belief of being a beggar in order to get a limited sustenance. Whether entitled or not, if given at all and it will be in some way, citizens receiving that benefit may as well be blessed with an uplift as to be made to feel degraded.

Very respectfully yours,

John M. Russ
Jacksonville, Florida

APRIL 30, 1935

Our Beloved President that God has placed over our own United States,

In your address over the Radio Sun. night you said anyone that had in mind any plan that might be of a benefit in their estimation in the management of the problems of today, you wanted them to feel free to write in, therefore I take advantage of the opertunity.

A year ago the Lord Layed it upon my heart to write you but I let the Devil talk me out of sending it. But this time I am sending it through. . . .

If you could bring about a three day fasting and prayer Service and get the Faith of the people as you do in other affairs, you would save more Souls for the Glory of God in three day than all the preachers in the United states in three years and, by that much food supply would be gained and all would be stronger at the end of the three day than they were the first, you try it and see.

From a Friend who believes in Prayer and the Power of God.

Mrs. Nellie Loch
Enid, Oklahoma

APRIL 30, 1935

I listened to you Sunday and believe you want to do the right thang. I relize you are the head & ruler of our cuntry you can govern for the good, or the eavle you can make thangs better or worse. By the help of our creator you can get help & knowledge to make thangs better. . . . I am a farmer live 23 miles back from town have famly of 10 children. I want to see you rule for the good. your friend & suporter

S. A. Allsup
Wilson, Texas

1. Crop & Seed Loan
Loan a man enough to by seed, and run him, and give him 4 years to pay same.
2. All Foods
Dont destroy any food at all. Lay up in store.

3. Relief

Let the relief run same There is as well qualified men & women on relief as run same That will do away with creads [?].

4. Cotton

Pass a law to restrect any from planting but one half of crop in cotton. If it take a vote we will vote it on. We are not babes, have to be paid to do right.

5. Law

Pass a law that USA dont protect no mans welth out of our cuntry.

6. Insurance

Let a man pay one cent on every dollar paid to any insurance company. Let company pay same. This will pay the ex soldiers.

7. Tax

Put a special tax on all new cars $5 motersckle $2 yats $20 Privet Plaines $10

Let suport relief

8. Special Tax

Silks Face lotions & Powders One cent on the dollar Silk Hose $100. be $101 yard goods To suport old people relief.

"AN ORDERLY ECONOMIC DEMOCRACY": SEPTEMBER 6, 1936

FDR WAITED UNTIL EIGHT WEEKS before the presidential election of 1936 to deliver his next Fireside Chat. More than sixteen months had elapsed since his last Chat, the longest he was ever to go without directly addressing the American people over the radio. In the interim, the century's worst drought, which had begun in the Great Plains in 1934, returned in 1936 to hold much of agrarian America from Texas to the Dakotas in its grip. At its worst, the drought displaced more than one million Southwestern tenant farmers — who came to be known collectively as Okies, though they came not only from Oklahoma but such states as Arkansas, Missouri, and Texas. The sense of bewilderment and frustration with which many of these tenants greeted their plight mirrored the spirit that had pervaded much of America when Roosevelt first took office. In *The Grapes of Wrath* (1939), John Steinbeck captured the sense of confusion and impotent anger that characterized so much of Depression America, as in the following dialogue between an outraged Oklahoma tenant farmer dispossessed from the land he and his father and grandfather had farmed and the tractor driver sent to knock down his house and fences:

> "[This house] is mine. I built it. You bump it down — I'll be in the window with a rifle. You even come too close and I'll pot you like a rabbit."
>
> "It's not me. There's nothing I can do. I'll lose my job if I don't do it. And look — suppose you kill me? They'll just hang you, but long before you're hung there'll be another guy on the tractor, and he'll bump the house down. You're not killing the right guy."
>
> "That's so," the tenant said. "Who gave you orders? I'll go after him. He's the one to kill."
>
> "You're wrong. He got his orders from the bank. The bank told him, 'Clear those people out or it's your job.'"
>
> "Well, there's a president of the bank. There's a board of di-

rectors. I'll fill up the magazine of the rifle and go into the bank."

The driver said, "Fellow was telling me the bank gets orders from the East. The orders were, 'Make the land show profit or we'll close you up.'"

"But where does it stop? Who can we shoot? I don't aim to starve to death before I kill the man that's starving me."

"I don't know. Maybe there's nobody to shoot. Maybe the thing isn't men at all . . ."[54]

FDR was more upbeat, less prone to explore questions of ultimate existential responsibility, and more inclined to use his political power to find solutions for those farmers who owned the land they were suffering on than for tenants and sharecroppers who did not own their own land. He began his eighth Fireside Chat by recounting his recent trip through nine agricultural states to inspect the results of the drought.[55]

> I talked with families who had lost their wheat crop, lost their corn crop, lost their livestock, lost the water in their well, lost their garden and come through to the end of the summer without one dollar of cash resources, facing a winter without feed or food — facing a planting season without seed to put in the ground.

He spoke also of those farm families who had not lost everything but who needed help to supplement their partial crops if they were to be able to continue farming in the spring. But he seemed haunted by the extreme scenes of want he had witnessed:

> I shall never forget the fields of wheat so blasted by heat that they cannot be harvested. I shall never forget field after field of corn stunted, earless, stripped of leaves, for what the sun left the grasshoppers took. I saw brown pastures that would not keep a cow on fifty acres.

He took care not to let this litany of disaster become a litany of despair:

> No cracked earth, no blistering sun, no burning wind, no grasshoppers, are a permanent match for the indomitable American farmers and stockmen and their wives and children who have

carried on through desperate days, and inspire us with their self-reliance, their tenacity and their courage. It was their fathers' task to make homes; it is their task to keep these homes; and it is our task to help them win their fight.

The choice for farm families "who need actual subsistence" was to put them on the dole or to put them to work. "They do not want to go on the dole and they are one thousand percent right. We agree, therefore, that we must put them to work, work for a decent wage." This would allow farmers to buy food for their stock and seed for next year's planting and thus to remain farmers in the future. The work supplied to those farmers needing help would be "directly aimed at the alleviation of future drought conditions" — projects that would mitigate future water shortages and soil erosion, projects that would build roads to markets. "Spending like this is not waste. It would spell future waste if we did not spend for such things now."

Underlying his Chat was a didactic message that FDR had stressed since the establishment of the Tennessee Valley Authority in 1933: the interdependence of every group of people and every geographical area in the nation:

> Every state in the drought area is now doing and always will do business with every state outside it. The very existence of the men and women working in the clothing factories of New York, making clothes worn by farmers and their families; of the workers in the steel mills in Pittsburgh and Gary, in the automobile factories of Detroit, and in the harvester factories of Illinois, depend upon the farmers' ability to purchase the commodities that they produce. In the same way it is the purchasing power of the workers in these factories in the cities that enables them and their wives and children to eat more beef, more pork, more wheat, more corn, more fruit and more dairy products, and to buy more clothing made from cotton and wool and leather. In a physical and in a property sense, as well as in a spiritual sense, we are members one of another.

This interdependence did not mean dependence. "The people in the drought area do not want to be dependent on Federal or state or any other kind of charity. They want for themselves and their families an opportunity to share fairly by their own efforts in the progress of America." Nevertheless, there was need for a sound national agricultural policy — implemented by the federal, state, and local governments — which would create a permanent land use program, would maintain farm prices in times of drought and times of bumper crops, would maintain a fair equilibrium between farm prices and the prices of industrial products, and would devise a means of guaranteeing sufficient food supplies in good years and lean years.

He admitted that when the drought began in 1934 "none of us had preparation; we worked without blue prints and we made the mistakes of inexperience. . . . But as time has gone on we have been making fewer and fewer mistakes." For FDR, responses to the drought illustrated what he considered to be two of the pillars of his Administration. First, to prevent the growth of a Leviathan state, the administration of New Deal policies should be kept as local as possible. "Remember that the Federal and state governments have done only broad planning. Actual work on a given project originates in the local community. Local needs are listed from local information. Local projects are decided on only after obtaining the recommendations and the help of those in the local community who are best able to give it." Second, he stressed experimentation and pragmatic responsiveness to the specific needs of a given situation:

> In the drought area people are not afraid to use new methods to meet changes in Nature, and to correct mistakes of the past. If over-grazing has injured range lands, they are willing to reduce the grazing. If certain wheat lands should be returned to pasture, they are willing to cooperate. If trees should be planted as windbreaks or to stop erosion, they will work with us. If terracing or summer fallowing or crop rotation is called for, they will carry them out. They stand ready to fit, not to fight, the ways of Nature.*

Turning to the problem of industrial employment, FDR praised "the brave spirit with which so many millions of working people are winning their way out of depression." Dependable employment at fair wages was the city and town equivalent to good farm income. He announced that "re-

---

*Although the drought was one of FDR's two major themes in this address, we have been able to find only two letters responding to this Fireside Chat that refer to the drought.

employment in industry is proceeding fairly rapidly" and pointed to government spending as the reason. "Government orders were the backlog of heavy industry; government wages turned over and over again to make consumer purchasing power and to sustain every merchant in the community. Businessmen with their businesses, small and large, had to be saved." Private enterprise was necessary to maintain democracy, and by saving business the government had saved private enterprise no less than it had saved drought-stricken farmers. It was now the "deep responsibility" of businessmen "to take men off the relief rolls and give them jobs in private enterprise." The United States Employment Service, established in 1933, was available to enable business to find workers with the skills they needed and workers to find jobs they were qualified for. Government relief programs like the Works Progress Administration (WPA) and the Public Works Administration (PWA) would continue "until all workers have decent jobs in private employment at decent wages. We do not surrender our responsibility to the unemployed." Still, it was the New Deal's intention "to use every resource to get private work for those now employed on government work, and thus to curtail to a minimum the government expenditures for direct employment."

"Tomorrow is Labor Day," he reminded his listeners:

> Labor Day in this country has never been a class holiday. It has always been a national holiday. . . . In this country we insist, as an essential of the American way of life, that the employer-employee relationship should be one between free men and equals. We refuse to regard those who work with hand or brain as different from or inferior to those who live from their own property. We insist that labor is entitled to as much respect as property. But our workers with hand and brain deserve more than respect for their labor. They deserve practical protection in the opportunity to use their labor at a return adequate to support them at a decent and constantly rising standard of living, and to accumulate a margin of security against the inevitable vicissitudes of life.

It was those who "would try to refuse the worker any effective power to bargain collectively, to earn a decent livelihood and to acquire security . . . who threaten this country with that class dissension which in other countries has led to dictatorship."

He concluded by emphasizing the need to build "an orderly economic democracy in which all can profit and in which all can be secure from the kind of faulty economic direction which brought us to the brink of common ruin seven years ago."

The Fourth of July commemorates our political freedom — a freedom which without economic freedom is meaningless indeed. Labor Day symbolizes our determination to achieve an economic freedom for the average man which will give his political freedom reality.

SEPTEMBER 7, 1936

Dear President Roosevelt,

We listened with great interest to your "fireside chat" last evening, and are in accord with your plans and ambitions for the Farmer and the less fortunate of our people in this United States.

The fact that you go about and observe personally and take the keen interest and have the intelligence to know how to correct the evils which exist, make you the outstanding President of all History. It is such a relief to hear about human beings and natural resources, and not "gold" & "statistics" by the yard.

I am one former Republican who has voted for you, and been your most devout follower. Your indomitable courage; your never finding any problem insurmountable is a guiding spirit to this nation;

We must win next November — and you will!

Most Sincerely yours

Gertrude Irene Falk
Waltham, Massachusetts

SEPTEMBER 6, 1936

Your Excellency: —

Just heard your wonderful speech in which you made yourself another 1,000,000 Votes. One of the very best you ever made. Also it came over fine all was perfect including the local weather. Thot you would like to know of this. Kindly excuse pencil.

Sincerely Yours,

Leo Weiler
El Paso, Tex.

SEPTEMBER 6, 1936

SPEECH TOUCHED WITH THE THRILL OF GREATNESS. NO LEADER IN EUROPE WOULD HAVE MADE IT; NONE IN AMERICA COULD HAVE MADE IT. UT-

TERLY UNMARKED BY PARTISANSHIP IT MADE ALL WHO HEARD IT YOUR
PARTISANS. . . . AFFECTIONATELY.

HERBERT BAYARD SWOPE
PORT WASHINGTON, N.Y.

SEPTEMBER 7, 1936

My Dear President —

My President I together with an elderly friend of Yours and Mine — listened to Your Radio speech over Radio Station W.B.B.M. and We thoroughly approve Your program of spending federal money in Your effort to
bring about better times but Industry is not doing Their part therefore I put
the blame on Industry for prolonging recovery but I believe You will succeed regardless of their policy on hinderance they blamed the N.R.A. for
retarding recovery but soon as the Supreme Court declared the N.R.A. Ille-
gal They cut wages & lengthened working hours so I predict you will be
elected President again I voted for You in 1932 and do not regret it and am
going to vote for You again in November and hope You can find some way
to induce or force industry to do their part

I lost My Job at Stewart-Warner factory after 6 years of continous work
in 1929 and was idle untill you gave Me a Chance Oct - 29 - 35 on the
W.P.A. And am still working and thanks to You but the wages of $55.00 per
month do not seam to be hardly enough for prices of food and clothing are
mounting in price right along and it is pretty hard for a family of 5 or 6 or
more get along without going into debt but even as it is it is better than direct relief count on Me in November

Respectively,

E. L. Emerson
Chicago, Ill.

SEPTEMBER 7, 1936

Dear Friend:

We listen in to your fire side address yesterday and it was wonderful. I
am sure that you made friends amongst the thousands of listener. you deliv-

ered a constructive address and you didn't abuse republican. I think the public appreciate listening to good constructive addresses.

I attended a movie theatre patronized by the poorest people. They showed new reel of one of Coughlin meeting. The audience remained silence during the Coughlin address. One person tried to get the people to applause but he couldn't get a response.

I listen to the Richfield new commentator and he claimed there were 46000 straw ballots voted in Washington, Oregon and California. He gave you 10,000 more votes than the combine candidates. The labor day parade here was the largest in the history of L.A. The marcher yell your name throughout the parade.

Wishing you and your family the best of health.

Yours very truly

Homer C. Allison
Los Angeles, California

SEPTEMBER 6, 1936

Dear Sir:

Just a few minutes ago, you finished your Fireside Chat. From the time I learned that it was scheduled, I have been looking forward to what you would have to say. After your recent trip over this part of the country, I felt you would talk on subjects which are very close to me and mine: the wonderful things you said leaves me without adequate words to express my opinion of your tonight's talk.

May I introduce myself. Indiana is my home state. I spent my entire life here up to the time that I came out of college and went to Washington, D.C. to seek — and find — employment in January 1935. From that time until just last Friday, I have lived in Washington. I am employed in the Resettlement Administration, and effective 9-8-36 I have been transferred from the Administrator's Office in Washington to the Audit Division here in Indianapolis. I am just 22 years old — I cast my first vote this year. . . .

I daily gain inspiration in my work in the Resettlement Administration from the thought that I am playing a small part in your effort to establish a fuller life for the citizens of our great Country. I sincerely believe that in

years to come, I shall point to the pages in a history book covering this period and your work and proudly say: "I was a part of that — he was MY
BOSS!"

May God bless and strengthen you for the work you are doing and will
continue to do for the benefit of us all.

Respectfully yours,

J. Murray Parker
Indianapolis, Ind.

SEPTEMBER 9, 1936

My Dear Mr. President,

Listened to your talk Sunday night. It was an address quite worthy of
you and should create new courage in the down-hearted and remind them
that they have at least one friend in this rather selfish-laden world of ours.
Having never taken up your time before, as I know 24 hours aren't enough
to perform your many duties, am prompted to do so because of a personal
collision with what I think is a very short-sighted attitude of corporate
business.

Am 39 year of age, and therein lies the tragedy. Was just old enough to
be in the army six months. Have a college degree in Civil Engineering, and
some 18 years experience in the oil business, in geological and land department work. Entered oil company work with Senator Guffy's company in
Oklahoma in 1918. Later was in the oil business for myself till that "mild
Hoover boom" wiped me out. Worked in the topographic division of the
U.S.G.S. [United States Geological Survey] from Nov. 1933 to June 1935,
being paid out of PWA funds, for which employment, I'll always be most
grateful to you. In July 1935 started to work for a large oil company at a low-
paying job considering my experience. On Jan. 1, 1936 changed companies
to get a little better paying job. Now, after 8 months of work, of which they
were quite lavish in their praise, and only offered minor criticisms, they
"resign" me despite the fact, that the corporation is showing a profit for the
first time in several years, and tell me that there is no hope of any further
work there, as when that position is re-filled, it will be with a younger man.
The man firing me intimated that insurance rates and pension rules influ-

ence this tendency toward younger help. Friends of mine say 40 is almost a deadline, which prevents entrance into company employment.

It appears that I will have to create my own job, or become an "odd-job" man. With so many people unemployed, the employers have a tremendous advantage and do not hesitate to use it. The golden rule has been suspended for some time. If there were no labor unions, I'd hesitate to predict the wage levels.

It is rather difficult to enter on a business venture of your own today due to the tremendous competition from corporations, that can operate at a loss more than half the time and still stay in business. There is no lack of confidence among people today, as I see it, but a fear of competition from entrenched corporate wealth, which has never hesitated to be just as ruthless as necessary to hold their ground.

These same corporations also showed this same short-sightedness in using so much machinery and eliminating man-power faster than new uses of labor could absorb it. Reminds me of a man trying to eat three beefsteaks a meal, when one is all he can digest.

The management of this corporation as well as others, constitute your chief opposition to-day, as to both recovery and you re-election, showing absolutely no gratitude for your efforts in their behalf. Rich men aren't always smart. Their selfishness often consumes them.

I appreciate your efforts in behalf of humanity and you have my whole-hearted support.

Sincerely,

Tell T. White
Tulsa, Oklahoma

SEPTEMBER 6, 1936

Dear President Roosevelt: I listened with great interest to your address from the White House, to-night (E.S.T. 9:45 p.m.) and agree with every word of your plan with reference to employment of drought stricken farmers, and the employment of persons living in town and cities — and the general welfare.

One trouble confronting many is the age limit placed upon workers, no matter what their ability may be, no matter how needy they may be, by industry, and the government, may I say as well — and I feel that you would correct that situation, if possible, and I am writing in the spirit of Constructive Criticism, no person with any ambition, possessing at least, some pride wants to go on Charity or government Relief.

The idea of refusing employment to capable persons who are more than 40 years of age is all wrong, as you know, and will bring its own just reward, in just what way I do not know. Women over 25 or 30 not wanted — I refer to stores factories, etc. I hope every one in this country heard your remarks, and will profit by them.

You have my thanks, and appreciation — and congratulations.

Certainly my support and sincere Congratulations,

Very Respectfully,

Ralph E. Race
[illegible], O.

SEPTEMBER 6, 1936

My Dear Mr. President. —

I have long wanted to write you a note of thanks and appreciation. —

I so enjoyed your talk tonight, the sound of your voice gives one so much courage I hope and pray you are our President for the next-term. When I look back & allow my thought to dwell on the condition that this country was in when you first took office, I think every American should thank God that we had a man like you to bring us out of these terrible times. All during your term of office as our President I have felt you were the right man in the right place. A man who loved his Maker & loved his fellow creatures.

Moses was choosen by God to lead the children of Isarel out of bondage. —

I also know that God the God of love was working in the American people when they choose you in 1932 to lead them out of these terrible times. —

To day we need more love in our hearts towards God & our fellow man, more gratitude towards those who are trying to make this a better world to live in. —

"If a man is not thinking about himself he is himself," no great man ever yet lived for himself alone.

Yours gratefully,

Mrs Wm. Semple
Cleveland, Ohio

SEPTEMBER 6-7-8, 1936

My Dear President Roosevelt:

After your talk tonight this thought came to me, "Let your light so shine that men may see your good works and glorify our father which is in heaven." In this world of ours we can not ignore the great problems that confront us each day and so we pledge our selves anew to the task of demonstrating the brotherhood of man.

You remember how Jesus went about teaching the people; He didn't do much preaching He walked among them and spoke as one having authority. when you go among the people, they have the joy of seeing you and hearing you say just what the Federal Government can and will do.

That harmony and peace for which I have been praying and working is coming here and now and I know your burden is much lighter for "where there is peace there is God."

I am wearing three out-ward signs for you. First a little gold cross that my father wore from birth, he was born an Episcopalian. A stirling silver ring on the third finger of my right hand made by my daughter of Hyde Park High School in Chicago and a handpainted medallion broach, which I painted in 1931 after the snap shot was taken; there are two roses with folage painted on the pin. Each article plays its part in your re-election. I have worn them all constantly.

Faithfully,

Margaret H. Moore
Normal, Illinois

PART TWO

THE CONTINUING CRISIS: 1937–1938

... constantly I seek to look beyond the doors of the White House, beyond the officialdom of the national capital, into the hopes and fears of men and women in their homes. . . . My friends, my enemies, my daily mail, bring to me reports of what you are thinking and hoping. I want to be sure that neither battles nor burdens of office shall ever blind me to an intimate knowledge of the way the American people want to live and the simple purposes for which they put me here.

FDR, Fireside Chat, April 14, 1938

Our only means of expression is a ballot and a three cent stamp.

Anthony N. Rodrigues, Springfield, Massachusetts, to FDR, March 9, 1937

"PACKING"
THE SUPREME COURT:
MARCH 9, 1937

"ROOSEVELT IS THE ONLY PRESIDENT we ever had that thought the Constitution belonged to the pore man too," George Dobbin, a recently unemployed sixty-eight-year-old Southern millworker, proclaimed during FDR's second term of office. "The way they've been areadin' it it seemed like they thought it said, 'Him that's got money shall have the rights to life, freedom and happiness.' . . . Yessir, it took Roosevelt to read in the Constitution and find out them folks way back yonder that made it was talkin' about the pore man right along with the rich one. I am a Roosevelt man."[1]

There were, as the elections of 1936 demonstrated, a great many Roosevelt men and women — enough to give Roosevelt one of the most lopsided victories in the history of the American presidency. He received almost five million more votes than he had in 1932, winning 60.8 percent of the popular vote and 523 of the 531 electoral votes — only Maine and Vermont went to his opponent, Governor Alfred M. Landon of Kansas. The already swollen Democratic majorities in Congress increased, with Democrats winning 331 House seats to the Republicans' 89 and controlling 76 of the Senate seats to the Republicans' 16. When Alf Landon was asked how his defeat felt he told the story of the Kansas farmer who watches a tornado engulf first his barn, then his out buildings, then his home, reducing them to splinters, and begins to laugh. "What are you laughing at, you darned old fool?" his wife asks him. "The completeness of it," her husband replies.[2]

If FDR had been similarly tempted to mirth at the completeness of his own political tornado in 1936, he would have laughed too soon. As it turned out, his victory was not quite as complete as it appeared. In the light of George Dobbin's praise for Roosevelt's constitutional acumen, it is ironic that FDR's most stunning electoral victory preceded by only several months what was undoubtedly his most striking political blunder: he gave the appearance, to millions of foes and supporters alike, of placing himself above the Constitution. The problem was that FDR's successes at the polls and in Congress were not duplicated in the federal courts. From the beginning of his presidency, FDR worried that the conservative Republican composition of the Supreme Court was a potential threat to the reform legislation that he deemed necessary to bring the nation out of the crisis. He himself believed, as he had proclaimed pointedly in his First Inaugural Address, that the Constitution was "so simple and practical" that it was entirely feasible "to meet the extraordinary needs" imposed by the Depression "under the form of government which we have inherited from our ancestors."[3]

On what came to be called "Black Monday," May 27, 1935, FDR's worst fears were realized: the Court in three unanimous decisions found against the New Deal, most importantly invalidating the National Recovery Administration. During his press conference four days later, Roosevelt, reading from a pile of telegrams sent by panicked businessmen pleading with him to take some action to revive the NRA, referred to the Court's "horse-and-buggy definition of interstate commerce" and spoke about what he called "the very great national non-partisan issue . . . whether we are going to relegate to the forty-eight States practically all control over economic conditions — not only State economic conditions but national economic conditions; and . . . social and working conditions throughout the country," or restore to the United States government "the powers which exist in the national governments of every other Nation in the world to enact and administer laws that have a bearing on, and general control over, national economic problems and national social problems." It was, he insisted, "the biggest question that has come before this country outside of time of war, and it has to be decided." "We are the only Nation in the world that has not solved that problem," he told the assembled reporters. "We thought we were solving it, and now it has been thrown right straight in our faces."[4]

Following the press conference, Roosevelt maintained a public silence regarding the Court, but in private he continued to express his fears. After a Cabinet meeting in December, Secretary of the Interior Harold Ickes noted in his diary: "Clearly, it is running in the President's mind that substantially all of the New Deal bills will be declared unconstitutional by the Supreme Court. This will mean that everything that this Administration has done of any moment will be nullified."[5] On January 6, 1936, the Court by a vote of six to three overturned the AAA, depriving farmers of billions of dollars in benefits. The previous August FDR had told a member of his Administration: "If the Court does send the AAA flying like the NRA there might even be a revolution."[6]

While bullets did not fly, words certainly did. Throughout all the turmoil, the President maintained his public silence, though he continued to explore with his Attorney General and others means of reforming the Court. Hopes were raised in February when the Court validated the right of the Tennessee Valley Authority to distribute power generated by the Wilson Dam, then were dashed in the spring by a series of decisions striking down several pieces of New Deal legislation and overturning the New York State minimum wage law. "The sacred right of liberty of contract again — the right of an immature child or a helpless woman to drive a bargain with a great corporation," Secretary Ickes fulminated in his diary. "This is positively medieval, and I am frank to say that if this decision is constitutional, we need either an entirely new or a radically amended Constitution. If it isn't constitutional, then we need a different Supreme Court."[7]

The President was increasingly reaching the latter conclusion: that the problem lay not in the Constitution but in the Supreme Court. On June 2 he spoke of the creation by the Court of a " 'no-man's-land' where no Government — State or Federal — can function," but refused a reporter's invitation to say what should be done about it.[8] While the 1936 Democratic platform called vaguely for an amendment if the constitutional problem could not be solved by legislation, FDR, though clearly worried that such reforms as the Social Security Act and the National Labor Relations Act as well as his relief agencies and such regulatory bodies as the Securities and Exchange Commission were in jeopardy, remained silent on the issue throughout the 1936 campaign. Once reelected, he turned his full attention to the Supreme Court. At his first postelection Cabinet meeting, he referred to the fact that the present Court was the most aged one in our history, with six judges over 70, remarking that he expected the arch-conservative Justice James C. McReynolds to still be on the bench when he was 105, to which his Solicitor General laughingly responded that McReynolds appeared to be in the best possible health. FDR resented the fact that he was the first President in American history to go through a full term without having an appointment to the Supreme Court and had suffered more severe defeats at the Court's hands than any of his predecessors. As far as he was concerned, the Court already was packed — with elderly conservative Republican Justices who, he was convinced, clung to their places "to block our social and economic progress." He now sought to remedy that situation.[9]

Throughout these months, there was a sense of growing anxiety. According to the future Supreme Court Justice Robert H. Jackson, the problem plaguing the New Deal was that if the Court continued to make it impossible for a popularly elected government to regulate capitalism, anarchy and ultimately revolution seemed inevitable.[10] Roosevelt was convinced that democracies abroad were "yielding place to dictatorships because they had proven too weak or too slow to fulfill the wants of their citizens."[11] In his Annual Message to Congress on January 6, 1937, Roosevelt invited the Supreme Court to join him and the Congress in the attack upon the Depression and advised it that "the process of our democracy must not be imperiled by the denial of essential powers of free government." He added pointedly that cooperation could only be based upon "mutual respect for each other's proper sphere of functioning in a democracy."[12] But FDR was not about to wait for the Court to reform itself. His fear that the potentially excrutiatingly slow process of amending the Constitution would squander precious time needed to combat the Depression, and the great popularity he enjoyed following his extraordinary electoral victory emboldened him to attempt a legislative solution.

The notion of appointing enough new Justices to the Court to alter its spirit of constitutional fundamentalism had been discussed since 1935 and was advocated by Attorney General Homer Cummings. The bill crafted by Cummings and Roosevelt, without consulting other members of the Cabinet or of Congress, was cast as a general reform of the federal judiciary, with its extremely crowded dockets and need for greater efficiency. The main provisions of the judiciary reorganization bill FDR submitted to Congress on February 5, 1937, provided that when a judge of a federal court who had served ten years or more did not resign or retire within six months after his seventieth birthday, the President might name an additional judge to the court, but in no case should the Supreme Court have more than six added Justices nor any lower federal court more than two.[13]

The instant furor this proposal generated is demonstrated by the letters below.[14] In spite of the deep divisions in the country, at the outset it was taken for granted that the President, with his control of both Houses, would prevail. But it was not to be. Although the number of Supreme Court Justices was set by legislation and not by the Constitution and had varied — with six in 1789, five in 1801, seven in 1807, nine in 1837, ten in 1863, eight in 1866, and nine in 1869 — it seemed impossible to shake the deeply ingrained belief that nine Justices had been the norm from the beginning and that in changing the number FDR was tampering with sacred tradition. Polls taken throughout the period of contestation over Roosevelt's plan showed a consistently negative majority. In May, a Gallup poll found 54 percent opposed, and by September less than one voter in three thought FDR should continue his effort to enlarge the Court.[15]

Paradoxically, this was in part the result of the fact that while Roosevelt was losing the battle he was winning the larger war, which in the eyes of many rendered his proposal less and less necessary. FDR's Court-packing threat stimulated one crucial swing vote — that of Justice Owen Roberts — to change direction, and in a series of decisions in the spring of 1937, the Court validated the Social Security Act and the Wagner Labor Relations Act and reversed its recent decision against a minimum wage law in New York by upholding a similar law in the state of Washington. One wry comment summed up the Court's reversal: "A switch in time saved nine."[16] At the same time, Willis Van Devanter, one of the more conservative Justices, announced his retirement, allowing FDR to make his first appointment to the Court — he was ultimately to make eight — and change its balance and its approach so that no New Deal statute was found unconstitutional for the remainder of his presidency.

While Roosevelt's Court plan did help to initiate what William Leuchtenburg and other scholars have called "the Constitutional Revolution of 1937," resulting in a Court that took a much broader view of the powers of the central government to regulate business and dispense social welfare, the President did pay a political price.[17] As the letters below also demonstrate, he disillusioned and bewildered significant numbers of his constituents. More than that, he helped consolidate a coalition of conservatives in both parties destined to frustrate many of his future reform attempts, and the constitutional debate with its fear of encroaching presidential power worked to undermine the remarkable pragmatic acceptance of the New Deal that had marked FDR's first term. Nevertheless, until the final defeat, FDR remained convinced that his Court plan was essential for the effective functioning and even the survival of democracy, and he fought for his doomed bill with all of his formidable powers. "The President felt very confident — almost 'cocky' — that he could win, and was in no mood for compromise," his speechwriter and friend Sam Rosenman commented.[18] Though FDR was apprised of the content of the huge number of letters he received on the Court issue, the majority of which supported him, had he paid closer attention to the *tone* of that flood of letters, his mood might have altered.

On March 4, he addressed a Democratic Victory Dinner in Washington's Mayflower Hotel and roused his large audience by making it clear why the nation could not afford the impasse imposed by the Court:

> Here is one-third of a Nation ill-nourished, ill-clad, ill-housed — NOW!
>
> Here are thousands upon thousands of farmers wondering whether next year's prices will meet their mortgage interest — NOW!
>
> Here are thousands upon thousands of men and women laboring for long hours in factories for inadequate pay — NOW!
>
> Here are thousands upon thousands of children who should be at school, working in mines and mills — NOW!
>
> Here are strikes more far-reaching than we have ever known, costing millions of dollars — NOW!
>
> Here are Spring floods threatening to roll again down our river valleys — NOW!
>
> Here is the Dust Bowl beginning to blow again — NOW!
>
> If we would keep faith with those who had faith in us, if we would make democracy succeed, I say we must act — NOW![19]

Five days later, FDR took his case to the American people in his first Fireside Chat since his reelection.[20] He reminded his listeners of the conditions that prevailed when he had taken office just four years earlier. "In 1933 you and I knew that we must never let our economic system get completely out of joint again . . . that the only way to avoid a repetition of those dark days was to have a government with power to prevent and to cure the abuses and the inequalities which had thrown that system out of joint." The Court, however, has "cast doubt on the ability of the elected Congress to protect us against catastrophe by meeting squarely our modern social and economic conditions."

> We are at a crisis, a crisis in our ability to proceed with that protection. It is a quiet crisis. There are not lines of depositors outside closed banks. But to the far-sighted it is far-reaching in its possibilities of injury to America.

He repeated the homey metaphor he had used in his Mayflower Hotel speech calling the U.S. government "a three-horse team . . . the Congress, the Executive and the Courts. Two of the horses, the Congress and the Executive, are pulling in unison today; the third is not."

> When the Congress has sought to stabilize national agriculture, to improve the conditions of labor, to safeguard business against unfair competition, to protect our national resources, and in many other ways to serve our clearly national needs, the majority of the Court has been assuming the power to pass on the wisdom of these Acts of the Congress — and to approve or disapprove the public policy written into these laws.

The Supreme Court, he charged, "has improperly set itself up as a third House of the Congress."

> We have, therefore, reached the point as a Nation where we must take action to save the Constitution from the Court and the Court from itself. We must find a way to take an appeal from the Supreme Court to the Constitution itself. We want a Supreme Court which will do justice under the Constitution and not over it. In our Courts we want a government of laws and not of men.

In this Chat, as well as in earlier pronouncements, FDR committed what he himself later thought was a blunder by stressing not only policy but age — which older Americans, in and out of Congress, resented and which many of all ages thought disingenuous. He praised his plan as a system that would bring into the judiciary "a steady and continuing stream of new and younger blood, . . . younger men who have had personal experience and contact with modern facts and circumstances," thus saving "our national Constitution from hardening of the judicial arteries." He went out of his way to inform his listeners that Supreme Court Justices could retire on the generous pension of $20,000 a year for life. He struck an uncharacteristic defensive note in his refutation of the charge of "packing" the Court, invoking his record as Governor and President, which had proved his "devotion" to liberty. "You who know me can have no fear that I would tolerate the destruction by any branch of government of any part of our heritage of freedom." He explained in detail why a constitutional amendment would not solve the problem. There was vast disagreement on what kind of amendment was needed and the process of amending the Constitution was too cumbersome to meet the nation's current needs:

No amendment which any powerful economic interests or the leaders of any powerful political party have had reason to oppose has ever been ratified within anything like a reasonable time. And remember that thirteen states which contain only five percent of the voting population can block ratification even though the thirty-five states with ninety-five percent of the population are in favor of it.

He concluded by invoking the Constitution itself:

During the past half century the balance of power between the three great branches of the Federal Government has been tipped out of balance by the Courts in direct contradiction of the high purposes of the framers of the Constitution. It is my purpose to restore that balance. You who know me will accept my solemn assurance that in a world in which democracy is under attack, I seek to make American democracy succeed. You and I will do our part.

MARCH 13, 1937

Respected President: I have written both of our Iowa Senators urging them to oppose you in your effort to bend and shape the Supreme Court to your liking and thus in the future if not at once make it possible for a president and a Congress to pass any law that appealed to their ideas — The very Supreme Court and Constitution that makes it possible for me as a citizen to write and urge you to Stop — Look — Listen is the very Court and Constitution that you with your fine mind but human seem determined to undermine —

I love my freedom and realize that did I live in Russia, Spain, Italy or many another country where the court is subservient to the ruler that this frank yet respectful letter would probably mean the loss of my physical freedom if not worse —

I along with 99% of the Iowans who voted for you did not give you a mandate to change the Constitution or Supreme Court — You have made a wonderful record for yourself as President and I am urging our Iowa representatives to save you from yourself in this crisis. . . .

The Supreme Court is highly respected in Iowa as are you — All this from a democrat —

Very respectfully,

Mrs. N. E. Richardson
Delta, Ia.

* * *

Dear Mr. President:

Never before have I written to a President of the United States, but never before have I been so strongly moved by a pending measure as the Judicial Reform Bill proposed by you.

I have not the slightest idea that you will see this letter, but it will act as a safety valve for me any way.

Surrounded as you are by "yes" men — and fawning subordinates — I wonder if you are really able to discover what the sentiments of the people are on this measure? Would it not be a wonderful thing for you to have honest, frank, disinterested and intelligent people to turn to for opinions — rather than to rely upon politicians & dependant office-holders?

I have been a great admirer of yours in the past, Mr. President, altho' not a Democrat. You probably realize that you would never have been elected by the votes of dyed-in-the-wool Democrats alone & it seems to me that you should be interested in the views of that great body of independent voters, of the middle class, who hold the balance of power.

The small merchant, the small professional man, the small salaried man, the small farmer were largely with you in the past, but they are not with you on this Supreme Court issue. Because the classes I have enumerated are not organized and are not particularly articulate — does not mean that they are not thinking. The Labor unions constitute a minority, but a very noisy & powerful one. Same with the farmers — But the hard back-bone of the country belongs to neither group.

We are not willing to turn over to you the dictatorship of the Supreme Court. You now have Congress under your thumb, in spite of us — but that has happened before & probably always will happen with a popular & powerful executive. We have been told by professors that a benevolent despotism is the best form of government — but we do not want despots — benevolent or otherwise.

Oh! Mr. President you have an opportunity to go down in history as one of our great presidents — along with the Great Theodore. Do not throw it all in the discard because of a personal pique & a personal quarrel with the Supreme Court. If you can trust the people — & you always have said you did — why not submit the question in an open way to the people & accept the verdict. Why descend to the contrivances of the petty politicians to gain your desires?

The elderly people will not soon forget your cruel flings at old age. They notice that you do not suggest that the elderly statesmen — such as Borah, Norris, McAdoo, Robinson & others retire. They wonder at your inconsistency.

They believe, as I believe, that the three co-ordinate branches of our government should be retained in their original dignity & power — until such time as the people decide otherwise.

In other words, however desirable the enactment of your social legislation may be, & I do not dispute that at all, it should not be accomplished by trampling on the Constitution.

The people will support the Supreme Court. In North Dakota & Wisconsin all through the years that the liberals have had control of the executive & legislative branches — the people have stood by the old judges & re-elected them in spite of the attempt made by partisans to control the judiciary.

Now, I have had the pleasure of writing this & you will never be bothered by having to read it.

I wish you well — I respect & admire you greatly — do not spoil it all now — do not give way to partisan motives in a matter so fundamental.

Respectfully yours,

W. H. Gurnee
St. Paul, Minn.

MARCH 10, 1937

Dear Mr. President:

. . . The desirability of obtaining expeditiously the social legislation which the President has in mind cannot in my opinion compensate us for the price we would be paying. In our zeal to accomplish what we may consider advantageous or important now we should not scuttle the American system, destroy our checks and balances, and throw overboard the protection of a free untrammeled Supreme Court.

I once heard you say very aptly, Mr. President, that you laid no claim to infalibility, but what you strove for was a good high batting average. You surely have that. What if the umpires have given you some unfavorable decisions, and even though you feel that they may continue to cut the corners against you, don't throw down your bat and demand the privilege of appointing your own umpires. That isn't cricket, it isn't baseball, and it is not American. Such procedure might improve ones batting average, but it would also kill the game.

There is no clear outspoken command from the people to accomplish this thing. Even the tremendous personal popularity of the President, which would write a blank check for him on most issues, is apathetic and in many cases revolted by this proposal. The President himself must have been surprised at the lack of spontaneous support which this issue has evoked. The reason is not difficult to find, the people don't want it.

I think it is very regretable that in placing this issue before the people it was found expedient to cast an unfavorable light on our Supreme Court. The spectacle of the Nine Silent Men, striped of the traditional reverence with which we have been accustomed to regard our highest tribunal, and held up to public disesteem, is to me a sorry sight. I venture to believe that there are other Americans who feel as I do.

Respectfully yours,

Lewis W. Berghoff
Chicago

MARCH 12, 1937

Mr. President: —

I understand that the right of sorvegnty [sovereignty] in this cuntry belongs to the People. Not to anney or part of the constuinal goverment That the constunial goverment is the President, House of Representives, Sennet, and the Surpream Cort. Now the point I can not understand is how the surpream coart came to the right to declair anney act of congress unconstutinal. as they are only a part of the constutinal Goverment. Rising themselves above congress and usupering the Sorvergn rights of the people is I think going beyond thire juresdiction. The people of this cuntry do Not send over 500 of thire best talanted peopel to Washington to make Laws for them jest to have a Dictorial supream cort knock them out the First round.

When a constutinal Goverment makes a Law it is constutnial. The surpream cort has Nothing els to do onley to see that it is put into use when or where Needed. Would you point out whire I am Rong thanking you in advance I remain a citisen by Berth.

Charles A. Nelsen
San Pedro, Calif.

MARCH 15, 1937

Pres. Roosevelt

I am just a poor uneducated farmer but want you to know I am with you on your changes on the Supreme Court it has always been constitutional when the government helps the industries or Big Business But when we have a president and congress that want to help and serve people the court says unconstitutional.

. . . it seems that some of our officials are crooked and some crippled in the head when you are just crippled in your legs Hats off to the greatest president we have ever had. . . .

Very Respectfully,

R. T. Hanners
Hartselle, Ala.

MARCH 11, 1937

Dear President Roosevelt:

I am for your plan all the way. Those men on the Supreme Court never were hungry. That's why they have no feelings for the lower third of our population.

Good Luck

Daniel Geller
Cleveland, Ohio

MARCH 10, 1937

My dear President Roosevelt:

I want to write and thank you for the enjoyment and satisfaction I derived from your "Fireside Chat" last night.

My husband and myself have supported you from the beginning. Altho' we have not suffered greatly from the depression, we have seen and feared the danger to our beloved country. . . . from the greed and increasing misuse of power by intrenched wealth; also the dishonesty, political bias and inefficiency of our Courts and lawyers. I have been a legal stenographer for many years and have seen many things in the courts and legal procedure which has disturbed me greatly. My husband's employment brings him into contact with every type of people, from bank presidents to janitors and elevator men, and he sees misery and injustice on every hand. . . .

Therefore, you can see why we are your ardent supporters in your war against special privilege which is creating a deadly hatred among the people, and which condition inevitably leads to serious consequences to the nation involved.

. . . I believe you are exactly right and that it is intolerable for a lot of prejudiced, jaundiced old men to nullify the wishes of the people. We will never have any progressive legislation if they are left in power, and Heaven only knows what an incensed people will do under the circumstances. We surly do not want conditions here to be as they are in Europe, but that is exactly what we will get if the majority of the people cannot have the necessities of life and some of the luxuries. . . .

Hoping God's blessing may rest on you, and that you may be able to keep our country intact without bloodshed, I am

Very Sincerely

Ethel H. Smith
Walworth, N.Y.

MARCH 17, 1937

My Dear President:

I am taking this opportunity of giving you some facts in the middle west, which I presume are true all over the country, showing the absolute necessity of some kind of government action in regard to the labor situation. I have read of the sit-down strikes in the east and if conditions there are as they are here, I cannot blame them one bit, and you would not either if you were placed in a like position. We, here in the middle west, whenever we are in a gathering of working people, the story is the same, viz: "I am being driven like a slave, made to do two mens work and receive one man's salary." Unless someone can get industry to awaken itself, there will be a revolution in United States, just as surely as the sun comes up in the morning, Men are being driven to desperation. For instance; . . .

I am working in the law office of one of the most influential firm of lawyers in Northeast Kansas. There are four lawyers. We have one stenographer who does nothing else; I am the Chief Clerk, and supposed to take all the responsibility of the outer office, keep about four sets of books, take dictation for two of the lawyers, etc. etc. We are compelled to work from 8 to

10 hours a day 6 days a week, and then we alternate on Sundays. She draws $105.00 a month and I get $165.00 a month. We are driven so hard that finally we are exhausted and have to go to bed and be out of the office from a week to 10 days resting up. These men draw all the way from $10,000.00 to $15,000.00 a year. You may say, "why dont you quit"? I have a family to support and where could I go to better myself. It is the same all over. This young lady has an aged father to help support. These lawyers seem to think you should be satisfied and glad that you have a job. Perhaps that is true, but they are not satisfied with what they are making.

I am hoping and praying that you will be successful with your Supreme Court fight and get men in there who will be a help instead of a hinderance. The only objection that I have to the whole thing is the fact that they would retire on full pay. I ask you this question: Why should they be pensioned anymore than the man who does any other kind of work. What act of God entitles these men to an easy seat the rest of their lives? If they can't save enough from their salaries of $20,000.00 a year while they are on the bench, to take care of them the rest of their lives, then how can a man drawing $100.00 or $150.00 be expected to save up enough to take care of him when he gets to be 70 years of age. Is it any wonder that we are having these uprisings. I am not a radical, a red, or an agitator, just an honest, hardworking American Citizen who would like to see a semblance of a square deal to the middle class of people. . . .

They can call you a Dictator if they want to, but if you are a DICTATOR then power to you.

If I can give you any further information as to the conditions in this state, I shall be only too glad to do so.

With the kindest personal regards, I am

Very sincerely,

Eugene S. Simmons
Atchison, Kansas

MARCH 11, 1937

Mr. President: —

After listening to your talk last night I just have to write you a note telling you how much I really appreciate your talks, and your courage. I no you are gaining thousands of friends daily. At the plant where I work The Sinclair Refinery East Chicago Ind. Conditions are 90% better since you came into office and gave us the write for collective bargaining. And the men in that plant are 97% for you. We talk of you often. Many remarks are made as to your fearless courage and your continued fight against organized capitalist. We no it is a hard uphill fight but we are with you. We are all for your Supreme Court change and several of us have written our representatives to vote for it. I am encouraging them to do this. . . .

The workers of America are praying for your success and your health so you can carry on to free the white Slaves of America.

There is lots I would like to tell you but I can't take up your valuable time explaining it in a letter. Sure wish all of us workers could no you personally. We all no you are our friend.

So we will continue to hope and pray for your success.

If there is any thing I can do to help in any way please let me no. I will be happy to do any thing in my power.

Thanks a thousand times for all you have done and for what you will do. May God bless you and keep you well.

Wishing you all the luck in the world.

I am
A Born American

Clyde Lowrance
and wife Bessie
Hammond, Indiana

MARCH 10, 1937

our President Mr. Roosevelt Dear Sure I lisen in to your wonderful speech on the 9th of March and i think they was the wonderfuls speech off our history your problum should have tuch the hart of all worker & men and women Just as it Did mine. We have neve befor had a president to take any step to help the progress of the worken class and it looks like it is un posable for you to pull us up buy the head when the Cort pull us Dawn buy the feet you are only one man and there is nine holding us Dawn We working class was with you in the start and we are with you to the ind in any under taken that you think will make the standed of liven better for us working class it is Just left up to you to Do your will we workers are with you from start to finish what wood we Don from 33 untell now if it had not been for you so i wish you all the sucsess from Richard. Cruse. Col.[ored] Chicago, ill

MARCH 26, 1937

Dear Mr. Franklin D. Roosevelt
Hon. President of the U. States.

As a citizen of this Country permit me to voice my opinion in favor of your plan in regard to the Supreme Court.

Every worker in this Nation is eagerly anticipating legislation to protect his right to live decently according to the present standards of living.

I work for a railroad 7 nights per week, 10 hrs. per night, a total of 70 hrs. per week, and watchmen for the same railroad work 84 hrs per week. There is no sunshine, no recreation of any sort for us, and millions of others like us throughout the Country. In face of so much unemployment this is intolerable.

Only the Federal Government can put a stop to such abuses, and may God give you strength to conquer all opposition.

We workers are with you to the bitter end of this fight. Wherever a group of citizens is found, no other topic interests them so much as this, and the dissappointment would be great should you fail in your great endeavor to protect the American people.

I am sending a similar letter to Senator Wagner of New York urging him to use his influence in this matter.

Yours Sincerely,

Manuel Mendes
New York, N.Y.

MARCH 12, 1937

Dear Mr. President:

I am writing you to say that the working men of California and of the Nation are behind you just as strong now as we were when we elected you to your high office. We elected you by an overwhelming majority and we feel that we are paying you a good salary to work for us and we feel that you are working for us but we did not vote for nor appoint the Supreme Court and we do not feel that they have worked for us but, rather have worked for the newspapers and the corporations that told us that if we voted for you that we would not have any jobs. The vast majority of working men have learned that we can produce everything in abundance that is needed for human welfare and if this Supreme Court and the corporations do not care to co-operate to this end we are willing to do without them and work for the federal government and the nation but we demand a few of the necessities of life.

I attended a meeting of 350 oil workers last night who are just 100% behind you and your plans to reorganize the Supreme Court. We admit that we are dumb but we know enough to know that this court has over ruled everything that would be of any benefit to a worker. . . . You do not have to be very smart to see that these recent decisions have nothing to do with the constitution but rather are the results of the private thoughts of these men who have been raised up under the false theory that the wealth of the nation is produced by the corporations instead of the workers.

Mr. President we are behind you. If you do not think so just send agents out into any bunch of working men and let him ask.

Very truly yours,

L. A. Duncan
Long Beach, Calif.

MARCH 13, 1937

My Dear Sir.

The English vocabulary fail to contain sufficient words to express our gratitude to you, for your great leadership.

We are hoping and praying, that congress may see the wisdom and abide your judgement; in the reorganizing the "Supreme Court."

The world has changed, and the onward march of civilication necesset-ate a change in laws, homes and most every pursuit of life.

We nine millions of Negros down South have watched your move from the first year you was elected President of these United States, we find that you emulate the Blessed Savior, when He was on earth You have fed the poor, clothed the naked and establish away by which those that are born afflicted could be healed. You have healed broken hearts.

I have in mind, the "Infantile Paralysis institutions" establish in a way that every loyal citizen can help. Its miraculus. We Negroes see things in the Democrat party, that we had never seen before. . . .

You have done more for the Negroes since you have been elected President, than the Republican did in a quarter of a century. You are the next "Moses" that "God has sent to lead the country to the promise land. There are no other country in this World, that gives the privilege to their minority and exslave race, as this country of ours; gives us. (No kick due us.)

Why, I write, you, I dreamed, that I saw you standing on a high mountain. You were called a Shepherd, there were millions of sheep down in the vally in a pasture. Some were White and some were black. as you stood with a staff in hand, you gave orders to the men to drive them all to the right. You was ask "must we separate them," You said no. They are all sheep; put them togather in this larger pasture; to my right. This point, I awoke and it bothered me. I promised myself to write you and express our thanks for your kind deeds done for our race.

I am an old school teacher, teaching now in the public Schools of Natchitoches Parish. I am in my sixties. Finally, Mr. President go on, God is leading you. . . . The unborn athousand years from now; will see your foot print on the sand of time by reading your history.—Your obedient Servant.

Matthew C. Harrison
Natchitoches, La.

MARCH 10, 1937

Dear Sir:

You want six extra judges so the court will interpret the Constitution and give your social laws a clean bill. . . . You talk about helping the lower third but the people worst off in the United States are the Southern Sharecroppers. I haven't heard you speak about the situation or do anythink about it. Talk about the workers in the factories, they get 600 to 700 dollars a year while down south 150 to 300 dollars is very common. Of course with Southern Senators being the main support of the Democratic party and they being elected by the Southern version of the "Economic Royalists" as only 30% of the southern people vote you cant do anything for the sharecroppers without stepping on your southern friends toes. And talking about liberty as you did last night the Southern Democrats have always been the ones who took away the right to vote of about 70% of the southern voters. If you appointed six democrats some would be southernors and the southern courts have a nasty habit of taken away the liberties of a man and we can assume that any of them appointed are liable to bring the habit to the Supreme Court of the United States. This court is the only court that has stood between the southern citizens and unjust laws and trials. . . .

Yours for a court that will say what it thinks and not what you think.

Tom Stryker Rice
Oshtemo, Michigan

* * *

My Dear Mr. President —

May I introduce myself to you as a man of about your own age raised on a corn farm in Nebraska and now farming in California. I am registered a Democrat and my entire education was acquired in a Little Red School House 14′ × 22′ located in the country. . . .

The use of your "three horse team" as you used it was wrong, which you would have known if you had ever been a real dirt farmer and not a gentleman farmer. You know you hitch the three horses to a three horse evener so that each horse has to do its part.

The Supreme Court as I see it corresponds to the horse in the furrow or the horse in the middle which keeps the other two bronchos going straight and also keeps the two mavericks from running away with the plow and breaking things up.

Please look into the working of a three horse team before you make another talk because any real farmer knows that your example of a three horse team really proves that the Supreme Court the odd horse or the horse in the furrow is the most important animal in the team.

Please get right on this Supreme Court and Federal Judiciary question. You are more often right than wrong. Get right on this question. You will be the greatest man in history. Do not listen to the politician. He has his ears to the ground for reelection.

Trusting you will get right on this question and make it an even 100%. I am

Very respectfully yours

D. E. Wilson
Chatsworth Park, California

MARCH 11, 1937

Mr. President

Too bad your fireside speech of last night didn't fall into the fire before you got a chance to deliver that masterpiece of hypocracy and deceit!

Yes our government is DIVIDED into 3 branches, but they are not supposed to PULL TOGETHER — that is the very thing they are not supposed to do if they are going to achieve the purpose of the framers of our constitution. What sense would there be in dividing the government into three branches if those branches are going to work in collusion???

. . . may I suggest that your reference to our revered elderly Justices who have given their best to the service of our country, as old foggies with "HARDENING OF THE ARTERIES" comes with exceedingly bad grace from one who can't stand on his own two feet unassisted!!! Shame on you, Mr. President! That remark hurt me more than anything you have ever uttered. How about making a MUST LAW which will require candidates for the presidency to be physically and mentally fit for the high position?

Sincerely yours

Leo P. Hansen
Democrat
Lacey, Washington

*   *   *

My dear Mr. President,

I, at least, am not of the number who can follow you in your assault on the Supreme Court. In fact, while a Democrat, the things you are now proposing and trying to rush through a "yes-man" Congress are so dangerous that I now have reluctantly to regard you as the most dangerous man who has ever been president. Nor am I a man out of touch with the common people. I know farmers and men of other businesses all over this county and in many other places, — and I know that I am not the only man who is now desperately afraid of you.

Yours, with sadness,

Daniel S. Gage
Fulton, Missouri

*   *   *

FRANKLINSTEIN 1937
By, Erwin Clarkson Garrett.

They raised them up a towering form —
A fearful Frankenstein;
They placed him in the highest seat —
All powerful — divine.

He bore a hypnotizing smile —
(That many called absurd) —
And tossed his chin with sparkling glance
And sweetly crooning word. . . .

Twain hands — that have with tyrant grasp
Choked Senate — crushed the House —
Till manhood and initiative
Bespeak the frightened mouse —

Twain hands are reaching now to raze
Democracy's last tower,

Which through the storm and stress of years
Has stood in righteous power. . . .

And you men call "Americans,"
And heroes' praises sing,
Will ye stand idly by and let
Him do this fearful thing?

Erwin Clarkson Garrett
Philadelphia, Pa.

MARCH 10, 1937

Dear Sir:

As a plain American citizen (I was not born an economic royalist on a Hyde Park estate) I think your attacks on the Supreme Court the most contemptible speeches ever uttered by a President of the United States. . . .

I understand on good authority that your speeches are written by a clever Jew and I can well believe it for only a shifty Oriental could write such a tissue of distortion and, in my opinion, only a traitor could get up and mouth it.

We, who know you, know that your purpose is unholy and that you lust for ever greater power. As a demagogue and as a dispenser of patronage you are without equal but no American President should be proud of these attributes. . . .

I am a Democrat and my father who is now 70 years old has been a Democrat his entire life (would you like me to chloroform him as an obsolete dotard?)

In my opinion, your undemocratic proposal has, indeed, rendered you unfit for the honorable office you hold. I cannot remain in any party that deliberately seeks to undermine our American system of government.

Karl Young
New York, N.Y.

MARCH 14, 1937

Pipe down, you with the Julius Caesar complex.
You may be MUSSOLINI, but we, thank God, ARE NOT WOPS!

> Decent American
> New York, N.Y.

MARCH 11, 1937

Mr. President:

Keep right on giving 'em hell. The great majority are with you in your attempt to put some much needed new blood in the Supreme Court.

. . . I have a wife and 3 fine, healthy children and fire a boiler for a gas company for our living. . . .

I am not alarmed in the least about a dictatorship because the American people just aren't, "built that way." I have previously mentioned having 3 children (from 3 yrs old to 12 yrs.) and I am firmly convinced that your course is the only one that will save America for them.

In my humble opinion the worst dangers in America today are the large corporations and I know you are handicapped now by the court in your effort to bust 'em up.

I want to congratulate you on your 2 fine speeches on the court issue and with the help of God I hope you succeed.

> Very truly yours,
>
> W. W. Boals
> Pavonia, O.

MARCH 10, 1937

My Dear Mr. President: —

I listened to your chat last evening and I quite agree with your conclusions, action is necessary and leave the past dead bury the dead. . . .

We must have reform along with recovery otherwise we will go stumbling along until we go head long into the ditch.

Frankly if I were in your place I would have this reform at all cost, in other words I would put this Nation under martial law and remove all those old fossils from the bench the Country over, and with them gather in all the International Bankers, and big industrialists and if need be stand them up against the wall and shoot them.

I believe in constitutional Government and real Democracy and not a Democracy of special privilege which is slowly but surely bringing us to a revolution. and believe me Mr. President that if it comes to that point wher we have once more to fight for our freedom, I will be on the side for freedom.

Yours respectfully.

M. A. Cypher
Butler, Pa.

MARCH 15, 1937

Dear Sir. I am heartily in favor of your plan to curb the Szarist policies of the Supreme Court, the opponents of curbing them argue that we had just as well do away with the court as to curb it on the other hand if the present policy is continued we in reality have no Congress, no Senate, no President, and in reality have already an absolute monarchy, composed of nine men who are not the real rulers in fact. the real rulers are the heads of the big corporations for whom they formerly worked in fact J. P Morgan aught to be called Emperor, for he is the real ruler and these old men always do his will regardless of the constitution. for in fact the constitution is not the complicated document these hired spellbinders claim it to be any tenth grade schoolboy can understand it and any adult who cannot comprehend it has no business on any court bench and any nine men who cannot agree unanimously when the facts are squarely before their eyes should be impeached for they have made up thier minds before the case comes before them. . . .

You have been too fair to these men by inferring that they are old fashioned and cannot change with the times. if those consistently stubborn members of the court were investigated you would find that their relatives are holding highly paid corporation jobs who would be fired if the Judge decided against them. in fact we have a Nazi or Facist government here now. and if something isnt done to curb the infallible, omnipotent pose of the Judges trouble is sure to come. . . .

Your friend

T. W. Howell
Okolona, Miss.

MARCH 12 AND 13, 1937

Dear Sir —

I listened carefully to your speech on Tuesday, and read carefully the one of last week, and have waited to cool off before writing. You may never see this, but I hope you will know what people are thinking, probably not the majority who usually follow the crowd without thinking but the thinking minority who seem to have little to do with your thoughts.

Naturally things should be better in a few years, no matter who would be president, so you could not possibly brag about that. But are they so much better? Many are still on relief and it seems in the present order of things they will forever be. . . . You had a landslide election, not because of your popularity, but because of all the benefits the so-called "poor working man" and laborers received and which they credited you for. Men think more of their pocketbooks than of principles. Who wants to get paid high wages by the hour to strike a small tree in the ground or wave a red flag of danger on a road being built? I mean who wants to live that way who is honest? No one. . . . Why are you always for the employees, never for the employers? Don't you sometimes wonder how long people will be so dumb as not to see through what you are doing? Whoever heard of a "free?" country allowing strikers sitting down in a plant owned by the ones who pay them, and wrecking it unless their wants are satisfied? Who has ever heard of so many strikes and so very much unrest as there is now? The unlawful element in the country have found they can almost get away with murder and nothing is done about it, so they go ahead and do almost anything under the sun. You can thank yourself, and no one else for the bitter class hatred you have stirred up. And what for? Popularity? Votes? And you are in the Capitalist class yourself! That is what makes it so funny if it were not so tragic! To think you always pose as being for the poor man and what do you know about being poor! You have never had to earn a dollar in your life and never will have to. Your sons have done many unlawful things and seem to be able to get away with them because they are your sons. What kind of example is that for the young people of the country? Where is your idea of fair play?

And now you are after the Supreme Court. . . . Why not think of the men who own small business places or the much maligned white collar man who has his Social Security money taken from him when he is earning less than the poor working man, but has no union to help him strike? I'd call him the "forgotten man" and not the strikers. . . . how can you pose as being for the "poor under dog" when you take money away by taxes from honest, hard working people who are middle class (so called) the backbone of the country, to pay for some of the worthless ones who get their money from those taxes? And they are even getting so they won't work otherwise knowing they can get government jobs from the Alphabet Soup and not have to hurt themselves working for it. We are getting to be a nation of spineless saps, and when I think how our forefathers worked to make this country what it has been and may never get to be again, I simply boil! . . .

Yours truly

(Mrs. C. O.) Mabel Young King
Berkeley, California

MARCH 10, 1937

Dear Friend: I am writing this letter to let you know that I agree with you in all you said last night about the supreme Court. . . .

It is said that you are causing class hatred but you are not. Class hatred was started before you were born. The very ones who are fighting you at every turn: such people as J. P. Morgan Rockefellers etc etc are the ones who are causing class hatred. There is class hatred most of us poor folks hate the rich class with a bitterness that hurts. You are doing more than anyone I know to do away with this feeling. You are trying to get them to stop doing the things which cause us to hate them. . . .

As I see it the supreme Court as it now stands is just like Old King George of England only there are nine Kings instead of one.

I sincerely hope you can win in your fight to subdue them. No one should be appointed for life and they certainly should not have power to overrule elected representitives of the people. . . .

Yours truly,

Ruskin Tansel
Swanton, Ohio

MARCH 10, 1937

Dear Sir;

I was somewhat uncertain as to the advisability of the proposed change in the Supreme Court, but after hearing you talk on the radio Tuesday night, I am convinced that such a change would be a disaster to the American form of government.

. . . You know as well as I do that it was only those millions who are on your pay roll in some way or another who re-elected you and not the popular vote. I do not know of any one person who voted for you who was not receiving money from some source or other or were promised money or jobs by the government.

Your talk of child labor makes me tired. My father died when I was four and my mother when I was eleven years of age. A maiden aunt, my brother who was two years older, and my self worked to keep the home to-gether. My brother worked in a grocery store after school, Saturdays and vacations, and I cared for babies, ran errands until I was thirteen and then worked during vacations in a shoe factory at Nyack, N.Y. which was our home town then. We both graduated from High school, and both upon graduation went to work in a large bank in N.Y. City. I was seventeen at the time. My brother is now an official of that same bank. I worked there for years and then became a reporter for some of the largest newspapers in New Jersey. . . . Had you been president at the time of my mother's death we would probably have been placed in an institution and to-day I would probably be on your relief rolls.

It is sad but true that you who would have been one of the most beloved of presidents, has brought so much sorrow and sadness on the middle class, that now the mere mention of your name sends the chills down our spines. Both my father and mother's families came here a hundred years or more before the Revolution, I am a member of the Society of Mayflower Descendents in the State of New Jersey, the D.A.R. and the New England Women, and I weep for the future of my beloved country. Fortunately I leave no children behind me who will not be able to enjoy the freedom of the loved country, as I knew it, but who would live and serve a Dictator in a Communistic Country, for as you say "we are on our way."

Very truly yours.

Edith H. Frank
Chicago, Ill.

*　　*　　*

President Roosevelt —

Who do you think you are to undertake disrupting our Supreme Court which has rendered unquestionable service to the public for 150 years, while you in four years have brought nothin but distruction, poverty, and misery of all kinds upon the Nation with the exception of the thousands and thousands of paid parasites which you unnecessarly mentain at Washington at the expense of the tax payer. . . . Like Hitler you imagine you know more than God Almighty. — You are crazed from the effects of the rotton disease your old carcass has been carrying around for the last fifteen years. — Now you want to dictate to, and dominate the nation at large. — The American people have tolerated you too long, you will get your desert one of these days. You damn traitor, liar and hypocrite of the deepest dye. — The very knowledge that you had the audacity to place your hand on the Holy Bible and swear allegiance to your country and people, which you failed to do is enough to disgust even Stallan. There is nothing too base for an animal like you to do.

. . . We are thoroughly disgusted with your whole tribe. You and your family have been a menace to the American standard of cilivization. Your son and daughter with two wives and two husbands. What an example placed before a Nation. Never have we had such rubbish in the White House.

Think of the condition of the country today from strikes and you don't say one word. Why? because you are a coward, you are afraid of John L. Lewis. I hope he will lick hell out of you before he gets through. You are nothing but a dirty lowdown Communist of the lowest grade. You, Farley, Wallace, Hopkins, Tugwell and the whole ring of vampires at Washington should be tared, feathered and set on fire. You are a marked man, you won't escape much longer. The dungeon of Hell will never be filled until you and your diabolical gang are dangling on pitchforks over the flames. It would be a real pleasure for the people whom you have deceived, ruined financially and physically to witness the scene which will surely take place. — You pretend to be a great philanthropist. You are worse than a highway robber stealing the hard earned pennies from the poor under the guise of your deceitful Security Act.

Not being satisfied with all this damage, you now want to regiment the children like Hitler and Stallan.

We all know your Communistic aims. — You old feather duster.

These are the sentiments of every decent American today, which you are not.

[unsigned]

MARCH 11, 1937

Dear Sir, I am now past 61 and have supported the Democratic ticket about all my life. . . . all the people I talk to say they think Judges on the U.S. Supreme Court should be retired at 70 but seem to feel that $20,000 a year is a big Pension to grant to men that have a plenty when there are so many old folks that are half fed and half dressed through the Country to day I have talked to a good many farmers and Factory workers and they tell me that the AAA and the N.R.A. was the only thing that ever done anything for them. . . . Economic Royalists who say that a Judge is in his prime of life when he is past 70 are the same boys who throw there own workers on the scrap heap at 40

Frank Deacon
Belding, Mich.

MARCH 11, 1937

THE SUPREME COURT IS PULLING OFF THE BEST SIT-DOWN STRIKE. THE COUNTRY OFFERS THEM 20 GRAND TO GO HOME PERMANENTLY. STILL THEY SIT.

JOE FERGG
CHICAGO

MARCH 16, 1937

Dear President: —

. . . You are the finest President we have ever had since Lincoln, and all the poor people love you dearly and have complete faith in you. If it were not for that love and faith, I believe America would have had a revolution before this time. We may have it yet if your hands are kept tied by the Conservative Supreme Court. I think the old Grandpas ought to be sent home to their rocking chairs where they can learn to knit stockings. It would be of more benefit to humanity than what they are doing now.

. . . I cannot agree with you about paying them for retiring. They have been dictators in this country too long, and should be retired forcibly. If they do not know how to knit let me know, and I will instruct them by mail free of charge. There is nothing like knitting to keep hands out of mischief and minds out of politics. Wouldn't dear old Willy Van Devanter look comical with a bunch of yarn held in his 77 year old Tory hands? How in the world do you suppose he could ever be comfortable in Heaven, associating with millions of poor trash like the common people? Or do they have a separate, exclusive heaven for conservative lawyers?

. . . God bless you always dear Mr. President, and may He comfort, guide and protect you in your hours of need. I send you also my deepest gratitude for the work you have given my husband on the W.P.A.

Mrs. Frank Taylor
Portland, Ore.

MARCH 10, 1937

Dear Mr. President,

Enjoyed and approved every word of your masterful "fireside chat" last evening. . . .

I am enclosing some nonsensical little nursery rhyme parodies I thought you might be able to put in the hands of some clever cartoonist, who would be in a position to capitalize on them.

Again assuring you of my complete approval of what you are trying to do for our Country, I remain,

Very respectfully yours,

H. C. Brown
San Diego, Calif.

"GRANDFATHER GOOSE RHYMES"

Hickery-dickery-dock
Old Age holds back the clock,
By votes of one, are laws undone,
Hickery-dickery-dock

. . .

Fe-fi-fo-fum
Judges as old as Methuselum,
Cast their votes as in days gone by,
Viewing tomorrow with yesterday's eye.

. . .

Ancient Judges, sat in the Hall,
Ancient Judges, due for a fall,
Our country's Great Leader thinks some younger men,
Would see that the Court gave us justice again.

. . .

MARCH 5, 1937

Mr. President;

Not knowing the correct form one addresses the Cheif Executive which I believe in this instance to be a fortunate one as my thoughts will not be stilted or modified by form. . . .

I feel secure in asking the folowing question and your answer will be highly appreciated and considered personal. Would you consider the appointment of a Negro to the Supreme Court and is there one to your knowledge possess of the necessary qualifications?

Perhaps I should have stated before that I am a Negro and beleiving Democracy being a Government representative of all the people. Having faith in your fairness I submit this question without qualms.

The fact that I am writing this will show I hope, the gap you have bridged when a member of a minority group can with confidence submit this question and be correctly understood more especially so when the question is address to one who occupies the highest post civilization can offer. I feel you are interested in problems that confront a large group of American citizens.

Thanking you for this privilege and wishing you continued strength and sucess to carry on.

Truly yours,

Leon Wadlington
Philadelphia, Penna.

MARCH 16, 1937

Honorable President Roosevelt:

Your idea to increase the No. of members in the Supreme Court, if the Justices over 70 years of adge will not retire, is a very good idea.

All over the world it is known, the unjustice, done by the American court, to the american common people, cries to the heaven.

It is a nessesety to get more justice in the court. . . .

New blood shall fill the arteries of the Justice-Department. to change the condition. But honorable Mr. Roosevelt please do not fill this arteries with Jewish or Negerblood.

We are 100 Millionen Arier [Aryans] in this country and I think these 100 Millionen Arien should have the right they claim, neamly to be ruled and justivied by Ariens. Don'd you think so too?

Respectfully signed by an American Citizen

Marta Schmidt
Philadelphia, Penn.

MARCH 19, 1937

Dear President Roosevelt!

The statement was made here at the A.A.U.W. National Convention by Mary Ritter Beard that more women than men were writing to you in protests against changing the Supreme Court.

For some weeks I have been thinking I should like to write & say that I am with you. Moreover, many of my friends, all college women are with you.

We do hope however, that you put a woman or two on the bench.

Very sincerely yours,

Sonia Pickett
Kirkwood, Missouri

MARCH 11, 1937

Your Excellency:

The logical argument in the matter of the Supreme Court is not that it is composed of nine old men, but that the Document they are called upon to interpret and apply is outmoded and no longer suits the conditions prevailing in the United States. This has been partially recognized by various amendments.

When the Constitution of 1789 was adopted:

The land of the country was practically unlimited and free for use to all who desired to settle upon and till it. . . .

There were no huge Corporations with "plants" in various States, employing hundreds of thousands of citizens, exceeding in some instances the population of certain States, and forming Industrial Empires within a Republic.

There were no huge Department Stores absorbing all the business of small independent Store-Keepers, and turning those independent dealers into employees.

There were no Bankers, National or International, having sole control of what is called the "circulating medium", the money of the country. . . .

To day there are few independent workers; the mass of the people are dependent on these huge Corporations for the privelege, and the right, of working to gain a subsistence.

And where does the profit earned by these great Corporations go? As huge salaries to the high officials. The common stockholders, the real owners of the Plants, may, or may not, get a trifling dividend.

Is it any wonder that men shut out from independent means of support should turn to criminality?

The logical need of the Country is a new Constitution that will make the People of the Country, and not the individual possessors of its money, supreme; and to that end the Government, representing the people, should own and control the industries of the Nation that are not strictly personal; and be the sole owner of the circulating medium, Money. And no individual should be allowed to accumulate money for the purpose of loaning it out at interest. . . .

When industry gets to the stage that the co-operation of thousands of men is required to produce the things desired, the Government should take it over. The welfare of the people as a whole is dependent upon it, and through its intimate relations with other and equally large industries the welfare of the Nation is affected.

As matters stand now there is a contest being waged for mastery between Capitalists and the so-called Labor leaders, while the Government stands by as a spectator having no interest in the conflict, or making feeble attempts at conciliation. But its own existence is at stake whichever of the constestants wins, for the victor will be the ruler of the people, a function that belongs solely to the Government as the representative Executive for all the people and their manifold interests.

Respectfully submitted.

Gustavus Harkness
Spring City, Pa.

MARCH 10, 1937

Dear Mr. Roosevelt,

. . . You complain that the Constitution, as interpreted at present, blocks "the modern movement for social and economic progress through legislation." But after all, the method of that modern movement, a strong centralized government, is one that its framers thoroughly distrusted; and so not only did they grant to government a minimum of specified powers, but made restrictions, in the form of a Bill of Rights, on the use of those powers. The fathers of the Constitution looked upon governments as potential tyrants. They established a system of checks and balances, so that one branch could not dominate the others, or a majority oppress a minority. They did not intend that the three branches, like three horses, should pull in unison.

You may sincerely believe that government is competent to direct a planned economy in the general interest. But that cannot be done without distorting or amending the present Constitution. The course of candor would be to submit the question to the people for their decision.

You have not done this, I take it, because you do not see the issue clearly. The choice is between historic liberalism and collectivism of one form or another. The record of your administration has shown that you want to combine incompatible elements of each. . . . Sooner or later, one or the other method must give way. We must either have an authoritarian state, with destruction of civil liberties, subverssion of democracy, and economic nationalism; or we must return to the methods of liberalism, which seeks prosperity by favors to none, rather than favors to all.

It is a tragic bit of irony that the party of Jefferson should be the party that has betrayed the principles he stood for.

Sincerely,

Conrad Wright
Cambridge, Massachussetts

MARCH 11, 1937

Your Excellency,

. . . I didn't think it necessary for ordinary folks to write to you. However, I learned my husband had written a very disrespectful letter to you and I feel it my duty to write that our daughter (a voter) and I are entirely in favor of this reform. . . .

Respectfully yours,

(Mrs.) Katharine Kandler
Chicago

MARCH 10, 1937

Sir — Attached copy of telegram sent you I as the telegrapher at the railroad station had to handle this in as much as it was against my will.

I cannot picture in my mine a woman so low in her walk of life lowering herself to stoop to such a cowardly act to belittle her President of her United States.

Never the less please confide in me when I say that I and hundreds of other railroad men are back of you one hundred percent and hope you remain in your present office the third term.

We appreciate you as a true friend of labor.

Most respectfully yours.

Charles E. Freeman
Beverly, Mass.

MARCH 10, 1937

IT IS COWARDLY TO TAKE ADVANTAGE OF YOUR POSITION TO BROADCAST STATEMENTS AGAINST THE JUSTICRATS OF THE SUPREME COURT TO WHICH YOU WILL REALIZE THEY MAY NOT REPLY BECAUSE OF THEIR RESPECT FOR THE OFFICE YOU OCCUPY IT IS AN INSULT TO EVERY CITIZEN

GRACE UNDERWOOD PERRY
IPSWICH, MASS.

MARCH 10, 1937

Dear Mr. Roosevelt I am the Hotel Man that wrote you good letters while you was a candidate for the Presidency You remember sending me a picture of you and your good Wife.

Mr President We are for you 100% for your Court change and dont weary you will get it all OK.

Now Mr Roosevelt I notice in the paper a few days ago that you was the best dressed man in the land I have always noticed you was so well dressed I am just a little Hotel Man but I am a real Roosevelt man and always speak a good word for you how about you sending me a suit of your clothes that you have discarded it would make me dressed up.

You owe it to me for all that I have done for you and you dont know how it would be appreciated.

We are the same size and the same age.

Your best friend.

J. C. Winder
Sulphur Springs, Texas

MARCH 9, 1937

Beloved President:

. . . I have never voted for you, though my wife has. When you were elected President the first time I obtained one of your pictures and rolled it up — I had seen the workers fooled SO many times — and said to my wife "put this picture away in a secure place and if and when this man has done half what he has promised the people I shall have it placed in a frame suitable to a great man and the accomplishment of a heroic undertaking and it shall be given an honored and conspicuos place in our home." I shall have it framed tomorrow; for I am convinced that under your leadership and with the cooperation of a liberty loving people, "It Can't Happen Here." May God Bless, strengthen and continue to guide you.

Most sincerely yours,

James W. Miller
Eldon, Mo.

BALANCING THE "HUMAN BUDGET": OCTOBER 12 AND NOVEMBER 14, 1937

FDR DELIVERED TWO MORE Fireside Chats during 1937.[21] The first came on October 12. Earlier that day, the President called for a special session of Congress to convene on November 15 to consider passage of legislation made necessary by the Supreme Court's nullification of several of his basic reform measures. That evening he spoke to the American people about the nature of the proposals he would place before Congress in the hope that his listeners would exert pressure for reform on their Senators and Representatives, who, with Congress adjourned, were then in their home states and districts. Indeed, Sam Rosenman called this Fireside Chat "an appeal to the people over the heads of the Congress."[22]

Roosevelt began by explaining — and defending — his decision to call for an extraordinary session: "I have never had sympathy with the point of view that a session of the Congress is an unfortunate intrusion of what they call 'politics' into our national affairs. Those who do not like democracy want to keep legislators at home. But the Congress is an essential instrument of democratic government."

Considering that the nation was on the brink of a recession which would plunge it into conditions not seen since the beginning of the New Deal, FDR spoke more prophetically than he knew when he warned of the dangers of "a merely temporary prosperity" and proclaimed: "The kind of prosperity we want is the sound and permanent kind which is not built up temporarily at the expense of any section or group." Without mentioning the Supreme Court, he made it clear that their recent decisions had undercut efforts to create a stable prosperity:

> The people of the United States were checked in their efforts to
> prevent future piling up of huge agricultural surpluses and the
> tumbling prices which inevitably follow them. They were
> checked in their efforts to secure reasonable minimum wages
> and maximum hours and the end of child labor. And because
> they were checked, many groups in many parts of the country

still have less purchasing power and a lower standard of living than the nation as a whole can permanently allow.

Therefore, in spite of the fact that 1937 had thus far been a good year with steadily returning prosperity, the people didn't want the government to stop governing. Americans, he asserted, "do not look on Government as an interloper in their affairs. On the contrary, they regard it as the most effective form of organized self-help."

> Sometimes I get bored sitting in Washington hearing certain people talk and talk about all that Government ought *not* to do — people who got all *they* wanted from Government back in the days when the financial institutions and the railroads were being bailed out in 1933, bailed out by the Government.

FDR had just returned from a trip to the Pacific Coast, and he was impressed by how well the "average citizen" understood the issues before the nation: "They want the financial budget balanced, these American people. But they want the human budget balanced as well." They "want a national economy which balances itself with as little Government subsidy as possible. . . . They are less concerned that every detail be immediately right than they are that the direction be right." Even though he himself proclaimed a third of the American people "ill-nourished," he remained concerned about agricultural overproduction. He criticized those who charged that he had created an "economy of scarcity." If Americans kept their shoe factories running twenty-four hours a day, seven days a week, they would duplicate the conditions now prevailing in agriculture. Those businessmen who condemned crop control "never hesitate to shut down their own huge plants, throw men out of work, and cut down the purchasing power of the whole community whenever they think they must adjust their production to an oversupply of the goods that they make. When it is their baby who has the measles, they call it not an 'economy of scarcity' but 'sound business judgment.' " He called for legislation that would protect farmers and consumers from alternating crop surpluses and crop scarcity. He advocated policies "to stop soil erosion, to save our forests, to prevent floods, to produce electric power for more general use, and to give people a chance to move from poor land to better land by irrigating thousands of acres."

His recent trip led him to stress again the interdependence of the entire nation. In the Boise Valley of Idaho, he visited a newly irrigated district being farmed by families who had recently been displaced by the dust storms that had affected ten states. "And, year by year, we propose to add more valleys to take care of thousands of other families who need the same kind of a second chance in new green pastures." He had also visited the Grand Coulee Dam in the state of Washington, where he learned that "almost half of the whole cost of that dam to date had been spent for materials that were manufactured east of the Mississippi River, giving employment and wages to thousands of industrial workers in the eastern third of the Nation, two thousand miles away." He called for legislation that would create seven planning regions — quickly labeled the "little TVA's" — in which local people would originate and coordinate recommendations as to what types of development and projects their areas needed. "To carry out any twentieth century program, we must give to the Executive branch of the Government twentieth century machinery to work with." Thus he called for the reorganization of the executive branch of the federal government.

On his trip, he learned of "the millions of men and women and children who still work at insufficient wages and overlong hours." Business had it within their power to improve their condition by paying better wages: "A few more dollars a week in wages, a better distribution of jobs with a shorter working day will almost overnight make millions of our lower-paid workers actual buyers of billions of dollars of industrial and farm products." Adequate wages and fair hours had to spread throughout the entire country if the demand for industrial and farm goods was to be revived and that spread was not the sole responsibility of business but also of the executive branch and the Congress as FDR made clear when he sent a minimum wage and maximum hours bill to the special session. While he believed in adequate pay for all labor, he explained to his listeners, "right now I am most greatly concerned in increasing the pay of the lowest-paid labor, those who are our most numerous consuming group but who today do not make enough to maintain a decent standard of living."

Whatever danger there was to property and profits "comes not from Government's attitude toward business but from restraints now imposed upon business by private monopolies and financial oligarchies." Thus the government was studying means of strengthening antitrust laws in order "to free the legitimate business of the Nation."

He closed his October 12 Fireside Chat by acknowledging that the prosperity of the United States was deeply affected by outside events: "we know that if the world outside our borders falls into the chaos of war, world trade will be completely disrupted. Nor can we view with indifference the destruction of civilized values throughout the world. We seek peace, not only for our generation but also for the generation of our children."

> We seek for them, our children, the continuance of world civilization in order that their American civilization may continue to be invigorated, helped by the achievements of civilized men and women in all the rest of the world.
> . . . In a world of mutual suspicions, peace must be affirmatively reached for. It cannot just be wished for. And it cannot just be waited for.

It was a theme he was to return to again and again in the coming years.

A month later, on the evening of November 14, he returned to the air with a Fireside Chat that was brief and on the surface narrow in scope. From the outset, one of the prime difficulties in combating the Depression was the appalling ignorance concerning how many Americans were actually unemployed and underemployed. In the initial years of the crisis, President Hoover provided a classic example of how ideology can rearrange facts to confirm one's sense of the way the world works. He ruthlessly edited the latest unemployment figures to reach his desk, cutting those workers he decided were jobless only temporarily and those he somehow convinced himself were not seriously searching for work. Even after he left office, Hoover continued to maintain that the apple sellers, who quickly became a familiar sight on street corners in cities throughout the nation, represented not the unemployed — even though many of them placed signs reading "UNEMPLOYED" on their box of fruit — but rather those who had "left their jobs for the more profitable one of selling apples." As late as 1936, Harry Hopkins, FDR's chief welfare adviser, conceded that his information on unemployment was not "adequate," and admitted that whether there were eight million or eleven million jobless depended on whose figures were consulted.[23]

To end the confusion and gather reliable figures, Congress decreed that a National Unemployment Census should be undertaken. In his Fireside Chat, FDR appealed to those who were unemployed or "insufficiently employed" to respond to the Unemployment Report Card they would receive in the mail the following Tuesday. If they would "conscientiously fill out these cards and mail them just as they are, without a stamp, without an envelope, by or before midnight of November 20, our nation will have real facts upon which to base a sound reemployment program. . . . we will know not only the extent of unemployment and partial unemployment, but we will know also the geographical location of unemployment . . . what age groups are most severely affected . . . we will know the work qualifications of the unemployed . . . in what industries they are suited to function, and we will be equipped to determine what future industrial trends are most likely to absorb these idle workers."

The President went beyond this appeal to discuss unemployment itself.

> Enforced idleness, embracing any considerable portion of our people, in a nation of such wealth and natural opportunity, is a paradox that challenges our ingenuity. Unemployment is one of the bitter and galling problems that now afflicts mankind. It has made necessary the expenditure of billions of dollars for relief and for publicly created work; it has delayed the balancing of our national budget, and has increased the tax burden of all our people. . . .
>
> It is a problem of every civilized nation — not ours alone. It has been solved in some countries by starting huge armament programs but we Americans do not want to solve it that way.

As a nation, "we adopted the policy that no unemployed man or woman can be permitted to starve for lack of aid." Nevertheless, unemployment relief was a temporary cure. The permanent solution lay in cooperative effort and planning involving industry, agriculture, and government. He expressed his conviction that the United States had "the genius to reorder its affairs" so that "everyone, young and old," could "enjoy the opportunity to work and earn." There was neither logic nor necessity "for one-third of our population to have less of the needs of modern life than make for decent living." Our "far-sighted industrial leaders," he said with perhaps more hope than conviction, "now recognize that a very substantial share of corporate earnings must be paid out in wages, or the soil from which these industries grow will soon become impoverished. Our farmers recognize that their largest consumers are the workers for wages, and that farm markets cannot be maintained except through widespread purchasing power." Unemployment, thus, was a problem "in which every individual and every economic group has a direct interest."

The President's attitudes toward unemployment reflected those of an increasing number of Americans. In July 1935, *Fortune* magazine, in the first of its influential series of quarterly national surveys, asked: "Do you believe that the government should see to it that every man who wants to work has a job?" It is not surprising that 88.8 percent of poor, 91.1 percent of Black, and 81.1 percent of lower-middle-class respondents answered yes. What is striking is that 69 percent of upper-middle-class and almost half of prosperous respondents did the same. Public opinion, *Fortune* concluded, "overwhelmingly favors assumption by the government of a function that was never seriously contemplated prior to the New Deal." National polls taken by the American Institute of Public Opinion (AIPO) in the months before Roosevelt's November 1937 Fireside Chat revealed that 76 percent felt that unemployed persons taken off relief jobs would have a "hard time" finding work (January 3); 67 percent were convinced that private business could not "absorb the able-bodied persons on relief during the coming year" (January 18); 73 percent supported a national census "to find out how many persons are unemployed" (June 20); 57 percent thought "there will always be as many as five million unemployed in this country" (July 12); and 68 percent opposed dropping WPA workers from relief before they have found jobs in private industry (August 9). A month before FDR's Chat *Fortune*, in its tenth quarterly survey, found that 63.8 percent agreed with the President "that one-third of the population of the U.S. has less than a minimum of the necessities for a decent life." More of those polled (34.8 percent) felt the federal government "should take care of relief" than state (17.6 percent) or local (28.4 percent) governments, and only 2.5 percent responded: "none of them."[24]

FDR understood better than any of his predecessors that in the complexities of a modern industrial world full employment could no longer be taken for granted; it had to be achieved. "The inherent right to work is one of the elemental privileges of a free people," he proclaimed in concluding his Fireside Chat:

> Continued failure to achieve that right, that privilege, by anyone who wants to work and needs work is a challenge to our civilization and to our security. Endowed, as our nation is, with abundant physical resources, and inspired as it should be with the high purpose to make those resources and opportunities available for the enjoyment of all, we approach this problem of reemployment with the real hope of finding a better answer than we have now.

OCTOBER 14, 1937

Dear Sir, — Your fireside chat on the evening of Wednesday Oct 13, was by far the most inspiring address of the several we have heard to date. It has proven to me that you are still the popular president of the millions of citizens in these United States. It has also shown that your principles and ideals remain the same as prior to your election which has made you the most popular president of all time. Your waning support and esteem is just so much "newspaper print" which is constantly aiming to hoodwink the public from actual facts. A true census of public opinion would still reveal that you are the same popular president that acclaimed you in 1932. I dare say if a vote were taken in my own little plant which employs approximately 300 people you would be chosen by at least 95% and I am reasonably certain that our plant is representative of the nation.

Your decision to call the Congress into special session on Nov. 15 is a masterful stroke, indeed, and is certainly approved by all fair minded and level headed citizens. Why shouldn't these men work when there is work to be done? You and I pay them to accomplish things, — not dilly-dally and after accomplishing little or nothing, declare a recess. You are the chosen captain and Congress is expected to enact legislation in accordance with your demands. When we, the public feel that your proposals are wrong or ill-timed we will soon put a stop to it at the ballot box. Until then let the work go on without fillibuster and shameful waste of public funds for doing nothing.

The public is still in back of you 100%, honorable President, and welcomes your fireside chats to let them know where you stand on matters of vital interest. We would welcome more such talks, especially now that we are constantly given nothing but biased opinions by our "press".

Yours Sincerely,

Benjamin B. Weiss
East Cleveland, Ohio

OCTOBER 13, 1937

Dear Mr. Roosevelt:

I heard your speech last night and I say right now that I agreed with everything you said. I'm glad that you called a special session of congress and I hope that now that you have the congressmen and women will cooperate with you as they should.

Your speech last night was very thorough, I thought, and one of the cleverest and truest parts about it was when you pointed out that if a shoe factory was faced with over production they would not hesitate to close their doors and then you said why not do the same with farm products. Why not indeed I would like to know.

As for your stand on the international situation — three cheers! I knew when you made your speech one week ago yesterday that you did not mean to imply that we would enter any war wherever it may be unless it was right here on our own shores. After your speech last week my father, who is a World War veteran, and my Grandfather were sure that we were heading for another war but I told them, without any luck at convincing them, that you had seen war and what it could do. Therefore, I told them that you would do nothing to get us into it. You convinced them last night. Frankly I don't see how they could possibly have had any doubt at all after watching you for almost five years.

I agree, too, with your stand on wages and hours and hope with all my heart that you will be able to get your legislation on that subject passed. As a matter of fact I hope that you will get all your legislation passed for I know that it would be best for the nation and after all you were elected to finish the job you began so splendidly. I still think, and always will, that your Court Reorganization was a fine idea and I hope that you will be able to attain it.

I would be deeply grateful if you would send me a copy of last evenings address.

I noticed that you sounded very tired last night Mr. Roosevelt. Please for your own sake and the sake of the country don't work too hard. I know you are earnestly striving to do the job you were elected to do and you are doing it in spite of all the silly opposition you have met with. Don't strive too hard for that would only lead to illness for you and that of course would never do.

You have earned and will keep forever my sincere gratitude and admiration and I will always do my utmost to cooperate with you in whatever small way I can.

A Sincerely Grateful citizen,

Beatrice Godin
Chillicothe, Ohio

OCTOBER 14, 1937

Gentlemen.

We have had another "Fire side chat" And I cannot help but wonder what manner of man our President really is.

He apparently imagines a great many things and seems to take it for granted that he is really doing some thinking. When in reality he is just letting his imagination run riot. A restless soul.

Nothing but "Front page Headlines" meets his ideas of life. So we must have another session of Congress. For no particular reason only his restlessness.

It is unfortunate that the idea of "Crop regulation" cannot be applied to the doings at the White House.

Very truly yours,

Robert Burgess
Brookline, Mass.

OCTOBER 14, 1937

Dear President Roosevelt:

My family and myself wish to write you a line to thank you for what you said in your recent fireside address.

I was not fortunate enough to hear it on the radio but I have just finished reading it in the Minneapolis Star.

We liked what you said about agriculture. As farmers we do not want doles, but we want to find our rightful niche in the economic plan of this nation. The Agricultural Adjustment Act was a great guide in that direction until it was taken away from us.

... The immediate concern is to get Congress to useful work. A subcommittee of Senators from the Agricultural Committee are holding hearings in St. Paul tomorrow. A number of us farmers are going down to ask for enactment of the ever normal granary, crop insurance, etc. ...

We are glad for the guidance and the courage generated in all of your addresses. We hope that many, if not all, of the objectives you seek will be attained soon. But if they are not we desire that all of your addresses be compiled in convenient form for coming generations to study. They are fountains stirring new hopes and new ambitions in the people down and out.

In closing will say that we have had a fairly good year. We have nothing to complain about, since we are comfortable. The only thing that worries us is that we can not see any program of national scope enacted thus far to prevent a debacle like the one in 1932 and 1933. But we shall tell the Senators tomorrow of that fear. Perhaps they will go then to the special session of Congress and work for such programs as will assure to all of our people, — laborers and farmers alike, — a sense of security in this land which is the best in all the world.

Sincerely yours,

Mr. and Mrs. J. Edward Anderson
Buffalo, Minnesota

OCTOBER 16, 1937

Dear Mr. Roosevelt:

I take this means to extend to you my appreciation of your speech the other night. I assure you it gives me a feeling of the greatest security to know that we have a President that has the foresight and wisdom that you have shown.

Please understand that I am an ex-service man and in a CCC camp drawing thirty six dollars per month and that before I came here have worked for three bushels of turnips per day boarding myself. Might I add that I am the father of six children, three of which are in high school. Of course I am not satisfied with the condition we are forced to live in because of the depression. Having been fortunate enough to have been with a firm for some eleven years previous to 1932 my family was used to the average standard of living, (1800. Annually). This is mentioned that you might know the drop in our living condition.

If we were to be faced with the continued circumstances we find ourselves in, life would be hopeless indeed BUT what cheers us is the thought, not of the petty errors of petty politics, but the splendid vision you have and the progress you have made. It is very easy to visualize what would have happened these past years when at the time you took over the ship of state the waves of dispair was washing over the whole country, had we not some one with courage enough to do the things you have done.

Your speech encourages us to "saw wood" and pull for the future you so courageously plan. It seems very dark indeed to us at times and personally I would like to hear you broadcast more often. It brings us out of the "Blues".

May our God watch over your every move and word and be with the leaders of our Nation.

Very respectfully,

Lawton L. Brown
Miller, Missouri

OCTOBER 16, 1937

My dear President Roosevelt:

Shades of Woodrow Wilson! The poor fellow must have stirred in his grave in efforts to warn you not to make the same mistake he did. He wanted to "make the world safe for Democracy" — you want to make the world safe for "civilization." Heaven preserve us from our heroes! I'm rapidly coming to the conclusion that this country, at least, is in far greater danger from people who want to be "noble" than from rascals.

If one can help to avert hostilities of any kind before a shot is fired, no one should refuse to negotiate. But after the conflagration has started then there is little one can do but try to keep it from spreading to one's own shores.

Haven't you heard that one must never argue with those who are angry, when they are angry? Always wait until they've cooled down, my teacher used to tell me. That applies to nations, I'm sure. Japan and Spain are already warring savagely. Do you really think you, or the rest of the world, or both, can shake a finger at them and say: "You naughty children, stop fighting at once. If you don't, I'll spank you; if you do, I'll give you a lolli-pop." — and presto! the wars will stop!? It's by far more probable that the harrassed warring nations will turn on their admonishers.

What possible harm could come to this country if it sat tight within its shores and attended to it's own domestic problems (numerous enough, as you know)? Under those circumstances, can you picture an enemy sending ships, planes or troops to molest this country? On the other hand, I can imagine so many complications arising out of a positive policy such as you advocate that I shudder away from really contemplating it.

After listening to your speech Columbus Day I'm sorry, for the first time since your election, that you are at the head of the government of this coun-try. Fear shakes my heart at the thought that one with your views of the sub-ject should hold the most important and influential position in the United States at this serious and turbulent time. And this fear will be my most con-stant companion unless something — perhaps Congress — checks your too ambitious course. Maybe neutrality laws should be mandated after all!

I'm not impugning your motives, which I still respect, your personality being such that one is somehow emotionally loyal even at a time when rea-son refuses to be loyal! (Of such personality stuff are dictators born, I sup-pose, even benevolent dictators such as you would be — not that I think you want to be. But I, and "the four million" like me who would suffer most in the cataclysm, pray that you have a change of heart. You have enough on your hands taking care of America — a job which, barring a few errors like the Supreme Court bungle, you are doing well. Please don't try to "save the world!"

I hope you will pardon this outpouring from an admirer, on the grounds of sincere anxiety which would not be stilled.

Respectfully,

Brownie Dressler
New York, N.Y.

OCTOBER 13, 1937

Dear President Roosevelt:

. . . Last night you sounded so weary, so different from the time before, when you sounded so proud to be able to tell the American people that you were protecting them, and when I saw you on the screen, (and for once they really let us hear your whole speech,) you looked so proud and sounded so happy, that last night I could have cried when I heard you sound so terribly weary — weary with the weight of having to actually use a sledge hammer to knock simple truths into the American people — who think they are so wise. — weary with constantly having your speeches misconstrued, deliberately misunderstood — weary with the WHY of it all. I felt so sorry for you — wished I could ease your burdens — wondered how you keep on — where you get the power to keep your vitality from being drained by an ungrateful populace. Glad — with a fierce gladness for the powers that be that gave us a MAN who could and would face the world for a CAUSE that HE KNEW was JUST & FAIR.

You promised America a NEW DEAL — well, you sure gave it to us. While so-called Brainy and highly educated people are really small-minded — you have taught others to THINK — you have succeeded, even if at times you may think it is useless — You HAVE given American people a NEW DEAL. . . .

I've wished many times there was some job I could fill to help you with your wonderful work, to be a part of the greatest thing in the world, to be able to feel that I was helping GOD'S MAN, then I realize I am a nonentity, just a scrub oak, looking up at the mighty great Oak. I realize you don't need my help, that you are backed by splendid people — first of whom are your Wife and Mother, and then I'm glad — but, still, I want to help.

Don't ever let them lick you — Always keep your smile — and lets hear from you more on the radio — and may God keep you in strength and health to finish the marvelous task you set out to do, for your pattern is so beautiful, some day, I know it will be hung in THE HALL OF FAME — finished — lovely — and INSPIRATION.

Sincerely,

Emma E. Wright
Roosevelt, N.Y.

*   *   *

Dear Mr. President:

I have just listened to your radio address of even date and wish to take this occasion to congratulate you on your talk. I enjoyed it immensely.

I was particularly impressed by the way you brought out the fact that in 1933 certain elements within our borders, and possibly outside our borders, were very happy for the so-called government intervention, which was accompanied by cash, stabilization of credits, and a general reduction in the feeling of fear by the people at large.

To-day, these certain elements would gladly like to take the reins again into their hands. Needless to say, if this should occur, I am of the opinion that within a very short time we would be back to the same condition which confronted our citizens when you first took office as President of these United States.

I believe that the majority of the people see eye to eye with you on your statement that a "reduction in hours, increases in salaries, stabilization of production, and distribution of certain consumer materials, dissolution of trade barriers within our shores" would soon produce such a tremendous market of home consumption that an unbounding prosperity would make us the most envied people of the world.

At the same time such a situation, if properly handled, would not only aid our export as well as import business but would materially decrease international jealousies, and set up a new standard for other nations of the world to follow, and we would still be preserving the great ideals of democracy.

We would move forward with a new spirit of hopefulness because as you expressed it "one part of the country cannot have prosperity if the other part of the country is exploited;" This cannot be stressed too often, as I believe there are certain elements still with that "rugged individual" strain running through them who believe they are not interdependent upon the prosperity of others for their own share of worldly goods.

Again I wish to state, believe me, when I wish you good health to carry on for democracy.

Sincerely,

D. P. Alterman
Mount Vernon, N.Y.

OCTOBER 12, 1937

SHOE PRODUCTION CAN BE CONTROLLED BY HUMAN HANDS. CROPS ARE
CONTROLLED BY NATURE AND SHOULD BE LEFT ALONE. . . .

HILDA ARIAS
NEW YORK, N.Y.

OCTOBER 12, 1937

IN YOUR SPEECH TONIGHT YOU FORGOT TO TELL US HOW YOU ARE GOING
TO CONTROL THE WEATHER AND INSECTS. I SUGGEST YOU DEVELOP A
PLAN TO GROW HAIR ON BALD HEADS.

J. D. GOODMAN
PHILADELPHIA, PENNA.

OCTOBER 12, 1937

PLEASE SPEND YOUR EVENINGS ATTENDING "I'D RATHER BE RIGHT" THAN
MAKING FIRESIDE CHATS AND POSSIBLY YOU MIGHT LEARN SOMETHING.

H. S. BABCOCK, STILL A REPUBLICAN
MYSTIC, CONN.

OCTOBER 12, 1937

MY REACTION: THIRTY MINUTES WORSE THAN LOST.

W. A. BLACK
OAKLAND, CALIF.

OCTOBER 13, 1937

Dear Mr. President:

For sometime I have wanted to write and tell you that I am very much in
accord with your entire program and after your speech of last night I could
not resist the impulse.

I suppose that if any one [of] my elders knew I was doing this they would advise me not to waste your time because they feel that I am too young to know much about politics. But on the contrary, I flatter myself that we young people of the coming generation know a great deal. Circumstances have forced us to understand and observe what is going on in the world about us, and I know from my contacts with young people that I am only one of scores who are standing firmly behind you.

While you were in Chicago . . . passing down La Salle Street everyone was at the windows and in the excitement some sneak-thief stole my purse from my desk. This occurrence made me the butt of many of my Republican friends jokes. But I think it was well worth all the tormenting I received, and the loss of my nice new black purse, of which I was very proud, to have been able to see you again.

But be that as it may the important thing which I wanted to convey is that we, the young people are with you all the way up that road which will lead us back to prosperity.

More power to you Mr. President.

Yours very truly,

(Miss) LaVergne E. Hintze
Chicago, Illinois

OCTOBER 12, 1937

Dear President:

I wish to take this opportunity of complimenting you on your radio speech this evening, it was wonderful!

However, there is one slight criticism I have to offer. After your hearty cough you overlooked pardoning yourself. I sincerely trust you will accept this jest in the right spirit.

Yours, as a public spirited citizen,

Henry Black
Rahway, N.J.

NOVEMBER 16, 1937

Dear Mr. President:

I listened, as I always do, to your radio speech of the 14th. You have a pleasing radio voice.

You are asking, and are going to ask, business to help you in reducing unemployment. Is it possible you have not heard that business is deceased? The death certificate gives "starvation" as the cause. Business had been ailing more or less since the New Deal policies got well under way. At first its health was very good. Your promises, before the election of 1932, to balance the budget, and to reduce government expenses 25% acted like a tonic, and everybody thought the patient was on the way to recovery. I remember your words: "I have a way of getting things done in Washington." But when these promises went sour, the body of the patient became heavily acidulated, aggravated by a malignant infection of taxeatus, the decline set in, which resulted in the recent demise of the patient.

Life might have been prolonged without the budget being balanced; but instead of the government expense being reduced, it has been so drunkenly increased, that the patient became afflicted with high blood pressure and dizzyness, resulting in heart failure.

Had you been willing to take business into your confidence, instead of by the scruff of the neck and the seat of the pants, we feel that the result might have been different. I fear it is too late now, even for resurrection. As the new deal resulted in death, we are looking forward to a new birth three years hence that will give us life again.

Yours respectfully,

W. B. Ladd
Denver, Colorado

NOVEMBER 14, 1937

Dear Mr. Roosevelt:

Five minutes ago you finished your epoch making explanation of the reason and purposes for the Unemployment Census. It was SUPREME! God bless you for it, and all of those who are with you. May you meet with the highest success!

That is the kind of work that will quickly put your knockers and opponents — the enemies of humanitarianism — under the table where they should stay and hide their faces in shame until they will apologize and promise to be good.

I am not one of the unemployed. I am working full time at sufficient pay to keep the wolf from the door, with a little to spare for needy relatives, etc., but I can well imagine the courage and gratitude which your promise of help must have brought to millions of homes this night. For that you have won my gratitude also. If I can be of help to you, just say the word.

Very truly yours,

W. E. Hendrickson
Alameda, Calif.

COMBATTING RENEWED
DEPRESSION: APRIL 14, 1938

NOTHING IN FRANKLIN ROOSEVELT'S second term seemed to
rise to the heights of the magnificent electoral victory that so auspiciously
placed him in office for an additional four years. The struggle over the Supreme Court was only the first of the setbacks Roosevelt faced after his second inauguration. More troubling for the President and his people was the
so-called recession of 1937–38, which was in reality a renewed depression
and threatened to bring back the perilous conditions that had gripped the
nation when FDR first took office in 1933. The President's opponents were
quick to use the renewed economic woes — which began in the late summer, accelerated in the latter months of 1937, and grew worse in early
1938 — as proof of the failure of the approach at the heart of the New Deal.
In fact, the severe economic setback — which was indeed largely self-
inflicted — was created not by Roosevelt's reform program but by his ambivalence toward that program.

FDR liked to see himself as a bridge between traditional America with
its ethos of individualism and a modern America characterized by huge organizations and enterprises and the new spirit of collectivism. Spanning
two historical stages, the first of which was not yet completely erased from
and the second not yet completely born in the popular consciousness, may
have been a necessary role but not an easy one. It was particularly difficult
for Franklin Roosevelt, who, as flexible as he proved to be, was himself in
many ways still in the grasp of the assumptions and beliefs of traditional
America. As FDR's adviser Rexford Guy Tugwell said of his chief: "And yet
he too had not been immune to our national myths. He, like others, would
spend a lot of time in the coming years planting protective shrubbery on the
slopes of a volcano which was by no means finished with eruption." Roosevelt, Tugwell maintained, "like all of us, had a weakness for what was familiar and trusted which led him to overestimate their sufficiency and to un-
derestimate their irrelevant antiquity." Tugwell, who often understood
FDR more profoundly than most of his other advisers, thus comprehended
more acutely than they the price the President paid for deviating too
sharply from tradition.

The serious student is forced to conclude that this man deliberately concealed the processes of his mind. He would rather have
posterity believe that for him everything was always plain and
easy, that he undertook all his projects with certainty and pursued them serenely, than ever to admit to any agony of indecision, any serious study of alternatives, any misgiving about mistakes. But it was not so. Not less for him than for others, his
burdens were burdens, carried with pain and endured with fa-
tigue.[25]

FDR's actions prior to the economic crisis of 1937–38 bear out Tugwell's
insight. Roosevelt's policies during the early months of his first term, as
necessary as he conceived them to be, had left him uneasy. That disquiet
was manifest as early as the summer of 1935, when the President responded
to a letter from the publisher Roy Howard warning FDR that business was
becoming edgy in the face of all the New Deal's reforms and asking him to
grant "a breathing spell to industry, and a recess from further experimentation." Roosevelt responded by assuring Howard that the New Deal's "basic
program . . . has now reached substantial completion and the 'breathing
spell' of which you speak is here — very decidedly so." That FDR was no
enemy to the fundamental structure of the American economy is revealed
by the fact that he liked one of Howard's concluding sentences so much he
repeated it in his own letter: "With all its faults and with the abuses it has
developed, our system has in the past enabled us to achieve greater mass
progress than has been attained by any other system on earth," and agreed
with the publisher that what the New Deal was about was not "revolution"
but the "orderly modernization of a system we want to preserve."[26]

The confusion, vacillation, and meandering that often characterized
New Deal economic policies was produced by the tension created between
what Roosevelt believed in and what he found himself having to do to bring
about recovery. Much of Roosevelt's heralded pragmatism stemmed not
from an absence of a prior faith but rather from the fact that the prior faith
he held was inadequate to deal with the situation he found himself in, and
he was constantly searching for solutions that would alleviate the situation
and do the least violence to those things in which he believed. Thus, as we
have seen, FDR never went as far as he could have in those crucial early
days of the New Deal. Thus many of the steps he took — such as his support of labor legislation and Keynesian pump-priming — he took with

some reluctance. Thus he did not give up on business support until it gave up on him — and he never gave up on it entirely. He made this clear in a speech in Chicago during the campaign of 1936 when he insisted: "It was this Administration which saved the system of private profit and free enterprise after it had been dragged to the brink of ruin by these same leaders who now try to scare you," and then turned to humor to deepen his point:

> Some of these people really forget how sick they were. But I know how sick they were. I have their fever charts. I know how the knees of all of our rugged individualists were trembling four years ago and how their hearts fluttered. They came to Washington in great numbers. Washington did not look like a dangerous bureaucracy to them then. Oh, no! It looked like an emergency hospital. All of the distinguished patients wanted two things — a quick hypodermic to end the pain and a course of treatment to cure the disease. They wanted them in a hurry; we gave them both. And now most of the patients seem to be doing very nicely. Some of them are even well enough to throw their crutches at the doctor.[27]

While Roosevelt's statement to Roy Howard was premature in 1935, the relative prosperity of 1937 seemed a more propitious time to act as if the New Deal were in fact complete. The economy had made an impressive recovery, with industrial production almost 80 percent greater than it had been in 1932 and agricultural income almost matching that of 1929. "The emergency," Senator James Byrnes of South Carolina announced in May, "has passed."[28] Although FDR was reviled by conservatives for reckless and irresponsible spending, and although he did proclaim that a "balanced economy rather than a balanced budget" was his goal, at no point did he accept deficit spending as normal policy or abandon his desire to balance the budget. He promised to do so during the campaign of 1936, and early in 1937 he reiterated his desire. "I have said fifty times that the budget will be balanced for the fiscal year 1938," he exclaimed to his conservative Vice President, John Nance Garner. "If you want me to say it again, I will say it either once or fifty times more. That is my intention."[29] He took an important step in this direction by substantially reduced funding for work relief, cutting the number of people working on WPA projects in half. In addition he decreased farm subsidies and encouraged the Federal Reserve to tighten credit, thus further reducing the circulation of money in the economy.

The times proved to be less propitious than FDR — and many of his supporters and opponents — had assumed. Indeed, while production, income, and profits had increased, the fact that 1937, with its seven million unemployed women and men — representing some 14 percent of the workforce — could have been considered prosperous in the first place, is a testament to the lowered expectations of the period and the deepening resignation that the United States would never again regain the buoyant abundance of the past. In his 1936 book *Spending to Save,* Harry Hopkins, the nation's relief administrator, wrote: "Intelligent people have long since left behind them the notion that under fullest recovery, and even with improved purchasing power, the unemployed will disappear."[30] In July 1937, 57 percent of those polled by the American Institute of Public Opinion agreed that "there will always be as many as five million unemployed in this country."[31]

By August 1937, the effects of FDR's policies of reducing the federal government's role in the economy were felt dramatically. Although many businessmen had called vigorously for a diminished federal presence, they proved unwilling or unable to step into the gap left by the withdrawal of government monies from the economy. The results were inevitable: the stock market plunged, along with production and sales, while unemployment soared to 20 percent of the workforce. Roosevelt, reluctant to increase government spending and debt, chose to wait the recession out, but waiting availed him no more than it had Herbert Hoover after the crash of 1929. He was besieged on all sides with contradictory advice: retrench further urged the conservatives; increase government spending counseled avid New Dealers; attack the trusts suggested the old Wilsonian progressives among his advisers. During his press conference of October 29, 1937, FDR told reporters of letters he had recently received from two distinguished economic experts: "One says the entire question is one of the velocity of capital turnover credit, so do not pay any attention to purchasing power. The other one says: forget all this algebraic formula about the velocity of capital turnover credit; the whole question is purchasing power on the part of one hundred and thirty million people." "It is," the President concluded wryly, "a fascinating study."[32]

It was not doctrines but circumstances that determined the President's course. He might have been ambivalent about unbalanced budgets but never about human suffering and want. Unlike his predecessor, he could find no rationale for tolerating the misery of his fellow citizens or blinding himself to their ordeal. He had been visibly moved when he told Secretary of the Interior Ickes that during his 1936 campaign stops in the West he heard voices from the crowds that lined the streets exclaiming: "He saved my home," "He gave me a job," "God bless you, Mr. President."[33]

When in March 1938 stocks took a frightening plunge, business conditions deteriorated further, and there were several million newly unemployed workers, FDR's decision was made for him. On April 14, he sent a message to Congress urging the appropriation of billions of dollars for work relief agencies and farm subsidies, which, along with more liberal policies governing credit, would help restore the economy and diminish the massive new suffering.

These were difficult days for the President. The day before he was to send his message to Congress, his Secretary of the Treasury and old friend, Henry Morgenthau, told him, "if you insist on going through with this spending program I am seriously thinking of resigning." In an emotional scene, FDR was able to dissuade him, but this encounter typified the pressures he was laboring under; pressures that emanated not only from his opponents but from within his own Administration and party as well. Not long after his confrontation with Morgenthau, he met with a group of his advisers and read them a first draft of his message to Congress, and then with a group of his speechwriters he worked on the final version until one o'clock in the morning and announced his intention to go to bed. His secretary, Missy LeHand, reminded him that he had scheduled a Fireside Chat for the next evening. "Oh, I'm tired, let me go to bed," he responded, but LeHand insisted: "You just have to get something down on paper tonight." Sam Rosenman, who was present, described what happened next:

> He leaned back on the sofa with an air of resignation and shut his eyes for a long time. We sat there very quietly; after a while we thought he had actually fallen asleep. But finally he opened his eyes and, starting to dictate, said, "Mah F-r-a-a-nds" in such an exaggerated drawl of "My friends" (with which salutation nearly all his fireside chats started), and with such a comic expression, that we all broke out laughing. That perked him right up, and he dictated steadily until 2:15 A.M., when we let him at last go to bed.[34]

That afternoon he joined Rosenman, Harry Hopkins, and Thomas Corcoran and worked on the final draft until six. He then took a nap, as he often did before a radio speech, had a light dinner in bed, and at ten-thirty in the evening, in his twelfth Fireside Chat, he addressed a beleaguered, apprehensive American people in an address that the *New York Times* found "strikingly reminiscent . . . of the dark days of 1933, when Mr. Roosevelt first came into power and in rapid-fire fashion set in motion a series of governmental actions to halt the economic depression which started in 1929."[35]

He opened by apologizing for intruding upon Holy Week but explained that what he had to say "to you, the people of the country, is of such immediate need and relates so closely to the lives of human beings and the prevention of human suffering that . . . I have been strengthened by the thought that by speaking tonight there may be greater peace of mind and that the hope of Easter may be more real at firesides everywhere."[36] In the past seven months, he said, the country had suffered a "visible setback." He had waited "patiently to see whether the forces of business itself would counteract it," but it had become apparent "that Government itself can no longer safely fail to take aggressive Government steps to meet it." He assured his listeners that the nation had not returned to the disastrous conditions that had prevailed when he first took office: banks were safe, stock speculation was minimized, farmers and workers had greater income, government had "an established and accepted responsibility for relief."

> But I know that many of you have lost your jobs or have seen your friends or members of your families lose their jobs, and I do not propose that the Government shall pretend not to see these things. . . . I conceive the first duty of Government is to protect the economic welfare of all the people in all sections and in all groups.

He spent a good part of his hastily prepared Chat quoting and summarizing passages from the message he had sent to Congress earlier that day. At the heart of his message and his thought were the people's "human problems of food and clothing and homes and education and health and old age." He had told the Congress that neither it nor the Chief Executive could afford

> to weaken or destroy great reforms which, during the past five years, have been effected on behalf of the American people. In our rehabilitation of the banking structure and of agriculture,

in our provisions for adequate and cheaper credit for all types of business, in our acceptance of national responsibility for unemployment relief, . . . in our encouragement of housing, and slum clearance and home ownership, in our supervision of stock exchanges and public utility holding companies . . . in our provision for social security itself, the electorate of America wants no backward steps taken.

On the contrary, the federal government had to move forward, and he proposed three groups of measures for Congress to act upon. First, to appropriate a billion and a quarter dollars more than he had asked for in January for the Works Progress Administration, the Farm Security Administration, the National Youth Administration, and the Civilian Conservation Corps. Second, to make some two billion dollars of gold reserves and bank reserves available for the credit needs of the country. Third "to make definite additions to the purchasing power of the Nation" by enabling the United States Housing Authority to undertake the immediate construction of three hundred million dollars worth of additional slum clearance projects; to renew public works projects by making one billion dollars worth of needed public improvements in states, cities, and counties; to add to his original requests an additional one hundred million dollars for federal aid to highways, thirty-seven million dollars for flood control and reclamation, and twenty-five million dollars for federal buildings in various parts of the country.

> In recommending this program I am thinking not only of the immediate economic needs of the people of the Nation, but also of their personal liberties — the most precious possession of all Americans. I am thinking of our democracy. . . .
>
> History proves that dictatorships do not grow out of strong and successful governments but out of weak and helpless governments. If by democratic methods people get a government strong enough to protect them from fear and starvation, their democracy succeeds, but if they do not, they grow impatient. Therefore, the only sure bulwark of continuing liberty is a government strong enough to protect the interests of the people, and a people strong enough and well enough informed to maintain its sovereign control over its government.

> We are a rich Nation; we can afford to pay for security and prosperity without having to sacrifice our liberties into the bargain.

As he often did, Roosevelt assumed the role of historian and teacher, explaining that during the first century of our existence the federal government had distributed its vast holdings of land, timber, and other resources to the American people in order to promote business and economic growth. "Thus, from our earliest days we have had a tradition of substantial Government help to our system of private enterprise." It is therefore "following tradition as well as necessity, if Government strives to put idle money and idle men to work, to increase our public wealth and to build up the health and strength of the people — to help our system of private enterprise to function again." It was crucial that these public expenditures be fairly distributed among all the people. "Consequently, I am again expressing my hope that the Congress will enact at this session a wage and hour bill putting a floor under industrial wages and a limit on working hours — to ensure a better distribution of our prosperity, a better distribution of available work, and a sounder distribution of buying power."

He reminded his audience that the increase in the national debt of some sixteen billion dollars included billions of dollars worth of assets: "schools, roads, bridges, tunnels, public buildings, parks and a host of other things that meet your eye in every one of the thirty-one hundred counties in the United States." Government spending not only added wealth, it also acted "as a trigger" to stimulate private spending of vast proportions. He concluded with what he called "a personal word to you."

> I never forget that I live in a house owned by all the American people and that I have been given their trust.
>
> I try always to remember that their deepest problems are human. . . . I try not to forget that what really counts at the bottom of it all, is that the men and women willing to work can have a decent job, — a decent job to take care of themselves and their homes and their children adequately; that the farmer, the factory worker, the storekeeper, the gas station man, the manufacturer, the merchant — big and small — the banker . . . that all of these can be sure of a reasonable profit and safety for the earnings that they make — not for today nor tomorrow alone, but as far ahead as they can see.

... I always try to remember that reconciling differences cannot satisfy everyone completely. . . . But I know that I must never give up — that I must never let the greater interest of all the people down, merely because that might be for the moment the easiest personal way out.

I believe that we have been right in the course we have charted. To abandon our purpose of building a greater, a more stable and a more tolerant America, would be to miss the tide and perhaps to miss the port. I propose to sail ahead. I feel sure that your hopes, I feel sure that your help are with me. For to reach a port, we must sail — sail, not lie at anchor, sail, not drift.

"I heard Roosevelt deliver this speech," Rosenman has written. "His voice seemed to reach out right into every home in the United States. Those paragraphs, spoken badly, could have sounded very 'corny'; but, as he delivered them, they expressed the deep, sincere, warm emotions of a leader who was terribly concerned about the millions of human beings whose welfare was so greatly affected by the policies of the government he led."[37]

APRIL 14, 1938

Dear Mr. President,

My wife and I stopped in the middle of drying our dinner dishes tonight to sit down in the kitchen beside the radio to hear your talk. I know the many hundred men who work where I do have also listened.

We cannot afford telegrams and too many of us feel that letters are of no consequence. Yet knowing how you have been harrassed by the loud voice of a selfish minority I am certain that a word of warm encouragement is not amiss.

You have not let us down. We know that. All the forces of propoganda in the world can't keep from us that knowledge. We know that you have kept the pledge you gave us. That you have justified the faith we have placed in you. We aren't very articulate about it. The men at my plant like men elsewhere were beginning to take you for granted — sort of the way a man takes health for granted until he gets sick. But it's now become obvious that the fight wasn't over with our 27 million votes in 1936 — it's obvious that we must make our voices heard again. We know that you are carrying on the program we voted for — and we mark well those delegates of ours who are letting us down, who are blocking our program and our will.

We have gained a better life — we mean to maintain this better life and extend it to others. Our wishes that you have so persistantly fought for have materialized. We used to leave work at nine o'clock in the evening. Now every day we go home at five! We used to live in a one room shack. Now we live in a flat with a kitchen, living room and bedroom — and best of all — with plumbing! Before we didn't dare hope for children. Now it's not such a bad idea as we can afford orange juice and cod liver oil. We even have a few extras such as a pork roast some Sundays and perhaps ice cream.

It's not important that this has happened to just us. But it is important that this has happened for so many millions of us, important that you are trying to extend this to many millions more.

And we do not forget that we have these things only because you did not let us down!

How necessary it is that you know these things. You have hurled at you every day the clamoring voices of self seeking individuals. How often, though, do you hear the voice of the people? Believe me, Mr. President it is the people speaking now. You must know that we are for you and with you.

Sincerely,

Mark F. Hawkins
San Francisco, California

APRIL 15, 1938

Dear Mr. President as a Citizen and a Colored American of this Country; also a veteran of the World War and an earnest listner of all your chats especially the last one made. In this regard I am attempting in these lines to express my sincere feeling toward you as a leader. I first wish to state I am unable to say to you and about you in words what is in my heart toward you. But as a man you are human, kind and sympathetic; as a Leader, you are Courageous Fearless and yet Gentle; and as an excutive thou art full of thoughts and masterful. God has truly sent you to the Seat of this Government to preside at such a times as these.

I am praying that you overcome oppositions confronting you and accheive in your efforts, that from 1933 until now, can be clearly seen have all been based on the needs of the people. May God Bless you and your household.

A true friend.

Rev. William White, Sr.
Venice, Ill.

APRIL 17, 1938

Dear Sir:

I want to register my emphatic protest against your proposed program.

Your policies have already begun to undermine the most precious possession of a people — its morale. They are stultifying the ideals of individual independence and integrity which gave this Nation whatever leadership it had. They are reducing the people to shame-faced alms-takers and grafting idlers. Your leadership along the lines you are following are deleterious.

I write only because of an earnest desire to arouse you from your error. . . .

The production and distribution of wealth, supply and demand of commodities, rent, wages and interest; price, etc., are all governed by Natural Laws — Laws which neither Presidents, nor Congress, nor Dictators can circumvent, Laws which are no respecters of men or measures. We may disobey them as we are doing and we can reap the consequent "depressions", "recessions", unemployment, poverty and all the horrors of life by "trial and error" with eventual chaos.

Therefore I beg of you since you have the position of leadership to seek the Law and follow it. It has been discovered and expounded and called to your attention more than once since you became president. You haven't the moral right to neglect it and lead a people to ruin.

Very truly yours,

Olive Maguire
Berkeley, California

APRIL 18, 1938

Dear sir:

I missed listening to your "Fireside Chat" last Friday, so I read it in the papers.

Your alibi for the present "re-cession" may get by a lot of people who dont know what it is all about, but some of us cant swallow it. . . .

Why cant you and your New Dealers recognize the truth that too much of the wealth is concentrated in the hands of the few for any ordinary activity, "pump priming" or what not, to balance our economic system so that human activity can ebb and flow according to the needs, desires, and aspirations of humanity. . . .

Your "pump priming" plan now, if it goes thru, will have the same effect as your first one — it will set the machinery going for a while, how long remains to be seen, but if you and your New Dealers dont do something that MUST BE DONE meanwhile, you will be going out of office about the time when the second re-cession comes along.

If a man has been robbed of everything he has, you cant make him normal economically, nor mentally, spiritually or physically, by giving him a WPA job, or a $30 per month pension. That is not restoration. That is TOLERATION of the crime, especially when nothing is done to make a repetition of the crime impossible. . . .

We dont want fine words, sympathy, and assurance that no one shall go hungry. It takes more than that to make a normal human being. We want RESTORATION of the rights that we know are ours. We want an equitable distribution of the wealth that humanity has produced. . . .

Sincerely yours,

J. EMIL NELSON
Willmar, Minnesota

APRIL 15, 1938

Sir —

I am amazed that after the "pump priming" you have already poured into the Country you should have nothing better to offer than a repetition of the same old dose. Surely it is apparent that this method is no good and cannot possibly take the place of the business methods this country has always followed. This proposed expenditure will bring the U.S. debt above $45,000,000,000. How can any apparent taxation possibly take care of the interest on this amount of money? To say nothing of reducing the principal?

My forefathers fought in the Revolutionary war, my father four years on the Union side in the Civil war and I certainly am opposed to the prospective ruin of this country by such methods as you are pursuing. There is no doubt that our present depression has been brought about entirely by your own false measures in combatting business with one hand while distributing political largess with the other.

I am 63 years old; have been out of work for several years, but my wife and I have managed to get along on a little tea-room business without one cent from the Government at any time. You are making it increasingly hard for every one in any small business to exist: to say nothing of what you are doing to larger businesses. Of course there is lack of confidence; how could it be otherwise with your vacillating policy?

It was a sorry day for America when you were elected. You will go down in history as the man who ruined America.

Yours.

Harry H. Rung
Waynesville, N.C.

APRIL 28, 1938

Dear Mr. President:

I should like to voice my humble approval of your plan for recovery as expressed in your recent radio address. Such forward-looking, courageous words seem to me in the best traditions of American leadership.

This plan must be put into immediate action. The plain people of America, and especially those whom you have designated as the ill-clothed, ill-housed, ill-fed "one-third" — these people cannot wait. The farmers cannot wait. The youth of the land cannot wait. None of us can hold out very long in the face of this devastating new recession.

That is why we urge you, Mr. President, to act upon your words. That is why I and the majority of my friends promise you our utmost support in your program.

I am not interested in balanced budgets and government interference in business. I am asking to see America — including myself — at work once more, if not in private industry, then on WPA. I am not interested in "rugged individualism". I am interested in the life and health of the average person — and that includes myself.

Sincerely yours,

Hellen Tenney
New York

APRIL 15, 1938

Dear Mr. President:

This being our 25th Wedding Anniversary I would like to celebrate it by doing something so different, that even to me it seems just a little forward and brazen.

But lets forget it at the present, for after hearing you talk last night over the radio, I made up my mind that I could talk to you as sincerely as to my own brother. Do you think Mr. President, that if you appealed to the people of our country, to play fair in every respect, I mean this, that if every man financialy independent and holding a job some other man could fill (propably just as good) would give this said job up, and if every woman employed that really does not have to work, would stay home and raise a family or take up some hobby (she would be much happier too) Im positive there would be plenty of work to go around and hence end the depression. Im not saying this to criticize any of your work, for to my estimation, there is no person living or dead that has accomplished as much as you have, you have saved our home from foreclosure, and helped us throu direct relief in 1933 and even now my husband got a job on the W.P.A. after being off steady employment 6 years, so you see, dear Mr. President, there's no one more gratefull than I am, but Im a woman past 45 and mother of 7 children, — ranging from 23 to 10 years of age — 5 of which are boys, so naturally Im a little concerned about their future, and also the future of all the younger generation.

Forgive this letter dear Mr. President, I just had to do it.

Sincerely and
Humbly
yours

Mrs. Agnes Drufke
Chicago, Ill.

*   *   *

Dear Mr Presdent

After listening to you speach over the Radio I have allways said <u>You cant borrow you self out of debt</u>, as I never buy enything unless I have the money <u>or know where its coming from</u>. <u>Credet</u> is the <u>Curse</u> of this country as its over done

As there is no steady work in the factory any more

Working man buys Cars on time Elec stove etc. and then the're laid off, and they cant Pay and the man take his car or what ever he <u>cant pay for</u> after he has <u>Put $100.00</u> or <u>more</u> into it. . . .

Real astate Insurrince & the Auto Business are three of the crookest business in this country All these things should be controlled by the Government as this is part of Wall St. dirty work on the poor working man. . . .

Stop the Recession
by
No. 1 cut White House expenses and do away with strikes all over the country. . . .

No. 3 stop married Women from working when there husbands are working. Put more men to work. let the Women stay home where they belong. . . .

No. 5 Welfare is demorolising the hole country give us work. not Welfare let keep our honer & Liberty. . . .

No. 7 Pass the Townsend Plan to take the old men out of factory and give the young men a chance to work. . . .

These are a few things for you to think about to make it a better country in which to Live

a good Citizen
Your. Truly

Wm. Mackintosh
Mt. Morris, Mich.

APRIL 16, 1938

Dear Sir: I heard your fireside chat and it made me sick at heart, to think you have nothing on your program only the same old thing you have had for 5 yrs. just giving to those who will take it. You have tried nothing else for 5 yrs and we are worse off then we were before. You speak of another depression. We have never been out of the first one and anyone knows it. The people around here have just been living off the Government, and the rest of us people ever since this started. You spoke of certain businesses making more. Yes the car business is making more because you are giving W.P.A. workers and others our money to buy them with, the mail order houses are making more because you are giving people money to order, the saloons and pool halls are flourishing because that is where the W.P.A. workers spend their time only what few hours they have to works. None of these wouldn't sell much if it were left up to us who just have what we make ourselves. The reliefers and W.P.A. workers and Farmers who draw big checks just laugh when we cant have the things they have. . . . You have enough bribed to put over anything you wish for they have come to the place where they wont vote against a dollar but God only knows what is to become of us few who aren't getting anything. It is taking all we have for taxes to just exist. We have little children ready for high school we cant send them for we haven't the money. We cant do anything the governments favorites are doing and yet I guess we will have to drag along for we wont sign a paper and say we are destitute, can't make our way, can't get any credit, to get on the W.P.A., till you take everything we've got.

Yours

Mrs. A. M. Jones
Inka, Ill.

APRIL 14, 1938

Dear Sir:

We heard your radio address and have concluded that we're all out of step but Jim.

I travel the state of Georgia continuously and if your ideas of recovery are right all of us down here are crazy.

Did it ever enter your head that the country ran before your time and will after your gone? Try dipping your head in a pail of water three times and just bring it out twice. Then the country will really recover.

Yours truly,

Harry Spencer
Atlanta, Ga.

APRIL 15, 1938

AS A NATIVE BORN AMERICAN WHO FOUGHT FOR 18 MONTHS IN THE FRONT LINE TRENCHES TO PRESERVE WHAT I CONCEIVED THEN AND NOW ASSERT TO BE OUR TRADITIONAL SYSTEM OF REPRESENTATIVE GOVERNMENT I

WISH TO SAY THIS. I WOULD RATHER HAVE DIED BY AN ENEMY BULLET
THAN TO HAVE LIVED TO SEE THE DAY WHEN THE PRESIDENT OF MY COUN-
TRY CAN SERIOUSLY ADVOCATE DOCTRINES AS EXPRESSED IN YOUR FIRE-
SIDE TALK TONIGHT WHICH ARE SO COMPLETELY OPPOSED TO THE
THINGS FOR WHICH I FOUGHT THAT I SOLEMNLY PROMISE YOU THAT I
WILL GIVE WITHOUT STINT OR LIMIT ALL OF MY FREE TIME AND ENERGY
TO DEFEAT AT ELECTION YOU AND ALL CANDIDATES FOR OFFICE WHO SUB-
SCRIBE TO YOUR SPECIOUS DOCTRINES.

> DONALD A. HOBART
> BRONXVILLE, N.Y.

APRIL 14, 1938

Dear Mr. President.

Your talk over the radio Thursday was wonderful. . . .

We should have a "Wage and Hour" Bill by all means. Right here in
Dade County, the richest county in Florida where millions are spent every
winter for pleasure there are many families living in one and two room huts
with no electric light or bath. A little woman whose child I teach in Public
Schools works six days a week for 6.00 and seems glad to have the work.
She is a nice sensible woman too, not much education, but an honest up-
right person trying to rear three children. It is a shame yet nothing is done
about it. There are men with families working for 1.50 to 2.00 per day. They
cant live decently or give their children proper food. It must be changed by
Congress and those who have the authority to do it.

> Your friend & supporter,
>
> Sarah M. Cobb
> Miami, Fla.

APRIL 14, 1938

My dear President: —

. . . The night before your radio talk, while sitting in a restaurant, I listened to such unjust criticisms of your theories and policies by some of my

friends, most of them quoting your personal enemies, that I resented them as tho they were criticising me personally. I thought to myself, "What a fool our president is to be working so hard to please such ingrates." But to-night, as I listened to your words which I know and feel come from your heart, I was again moved as I was on that famous night in March 1933.

Carry on, in spite of the fools who know not what is good for them. May God bless you and yours.

Very humbly yours,

Nat Baumann
New York, N.Y.

* * *

Dear President Roosevelt:

As staunch believers in your interpretation of the American way, We, the undersigned, feel it to be our duty to leave the vast ranks of the inarticulate and give voice to our approval of your humane program.

We have followed with admiration your capable leadership in lifting the nation from the gloomy depths of despair into which it had been plunged by the laissez-faire policies of a decade.

We have witnessed the tragic destruction of the earning power of many — either from technological inroads, or because of other factors — and have seen men so displaced, unceremoniously thrown into the lap of Government for food, clothing, and shelter, and, for the first time in our history, have seen Government accept that responsibility by creating "W.P.A." "P.W.A." "C.C.C." and other worthy work-relief agencies.

We have witnessed, too, the most vociferous criticism of such Government action emanating from those who were instrumental in creating the burden. Even during the period of recovery, the destruction of earning power, through the installation of labor-saving devices, goes feverishly on aiding in creating a recession, because the ability to produce exceeds the ability to consume because the ability to buy has been destroyed, and always the Government has been required to shoulder the added burden.

Needless to say, we wholeheartedly accept Social-Security; visualizing the economic security and attendant contentment it will afford us and millions like us, who otherwise, in an age where the productive years of the average worker is gradually diminishing, would be forced to face an insecure old age not pleasant to contemplate.

We have recently had occasion to witness the wisdom and soundness of "F.D.I.C." when an economic setback has failed to follow historical precedent, in that it failed to produce long lines of panic-stricken, desperate, people; storming the doors of failing banks, and in its stead, see complete confidence existing in the security of insured deposits, speaking eloquently of the fact that "F.D.I.C." is a perfectly functioning being.

We are convinced that the inexorable hand of time will bring into full view the magnificent import of the reform and social legislation enacted by your administration whereby the common man, championed as never before, will have the opportunity to share equitably in the bountiful beneficence of a kindly provider.

The tortured interpretations presented to the public, through the misuse of the Freedom of the Press, and through other sources, seeking to belittle your sound program, has reacted quite favorably from many, for it has spurred us to seek and find more reliable channels of information in quest of the facts, and the result is the greater ease with which to recognize propoganda.

Accordingly, we feel that we owe you and your administration a deep debt of gratitude for what has been achieved, and a pledge of our unwavering loyal support in your splendid objective to rid our country of the stigma that one-third of our population is still ill-nourished, ill-clothed, and ill-housed.

We are confident that when the true history of our generation has been written and the names of your detractors will have disappeared in the maw of mediocrity, yours will stand immortalized as a true friend and leader of man, as one, indeed worthy of his generation.

It is our sincere hope that you may enjoy continued good health, and retain your indomitable courage to chart our course along the road that you have so ably mapped out.

> [signed by Henry G. Steinbrenner and
> forty-one other men and women]
> Chicago, Illinois

APRIL 17, 1938

Dear Mr. President:

Your splendid talk given on the evening of Holy Thursday cannot but make the working man feel secure as long as you are in the White House. In a very small but temporary job as claim clerk with the Unemployment Compensation Bureau, I can see the suffering in the faces of the men and women who are receiving their small checks.

The Collins & Aikman Corp. where most of these people have been working have enough orders to work twenty four hours a day, just as they have been doing for years; but I know that they are purposely closed in an attempt to break the spirit of the people, and to embarrass your administration. They are attempting to impress the public that you and your Congress have imposed too many taxes on them, and that shall stay closed unless you lessen their burden of taxation.

I want you to know Mr. President that the workers still have faith in you, and that they do no believe the bunk handed to them by Charles B. Rockwell and his Collins & Aikman Corp. I do not know how much longer they can endure it. The compensation checks they are receiving weekly are diminishing, and the Lord only knows what will happen to them.

Please Mr. President do not let them down, If big business is retarding your program, crack down, and crack down hard. I feel certain that most of them could open their factories to-morrow, but they purposely are trying to make the people lose faith in you, don't let them do it.

Call me a Fascist, Bolshevist, Anarchist, Socialist, or a nut (one of your secretaries will probably call me that anyhow) my solution would be for you to declare that an emergency exists, take over all the mills and factories and have the government run them. If you had a few more able men like my Senator Green to help you I believe you could do it. Although it may be unconstitutional, when a man and his family is hungry, get him a job, he doesn't care how you do it. . . .

Sincerely yours,

Dominic J. Langello
Bristol, R.I.

APRIL 28, 1938

Honorable Sir:

For the last thirty years I have been actively engaged in the Real Estate business in this section, and I am addressing you as disapproving the $4,500,000,000 relief expenditure which you propose to make. . . .

If I had you out here for an hour, I could show you miles and miles of river and creek beds where W.P.A. workers spent millions of our hard earned cash on putting in inadequate, poorly constructed, poorly planned flood control work, and what is left to show for all this time, labor and money? Nothing! Miles and miles of river bank covered with rock work laid in sand, when concrete was absolutely necessary. Any eleven year old child could have predicted it would go out with the first hard rain and it did. No wonder we are all heartsick.

Another point I wish to get across to you, is that you can never win, barter or steal the confidence of thinking people in this country as long as you try to fool them. Some Americans may be dumb, but not the large majority of them. You can't take the laboring man with his limited mental capacity, and put them over or on a par with live thinking, brainy business men. If you don't play ball with business men who furnish labor with jobs you are due to learn a harder lesson than you have already learned. . . .

Thanking you, I am

Respectfully,

Colin Stewart
Pasadena, Cal.

APRIL 14, 1938

Dear Sir:

. . . In June, 1935, my husband and I motored from Portland through Washington, Idaho, Montana, North and South Dakota to St. Paul, Minn., and returned home by way of Iowa, Nebraska, Wyoming, Idaho, into Oregon. It was hot and dry even then in most of the states just prior to the drought spell. In everyone of the most insignificant, barren little towns, the only work that appeared to be available was a WPA project and every one of these projects was a most necessary one and perhaps the outstanding civic accomplishment in that particular place. Without these, I doubt if people could have carried on. In Portland, we have many wonderful projects that have been accomplished through the WPA throughout the state of Oregon. The CCC boys have beautified natural scenic points of interest by their handiwork almost unbelievably and it is a joy to all who have the privilege of using these facilities. I have an elderly Uncle, and if it wasn't for WPA work, he and his wife would be without funds and would lose their home. So with any criticism that comes, you will know deep within yourself the goodness you have wrought.

Your devoted and humble servant,

(Mrs. E. H.) Marguerite McMahill
Portland, Oregon

APRIL 15, 1938

Dear President Roosevelt:

. . . I believe your speech was most helpful and inspiring at this time. How can anybody be against you?! You have kept so many parents and children together through W.P.A.

My husband is working under W.P.A. and what would we, including two small boys, four and three years, do without it! My husband is a strong, healthy man used to outside work. As you know all the work, outside, not under W.P.A., is or has all the men they want.

You have made it possible for us to lead a respectable life. We live in four rooms upstairs which I try to keep clean and orderly by using plenty of soap and water freely. I try to buy and prepare good food so that we stay healthy and strong.

My husband helps put up small bridges over creeks in this county. He enjoys the work very much.

I think your ideas and plans are very good if you only can carry them out. You have my loyal support as everyone I come in contact with I am in your favor.

May W.P.A. continue for a long time!

Yours very truly

Mrs. Albert Downs
Rochester, N.Y.

MAY 10, 1938

Dear Mr. Roosevelt,

. . . I am a student on the W.P.A. Music Project I am also a wife & a mother of a high school son.

Ive wanted to play the piano since I was a child I could only take a few lessons when I could afford them that was rarely.

When I heard of the W.P.A. Music Project I immediately joined one of the classes It has given me hope Art helps one to live.

The art projects should be broadened The American people should be made art concious No wage cuts The 25 dollars the artist gets is far too little My husband makes 25 dollars a week Its a terrible struggle to live Its borrowing here & borrowing there, then the worry of how to give back

One consolation We have these days is that we have a president that is fighting on the side of the have nots.

Friends & I are looking forward to hearing more of your fireside chats Its the only way that you can get the American people to understand what you are trying to do The newspapers generally distort the news to suit certain interests and play down your effort on behalf of the people.

Wishing you and Mrs. Roosevelt the best of health

I am

Yours sincerely

Etta Rich
New York, New York

APRIL 21, 1938

Your Excellency:—

After hearing your "Fireside talk" over our local station W.S.M.B. on Thursday evening, I feel privileged to write to you. . . .

We are indeed indebted to you to the fullest extent for enabling us to lead a useful, pleasant and normal life. For instance, what should I do, if it were not for the W.P.A. A woman past middle life, lately widowed, and with no income other than my salary as Senior Translator and research worker? I have been assigned to one of your projects at our local "Historic State Museum" in the heart of the "Vieux Carre" I spend six hours each day, delving in old documents, yellow with age, moth eaten, water stained, partially burned in a fire which threatened to destroy Our City in 1788 — reading the history of our Metropolis in the French vernacular, and translating it. These hours which I spend in quaint surroundings, in an environment replete with historic relics and memories, are in contrast to my home where I repair every evening to a comfortable, well kept house, to be greeted by my Mother and Sister who are ever gracious and happy to welcome my return to the fireside. Incidentally those ladies feel very much indebted to you for the joy and pleasure they enjoy.

. . . There had been propaganda talks of a depression worst in it's effects and ravages than the one from which we were emerging; and no words of encouragement, comfort and solace were ever spoken until you delivered your address Thursday night. I was enveloped so to speak in a mantle of insecurity and mental anguish until you lifted the pall from my shoulders. . . .

With the assurance of my deep appreciation for all you have done for me, and asking God to bless and protect you Our Beloved President, I remain,

Very respectfully yours,

(Mrs.) Marie Louise Charbonnet
New Orleans, La.

APRIL 15, 1938

My dear President Roosevelt:

You have just finished your 'Fireside' talk over the radio. Somehow, since your voice came out so clear and distinct it seemed as though you were speaking individually to me, hence to each of the millions listening in! individually!

Your message had an especial message to me, since my work as an Investigator for New York City Relief, in what might be termed one of the worst housing sections of this city. Most of these buildings are condemned and will come down, and as you spoke and have spoken before — I realized afresh that you are the first President we have ever had who has been so thoroughly awakened to the situations that exist to-day, among and in the under-priveleged classes.

. . . I have been since the begining deeply interested in your program —

saw you at the first Inauguration within the Capital, as I also saw your wife — and I felt then as I still do that both of you were sent by an all wise Providence to help this country and its people to a new and better and more unselfish day!! One of the reasons also, that I think you must have been a great men even in your youth, was that you had the vision, perception and intelligence to choose Elanore Roosevelt for your life-partner!! She is certainly a great spirit and a great soul, unselfish with a big and noble heart. . . .

I do not know exactly where you and Mrs. Roosevelt get all your broad and basic understanding and philosophy from, coming from the homes you both did — but to me it is remarkable you have the character and insight and understanding to stand up (despite many of your wealthy friends) and say and plan and do as you both have since you came to Washington! . . .

With my social-work case load I see only the poorest and the unskilled but their families are large and increasing, even tho' men have not had work for many years — these large families fostered from relief and other charity organizations. If these people could grow up to be rugged and healthy citizens I would not care, but the health conditions even with better housing will never fully take care of the rapid increase in the birth-rate! When will Birth-Control have real planning thru' the Government so as to reduce the population in these quarters. . . . I can see where Birth-Control Clinics have already helped many plan for and 'space' their children, but this is not carried to those among the very poor and less intelligent groups — many of whom are in fear of the laws of their Catholic Church! You have been so wonderfully forceful and creative in going ahead with your program in face of opposition; perhaps you may be able later on to give this issue some of your attention!! . . .

From one of many who sends out a prayer for renewed strength and courage, for the daily battle! to go on, despite all adversity and opposition. These are sincere words.

Janet Speakman
New York, N.Y.

APRIL 20, 1938

Dear Mr. President Roosevelt: —

After hearing your radio address to the public and pondering it a few days I am impelled to write you . . . not since Abraham Lincoln have we had a president with such zeal behind his efforts to help the enslaved man. To be sure it's a different form of slavery but non the less tyranneous.

. . . I am a Sunday school teacher in a local church here in Detroit and was endeavoring to teach one of my 5 year old boys about Moses and the children of Israel in their pilgrimage through the Red Sea. Later during the week the little fellow, who lives near me, was playing in the street with another neighbor boy. They came dashing in to me to settle an argument they were having. Frankie said to me, "Auntie, was it Moses or President Roosevelt who led the children of Isabel through the Red Sea? Freddie said it Moses but I said it was President Roosevelt." So you see even the little children have the greatest confidence in your ability and we larger children pray that you will be successful in leading the children of this great Democracy through the great sea of labor's troubled waters. May we all pull together and reach the shore in safety.

Thank you and sincerely
Yours

Mrs W. E. Lange
Detroit, Michigan

GOOD FRIDAY, 1938

My dear Mr. President:

I am only one of the hundreds of thousands of ordinary people for whom you are striving so nobly. But your fire-side talks have come to our home and made us feel that you are not only a great leader, but a friend as well.

Last night it seemed to us that, in spite of your superb courage and gallantry, there was a note of weariness and a trace of discouragement. I should think this might well be so, and I felt that we, for whom you are fighting, must some how reach you quickly with a word of faith and encouragement.

I am the mother of a family of growing boys, and I would give my children something even more important than food and good physical care. They need faith and ideals of service, and examples of heroism. To them you are a great living hero, fighting against the tremendous forces of greed and fear and tyranny. For them your struggle has all the poetic glamour of the old epics, as well as the fascination of an actual contest in which some day they must take part. The contest which will mean the life or death of democracy. And they feel for you all the whole-hearted loyalty a boy gives to a great warrior.

My husband is a newspaper man, whose task is studying foreign affairs. Sometimes, I am afraid, the world looks to him like a quaking bog of deceit and hate and lost illusions.

To him you are a beacon of light. You have given him something much finer even than economic security. You have given him back a faith in decent, sane government — a faith which he lost somewhere in France during the war.

I hope you will forgive my writing to you of my family, but I'm sure the same things are true in many, many families, from whom you never hear.

The newspapers are full of bitterness and criticism. The columnists scream with hate. But I'm afraid you don't hear from all the little homes where you are loved and honored, and where your cheerful courage is an inspiration.

This is Good Friday and we are recalling the supreme sacrifices of the Great Leader, who was betrayed and crucified for our sake.

May Easter time bring you renewed strength and courage to carry your great burdens. You have our gratitude and love.

Very sincerely yours,

(Mrs. James H. Powers) Anne Campbell Powers
Sudbury, Mass.

APRIL 15, 1938

Dear Mr. Roosevelt,

In listening to the opening words about Holy Week in your radio speech last night, I felt sorry that you had not also recognized that your Jewish listeners were celebrating Passover. Mention of their Holiday would have included instead of excluding a large group of your people and would have added to the sense of unity which your talk stressed.

Very sincerely yours,

Caroline F. Ware
Vienna, Virginia

"PURGING" THE DEMOCRATIC
PARTY: JUNE 24, 1938

IN RESPONDING to his Fireside Chat of April 14, Harriette Ashbrook of New York City wrote FDR: "In 1938 we'll try to give you a Congress that will give you better backing than the present one has done, but in the meantime be up and at 'em, and we'll back you up." Charles M. Flaig of Richmond, Indiana, agreed:

> We must also purge our party of these demagogue Democrats. These few who have not only betrayed you but the people who made it possible for them to be in Washington. It is much harder to fight back when we have members within our own party, aligning with reactionaries and fighting us. The party cannot keep the confidence of the people with such traitors in the party. They all should have opposition at the primaries.[38]

As the midterm elections of 1938 approached, FDR came to the same conclusion.

The Supreme Court had not been FDR's only concern in his quest for recovery and reform. He understood that the nature of the American party system constituted a potential bulwark against political innovation as well. Political parties as they evolved in the United States were less programmatic or ideological entities than coalitions of diverse groups and interests. In a country as large and heterogeneous as the United States, this type of party system meant that Democrats elected from different geographic regions, different states, indeed even different parts of the same state, county, or city, often had little in common, representing as they did divergent constituencies, cultures, and belief systems.

This became manifestly clear during Roosevelt's First Administration, when, in reaction to an increase in lynchings of Black Americans, two Democratic Senators, Robert F. Wagner of New York and Edward P. Costigan of Colorado, sponsored a bill in Congress that made lynching a federal crime. Introduced in 1934, the anti-lynching bill was reported out of the Senate Judiciary Committee and sent to the floor of the Senate only to be met by a filibuster conducted largely by Democratic Senators from the South. In

1935 the Judiciary Committee once more sent the bill to the entire Senate, where it was again waylaid by a filibuster. On a Sunday afternoon in May of 1935, while the Wagner-Costigan bill was drowning in the oratory of its determined opponents, Eleanor Roosevelt, who played an important role in making her husband aware of the plight of Black Americans, invited Walter White, the Executive Secretary of the National Association for the Advancement of Colored People (NAACP), to the White House to confer with the President. FDR had already spoken out against lynching in his Annual Message of January 1934, including it among those crimes that "have threatened our security [and] call on the strong arm of Government for their immediate suppression."[39]

With majorities in both the Senate and House reportedly in support of the Wagner-Costigan bill, had the President intervened strongly to break the Senate impasse, he might have saved the bill. But this he refused to do. "I did not choose the tools with which I must work," he told White during their meeting. "Had I been permitted to choose them I would have selected quite different ones. But I've got to get legislation passed by Congress to save America. The Southerners by reason of the seniority rule in Congress are chairmen or occupy strategic places on most of the Senate and House committees. If I come out for the anti-lynching bill now, they will block every bill I ask Congress to pass to keep America from collapsing. I just can't take that risk." When Eleanor Roosevelt pushed her husband to give his "all-out support" for the anti-lynching bill and the removal of the poll tax, she received a similar response: "First things come first, and I can't alienate certain votes I need for measures that are more important at the moment by pushing any measure that would entail a fight."[40]

At the same time Roosevelt — and White — understood the Democratic Party's need for the Northern Black vote. If FDR couldn't afford to alienate powerful Southern Senators, neither could he risk driving African Americans back to the party of Lincoln to which they had remained loyal from the Civil War until the advent of the New Deal. During the 1932 campaign, Robert Vann, the publisher of the influential African American newspaper the *Pittsburgh Courier* told his readers to "turn Lincoln's picture to the wall. That debt has been paid in full." But Black voters were not yet ready to forget the past, and their vote went to Hoover and the Republicans in 1932. Two years of the New Deal changed that: a majority of Black voters supported the Democrats for the first time in the congressional elections of 1934, and by the presidential elections of 1936 they had become an important part of the Democratic coalition that helped Roosevelt win an unprecedented four terms in the White House. Leaders like Walter White never tired of reminding the Democrats that their inattention to the needs of Black Americans could reverse the direction of their votes.

While FDR, unlike his wife, was no crusader for racial justice, considerations of fairness and of political necessity led him to triple the number of Blacks in federal employment, to begin desegregation in the federal workplace, to appoint more Blacks to administrative jobs in the New Deal and invite more Blacks to the White House than any prior President, to see that Blacks were accredited as delegates to the Democrats' national conventions, and to help ensure that Black Americans received a fairer share of New Deal benefits than they had in the first two years of his Administration. Above all, what attracted and held Black Americans to the Democratic Party was the fact that through such New Deal policies as support for the right of workers to organize, minimum wages and maximum hours legislation, low-income housing, work relief, social security, aid to young people through the Civilian Conservation Corps and the National Youth Administration, and help for marginal farmers through such agencies as the Farm Security Administration, FDR brought immense aid to *poor* people among whose ranks Blacks held a disproportionate percentage. As the NAACP concluded, while FDR did not ring in "the millennium in race relations" — there remained rank discrimination in many New Deal agencies as well as his tepid response to the legislative assault on lynching and the poll tax — under his aegis "the great body of Negro citizens made progress."[41]

Thus while Roosevelt was loathe to confront the White South directly, he did many things to nettle it. For the first time in its history, the Democratic National Convention in 1936 seated Black delegates. FDR chose a Black minister to give the invocation and Representative Arthur Mitchell of Chicago — the first Black Democrat ever elected to Congress — to deliver a major address. As the minister rose to speak, Senator Ellison "Cotton Ed" Smith of South Carolina bolted for the doors muttering: "By God, he's as black as melted midnight! Get outa my way. This mongrel meeting ain't no place for a white man!" Smith later related the incident to his constituents: "And he started praying and I started walking. And as I pushed through those great doors, and walked across that vast rotunda, it seemed to me that old John Calhoun leaned down from his mansion in the sky and whispered in my ear, 'You did right, Ed.' "[42]

As this dramatic but by no means exceptional example illustrates, it was no easy task to navigate the waters of the Democratic polity. Although Roosevelt prided himself on his abilities as a political broker, it became more and more difficult to balance the fundamental contradictions and dualities within his own party in order to achieve his reformist goals. FDR had understood the need for restructuring his party from the beginning. As we have seen, as early as 1932 he told Rexford Guy Tugwell that "in eight years we might not any longer have a Democratic party; but we will have a Progressive one." In 1936 he assured Harold Ickes that the defections from the Democratic Party of such conservatives as Al Smith, the 1928 Democratic presidential candidate, and Governor Eugene Talmadge of Georgia were clear signs that there would be a realignment of parties.[43]

Roosevelt may have understood the need to restructure the organizations that dominated American politics from the outset, but until 1938 he made no concerted effort to transform his comprehension into action. Indeed, in the beginning of his presidency it might be argued that he had little need to. The depth of the crisis and the national hunger for leadership were converted by FDR's political and temperamental genius into instruments of almost unprecedented popularity and power. Thus he could function — or at least seem to function — during his first term as a *national* leader above such mundane considerations as party politics. It was Roosevelt's pleasure in those early years to assume the role of the bipartisan champion of all the people. He saw himself as the great broker unifying and balancing the nation. Like many of those whose politics were nurtured during the Progressive Era at the turn of the century, FDR never put much store in the notion of class divisions or conflicts. He believed there was often a struggle for power among aggregations of interests but that these were various and temporary. At root, the interests of all groups, rightly and fairly understood, were complementary. He stressed harmony of interests and mutual dependence. As he said in his final speech of the 1932 presidential campaign:

> There is an interdependence in economics, just as there is a brotherhood in humanity. Loss to any is loss to all. . . . The next Administration must represent not a fraction of the United States, but all of the United States. . . . Our real enemies are hunger, want, insecurity, poverty and fear. Against these there is no glory in a victory only partisan. The genius of America is

stronger than any candidate or any party. . . . Today there appears once more the truth taught two thousand years ago that "no man lives to himself, and no man dies to himself; but living or dying, we are the Lord's and each other's."[44]

In this mood, Roosevelt did not play a particularly partisan role in his early days of power. In the midst of the extreme crisis of 1933, he could generally get what he wanted from a compliant Congress. It became apparent very shortly after his first election that FDR had established a binding hold on the American people and could exercise power and win reelection without the benefit of a new party structure. Added to this was the President's tendency to seek advice from extremely disparate kinds of people, conservatives as well as liberals. He insisted that party labels were less important than surrounding himself with what he liked to call "the right kind of people." Initially, he declined to participate in traditional Democratic Party Jefferson Day dinners, suggesting nonpartisan dinners instead. In 1934 he even went so far as to support such Republicans or Progressives as Robert La Follette of Wisconsin and George Norris of Nebraska in their campaigns against conservative Democrats for Senate seats, but he made no move to enlist them in the Democratic Party. At the same time, he withheld his support from such outspoken reformers as the Progressive Philip La Follette of Wisconsin, the Democrat Upton Sinclair, and the Republican Bronson Cutting of New Mexico. When FDR did desert his party's nominees, it was to support a progressive Republican or independent candidate, but he did so inconsistently and with what appeared to be no clear plan to create a truly progressive party. Nor could he invariably be counted on to support a liberal Democrat's attempt to win renomination.

Thus the Democratic Party that won such an overwhelming victory in 1936 was as divided and disparate as it had ever been. What had changed by FDR's second term was not the nature of the major parties but the President's ability to transcend the party structure. This became clear during the struggles over the Supreme Court and Roosevelt's attempt to combat the recession of 1937–38. Major defections within his own party caused the defeat of his Court plan and either killed or emasculated much of his proposed reform legislation. It is fair to say that the final major social reform of the New Deal — at least until the GI Bill of 1944 — was the Fair Labor Standards Act of 1938, which abolished child labor in interstate commerce and established minimum wages of twenty-five cents an hour and maximum hours of forty-four a week — which would change to forty cents and forty hours in two years. And this important bill passed only after conservatives in both parties weakened many of its provisions and exempted some of the most needy groups — domestic workers, retail clerks, seasonal employees, and farm laborers — from coverage. So even this crucial victory, which almost immediately raised the wages of some 300,000 workers and shortened the work weeks of about 1.3 million, was not as sweet as Roosevelt had hoped in spite of the overwhelming Democratic majorities in both houses.

It is perhaps the greatest irony of FDR's career that at his death this master politician would leave behind him a Democratic Party that had enjoyed many years of power and had undeniably accomplished much but that was as inherently unstable and as prone to ideological and political stalemate as the day Roosevelt became its leader. That FDR desperately did not want to leave that type of legacy became clear in 1938 when, with little consultation, he decided at long last to begin the reconstitution of his party by opposing a number of his fellow Democrats in the forthcoming party primaries.

He first revealed his intentions on the evening of June 24, in his Fireside Chat to the nation.[45] Roosevelt opened his controversial chat innocently enough with wry humor:

> The American public and the American newspapers are certainly creatures of habit. This is one of the warmest evenings that I have ever felt in Washington, D.C., and yet this talk tonight will be referred to as a fireside talk.

His ostensible purpose was to report on the progress made by the Seventy-Fifth Congress, which had been elected during the Democratic landslide of 1936 "on a platform uncompromisingly liberal," and had just adjourned. He admitted that it had "left many things undone." FDR specifically cited its failure to reform the nation's railroads or pass his proposed act reorganizing the executive branch. He chose not to speak of the difficulty he had experienced in pushing reform legislation through the Congress and the many ways in which he was forced to weaken such acts as the Revenue Act of 1938, which Congress so altered by drastically reducing the tax on undistributed profits and discarding the graduated corporate income tax, that for the first time in his presidency he allowed an act to become law without his signature. Mistakes, he conceded, "were made by the leaders of private enterprise, by the leaders of labor and by the leaders of

Government — all three." Rather than dwell on these painful episodes, he praised the Congress for providing additional funds to create jobs for the unemployed and for passing a number of significant acts, such as the Agricultural Adjustment Act of 1938, replacing the earlier AAA found unconstitutional by the Supreme Court, and most especially the Fair Labor Standards Act, which Congress passed "after many requests on my part," and which, with the possible exception of the Social Security Act, Roosevelt proclaimed "the most far-reaching program, the most far-sighted program for the benefit of workers that has ever been adopted here or in any other country. Without question it starts us towards a better standard of living and increases purchasing power to buy the products of farm and factory."

> Do not let any calamity-howling executive with an income of $1,000 a day, who has been turning his employees over to the Government relief rolls in order to preserve his company's undistributed reserves, tell you . . . that a wage of $11.00 a week is going to have a disastrous effect on all American industry.

Anticipating the charge that his decision to oppose the renomination of certain Democratic Senators would be attributed to his desire to revenge their defection during the Supreme Court fight, he was quick to pronounce that struggle "a lost battle which won a war." The "real objectives" of his attempt to reform the Court, he claimed, "have been substantially attained." The Court's attitude "towards constitutional questions is entirely changed. Its recent decisions are eloquent testimony of a willingness to collaborate with the two other branches of Government to make democracy work."

He then gradually unfolded his momentous political decision, pointing to "that small minority which, in spite of its own disastrous leadership in 1929, is always eager to resume its control over the Government of the United States." Never, he charged, "has such a concerted campaign of defeatism been thrown at the heads of the President and the Senators and Congressmen as in the case of this Seventy-Fifth Congress. Never before have we had so many Copperheads among us." Here Roosevelt took the term that had been used to characterize Northerners who had sided with the South during the Civil War and applied it to those in his own party who opposed the New Deal program. He criticized those who from the beginning of the New Deal had ceaselessly raised a cry "to do something, to say something, to restore confidence."

There is a very articulate group of people in this country, with plenty of ability to procure publicity for their views, who have consistently refused to cooperate with the mass of the people ... on the ground that they required more concessions to their point of view before they would admit having what they called "confidence."

... It is my belief that the mass of the American people do have confidence, do have confidence in themselves — confidence in their ability, with the aid of their Government, to solve their own problems.

It is because you are not satisfied, and I am not satisfied, with the progress that we have made in finally solving our business and agricultural and social problems that I believe the great majority of you want your own Government to keep on trying to solve them. In simple frankness and in simple honesty, I need all the help I can get.

Then, without warning, he launched into "a few words about the coming political primaries." An election, he asserted, "cannot give a country a firm sense of direction if it has two or more national parties which merely have different names but are as alike in their principles and aims as peas in the same pod." In the coming primaries, in all parties, there would be clashes between two schools of thought: liberal and conservative. The liberal school of thought "recognizes that the new conditions throughout the world call for new remedies."

Those of us in America who hold to this school of thought, insist that these new remedies can be adopted and successfully maintained in this country under our present form of Government if we use Government as an instrument of cooperation to provide these remedies. We believe that we can solve our problems through continuing effort. . . . We are opposed to the kind of moratorium on reform which, in effect, means reaction itself.

Be it clearly understood, however, that when I use that word "liberal," I mean the believer in progressive principles of democratic, representative Government and not the wild man who, in effect, leans in the direction of Communism, for that is just as dangerous to us as Fascism itself.

The conservative school of thought "does not recognize the need for Government itself to step in and take action to meet these new problems."

> It believes that individual initiative and private philanthropy will solve them — that we ought to repeal many of the things we have done and go back, for example, to the old gold standard, or stop all this business of old age pensions and unemployment insurance, or repeal the Securities and Exchange Act, or let monopolies thrive unchecked — return, in effect, to the kind of Government that we had in the nineteen twenties.

The important question that every primary voter had to ask was: "To which of these general schools of thought does the candidate belong?"

> As President of the United States, I am not asking the voters of the country to vote for Democrats next November as opposed to Republicans or members of any other party. Nor am I, as President, taking part in Democratic primaries.
>
> As head of the Democratic Party, however, charged with the responsibility of carrying out the definitely liberal declaration of principles set forth in the 1936 Democratic platform, I feel that I have every right to speak in those few instances where there may be a clear-cut issue between candidates for a Democratic nomination involving these principles, or involving a clear misuse of my own name.

He was asking for the defeat not only of "outspoken reactionaries" but also of the type of candidate he labeled "a 'yes, but' fellow" — those Democrats who "say 'yes' to a progressive objective, but who always find some reason to oppose any special specific proposal to gain that objective."

"The rich voice, the calm assurance, the adroit catchwords," the *New York Herald Tribune* editorialized the next day, "the note of simple sincerity and of genial friendliness to all mankind — punctuated by neat jabs at all who oppose him — all the old magic was there without a flaw."[46] This time, however, the "old magic" had lost its potency. FDR's campaign, which his opponents and the nation's press quickly dubbed a "purge," won him more publicity than success. A number of the liberal Democrats he campaigned for, such as Senators Alben Barkley of Kentucky and Hattie Caraway of Arkansas, were renominated, but all of the conservative Democrats he most openly opposed — Walter George of Georgia, Millard Tyd-ings of Maryland, and Cotton Ed Smith of South Carolina — were also re-nominated, which in the South of that time was tantamount to reelection.

The President had chosen a poor moment to inaugurate his plan to re-structure his party. The "Court-packing" fight, along with the reces-sion, had weakened him politically, and he was further hobbled by what appeared to be his lame-duck status since it was widely assumed he would adhere to the two-term tradition. FDR was, of course, politically savvy enough to understand these disabilities, but as Rexford Guy Tugwell has argued, by 1938 he "was as nearly desperate as he had ever been in all his political life." Loss of control of his party in Congress augured the potential loss of power within the party itself and thus an inability to ensure that the Democratic candidate in 1940 would be a progressive who would protect and expand New Deal reforms. He was in a corner, Tugwell has argued, from which there was no other escape: "He had either to give up his dreams of a transformed nation, of new and higher levels of well-being, of an econ-omy managed in the general interest, or he must gather behind them a polit-ical support sufficient for the purpose." A deeply divided Democratic Party was incapable of providing such support. Indeed, Tugwell was convinced that had Roosevelt lived after the war to run for a fifth term, "it would not have been as a Democrat, but as a Progressive."[47]

JUNE 25, 1938

My Dear Mr. President:

I was very much displeased with your speech last night.

No great leader can ever afford to stoop to do what you proposed regarding your opposition: This is a democracy and it is healthy to have a strong opposition. No man is always right. You need criticism for your own good.

I am not a politician, only so far as my own vote is concerned. And yet I know your speech of last night was poorly timed, illy advised, and certain to strengthen your opposition.

Hoping this straw may be of value.

I am yours

Allen B. Rice (Methodist Minister)
Kokomo, Indiana

JUNE 25, 1938

AS A CITIZEN OF THE UNITED STATES I RESENT BEING CALLED A COPPER-HEAD BY ONE WHOSE EGOTISM FAST APPROACHES MANIA AS WAS AGAIN EVIDENCED BY THE EXTENSIVE USE OF FIRST PERSON SINGULAR PRONOUNS HALF TRUTHS INCONSISTENCIES AND NAME CALLINGS IN YOUR FIRESIDE CHATTER LAST NIGHT.

WM. A. STARK
CINCINNATI, OHIO

JUNE 25, 1938

Our dear Mr. President,

We have listened to all of your fire-side chats.

All of them sermons and each one a message of sympathy and understanding.

Like Christ, going into the homes of the people, giving them comfort and restoring their faith.

You have fed and clothed those in need and furnished jobs for the unemployed.

Your accomplishments and good deeds have been too great to be enumerated.

You have had and will continue to have our support to the limit. . . .

Your friends and admirers

Curtis M. Field
Mrs. Helen Field
Kansas City, Mo.

JUNE 27, 1938

Dear Mr. Roosevelt,

As usual I listened to your last Friday's speech because I enjoy your artistry on the radio. You must be too intelligent to believe what you say — but you do say it in a most appealing and convincing way.

Just what good do you hope to accomplish by your continuing tactics that can only make the poorer classes hate those who have more of the good things of life? The only real sower of wealth can be the Nation's industries, and through your over-paternalistic WPA, Home Relief and Labor policy, you are at the one time making private employment less inviting than "something-for-nothing" and making it difficult, if not down right impossible for Industry to carry on.

A review of where your strength lies — 87% of the Negros for you — must comfort you. Come to this section and try to hire a negress to do general housework! As the intelligence of the various groups increases (barring outright gifts to the farmers etc.), your popularity decreases.

For a modern version of "Bread and Circuses" you are doing famously. But why run the country into a hole? Nothing was ever permanently bettered by your procedure. The piper always has to be paid.

Please do come down to Earth.

Very truly your

R. A. Johnson
Glenside, Penna.

JUNE 24, 1938

My Dear Mr. President; —

. . . I am a Southern man and naturally proud of the traditions of the
Southland, but I have no sympathy for the attitude shown by our misrepre-
sentative in the United States Senate and Congress, who in their eagerness
to serve the Mammon of unrighteousness have used every reprehensible
method known to hamper and defeat your program of recovery. The North
and East have no monopoly of political crooks and traitors. I have seen men
claiming to be liberal in their views from the South who have brazenly and
openly betrayed the people in congress in order to curry favor with Money
Kings of the nation. Most of these men owe their election to you and in the
coming campaign they will be on the political platforms throughout the
South proclaiming in thunder tones their loyalty to you and liberalism. All
they are interested in is their own reelection and as soon as they win they
will again emulate the Dog who returned to his vomit. . . .

I do hope you will decide to run again as there is not another man on the
top side of this earth who can fill your shoes. If you accept a Third nomination your election will be even more overwhelming than it was Two years
ago. Your work is not complete and if you step aside at this stage of the game
our last estate will be worse than the First as the reactionaries will run away
with the Government. Thanking you from the bottom of my heart for your
great address which I believe will touch the heart of the entire world,

Sincerely Yours,

James H. Holloway
Raleigh, N.C.

JUNE 29, 1938

My Dear President:

As one who represents the average citizen let me congratulate you for
your fighting speech of June 24th.

The recent Fortune poll clearly indicates the popularity of you and your
objectives. It will be a tough fight before those objectives are reached.

Therefore, I think you should run again in 1940 because no one but you can complete the job.

Above all, do not permit Joseph Kennedy or any other Catholic to run in 1940 for they will be decisively defeated. Do not forget that 80 per cent of our people are Protestant and will not stand for any President who must bow to kiss the hand of another man.

Yours for success in 1940,

Everett H. Wallace
Chicago, Illinois

JUNE 30, 1938

Dear Sir:

I was shocked at the gratuitous red baiting contained in your fine radio address on the evening of June 24th.

I am sure, President Roosevelt, however you may feel about the economic policy of the communists and of the fascists you will admit there is a difference between the leading advocate of international peace in the world, the Soviet Union, and the Rome-Berlin Axis with its disregard of all international obligations and its glorification of brute force; between a system of society where racial discrimination is a crime and one where racial persecution is an avowed policy.

The reason for these great differences is inherent in the systems themselves, systems which, I am sure, you have no interest in discussing. But such a statement as "Communism, for that is just as dangerous as Fascism", is loose and calculated to destroy the force of some of your other statements in the minds of thoughtful people.

Respectfully yours,

E. M. Pierson
(Emily M. Pierson, M.D.)
Cromwell, Connecticut

JUNE 24, 1938

Dear Mr. President:

We listened with interest to your radio talk tonight and wish to express our agreement and thanks anent the advice you gave on how to choose candidates in the primaries. . . .

But we feel that we must express ourselves to you on two of your statements. From our experience as working citizens, we feel it is inaccurate and dangerous to say "We have as much to fear from Communism as from Fascism." This is the theme-song of the Chicago Tribune and the Hearst press which are the most bitter enemies of all the progressive legislation that you have proposed on behalf of the people. On the contrary, we interpret the events in Spain, China, and Mexico to mean that Democracy is threatened only by Fascism. And here in Hyde Park we see the growth of Fascism: a newspaper, "Dynamite", has been started in the Negro district with the deliberate intent of building Anti-Semitism among our colored neighbors. And the only violence of a political nature in our neighborhood is coming from a gang of hoodlums who have been organized to break windows of the "Co-op", a cooperative restaurant.

Likewise we do not feel that such a term as "Wildmen" is up to your usual standards of statesmanship. We have heard Mr. Browder speak, and have known many Communists (party members) and nothing in their speech or action bears out such a caption.

Mr. President, you are our leader — the representative of all the people who believe in Democracy — the majority. We want you to keep up the good fight against the monopolies, for minimum wages, maximum hours, and for jobs for the unemployed. But don't let us down by using such a tactic so characteristic of the fascist-minded as Red-baiting.

Respectfully yours

Timothy Burr
Mary Burr
Chicago, Illinois

JUNE 24, 1938

Mr. President

I have just listened to your fireside chat — it seemed to me we were getting along fairley well and just why you have deemed it wise to lower the dignity of your office and the white house by telling folks how to vote is beyond me. It looks suspicious that things are not going as well for you individually as it looks from outside for the people certainly have given you free range to carry out your plans and now you reflect on their intelligence by insinuating they must vote as you dictate or else. I have never written any criticism before but it looks to me from this cheap political urge the charge of your wanting dictatorial power is plain and you are practically warning politicians to do as you bid regardless of any individual or personal ideas — Your political boldness has excited my state of mind and caused realization that we are in the hands of selfish politicians instead of the sincere leader it once seemed — Its a big disappointment to see what seemed like "greatness" reduced to cheap politics at the peoples expense in 30 minutes.

Respectfully

J. V. Cowart
Birmingham, Ala.

* * *

Dear Pres. Roosevelt,

I know you have the cares of a nation on your back but I'm writing to get to the point, your latest fireside chat was a nifty speech and will bring you what you want. I'm for you tooth and nail even if my family aren't. There rather stupid, not realizing that you're just a human being and for one you've done a remarkable job. I'm 13 and at school whenever your name is mentioned, Joan Leffert a good Republican and I argue about you and your policies. After 2 long yrs of this, she admits being ¼ Democrat. Chalk up one for you. If you want a perfect description of yourself, read "IF" by Rudyard Kipling. I think you might get a lot more cooperation if you did something for Wall Street. Thats only a suggestion.

Sincerly Yours

Mary Jacoby
New York, N.Y.

P.S. Your the tops

JUNE 25, 1938

Dear Mr. Roosevelt:

Last night's Fireside Talk may not rank among the greatest of your fireside reports to the nation, but it had in its content and confident delivery a quality of high courage and moral earnestness that should earn for it permanent place among your many notable utterances as the Chief Executive of our country.

I preferred to hear it not at home but at a downtown lunchroom frequented by railroad and other workers. Slot machines and pin games suspended for the greater part of your talk; heads nodded in agreement as important points went home; bronzed men smiled and nodded to one another as you . . . defined the liberal.

"That's telling them. I knew he'd do it," said an elderly man to the group leaning over the counter.

"And right from the shoulder," someone responded. "He's not letting them get away with anything."

And that seemed the concensus of this crowd. . . .

It's a proud thing to be living today in an America attaining its true destiny under the ablest administration since Washington's

With deepest respect and admiration

E. E. McLeish
Alexandria, Va.

JUNE 26, 1938

Dear sir [Secretary McIntyre]:

I listened with much pleasure to our President's "fireside chat."

It was gratifying among other things to hear what he said about the steel company. Yesterday's Chicago Tribune left that paragraph out. I am enclosing their text of the President's speech.

I have written their editor the following: "Regardless of your political affiliations or your dislike of the President of the United States, the leaving out of part of his speech was about the smallest thing you have yet done. Your readers have the right to have the news as it is given. The St. Louis Globe-Democrat and the Indianapolis Star published his speech in full."

This is as the President said a country where "free speech and freedom of religious belief is the only thing" — but — There is of course nothing that can be done about it, but it does seem a pity. So many people in this state read nothing but the Tribune, and it does not seem fair that the news they receive is so unsatisfactory.

Very truly yours,

(Mrs.) Mary B. Graham
Danville, Illinois

JUNE 25, 1938

My dear Mr. President:

I with the nation appreciated your "chat" yesterday, and since feel impelled to suggest a two-point program that will at once solve the deplorable lack of cooperation by business in general, which maintains our unemployment dilemma. . . .

I — Between now and the next Congress in January if business will not at least double its working personnel, then let down the bars of W.P.A., P.W.A., and the whole alphabet; employ every available worker and assess business the necessary taxes to foot the bill!

II — Absolutely prohibit all foreign made goods from import until local factories are normal, at least.

IIA — Make the wages adequate. . . . If this is state socialism let's have it once and for all. Business is only practicing its old game of bluff and exploitation.

More power to you.

Sincerely,

O. C. Bond
Portland, Ore.

JUNE 27, 1938

Mr. Franklin D. Roosevelt

Just a few lines to let You know that I like Your last Speach Very Much, and I can say that You are One of the Best Presidents this Cuntry is got, in My length of life and that is 53 Years, and I would be very very Glad to have You come in to see our Music Shop and Store when the next time You will be in Milwaukee Wis. then I and My Wife and My Son Frank will Play You a few nombers some of the old time Music that You and Your Wife and Your Father and Mother injoyed dancing in them Days on My Own Home Made Instruments. and Weel Play them Perfect, and will show You a Picture of Your Self a infant in Your Mothers Arms.

Yours very Truly —

Anton Hudy
(Maker of High Grade Violins & Concertinas)
Milwaukee, Wis.

Please answer Soon.

PART THREE

LOOKING ABROAD: 1939–1941

This nation will remain a neutral nation, but I cannot ask that every American remain neutral in thought as well. Even a neutral has a right to take account of facts. Even a neutral cannot be asked to close his mind or close his conscience.

FDR, Fireside Chat, September 3, 1939

I wonder whether you can realize what it means to be one of the "little people", and see a holocaust like this moving down upon you, without any apparent means of preventing it.

Helen Norton, Naperville, Illinois,
to FDR, September 1, 1939

"TRUE NEUTRALITY":
SEPTEMBER 3, 1939

FDR HAD BEEN PRESIDENT for little more than two months when Ben Fortin of Butler, Wisconsin, sent him a newspaper clipping speculating that "there is imminent danger of another war in Europe," and scribbled below the clipping, "Whatever happens in Europe dont let our boys go to war again, please Mr. Roosevelt dont ever think of it."[1] It was, as it turned out, a futile plea. The Fireside Chat of June 24, 1938, was the last fully domestic one FDR was to deliver. Once again in our history, a domestic crisis and the resulting reform movement were eclipsed by the crisis of war. War had intruded upon Jeffersonian and Jacksonian democracy, upon the multifaceted reform movements of the 1840s and 1850s, upon populism and progressivism at the turn of the century, as it was about to intrude upon the New Deal, and as it would in more recent years intrude upon Harry Truman's Fair Deal, the civil rights movement, and Lyndon Johnson's War on Poverty.

As he accepted his party's renomination for the presidency in Philadelphia on June 27, 1936, Roosevelt had exhibited a sense of unease when he surveyed the world. "I cannot, with candor, tell you that all is well with the world," he told his fellow Democrats. "Clouds of suspicion, tides of ill-will and intolerance gather darkly in many places." Even as he spoke in his acceptance speech of the continuing domestic obligations of the federal government to its citizens ("the protection of the family and the home, the establishment of a democracy of opportunity, and aid to those overtaken by disaster"), even as he spoke of "the resolute enemy within our gates" (those protectors of privilege he termed "economic royalists"), his gaze moved beyond America's borders:

> In this world of ours in other lands, there are some people, who, in times past, have lived and fought for freedom, and seem to have grown too weary to carry on the fight. They have sold their heritage of freedom for the illusion of a living. They have yielded their democracy.

Only the United States could "stir their ancient hope" by making them understand that the struggle in America "is not alone a war against want and destitution and economic demoralization. It is more than that; it is a war for the survival of democracy. We are fighting to save a great and precious form of government for ourselves and for the world." It was clearly this dual purpose that underlay the memorable and oft-quoted declaration he made toward the close of his acceptance speech:

> There is a mysterious cycle in human events. To some generations much is given. Of other generations much is expected. This generation of Americans has a rendezvous with destiny.[2]

In spite of these impressive words, it was hard to discern whether FDR literally thought his nation's destiny was entwined with that of the world. During the 1932 presidential campaign, he placated isolationists by promising that he would not lead the United States into the League of Nations, and throughout his first term and the first half of his second term, his focus remained on his program of internal recovery and reform. His only mention of foreign policy in his First Inaugural Address was his initially vague Good Neighbor Policy toward other nations of the Western Hemisphere, and his major early foreign policy initiative was the recognition of the Soviet Union, which he did primarily at the behest of corporations that wanted to do business with the Communist power.

During these years, he won a reputation as an economic nationalist. He refused to accept Herbert Hoover's insistence that the Depression was a worldwide phenomenon that could not be attributed primarily to the failure of American institutions and that demanded international action. Roosevelt proceeded on the contrary assumption that the profound suffering imposed by the Great Depression could indeed be understood as stemming from the internal failure of certain American institutions and the blind greed of certain American citizens and could be reversed most effectively by correcting the failures and combating the greed. Accordingly, several months after Roosevelt took the United States off the gold standard, he refused to join European nations in an international plan to stabilize national currencies, and he helped to undercut the London Economic Conference, which was meeting for this purpose, by wiring it a message on July 3, 1933, that he himself later referred to as a "bombshell." "The sound internal economic system of a Nation," he lectured the European states gathered in London, "is a greater factor in its well-being than the price of its currency in changing terms of the currencies of other Nations."[3] While in early 1935 he advocated American entry into the World Court, before the year was out, in a major speech in San Diego, he declared: "despite what happens in continents overseas, the United States of America shall and must remain, as long ago the Father of our Country prayed that it might remain — unentangled and free."[4]

These actions and proclamations were in tune with the sentiment of the country at large. By the time FDR assumed office, negative reactions to America's participation in World War One had become deeply ingrained and cast a controlling influence over foreign policy. In 1934 a Senate committee chaired by Gerald Nye of North Dakota set about aggressively investigating the armaments industry and its role in fostering war, and then expanded its inquiry into the ways in which leading bankers and industrialists like J. P. Morgan and the du Pont brothers had manipulated American involvement in 1917 to protect their own economic interests. Even had Roosevelt advocated a more internationalist stance during his first term, he would not have prevailed. His largely symbolic support of American entry into the World Court in 1935 was decisively defeated by a Senate in which twenty Democrats deserted their leader. Pacifist sentiment rose among the young as students on campus after campus protested against the ROTC and reacted against what they considered to have been the needless sacrifices of their parents' generation. A student protest chant from the mid-thirties put it succinctly:

> In seventeen we went to war,
> In seventeen we went to war,
> In seventeen we went to war,
> Didn't know what we were fighting for.[5]

It should have surprised nobody that these feelings of disillusionment and anger, coupled with the growing instability in Europe, Africa, and Asia, led to demands for some mechanism that would prevent America's involvement in world carnage. Congress's answer was a series of neutrality laws, passed between 1935 and 1939, designed to prevent the repetition of those conditions popularly believed to have led to America's entry into the first world war — particularly the involvement of our government and our citizens with countries at war with one another. Thus American loans and credits to belligerents were banned; an embargo on arms shipments to belligerents was made mandatory; American citizens were forbidden to take passage on the ships of belligerents; American vessels trading with belligerents were forbidden from being armed or carrying munitions. Motivated in part by his need for congressional support for his domestic program, Roosevelt signed these bills but never with enthusiasm. The one provision he fought for consistently was presidential discretion in making qualitative distinctions between belligerents and thus utilizing the punitive embargoes to penalize aggressor nations rather than all belligerents indiscriminately. As he signed the first Neutrality Act in 1935, he warned that its "wholly inflexible provisions" on this issue "might drag us into war instead of keeping us out."[6]

But FDR should not be viewed as a mere victim of circumstances. He shared many of the views prevalent in the nation at large. He signed each new neutrality act as it issued from Congress and enforced them without protest, even in such cases of clear-cut aggression as Italy's invasion of Ethiopia in 1935 and General Franco's assault on the Spanish Republic in 1936. In the latter case, the President outdid the isolationists by treating an internal insurrection supported by Hitler and Mussolini against a democratic government as a war between two foreign states and invoking the embargo provision of the neutrality acts against both sides. He even went so far as to denounce an American businessman who exported planes to the democratic Spanish government as "thoroughly unpatriotic" and prodded Congress into extending the embargo on munitions to civil wars. Although such isolationists as Senator Nye came to advocate repealing the embargo on arms to the Loyalists in order to preserve Spanish democracy and thousands of Americans went to Spain to fight and many to die for the Republic, Roosevelt maintained his position.

It was difficult to fathom completely or to find consistency in Roosevelt's foreign policy in the years preceding the outbreak of World War Two. It was never clear whether he was being driven by international or domestic issues. Even while he was refusing to act against fascist aggression in Spain, he told the nation in a Chicago address in the fall of 1937 that an "epidemic of world lawlessness" was spreading and that, as with a medical epidemic, the way to halt it was through "a quarantine" of the aggressors.[7] The voice of Roosevelt the statesman was never easy to separate from the actions of Roosevelt the politician. In May of 1938, only half a year after the quarantine speech, Harold Ickes noted in his diary that FDR "said frankly that to raise the [Spanish] embargo would mean the loss of every Catholic vote next fall." This, Ickes concluded, "was the cat that was actually in the bag, and it is the mangiest, scabbiest cat ever." Only four months later, Ickes recorded the President as saying that in the event of war in Europe "even if we had to enforce our neutrality laws, there would be a large outlet . . . for munitions to flow toward England and France by way of Canada and otherwise." The President speculated, "There could be bought in this country materials, nonmilitary in themselves, such as pipes . . . which could easily be turned into shells and bullets and airplanes." In carrying out our neutrality laws, Roosevelt told Ickes, "we would resolve all doubts in favor of the democratic countries," a policy he certainly hadn't followed with regard to Spain.[8]

Only several months after that, on January 4, 1939, FDR opened his Annual Message to Congress with warnings about "storm signals from across the seas," and in effect called Congress's passage and his acceptance of neutrality legislation an error: "We have learned that when we deliberately try to legislate neutrality, our neutrality laws may operate unevenly and unfairly — may actually give aid to an aggressor and deny it to the victim. The instinct of self-preservation should warn us that we ought not to let that happen any more."[9] Congress obviously failed to share his "instinct." A bill with the discretionary provisions FDR requested failed to even get to the floor of the Senate.*

Although the impasse and inconsistency continued, 1939 was a momentous year whose events brought some degree of resolution to a number of these issues. Like most Western leaders, Roosevelt had been relieved at the Munich agreement in September 1938, which preserved peace at the expense of Czechoslovakia. He wrote Mackenzie King of Canada: "We in the United States rejoice with you, and the world at large, that the outbreak of war was averted," but in the same letter he spoke of his fears for the future.[10] Those fears proved justified. Despite American protests, the Japanese intensified their campaign to conquer China and establish a "new order" in Asia. In March of 1939, Germany invaded and conquered Czechoslovakia. The following month, Italy occupied Albania. The pattern of events was clear. In early April as he prepared to leave Warm Springs, Georgia, where

---

*In July 1941, in his introduction to the volume of his public papers dealing with the year 1939, Roosevelt wrote of the neutrality acts: "Although I approved this legislation when it was passed originally and when it was extended from time to time, I have regretted my action" (*The Public Papers and Addresses of Franklin D. Roosevelt* [New York: Macmillan, 1941], vol. 8).

he had established a treatment center for the victims of polio and where he spent several weeks every spring and autumn, FDR told the residents: "I have had a fine holiday here with you all. I'll be back in the fall if we do not have a war."[11] On August 4, 1939, Germany and the Soviet Union signed a nonaggression pact, leaving the Nazis at liberty to attack Poland, which they did on September 1 in the face of Britain's guarantee of Poland's independence. The following day, while FDR was enjoying a Saturday evening poker game with several advisers and aides, he read a dispatch that arrived about eleven o'clock, looked up, and informed his colleagues: "War will be declared by noon tomorrow."[12]

On September 3, just hours after Great Britain and France had declared war on Germany, FDR spoke to the American people in a Sunday evening Fireside Chat.[13] Throughout the address, he walked a thin line between reassuring his listeners that the nation would remain neutral and expressing solidarity with the democratic Allies. He announced that in accordance with the provisions of the 1935 Neutrality Act he would soon issue a proclamation of American neutrality in the European conflict. But he spoke of what he called "true neutrality" that would allow every American to "take account of facts" and not "close his mind or close his conscience." The national goals he outlined in this moment of renewed world war were more spiritual than concrete: "to maintain as a national policy the fundamental moralities, the teachings of religion, the continuation of efforts to restore peace — because some day, though the time may be distant, we can be of even greater help to a crippled humanity."

He stressed the need for the United States to remain unified, preceding his usual salutation, "My Friends," with the phrase, "My Countrymen," and emphasizing his "single duty . . . to speak to the whole of America." He assured the American people that because of the news they received from their radios and newspapers "at every hour of the day," and because they had a government that imposed no censorship and withheld no facts, they were "the most enlightened and the best informed people in all the world at this moment," and pleaded with them to "discriminate most carefully between news and rumor. Do not believe of necessity everything you hear or read. Check up on it first."

He admonished his listeners to remember, "When peace has been broken anywhere, the peace of all countries everywhere is in danger." It is easy, he said, "for you and for me to shrug our shoulders and to say that conflicts taking place thousands of miles . . . from the whole American hemisphere do not seriously affect the Americas — and that all the United States has to do is to ignore them and go about its own business. Passionately though we may desire detachment, we are forced to realize that every word that comes through the air, every ship that sails the sea, every battle that is fought does affect the American future." If it was our national tragedy "to live in a world that is torn by wars on other continents," it was "our national duty to use every effort to keep those wars out of the Americas." And he intimated that the best way to accomplish that was not necessarily to isolate ourselves.

He concluded his brief Chat with a pledge that was to become familiar to the American people in the next two years:

> I have said not once but many times that I have seen war and that I hate war. I say that again and again.
>
> I hope the United states will keep out of this war. I believe that it will. And I give you assurance and reassurance that every effort of your Government will be directed toward that end.
>
> As long as it remains within my power to prevent, there will be no blackout of peace in the United States.

As the President's voice faded, it was replaced by that of an announcer who reminded the audience that they and their President were now players on an expanded stage by informing them that the Fireside Chat they had just heard was carried to the world in French, Spanish, Portuguese, German, and Italian. This revelation was followed by a studio rendition of excerpts from Beethoven's *Moonlight Sonata*. It was a sobering close to a somber speech that was in fact not one of Roosevelt's best performances. It was short and contained little substance besides his declaration of devotion to peace in a world in which peace was fast disappearing. It was more the tone of his speech than its contents that was important. His words were suffused with the notion that the United States had a responsibility not merely to itself but to a world that was once again engulfed in war. Precisely what that responsibility entailed remained to be articulated.

SEPTEMBER 3, 1939

Dear Mr. President,

My wife and I have just heard your great speech over the radio. We cannot refrain from expressing our deepest appreciation of your statement that you and the rest of our great government will do everything possible to keep this country neutral in this horrible struggle. I, personally, was a medical officer in the World War in 1918 in France. Though a member of the Society of Friends, I believed then, mistakenly, that it was a war to end war and a war to make the world safe for democracy, and while I could not conscientiously go to take life, I felt I could go in such a noble cause to save life. Now I know there is no such thing, and we all know it.

The light of reason has gone out over a large part of Europe and will be replaced by hate and fury. May God uphold your powerful arm in keeping that light burning steadily, clearly and brightly in this country, and keep you firm in your resolve that millions of our young men will not be condemned to death because of selfish Old World diplomacy that is bringing a large part of mankind to death and destruction.

On behalf of our two sons, on behalf of all the people of this great nation, on behalf of humanity, and in the name of Him who said, "Father, forgive them for they know not what they do", we thank you for your great stand which you have voiced this day.

Most sincerely yours, with deep gratitude,

Frederick R. Taylor, M.D.
Rachel F. Taylor
High Point, N.C.

* * *

Dear President Roosevelt:

Ever since I heard you speak over the radio a couple Sundays ago I have been wanting to write you a few lines of appreciation for the very friendly and sincere speech. It made me wish that I might pick up my telephone and talk to you. You DO seem like a friend to each of us and oh I do hope that you will keep us out of War!

I will be 35 years old next month and I have a fine son who is 15 years of age and I'd die if he had to go to War, I also have three other sons and a daughter. My hubby was in the last War, he is only 41 now and I wrote you once before telling you that I'd rather shoot him myself than let him go to War and I mean it. I've brought my sons up to hate War and all it does and they do not want to fight and kill other mother's sons. My hubby won't allow the boys to play with guns, etc. like some of the other boys around here, we believe that if all parents would teach their children the horrors of War instead of making them believe it is wonderful and heroic that there wouldn't be so many youths raring to go to War. My boys aren't sissies either but my hubby and I believe that THE UNITED STATES OF AMERICA SHOULD NOT FIGHT UNLESS THE ENEMY COMES OVER HERE AND ATTACKS US!

I hope that you will see this letter and thanks again for the grand talk of two Sundays ago. We are for you 100% in this family. In fact, all our friends are for you.

Very sincerely,

Mrs. J. A. Ringis
Detroit, Michigan

SEPTEMBER 3, 1939

THE PRESIDENT.

CONSENSUS OF OPINION SEEMS TO BACK YOUR STAND FOR PEACE WITH HONOR AND YOUR REQUEST FOR AMENDMENT OF NEUTRALITY LAWS. SHOULD DISASTER BEFALL, AND THE UNITED STATES BE FORCED INTO WAR, I HEREBY OFFER MY SERVICE IN ANY CAPACITY IN WHICH I CAN BE USEFUL.

WYNDHAM MANNING, EX LIEUT. COLONEL
SUMTER, SOUTH CAROLINA

SEPTEMBER 3, 1939

Dear Sir: — Like a soothing hand to a sick body, so your radio broadcast was felt to me — soulsick — heartsick mother, and may I add to many a mother and father of sons and yes daughters who live in such frenzied hours. You may not think that on a little stump farm in the western hills we may not realize the anxiety of war. But as I write, it is hard to choke back the tears, because men will not love their neighbors as themselves. War knows no love — no — compassion. Misery, hate and greed are its companions.

As I am sitting here writing this letter I see the cows leisurely walking to the barn for the evening milking Symbol of peace and security — A boy was raised on these hills & on this little farm — A boy whose first lesson in life was to love his fellow man, to attain that which brot happiness and peace. And who now is struggling to gain knowledge so he can teach others to better living.

Oh Sir, can not, will not the people of the world realize that "one soul is worth the whole world" That all things can be gotten with love; that propoganda, greed, self justification and so forth are no excuses to shatter the souls and lives of humanity. . . .

We shudder as we read the stories of old. Of the Druid maidens that were thrown in the well to appease the Sun God. But are we so different? Is it so different to thro the flour of youth into the mouth of the cannon then the maidens into the well. We think of ourselves as super intelligent — But do we use intelligence when we say might makes right?

The Great Master has given you much power. So dear Sir, it is my humble plea that you will ask of Him in all your undertakings; that you may have the judgement of Solomon, to lead the world to peace and security,

Sincerely your humble citizen,

Valesta Whall
Kent, Washington

SEPTEMBER 4, 1939

Dear President:

Immediately after hearing your speech I had to let you know how thankful I am you will do everything possible to protect us from being drawn into the foreign conflict.

You must be successful in the greatest battle you ever had.

Dear President this is the plea of a 18 year old girl who loves life and her brother, I am sure you understand my anguish.

The 12 members of our family breathed a prayer of relief when you annouced your firm stand for peace, I know God has guided you.

Yours thankfully,

Beatrice Unger
Philadelphia, Pa.

SEPTEMBER 3, 1939

DEAR MR. PRESIDENT: I WAS GREATLY HEARTENED BY YOUR STATEMENT THAT YOUR ADMINISTRATION DEDICATES ITSELF TO THE TASK OF KEEPING THE UNITED STATES OUT OF THE WAR THAT SEEMS TO BE ENGULFING EUROPE. LAST SATURDAY I PASSED MY 25TH BIRTHDAY. I HAD LITTLE TIME TO NOTICE IT AS I AM VERY BUSY RIGHT NOW STARTING A BUSINESS. WITH SEVERAL OTHER YOUNG FELLOWS MY OWN AGE I AM PREPARING TO LAUNCH A NEW CIVIL SERVICE NEWSPAPER. IF THE UNITED STATES WERE TO BECOME INVOLVED IN A EUROPEAN WAR WE WOULD ALL HAVE TO GO. WE DON'T WANT TO GO TO WAR. THERE IS SO MUCH TO BUILD UP RIGHT HERE IN THIS COUNTRY. WHY SHOULD WE DESTROY? WE ARE VERY GLAD TO HAVE THE OPPORTUNITY TO START IN SOMETHING WORTHWHILE, AND MAKE JOBS IN THE PROCESS. THERE MUST BE MILLIONS OF YOUNG PERSONS IN THIS COUNTRY STARTING ON CAREERS EQUALLY WORTHWHILE. IT IS MY EARNEST HOPE AND THE HOPE OF MILLIONS OF YOUNG AMERICANS THAT THE UNITED STATES NOT BE DRAGGED INTO BLOODY CONFLICT, AND THAT YOU RETAIN THE STRENGTH TO LEAD US SO THAT WE DO NOT STUMBLE.

RESPECTFULLY,

SEWARD BRISBANE
NEW YORK, N.Y.

SEPTEMBER 3, 1939

DARE PEACE MR. ROOSEVELT AND HISTORY WILL RECORD AMERICA'S PRESIDENT AS THE WORLD'S GREATEST HERO. YOUR PEOPLE KNOW IT WILL NOT BE EASY FOR YOU TO WITHSTAND THOSE WHO PROFIT THRU DESTRUCTION AND THOSE WHO HONESTLY BELIEVE ANY GOOD CAN BE ACHIEVED THRU

WAR. MILLIONS OF AMERICANS ARE PRAYING THAT YOU HAVE COURAGE
NOT ONLY TO KEEP AMERICA OUT OF WAR BUT TO REFUSE THAT SHE HAVE
ANY SHARE IN THE DEALING OF DEATH. I AM BUT ONE OF THOUSANDS OF
YOUNG AMERICANS WHO WILL ACCEPT PRISON OR DEATH IN PREFERENCE
TO WAR PARTICIPATION. DARE PEACE, MR. PRESIDENT.

GERALDINE GREGG
EVANSTON, ILLS.

SEPTEMBER 4, 1939

THE PRESIDENT:

YOUR NEUTRALITY DECLARATION CONDONES HITLERS BRUTALITY.

GEORGE ARNOTT
BIRMINGHAM

SEPTEMBER 3, 1939

THE PRESIDENT:

DID NOT CARE FOR SPEECH. IS HITLER LAUGHING.

MABEL S. BUELL
SAN DIEGO, CALIF.

SEPTEMBER 10, 1939

Mr. President:

If you were sincere in your promise over the Radio; to keep the United
States out of this European war, and I must say you sounded sincere, you
will have the gratitude and blessings of this generation of Americans, and
of generations to follow. If you were merely trying to gain time to fool the
American public, you will be criminally guilty of the murder of millions of
American and European boys and men.

We were deceived before within living memory by a Democratic President, who was more English than American. Let us not be betrayed again by another Democratic President. It will mean that the Democratic party will be anathema, and rightly, by all true Americans. And I am a Democrat who says this.

. . . if you plunge us into a second world war there will be no Democratic party to vote for.

We are not an English colony. Most of us will not swallow English propoganda, even in the thick doses it is given us. We are Americans only, first and last, and we are willing to fight only if our own shores are attacked. Please prove to us that you are an American President, with only the interests of your own country at heart. And do not let us get rich on the blood money that we would gain by selling arms and ammunitions to any of the belligerants.

Sincerely,

Catherine McD. Larkin
New York, N.Y.

SEPTEMBER 5, 1939

My dear Mr. President:

. . . May I suggest that this is the time when we should deport from our Country every undesirable alien.

With all good wishes for our Country and you, I am

Yours very truly,

D. P. Hopkins
Beverly, N.J.

SEPTEMBER 4, 1939

Honorable Sir: —

I had listened patiently to your speech of last evening Sept 3. 1939 at 10 P.M. and I dare say it was a masterpiece. . . .

How extremely fortunate the "American People" are to live in a century when they can live as freely as the birds that live in the air. Did you ever stop to think that here in little old New York that Father Knickerbocker's children are descendents of every race of people that God ever created, that every language spoken under the sun, is spoken here in N.Y. that every religious faith known to mankind or preached, is preached here in N.Y. City. NY. is this not cold positive proof that in all this cold indifferent World what is needed is just a few drops of the milk of human kindness? I thank almighty God that here in the good old U.S.A. I can work hard and sweat blood to give to myself and my children a far better chance and opportunity than I had myself. My children are now full grown the babies (twins) just past 25. and yet I would hate to see my boy or any other mother's or father go to war. I would gladly give my own full measure of devotion if need be to save this Nation from ruin.

Assuring of faithful devotion to my country I am sir

Sincerely and Respectfully

Joseph M. Steinberg
New York, N.Y.

SEPTEMBER 8, 1939

Dear Mr. President:

I doubt whether this letter is even called to your attention. I am writing it only because I suppose there is a bare possibility that it might be.

I am a ticket agent for the Florida Motor Lines, a college graduate and former school teacher. I am just the age for soldiering.

I have been a strong critic of many of your ideas. However, the success or failure of many of these social and industrial plans matters so little compared to whether we as a people are drawn into another useless war.

Your talk on America's position last Sunday Evening gave me new faith and courage in the future. It was one of the most thoughtful and Christian speeches I have heard a man in public office deliver.

Since last Sunday Evening I have noticed that the average person has calmed his war talk. I attribute this fact largely to your talk.

I, and thousands like me, who may disagree with you on domestic questions, turn with all our faith to you as the leader of our Country and hope that you with calm determination will continue to lead us in the paths of peace.

Most sincerely

John K. Davis
Ocala, Florida

SEPTEMBER 4, 1939

Dear Mr. President:

Last night I listened to your radio address with much pleasure. I enjoyed and endorsed every sentence of it.

Since I have taught in our public Schools of Texas for 44 years, I have formed a habit of correcting grammatical errors. Will you pardon me if I tell you to pronounce "again" agĕn instead of again.

The treats are on you. I will expect you to "come across" the first time I see you.

May God bless you in your good work.

Respectfully,

J. B. Jordan
Monahans, Texas

*   *   *

Dear Mr. President,

I listened to your talk last night and thought it was wonderful. It reminds me of the time I stood behind you when you dedicated the Merryweather Fire tower in Warm Springs, though I was little I can well remember it. I came out of my Polio very well it left me with no defects, and I am always very happy to do what I can for the instution at Warm Springs.

After hearing your speech, I resolved to live for my country, and live the best I can, you know that's a harder job than to die for it in war.

Sincerely,

Phil Kennedy
Rochester, N.Y.

SEPTEMBER 1, 1939

Mr. President:

Thank you so much for you reassuring talk of Sunday evening. You may well believe that it was exactly what we wanted to hear. I wonder whether you can realize what it means to be one of the "little people", and see a holocaust like this moving down upon you, without any apparent means of preventing it. That is why it came as a great comfort to know that there is a strong arm and will at the head of our State, ready to stem the tide of hate and greed and fear that seemed to be moving down upon us.

There are millions of us, the little people of the United States, and our prayers are with you daily that God may give you the wisdom and strength to keep us from war, for the price is too great for America to pay.

Respectfully yours,

Helen Norton
Naperville, Illinois

"THE APPROACHING STORM":
MAY 26, 1940

IN LOOKING BACK on the first six months of the European war, the President characterized the attitude of his fellow citizens as "one of sympathetic aloofness." He had no doubt that his people's sympathies were with England and France. Nevertheless, "they seemed determined not only to remain out of the war, but also to maintain a strict neutrality in the fullest sense of the word. Their attitude was merely that of a very interested spectator."[14] Though there was doubtless some degree of oversimplification here, FDR seems to have been essentially correct on both scores.

The number of polls and surveys querying the American people about foreign policy issues increased dramatically as events in Europe and Asia escalated. In addition to the letters he received, FDR gauged the attitudes of the American people by paying close attention to the polls, especially those on foreign policy. Throughout 1939 and the first half of 1940, the American people expressed their preference for England, France, and China over Germany, Italy, and Japan. In March 1939, 65 percent said they would approve of a boycott on German-made goods and 57 percent felt the neutrality laws should be changed to allow the United States to sell war materials to England and France in the event of war; in May, 74 percent expressed sympathy for China and only 2 percent for Japan; in July, 70 percent listed Germany and Italy as the European countries they liked the least; in September, 82 percent held Germany responsible for causing the war and only 3 percent blamed England and France. In January 1940, 75 percent supported a ban on the sales of war materials to Japan; in February, 55 percent favored loaning money to England and France rather than see them defeated; in March, 84 percent expressed a desire to see England and France win the war as opposed to 1 percent for Germany; in April, 66 percent said they would support a presidential candidate willing to give England and France "all the help they want, except sending our army and navy."[15]

As this last poll indicates, in spite of their sympathy for the Allies, Americans made it clear that they desired no direct involvement. In September 1939, a *Fortune* Survey asked whether there were international issues so important to the United States that our government should take a stand on them even at the risk of getting into war, and less than 20 percent answered affirmatively while 54 percent said no. That same month, 95 percent of those polled by Gallup were opposed to sending our army and navy abroad to fight Germany. In October, although 84 percent wanted to see an Allied victory, 71 percent said that even if Germany were defeating England and France we should keep our troops at home. In November 1939, 47 percent thought keeping out of war was "the most important problem before the American people today," twice as many as those who listed solving unemployment as paramount.[16]

Running through all of these sentiments there seemed to be a sense of reprise, of having been through this before, as well as a sense of imminence, of being on the brink of having to go through it again. In April 1939, 57 percent of those polled told the American Institute of Public Opinion that FDR's foreign policy would not be able to keep war from breaking out in Europe. In July and August, 76 percent answered yes when Gallup pollsters asked: "If England and France have a war with Germany and Italy, do you think the United States will be drawn in?" In September, 63 percent thought that if Germany defeated England and France it "would start a war against the United States sooner or later." In May 1940, 65 percent agreed.[17] In 1940, a correspondent in the *Atlantic Monthly* compared the "average American" to a figure in a Greek tragedy: "his will was set one way, but he felt that the gods would be stronger than his will."[18]

If the situation *was* tragic, the tragedy was more Shakespearean than Greek. Americans were hardly blindly lost in the webs of the gods; they understood their situation. Increasingly, large numbers of Americans came to see their fate tied to that of the Allies but were ambivalent about embracing consequences that seemed to involve repeating what many of them felt were the mistakes of 1917–18. "It is no more than exact to say that many Americans were divided in their own minds," Rexford Guy Tugwell noted, "one moment intent on peace, the next indignant to the point of wanting to act."[19] If Americans resembled any classic dramatic figure, it was Hamlet, not Oedipus.

The months following the onset of war in September 1939 had been largely a period of inaction, dubbed by some as a "phony war." With the end of winter, reality set in. Beginning in April 1940, Germany invaded Denmark and Norway and then swept through Holland, Belgium, Luxembourg, and France. Great Britain, as FDR put it, was now left "alone to face the terror."[20] The President was determined not to allow them to remain abandoned for long. The previous November, two months after the war began, Congress had finally passed a new neutrality law that embodied the provisions FDR had urged upon it: the mandatory arms embargo was lifted and the President could authorize sales of arms to a belligerent on a "cash and carry" basis. The President now had at least the beginnings of the means to help Great Britain; what he needed to do was to create the will to help Britain in the country at large. An important instrument toward that end was to convince the vast majority that the European war both involved and threatened them and that the build-up of American readiness for war was essential, as was aid to Great Britain. Hitler's easy conquests in 1939 and 1940 certainly helped, as did England's stubborn resistance to the Nazi airborne onslaught.

Several polls held in May 1940, just prior to FDR's Fireside Chat, reveal the intricacy of American attitudes. Eighty-six percent answered no to the question, "Do you think our country's army, navy, and air forces are strong enough so that the United States is safe from attack by any foreign nation?" The same percentage of those polled supported the President's request for billions of dollars for building up our armed forces. But although the previous month 65 percent agreed that if Germany defeated England it "would start a war against the United States," 93 percent of those questioned by Gallup between May 18 and May 23 opposed war with Germany, and 64 percent surveyed by the American Institute of Public Opinion on May 23 thought it was more important to stay out of war than to help England win.[21]

This was the complex state of public opinion when Roosevelt delivered his Fireside Chat on Sunday evening, May 26.[22] At the time FDR spoke, Denmark, Holland, and most of Norway were in German hands; Belgium would surrender two days later; and France, whose premier had called vainly four days earlier for the United States to send its Atlantic fleet and air force to defend it, was less than a month away from capitulation. Sam Rosenman has left us a picture of the President's mood in the hours before he spoke to the American people:

> I remember very well the small group in the President's study in the White House before dinner on the evening of this broadcast. Tonight there was no levity. There was no small talk. The President was reading dispatches which were being

brought in to him from time to time by a White House usher. He mixed cocktails rather mechanically, as though his mind were thousands of miles away — as, of course, it was. The dispatches all painted a complete rout of the Allied armies.

"All bad, all bad," he muttered as he read one dispatch after another and handed them to Mrs. Roosevelt, who stood by his side. She read them and silently passed them on to us. It was a dejected dinner group.

It was a grim-looking President — but a very determined one — who took the microphone that night.[23]

FDR's mood was evident in the opening paragraphs of his Chat as he spoke of "this moment of sadness throughout most of the world," and pleaded "in behalf of women and children and old men who need help . . . from us who are still free to give it."

> Tonight over the once peaceful roads of Belgium and France millions are now moving, running from their homes to escape bombs and shells and fire and machine gunning, without shelter, and almost wholly without food. They stumble on, knowing not where the end of the road will be.

He implored his fellow Americans to extend help through the Red Cross: "Please — I beg you — please give according to your means . . . give as generously as you can. I ask this in the name of our common humanity."

"Let us sit down together again, you and I, to consider our own pressing problems that confront us," he said in words reminiscent of those with which he had opened his first Fireside Chat during the banking crisis. In a message to Congress ten days earlier, he had tried to demonstrate that the Atlantic and Pacific Oceans were no longer the barriers they had been before modern warfare. He pointed out that from the fiords of Greenland it was only six hours to New England; from a base in the outer West Indies, Florida could be reached in two hundred minutes; Alaska was only four or five hours by air from Seattle; the west coast of South America was "not too far removed" from the islands of the South Pacific, while its east coast was equally vulnerable from the Cape Verde Islands off the coast of Africa, and the whole of the United States was accessible from South America.[24] Building on this theme in his Fireside Chat, he spoke of the myths and illusions that blinded so many in the current crisis just as they had prevented millions from comprehending events in the crisis of 1933:

> To those who have closed their eyes . . . to those who would not admit the possibility of the approaching storm — to all of them the past two weeks have meant the shattering of many illusions.
>
> They have lost the illusion that we are remote and isolated and, therefore, secure against the dangers from which no other land is free.
>
> In some quarters, with this rude awakening has come fear, fear bordering on panic. It is said that we are defenseless. It is whispered by some that, only by abandoning our freedom, our ideals, our way of life, can we build our defenses adequately, can we match the strength of the aggressors.
>
> I did not share those illusions. I do not share these fears.

FDR launched into an extended and very detailed exposition attempting to show how dramatically our armed forces and materials had increased from 1933 to 1940. His comparison was strengthened by his strategy of combining war materials on hand and *on order* in giving the 1940 figures. Sam Rosenman, who helped to write this Chat, received the 1940 figures from Major Walter Bedell Smith, who wrote him: "If limited to materiel actually on hand the figures would not be particularly impressive since we are just now beginning to get the benefit of the large appropriation for materiel authorized in 1940."[25] Even if his statistics were optimistic to the point of being misleading, FDR spoke forcefully and skillfully both to calm the fears of the American people and to stimulate their support for accelerating the build-up of American preparedness. He asserted that the nation would build up its armed defenses "to whatever heights the future may require." He assured business that because the international situation could change swiftly, the government would aid them in enlarging factories, establishing new plants, locating resources and raw materials, developing mass transportation, and training workers for the manufacture of arms.

Having assured industry of government aid, he quickly turned to assure the people forcefully and eloquently that there would be "no breakdown or cancellation of any of the great social gains which we have made in these past years."

> There is nothing in our present emergency to justify making the workers of our nation toil for longer hours than those now

limited by statute. As more orders come in and as more work has to be done, tens of thousands of people, who are now unemployed, will, I believe, receive employment.

There is nothing in our present emergency to justify a lowering of the standards of employment. Minimum wages should not be reduced. It is my hope, indeed, that the new speed-up of production will cause many businesses which now pay below the minimum standards to bring their wages up.

There is nothing in our present emergency to justify a breaking down of old age pensions or of unemployment insurance. I would rather see the systems extended to other groups who do not now enjoy them.

There is nothing in our present emergency to justify a retreat, any retreat, from any of our social objectives — from conservation of natural resources, assistance to agriculture, housing, and help to the under-privileged.

He went even further, promising labor that its rights of collective bargaining would be protected, and assuring consumers that their rights would be similarly protected "so that our general cost of living can be maintained at a reasonable level." He declared that "no new group of war millionaires shall come into being in this nation as a result of the struggles abroad. The American people will not relish the idea of any American citizen growing rich and fat in an emergency of blood and slaughter and human suffering."

Perhaps with recent instances in Europe in mind as well as the deeply troubling campaign being waged against his foreign policy by those like Charles Lindbergh, FDR devoted a surprisingly substantial section of his Chat to the internal dangers the country faced: "The Trojan Horse. The Fifth Column that betrays a nation unprepared for treachery." He had in mind not only "spies, saboteurs and traitors" but also "the dissemination of discord" by those who exploited the prejudices of sectional, racial, or political groups. "The aim of those who deliberately egg on these groups is to create confusion of counsel, public indecision, political paralysis and eventually, a state of panic." His charges were as strong as they were vague. He condemned the "undiluted poison" of "deliberately planned propagandas to divide and weaken us in the face of danger as other nations have been weakened before," and called for "singleness of national purpose," confidence, faith, and unity. "Our moral, our mental defenses must be raised up as never before against those who would cast a smokescreen across our vision."

He concluded his Chat on a visionary and spiritual note:

> For more than three centuries we Americans have been building on this continent a free society, a society in which the promise of the human spirit may find fulfillment. Commingled here are the blood and the genius of all the peoples of the world who have sought this promise. . . . We defend and we build a way of life, not for America alone, but for all mankind. Ours is a high duty, a noble task.
>
> Day and night I pray for the restoration of peace in this mad world of ours . . . all of us beg that suffering and starving, that death and destruction may end — and that peace may return to the world. In common affection for all mankind, your prayers join with mine — that God will heal the wounds and the hearts of humanity.

Two days later, at his press conference, the President told the assembled reporters of "the flood of mail and telegrams that has been coming in since Sunday night . . . from people offering help, almost every known way." Not only were numerous checks for the Red Cross sent directly to FDR, but there were offers of service from "retired officers of the last war, dollar-a-year men, other experts, engineers, physicians, pilots, chemists, et cetera, and a very large number from local labor unions, Chambers of Commerce, and various business associations, offering the services of their groups." Letters offered the government factories, mines, airplane plants, aviation training schools, "a cigar company, a publishing company, a motion-picture company, [a] yacht, . . . et cetera and so on."[26]

This enthusiastic volunteerism hearkened back to the spirit that had prevailed after his early Fireside Chats appealing to the people to enlist in the fight against the Depression. Now, as then, people offered not only their aid but their opinions and advice, as the letters below amply demonstrate.

MAY 26, 1940

Dear Mr. Roosevelt —

May I express my personal gratitude for the radio talk you have just finished? The note of confident inspiration you have just given me has made a
big impression, and this must certainly be shared by others.

This is the first speech in a long time that has affected me so profoundly,
and it is most timely if I am to judge the feelings of others by those of mine.
The emotional strain under which we have laboured the last few months
is probably responsible for this outburst, for while I don't consider myself
among those suffering panic, I confess that I have been bothered by the
present wave of sensationalism.

May I emphasize the fact that while I don't agree with many of the policies and ideals of your administration, I do wholeheartedly support you in
your foreign policy and defense program. The question in my mind is, can
we prepare our defenses in time? A lot of things can happen in the next
year. What with the alarming rapidity of events the last few weeks, as well
as the unpredictable whims of a Hitler, might we not become embroiled
before then?

Please don't go to the trouble of answering this as I wish to thank you
for myself and others, the confidence and inspiration your words carried
tonight.

Sincerely yours,

Charles E. Baker
Cambridge, Mass.

MAY 27, 1940

Dear Sir

I am just an old Kansas farmer and stockman I have been A Republican
all my life I admit I have been so prejudiced I could see no good in the Democrat party. but Democrat or no Democrat my heart warmed to you last
night for the first time in my life it ever warmed to a Democrat I am with you

one hundred percent in what you said last night. may God be with you. Lord God of hosts be with us yet lest we forget, lest we forget.

Respt yours

C. H. Russell
Redfield, Kans.

MAY [29], 1940

Dear President:

My congratulations! What a wonderful speech! As I listened to you after a very busy day, not a hard day for when I think of how lucky I am just to be alive nothing is hard, somehow I thought I was listening to Abraham Lincoln also. I know that hard work and many of the precious hours of your life doing things for others has made you the successful person you are. In some way some day, in some little way I hope I can do something to show you how much I appreciate living in the America, of which you are the Peacemaker.

If I do not get that chance beleive me — when I have children and grandchildren, I am not going to cease telling them how proud I am to be living during the time that Franklin Delano Roosevelt was President and Eleanor Roosevelt was the First Lady of the Land of America.

Very sincerely yours,

Carnation Marin
Martinez, Calif.

MAY 30, 1940

My dear Mr. Roosevelt:

As an ardent supporter of most of your policies and opinions, I feel impelled to tell you that certain phases of your recent "Fireside Chat" have left an unfavorable impression in this region, even among those strongly inclined to follow and to defend you. After having considered that speech rather carefully and after talking it over with several thoughtful persons, I too have come to the conclusion that it was one of your least successful or creditable efforts in the shaping of public opinion. . . .

Undoubtedly you know that your frequently recurring phrase "on order" is not very revealing. Thus, for example, one does not get much precise information from your statement that "we now have on hand and on order more than 1,600" modern infantry mortars. Considering the billions of dollars that have been allocated to the national defense during recent years and considering also the present state of the world, tax payers and citizens feel a natural curiosity to know whether at this moment we actually possess anything like an adequate supply of this weapon; but there is nothing whatever in your words to suggest what an adequate supply would be or whether just now we really have ready for use even so many as two of these mortars. . . .

The present emergency in America is serious enough, in your belief, to justify a great increase in public expenditure, and, ultimately, in taxation. No patriotic American is likely to object to that so long as it is made clear that this expenditure is economically administered in the public interest. The taxation must fall in large part, however, upon the propertied classes — to which, as it happens, I do not belong. Now of course those classes will quite reasonably expect that labor will bear its share of the exceptional burdens laid upon the country, just as it has recently been called upon to do — one fears, too late — in France and England. Labor can do its share just now chiefly by working longer hours. And labor, I think, should be told just this, without regard to the fact that this is an election year. — I know of course that such a statement would take great courage, coming from an American President with a "liberal" background and record; but we are expecting courage in these days from all men. Why not from politicians, even? We are expecting temporary sacrifice of all Americans. Why not from labor?

This letter, however it may sound, comes from a man who has deeply and gratefully admired the work you have done in your administration. It stands, I think, for the feeling and opinion of more than one man. My present hope is that our next President will be Franklin Delano Roosevelt. Toward this leader of my country I feel a strong sense of personal loyalty. Yet I am loyal only to what I consider the best that there is in him. I feel that he may be not only an agile, nimble-witted, clever, charming, and versatile President but that, under the stress and strain of the times now upon us, a

President really great. Just that is what his really loyal followers demand of him. Nothing less will suffice.

Do try to pardon me, sir. I had to say these things.

Respectfully yours,

Odell Shepard
Hartford, Connecticut

MAY 27, 1940

Dear Franklin

. . . The roosters woke me at four and I opened the May atlantic [*Atlantic Monthly*] where Eva Curie stated French women in the last war worked 10, 11, even 14 hours a day in munitions factories. So I think it was wrong to tell our labor people their hours would not be increased. Those communists are likely to all go on strike because you promised them no longer hours, as if going around [Cape] Hatteras in a storm the seamans union struck because the storm made long hours necessary.

Suppose we small farmers struck for equal pay and hours with railroad unions?

I would feel more confident if you didn't have so many smart alex young Jews and Irish around you. Good at massaging you with oil, but lacking in all ideas of government as centuries of time have proved.

. . . Aren't there any Smiths, Browns, Jones', Robinsons who can help you? Or Lees or Jacksons?

Well it is 5:10 and time to pail the cows. And remember Frank the old American revolution saying. "Trust in God but keep your powder dry." The British have merely trusted in God. . . .

Robert D. Kellogg
Richfield, California

JUNE 10, 1940

YOUR SPEECH IS LIKELY TO ENDANGER AND SACRIFICE AMERICAN FREE-
DOM BY PROVOKING AN ENEMY WHO IS STRONGER BETTER ARMED AND AL-

READY VICTORIOUS BEFORE WE ARE READY ARM TO TEETH IMMEDIATELY
AND NOT IN SIX MONTHS AND PRESERVE OUR AMERICAN INDEPENDENCE
EVERYTHING ELSE IS SECONDARY.

A. O. SMITH

AKRON, OHIO

MAY 28, 1940

Mr. President: —

Your "Fire Side Chats" and other speeches have always been events of
importance to me. Although I have always been an ardent adherent of yours
I have not always been able to subscribe to every one of your policies. Until
now I should have considered it presumptuous to write to you and express
criticism or tender advice. But the present situation is so desperately serious that I cannot keep still and must tell you how one patriotic citizen feels
about it.

... your Fire Side Chat on Sunday was an absolute let down. I had
looked forward to it all day and now I must make the uncomplimentary
confession that I fell asleep in the midst of it. I queried 27 persons yesterday,
all of them admirers of yours and not one of them listened to it all the way
through. And now that I have read it I feel so discouraged that I could weep
with anguish and pain. A purely political speech, defending the administration and it's disbursements during the recent past for our defensive
forces. But what we really need is to be told that we must be done with such
petty dilly-dallying and must boldly begin to arm ourselves as no country
ever has before and train all our citizens, male and female in the grim arts
of war; that we must subordinate all our aims, aspirations and activities to
this one task and dedicate our lives and fortunes to it. For unless we can do
so quickly and adequately we shall not be able to preserve much of anything
that has value and meaning for us to-day.

Mr. President, perhaps you don't know fully the danger we are in. I cannot believe that you have not acquainted yourself with the writings and say-
ings of the men that dominate Central Europe to-day and are in a fair way
of dominating all of it very shortly. Surely you must know that only force,
superior force can protect us and save us from their encroachment into our
hemisphere. I am sure they rubbed their hands in joy when they read your

speech or those of your opponents for they know that no country that fiddles around that way in a time of grave emergency will be able to cross their plans.

. . . I am afraid you are mistaken when you stress the importance of social gains made during your administration. These must gradually be suspended and given up willingly, gladly. Surely people cannot be so blind as not to see what happens in war times; it seems so silly to think of wages and hours and profits and collective bargaining for what meaning have such words against a background of smoldering cities and hamlets, of mangled bodies, of death to hundreds of thousands of men, women and children? Let us get started today, not to-morrow on a bold and far reaching program of rearmament; we have so much that is worth saving and we are ready for every sacrifice. . . .

I am, Mr. President,

very respectfully Yours:

John C. Benedict
New York, N.Y.

MAY 29, 1940

Dear sir:

I heard your fireside speech on defense last Sunday (May 26, 1940). I agree with most of it, but I am inclined to believe that more stress and attention should be put on the "secret weapon" end of it. . . . Our enemies are always on the alert for secret weapons. They betray confidence and get themselves into our factories where secret weapons are made. None should work in a weapon factory who cannot trace his ancestry back about five generations in America; and his record for patriotism should be unstained. . . .

I have three secret weapons designed. I know war. I fought in three offensives. One of these weapons should be in the hands of the government right now. It takes time to design and build it. But I will not run the risk of exposing my name and address (which is neither on the outside of this envelope nor at the heading of this letter). As I know how alert some nations are for such things. I am trying to find a way to get this into trustworthy hands. Even the mails are unsafe for such plans. If either fighting army had the above weapon today, the fate of those trapped allies would now be decided.

The other two weapons are effective and cheap. Terrible too. But they can be made quickly and put into use in less than ten days after I should turn over the plans. Either of them would speak in Europe today.

A GENUINE AMERICAN
Fremont, Nebraska

MAY 26, 1940

Dear Mr. President.

Thanks for your Speech or Chat tonight — it was very EMPTY — a flop.

I was bitterly disappointed.

You seem to be weakening. — <u>FAST</u>.

One would appreciate a little more of the <u>Winston Churchill spirit</u> against the rank rottenness of Hitlerism — the major cause of World chaos today.

<u>Not one Word mentioned about the main thing at issue.</u>

<u>Hitler versus Americanism.</u>

I must confess I am totally at loss to understand the confusion & mudelling at Washington. . . .

Cant America Wake up & <u>do something Now</u> — not tomorrow. That will be too late.

Let the World know by direct action America & its spokesmen are not mere bags of hot air — plain wind.

Please for God's Sake <u>Wake Up & do something to stop HITLER.</u>

Yours Very Truly

Harry C. Armin
Brooklyn, N.Y.

MAY 26, 1940

My dear Mr. President: —

. . . I cut short my church service tonight and brought a crowd over to my house and told the others to hurry home and listen to your address.

I wish to thank you for your noble deliverance; its solid and sane Americanism and its lofty Christian spirit. Every true American will rally to it and those who will not should be shipped out of the country.

I have written you before and I now say again that it is my candid opinion that this nation should build the greatest fleet for sea and air and the greatest land and coast defense of any nation in the world. Brotherly love is a fine appeal to those who have the character to appreciate it is a fine thing but International robbers and plunderers can be silenced only with bullets, sad as the fact is.

Real Americans are behind you and you may be sure that you have my hearty approval and support.

Most sincerely,

W. G. Beasley
Pastor Methodist Church
Marietta, Oklahoma

MAY 27, 1940

My dear President Roosevelt,

I can see that if one frankly discards the teachings and spirit of Christianity, he can make a strong logical case for building up enormous defenses against agressive nations. I cannot see however how you can conclude a speech urging and detailing the establishment and maintenance of vast numbers of military planes equipped and intended to kill other human beings, and then call on your fellow countrymen to pray to God for all humanity. War hysteria undoubtedly enfeebles many minds, but there are still some Americans who can detect such confusion of thought, and beg you to leave God out of your fireside chats.

Sincerely yours,

(Mrs.) Marcia J. Lyttle
Chicago, Illinois

JUNE 1, 1940

Dear Mr. President:

May I presume to write a note of commendation on your speech of last Sunday night? I thought it was very fine and am wholeheartedly in favor of preparedness — but for defense. The thing that particularly pleased me about your remarks then was that you made no virulent attacks on the so-called dictatorships. The United States, from what I see in the papers, is in no position to pick a fight with anybody, and I urge that our remarks to foreign nations be accordingly restrained.

It seems quite possible that we are going to have to live in a world in which Germany will be one of the dominant powers, and I believe that calling their political leaders names will not assist us in getting along with them peacably.

Your great relative, Theodore Roosevelt, referred to "talking softly with a big stick", and I respectfully submit that some of the utterances coming out of Washington have reversed Roosevelt the First's admonition, because we have no big stick to wield.

Respectfully,

Granger Hansell
Atlanta

MAY 18, 1940

LETS APPEASE HITLER. GIVE HIM ENGLAND FRANCE. KEEP AMERICA OUT.

VIRGINIA HARVESTER
NEW YORK, N.Y.

JUNE 10, 1940

MR PRESIDENT, IF YOU SPOKE THE TRUTH IN YOUR RECENT BROADCAST ON NATIONAL DEFENSE AMERICA CANNOT SPARE ONE GUN OR ONE AEROPLANE TO A FOREIGN BELLIGERENT. IT IS YOUR DUTY TO SAVE THE UNITED STATES OF AMERICA AND NOT THE BRITISH EMPIRE.

ALICE PRIEST
PHILADELPHIA, PENN.

MAY 19, 1940

YANKS ARE NOT COMING WE WILL NOT DIE FOR WALL STREET.

[SIGNED BY 167 STUDENTS
FROM THE COLLEGE OF THE CITY OF NEW YORK]

MAY 18, 1940

THE PRESIDENT:

BANKERS CAN BUY THEIR SONS OFF THE DRAFT. WE WON'T GIVE OUR
FLESH AND BLOOD TO FATHER WALL STREET PROFIT. NATIONAL INTEREST
MEAN MORE JOBS, MORE HOUSING, MORE HOSPITALS, MORE SCHOOLS —
NOT GUNS.

GROUP OF BROWNSVILLE MOTHERS
NEW YORK, N.Y.

MAY 18, 1940

THE PRESIDENT:

TAKE YOUR OWN FAMILY AND FORTUNE AND FIGHT FOR YOUR FRIEND KING
GEORGE. WE WANT NO PART OF IT.

LEWIS HILL
UNION CITY, N.J.

MAY 18, 1940

THE PRESIDENT:

AFTER YOU HAVE DRIVEN OUR COUNTRY DOWN THE HYSTERIA PATH AND
INTO THE WAR, WILL YOUR FOUR SONS BE CANNON FODDER ALONG WITH
US?

THREE MILITARY AGE BROTHERS
YONKERS, N.Y.

MAY 18, 1940

MR PRESIDENT: "WE ARE AMERICANS WE ARE NOT THE HUMBLE SUBJECT OF AN ALL POWERFUL GOVERNMENT WE ARE THE PEOPLE WE ARE THE SOVEREIGN CITIZENS OF THE U S OF AMERICA WE ARE THE GOVERNMENT WE DO NOT BEG FOR PEACE LIKE SLAVES WE DO NOT PLEAD FOR IT LIKE SERFS WE COMMAND IT."

LOUIS GILBERT
EDDIE BALCHOWSKY
RAY HOCHMAN
IRV SOLTKER
DAVID DEKOVEN
ISADORE MARKIN
WILLIAM KEE
LOUIS TERKEL
GERTRUDE GUNTER
TILLIE SACKS
CHICAGO, ILL.

MAY 28, 1940

Mr. President,

. . . As the daughter of one, who actually kept the torch of Liberty aglow for a number of years, in New York Harbor, perhaps it is fitting that in a small way, the following may light the fires of loyalty — make them burn more brightly, with greater love for our National Emblem.

THE FLAG OF FLAGS

. . .

Do you love 'The Stars and Stripes'?
Do you love its field of blue?
Do you love its 'red and white'
And all they stand for, too?
Are you proud that you were born
Where there's a Leader, tried and true?
Then back our Leader — and that flag —
Our own 'RED, WHITE AND BLUE!'

... With the approach of Flag Day, the thought occurred that you might enjoy this new salute to our banner. Within the next two weeks, I have been asked to present it before the Veterans of Foreign Wars, The American Legion and The American Legion Auxiliary. In a small way, I hope to counteract some of the 'insidious poison' that has been spread throughout the country, to destroy our national spirit!

Thanking you for a few moments of your precious time, I remain,

Sincerely,

(Mrs.) Stella Watts Hollowell
Santa Barbara, California

MAY 27, 1940

Dear Mr. President,

... We all look with horror upon the economic as well as the aggressive territorial policies pursued by the dictator nations. In spite of their short comings there is one good trait, however, which we can learn from them. That of undying loyalty. I believe that every effort should be made daily in our Schools, Churches, Theatres, Publications, and over our Radios to instill in the conscienceness of everyone the patriotism which is so rightfully due these United States. The National Anthem should be sung, the Oath to the Flag should be given, etc., until unity of thought in this country should be such that it is incomparable.

Again, let me thank you for your "Fire side chat".

Yours very truly,

E. V. Dunphy Jr.
Evanston, Ill.

MAY 26, 1940

THE PRESIDENT:

WHY DON'T YOU ORDER THE FBI TO ACT UPON THE INFORMATION DISCLOSED ON RADIO PROGRAM, "CONFIDENTIALLY YOURS," MUTUAL

BROADCASTING CHAIN, 9:30 THIS EVENING AND DEPORT ALL ALIENS BE-
FORE THEY CAN COMMIT SABOTAGE AND DESTROY OUR MUNITION PLANTS
AND BRING ON A REVOLUTION. IT CAN HAPPEN HERE.

HENRY G. BONNELLE
NEW YORK, N.Y.

MAY 29, 1940

My Dear Mr. President

Your Radio Chat of May 26 was splendid, and the Citizens of USA.
should wake up to the actual facts and conditions that we face. In my opinion what is needed is the solidity of this Nation which I am afraid does not
exist today as it should. This is an English Speaking Nation and the English
Language should be required by Law, to be spoken in all Public places,
Business and social & etc. Only in the Homes of Foreigners and their De-
cendants any Foreign Language be spoken. In all part of this Country, there
are Towns, Villages & Cities of German, Polish Italian Bohemian, Mexicans and others, that speak their own tongue and not ours. That state of
affairs only goes to keep up those Old Country Idears (although they left
there to get an even chance Life) Freedom of speech mean the English Language. I consider you are the only one who can broach the subject without
Fear or Favor.

Your sincere citizen,

W. F. Courtenay
San Antonio, Texas

* * *

Honorable President Franklin D. Roosevelt

Your speech dispelled doubts and fears from our hearts — God bless
you.

We realize democracy is on the defensive. The greatest danger is to our
Democratic system and Democracy is the only good form of government.

The whole world is in such a state of flux.

Can't something be done As our emergency need — to control Immigration?

We should not be so democratic in the way we apply it — but keep more out! We could improve the cultural level of this country by selective immigration. I thank God for the Judgment our ancestors showed in leaving Europe — I shall always be grateful for that. God bless you and give you strength to carry your many burdens — Sincerely,

(Miss) Berenice Boyer
Dayton, Ohio

MAY 26, 1940

MR PRESIDENT THE MOST IMPORTANT DEFENSE OF OUR DEMOCRATIC SYS-
TEM IS THE DEFENSE OF ITS BASIC PRINCIPLES AND ATTITUDES. WHEN
THEY GO WE ARE DEFEATED EVEN THOUGH NO ENEMY HAS SET FOOT UPON
OUR SOIL.

IF OUR OFFICIAL INVESTIGATING AGENCY LIST MEN ACCORDING TO
THEIR BELIEF AND POLITICAL AFFILIATIONS, THAT IS SIMPLY THE CONTI-
NENTAL SYSTEM OF POLITICAL OFFENDERS AND AN IMMITATION OF HIT-
LER. CITIZENS VIGILANTE GROUPS WOULD BE EXACTLY THE SAME CLASS
OF INSTITUTION AS HITLER'S STORMTROOPERS . . .

I WAS IN THE DEPARTMENT OF JUSTICE DURING THE WORLD WAR IN THE
DIVISION IN CHARGE OF ESPIONAGE ACT AND PLAINLY THERE ARE TODAY
APPEARING ALL THE MANIFESTATIONS WHICH PRODUCED SUCH DAMAGE
TO OUR DEMOCRACY IN THE LATER WORLD WAR AND POST ARMISTICE PE-
RIOD. THE EXPRESSION SUBVERSIVE COMMUNISM AND FIFTH COLUMN ARE
EASILY RECOGNIZED AS THE CONTEMPORARY SUCCESSORS OF THE CRY OF
BOLSHEVISM IN 1918 AND THE CRY OF JACOBINISM AT THE END OF THE
18TH CENTURY AND BEGINNING OF THE 19TH; THE VERY SORT OF THING
AGAINST WHICH OUR BILL OF RIGHTS WAS CONSCIOUSLY DIRECTED. OUR
DEMOCRATIC PRINCIPLE IS SIMPLE. ACTS ARE PUNISHABLE BUT BELIEFS
AND THEIR EXPRESSION ARE FREE AND EQUAL.

PLEASE MR. PRESIDENT IN YOUR ADDRESS TONIGHT TELL US THAT
LISTS OF POLITICAL OFFENDERS, VIGILANTISM, PRIVATE SPYING AND IN-
FORMING, ALIEN AND SEDITION LAWS AND OTHER LIGHT [LIKE] METHODS

OF HITLER AND OTHER ENEMIES OF DEMOCRACY SHALL NOT BE INSTI-
TUTED OR TOLERATED IN OUR GREAT DEMOCRATIC COUNTRY.

ALFRED BETTMAN

CINCINNATI, OHIO

MAY 26, 1940

THE PRESIDENT:

HAVING JUST LISTENED TO YOUR BROADCAST I AM MOVED TO REMARK
AREN'T YOU LUCKY, MR. PRESIDENT, TO HAVE A REAL EMERGENCY PRES-
ENT THE POSSIBILITY OF RE-EMPLOYMENT FOR THE MILLIONS WHICH
YOUR DOMESTIC POLICIES HAVE PLACED IN THE HUMILIATING POSITION
OF ACCEPTING GOVERNMENT CHARITY. YOU WHO HAVE DELIBERATELY
CREATED CLASS FEELING IN THIS COUNTRY ARE HARDLY THE ONE TO
SOUND THE BATTLE CRY OF UNITY. MAY WE NOT LONG ENDURE THE HY-
POCRISY OF YOUR DIATRIBES.

I. B. WOOLLEY

SANTA FE, N.M.

MAY 18, 1940

DEAR MR. PRESIDENT: WE, AS AMERICAN CITIZENS, DEMAND THAT YOU
CEASE THIS CRY OF WAR, AND STOP SHIPPING WAR PLANES AND MUNITIONS
TO THE ALLIES WITH WHICH TO MASSACRE THE MOTHERS AND CHILDREN
OF THE WORLD, ALL FOR THE SAKE OF PROFIT. OUR LIVES DEPEND ON DE-
MOCRACY, WHICH IN TURN DEPENDS ON THE MAINTENANCE OF JOBS,
SECURITY AND PEACE. WE DEMAND AGAIN THAT YOU FEED AMERICA AND
STARVE THE WAR.

CLIFFORD GREENE

ARTHUR VOGEL

HANNAH MOYER

DOMENICK MIRABILE

NEW YORK, N.Y.

MAY 28, 1940

Dear Sir,

I heard your Speach on Sunday 26, 1940 and I am Veary Suprise at Such.

I would think that you Should Do Sompthing for the poor people of this country instead of Giving our money to the other country.

. . . Mr. President they ar women and children walking the Road crying for Bread hear in Tishomingo Co. Miss. . . .

Bart G. S. Defoare
Bernsvill [Burnsville], Miss.

"THE GREAT ARSENAL
OF DEMOCRACY":
DECEMBER 29, 1940

"WHAT WORRIES ME, especially," FDR wrote to the Kansas editor William Allen White at the end of 1939, "is that public opinion over here is patting itself on the back every morning and thanking God for the Atlantic Ocean (and the Pacific Ocean). . . . Things move with such terrific speed, these days, that it really is essential to us to think in broader terms and, in effect, to warn the American people that they, too, should think of possible ultimate results in Europe and the Far East."[27] Throughout 1940 this worry remained very much in the forefront of the President's mind.

In the months after his Fireside Chat of May 26, conditions in Europe had grown even more dire. France had fallen and England was under siege. While the endless rain of bombs on English cities received the most publicity in the United States, the withering German attack on the British fleet, which destroyed substantial numbers of England's warships, especially its destroyers, threatened England's primary line of defense: its control of the seas. Preoccupied with his unprecedented and controversial bid for a third presidential term, and burdened by the delicate political situation attending a presidential campaign, Roosevelt was unable to provide the kind of leadership in world affairs that corresponded to the fears he felt. He warned White in the letter quoted above that should "Germany and Russia win the war or force a peace favorable to them, the situation of your civilization and mine is indeed in peril." Although he felt increasingly certain that England's cause was America's and that Churchill was correct in predicting that a British defeat would inaugurate a "new Dark Age," the domestic political situation continued to constrain the President. With his Republican opponent, Wendell Willkie, gaining in the polls and warning the nation that if Roosevelt was reelected he would "send our boys over there again," FDR in a Boston campaign speech six days before the November 5 election repeated a promise he himself doubtless had lost faith in:

> I have said this before, but I shall say it again and again and
> again:

Your boys are not going to be sent into any foreign wars.

They are going into training to form a force so strong that, by its very existence, it will keep the threat of war far away from our shores.

The purpose of our defense is defense.[28]

Three days before the election, in extemporaneous remarks he made in Buffalo, he reiterated the need for building up America's defenses and again promised: "this country is not going to war."[29] But political constraints did not equal paralysis, and FDR took the initiative in those areas where he deemed it possible.

In June 1940, in order to pave the way for more bipartisanship in his attempt to aid England, FDR appointed two Republicans to his Cabinet, including, as Secretary of War, Henry Stimson, who had held the same post under Taft and had been Secretary of State under Hoover, and whose enthusiasm for aiding England led him to go so far as to advocate that American warships escort British merchant vessels carrying war supplies across the Atlantic. That same month, the President addressed the graduating class of the University of Virginia on the day Italy declared war on France, which led Roosevelt, who had tried to dissuade Mussolini from entering the war, to make his dramatic proclamation: "On this tenth day of June, 1940, the hand that held the dagger has struck it into the back of its neighbor." America's course would now be to arm itself and to "extend to the opponents of force the material resources of this nation." He spoke to the graduates of the "obvious delusion" that the United States could become "a lone island in a world dominated by the philosophy of force." Such an island might appeal to isolationists, FDR asserted, but to him, and he was certain to the vast majority of Americans, that type of total isolation represented "the nightmare of a people lodged in prison, handcuffed, hungry, and fed through the bars from day to day by the contemptuous, unpitying masters of other continents."[30]

Before June ended, the President had sent to Great Britain more than forty-three million dollars worth of mostly World War One–era machine guns, field artillery, ammunition, along with some modern aircraft, which helped to replace the cache of arms the British army had to abandon when its soldiers were evacuated from France earlier that month. In September, the United States transferred fifty overage destroyers to England in exchange for ninety-nine-year leases on bases in Newfoundland and the Caribbean. September also marked the passage of the first compulsory peace-time military draft in our history.

FDR was convinced that important as these acts were in extending some aid to Britain and beginning the process of readying America for defense or war, they were insufficient to prevent the Axis powers from conquering Europe. "As 1940 drew to a close," he later recalled, "Britain's financial assets reached a dangerously low point. In her heroic fight to repulse the Nazis, her gold reserve and dollar exchange assets left small leeway for additional purchases in this country. Action became imperative to bolster her position and at the same time strengthen our own defenses."[31] The "cash and carry" provision of the Neutrality Act prevented Britain from obtaining the arms it needed to repulse the Nazis without the dollars that Churchill warned the President Britain would soon no longer have. "We must find some way to lease or even lend these goods to the British," Roosevelt told Robert Sherwood.[32] His reelection on November 5, 1940, left him freer to work for ways to solve this dilemma.

In his press conference on December 17, FDR asserted that "the best defense of Great Britain is the best defense of the United States," and surmised that the war materials being produced in the United States "would give us greater protection if they were used in Great Britain than if they were kept in storage here." As he had in the domestic crisis, he derided those "who can only think in what we may call traditional terms about finances." "Now, what I am trying to do," he told the reporters, "is to eliminate the dollar sign. . . . get rid of the silly, foolish old dollar sign." He then launched into a homey allegory that proved to be one of his most widely repeated and effective public arguments for the plan of lending or leasing Great Britain the implements of war it needed to stave off the German attack:

> Suppose my neighbor's home catches fire, and I have a length of garden hose four or five hundred feet away. If he can take my garden hose and connect it up with his hydrant, I may help him to put out his fire. Now, what do I do? I don't say to him before that operation, "Neighbor, my garden hose cost me $15; you have to pay me $15 for it." . . . I don't want $15 — I want my garden hose back after the fire is over. . . . But suppose it gets smashed up — holes in it — during the fire. . . . He says, "How

many feet of it were there?" I tell him, "There were 150 feet of it." He says, "All right, I will replace it." Now, if I get a nice garden hose back, I am in pretty good shape.[33]

Twelve days later, he took his arguments directly to the American people in the final Fireside Chat of his second term.[34] He spoke in the White House before a small audience, including several members of his Cabinet and the actress Carole Lombard and her husband, Clark Gable. FDR opened by comparing the present crisis with that which beset the nation when he first took office and warned his listeners that the current situation was even more grave than the previous one: "Never before since Jamestown and Plymouth Rock has our American civilization been in such danger as now." We were able to proclaim the Monroe Doctrine in 1823, warning European nations not to interfere in the Western Hemisphere, because of our "unwritten agreement" that the British fleet would help to enforce it. "Does anyone seriously believe that we need to fear attack anywhere in the Americas while a free Britain remains our most powerful naval neighbor in the Atlantic? And does anyone seriously believe, on the other hand, that we could rest easy if the Axis powers were our neighbors there?" If Great Britain went down, the Axis powers, who avowed "that there can be no ultimate peace between . . . their philosophy of government and our philosophy of government," would control Europe, Asia, Africa, Australasia, and the high seas. The Americas "would be living at the point of a gun — a gun loaded with explosive bullets, economic as well as military." We would enter upon "a new and terrible era" in which we would be forced "to convert ourselves permanently into a militaristic power on the basis of war economy."

He tried again to demolish the notion that the vast expanses of the Atlantic and Pacific protected us by pointing out that modern weapons had reduced the spaces that separated nations. "Why, even today we have planes that could fly from the British Isles to New England and back again without refueling. And remember that the range of the modern bomber is ever being increased." He warned the American people, "Frankly and definitely there is danger ahead. . . . But we well know that we cannot escape danger, or the fear of danger, by crawling into bed and pulling the covers over our heads."

Again he turned to the internal menace that beset our country. Without supplying any specifics, he spoke of "secret emissaries" who "try to turn capital against labor, . . . to reawaken long slumbering racial and religious enmities which should have no place in this country . . . to divide our people, to divide them into hostile groups and to destroy our unity and shatter our will to defend ourselves." There were also loyal American citizens, "many of them in high places, who, unwittingly in most cases, are aiding and abetting the work of these agents. I do not charge these American citizens with being foreign agents. But I do charge them with doing exactly the kind of work that the dictators want done in the United States."* These people, Roosevelt continued, "not only believe that we can save our own skins by shutting our eyes to the fate of other nations. Some of them go much further than that. They say that we can and should become the friends and even the partners of the Axis powers. Some of them even suggest that we should imitate the methods of the dictatorships. But Americans never can and never will do that."

His reelection made it possible for him to speak his mind more forthrightly on Germany than he had before:

> The experience of the past two years has proven beyond doubt that no nation can appease the Nazis. . . . There can be no appeasement with ruthlessness. There can be no reasoning with an incendiary bomb. We know that a nation can have peace with the Nazis only at the price of total surrender.
>
> . . . The history of recent years proves that the shootings and the chains and the concentration camps are not simply the transient tools but the very altars of modern dictatorships. They may talk of a "new order" in the world, but what they have in mind is only a revival of the oldest and the worst tyranny. In that there is no liberty, no religion, no hope.

He asserted again what he had told the reporters earlier, that "there is far less chance of the United States getting into war, if we do all we can now to support the nations defending themselves against attack by the Axis than if

---

*When a draft of this Chat was submitted to the State Department for suggestions, it came back with a red line through the phrase, "many of them in high places." When Roosevelt asked "Who put this red line in here?" Sherwood and other advisers explained that the State Department suggested it would be well to delete these words. "Oh, *do* they," FDR replied. "Very well. We'll change it to read — 'There are also American citizens, many of them in high places — *especially in the State Department* — and so forth.'" The original version was left uncut (Robert E.

we acquiesce in their defeat, submit tamely to an Axis victory, and wait our turn to be the object of attack in another war later on." The people of Europe defending themselves against the Axis were not asking us to do their fighting, but to supply them with the implements of war "which will enable them to fight for their liberty and for our security . . . so that we and our children will be saved the agony and suffering of war which others have had to endure." We must, Roosevelt insisted, "have more ships, more guns, more planes — more of everything." In a phrase that was to become one of his most memorable, he proclaimed: "We must be the great arsenal of democracy." We must, he continued, "apply ourselves to our task with the same resolution, the same sense of urgency, the same spirit of patriotism and sacrifice as we would show were we at war."

Though his focus was resolutely on the world situation, Roosevelt did not completely ignore the domestic repercussions of the defense program he was promulgating. As he had in May, he insisted that there would be no rollback of the New Deal. "I would ask no one to defend a democracy which in turn would not defend everyone in the nation against want and privation," he asserted. "The strength of this nation shall not be diluted by the failure of the Government to protect the economic well-being of its citizens." He promised that the rights of the workers would be protected but in turn he expected them to shoulder the great responsibility of their obligation to the defense of the nation. "The nation expects our defense industries to continue operation without interruption by strikes or lock-outs. It expects and insists that management and workers will reconcile their differences by voluntary or legal means, to continue to produce the supplies that are so sorely needed." And he warned industry that he would tolerate none of their fears about the future consequences of possible surplus plant capacity caused by conversion to the manufacture of the weapons of war. "The possible consequences of failure of our defense efforts now are much more to be feared."

During the afternoon of December 29, FDR sat in the Cabinet Room with his speechwriters and advisers, Sam Rosenman, Robert Sherwood, and Harry Hopkins, making last-minute changes to the Chat he would deliver that evening. "Mr. President," Hopkins asked, "do you feel that you could include in this speech some kind of optimistic statement that will

Sherwood, *Roosevelt and Hopkins: An Intimate History* [New York: Harper and Brothers, 1948], 227).

hearten the people who are doing the fighting — the British, the Greeks and the Chinese?" The President, Sherwood remembered, "thought that over for a long time, tilting his head back, puffing out his cheeks as was his habit." At length he dictated: "I believe the Axis powers are not going to win this war. I base that belief on the latest and best information." In fact, his only "information" was his conviction that the lend-lease program would be implemented and make it impossible for Germany to defeat Great Britain.[35] This spirit of optimism infused the final paragraphs of his Chat:

> We have no excuse for defeatism. We have every good reason for hope — hope for peace, yes, and hope for the defense of our civilization and for the building of a better civilization in the future.

From the outset, the December 29 Chat was seen as one of FDR's most noteworthy. On the day of the Chat, the *New York Times* predicted that it would draw the "largest radio audience in history," estimating that as many as eighty million Americans would be listening.[36] Its predictions turned out to be accurate. A huge audience gathered around their radios in almost forty-four million American homes, some 60 percent of the total.[37] Walter Compton, the radio announcer who introduced the Chat, told the listeners that they were about to hear FDR "discuss measures of great import to the nation and to the world. . . . it has been disclosed that the American President will speak firmly concerning national defense and aid to Great Britain." At the Chat's end, Compton announced: "Ladies and Gentlemen, you have heard a profound pronouncement by the President of the United States. This broadcast was heard over the 165 stations of the Mutual network and was broadcast via shortwave radio to South America."[38]

The address, which was the most oratorical and least conversational of the Fireside Chats, was FDR's most comprehensive and forthright statement on the world situation and the nation's role in it to date. "Roosevelt really enjoyed working on this speech," Robert Sherwood has written, "for with the political campaign over, it was the first chance he had had in months and even years to speak his mind with comparative freedom." He could finally discard "namby-pamby euphemisms in all references to the international situation. Now, for the first time, he could mention the Nazis by name. He could lash out against the apostles of appeasement. . . . He could speak plainly on the subject which was always in his mind — the disastrous folly of any attempt at a negotiated peace."[39] Secretary of War

Stimson, who had already decided that American entry into the war was inevitable, wrote in his diary shortly after FDR's Chat: "the President went as far as he could at the present time."[40]

"It is difficult," Sam Rosenman reflected twelve years after helping to write the Chat, "to put ourselves back in the atmosphere of 1940 when so many people really believed . . . that we were fully protected by the Atlantic and Pacific oceans. . . . Those who are now too young to have lived in maturity through those days will find it hard to realize how startling some of Roosevelt's statements sounded to a great many American people in 1940." Rosenman insisted that what he called Roosevelt's "bold leadership" was necessary "to awaken the American people to the danger abroad and to prepare them to meet it, even though it was still three thousand miles away."[41] It was an "awakening" that met with a mixed reaction from the American people.

JANUARY 5, 1941

Dear Sir:

I am just one of the common folks to whom you spoke last Sunday eve-ning. Some might consider me the commonest of common for, though I graduated from our local high school several years ago, at present, I am obliged to do laundry work at home while caring for my family and an in-valid mother. I have 3 daughters. One of them has a 23 yr. old husband; the other two have boyfriends aged 18 & 19. My own son is just 10. You can see from these facts I am vitally interested in this war of wars. In spite of that I hardly ever read war news or listen to war talks on the radio. Not because I think it wise to play "Osterich" but I feel if I assumed managership of this war along with my own personal worries I would soon suffer nervous col-lapse and not be of use to anyone. With this in mind I spun my Dial from station to station to tune out your speech. Wherever I tuned "there you were before me" so in spite of myself I listened and I have been thankful ever since that I did.

No ranting, no raving — no bullying, no bragging but logical, under-standable facts, told in a calm, unruffled voice that carried conviction, con-fidence and courage right into my heart. A feeling of peace and serenity stole over me. . . . I do feel that as long as "God's in His Heaven," stretching out a guiding Hand and we have God-fearing men like yourself at the head of our country, willing to be guided by Him, we'll never be hopelessly lost even though the going may be rough. I feel as though I have had a personal interview with you and I want to thank you for your Fireside Chat.

Sincerely Yours,

Mrs. Helen J. Quinn
Corning, N.Y.

DECEMBER 31, 1940

Your Excellency:

. . . George Washington made us a nation, Abraham Lincoln preserved the nation from itself — and now it is your fearful and solemn duty to pre-serve for us against the threat of international banditry the priceless heri-tage that belongs to me and my fellow countrymen and our children, won and preserved with our fathers' blood. The nation can feel safe with your hand at the helm. . . .

Respectfully yours,

James M. Saunders
Annapolis, Maryland

DECEMBER 29, 1940

Dear Sir:

While attending the Vesper Service at the Navy Y.M.C.A. this evening, a group of young Navy men and civilians, were listening to your beloved voice. . . .

I am one of a group of Navy Mother's, whose son's are serving in the finest service, or should I say Navy in the world. I am not speaking for them, but my desire to let you know we have the utmost confidence in your ability to lead us thru these trying times, that we are, in other words, putting our sons in your care, proud and happy to know that part of us, our sons, are ready and willing to protect these United States, because it belongs to them, they were born here, have married and are having their children born here, many reasons why they will not tolerate the thot of being invaded by foreign "beasts".

God gave me two fine sons, several years ago, who have given 13 and 9 years, respectively, of service in our magnificent Navy. studying, and making their way up the ladder of success, with the help of their young wives who are bearing little sons and daughters to them. I'm proud too, to have the distinction of a son serving in both the Atlantic and the Pacific Fleet.

We all know you will not send our sons to foreign lands, to be destroyed by those "beasts", but we all do know that every one of us will fight to keep them from coming here, By giving all the aid possible to Great Britain will be the one way of doing that.

. . . your assurance that we will not go to war, in the near future anyway, gives us courage to prepare for what might come later. God bless you.

Respectfully and faithfully yours,

Mrs. Ruth N. Morris
Long Beach, California

DECEMBER 27, 1940

MR. PRESIDENT: YOUR FIRESIDE CHAT SHOULD TELL THE NATION THE
PARENTS OF AMERICA WANT NO HELP TO ENGLAND THAT WILL LEAD US
INTO WAR. I HAVE TWO SONS 18 AND 20 YEARS OLD. I DO NOT WANT
THEM SLAUGHTERED IN EUROPE TO PRESERVE THE BRITISH EMPIRE
THEY GOT THAT EMPIRE THE SAME WAY HITLER IS GETTING HIS. LET US
KEEP AWAY FROM THEM ALL AND PREPARE OUR OWN DEFENSE.

J. B. NEVIN
SPRINGFIELD, ILLS.

DECEMBER 30, 1940

My dear President

I was very much disappointed in your talk last evening. It would appear
that you have about decided to repeat our disastrous experience of 1917.
You solemly promised during the campaign that no mothers son would be
sacrificed in any expeditionary force to any foreign country but if I understood you correctly you are not so sure of this now. Wilson also kept us out
of war — until after the election.

Why should we guarantee England's title to 20 percent of the earths surface. England acquired her empire thru wars, murder and rape which you
now ask us to underwrite. . . .

Lets keep our planes and munitions at home so that if England goes
down they will not be used against us.

Yours sincerely,

Louis R. Fehl
Laona, Wisconsin

DECEMBER 29, 1940

Dear Sir:

. . . I voted for you the first two times, but now I am in a confusion as to
what and whom I voted for. Was it for President of the United States or was
it for president of Great Britain and her colonies? . . .

Well, I still consider myself an American and so do many millions of other Americans, and we don't intend to do anymore fighting for Great Britain. We did enough of that in the last World War.

It so happened that I was sent to France in the last World War with the 77th division We were told to fight for democracy. England was in that war. Now, twenty-three years later, England is in another war and we have to hear the same bunk again. Cut out the bunk!

I now have two sons, and if you or Churchill or anyone else thinks that we Americans are going to have the wool pulled over our eyes, guess again. . . .

Suppose you try helping the American people with all possible aid. Try a policy of staying on our own side of the fence. Let Europe and the rest of the world look out for their side, and you will find that that policy fits verry nicely into the constitution.

I hope I have made myself clear, I remain

> A loyal American
>
> Andrew Baier
> Cicero, Illinois

DECEMBER 30, 1940

Dear Mr. President,

Your talk Sunday was what I have long been waiting for. If England is willing to do the dying and suffering to save our civilization the least we can do is to give her all possible aid. We cannot afford to let her fall.

> Yours respectfully,
>
> (Mrs.) Dorothy M. Kuehnl
> Monrovia, Calif.

DECEMBER 30, 1940

My dear Mr. President:

After hearing your speech and then reading it permit me (a Republican) to add without reserve my congratulations to you on the superb accomplishment of a stupendous task.

In speaking to persons in every walk of life in and around Philadelphia it may surprise you to learn that I find an ever increasing number, . . . who feel profoundly convinced, as I do, that it is in the best interests of the United States to declare war now on Germany and Italy. If we accept your thesis, and almost the entire nation does accept it now, that the utter defeat of Hitlerism is as vital to the United States as it is to Great Britain, that it is our fight as much as hers, then there remains no conceivable reason why her sons alone should risk their necks while we confine ourselves to the civil jobs.

I find that it is a distinctly uncomfortable feeling, and one quite uncongenial to the American turn of mind, to have someone else fighting our fight for us and bearing all the immediate risk and physical danger. . . .

Yours respectfully,

Warwick Potter Scott
Philadelphia

DECEMBER 30, 1940

DONT MEDDLE IN TREACHEROUS EUROPE. ENGLAND WOULD BETRAY US AS SHE HAS BETRAYED RUSSIA FRANCE ITALY THE ARABS AND THE JEWS. DONT FORGET WHAT THEY DID TO THE BOER REPUBLIC. WE CAN ALWAYS TAKE CARE OF OURSELVES. KEEP OUT OF WAR. WORK FOR PEACE.

FREDERICK SIEFKE
NEW YORK, N.Y.

DECEMBER 31, 1940

Dear Mr. President:

Your speech on Sunday night was an historic address. We want you to know that we are with you all the way in your expressions as to the necessity of aid to Great Britain.

Some of us who sign this letter fought in the last war in Europe; some of us have sons of military age; some of us are of military age, and all of us want peace. But peace under an Axis dominated World would be a return toward the Dark Ages — a going away from the bright light of Liberty and Freedom which has become the heritage of all of us in our Country. If fight we must, fight we will. But now, this minute, we want to give Britain everything possible for her gallant defense. Ships, guns, planes, supplies, ammunition and all the necessities for war. We are willing to lend or give all these and more. Forget any future payment — we will gladly bear our share of the burden. Britain is assailed by the noonday terror and the pestilence by night. Her women, her children, her gallant sons are giving their lives — lives which are keeping the vandals from threatening us. Lives which are giving us precious time to grow strong.

We realize that the threat of invasion of our shores is not now present. But we also realize that with Great Britain defeated, we, as a nation, can be squeezed and isolated, our economic life so restricted that our American standards would topple like ninepins — farm prices at unheard of lows — unemployment at unheard of highs — the gains of labor so long in building up swept away in a moment. These things a victorious Axis could, and would, effect in a very short time.

Lead us, Mr. President, to strength and unity. Keep telling us of the perils of this hour. Never let us forget that the things we cherish as our rights are worth sacrificing for and fighting for. If we have become soft, help us to get hard — the hardness of a strong right arm, as the Bible says. Lead us boldly, fearlessly and unerringly with the knowledge that we are behind you to a man in this crusade of righteousness.

[signed by twenty-six employees
of Chatham Manufacturing Company]
Elkin, North Carolina

JANUARY 3, 1941

Dear Sir:

The people speaking. I listened carefully to the President's speech Sunday night. . . .

Mr. secretary, that was a declaration of war. We have begun the downward rush. It was for this the President broke tradition and insisted on a third term. Before, when we went to war we were strong and solvent. Today we are weighed down by debt and the end not in sight. Before, we were a united people, today we are disunited, torn by industrial strife and by class hatreds. Before we were a productive nation, producing in abundance all we needed. Today, we are a stalled, hampered unproductive nation, — enterprise is stalled by government restrictions and by strikes. Even the aid we have given Britain was not produced in this administration. This administration has produced nothing — it has only spent the products and labors of the thrifty productive 150 years now gone and boasted of itself and maligned every force which has made us strong and might again have done so. Before, we had a wise, statesmanlike man at the head who put production and authority into the hands of the experts and left them there. Today, we have a stubborn, egoistic man who neither understands how to produce and defend, but refuses to let any one else do so.

Our destiny is upon us and we are not ready. Like France we are not ready. We have only blue prints. And we are led by unready men. It does not seem possible this could have happened to us, us who had everything, — youth, strength, liberty, rich raw materials, genius for organization.

God help us in our time of need!

> From one of the people
> Bellingham, Washington

DECEMBER 29, 1940

Dear Mr. President:

I have just finished listening to your frank and sincere radio talk. I do not doubt the honesty of your purpose and motives. However, may I say that I feel you are largely mistaken. I am not at all clear how we can save democracy and our American way of life by adopting the very methods and characteristics of fascism against which we are defending ourselves. For instance, we have adopted their technique of militarism. We are rapidly becoming an armed camp. You say that labor has no right to strike. How different is that from Nazism?? In fact, it is my contention that war leads us rapidly into fascism not rapidly away from it!

Furthermore, I regret to see that you have lost much of your old prophetic vision and courage. It would seem that events have warped your thinking and basic analysis of the trend of the times. Can you not see that all this conflict is the attempt of an outworn capitalism to save itself? That form of economic organisation can no more take us down the intricate modern industrial road than can the old-fashioned buggy take us down Fifth Ave., New York City. You have made valiant attempts to make it work and have made some small progres. But we are still not solving the problem of meeting the needs of the majority of our people. We have the resources to make this a great nation. But this cannot be done by tuning our industry to production of goods which are made for destruction!

To my way of thinking there is only one sure way to future security and peace for our country and the world. That is — for us to work out an American solution of our economic system based, not on profit but on service and brotherhood. This is Christian to me. . . .

Sincerely yours,

James K. Morse, Ph.D.
Hackensack, N.J.

DECEMBER 30, 1940

Dear Mr. President:

I want to express my deep appreciation of your magnificent address yesterday evening. . . .

I appreciate also particularly the statement that labor's rights will be protected. The test of democracy is not in the wealth of the wealthy but in the liberties and character of the common people. We know that abuse by labor of labor's privileges will not and must not be tolerated, but there are plenty of men who for selfish purposes would use the emergency as an excuse to destroy the social gains which you more than any other man have helped to win and which they feel hinder their lust for power. . . .

Yours sincerely,

Robert Weston
Schenectady, N.Y.

DECEMBER 31, 1940

Dear Sir:

We listened to your speech over the radio and are very much afraid such talk will get us into war. We are the parents of five sons and have told them to give the last drop of their blood in defense of their country but to refuse to leave these shores to fight the battles of European countries. All the people we know feel the same so you might have some difficulty in raising an army to send so would advise you to be more careful about antagonising those nations now at war. You seem to forget that we are not all of English descent, many of us are of German descent, and while we have no admiration for Hitler or any other dictator, our hearts sympathize with the sufferings of the German people as well as the English people. We would admire you more had you, as the head of a great nation, tried to make peace instead of calling ugly names and thus arousing hate toward this country.

Very Truly,

George Messinger
Martha Messinger
Bowmansville, N.Y.

DECEMBER 30, 1940

Dear Honorable President F. D. Roosevelt:

Conspicuous, in your forceful fire-side chat, was the minus-quantity of condemnation for the Christian-killing atheistic leader of Communist Russia. May I ask you dear Mr. President if you think that Russia is good company for our United States to keep? You pledge our people to fight against a band of out-law nations, — fine!, but why fight or help to fight one band, when the other band is free to help the first and then deal Christian Civilization a death blow by taking all the spoils of the whole world including our own beloved country!?

... Russia is our arch-enemy and the greatest force for disorder in the world to-day. Who is helping the Nazi now? Who egged Germany on to attack Poland, and thus to get the British to declare war!? If you wish to be consistent, dear Mr. President, why not put Russia in the same category as you put Germany and the Axis nations!!?

... I am for stopping Russia immediately, by war if no other way. We have plenty of excuses to declare war right now. If Russia were in our hands we could tell Germany where to jump and Japan would string along like a good boy. In a military way we could win a war with Russia quicker and more easily than from any other Eastern Hemisphere power. At present I am figuring out a campaign that could be followed to a successful end, putting our Armies east of Germany and in a position where you, dear Mr. President could tell the leader of the Nazi where to go. I was a former first-class private in Co. A. 163 Infantry, National Guard; and, so, you see I have 'some' training in military thought. Here is for fighting all Satanic-controlled nations with the help of God and the Holy Angels and not just one gang. . . .

Faithfully,

John B. Schmitz
Elizabeth, N.J.

DECEMBER 29, 1940

Dear Mr. President,

I am going to address my remarks as though you were to actually read this, although I am certain it will never reach you.

As I sat listening to your talk tonight, realizing how much hope and courage it was bringing to some people, I was so deeply moved by the crystal clear presentation of our situation today, together with the sincerity and honesty of your picturization, that I feel obliged to try in a small way to convey to you the faith and hope I know the great masses of we Americans have placed and shall continue to hold in you.

What nation could fail to be great with a leadership such as this!

I have just passed my twenty-second birthday and am the holder of a low draft number. I expect to be in service very shortly and I am proud to have this privilage — humbly grateful to God that I am an American.

Respectfully yours,

David W. Flanzbaum
Somerville, New Jersey

DECEMBER 31, 1940

Most Wisest. And Most Loveing President.

Mr. Franklin Delano Roosevelt. I am so very glad to have so much Love in my heart for you to let you know just how just how Great your speech was

Sunday night that you made to the Whole World for Our Great Nation. Our Great President Everyone in Our Country should stand hard By your side. Because you are a Presidint for the Rich for the Poor. For the White Man. And the Black Man Too. Please except this letter from a Poor Colored Man that Loves you Dear to my heart. Because you have Done so much for Our Nation. . . . I want to Thank you for all these Buildings that you have put in Tallahassee. I want to Thank you again for that gieft for Our Colored College The A. & M. College. I shall always Prove True to Our God. And Our Country. Even if it should Cost me my Life. May the God of Heaven Prolong your Life and Bless you. And your whole Family always.

from a True. And Loveing Friend,

William Washington Jr.
Tallahassee, Fla.

DECEMBER 29, 1940

My dear Mr. President:

You have just concluded taking the American people into your confidence, and I, as one who will be called upon to make sacrifices, as well as 130,000,000 and some odd number of American citizens, naturally missed any reference to the one third of the ill fed and ill clad who are still among us. Can you vision what a happy and united land the United States of America would be today if the same concern had been shown them as is now being shown Great Britain? The billions of dollars being loaned or given, which, we do not know but can quite accurately guess, could much more profitably be spent to make this a truly democratic and united nation and would make conscription unnecessary.

Believe me when I say I am opposed to any action which will further involve us in a foreign war and until I am convinced that the foreign policy of this country is not rapidly taking us into this war I shall utilize my fundamental rights as an American citizen to most vigorously disagree and oppose you.

Respectfully yours

Paul F. Axelson
Hermosa Beach, Cal.

DECEMBER 30, 1940

Dear Mr. President:

. . . Most of my business and personal acquaintances have felt during the past 8 years that your contradictory speeches and acts have not been for the good of the country as a whole, but for political expediency only. Now you have an opportunity to prove your sincerity.

In your "Fireside Chat" last evening you told the most of us what we had to do to prepare for total defense. You told industry, capital, Government employees and the people, but why did you omit similarly emphatic instructions to labor and executives of the Government. Isn't it about time to:

Abandon your WPA and CCC so men will have an incentive to go to work?

Modify your Wage and Hour Law and Wagner Act so men can go to work?

Discontinue your subsidies to AAA, REA, PDQ and XYZ so that the country can afford defense?

You can't make a country strong by continuing to promote class hatred, expand the bureaucracy of Government and juggle alphabetical soup with your right hand and try to manufacture bombs and ships with your left hand. Your personal, political and economic future is even more at stake than that of some of the rest of us. Here is a chance for you to save yourself and at the same time prove your integrity and ability to the 130 odd million people of this United States of America which still is the best country on earth.

Can we count on you now?

Yours respectfully,

Russel D. Baker
Decorah, Iowa

*   *   *

Dear President;

I heard your speech last night and am with you a hundred percent on all you say.

We must get air planes, guns, tanks, and other war equipment to England and quickly I think. And if "Big Business" will not produce as it should, then I say you — our government — should take over their plants and operate them ourselves in the interest of self protection.

I think that the Industrial World has "Held out on you" long enough and if they are not ready to go, lets get the production from their plants just the same. . . .

I am yours for greater social and other progress,

Frank Holcombe
Oneonta, Ala.

DECEMBER 30, 1940

Honorable Sir: —

Your radio speech of yesterday certainly will find the American people in a very disturbed state of mind.

You speak of labor forgoing the right to strike and capital giving up the lockout. Without the right to strike Labor is deprived of the only weapon that management understands.

Labor uses the strike weapon in industrial disputes only as a last resort. Workers do not relish the idea of coming home to hungry children and a tired wife and telling them they are going to strike.

When defense contracts are given to enemies of labor like Henry Ford what can labor hope for from "impartial" labor arbitration boards?

Yours truly

John S. Quinton
New York, N.Y.

JANUARY 2, 1941

Your excellency:

I'll bet the boys here at the plant would call me plain screwy if I told them that I had written the President of the United States, but I don't believe I am, particularily when I am writing him to express my admiration of your address the other evening and for you yourself.

I'll tell you, Mr. President, I cast my ballot for Mr. Wilkie and I am a Republican what's more, but I'll wager there isn't a day goes by now that I don't thank God you were elected.

My mother who voted for you despite the arguments against it on the part of my editor father, is constantly smiling, intimating to my father by raised eyebrows, that perhaps he figures she had a right smart idea at that when she voted for you.

And Mr. President, knowing my father as I do, there's not a man in our America today who is prouder of you as "his" president than Dad.

Thank you sir for all that you have done, all that you are striving to do and for telling the rest of the world in so many words, "Boys, there's no bluffing in this poker game".

Sincerely,

MacLeod Williams
Dunkirk, N.Y.

DECEMBER 30, 1940

Dear President Roosevelt:

I am a young woman intelligent and well bred, I listened to your last broad cast in which you called upon us all to help with the defense program and I am most willing. . . . Let me assure you that there are still millions of us red blooded Americans who are willing to lay down our lives and even the lives that we love, for our country and freedom. We understand that there is no compromise with dictators; with a nazi or facist world, no freedom. I am offering you and my government my services for whatever they are worth and I can make them <u>ten</u> times their usual worth for defense. Just call on me.

Ann Patton Brown
St. Louis, Mo.

P.S. God bless Eleanor, too.

DECEMBER 30, 1940

Dear Mr. President:

. . . To-day the day after your wonderful speech, I am still elated by it. There is suddenly hope again for all of us, especially for us younger men. We all must follow your course which is the only possible one. . . .

Hitler's great success was partly due to the fact that he challenged the youth of his country; he gave them tasks to master, tasks which we regard as criminal, but which gave content to their empty lives. I wish you too would give us tasks, tasks for a democratic nation and for freedom of the spirit, so that we can master them individually or with others. You talked to the workers and to the engineers and to the managers of the factories — but others are burning too to help you in this gigantic fight.

Most sincerely

Richard Ettinghausen
Ann Arbor, Michigan

DECEMBER 29, 1940

Dear sir:

I am colored & have listened to your message today. Altho I am colored & am out of the conscription age at present, you will find me ready to serve anytime men of my age are needed, either in peace or in war.

Respectfully

Chas. Fisher
Chicago, Ill.

DECEMBER [1940]

Dear Mr. President,

Fully aware that millions of messages will pour into the White House after your Fireside Chat, and that mine is only one very small voice, I must yet give utterance to that which will no longer be constrained.

Bravo, Mr. President!

... We have four sons. If they are not man enough, each one of them, to fight for that which this glorious land gives to the children of those who have sought its shores, — who sacrificed all they held dear, all that was familiar and beloved, their background, the companionship of relatives and friends, their very identity, to gain that which America held out — they are not worthy of it!

And we, who have grown up in Europe, with its class hatred, its stiffling conservatism, its inhibitions, its inbred narrowness, we wonder whether they realize to what they were born. . . .

(Mrs. M.) Gertrude E. Hettinga
Vicksburg, Mich.

DECEMBER 30, 1940

Sir: —

Having listened to your speech of Dec. 29th most carefully, I, (with millions of other mothers I am sure), am filled with horror and dread, that you are surely and unremittedly driving us into a war, that is not of our making.

We have broken almost every law of neutrality that ever existed and if the tables were turned and Italy and Germany had done to us, what we have insistently and continuously done against them, we would have declared war against them long ago.

Why all this solicitation for England? Why not America first, last and always? We haven't even begun to prepare ourselves for defense!

What has England ever done for us, that we owe her such enormous consideration? And what would England do for us, should we ever cry for help?

I am a widow with one son, and he is all the world to me. If war came to our shores, my son, would fight for his country, with the best of them; but I absolutely refuse to sanction any move that might mean his leaving the United States to fight the battles of foreign countries. . . .

Yours most respectfully

(Mrs. F. Wm.) Lisette M. Wessel
New York, N.Y.

JANUARY 2, 1941

Dear Mr. President:

. . . I am 65 years old and never have written a poem, but was inspired to write the enclosed after listening to you.

Maybe you could make use of it. I have thought if copies were printed and placed in the industrial plants of the Country, it might inspire the men to work faster and more cheerfully. . . .

Respectfully yours,

(Mrs) Cecilia Blade DuBois
Chepinanoxet, R.I.

THE GOOD OLD U.S.A.

CHORUS

Now, come all you Irishmen, you Scotchmen and Swedes,
     All pull together, your Country's in need
Portugese, Polish, Italians and Danes,
     Austrians, Germans and Spaniards from Spain,
English, Norwegians, Canadians and Turks
     All get together, we've got lots of work
Finnish and Russians, Frenchmen and Chezs,
     Hungarians, Romanians, Chinese and Japs,
Dutch and Bulgarians, Albanians, and Greeks
     Shoulder to shoulder we'll stop up the leaks
Belgiums, Australians, Indians and Jews
     Egyptians, Ethiopians, Africans, too
Why should we worry, with such an array
     From the old melting pot of the good U.S.A.

DECEMBER 30, 1940

Dear Mr. President,

Your fireside talk on Sunday evening made us very happy. . . . My husband and I are both born in Germany, but for about 25 years we are proud and thankful American citizens. We feel the shame of our old homeland deeply and hope and pray, that one day, over there the people will return to reason, to religion and humanity. We are a little worried over the Nazi's in this country, but we have confidence that our government is well informed and will take care of the situation before too much harm is done. God bless you, Mr. President!

Luise Feistel
New York, N.Y.

DECEMBER 29, 1940

Dear Mr President.

I have just listened to your speech, & I want you to know, you have my full support. . . . I feel we should not, let the mad Dictators, of Germany & Italy, win, even if we have to send troops, to prevent it. Neutrality or no neutrality, come what may. . . .

In 1923, I married a Girl of German parentage her folks had come to the U.S. direct from Germany. Since 1923, I have been closely associated, with people's of German decest. my best friends, my farm neighbors, all most with out exception are German. I am sorry to say, 95 per cent of them are for Hitler & Nazi Germany.

It is not all uncommon to hear of a father of German boys, state his sons, can go to jail, before they will be drafted for military training. I know, what I am talking about, for I've lived around Ricketts, Schleswig, & Charter Oak, Iowa since the last world war. I say such people do not represent, the real American viewpoint, & no attention should be paid to their pleas for America to stay Neutral. Many letters are written to represenitives & senators by these German people, urging them to keep this country out of war, when there real, objective, is by so doing, help Germany! . . .

Yours Truly.

J. D. Chedester
Mapleton, Iowa

DECEMBER 29, 1940

My Dear Mr. President:

I sat by my radio this evening listening to your splendid talk to our beloved America. It was splendid as far as it went but it did not go half far enough. Of what use is any talk or any plan that deliberately leaves God out of the picture? I waited breathlessly to hear you give a call to your people to turn to God to direct this nation, and the people of Great Britain.

Surely you leaders must know by this time that He is the Councellor, and the government is upon His shoulder and all that will not embrace this blessed Truth and shout it from the house top (or radio) is undone!

. . . If every gun and means of defense were spiked with a prayer for Divine help and guidance as King David asked before he went to battle, we would win and save Christianity for the world. But it has to be on God's plan, led by God-men and God-women. Nothing else will eventually prevail for ourselves and our children's children to come. In His Name,

Yours very respectfully,

(Mrs.) Maude I. Armstrong
Roseville, Mich.

DECEMBER 30, 1940

NINETEEN HUNDRED YEARS OR MORE AGO AN ANGEL FROM HEAVEN SPOKE TO THE SHEPHERDS ON DECEMBER 25TH AT BETHLEHEM SUNDAY EVENING DECEMBER 29TH 830 PM 1940 A VOICE FROM THE HEAVENS SPOKE A SECOND SAVIOUR OF MANKIND HE IS FRANKLIN D ROOSEVELT PRESIDENT OF THE UNITED STATES.

THE HOLLEARING FAMILY
ST. LOUIS, MO.

JANUARY 8, 1941

My dear Mr. President:

I am a Quaker by tradition and rearing and you know what that means as regards my attitude toward war. Yet I feel that I must thank you for your fire side chat of Sunday evening, December 29th and also for your message to congress on January 6th.

The time has long since passed when we must all realize that bombs cannot be answered with kind words. And much as we should like to believe that "A soft answer turneth away wrath," events of the past years have abundantly proved that such is not the case.

. . . I say this even though I have a son, twenty-two who might be among the first to be called upon to defend his country should the need arise. Should such need arise, I would want him to have every physical means at his disposal as well as deep spiritual conviction that he is doing the right as "God gives him to see the right." . . .

Sincerely yours,

Mrs. David Stevenson
Downers Grove, Ill.

DECEMBER 29, 1940

My dear Mr. Roosevelt: — You made a notable speech to-night; one that will go down in history as truly as has the Emancipation Proclamation done. . . . There is only one thing for which I regret our mildness, our humanity, our generosity towards any members of Bunds, or 5th columns, or Coughlinites et cetera. If we know who they are, why waste time on them. Line them up before a firing squad, and such nonsense will soon stop. I well know that this isn't the American way; but neither are these normal times. Don't get the idea that I'm a woman who loves force. I'm an old (in my 78th year) frail woman who loves peace, brotherly love, being a good neighbor, and above all who thanks God that she is an American. . . .

Very cordially yours

Anna G. Baer
Chicago, Illinois

DECEMBER 30, 1940

Dear President: —

I have heard your radio-speech last night appealing to the peoples of our grand and glorious united States for "National Defense." . . . We should do the utmost to aid and extend credit to England.

After all; England is fighting our battle as well as their's to save civilization and democracies of the world. . . . I would rather defend and die for the only flag and that is the American flag which stood the test for one hundred and sixty four years. The national Congress should make a law with teeth in it not loop-holes, to outlaw the Communist party or any other party which is directed by foreign Governments. We dont need them here and that foreign'isms do bawled out like a grown calf when they get into trouble. They squawk about the bill of right freedom of speech, liberty and so on. Those class of peoples are a menace and a pest to our community. They give you a pain in the neck. Get them out of here if they dont like our form of government. . . .

I am just an ordinary native Oklahoma Indian who did his part twenty-two years ago with the famous Fourth Division Battery "B" 16th Field Artillery. I received my education at Chilocco Indian school in Kay County, Oklahoma. I am willing to do my part again if it is necessary. I am as ever your humble servant and friend.

Yours respectfully

John B. Pambogo
Oklahoma City, Oklahoma

DECEMBER 30, 1940

Dear Presidend Roosevelt. I am a girl of seven. My name is Joan Bagnel. I heard your Speech Sunday night I liked It to. I have two guns I want to give one to you.

Joan Bagnel
[no address]

* * *

Dear Mr. Roosevelt

I am just writing you a few lines to tell you What a wonderful thing you are doing. I wish I could join the army. My addrass is on the front of the letter if you want some of the steel that I have you may write me back.

My name is Harold Willis I am 8 years old.
[no address]

DECEMBER 29, 1940

Dear Mr. Roosevelt:

I am only twelve years old and I am in the seventh grade. The reason I am writing this letter is because we have to write one in school and send it to someone so I am sending mine to you.

Our gang listened to your fireside chat tonight and we really enjoyed it. . . .

We don't want war, if we did go to war then the boys in our gang would have to go in about six years but if you think we should, Mr. Roosevelt we are ready.

You'r right when you say that we'll give all we can spare to England but the only thing thats wrong is that the Nasis will bomb our ships carrying supplys and I think that we should send them by submarine.

I hope that I haven't taken up to much of your time and you must hurry and write to me. Please do, nobody has ever recieved a personal letter from you and I surely will be thrilled to get one from you.

Your friend,

Elaine Albred
Provo, Utah

DECEMBER 30, 1940

Dear President Roosevelt,

I am an American girl of fourteen. I am in Junior High School of Marlow. I heard your speech on December 29, 1940; and so I decided to write to you. I am very intrested in the problems of the United States and how we can solve these problems.

I am proud that I am an American; everyone should be proud of the fact that they are an American. It is not every person who can talk freely, & vote as they wish. It makes me very angry to hear Americans talk about things that they don't have. God gave them something worth more than all the riches of the earth. "American Citizenship."

My father fought in the last world war and is now a disable veteran. I had to give him up three years ago because he was insane. We had lived in Fort Sill for quiet a while. We hated to move off that Post because we loved the Army life. But we kept up our chins; and let me tell you this my mother is the best pal and manager there is in the world. She kept us with food and clothes till the bill was passed to give the World War Veterans a check every month. She has money left over every month; And it's too bad other people don't try to save; for if they would, the United States would have a lot more than they do.

I hope that soon people will relize that they are better off than they think they are; and I know their going to keep their chins up and fight for liberty. I'll keep my chin up for the good old U.S.A. and for you.

A citizen of the U.S.A. and friend to you

Mary Cecil Dukes
Marlow, Oklahoma

PS: Write too me when you have time.

DECEMBER 29, 1940

Dear President Roosevelt:

Your fire-side chat on national defense, which I heard a few moments ago, was in my opinion the strongest speech you have ever made. You evaded no issues, pulled no punches, but pointed precisely the alternatives which the future offers.

I hope your speech does not mean war for this country, yet if it does then most of us are ready. A proclamation of full emergency is greatly needed, in order to underline the urgent demands on us of all possible aid to England. All ships idle in our ports should be lent to England for the duration; all financial aid required by England should be advanced without haggling over the question of loan or gift. You have identified, as any clear-sighted person must identify, England's defense with our own.

No one knows to what extent the next Congress will support you. All too often you and your advisers and most of the nation have been far ahead of Congress in grasping situations and in preparing to cope with them.

So many of us, who are old enough to remember, prefer to forget that in 1919 the die of a cynical future was cast by the American Senate, when it told the world, then looking to us as its saviour, that it must get along without us as best it could. Now England alone holds the precipice, which so narrowly separates us from the world we told to get along without us. Thus a tide in the affairs of men, sweeping away all values we have known, has turned full cycle upon us. Isolation is not splendid, it is not even sane; I never thought it was. It is a mythos fit only for the moon.

Sincerely yours,

C. F. DeGaris, M.D.
Oklahoma City, Oklahoma

AN UNLIMITED NATIONAL
EMERGENCY: MAY 27, 1941

IN THE FIVE MONTHS between Roosevelt's final Fireside Chat of 1940 and his first one of 1941, the Nazi war machine continued to roll into Greece, Yugoslavia, and North Africa and maintained the punishing air and sea war against England. FDR accordingly escalated his support of Germany's opponents. In the eyes of many, the President's actions in 1940 and 1941 brought him decisively across the line of neutrality into the circle of the belligerents. "The transfer to Great Britain of fifty American warships," Winston Churchill later reflected, "was a decidedly unneutral Act. It would, according to all the standards of history, have justified the German Government in declaring war upon them. . . . It was the first of a long succession of increasingly unneutral acts in the Atlantic which were of the utmost service to us." "All the world," Churchill added, "understood the significance of the gesture."[42]

Certainly, the opponents of intervention in the United States understood the significance very clearly. FDR's increasingly overt Allied sympathies and his frequently expressed hostility to the Axis — especially Nazi Germany — helped generate organized opposition, in particular the creation of the America First Committee in the summer of 1940. Led by General Robert E. Wood, head of Sears, Roebuck, and other conservative Midwestern businessmen, and soon featuring Charles Lindbergh as its best known and most effective proselytizer, by early 1941 America First had some 450 chapters and 850,000 members, including such luminaries as Teddy Roosevelt's daughter Alice Roosevelt Longworth, the aviator Edward Rickenbacker, the author Kathleen Norris, and the actress Lillian Gish.

It was in the face of this formidable opposition and its strong contingent of congressional isolationists, among whom were Midwestern progressives who had supported the President's domestic reform, that FDR had to act. His first impulse concerning the transfer of fifty American destroyers to Britain in return for bases in Newfoundland and the British West Indies in September 1940, for example, had been to pursue it through legislation, but he soon realized the impossibility of that avenue and resorted reluctantly to executive fiat. That road was not open to Roosevelt when he decided to implement his plan of lending or leasing Britain the implements of war, which could be financed only through congressional appropriations. In his Annual Message, delivered to Congress on January 16, 1941, the President announced his intention of presenting Congress with a lend-lease bill. He asked Congress to join him in saying to the democracies resisting aggression: "We Americans are vitally concerned in your defense of freedom. . . . We shall send you, in ever-increasing numbers, ships, planes, tanks, guns. This is our purpose and our pledge." He also reiterated the points he had made in his last two Fireside Chats: that "this is no time for any of us to stop thinking about the social and economic problems which are the root cause of the social revolution which is today a supreme factor in the world." The American people, he insisted, expected certain "simple, basic things":

> Equality of opportunity for youth and for others.
> Jobs for those who can work. Security for those who need it.
> The ending of special privilege for the few. The preservation
> of civil liberties for all.
> The enjoyment of the fruits of scientific progress in a wider
> and constantly rising standard of living.

Building on these domestic goals, the President, in phrases that soon became woven into American popular culture, articulated his vision of the world he wanted to emerge from the carnage. That world, he proclaimed, would be founded "upon four essential human freedoms."

> The first is freedom of speech and expression — everywhere
> in the world.
> The second is freedom of every person to worship God in
> his own way — everywhere in the world.
> The third is freedom from want . . . which will secure to
> every nation a healthy peacetime life for its inhabitants —
> everywhere in the world.
> The fourth is freedom from fear . . . a world-wide reduction
> of armaments to such a point and in such a thorough fashion
> that no nation will be in a position to commit an act of physical
> aggression against any neighbor — anywhere in the world.[43]

In articulating both his domestic and global ideals, and placing the latter in the simple, easily grasped and remembered "Four Freedoms," FDR was

clearly endeavoring to supplement the nation's and the hemisphere's practical need for security against Axis aggression (which thus far had been his
emphasis) with a vision of the kind of world "attainable in our own time
and generation." It was still another attempt to persuade the American people to see the current wars in Europe and Asia in larger perspective.

There were certainly tangible indications that he was succeeding, as evidenced by the polls and his successful campaign for the Lend-Lease Act.
In March 1941, the American Institute of Public Opinion found that 48 percent of those it queried thought the most important policy we could pursue
during the next few decades would be to take the lead in improving the
world, while only 24 percent thought we should primarily concentrate on
home problems. The Office of Public Opinion Research found that from
May 1940 to November 1941 the number of people who were willing to aid
Britain even if it involved the risk of getting into the war ourselves grew
from slightly over 30 percent to over 70 percent. Underlying this change
was a growing sense of involvement. Three-quarters of those willing to aid
Britain regardless of consequences were convinced by November 1941 that
if Germany defeated England they would attack us. Eighty-five percent felt
that if Hitler won, "he will be much harder to deal with than England ever
was." Sixty-eight percent told Gallup pollsters that "our country's future
safety depends on England winning this war." Polls by the American Institute of Public Opinion and the Office of Public Opinion Research found
that the last date on which a majority of Americans felt we could avoid
involvement in the war was October 1940. By March of 1941, more than 80
percent of those polled believed the United States would "go into the war
in Europe."[44]

These changing attitudes helped pave the way for the successful passage
of FDR's Lend-Lease Act. Indeed, 68 percent of those asked by Gallup between January 11 and 17, 1941, whether we should lease England war materials if they couldn't afford to buy them, answered in the affirmative, and a
month later Gallup pollsters found 59 percent in favor of the Lend-Lease
Act.[45] The debate over the bill was heated, with Senator Burton Wheeler
of Montana asserting that Lend-Lease was "the New Deal's triple A foreign
policy; it will plow under every fourth American boy." FDR responded
by calling Wheeler's remark "untruthful," "dastardly," and "unpatriotic."
"Quote me on that," he angrily told reporters. "That really is the rottenest
thing that has been said in public life in my generation." Charles Lindbergh
recited the isolationist case before Congress, testifying that the United

States could not save England in any event and did not need to since air power made the Western Hemisphere invulnerable to conquest by Germany, even if Germany and Japan came to command all of Europe and the oceans. "We are strong enough in this nation and this hemisphere to maintain our own way of life," he insisted. President Robert Hutchins of the University of Chicago predicted that with the advent of Lend-Lease "the American people are about to commit suicide." Prime Minister Churchill got into the act in a February radio address in which he assured the American people somewhat disingenuously that England was not requesting that America send its soldiers to Europe. "We do not need them this year, nor next year; nor any year that I can foresee." What was needed was an immense and continuous supply of war materials. "Give us the tools," he implored the American people, "and we will finish the job."[46]

On March 11, 1941, Congress passed and the President signed the Lend-Lease Act. "There are not many dates in the history of the world as important as that one," Sam Rosenman was to write in his autobiography a decade later.[47] Within minutes of his signing the bill, the President wrote, "army and navy war materials were speeding on their way to Great Britain and Greece."[48] Congress initially appropriated seven billion dollars and authorized the President to "sell, transfer title to, exchange, lease, lend or otherwise dispose of" war materials to "any country whose defense the President deems vital to the defense of the United States."*

Yet, having won this battle, and the enormous discretionary power the Lend-Lease Act gave him, the President seemed to lose direction. He took a number of further steps, such as placing Greenland under American protection, allowing unarmed American merchant ships to carry supplies to Britain, permitting British ships to be repaired in American docks and British pilots to be trained in American bases. But he hesitated to allow American naval and air forces to escort British convoys between the United States and England even though Secretary of the Treasury Henry Morgenthau, Secretary of War Henry Stimson, Secretary of the Navy Frank Knox, and Secretary of the Interior Harold Ickes felt such a step was essential if Lend-Lease was to be effective. What was the point of allowing England to

---

*By the end of World War Two, the United States had distributed approximately forty-eight billion dollars in material aid to its allies through the Lend-Lease Act, with Great Britain receiving between thirteen and twenty billion and the Soviet Union between nine and ten billion dollars.

lease or borrow the goods it needed, they asked, without also ensuring that the supplies reached England and British forces in Africa? "The President," Morgenthau wrote in his diary, "said that public opinion was not yet ready for the United States to convoy ships . . . he seemed to be still waiting and not ready to go ahead on 'all out aid for England.'" At a Cabinet meeting the week before he was to deliver his May Fireside Chat, the President was urged to use the occasion to announce further action to aid Britain against the increasingly effective submarine attacks on its shipping. "I am not willing to take the first shot," he responded. "So," Harold Ickes commented in his diary, "it seems that he is still waiting for the Germans to create an 'incident.'" Morgenthau also took note of this. He wrote that FDR had said "that he thought something might happen at any time, and I gather that he wanted to be pushed into the war rather than lead us into it." On May 17, according to Morgenthau, the President actually told him: "I am waiting to be pushed into this situation."[49]

While slightly over half of the respondents to Gallup polls in May agreed that the U.S. Navy should guard ships transporting arms to Britain, 80 percent continued to oppose going to war. Only 20 percent of those polled in May felt the United States hadn't gone far enough in helping Britain, 21 percent thought we had gone too far, and 59 percent thought the level of our help was "about right." At the same time, when people were asked, "Would you rather see Britain surrender to Germany than have the United States go into the war?" 62 percent said no.[50] The signals from the people continued to be mixed, and FDR's actions reflected this ambivalence. "I think that both the President and Hopkins are groping as to what to do," Morgenthau confided to his diary. "They feel something has to be done but don't know just what. Hopkins . . . thinks the President is loath to get us into this war, and he would rather follow public opinion than to lead it."[51] The President's strategy of waiting for one of the Axis powers to take the decisive step did not sit well with many members of his Cabinet. "I find a growing discontent with the President's lack of leadership," Ickes wrote on May 10. "He still has the country if he will take it and lead it. But he won't have it very much longer unless he does something . . . if I could have looked this far ahead and seen an inactive and uninspiring President, I would not have supported Roosevelt for a third term."[52] When at one Cabinet meeting FDR portrayed increased naval and air patrols against German submarines as "a step forward," Secretary of War Stimson exclaimed: "Well, I hope you will keep on walking, Mr. President. Keep on walking."[53]

In the face of the President's inability or unwillingness to take the decisive actions they advocated, several of his advisers urged him, at the very
least, to declare a state of national emergency during his Fireside Chat.[54]
FDR followed this advice in his May 27 Chat delivered in the East Room of
the White House before a large audience of ambassadors and ministers
from all the nations of the Western Hemisphere.* In the final paragraphs of
his talk, the President announced: "I have tonight issued a proclamation
that an unlimited national emergency exists and requires the strengthening
of our defense to the extreme limit of our national power and authority." In
spite of this declaration, the full significance and effects of which he did not
explain, the bulk of his Chat reflected his uncertainty about what course
to follow.[55]

Indeed, his Chat was largely more of the same things he had been saying
in 1940 and 1941, delivered, like his last Chat, in a more formal oratorical
style than had been the norm. Again he stressed the fact that the European
war was in fact a *world* war: "The war is approaching the brink of the Western Hemisphere itself. It is coming very close to home." Again he tried to
demonstrate that if the Nazis were not stopped they would soon threaten
"the ultimate safety of the continental United States itself," and went into
such detail that one of his advisers characterized the Chat as "calculated to
scare the daylights out of everyone."[56] Again he stressed the consequences
of a Nazi victory over England, which would force us to "curtail the funds
we could spend on education, on housing, on public works, on flood control, on health" and become a warrior nation, "permanently pouring our
resources into armaments; and, year in and year out, standing day and
night watch against the destruction of our cities." Again he stressed the
threat to American values and the belief in the dignity of the human being,
and asked: "Will our children, too, wander off, goose-stepping in search of
new gods?" Again he stressed that American rearmament was only for purposes of defense, but he explained how complicated the concept of defense
was in the modern world. Some think that we are not attacked until bombs
actually drop on the streets of our cities. "But they are simply shutting their

---

*The President had been scheduled to address the Pan American Union two
weeks earlier but had to cancel because of illness. The representatives of the member nations of the Union and their families were instead invited to his Fireside Chat
and to a dinner reception that followed it. This was the only one of FDR's Fireside
Chats delivered with so large a group in attendance.

eyes. . . . When your enemy comes at you in a tank or a bombing plane, if you hold your fire until you see the whites of his eyes, you will never know what hit you. Our Bunker Hill of tomorrow may be several thousand miles from Boston, Massachusetts."

Again he emphasized the importance of the freedom of the seas throughout American history and announced: "We shall actively resist [Hitler's] every attempt to gain control of the seas. We insist upon the vital importance of keeping Hitlerism away from any point in the world which could be used or would be used as a base of attack against the Americas." Again he stressed how imperative it was to aid England and revealed for the first time that "the present rate of Nazi sinkings of merchant ships is more than three times as high as the capacity of British shipyards to replace them; it is more than twice the combined British and American output of merchant ships today." He seemed to hold out hope for those advocating that American convoys protect British shipping by proclaiming: "Our patrols are helping now to insure delivery of the needed supplies to Britain. All additional measures necessary to deliver the goods will be taken."*

Again he criticized those "who say that we must preserve peace at any price," and condemned "the defeatist forebodings" of "the Bundists, the Fascists, and Communists, and every group devoted to bigotry and racial and religious intolerance." Again he asked for unity at home and for peace between capital and labor. "Articles of defense must have undisputed right of way in every industrial plant in the country." He concluded this by now familiar litany on a note of resolution:

> We reassert the ancient American doctrine of freedom of the seas.
>
> We reassert the solidarity of the twenty-one American Republics and the Dominion of Canada in the preservation of the independence of the hemisphere.
>
> We have pledged material support to the other democracies of the world — and we will fulfill that pledge.
>
> We in the Americas will decide for ourselves whether, and when, and where, our American interests are attacked or our security threatened.

---

*At a press conference the next day, the President explicitly denied that he planned to use the American navy to escort ships carrying war materials to Britain.

We are placing our armed forces in strategic military position.

We will not hesitate to use our armed forces to repel attack.

We reassert our abiding faith in the vitality of our constitutional republic as a perpetual home of freedom, of tolerance, and of devotion to the word of God.

But if FDR said little that was new, he spoke at a time when there was an increased sense of urgency among the American people, which created a more intense interest in his Chat than even he could have anticipated. He was heard in some 70 percent of the homes in the United States and attracted a total audience of eighty-five million people.[57] According to the press, the nation's largest city virtually came to a standstill while FDR spoke. There was scant traffic in Times Square; crowds gathered around taxicabs and storefronts to hear the address; the New York Telephone Company reported that phone calls dropped 50 percent; jukeboxes in bars and restaurants fell silent as bartenders, waiters, and customers listened to the President; at movie theaters audiences "walked out" on the films to assemble in theater lobbies where the Chat was broadcast; at the Polo Grounds the game between the New York Giants and the Boston Braves, tied one to one after seven innings, was halted while the ball players and seventeen thousand fans spent the next forty-five minutes listening to the President, before the game was completed.[58]

Secretary Ickes was one of the tens of millions listening to the Chat on the radio and commented afterward that the President "spoke well, with good delivery. . . . But there was no lift to his speech. It was not the kind of speech that I hoped he would make. . . . My own feeling still is that the President has not aroused the country; has not really sounded the bell."[59] FDR received a markedly different initial response from the American people. Robert Sherwood, who had helped write the Chat, remained at the White House during its broadcast and the dinner that followed. Just before his departure, he went to the President's bedroom to say goodnight: "He was in bed surrounded with telegrams. There must have been a thousand or more of them. He had looked at them all." "They're ninety-five percent favorable," the President told Sherwood. "And I figured I'd be lucky to get an even break on this speech."[60]

As the letters below demonstrate, there was certainly ample and heated opposition to the direction the President was moving in. And Ickes was correct in perceiving no strategic core to FDR's Chat, no clear plan of action. What Ickes seems to have seen less clearly than many of those in Roosevelt's vast audience was the Chat's ideological center. Toward the end of his address, FDR proclaimed: "We will not accept a Hitler dominated world. And we will not accept a world, like the post-war world of the 1920's, in which the seeds of Hitlerism can again be planted and allowed to grow." We will, he proclaimed, reiterating the Four Freedoms he had first enunciated in his Annual Message: "accept only a world consecrated to freedom of speech and expression — freedom of every person to worship God in his own way — freedom from want — and freedom from terror."

Roosevelt's close friend, adviser, and speechwriter, Harry Hopkins, comprehended the power of these words. Shortly after this Chat, he told Robert Sherwood, "You and I are for Roosevelt because he's a great spiritual figure, because he's an idealist. . . . Oh — he sometimes tries to appear tough and cynical and flippant, but that's an act he likes to put on, especially at press conferences. He wants to make the boys think he's hard-boiled. Maybe he fools some of them, now and then — but don't ever let him fool you, or you won't be of any use to him. You can see the real Roosevelt when he comes out with something like the Four Freedoms. And don't get the idea that those are any catch phrases. *He believes them!* He believes they can be practically attained. That's what you and I have got to remember in everything we may be able to do for him . . . it's your job and mine — as long as we're around here — to keep reminding him that he's unlimited, and that's the way he's got to talk because that's the way he's going to act."[61]

MAY 28, 1941

YESTERDAY THERE WAS ROOM IN AMERICA FOR DEMOCRATS AND REPUBLI-
CANS LIBERALS AND CONSERVATIVES AND FOR INDUSTRIALISTS WORKERS
AND FARMERS. TODAY AS THE RESULT OF YOUR MAGNIFICENT AND INSPIR-
ING LEADERSHIP THERE IS ROOM ONLY FOR AMERICANS. YOU HAVE UNITED
THE COUNTRY AS NO OTHER PERSON COULD HAVE DONE. . . . I AM YOURS
TO COMMAND.

J. C. TREES
PITTSBURGH, PENN.

MAY 28, 1941

TONIGHT YOU HAVE MADE THE WHITE HOUSE THE LIGHT HOUSE OF THE
WORLD. BLESS YOU.

EUGENE B. RODNEY AND FAMILY
BRANFORD, CONN.

MAY 28, 1941

SINCE 1933 I HAVE BELIEVED THAT THE WORLD WOULD ALWAYS SAY THAT
THE THREE GREATEST PRESIDENTS WE HAVE HAD ARE WASHINGTON LIN-
COLN AND YOURSELF AND AFTER YOUR SPEECH TONIGHT I BELIEVE THE
WORLD WILL SAY YOU HAVE SAVED ALL THAT WASHINGTON AND LINCOLN
STOOD FOR.

D. W. NORTHRUP
NEW HAVEN, CONN.

MAY 28, 1941

Dear Mr. Roosevelt:

I deeply regret that in your announcement on Tuesday night, you did
not speak for the people of America. We do not want to support Britain to
the point of war. We do not fear Hitler on our own shores. But we do weep
within our hearts for the horrible fate into which you are driving our sons.

349

What is going to become of Washington's United States, Jefferson's Democracy, Lincoln's Union, if every 20 to 25 years we slaughter the finest of our young men? Is our fate to be directed by Churchill of England? We, the American people, pray nightly for a strong man, to rise up to direct our destiny, not to war, but to the defense of the Americas. Why can't you be that man?

Sincerely

Mrs. H. H. Clark
New Hope, Pa.

MAY 28, 1941

Dear Sir:

After hearing your address last night, I felt that you had betrayed every promise you have made to Americans in general, and to American mothers in particular.

We do not want war — can't you realize that?

We brought our sons up to love, not to hate.

We raised them to live, not to be killed.

We are willing to defend American shores, but we want none of England's wars. In 20 years there'll be another. My husband left college to go into the last one, and this is no different.

I haven't one single ancestor who isn't of English extraction, or Canadian, but we had to fight off Britian 3 times to be Americans. Let us remain Americans, and mind our own business in our own country.

Sincerely,

E. C. Schmidt
[no address]

MAY 28, 1941

My dear Mr. Roosevelt:

Last night — here on an isolated ranch in Idaho — I listened to your radio address. I am wondering if history is going to repeat itself?

My memory goes back — to the year 1916 — to an entirely different setting. I was attending high school in one of our large steel manufacturing centers. President Wilson had been elected for a second term on the slogan, "He kept us out of war." Immediately after election, he broke his pledge to the American people and proceeded to get us in war. He too said, we were to save the world for democracy & save our country from German invasion.

I shall never forget the train loads of fine young men that left Youngstown, Ohio for over sea service nor can I forget the sorrowing parents. — President Wilson did not save the world for Democracy but he did cause this nation to lose thousands upon thousands of her finest young men.

Then I remember President Wilson's return from Europe, after the Versailles Treaty — a sadder and wiser man — also a man broke in heart, spirit and body. He lived a few years — a life of isolation — he died, "unwept, unhonored, and unsung."

Cannot you reap from President Wilson's experience? The American People have honored you with a third term, to the White House — an honor given no other man, I beg of you — do not break faith with us.

Very sincerely,

Marion W. Sullivan
Winsper, Idaho

MAY 29, 1941

Dear Mr. Roosevelt,

. . . I am a World War Veteran and have a son nearing military age. I think the last war was fought in vain and was meaningless unless we finish the job now. The German menace as we know it now under Hitler and his communist upstarts must be ended once and for all time. . . .

Sincerely and Respectfully yours

M. T. Rose
Highland Park, Mich.

MAY 27, 1941

Mr. President:

. . . I served before and with the full knowledge from experience of warfare would feel far better to bid my wife and daughter Godspeed and go three thousand miles away to fight in their defense — than to wait for an attack which would cause a final frantic, futile effort upon my part on a makeshift battle front with those loved ones just three miles back and subjected to all the hell of conflict. . . .

Respectfully,

L. G. Harries
Oklahoma City, Oklahoma

MAY 28, 1941

Dear President:

I just have to tell you how wonderful your speech was last night: You are the most briliant man in this big troublesome world: Every word you utered was of great wisdom: If you was to get killed, or die; This world will surley go to old Hitler, sure enough; — There is no other man living that can any where near keep us out of war. But you with God's help, you will longer than any one else ever can; Of course you hinted of war, to make us see more plainer what we might have to face. But you will steer us clear as long as it can ever be done by any one: You are so level headed and wise and quiet about every thing: — you are next to God with me. I can't just express with words my thoughts and feelings for you, our "Best President" when you are through we are all Sunk. And we are not alone in our esteem for you, for you know there are millions that love you for the man you are: my hubby and I extend you our best thoughts and wishes in all your efforts: —

I am —

Mrs. Art Le Tellier
Vallejo, California

My hubby is doing his bit helping build ships, "Shipfitter"

MAY 28, 1941

Dear Mr. President:

It was a great speech. Now America will make it.

Now comes the shooting — and let it come.

I speak as a midwesterner and a man of German ancestry. We have our stupid ones out here just as you have in the East — but the vast majority know that this war must come and are ready for it.

If I may, I should like to suggest something. When the guns begin to shoot, let us have a military leader who is tough. Maybe a loyal American with a German name and the German "will to win." A man who is not afraid to "spend" men, money and material. . . .

When I say "spend" men, I speak as one who intends to take part in this fracas and as one of the men possibly to be spent. But war is no pink tea party and the British, on land at least, have been inclined, it seems, to treat it as such. . . .

Time after time the British have retreated and have boasted about the "men they saved." This notion must be reversed. In the end it is more humane to "spend" the men. The war will end more quickly and more satisfactorily.

We must enforce our will upon the enemy. We must match and better the German will to win. I should say that, once in, no American army, no detachment should ever retreat. If and when blunders are made the men should stay there and die. It's the only way to win. And with that spirit grows the notion of invincibility that the Germans have grown to believe in and have got a lot of other people sold on. And they will be invincible until they run into someone more determined. That's our cue.

Let us have the toughest military leader you can find.

It is going to be a matter of leadership in the final analysis.

With profound respect I am your humble servant,

W. Clay Stearley
Brazil, Ind.

MAY 28, 1941

Dear Mr. President:

Your speech last night was splendid. I had hoped for an announcement of us taking a strong position even to ordering the Navy & air force into immediate collaboration with Britain & China. We can turn the tide if we act at once & strongly. Get bases in Azores, Cape Verde islands & at Freetown to watch Dakar. A few bombers from Manila would burn out Tokio, Yokahama, & other Japanese strategic centers. Let us do the job that needs doing & do it right. The Japanese started all this trouble in Manchuria. They have insulted us for years. Let us wipe them off the Pacific as a Naval power. Admirals Yarnell & Richardson can do the job & quick.

Best wishes,

R. Linn Crockett
Dallas, Texas

MAY 28, 1941

Dear Mr. President:

I voted against you in the November election, but now I would like to say that I am sincerely glad that the majority was wiser than I.

Many of us were beginning to be afraid that the organized shouting of the appeasers and traitors had frightened the leadership of this country. Your speech last night, and your proclamation of an unlimited emergency with the accompanying powers that gives you, came as a great relief.

Throughout our entire history, America has never played the part of a coward. The only thing that can frighten it now is evidence of fear and hesitancy in our leadership. If you will lead us courageously and unhesitatingly, America will follow in the same manner.

I hope you will use your new powers without fear of either the opposition within our borders, or the threat from outside our country. If we must fight (and I fear we must) it would be a thousand times better to fight while we still have the British as allies.

Every other country has resisted the aggressors too late. America is the last. America can not afford to be too late. It is your responsibility, Mr. President, to see that America is <u>not</u> too late, even if that means American soldiers on the battle line in Europe.

Sincerely,

Jack Beaver
Chadron, Nebr.

MAY 27, 1941

Your Excellency:

Your speech this evening was wonderful and a real and decisive challenge to Hitler and his cohorts. 110 million Americans are behind you Mr. President and fully approve your plan of action in aid for England. 20 million Catholics are against you and are opposed to American principles, and are traitors and arch enemies of this country as follows:

All Irish Catholics who are bitter enemies of England.

All Italian Catholics who are for Mussolini.

All other Catholics and all Germans who are for Hitler and his group of villians and murderers.

This 20 million multitude includes not only foreign born but very many native born. They are almost as dangerous as the Hitler fifth columnists.

Just one of the 110 million.

Herbert Swensen
New York, N.Y.

MAY 28, 1941

Honable President Roosevelt: —

I listened intently to your report of May 27th and I was very dissappointed in your utterence, I and my friends had so much faith in you, but you are just destroying that faith. Im a negro youth, the freedoms and libities you advocate carrying to the four cornors of the world and wont [want]

me and my friends to fight and die for, are denied me here, first lets estabi-
lish Demorcy here, then and not until then will we have something to fight
for. Please rekindle that faith with me and my friends again.

A staunch citizen
Yours Truly

Paul Durdin
New York, N.Y.

JUNE 2, 1941

Dear Mr. President:

After listening to your fireside chat on last Tuesday night, I've pondered
over it for three days and nights. Insignificant though I may be I too am considered an American human being, regardless of the color and pigmenta-
tion of my skin.

In your speech of last Tuesday night you declared an unlimited emergency existed. To my humble mind such a declaration calls for a United
front. As a negro woman I am prepared to say to you that such a thing does
not exist in this Democratic United States.

In event of actual warfare our men whom we love with every fiber of our
being, are going to be called on to fight and do their share to defend a Democracy which does not allow them the right to live like other human beings. I'm not going to point out to you the many deplorable conditions that
exist because I'm aware of the fact that you are quite familiar with them. I
am, however going to say to you that despite the fact you say Hitler and Hitlerism must be stopped, the negro as an unskilled man has no place in this
modern warfare. . . .

Our negro men will die, yes die like flies, but unless you train them, give
them technical knowledge they will all die without being any help to the
United States. This war calls for trained men. You cant give a man a mop
and say to him defend American Democracy. How absured. Sometimes I
cant understand our so called intellectual leaders, I've got to laugh at their
ignorance. Here you are condeming Hitler for something you yourselves
are embracing in this country. . . .

To call this America the United States in which we live a true Democracy is misrepresenting the truth. You do not want to defeat Hitler because he is dominating the minorities of the world because if that were true when Hitler's pal Mussolini decided he wanted to take over Etheopia you would have then acted but you were silent. You know why? That was a black country. Well now my friend we have nothing to fight for and I dare you or any of your brain trust to refute that statement. . . .

We're all called wishful thinkers and so are you so long as you stick to the age old policy of discrimination and race prejudices. Remember you are kidding yourselves not us. President Roosevelt you are helping Hitler by your silent acquisecence to jimcrowism.

Just this and I'm through, in order for the United States to defend Democracy it will have to be a 100% true Democracy.

Respectfully Yours,

(Mrs.) Mildred C. Fredericks
New York, N.Y.

MAY 28, 1941

Dear Mr. President:

I looked forward toward listening to your Fireside Chat, and like millions of other young people I listened with hope in my heart. I hoped that your words would soothe our hearts and prevent us from being dragged into the European war.

I think it entirely incorrect to assume that those millions of us who oppose being involved in this bloody mess are cowards. I want to refute such false statements with all my strength. We are the American people who are courageous enough to stand up for our rights and who will fight to the last measure to increase our wages, to fight for collective bargaining as you mentioned in your speech, and to better the American way of life right here in our own United States. Our jobs is right here!

. . . We want a life worth fighting for and we'll do this by building our trade unions and peace organizations.

It's easy for you who will not be going "over there" to talk so big, while we will suffer by sending our sons, husbands & sweethearts. I will exert every ounce of energy I possess to help build a true democracy here.

Very truly yours

Rose Rosenberg

[no address]

* * *

Dear Sir:

If there were any Americans who still believed that you were sincerely trying to keep this country out of war, your talk tonight must surely have dissipated any such illusions. Since you are forbidden by the Constitution to actually declare war you are seeking by inflammatory and un-neutral speeches to incite Germany to some overt act so that you can force Congress to declare war without too much fear of the reactions of the American people. You are also attempting, with your hysterical talk of "invasion", to stampede the people into line behind your program for war. . . . You talk of preserving democracy and stopping Hitler and while you talk thus you are attempting to strangle American Democracy. . . . you have declared that a state of emergency exists so that you may break strikes and use further dictatorial and un-Constitutional methods to silence and enslave the American people. These are exactly the same methods used by Hitler to establish his Nazi dictatorship in Germany.

Since you are suddenly so anxious to preserve "democracy against Hitlerism" why don't you explain to the people why you imposed the embargo against Spain when the democratic people of that country were fighting so gallantly against Hitler's stooge, Franco? . . . And, also, why you continue to allow scrap iron and oil and other materials to go to Japan to crush Chinese democracy. . . .

This is not a war for democracy and you know it is not. America is in no danger of attack and you know that also. England is fighting German imperialism in order to preserve British imperialism so that she can maintain her tyrannical ruler over the oppressed peoples of her colonies. Our own gallant forefathers had to fight to save America from British tyranny.

We want no part in Europe's war. While you talk of saving democracy you do nothing to stop the rise in food prices and the rise in prices of other basic commodities. You blandly allow profiteers to reap a fortune from the sufferings of the American people. You allow children to starve while great corporations receive huge profits from government war orders. You have completely forgotten the "one-third of the nation who are ill-housed, ill-clothed, ill-fed." The Roosevelt New Deal is a thing of the past. . . .

Very truly yours,

(Mrs.) Harriet Food
Oroville, Calif.

MAY 28, 1941

Dear Mr President:

I heard your speech last night along with millions of other serious minded and well thinking Americans. But somehow, you sounded more like a British official than an American. How can you say that this war in any form is good for us Americans; we did not start it; we had no part whatever in it and it is not a war for democracy — If it were we Americans would be 100% behind you instead of 10% as we are today. This war as you yourself indicated last night, is a war of imperialism — and imperialism is to be defended & is defended by Industrialists not by the working people — This is a struggle for power between two forces — We Americans want no part of it. We are not willing to go overseas again to defend a democracy that does not exist — I am a negro — and democracy has no meaning to me. The only word I understand is equality. Therefore I ask you in the name of the working people & middle class people all over America, not to involve us farther in this bloody struggle for power — Remember your campaign promises that no American boys would be sent overseas — We Remember!

Respectfully,

Ruth Hutman
[no address]

MAY 30, 1941

My President:

Congratulatory mail is probably coming to The White House now as a result of your speech of Tuesday Evening. My letter, however, is not in that category. . . .

As I believe in true Democracy, it is only fair that I write my President and tell him, honestly, that when people ask me what I thought of President Roosevelt's talk, I will say that I do not agree with my President and that I cannot keep silent. As I see it, to be truly democratic, my President should have said, "We offer a home in the United States to any man or woman who fought Hitler during the Spanish Civil War; we are stopping all aid to Japan and promise to increase help to China, which has fought against the dictators of Japan since 1931 with little aid from us thus far; we are proclaiming equal rights to the Negro, not only in the south and in defense industries in the north, but in the Army as well (I am a white person, but I do not see how any of us can have the gaul to ask a colored man to fight for democracy-as-we-know-it); we are asking Britain to grant independence to India and Northern Ireland at once; we are dismissing from the government of the United States all those who have fascist or nazi minds, who hate the Negro, the Jew, Labor, etc.; we are ending war profiteering, even to the extent that all munitions plants must be government-owned; and we are, by national democratic referendum, giving the people of the United States their vote on matters of vital importance to them — foreign policy and war."

This is Americanism; its arguments are indisputable!

Respectfully,

Jeanette Peterson Daronatsy
East Chicago, Indiana

MAY 28, 1941

Dear Sir:

To comment on your speech tonight. . . .
We were referred to all the small nations the Nazis seized. How about

Britain? Britain's seizure of Nigeria in 1886, of Somaliland in 1887, of British East Africa in 1888, of Rhodesia in 1889, of British Central Africa in 1893, of Uganda in 1896 and of South Africa in 1898 — seizures totaling more than 900,000 square miles; seizures which were instigated and conducted more ruthlessly than those accredited to Italy and Germany during the past two years. . . .

Did they inform you that France, the other great democracy, captured Tunis in 1878, Annan and Tonkin from China and Laos from Siam in 1887? Did they refer to the subjugation of Madagascar in 1896 and to the unjust aggressions committed against Djibouti, Dahomey and Morocco at a later date — aggressions which netted the French Empire more that 670,000 square miles? . . .

By reminding you of these lurid, historical facts which besmirch the pages of modern history, I am in no way condoning the conduct of the modern dictators. But I am reminding you that the same policy of seizure and exploitation is dominant in the world today as it was yesterday; the same catchwords are being used to deceive the common people; the same propaganda is issued by those who dominate both governments and nations — the hidden hand of the internationalists.

Let me repeat. The nazi's are like the British, the French, and the Italians. I repeat emphatically, let the snakes of Europe fight their own troubles. . . .

Respectfully yours,

M. A. Jans
Gibbon, Minn.

MAY 28, 1941

Dear President Roosevelt: —

Your speech last night made me shiver with fear and disgust.

Fine-sounding words to drag us into a war of spoils — What difference whether British fascism or German gets the bigger booty.

How about the menace of fascism here in America, with all the alien-baiting lynch law, poll-tax, Silver Shirts, Christian Fronters, Coughlinites (Anti-Semitic) anti-Union —

Give us a break — we want to live in a better America, not die for the British Empire.

Yours truly,

(Mrs) Rosetta Harris
New York, N.Y.

MAY 27, 1941

Mr. President:

I'm not waiting for you to finish your fire-side chat to type this note off to you and regester my disgust with you and all your re-actionary dark complexioned advisors.

We are not going to fight for your British and American Isrelites. Judge O'Brien was right when he said the streets of New York City would be red with blood.

You are the traitor to the American people, a pro-British Quisling!

A REAL AMERICAN
New York, N.Y.

MAY 27, 1941

My dear Mr. President:

I listened to your fire-side chat of Tuesday evening and found nowhere in it sufficient or valid reason for the United States to depart from the pledge you made to the American people last October 23 — the pledge to keep us out of this world war. . . .

You are our leader. Your word comes closer to being the law of the land than that of any other man this nation has elevated to the presidency. But please remember that it was the Forgotten man — the people in the lower income brackets — the lower middle class group which elected you to office in 1932, in 1936 and again in 1940.

It was not the newspapers of this country — the majority of them opposed you each time. It was not the Morgans or the Rockefellers and their ilk — they opposed you almost to the man. It was not the industrialists who flock to your banner now, urging war. It was the ever inarticulate little man of the country — the little man who is now, has been and always will be the pawn and the dupe in war, the little man who is now and at last opposed to this foreign venture, the little man who believed you on October 23 — who voted for you on the election day following and who now calls on you to stand by the pledge you made to him — which is a pledge higher than any given to Britain, to China, to Greece or to any other land.

Mr. President, this nation is united — firmly united on the twin proposition of building up our national defense so that no nation can attack us — and to stand with you in your pledge to keep us from being involved in this war.

May God grant you the strength and wisdom to keep us from this war —

Wilbert Bach
Miami, Fla.

MAY 27, 1941

My dear Mr. President:

. . . I could not sleep last night for thinking of how war-like you have become. Even the cocks crowed and the dogs howled as I was up, as if they too were disturbed by your speech. Tears were shed in America last night because of your speech. How many more will be shed before this is over I don't know. I thank God that only Congress can declare war, and pray that they will hold for peace as we want them to.

Yours respectfully,

Alice Wallingford
Princeton, W.Va.

MAY 29, 1941

My dear Mr. President; —

. . . When I listened to your speech Tuesday night tears filled my eyes — tears of joy — Now, I thought, the period of action has begun — Vain words and threats are of the past — That night I slept, feeling safer than in many months — relying upon the strength of our armed forces — in strategic places. . . .

I have done what I could to help enlighten public opinion in my own locality — to make the issue clear to those in my immediate neighborhood who are hopelessly muddled — Some have acknowledged utter inability to understand —

For weeks (while Rome burned!) only the small but very vocal opposition was heard — The front pages of all Tulsa newspapers were filled with the propaganda of the "America First Committee," as was the radio. . . .

Surely you will back up your words with deeds and not leave our people without hope. . . .

I thank you, Mr. President,

> (Mrs.) Margaret L. Trezevant
> Tulsa, Oklahoma

MAY 29, 1941

Dear Mr. President —

I listened to your speech of Tuesday evening.

For the first time, you seemed to be hiding a feeling of nervousness and emotion. You stumbled on three words — it is unusual for you as you usually sound confident and eloquent.

I feel as though I could read between the lines of that speech — you don't really want to take us into a war — you know that the people of our country dont want it and see no reason for it. . . .

Don't let those men around you push you into war-minded ideas — You have the ability to outsmart them. . . .

> Sincerely,
>
> Beatrice Schick
> [no address]

MAY 28, 1941

Dear President Roosevelt —

I listened to your fireside chat last evening and dear President it was wonderful but sad.

I could feel all you were suffering and know how sick your soul is with this awful task before you, and may God Bless you and give you Faith Strength and courage with divine guidance at all times.

Be not afraid dear President you are doing the right thing. . . .

Sincerely

Lillian Claycomb
Yonkers, N.Y.

To President Roosevelt:

1.

A lonely man sat in a chair
His eyes looked straight ahead
The shadows lengthened on the wall
E're he bowed that silvery head.

2.

He felt the sorrow's of a world
across and ocean wide
and knew just what his duty was
and never turned aside. . . .

MAY 28, 1941

My dear friend I listened with intense interest to your fire side talk last night. I am sending my hearty congratulations to you. I prayed to God to direct you and to give you a message to a troubled world. I believe he did. I am happy over the out come as it seems the whole American Nation is moved in the same way. Your words were beautifully put with the kind of force that all Christians should be careful to put them. There was not anything that you said that would cause any people to become offended. You have always had my prayers. I shall continue to pray for you. your family. and cabinett members. my two sons are already in the draft. my daughter in New York City stands ready to serve wherever you think what is the best place for her to serve. She is a musician. and a teacher. Mrs. Andrades Lindsay Brown. wife of the deceased Bishop W. Brown. and last but I hope not the least. I'll be 69 years of age in June. and I too stand ready to serve my country. I am a musician. I served at camps in the last worlds war. as long as I am able to stand or sit I am ready for servis to cheer the soldier. to shell beans. to peal potatoes. to play my music. With all good wishes. and prayers for all. I am your Loyal Subject.

Will Lindsay. colored
Greensboro, N.C.

MAY 28, 1941

Dear Mr. Roosevelt the President of the U.S.A. I am just a poor Negro woman with not much education. but I sit and cry meny days because of it. I am just a 9th grade scholer. but I just wont too write yo. for I Do think persons who can scratch a word. this respect Is due too yo. as I sit last night and listen too your Fire side chat. too U.S.A. giveing them facts. it please me so. there is no one as sorry as I am about this trouble. for I am a dezerted wider with 2 sons and I have give them too U.S.A. for National Defince. and I will pray God. Blessing too them all. if they cant do one thang I no they can Another. for the thang too do is try too stop it now. if we can. . . .

a colored woman an american Born and For american I live.

Sadie Kirven
Florence, S.C.

I will Keep an eye. on my Radio.

MAY 28, 1941

My dear Mr. President:

. . . The story of the Peyton family relates that my ancestors came to Virginia from England in 1623 and wherein it doesn't say so specifically, I am convinced that my family, like your family, came to America to get away from foreign persecutions and involvement in foreign wars. They did not run away, they moved away, and at great hazard to themselves.

Mrs. Peyton and I have, in her family and mine, five fine sons, ranging in age from fifteen to twenty-five; one is now an ensign in the navy flying corp and another a member of his naval science class in college. It seems to me that if any one of these boys, or any other son of a truly American family, is blown to bits in Europe or sunk off the coast off Iceland, that our families will have moved in vain. . . .

The discouraging part about this situation to me is that I honestly fear that you and the group surrounding you are not going to listen to those who disagree with your position and further, that those of us who may question you and your actions in this serious matter are to have their loyalty questioned. When we reach this point, certainly we can no longer claim that we are living under a Democratic form of government.

Yours very sincerely,

Harlan I. Peyton
Spokane, Washington

MAY 28, 1941

Dear Mr. President:

. . . You have forfeited the confidence of the people who placed their trust in you to keep us out of war. Last night you removed the mask. You have told the South American nations that we are unified here. You have created more disunity than ever existed here before. You are taking a peaceful people to war in Europe's fights.

Don't think that I like Hitler. I don't and can't. Being a Jew How could I like him? Being a veteran of the last war I don't like war either. Young men fought for a War to end all wars in 1918. We fought for a war to save democracy. Where is it in Europe now. Are our boys again going to die in Europe? Will your sons be in the front lines? Do you think we will come thru a war with any democracy left here? Thinking people don't.

You can make all the speeches you want and take us into this war with your power but the people won't have their hearts in it. . . .

Yours truly,

Norman C. Norman
New York, N.Y.

MAY 28, 1941

My dear President:

I, the father of six sons of military age, have been an ardent New Deal Democrat, proud of my party's social interest, proud indeed of my great President. . . .

In your campaign speeches, I heard you promise several times that you would never send our boys to fight on foreign soil. . . .

But last night, I listened attentively to your speech, and I now fear that you have changed your mind. I fear that we are near, very, very near to actual war.

Should one of my sons fail to respond in a run to defend our great country from actual attack, I would be much ashamed. But that could not be; they have been taught to love and honor and cherish all for which our Flag stands.

But, my dear President, for you to say that you intend to destroy Hitler and all for which he stands; for you to say that we are out to assure all people everywhere freedom of speech, freedom of religious worship, freedom from want, and freedom from fear — that is a big order. If that is what you mean to do, taking the law of averages, I shall have sons buried in the sands of Africa, in the wastes of Siberia, in the blood soaked soils of Europe. . . .

It is my honest opinion, my dear President, that by no stretch of imagination, can we be fighting for democracy if we are to restore to the thrones of Europe, King Albert, Queen Whilimina, King Haakon, King George, King Peter, Dictator Beck, and their like. . . .

It is my honest opinion that we could go over there, defeat Hitler, deliver all countries, supervise a free election in each; leave them for three election, return and find the same old selfish crews back in the saddle. No! it is not our fight. It will be in vain.

Hold to your social gains, build them higher; set such a shining example that all people will see the light and follow us. You can not shoot this into any of them. . . .

Sincerely,

Fred Langenkamp
Tulsa, Oklahoma

MAY 27, 1941

TONIGHT I BECAME 21. YOUR SPEECH HAS SENT ME AND THOUSANDS MORE
AMERICAN BOYS CLOSER TO OUR DEATH.

RUBEN COPPERMAN
PHILADELPHIA, PENN.

MAY 30, 1941

Dear Sir: —

On the evening of May 27th I returned to my family home to hear your
broadcast (though of course I have my own excellent radio here in my studio) because I wanted to be with my mother, my brother and his wife while
we all listened to our President. Had the "Fireside Chat" proved just another chat without full significance for the hour, I felt we could stand the
disappointment better if we were all together.

But, somehow, deeper than any such misgivings, was a conviction that
you would not, could not, disappoint us. And if you could have seen our
family circle about the radio in that humble farm sitting-room, you would
have realized that we were not disappointed! We clapped at various passages and our hearts were full and our eyes shining with a new light when
the great speech was over. And our Irish maid was as elated as any of us. . . .

The most noticeable break in the family circle was the eldest son's absence. He is nearly seventeen. . . . His reaction to glowing accounts of the
speech, later, was rather cynical. If this were exceptional, it would not be
worth mentioning, but in my contacts with young people (and I have many,
as a teacher) I have observed that many boys and girls of his age and a bit
older are cynical & defeatist, when they are not actually quite isolationist
or even pro-fascist. They admire the swift decisive action, even though bru-
tal, of Hitler. . . .

I realize they feel that they are the ones who will be called on to face the
brunt of it — to die — in the air, at sea, or on foreign shores. . . . They feel
that you have broken your promise not to send our boys to foreign shores,
and they are afraid of a nameless terror. — Can't you talk to them — soon
— and make it clear to them — fill them with courage, and call on them to

be as loyal in their defense of liberty and democracy as Hitler's youths are in their defense of their "Führer's"?

. . . At least, they abhor restrictions — but they do not yet realize what restrictions a Hitler-dominated world would impose upon them! — But the chief thing is that they need a cause which will enlist them heart and soul, and sweep them out of their cynicism, fears, and doubts, into a positive crusade.

I believe the majority of young people are already enlisted in the cause of freedom — but there is still too large a minority of the other type for real unity. Hence this letter.

Respectfully yours,

Elna Sherman
Providence, R.I.

MAY 27, 1941

Dear President Roosevelt,

Tonight I listened to your speech and I wish to express my admiration for you, both as my President and Commander in Chief — for I am a private in the United States Army. . . .

I enlisted in the Army four months ago — I quit a job, left my mother and Sweetheart behind, for there is something deep inside me that told me I had to help protect all of the fine things that America means to me. When I think of what other Americans before me have gone through in order to let me have the wonderful opportunities I have had, it seems I have really done nothing. But I'm where I can help now, and I'm willing to help in every way that I can.

. . . last week I was sent down here from Hamilton Field to study a course in Airplane Mechanics at California Flyers Inc. So I will at the end of six months be in more of a position to really help out in the defence work. When I think of what a wonderful opportunity this is, I feel humble to Uncle Sam. For if the war ends and I am still alive, I will be prepared to earn my living in a skilled trade — so I even owe my future happiness to the opportunity the Army is now offering me. . . .

I feel humble writing this letter to you — perhaps you will never see it. But I thought you might wonder how we soldiers feel. Were behind each other, were behind you, and were behind America, and we intend to remain there ready to give our lives if necessary. . . .

Truly yours —

Private Jerry Ryan
Ocean Park, California

MAY 28, 1941

HONARABLE SIR CONGRATULATIONS ON THE STAND YOU TOOK LAST EVE-
NING. WE ARE A GROUP OF COLORED GIRLS NEARLY 300 STRONG. WE ARE
WITH YOU 100 PERCENT. WE WERE ORGANIZED BY MRS MARIE REED FOR
HOME DEFENSE. HAVE DRILLED SINCE JANUARY AND ARE READY FOR FIRST
AID TRAINING ETC BUT NO TRAINERS. MAY WE NOT HAVE AN EARLY REPLY
FROM YOUR HONOR CONCERNING TEACHERS FOR OUR GROUP. THANK
YOU SIR.

MARIE REED (PRESIDENT VETERANS OF FOREIGN WARS AUXILIARY)
LOS ANGELES, CALIF.

MAY 28, 1941

Dear Mr. President,

I heard your speech Tuesday night & I feel I just must write you a line and tell you how I & any others that I know feel about all this war business. . . .

Please, do not listen to those in Washington who would like to see us at war. Think of the thousands — who, like myself are just newly wed and who have made such plans and whose life would be ruined if something happened to those they love. Not only their new husbands, but brothers as well. God forbid, but if we should go to war, I would rather go then let my beloved, for my life would not be worth any thing nor would I go on living.

So please stop for one moment and try & consider the feeling of the American people the people who would have to fight & lose their lives — or an eye — or leg or arm.

I beg you to keep us out of war. . . .

A loving wife & true American
[no address]

MAY 28, 1941

Honorable Sir:

. . . Yesterday you proclaimed the existance of a national emergency. You did this, we trust, only after careful consideration and fervent prayer for divine guidance. We are in no position to judge as to the wisdom of your action in this matter. At the same time, however, we feel that there exists in our nation an "emergency" even greater, but which you failed to mention. It is the emergency brought about by the sins of our nation. How can we expect God's blessing to rest upon our land when almost half the nation professes no faith in the true God, when God's name is constantly taken in vain in cursing and blasphemy by millions of our people, when God's Word is ridiculed and utterly disregarded, when respect for parental and all other authority has all but vanished from our land, when reports of murders constitute a large part of the news of the day, when the sanctity of marriage is flagrantly violated, divorce condoned and the immorality extant in the land reminds one of the Biblical description of Sodom and Gomorrah? . . . It will be well with us if we repent and turn to God. If we do not, nothing in all the world, neither planning nor armaments or confident claims on our part will prevent God from visiting His wrath upon us in His own manner and at His own time. We, therefore, truly believe that the fundamental emergency confronting our nation to-day is that of SIN.

In this manner we believe that you, Mr. President, have a very solemn obligation toward our nation. You ought by word and example, as a God-fearing leader, urge our nation to repent and to turn to God. This you can do without mixing church and state or violating the principle of religious liberty. It will do more for our nation than anything else you can possibly do and should do as the president of the United States.

Respectfully,

Edward J. Brott
Woodland, California

MAY 28, 1941

Mr. President:

I voted for you every time you ran, and have had more battles for you than for any other person I have known. . . .

I have said often that you are the closest thing to Christ (for you have fed the hungry) and then last night you come with your malicious, intolerant talk spouting hate like some ignorant columnist for all things and people Germanic. How could you who have always been so kind and sweet fall to such levels of ignorance and hatred. . . .

Stop and think of what a wealth of hatred your speech unloosed last evening against naturlized Germans and people of German decent in this country, fine citizens, but just let a speech like yours turn the masses and they will start their horrible persecution that leads to stoning to death of Dashound puppies.

Your talk last night sounded like anyone on earth but Mr. Roosevelt President of the United States.

Mrs Robert Olive
San Bernardino, Calif.

MAY 28, 1941

YESTERDAY I FELT THAT WE SHOULD STAY OUT OF WAR AND I TELE-GRAPHED THAT REGARDLESS OF THE INTERVENTIONISTS YOU WOULD KEEP US OUT OF THE EUROPEAN CONFLICT. AFTER HEARING YOUR INSPIR-ING AND REALISTIC SPEECH OF TONIGHT I HAVE CHANGED MY MIND. I AM NOW SATISFIED THAT I A FORMER SOLDIER OF THE WORLD WAR WAS TOO DEFINITELY INFLUENCED REGARDING MY SONS GETTING INTO THE NEXT WAR. YOUR FORTHRIGHT SPEECH HAS CHANGED MY IDEAS AND NOW I THINK THAT YOU OUR PRESIDENT KNOW WHAT IS BEST FOR OUR NATIONAL WELFARE AND I AM THEREFORE PREPARED TO ACCEPT YOUR LEADERSHIP IN WHATEVER COURSE YOU LAY OUT FOR US . . .

SINCERELY AND RESPECTFULLY.

ANTHONY J. KERIN.
NEW ROCHELLE, NY

THE ATTACK ON
THE USS *GREER*:
SEPTEMBER 11, 1941

A FEW DAYS BEFORE his May 27 Fireside Chat, FDR received reports that the giant German battleship *Bismarck* was on a course for Newfoundland and the East Coast of the United States. Roosevelt suspected that it was headed toward the Caribbean, perhaps to take possession of the French colony of Martinique. Sitting at his desk in the Oval Office, the President wondered out loud: "Suppose she does show up in the Caribbean? We have some submarines down there. Suppose we order them to attack her and attempt to sink her? Do you think the people would demand to have me impeached?"[62] On the day of the May Chat, the *Bismarck* was sunk in European waters by the Royal Navy and never made it to the Western Hemisphere, but FDR's dilemma concerning the thin line between legitimate defense and outright belligerency was hardly over.

The President's plight was exacerbated by the fact that he had not yet determined that American entry into the war was necessary to the defeat of the Axis powers. In this he differed markedly from a number of his closest advisers. On July 10, just weeks after Germany invaded the Soviet Union and exhibited every sign of being as invulnerable on the Eastern Front as it had been on the Western, Secretary of War Stimson confided his growing despair to his diary: "Altogether, tonight I feel more up against it than ever before. It is a problem whether this country has it in itself to meet such an emergency. Whether we are really powerful enough and sincere enough and devoted enough to meet the Germans is getting to be more and more of a real problem." The next day he wrote the President suggesting in effect that we go to war and supplying the draft of a war message to Congress.[63]

FDR had not yet crossed that bridge. He still had not given up the hope that he could help England withstand the German juggernaut short of entering the war. This is what accounts for his indecision, for his contradictory statements and actions. It was not really, as he blurted out in front of several advisers, that he feared impeachment; it was that he feared being wrong, feared leading the American people into bloody strife if he could find another path. He also feared getting too far ahead of public opinion as he had in the Court fight. For all the comparisons that were constantly made, positively and negatively, between the President and two of his more recent predecessors — Theodore Roosevelt and Woodrow Wilson — FDR was in certain profound ways unlike either of them: less headstrong and impetuous than the former, less coolly removed from the turmoil of democratic politics than the latter, and less serenely certain of the rightness — indeed, righteousness — of his actions than either. Although he has been accused by historians and politicians of maneuvering the United States into war, he was not so much Machiavellian as uncertain. When Helen Rogers Reid notified FDR that she had become a convert to strong action against Germany, he replied: "From what extremes do the pendulums swing for us as individuals. Governments, such as ours, cannot swing so far or so quickly. They can only move in keeping with the thought and will of the great majority of our people."[64]

If Roosevelt was simply waiting for "the accidental shot of some irresponsible captain on either side to be the occasion of his going to war," as Secretary Stimson believed, he had several opportunities, none of which he seized as an excuse to make the United States a belligerent.[65] In early June, survivors of the American freighter *Robin Moore* were picked up in the South Atlantic, halfway between Brazil and Africa, and reported their ship had been destroyed by a German U-boat. Harry Hopkins advised the President that the sinking "violated international law at sea; it violates your policy of freedom of the seas," and urged the President to respond aggressively.[66] Although he did close some German consulates in the United States, Roosevelt failed to take more drastic action.

On September 4, another occasion presented itself. Delivering mail and supplies to the American base on Iceland, whose defense the United States had assumed in July, the United States destroyer *Greer* learned from a British plane of the presence of a submerged German U-boat some ten miles ahead. Cooperating with the English, the *Greer* located and followed the submarine for several hours and reported its location to the aircraft. Running low on fuel, the English plane dropped four depth charges and departed. The U-boat commander, obviously confused as to who had attacked his vessel and uncertain as to the nationality of the ship above him, fired torpedoes that missed the *Greer*, which promptly released some eight depth charges and, after first losing and then regaining contact with the U-boat several hours later, fired an additional eleven depth charges, all of which missed their mark.

The President reacted to this incident more assertively but still short of the declaration of war Churchill had pleaded for when the two leaders had met a month earlier to issue the Atlantic Charter to affirm democratic and humanitarian ideals for the postwar world, including freedom of the seas and two of FDR's Four Freedoms: freedom from want and fear. Roosevelt determined finally to allow American warships to escort British merchant convoys from Newfoundland to Iceland, where they would be met by British warships that would guard them the rest of the way to England. He decided to justify this course in a Fireside Chat on September 8. The death of his eighty-five-year-old mother, Sara Delano Roosevelt, on September 7 postponed the Chat for several days, allowing ample time for protracted debate about its contents.

FDR took great pains with this address, asking the State Department to supply a draft and working closely with Sam Rosenman and Harry Hopkins in Hyde Park, Washington, and on the train between the two cities, on a draft of his own. He consulted with Cabinet members, resisting the last minute attempts of Secretary of State Hull to tone down his language, and on the morning of the Chat, he read his final draft to congressional leaders of both parties. On the evening of September 11, wearing a black armband in memory of his mother, the President sat before a bank of microphones and a group of his advisers and family members in the Diplomatic Reception Room of the White House, and spoke with impressive deliberateness to the American people about the ordeal of the USS *Greer*.[67]

The President was prepared to tell the nation the truth, but not quite the whole truth. Missing was any mention of the fact that prior to being attacked the *Greer* had been actively aiding a British plane to hunt down the U-boat or that it was the British who had fired the first shot. What he did say was accurate enough but misleadingly incomplete: "I tell you the blunt fact that the German submarine fired first upon this American destroyer without warning, and with deliberate design to sink her." FDR was not impressed by quibbles over whether the U-boat commander knew the nationality of the *Greer*. If he did, "then the attack was a deliberate attempt by the Nazis to sink a clearly identified American warship." If he did not, "the attack was even more outrageous. For it indicates a policy of indiscriminate violence against any vessel sailing the seas — belligerent or nonbelligerent." This, he proclaimed, "was piracy — piracy legally and morally."

FDR rehearsed the pattern of recent attacks on several American vessels, in spite of which "we Americans are keeping our feet on the ground. Our type of democratic civilization has outgrown the thought of feeling compelled to fight some other nation by reason of any single piratical attack on one of our ships. We are not becoming hysterical or losing our sense of proportion. . . . But it would be inexcusable folly to minimize such incidents in the face of evidence which makes it clear that the incident is not isolated, but is part of a general plan." That plan included the Nazi determination to abolish the freedom of the seas as a step toward

> domination of the United States, domination of the Western Hemisphere by force of arms. Under Nazi control of the seas, no merchant ship of the United States or of any other American Republic would be free to carry on any peaceful commerce, except by the condescending grace of this foreign and tyrannical power. The Atlantic Ocean which has been, and which should always be, a free and friendly highway for us would then become a deadly menace to the commerce of the United States, to the coasts of the United States, and even to the inland cities of the United States.

"No tender whisperings of appeasers that Hitler is not interested in the Western Hemisphere," Roosevelt proclaimed, "no soporific lullabies that a wide ocean protects us from him, can long have any effect on the hard-headed, farsighted, and realistic American people." If the world outside of the Americas fell to Axis domination, their shipbuilding facilities would be two or three times greater than that of all the Americas — "enough to win." It is time, he insisted, for "Americans of all the Americas to stop being deluded by the romantic notion that the Americas can go on living happily and peacefully in a Nazi-dominated world." The Nazis "are waiting, waiting to see whether the United States will by silence give them the green light to go ahead on this path of destruction." The time had now come to tell these pursuers of world conquest: "You seek to throw our children and our children's children into your form of terrorism and slavery. You have now attacked our own safety. You shall go no further." "No matter what it takes," he proclaimed, "no matter what it costs, we will keep open the line of legitimate commerce in these defensive waters of ours."

He then spoke the words that Secretary Hull had tried to modify: "We have sought no shooting war with Hitler. We do not seek it now. But neither do we want peace so much, that we are willing to pay for it by permitting him to attack our naval and merchant ships, while they are on legitimate business . . . when you see a rattlesnake poised to strike, you do not wait until he has struck before you crush him. These Nazi submarines and raiders are the rattlesnakes of the Atlantic. . . . They are a challenge to our own sovereignty. They hammer at our most precious rights when they attack ships of the American flag — symbols of our independence, our freedom, our very life."

According to what he understood as his "historic . . . clear . . . inescapable" obligation as President, he promulgated the nation's new policy: "our patrolling vessels and planes will protect all merchant ships — not only American ships but ships of any flag — engaged in commerce in our defensive waters. They will protect them from submarines; they will protect them from surface raiders. . . . From now on, if German or Italian vessels of war enter the waters, the protection of which is necessary for American defense, they do so at their own peril." The sole responsibility, he declared, "rests upon Germany. There will be no shooting unless Germany continues to seek it. . . . I have no illusions about the gravity of this step. I have not taken it hurriedly or lightly. It is the result of months and months of constant thought and anxiety and prayer. In the protection of your nation and mine it cannot be avoided."

The President's was not the only major address broadcast on the evening of September 11. Many of FDR's listeners also tuned into a speech delivered by Charles Lindbergh to an America First gathering at Des Moines, Iowa. Lindbergh furnished fresh fuel for those who charged that the ranks of the noninterventionists were riddled through with anti-Semitism, by identifying Jews as prominent among those "responsible for changing our national policy from one of neutrality and independence to one of entanglement in European affairs." In Lindbergh's view, "The three most important groups who have been pressing this country toward war are the British, the Jewish and the Roosevelt administration." Declaring that "No person with a sense of the dignity of mankind can condone the persecution the Jewish race suffered in Germany," he nevertheless concluded: "Their greatest danger to this country lies in their large ownership and influence in our motion pictures, our press, our radio, and our government."[68]

One of those Lindbergh doubtless was referring to, Sam Rosenman, who had helped draft FDR's Chat and had then left the capital for a trip to the Tennessee Valley Authority, was driving along the Tennessee River with his family when the President spoke: "We stopped the car and turned on the radio. . . . The atmosphere was quiet and peaceful down there on the shores of the Tennessee River on that still September night. It seemed so far away from the world of conflict and destruction, from the mass killing of civilians and the cruelties of the Nazis, that the bold, resolute — almost belligerent — tones of the President seemed a little like a voice coming from another planet."[69]

FDR himself was struck by this same dissonance. During the *Bismarck* episode, Roosevelt dreamed that he was at Hyde Park when the Germans bombed New York. The Secret Service whisked him away to a bombproof cave two hundred feet under a cliff on his estate where he remained until the German planes had passed over.[70] His dream was at once too pessimistic and too optimistic. The Germans, of course, never did manage to bomb New York. And FDR never did manage to find a shelter deep enough to secure himself and his people against the cruel vagaries of the times they lived in.

SEPTEMBER [11], 1941

My Dear President I agree with your speech of this evening 100% I am the Son of an Irish Catholic immogrant. He was proud and Boastfull of his American citizenship. I have gone though my life of 53 year's Proud and also Boastfull, that I was Born in the United States. There is something worse than war and that is that my thee son's would have to go through life with there heads bowed in shame in a Natzie domonated world Better be they Dead.

Resp. your

John J. Morris
Anaconda, Montana

* * *

My dear Mr. President:

I have been on the Republican side of the political fence for years until 1940. Your speaking voice is one of the most powerful forces in America today. Not only your voice but the thought behind your words, is so eloquently expressed that I find many of my republican friends are in absolute agreement with your views. Your speech of Thursday last was one of the most eloquent historical documents of all time.

We love America — my husband and I — As you will see if you note our address — we are in the service — I am proud to be here serving my country however I may — John had many exemptions from duty — he was the Quality Control Manager for Remington Guns — an exemption in itself — his salary was more there, than here — but we have two children and we feel so strongly for our countrys safety that we willingly came into the service when the request was sent over a year ago in July.

For this reason we both put our trust in you for we are the little people who make America, and realize that there is a man at the head of our great nation who is capable of making decisions on time and in time — the usual red-tape not with standing.

No one wants war less than I — and I know this is your feeling too — but neither do I believe in being "too late with too little." I have never written to anyone I did not personally know, before — but I felt so strongly about your speech on the Freedom of the Seas that I wanted to add my note of congratulation. I cannot but be vehement in my approval of everything you have done about this menace to our freedom.

Sincerely yours

Agnes D. Strong
Fortress Monroe, Va.

SEPTEMBER 12, 1941

My dear President: —

I listened to your broadcast of last evening and was impressed with its insincerity. Your Administration has been going about with a Chip on its Shoulder for a long time now, and it is little wonder it was knocked off — but you put it back on and dare the Germans to Knock it off again. Well, the Germans, or Nazis as you and Winsy say, are little hurt by your warmongering — only the common folks of the U.S. will suffer if you go too far. I am a veteran of the World War, and I know the English soldiers only too well — a bunch of Rats — and many a fight we boys had when we met up with that outfit.

I also listened to Lindeberg afterwards, and he said what Millions of Americans are saying to each other for the past two years — namely that the Jews of America want a war. More power to him, for he is the First in America, with any influence, who dared drag the thing out of the Dark and shed light on it. This country, within ten years is in for much trouble from that Race of People — it is rising gradually, and eventually will blossom out in full and then Beware Little Jew. We keep them out of our Best Hotels — Golf Courses and Organizations as it is now — eventually they are destined for the Ash Can in this Country, unless they mend their ways. . . .

Yours,

Frank Casey
Troy, N.Y.

SEPTEMBER 12, 1941

My dear President Roosevelt:

. . . Mr. Lindbergh's notorious speech seems very much to be the "formal opening gun" of a hate campaign in this country against the Jews (a movement which already is getting out of hand and needs no encouragement from such men as Charles A. Lindbergh).

Now, I am an American citizen, and I love and cherish my freedom more than the average person, but, if it will mean silencing such prejudiced persons as Lindbergh, I am willing at this time to sacrifice my right to free speech.

Something has definitely got to be done about this (up until now, whispering) campaign of hate against the Jews. It gains momentum every day, and the pattern it is following in America reeks of a foreign odor. . . .

The balance of Mr. Lindberghs speech also sounds as though it might have been written in Berlin, for it certainly runs true to form when it says "The Roosevelt Administration, the Jews, and the British"

I am not a Jew, or a Jewess, Mr. President, but I plead their cause — let's stop this hate campaign NOW!

Respectfully,

(Mrs.) Ruth N. Fishel
Philadelphia, Pa.

*   *   *

Dear Mr. President:

More power to you for your speech of last night. My only complaint is that it didn't come sooner.

I wonder if the unspeakable Lindbergh realizes that he is now in the only country in the world where he could talk as he did last night and not wake up the next day in a concentration camp or worse yet not wake up at all?

With all best wishes to you,

Sincerely,

C. Lee Curtis
Portland, Oregon

SEPTEMBER 12, 1941

Your Excellency:

I am a Jew. That is my faith in God.

I am an American. That is my faith in man.

I hate those that have brought suffering to all the world and have cruelly mangled the souls of those who share my faith in God.

But far more than I hate them, I love my country and hope and pray that we may remain at peace.

I am grateful that you, the Commander-in-Chief of our armed forces, desiring peace but valuing the safety of our country, have shown the courage to protect America from aggression.

You, our President, have kept faith with those who placed their trust in you —

Respectfully yours,

James Meyberg
Los Angeles, California

SEPTEMBER 12, 1941

My dear President:

Every right thinking American mourns the passing of your Mother. Millions of these Americans had hoped that in the passing of your Mother, a glimpse of the Infinite; a realization that, "God created man in His own image and likeness"; a better understanding of Lincoln's immortal phrase, "with malice toward none, with charity for all," would filter through the mind of our President.

From your speech of last night, it is evident that these millions of American citizens are doomed to disappointment.

To be sure, Germany has committed plenty of errors — so have we and Great Britain. The Germans and even Hitler have been created in the image of God — the same as we. Have we tried to see this perfect creation? Our actions do not say so. . . .

Two wrongs never have made one right!

Hoping that you may really get a better understanding of Christian principles. I am

Sincerely yours,

Ernest G. Woleslagel
Hutchinson, Kansas

SEPTEMBER 12, 1941

Dear Sir

. . . I listened in Thursday night to your address and I think it one of your master pieces because I think you were inspired by your mother who in spirit was beside you. . . .

Very Truly Yours

Edward J. Dwyer Sr.
Pittsburgh, Pa.

SEPTEMBER 12, 1941

My Dear President:

I liked your speech of last evening very much. I have a son serving on the U.S. Bellknap and assigned to the northern waters, also a son in the Air Corps, and being a veteran of the A.E.F. the import of what you said went deeply home to me.

Mr. President, I live in Rattle Snake Hollow out in the hills from Helena. I was awakened this morning by such a din as you've never heard. I stepped out to learn the cause and found my house surrounded by giant rattlers. I held up my hand for quiet and asked the cause of their complaint. The spokesman, a gent of some thirtyfive rattles, replied, "The President compared us to the Nazi's." "Now, wait a minute," I said, "The President simply does not know you Rattlers as I know you. He simply has you confused with the side-winders that bite people without warning. I will set the President right on this matter at once." This seemed to please the Rattlers and they turned to make their way back in the hills.

The rattle snakes on my farm are loyal and home grown Americans. You will remember that early Massachusetts flag, "Don't tread on me"? That has always been the attitude of the American people and of the American rattle snakes. The rattlers don't bother me. If I get too close to them they warn me just as you warned the Nazi's last night. If I don't heed that warning they do just as we are going to do if the Nazi's fail to heed our warning.

I have learned to admire the rattle snake above everything that crawls because he is bold, fearless, fair, and gentlemanly. Especially, have I learn to admire his readiness to fight unto death for his American right to the peaceful pursuit of his own happiness.

Sincerely yours,

F. F. Acree
Helena, Ark.

SEPTEMBER 14, 1941

Dear Mr. President —

. . . I protest vigorously, the stand taken in the Radio Speech of Thursday night. I consider the speech an unwarranted dangerous, veiled provocation, inciting to war.

I urgently ask for the removal of all U.S. troops from Iceland as long as British troops have not been removed from there. I protest the use of our ships as convoys — anywhere — and ask that they be recalled.

I urge strict neutrality and decry the attempts to align this country in anyway in Great Britain's desires to be the Ruler of the World.

I also seriously protest the disgraceful alignment of the United States with Communist Russia.

We Americans do not consider this our war and this nation is not, Mr President, as you mistakenly stated, ready to fight. For what, I ask, and Why?

There is nothing in the whole of Europe, including Great Britain, worth the life of one of our American boys, even the meanest of them. . . .

Very sincerely

(Mrs.) Rose G. Rockwell
New York, N.Y.

SEPTEMBER 11, 1941

Mr President: —

This effort is not to compliment you on your great speach of this Eve, nor is it to add my sympethies to those millions of other Americans, who bemoan the passing of your fine and noble mother.

It is however, my sincere attempt to add one more letter of appreciation, for your being a president to the majority of People, bracketing the middle & working classes, which, incidentally, includes my fellow American Negro.

Had you retired at the end of your first year, when my working day was from fifteen to twenty hours long, I would have reverently remembered and appreciated you for the Inception of the "Blue Eagle." But God through you had said, 'that wasn't enough,' you were to do bigger and greater things. From that point you turned to making our earnings safe, clearing Slums, Building nice homes for hundreds, for a rental they could easily Pay, giving work to those without jobs, Paychecks to those without work (S.S.), Facilate the owning of homes, and on down the list of benificial deeds, construed to make life happier for the majority of people. Yet with bowed head, it is noted that from this long list of social gains, no preceeding president had the foresight, inclination, fortitude or time to consider one of them. . . .

All in All the good has so outweighed the evil in your administration, I feel compelled to add this one more letter of thanks for Past Deeds.

As for your Foreign Policy and your latest declaration of Aims, there may be Argument, but there can be no debate, because — because it is believed, you have been and are inspired to do what is best for the people, and you alone in America <u>are best informed</u>, to manifest your best inspiration. . . .

I'm neither a crank nor am I vain enough to think I can write (as my many mistakes testify) but simply another person, taking this means of letting you know, the many needed reforms brought about by you and your Aids, have not gone unnoticed but have been appreciated by one more American.

I hope you will receive, in the spirit my heart dictates, this humble record of my thoughts for your past Eight Years of Service.

Sincerely,

Luther Rice
Cleveland, Ohio

SEPTEMBER 12, 1941

President Roosevelt —

. . . The American people are with you. The poor people will support you because of your social reforms. The people in comfortable financial circumstances will support you because it is to their interest to do so. Ignore the few isolationists among the extremely rich. Their numbers are so few, even though vocally they are so in evidence.

All the American people — regardless of financial standing, social standing, politics, or racial inheritances — who love this country and its institutions, will support you.

Be bold. People want to be led at a time like this.

Respectfully,

(Mrs. H. C. F.) Ethel W. Freeman
Houston, Texas

* * *

Dear Mr. President —

. . . All of my friends in the trades, i.e. railroad men, electricians, mechanics, etc., shook their heads heartily and exclaimed:- "The President — he told 'em, didn't he?" But what is the matter with the anaemic clerks, book-keepers, salesmen, adjusters, union office managers, accountants, actuaries, etc.? They were apathetic in my experience. They don't seem to understand it all. They think only of their cozy little houses in the suburbs and their auto and their theatre tickets and their summer place at the seashore.

You haven't gotten to the so-called "great middle-class," sir! Perhaps nothing but the trump of doom will awaken them. . . .

Mr. President, can't you blast them out of their false security soon? They are gumming the wheels of progress.

Very respectfully,

Tobias Wagner
Penllyn, Pa.

SEPTEMBER 17, 1941

Dear Mr. President: —

. . . Hoping that perhaps I may be of some slight assistance in helping to arouse my fellow citizens to the dangers by which we are surrounded, I have composed the enclosed lines, in which I have tried to picture the situation as it seems to be today.

Please feel free to make any use whatsoever you may desire of same, if you think it will help.

Respectfully yours,

George H. Ince
Bellport, N.Y.

"WAKE UP AMERICA"

America, awake! awake!
The foe is almost at our gate. . . .
What is it makes us hesitate
Until perhaps it is too late?
Must we wait till our loved ones die,
By bombs dropped on them from the sky.
Our Forbears did not cringe or shrink
Or yet resort to Printer's Ink,
Nor try the enemy to please
By futile efforts to appease.
When danger threatened to their lives
Grabbed up their muskets and their knives
Resolved their country to defend
If need be, to the bitter end.
Shall we waste time in endless talk
As perils all around us stalk?
What do we have a Navy for
If not to use in time of war? . . .

SEPTEMBER 14, 1941

Dear presedent

Sir I heard your talk. . . .

As you know that the black people of these U.S.A. are always loyal to this Country.

Dear Sir may God bless you and Mrs F.D.R.

Dear sir you are the first Presedent the black man can call our Presedent. . . .

I pray God of all men will let you live a long long time for the sake of humanity. not for black peope only but for every body.

I am an ex sirves man and may be too Old but I am ready to do so at any time.

Your cromade

William Kelly
Buffalo, N.Y.

SEPTEMBER 12, 1941

Mr. President —

After listening to your own personal declaration of war last night I have no hesitation in saying that I consider you a dangerous President and your foreign policy a menace to the peace and safety of this country. I fear you now as much as I do Hitler.

If our ships sail the seven seas loaded with contriband for a beligerant country, they may expect to be fired upon. If we give England ships planes money and arms, I think the least she could do would be to man the ships and sail under her own flag. I do not belong to any committee and I despise Hitler but after listening to your last speech I intend to join the America First Committee to day.

Sincerely,

Fred D. Decker
New Rochelle, N.Y.

* * *

Honorable Sir:

Your speech was magnificent. I have just one suggestion that should neatly kill 2 birds with one stone. On the first boat to attack the Nazi menace arrange to have all the members of the America First Committee. If they should get "dunked" no one could possibly accuse you of sacrificing the "cream" of the country — only the sour milk!

Can't the American people pass some sort of legislation insisting that candidates for Congress pass an intelligence test? I don't think morons should be put in asylums — but I certainly don't think politics should be one of their extra-curricular activities!

Devotedly yours

Martha Lee Lorenz
White Plains, N.Y.

SEPTEMBER 13, 1941

Dear President Roosevelt:

Congratulations upon making a wonderful talk to the nation and to the world Thursday. You were bold, but that was absolutely necessary.

We strongly support your order to the Navy to "shoot first". Infact, we strongly support ANY measures which are deemed necessary to defeat Hitler. These poor deluded fools in this country, who believe that it is a physical impossibility to invade America, have forgotten that Napoleon invaded Mexico during our Civil War; Pizarro invaded and defeated Peru (while the Incas were there); Cortez invaded Mexico; or for that matter, our Pilgrim Fathers invaded the United States, to be absolutely technical.

We're proud that we have YOU as our President, and are sure that you will not hesitate nor falter in doing what is right.

Most sincerely,

(Miss) Rosarah Campell
Los Angeles, California

SEPTEMBER 11, 1941

Dear Mr. President,

. . . I am against the Nazis as is any real American, but, Mr. President, when a submarine fires on a ship of ours, how are we to know whose submarine it is? In times like these our immediate and natural conclusion would be that the submarine, sight unseen, would belong to the Nazi government. But need that be necessarily so? I admire the British people. They have fought a valiant war. I do not trust them. . . . No nation so small and yet with such imperialistic scope as they have attained can be honest with other nations, for to acquire what they have took intelligence and cunning. . . . Surely now of all times she would not hesitate to do anything in her power to aid her crucial position in this war.

What actual proof have we that the ships that fired on our ships are acting under German orders? In every case the agressor ships were under seas craft. Might not they be English? Are the German marksmen so poor that they fire two torpedoes at an unsuspecting destroyer and miss with both shots? Does Germany want us in the war at the present time? I think not. She has her hands full and would scarcely be asking for more difficulties. . . . Her soldiers are scattered in many parts; revolt must be imminent in many countries; the Russians are not surrendering as was planned; winter is coming and the moral of the German populace must be low. Would not this, then, be the time for England to gather all aid by any means? . . .

. . . So, Mr. President, before we declare war on Germany, before we send our men and our dollars to destruction, lets make sure it's Germany who fires upon our ships.

Respectfully,

Mrs. Charles Trail
College Station, Texas

SEPTEMBER 11, 1941

Dear President Roosevelt: —

I heard your speech over the Radio and it was perfect, and God bless you for it. . . .

Dear, dear President words can not express my feelings for you. I know how your heart aches and how tired you are. I know how you are grieving every minute of the day and far into the night wanting so hard to do the right thing, for all. No one on earth will ever know the suffering you are going through.

So much depends on you and please do not lose faith, keep up your courage and all will be well.

Dear President I love you and I pray for you and our country each day and I know that only good can come of believing, having faith. . . .

So long for now and don't worry. Oh, I want to say that I was happy when you mentioned poor Abe Lincoln in one of your speeches. No one ever really gave him all the credit which was due him. He was a good man like your self. He suffered too.

May peace be with you.

Your loyal friend

Lillian Claycomb
New York, N.Y.

12 P.M. good night

PEARL HARBOR:
DECEMBER 9, 1941

IN HIS MAY 27 Fireside Chat, FDR had warned that "our Bunker Hill of tomorrow may be several thousand miles from Boston, Massachusetts." In fact it proved to be five thousand miles away when, just little more than six months later, Japanese bombs rained down on Pearl Harbor. It would be some time before the public learned that during the two hours the raid lasted, some 350 Japanese planes (only 29 of which failed to return to their carriers) sank or heavily damaged eight American battleships, three light cruisers, three destroyers, and four auxiliary ships; destroyed almost two hundred planes and seriously damaged more than a hundred more; killed 2,403 and wounded 1,178 soldiers, sailors, and civilians.

In spite of the distance from the Hawaiian Islands, the American people were in a number of ways closer to events than their counterparts in the American colonies had been a century and a half earlier. The second world war was the first war in history to be experienced as it unfolded by vast radio audiences. "Who could forget December 7, 1941," Allen Hilborn of upstate New York, asked, "when the football broadcast was interrupted for the Pearl Harbor announcement?" That afternoon in Kentucky, John Simms went to his grandfather's house for the weekly Sunday gathering of his extended family and found everyone "seated around that Stromberg Carlson listening to the war news. Everybody was hushed — in absolute silence." Thomas Fetters and his parents were eating lunch in a restaurant near Akron, Ohio: "The radio was on, when everyone suddenly jumped to their feet and gathered around the floor model radio as the announcer told of the attack on Pearl Harbor. There were gasps and startled looks. My parents returned to the table obviously very upset, but the idea of war was still a bit vague for me. But not for long."[71]

The following day, President Roosevelt addressed a joint session of Congress to ask for a declaration of war. His brief address, which was broadcast across the nation, began with the famous line: "Yesterday, December 7, 1941 — a date which will live in infamy — the United States of America was suddenly and deliberately attacked by naval and air forces of the Empire of Japan."[72] Many years later, Kathy Cunningham still remembered "the smell of the wooden, oiled floors in the school in North Platte, Nebraska," when she and her classmates "sat out in the massive entrance hall and listened to FDR declare war." In Marshall, North Carolina, Ellen Edmonds's seventh-grade teacher "took the class of about thirty or thirty-five students outside to her car, and we stood and listened to President Franklin Roosevelt declare that we were at war! It was a cold, gray day, and for us life changed." On a North Carolina farm, John Idol and his four brothers were gathered by their mother in front of the living room radio and asked "to listen quietly" to President Roosevelt's address to the Congress:

> I can't say that I remember his famous opening line. I do recall that I had never heard anything more solemn or so eloquently expressed. As a nine year old, I had sparse knowledge of the enemy my country was being called upon to fight, but I was moved to defend my own and to sacrifice for it.
>
> Mother had a profounder feel for the sacrifices American families would be called upon to make. Her response was not to flag-waving but to loss of lives. Whereas her sons were behaving like little patriots, she began crying.
>
> "Why are you crying?" we asked.
>
> "I think that this thing will go on for so long that you will all be in it," she said.[73]

Both of those responses — patriotism and anxiety — were salient throughout the war. In spite of the current reputation of World War Two as the "Good War," Robert Sherwood, writing in the years immediately after the war, expressed a much more muted view: "Morale was never particularly good nor alarmingly bad. There was a minimum of flag waving and parades. It was the first war in American history in which the general disillusionment preceded the firing of the first shot. It has been called, from the American point of view, 'the most unpopular war in history'; but that could be taken as proof that the people for once were not misled as to the terrible nature and extent of the task that confronted them."[74]

Regardless of the state of American morale, and there is evidence to document Sherwood's sense, what the Japanese attack did was to unify the American people and to render the opponents of war impotent. Sam Rosenman wrote that the assault on Pearl Harbor "did something that the Nazis and the Japanese should have feared more than the American fleet and the British fleet combined — it created a unified, outraged and determined

America."[75] Thus, while there is no convincing evidence for the assertions that FDR knew of the Japanese attack on Hawaii and took no measures to prevent it in order to precipitate American entry into the war — charges that several scholars have convincingly refuted* — this does not mean that the attack was not received, and by some even welcomed, as a useful door through which the United States could finally enter the war before the Axis powers dominated Europe and Asia.[76] With the casual acceptance of death and destruction that so often characterizes leaders in wartime, Secretary of War Henry Stimson noted in his diary after FDR phoned the afternoon of December 7 to inform him of the events at Pearl Harbor:

> When the news first came that Japan had attacked us, my first feeling was of relief that the indecision was over and that a crisis had come in a way which would unite all our people. This continued to be my dominant feeling in spite of the news of catastrophes which quickly developed. For I feel that this country united has practically nothing to fear, while the apathy and divisions stirred up by unpatriotic men have been hitherto very discouraging.[77]

Winston Churchill greeted the news with similar feelings. "This certainly simplifies things," he told FDR in a phone conversation. "England would live," he remembered thinking. "I went to bed and slept the sleep of the saved and thankful."[78]

The President himself was not immune to such reactions. Eleanor Roosevelt later observed: "I thought that in spite of his anxiety Franklin was in a way more serene than he had appeared in a long time. I think it was steadying to know finally that the die was cast."[79] Writing of the emergency Cabinet meeting held just six hours after news of Pearl Harbor reached Washington, Secretary of Labor Frances Perkins noted:

---

*Most recently, Joseph E. Persico, in his study of FDR and wartime espionage, concluded: "The inescapable, if prosaic, truth is that no evidence whatever exists that President Roosevelt wanted a war in the Pacific, and all the evidence demonstrates that he wanted to enter the war in Europe. A monumental distraction from that objective, a war with Japan, was the last thing he needed. All the secrets, the intelligence, the intercepted Japanese codes, the very stuff with which the historian works, supports this conclusion: Pearl Harbor was a catastrophe, not a conspiracy" (*Roosevelt's Secret War: FDR and World War II Espionage* [New York: Random House, 2001], 156).

A great change had come over the President since we had seen him on Friday. Then he had been tense, worried, trying to be optimistic as usual, but it was evident that he was carrying an awful burden of decision. The Navy on Friday had thought it likely it would be Singapore and the English ports if the Japanese fleet meant business. What should the United States do in that case? I don't know whether he had decided in his own mind. . . . But one was conscious that night of December 7, 1941, that in spite of the terrible blow to his pride, to his faith in the Navy and its ships, and to his confidence in the American Intelligence Service, and in spite of the horror that war had actually been brought to us, he had, nevertheless, a much calmer air. His terrible moral problem had been resolved by the event.

As we went out [Attorney General] Frank Walker said to me, "I think the Boss really feels more relief than he has had for weeks."[80]

For the first time since Germany invaded Poland in 1939, FDR did not have to face the question — which Churchill and some of his own advisers seldom let him evade — of whether the United States should enter the war. On December 7, 1941, war came to the United States. Within an hour of receiving the news about Pearl Harbor, the President convened a conference with his Secretaries of State, War, and Navy and with General George Marshall and Admiral Harold Stark. Harry Hopkins, who was present, took notes on what transpired: "I think that all of us believed that in the last analysis the enemy was Hitler and that he could never be defeated without force of arms; that sooner or later we were bound to be in the war and that Japan had given us an opportunity. Everybody, however, agreed on the seriousness of the war and that it would be a long, hard struggle."[81]

The congressional leaders with whom the President conferred directly after his Cabinet meeting on the evening of the seventh, asked whether, in his message to Congress the next day, FDR intended to ask for a declaration of war against Germany and Italy as well as Japan. From the outset FDR agreed that the United States could not turn its back on Europe to concentrate on the Pacific and allow Hitler to achieve final victory against England and Russia. But from the information contained in intercepted Axis documents, he was confident Germany and Italy would soon declare war on the United States. Thus he skirted the more divisive issue of asking Congress to declare war on two powers that had not as yet directly attacked the nation, and he devoted his address to Congress on December 8 to the request for a declaration of war against Japan, which the Congress passed thirty-three minutes later with one dissenting vote.

Until Germany and Italy declared war on the United States on December 11, the issue of becoming a belligerent in the European theater remained very much on FDR's mind. After his address to Congress, Roosevelt returned to the White House, where he lunched with Sam Rosenman and Robert Sherwood, whom he asked to begin drafting the Fireside Chat he was to deliver the next evening, December 9. "There was no small talk," during the lunch, Rosenman recalled; "there were no jokes or quips; the coming events of the war were the topic of conversation. The President emphasized the fact that Hitler was still the first target, but he feared that a great many Americans would insist that we make the war in the Pacific at least equally important with the war against Hitler."[82] It was hardly surprising, then, that this fear surfaced in his Chat, which was listened to by Americans in some eight out of every ten homes in the nation — one of the largest audiences FDR ever spoke to.[83]

> We are now in the midst of a war, not for conquest, not for vengeance, but for a world in which this nation, and all that this nation represents, will be safe for our children. We expect to eliminate the danger from Japan, but it would serve us ill if we accomplished that and found that the rest of the world was dominated by Hitler and Mussolini.

He spoke emphatically of Germany's complicity in the Japanese attack:

> Your Government knows that for weeks Germany has been telling Japan that if Japan did not attack the United States, Japan would not share in dividing the spoils with Germany when peace came. She was promised by Germany that if she came in she would receive the complete and perpetual control of the whole Pacific area . . . and also a stranglehold on the west coast of North, and Central and South America.

Germany and Italy, he assured his listeners, were Japan's close allies and "consider themselves at war with the United States at this moment just as much as they consider themselves at war with Britain or Russia."

Speaking in his gravest and most deliberate manner — only some 88 words a minute instead of his normal Fireside Chat pace of around 100 to 120 words per minute — Roosevelt focused on the trials that lay before the American people and the goals for which they now had to strive.[84] In preparing the Chat, there had been disagreement as to just how detailed the President should be in divulging the damage the Japanese had wrought in their attack. The poet Archibald MacLeish, who often assisted in drafting FDR's addresses, urged vehemently that the people be told in detail all that had happened at Pearl Harbor. Rosenman and Sherwood argued that because it was not certain that the Japanese themselves understood how devastating their blow had been, it would be foolish to inform them voluntarily of how many ships and planes had been put out of commission or the precise numbers of human casualties.

Although the White House had promised the press that in his Chat the President would make "a more complete documentation" of the Japanese attack than had yet been possible, after consulting his Chiefs of Staff, FDR decided to withhold details that the Japanese might not yet possess.[85] Nevertheless, he did not minimize the defeat the country had suffered: "Many American soldiers and sailors have been killed by enemy action. American ships have been sunk; American airplanes have been destroyed. So far, the news has been all bad. We have suffered a serious set-back in Hawaii. Our forces in the Philippines, which include the brave people of that Commonwealth, are taking punishment, but are defending themselves vigorously. The reports from Guam and Wake and Midway Islands are still confused, but we must be prepared for the announcement that all these three outposts have been seized. The casualty lists of these first few days will undoubtedly be large."

He urged Americans to guard against rumors and enemy propaganda and promised to share wartime facts as soon as they were confirmed and so long as the information did not prove valuable to the enemy. He spoke optimistically about the improvements in war production during the past eighteen months and gravely about how much remained to be accomplished. "It will not only be a long war, it will be a hard war. . . . The production must be not only for our own army and navy and air forces. It must reinforce the other armies and navies and air forces fighting the Nazis and the war lords of Japan. . . . On the road ahead there lies hard work — grueling work — day and night, every hour and every minute." There must be a seven-day week in producing the materials of war, and while there should be no need to curtail the normal production and use of food, there would be definite shortages of many materials for civilian use: "Yes, we shall have to give up many things entirely." He had, he said, almost spoken of the "sacrifices" that lay ahead. "But it is not correct to use that word. The United States does not consider it a sacrifice to do all one can, to give one's best to our nation, when the nation is fighting for its existence and its future life." It is not a "sacrifice" to serve in the armed forces, "to pay more taxes, to buy more bonds, to forego extra profits, to work longer or harder. . . . Rather is it a privilege."

"It is our obligation to our dead — it is our sacred obligation to their children and to our children — that we must never forget what we have learned. . . . There is no such thing as security for any nation — or any individual — in a world ruled by the principles of gangsterism . . . we cannot measure our safety in terms of miles on any map any more." Modern war "is a dirty business. We don't like it — we didn't want to get in it — but we are in it and we're going to fight it with everything we've got." Our goal, he insisted, must transcend the war itself and focus on the world that would emerge from it. "When we resort to force, as now we must, we are determined that this force shall be directed toward ultimate good as well as against immediate evil. We Americans are not destroyers — we are builders." These were "difficult hours" and there were "dark days" yet to come, but he assured the people that "we are going to win the war and we are going to win the peace that follows."

Among the tens of millions of listeners to the December 9 Chat were the cadets at West Point, who were requested to return to the mess hall a few hours after eating their six o'clock dinner to hear the President. Sitting in familiar surroundings with the same cadets he shared a table with during his entire time at West Point, and whom by now he knew quite well, Roulé Cole Mozingo, a second-year cadet from Selma, North Carolina, heard FDR confirm what he and his classmates already sensed: that this was not to be a conflict limited to Japan and the Pacific theater but one which would encompass Europe and much of the rest of the world and that when they graduated in 1943 their service would be marked not by the routines of peacetime duty but by the rigors and dangers of war. Returning to their quarters, Mozingo and his two roommates discussed FDR's Chat and its implications for their future. Pondering the statistic that as second lieutenant infantry platoon leaders one of the three would perish, the young men decided to peer into the uncertain future by drawing straws to see which one of them would not be around when peace returned. Years later, Roulé

Mozingo, who became a career army officer, shared with his five children the story of how he drew the ill-fated short straw though, as it turned out, he was the only one of the three roommates to survive the fierce fighting all three of them experienced.[86]

Following the Fireside Chat, while Mozingo and his buddies were contemplating the bleak future, FDR sat alone at his large desk in the Oval Office smoking a cigarette and working on his stamp collection. Sam Rosenman, returning to the White House after having driven his wife to the airport to catch a plane for New York City, poured himself a ginger ale and the President a beer, and they sat talking of local New York City politics, of the possible candidates in the next New York gubernatorial election, of the coming Christmas holidays, of anything but the war itself. "Pretty soon the telegrams began to come in about his speech," Rosenman recalled. "They always did after a radio speech; and until he went to bed, they would be brought over to him. Tonight, the usher brought them in large batches. During the time I was there, several hundred came. He read them hurriedly, and silently passed them over to me to read."[87]

The telegrams would be followed over the next days by streams of letters from a people who found themselves entering their second major crisis in little more than a decade.

DECEMBER 11, 1941

Dear President Roosevelt:

Your talk to us last night was just what we needed.

No task too great
No toil too hard
No cost too high
No blood too dear
Until the war is WON!

All selfish aims
All petty ills
All politics
Put on the shelf
Until the war is WON!

May God give you all the strength you need to lead us.

P. H. Ryan
Louisville, Kentucky

DECEMBER 10, 1941

Dear Mr. President:

Listening to your great speech last night prompts me to write you and say how much I trust you. . . .

It is too late to complain of those members of Congree who would not vote funds to fortify Guam and supply adequate protection to us in all departments as you requested and too late to complain of the isolationist, pacifist, etc. But if I lose some of my sons who are now in the service by reason of such inadequate preparation I am going to be hard to pacify by loud mouthed and half baked mentalities who believed we could isolate ourselves and get by. . . .

Respectfully yours,

James W. Densford
Shawnee, Okla.

DECEMBER 10, 1941

My dear Mr. Roosevelt:

Your speech last night was wonderful. Everyone I spoke to thinks the same. We, up here in the Bronx, love you as no other person could. I want you to know that your wish is our command. I am a high school girl, and that is probably why I am so bold. But just the same I love you. You are marvelous.

Respectfully yours,

Marilyn Schissel
New York, N.Y.

DECEMBER 10, 1941

Dear Mr. President,

I enjoyed your speech on Monday very much. I liked best the part where you said that the United States would come through with a complete victory.

I thought that everybody had heard you when I got back to school, because everybody was talking about it.

My geography teacher is talking about the war and at home I have the radio on all the time.

Your friend,

James Hall
Penn Wynne, Penna.

DECEMBER 10, 1941

Dear Sir:

I am writing you this few lines to tell you that once more the American flag is bent over with sorro and with madness to see that she is being attack once again by a group of bandits. We have all ways manage to handle bandits and believe me this time we will put an end once and for all. Last night

I sat by our radio and listten to your speach when you said that we were going to put in action every thing we got to whip Japan you were not a bit mistaken when ever we all get to the front line you are going to see that America is still the same as it ever was and this time a little tougher this morning I got my affidevits to get out of the army I destroyed them I don't wan't to get out of the army I wan't liberty as I always have had it and if it gets dangerous in to where I can't have it any more I don't wan't to live I wan't death. I prefer death then to live under a group of Bandits so you & my country and the american people can count on me I will never sorrinder I will fight too death I have a father 69 years old a mother 49 years and two sisters to soport but I also have a country to defend and if I don't put all my strengh to do so I will have a hungry family on my hand giving and working their last meal to a group of Bandits I and my family would rather Die and Die under a free country than to worship our selves for a group of rats that are trying to steel our food at night and with out warning. I am a man with out much Edjucation but I have Geat Sympathy I love my country. I was born here to Defend it. To fight for it, with Sympathy and as a man not as a coward my eyes are open and I will keep them open until we win the war.

God Bless America and God Bless Democracy. Give me Liberty or Give me Death.

Yours Truly Soldier till Death apart.

PVT Juan N. Cavazos
Camp Bowie, Tex.

DECEMBER 10, 1941

Dear Mr. President:

Since war was declared on Japan my husband and I have had many conflicting emotions. We were both born at the close of the last war and even though other nations of the world have been at battle since that time, we were unable to realize or comprehend the real meaning of war until last Sunday. The news, telephoned to us by a neighbor, first brought shock, then anger, and then slowly a despondent feeling which intermingled with confusion, bewilderment, and fear as the passing hours brought varied reports and rumors. These were the emotions with which we sat down last night to listen to your Fireside Chat.

As you spoke I forgot that you are our President, for as I listened to your words I felt as I used to feel at times long ago, when things seemed all wrong and my world gone bad, and broad-minded, fairminded, lawyer-daddy would sit down with me and talk, pointing out both sides of my problem, getting me to face the facts as they were, and giving me encouragement and the desire to make the best of things. An inner-peace, a calmer spirit, and a strong determination to make things right would come to me then, just as it did last night. That is why I forgot for a few moments that it was my President speaking to me — somehow it seemed as though it was my dad instead.

Thank you for making your Fireside Chat. Because of your talk last night I feel better equipped mentally and spiritually to do my part in this war. I sincerely hope that in the coming months it will be possible for you to talk to the people often. We have full confidence in you — we are all behind you 100%.

Sincerely yours,

(Mrs. C. T. Tew, Jr.) Mamie O. Tew
Wife — Mother — and Secretary
Gainesville, Florida

* * *

Dear Mr. President: —

Heard your powerful speech via radio at 10:00 P.M. Tuesday, December 9th. and can truly say: —

> You are the right man at the wheel,
> To pilot our Good Ship of State;
> And though some fools mock The New Deal,
> They'll praise it at a future date.
> Some men of old were brave and bold, —
> Our Lincoln, and our Washington;
> Yet their real worth had not been told,
> Until the setting of their Sun.
> But times have changed and people too,
> And when this flow of blood shall cease;

The world will know the worth of you,
And call you the Real Prince of Peace."

"God Bless You."

William H. Gramfort

Born Oct. 29, 1880
Jersey City, New Jersey

DECEMBER 9, 1941

LISTENED TO YOUR BROADCAST. THE SAME APPEARED WEAK AND CAV-
ILLATING. PEOPLE OF IOWA AND MIDWEST WANT TO KNOW WHAT LOSSES
WE SUSTAINED AT PEARL HARBOR AND WHO IS RESPONSIBLE FOR THIS
LOSS. WHY NOT PURGE YOUR NAVY AND ARMY OF BRASS HATS THE SAME AS
YOU DID THE SUPREME COURT. THE PEOPLE IN IOWA WANT ACTION.

J. T. DAHLSTROM AND N. N. QUINN
WATERLOO, IOWA

DECEMBER 10, 1941

Dear Mr. Early:*

That was a good speech the President made the other night, (last night)
but I do think he tends to be too idealistic. To Hell with ideals, until we
have licked these international thugs. Blast Hell out of them, and make
them cry 'Uncle'. Then blast em again. The treacherous yellow rats understand only one language, FORCE. Lets give them 10 times as much as they
gave us. Put them back to where they were when we discovered them. That
have no love for us, only hate, and will gladly bite the hand that feeds them.
That goes for Hitler and Muss, too. Everybody out here is willing to go the
absolute limit to give these mugs a sound beating.

yours truly,

A Michigander
Detroit, Michigan

*Stephen T. Early was FDR's press secretary, from 1933 to 1945

405

DECEMBER 10, 1941

Dear Mr. President:

God Bless you, sir, for the wonderful speech you gave to your people last night. Your frankness, honesty and sincerity makes us all want to fight to the bitter end for victory for this wonderful country of ours. . . . I can remember the terrible dark days and the horrible outlook we had on life back in 1933. After you spoke to us when you first became President, telling us not to give up hope and faith, it was like a fresh breeze in a hot room where the air is about to choke you. Your great faith in God and in this country is given to us through your talks on the radio from time to time.

I am a married girl of twenty-seven, working in a bank in Philadelphia, and if my husband is called to protect his country, I know I shall be glad to make the best of the situation even though it means losing him, and he feels the same way about it as I do. I believe the country is now united with one goal in mind and with you to lead us, we shall win, so help us God. You are truly a great man and the only one to lead our country at this time.

May God be with you always, and give you health and strength for this big ordeal.

Respectfully and sincerely,

(Mrs.) Lenore B. Parker
Llanarch, Pennsylvania

DECEMBER 9, 1941

Dear Mr. President:

Your message to the American people tonight carried so much sincerity of purpose and determination that I am impelled to, as no doubt thousands of others are doing, to thank you for your courageous words, while at the same time thanking God because we have you.

I am a partial stranger in Chicago, arriving from Denver a few weeks ago to obtain work as an engineer in one of the defense plants. I know how we of Colorado, make every effort to consume each word spoken by you over the radio. Naturally, it would be an interesting innovation to partake of the Chicago reaction. Purposely, I went to a large eatery and gin mill in one of the rougher sections, where the din of the constant shuffle of people and their voices precludes even one possible thought.

It is with pride that I can relate for even the lowliest bum, that when the first tones of your voice were heard over the loud speaker, that upon closing ones eyes you could believe all had vanished, it became so still. Yes, every once in a while some hand clapping, a 'God Bless You', or some other indication of respect was all that could be heard until you closed with the last syllable. Some jaws were set a little tighter, a tear could be seen coursing down a man's cheek now and then, looks of reassurance and determination were in abundance. That from men who looked like they had lost already, everything in this world, but who couldn't stand to lose anymore. It was a sight that shall be remembered as often as I hear your clear cut voice over the air and as long as I'll be able to remember anything. Yes, Mr. President, you placed your confidence in the American people. In Chicago you can feel assured that that good cause shall not lack a champion. . . .

Respectfully yours

James C. Hughes
Chicago, Ill.

P.S.: THOSE JAPS HAVEN'T GOT A CHINAMANS CHANCE WITH YOUR UNCLE SAMSON — J.C.H.

*   *   *

My dear Mr. President —

You have just concluded one of the most stirring and inspiring talks that we have listened to. . . .

It was your courage, & your foresight that brought the American people to realize our dangers against the forces of aggression during these past few years.

Despite isolationists, despite "copperheads" and despite a feeling of apathy that prevailed among too many people you insisted and persisted that safeguards be taken to protect our precious democratic inheritance. It is only now, since the forces of aggression have shown themselves in their true light, do these people who once opposed you, now realize the justification of your past policies. The future is grave and serious, and your burden will be heavy, but we are confident that you will guide us through these dark days with unerring wisdom so that the beacon of freedom and democracy will shine brighter than ever before when victory is won.

We are not very much given to prayer — but I do say — May God keep you in good health and protect you. America and the world needs you!

Respectfully yours

Arthur Gahiner
Riverdale, N.Y.

PART FOUR

AMERICA AT WAR: 1942–1945

December the seventh, nineteen hundred and forty-one,
The Japanese flew over Pearl Harbor, dropping bombs by
the ton. . . .

I turned on my radio, and I heard Mr. Roosevelt say,
"We wanted to stay out of Europe and Asia, but now we all got
a debt to pay."

Peter "Doctor" Clayton, "Pearl Harbor Blues"

It has been months since I wrote you last from my small Farm
in Missouri, and now as I write you again it is not with fear or
trepidation that I write but with a glorious feeling of a still free
Country where I can write my President when I feel inclined to
do so.

PS I heard you say once in a speech that people wrote you letters and you knew what was going on, so you really do read our
letters I know, and do we like it so.

William H. Nanz, Sr., to FDR, September 9, 1942

"THE BATTLE GROUND
OF CIVILIZATION":
FEBRUARY 23, 1942

SHORTLY AFTER Pearl Harbor, the radio commentator Elmer Davis observed on a CBS broadcast: "There are some patriotic citizens who sincerely hope that America will win the war — but they also hope that Russia will lose it; and there are some who hope that America will win the war, but that England will lose it; and there are some who hope that America will win the war, but that Roosevelt will lose it!"[1] In the spring of 1943, FDR amused his Cabinet with the story of the American marine being shipped home from Guadalcanal who was disconsolate because he hadn't killed even one Japanese soldier. His superior officer told him that if he wanted to flush the Japanese out of the jungle he should go up on the hill and shout: "To hell with Emperor Hirohito." Sure enough, a Japanese soldier immediately appeared and shouted back: "To hell with Roosevelt." "And of course," said the marine, "I could not kill a Republican."[2]

Davis's and Roosevelt's irony underlined the truth that while the Japanese attack may have unified the American people with regard to entering the war, it did not unify them on all things; it did not transform them into a monolithic political, social, and economic bloc, and by no means did it render Congress compliant. Only eight days after Pearl Harbor, for instance, a House committee declined to widen the military draft to men under the age of twenty-one. FDR's early wartime Fireside Chats reflected this reality. Twice in two months — in late February and again in late April 1942 — the President took to the air to bolster morale and to plead for unity, cooperation, and sacrifice.

The months following Pearl Harbor were difficult ones for the American people. Militarily, the period immediately after the Japanese attack was, in Robert Sherwood's words, "a winter of disaster," creating what Sam Rosenman characterized as an "atmosphere of black defeat."[3] Secretary of War Stimson explained to a press conference on December 11 that in the opening stage of warfare, "it is inevitable that the free government, the government which depends on the consent of the people, . . . should be at a distinct disadvantage." This momentary weakness and inability to seize the moment was endemic in democracies and, he assured reporters, was only temporary and would change, but not overnight.[4]

Events bore out his caution. Before December was out, the Japanese had conquered Guam, Wake Island, and Hong Kong; invaded Thailand, Malaya, and the Philippines; and sunk the battleship *Prince of Wales* and the battle cruiser *Repulse,* Britain's two largest warships in the Far East. In the opening months of 1942, the Japanese moved almost at will throughout the Pacific, defeating American troops in the Philippines, forcing the surrender of the last American strongholds on the Bataan Peninsula and the island of Corregidor in Manila Bay, and severely beating the American navy in the Battle of the Java Sea in late February. The British fared no better, retreating from Malaya, Singapore, and Rangoon in Burma. By the end of February, Japanese armies had also invaded Borneo, New Guinea, New Britain, and the Solomon Islands.

Rumor was rife: Japanese ships were returning to Hawaii, or were on their way to bomb the Panama Canal, or on a course to attack the West Coast itself. "We heard that the Japanese had destroyed our fleet and would come here by sea," Frank Keegan of Santa Rosa, California, remembered. "There was considerable talk of a Japanese midget submarine fleet. . . . We were dreadfully frightened of the Japanese. For years we were told of the yellow hordes. We had the Oriental Exclusion Act. Even before Pearl Harbor we were scared of them."[5] It was this combination of rumor, fear, and racism that led to an increasing demand from the most respectable and powerful corners of California society, characterized by General John De-Witt as "the best people of California" — Governor Culbert Olson and Attorney General Earl Warren, the Hearst press and almost all of the other newspapers of the state, most of California's congressional delegation, the mayors and other municipal leaders of most of the leading cities in California, and indeed, in Oregon and Washington as well — for the forcible expulsion and internment of more than a hundred thousand Japanese Americans, citizens and noncitizens alike, from the West Coast.

On February 19, 1942, FDR, over the objections of Attorney General Francis Biddle, issued Executive Order 9066 complying with those demands, an act that the American Civil Liberties Union characterized as "the worst single wholesale violation of civil rights of American citizens in our history." Once again, as during the campaign for the Wagner-Costigan anti-lynching bill, Roosevelt proved to be no pillar of protection for those whose race and ethnicity denied them the rights guaranteed to all Americans. "Through lack of independent courage and faith in American reality," Francis Biddle would later write in his autobiography, "a superb opportunity was lost by the government in failing to assert the human decencies for which we were fighting."[6]

This was the context in which Roosevelt made his first Fireside Chat since the United States had become a full participant in World War Two.[7] Because George Washington's birthday fell on a Sunday in 1942, it was celebrated the next day, Monday, February 23, which FDR chose for his address. This allowed him to open with an analogy between Washington's bleak prospects throughout much of the Revolutionary War and America's current situation.

> For eight years, General Washington and his Continental
> Army were faced continually with formidable odds and recurring defeats. Supplies and equipment were lacking. In a sense,
> every winter was a Valley Forge. Throughout the thirteen states
> there existed fifth columnists — and selfish men, jealous men,
> fearful men, who proclaimed that Washington's cause was
> hopeless, and that he should ask for a negotiated peace.
>
> Washington's conduct in those hard times has provided the
> model for all Americans ever since — a model of moral stamina. He held to his course, as it had been charted in the Declaration of Independence. He and the brave men who served with
> him knew that no man's life or fortune was secure, without freedom and free institutions.

The present war, he continued, taught us similar lessons on a larger scale: "freedom of person and security of property anywhere in the world depend upon the security of the rights and obligations of liberty and justice everywhere in the world." Thus, though the goals were similar, this was "a new kind of war. It is different from all other wars of the past. . . . It is warfare in terms of every continent, every island, every sea, every air-lane in the world."

To help his listeners understand this global scope, FDR planned from the beginning to ask them to refer to maps of the world as he spoke and to ask the newspapers to print world maps in that day's editions that could be used for this purpose. "I'm going to speak about strange places that many of them never heard of — places that are now the battleground for civilization," he told Rosenman. "I want to explain to the people something about geography — what our problem is and what the over-all strategy of this war has to be. I want to tell it to them in simple terms of A B C so that they will understand what is going on and how each battle fits into the picture. I want to explain this war in laymen's language; if they understand the problem and what we are driving at, I am sure that they can take any kind of bad news right on the chin." It was this objective that led Rosenman to compare this Chat to the President's first during the banking crisis of 1933.[8] Rosenman was doubtless correct. Both Chats had the same didactic purpose: to reassure the American people by explaining the situation to them, by ushering them into the circle of the informed. In his best Chats, FDR always took the role of professor-politician: informing, explaining, reassuring, persuading.

As with the first Fireside Chat, the amount of work that went into the February 23 Chat was immense, and the sense of urgency palpable. "If the American people ever needed a shot in the arm, this is the time," Sherwood commented as he, Rosenman, and Hopkins worked on the sixth draft around midnight of February 21. The President had already read and annotated the fifth draft, cutting out purple prose and overly optimistic predictions. "One thing the President does not want to do," Harry Hopkins commented, "is to kid the American people into believing that this is anything but a tough son-of-a-bitch war against the toughest and cruelest bastards on earth. He wants them to realize right at the start what they are up against." Bob Sherwood agreed, observing that "no one is as good as the President in fixing the line between keeping up morale and confidence on the one hand, and being too optimistic on the other. I'd take his judgment any time." His speechwriters, in their turn, had persuaded the President to temper his vindictive language about the isolationists, which they felt was out of place now that we were at war, and planned — successfully as it turned out — to talk him out of one long passage he had written that they found too defensive concerning recent British naval defeats. By two in the morning they had finished the sixth draft. Hopkins, who was ill, went to bed while his two colleagues immediately set to work on a seventh draft, "polishing, correcting, adding, deleting," as Rosenman explained the process. This was completed by three that morning, sent on to Army Chief of Staff General George Marshall for his comments, and used as the basis for the final draft, which they hammered out with FDR the next day.[9]

It was that draft FDR read from on the evening of the twenty-third as he asked his listeners gathered in 61,365,000 American homes (78.1 percent of the total) to turn to their maps "and to follow with me in the references which I shall make to the world-encircling battle lines of this war."

> Look at your map. Look at the vast area of China, with its millions of fighting men. Look at the vast area of Russia, with its powerful armies and proven military might. Look at the Islands of Britain, Australia, New Zealand, the Dutch Indies, India, the Near East and the Continent of Africa with their . . . resources of raw materials, and of peoples determined to resist Axis domination. Look too at North America, Central America and South America.

> It is obvious what would happen if all of these great reservoirs of power were cut off from each other either by enemy action or by self-imposed isolation.

He explained in patient detail the disasters that would befall the Allies if they allowed the Axis plan of divide and conquer to prevail. China would fall, freeing Japanese armies to dominate Australia, New Zealand, and the entire southwest Pacific, which in turn would free Japanese troops, ships, and planes to turn toward the Western Hemisphere "and launch attacks on a large scale against the coasts of . . . South America and Central America, and North America — including Alaska." At the same time, Japan could turn to India, and through the Indian Ocean to Africa and the Near East "and try to join forces with Germany and Italy." Similarly, if we stopped aiding the British and the Russians, the Nazis would overrun them and be free to turn to Turkey, Syria, Iraq, Iran, Egypt and the Suez Canal, and the whole coast of West Africa, "putting Germany within easy striking distance of South America — fifteen hundred miles away."

In order to carry "the war to the enemy in distant lands and distant waters — as far away as possible from our own home grounds," it was necessary to protect four main lines of communications: the North Atlantic, the South Atlantic, the Indian Ocean, and the South Pacific, which he asked his listeners to find on their maps so they could visualize them. To keep these "vital lines" open "requires tremendous daring, tremendous resourcefulness, and, above all, tremendous production of planes and tanks and guns and also of the ships to carry them. And I speak again for the American people when I say that we can and will do that job."

He rehearsed the many rumors about the magnitude of our defeat at Pearl Harbor — that there was no longer any Pacific fleet, that more than a thousand planes were destroyed on the ground, that eleven or twelve thousand men were killed, whose bodies "were about to arrive in New York harbor to be put into a common grave." He refuted these "damnable misstatements" and supplied figures to show the defeat was less cataclysmic than had been portrayed. "We have certainly suffered losses — from Hitler's U-Boats in the Atlantic as well as from the Japanese in the Pacific — and we shall suffer more of them before the turn of the tide. . . . We Americans have been compelled to yield ground, but we will regain it. We and the other United Nations are committed to the destruction of the militarism of Japan and Germany. We are daily increasing our strength. Soon, we and not our enemies will have the offensive; we, not they, will win the final battles; and we, not they, will make the final peace."

The Axis powers were close to their maximum output of planes, guns, ships, and tanks. We were far from it and with "uninterrupted production" we could create "not merely a slight superiority, but an overwhelming superiority." To accomplish this would entail full conversion of every aspect of the society and economy to war needs. There could be no stoppage of work for a single day. All disputes would have to be solved "by mediation or conciliation or arbitration — until the war is won." There would be no "special gains or special privileges or special advantages" for any group or occupation. Many conveniences and normal routines would have to be abandoned. "We can lose this war only if we slow up our effort or if we waste our ammunition sniping at each other."

> This generation of Americans has come to realize, with a present and personal realization, that there is something larger and more important than the life of any individual or of any individual group — something for which a man will sacrifice, and gladly sacrifice, not only his pleasures, not only his goods, not only his associations with those he loves, but his life itself. In time of crisis when the future is in the balance, we come to understand, with full recognition and devotion, what this nation is, and what we owe to it.

Axis propagandists had called Americans soft and decadent, "playboys" who hired other nations to do our fighting for us.

Let them repeat that now!

Let them tell that to General MacArthur and his men.

Let them tell that to the sailors who today are hitting hard in the far waters of the Pacific.

Let them tell that to the boys in the Flying Fortresses.

Let them tell that to the Marines!

The Atlantic Charter, he insisted, applied not only to the world that borders the Atlantic but to the whole world: "disarmament of aggressors, self-determination of nations and peoples, and the four freedoms — freedom of speech, freedom of religion, freedom from want, and freedom from fear."

Quoting Tom Paine — "These are the times that try men's souls" — he moved back to the time of Washington for his peroration:

> "The summer soldier and the sunshine patriot will, in this crisis, shrink from the service of their country; but he that stands it now, deserves the love and thanks of man and woman. Tyranny, like hell, is not easily conquered; yet we have this consolation with us, that the harder the sacrifice, the more glorious the triumph."

> So spoke Americans in the year 1776.

> So speak Americans today!

When FDR finished his broadcast, he and several advisers went to the Oval Office for a drink. While they were gathered there, word came from California that during the Chat a Japanese submarine had surfaced off the coast near Santa Barbara and fired more than a dozen shells at an oil refinery near the shore, causing little damage and no casualties.[10] The attack was little more than a symbolic act on the part of the Japanese — what the President called at his press conference on February 24 "an excellent example of political warfare."[11] Nevertheless, as the *San Francisco Examiner's* headlines the next day — "JAPS SHELL OIL PLANT NEAR SANTA BARBARA" — made clear, it stood as a graphic demonstration for the entire country that the days of all-out war had finally come.[12]

FEBRUARY 24, 1942

JUST HEARD YOUR SPEECH. IT CHEERED ME UP. RECEIVED NOTICE TODAY
THAT MY SON WAS KILLED IN SERVICE OF THE UNITED STATES AT PEARL
HARBOR DECEMBER 7TH.

J. B. MANUAL
BRIDGEPORT, CONN.

* * *

Dear Mr. President

I just heard your speech over the riado. I am a widow with 2 sons which
I love dearly. They are 26 and 24 years. But I would gladly give to the army
after I heard you talk to night.

. . . I went through the last war working on war work bringing up my 2
sons which was small then but this time it is different, I always said I would
never want my sons to go to fight but you talk tonight has made me see
things a lot different. Please Mr President please take care of yourself if we
lose you we are going to lose the fight. I pray evry night that God will keep
you well and stray to see us throught this turmoil.

Please excuse writing I never had no education I am just a poor widow
trying to be a honest American thank you for that excellent talk dear Mr
President May God bless you and keep you well throught this ordeal.

Sincerely

Mrs Bertha Braun
Waterbury, Conn.

FEBRUARY 23, 1942

HEARD YOUR BROADCAST. WAS SWELL. I AM MASTER PLUMBER 26 YEARS OF
AGE. WIRE QUICK WHAT I CAN DO.

JAMES A. BANDOEE
LINCOLN, NEBR.

FEBRUARY 26, 1942

My Dear Mr. President:

As an ardent supporter of the Administration and a long time New
Dealer, I would like to tell you how unsatisfactory your broadcasted speech
of February 23 was to me and my friends.

Your failure to be frank with us (the public) about the extent of our naval
losses (serious damage as well as complete loss) in other places as well as
Pearl Harbor during the first week of the war, has led to a considerable loss
of confidence in your leadership. It is true that many things must not be discussed, but the American people are entitled to know as much as the Japanese do about our reverses. Mr. Churchill has given us more information
about the size of our naval defeat at the onset of the war than has been forthcoming from any official of our own Government.

Constructively and respectfully yours,

Eaton M. MacKay, M.D.
La Jolla, California

FEBRUARY 25, 1942

Mr. President:

Referring to your Washington's Birthday address:
With the foreign interventionist policy you have pursued you should be
ashamed to look in the face that great leader's record.

Washington's army knew what it was fighting for, for AMERICA, this
continent —
not foreign imperialism, but against it,
not for Bolshevism
not for the Chinese
not to stop changes in yellow man's country
not to stay evolution in the continent of Europe.

Truly, "these are the times that try men's souls", under such basically
unsound and un-American leadership.

To my mind you have sold out the best interests of your own country in an attempt to stop changes abroad, many of them needed changes, sold out your country to Britain's world imperialism, itself a dying cause.

Sincerely,

Lloyd Espenschied
New York, N.Y.

FEBRUARY 24, 1942

Dear Mr. President —

Your speech last night depressed me. American strategy — to give up the Phillipines! I always thought Americans never gave up.

Every American's heart is breaking for our soldiers on Batan. What are we going to do with our battleships and aircraft carriers? Keep them in a vault? They might as well be at the bottom of the sea. Our planes can protect our coasts.

If you don't send the Pacific Fleet to blast their way to General MacArthur every American will bust.

Pardon my frankness but that's the way I feel. I'm not interested in bases, supply lines or statistics. I am only interested in victories or at least attacks. Let's stop talking about the offensive and take it. Those men on Batan are Americans. Right now I am interested in nothing about this war but that those men be saved and the Philippines be held.

Sincerely yours,

Benjamin Bloomfield
New York, N.Y.

FEBRUARY 30, 1942

Mr. President, —

. . . It was the same voice which has for so long lulled the nation into a sense of security, the same old Braggadocia which has characterized all of your fire side talks, but somehow there was a lack of the assurance which has been so pronounced in them. It was the speech of a man not sure of himself. In short it was the speech of a man great on promises but short on delivery, in otherwords it was a flop and left a bewildered public all the more befuddled. . . . Every thing in Washington, including your cabinet, is in a muddle, a real mad house, and your complacency is beyond understanding. Nothing like it has been known since Nero fiddled. I used to think this Nero tale pure fiction but now I think there may have been some truth in it. . . .

Respectfully Yours,

John M. Hart
Roanoke, Va.

FEBRUARY 23, 1942

AS FAR AS IM CONCERNED YOUR SPEECH HAS ALREADY WON THE WAR.

MOLLY MCDONALD
DETROIT, MICH.

FEBRUARY 23, 1942

Dear President Roosevelt: —

Many times before, after hearing you speak over the radio, I have wanted to write you, but realizing the volume of mail you must receive, I have hesitated.

Tonight, however, after hearing your address, I cannot resist telling you how splendid it was. — I liked your reference to each of our allies; I liked your quashing of the ugly rumors of disastrous losses, defection of our allies, and of our inability or disinclination to fight. I liked especially, your assurance that the battle of production shall be uninterrupted.

Here in the Northwest where isolationism was very strong before Pearl Harbor, where it still persists in some instances, I hear statements like the following every day; "I must confess I did not like the Chicago 'quarantine' speech, but now I see — "

"I was against the League of Nations, but now — "

"I didn't vote for President Roosevelt, but — "

The Historic sound of the American people making up its mind.

May God guide you in the many vital decisions you must make every day, and grant you the strength to carry on in the way you have been going.

Respectfully and Affectionately,

Stella N. Gale
Minneapolis, Minn.

FEBRUARY 24, 1942

Dear War President: —

This letter is — quite frankly — A FAN LETTER. It will be my first, and quite probably, my last. . . .

My Dad and I sat at our Radio last night listening to OUR PRESI-DENT. As we listened to your quiet voice I watched the face of my Dad. Slowly the wrinkles smoothed out of his brow — the tenseness of his whole face relaxed, as we listened to the one man in whom we can believe.

The rumors became things of the past — we believed you when you told us the correct casualty list. Quietly — compassionately you laid the ghost of the destruction of our Pacific Fleet. Not for the moment — but for Keeps.

As I watched my Dad — so little and gray and tired (he's 68) giving the last years of his life to the speeding up of this War Production I was glad that it was you to whom he listened. It is wonderful to believe in the man who is responsible for our destiny as a nation and as indi-viduals. . . .

I shall probably spend many sleepless nights because of my temerity in writing to the President — but on the other hand perhaps our own sincer-ity can reach out to you through these lines — it might even help a little to know how well-beloved you are. You and the gracious lady who is your wife.

I am the "Voice on the telephone" for this agency — and I contact thou-sands of men in defense industry each month who do the hiring for our huge plants in Cleveland.

There are no more differences of opinion — Mr. President — they are for you to a man.

Would you please — come to us in our homes more often? We need you but definitely —

Sincerely and humbly —

Doris E. Noble
Cleveland, Ohio

FEBRUARY 24, 1942

Dear Mr. President:

. . . Where I have been an ardent supporter of your administration with few exceptions, I am now speaking as a citizen interested in Victory only. No one in our land is more capable of handling this gigantic task than yourself, but time has proven all men enjoying our freedom are not willing to sacrifice to preserve it, therefore, iron hard-fisted measures should be put into effect immediately if we are to win, namely the appointment of Gen. MacArthur as a Military Dictator to force to their knees, those selfish corrupt snakes such as labor leaders, Congressmen, Senators, and heckling bystanders. In this crisis it is time we used some of our rock walls and long branched trees to impress on the non-interested and obstructionists, we mean business.

. . . You are a wonderful President but far too easy with those who cast thorns in your path.

May God bless our Country with your health to carry on.

Sincerely yours,

Leo P. Scanlon
Kansas City, Mo.

FEBRUARY 25, 1942

CONGRATULATIONS YOUR FIGHTING SPEECH, WE ARE IN FULL AGREEMENT THAT THERE MUST BE NO STOPPAGES IN WORK UNTIL WAR IS WON, 400

EMPLOYEES OF HEDSTROM UNION FORCED ON STRIKE SINCE FEBRUARY SIXTEENTH, BECAUSE COMPANY REFUSES ARBITRATION. ASK YOU EVOKE EMERGENCY POWERS TO PUT COMPANY BACK TO WORK PENDING ARBITRA- TION SO WE CAN CONTINUE BUY DEFENSE BONDS AND STAMPS AND SET- TLE DISPUTES.

UNITED FURN WORKERS OF AMERICA

GARDNER, MASS.

FEBRUARY 24, 1942

Mr. President:

We listened last night with great interest to your "report" to the nation, and now this small section of the nation makes its "report" to you, in all sin- cerity, loyalty and resolve to stand by you, but just now heard on radio a news caster state that C.I.O. (that treasonable body) and Bethlehem Steel at work stoppage because of differences of opinion on length of work day. "How long, O Mr President, how long?"

With his words still in our ears, a program of strong hearted men The Marines followed with the Diary of the heroic men at Wake Island if you but knew the feeling of disgust which came over us, when comparing the news & the Marines you would BEAR DOWN on these moneygrabber unions. For God's sake can't you do something about them? Is this to be a second France?

You in your message used the word "uninterrupted" three times, unin- terrupted production, and on your very messages heels comes this "treach- erous" action of the unions.

We of this section, as you know, are behind you 100 per cent willing to and are making sacrifices, as our $21 a month soldiers are, but more than one loyal citizen expressed fear again that you were being betrayed by labor.

If you don't want to handle them as they should be handled, why not ap- point a Secretary of Labor that will take off the gloves?

God Bless & keep you.

Yours in Democracy

Larry and Nell Powers
Clinton, North Carolina

FEBRUARY 25, 1942

Dear Mr. Roosevelt,

Permit me a word of thanks for your last radio address. It gave all of us renewed confidence in our government.

Is it possible to create magnets powerful enough to change the course of a bullet. They could be fastened to either side of the object we want protected by long prongs.

Couldn't we have sister ships manned by robot pilots on either side of our ships transporting troops, to intercept submarine torpedoes. We have robot pilots on land, why not on water.

You still have not appointed a single chief for the army, navy, and air forces and it is probable no one person qualifies. Couldn't you ask the existing heads of these departments in strategic areas to function as a board of administration, conferring every day and reporting on their activities to one member acting as chairman, who would in turn report to you or your secretary.

Breaking precedents should always be your ambition. . . . Last summer I wrote in to your office that tanks should have noses for ramming objects in their way. To-day I read that the Japs have V-shaped tanks as though it were an oddity. Do you wonder that I am thinking the Japs must be studying our mail more intently than we are. There are so many white people in sympathy with them and the Nazis it must be hard to weed them out.

Please keep well. With patience and faith we will triumph in the end.

Sincerely yours,

Esther D. Bookman
New York, N.Y.

FEBRUARY 24, 1942

Dear Mr. President:

Last nite you stressed with special emphasis the imperative need and urgency of our total war of production. . . .

In spite of a bad cold you carried on. But each time you coughed it hurt me. Evidently your efforts are too streneous, Be careful. But, dear President Roosevelt you need not have those colds. You can prevent their handicapping, depleting and "retarding" occurences. . . .

For several years I made repeated attempts to bring to your attention a very simple (old fashioned) remedy against colds. I wrote to you several times and to people of your entourage several times urging that you take pure lemon juice regularly. . . .

Now, dear President Roosevelt, permit me to take you on your word and invoke your own urgent instructions to the people: "We must see to it that our efforts remain UNINTERRUPTED."

. . . take that pure lemon juice. It POSITIVELY does p r e v e n t the recurrence of colds if taken regularly.

Sincerely,

Henri E. Verbinnen
Newark, N.J.

FEBRUARY 24, 1942

My Dear Mr. President

I listened to your nation wide talk last night. It was fine but you seem to have a bad cold and must take care of your self. Grease with musterole and use vicks drops because we need you verey much to win this war.

your friend

Charles Leslie Minnick
Signal Mt., Tenn.

Age 11
I go to Nathan L. Bachman School

MARCH 2, 1942

Dear President:

The omission of any reference whatever to a Deity in your "fireside chat" on February 22, makes this speech, in my estimation, one of the greatest orations ever delivered to our Nation.

The sooner we Americans are made to realize that this is a struggle of and for <u>humanity alone</u> — without any Providential intercession — the sooner will Peace and Victory become a reality.

Words cannot express my gratitude for your high tribute to Thomas Paine. I cannot help but compare this in contrast to another Roosevelt a quarter of a century ago who libelously referred to Paine as a "filthy little atheist", and he was neither.

Respectfully yours,

H. G. Hayes
Junction City, Kansas

*   *   *

Dear Mr. President:

I heard your message over the radio Monday night and I was very impressed over it.

I am now twenty-one years old and I just registered for the draft, I don't care when I have to go to the army, I am anxious to get in the service. — But please Mr President the next time you make a speech, please bring <u>God</u> in it, because if any-one can bring us victory it is the "Lord Jesus Christ", I never hardly heard you make a speech with-out bringing in the Lord, but I didn't hear it Monday night. — I am a Christian and belong to Zion Baptist Church, and I'm not afraid of dying in action if I have got the Lord on my side. — I haven't ever dreamed of writing to the President of the United States, but please don't hold this against me.

Your Friend:

Lewis Thomas Smith
Chillicothe, Ohio

FEBRUARY 24, 1942

Dear Mr. Roosevelt.

What is the matter, are you loosing your punch, it sure was a weak speach you made last night, hell boy why dont you tear em apart, we are in this war now, to win, so lets give em hell. . . .

Remember us old Americans dont like England it is in our blood we cant help it, we just cant forget what they did in the past and we dont trust them. And we have not forgot how Loyd George done when the last peace treaty was drawn up. Most every body is afraid their promises are faithless we can see with our own eyes how they treat India. In fact most everyone I talk to has no faith in English talk or promises. . . .

Yes sir kid we are with you so get in there and start swinging, if the young whiper snapers cant lick them dear little Japs why just call on the papies of these squirts.

And another thing lets get something out of this war, yes sir I mean possesions thats got ruber trees and oil wells on them. It is time we stop being a sucker and start grabing something for our selves, I think we can run any country better than any other Nation can, the Filipinoes will alow that am the truth. We should take all the islands between us and Europe and between us and Asia and Africa, also the Malay peninsula. If we would keep them well fortified we could rule the world, we would be right smack dab in their front yards all the time. And another thing when this war is over lets face facts and be prepared for war all the time. Past experience has proved this is the only way to really live in peace, we just had a sample from Japan.

All right Franklin get up there and start swinging the old hickory. We want a home run.

Best regards,

P. G. Maxwell
Burbank, California

FEBRUARY 24, 1942

My Dear President: —

I listened to your Radio Speech on Monday night with a great deal of interest. You mentioned again your idea of the so called Four Freedoms for the whole World. This is all very well in theory and sounds very nice over the Radio, but it will never work out practically which we will learn sooner or later to our sorrow.

I feel that it is not up to us to try to force our ideas and ideals on the Whole World. The Whole World may not appreciate them or want them, and anyway it is not our job to impose our ideas on others any more than we would permit Hitler to impose his ideas on us.

Very truly yours,

Frank A. Harden
New York, N.Y.

"HARD WORK AND SORROW
AND BLOOD":
APRIL 28, 1942

LITTLE MORE than two months later, the President was back on the air with another Fireside Chat. Its purpose was the same as the February Chat — to bolster morale and help forge a unified people — but its method was different. This time FDR was less the professor with his maps and explanations of global geopolitics and strategies than the preacher with his exhortations to a still troubled people that the war had to be fought on the domestic as well as the international front. "It is nearly five months since we were attacked at Pearl Harbor," he told them, and yet the "dislocation" in most American lives was still minimal. That was about to change.[13]

"War costs money," he had told Congress in his State of the Union Address on January 6. "So far, we have hardly even begun to pay for it." In the current fiscal year, he informed them, the war would cost fifty-six billion dollars — which constituted more than half of the estimated annual national income. "That means taxes and bonds and bonds and taxes. It means cutting luxuries and other non-essentials. In a word, it means an 'all-out' war by individual effort and family effort in a united country."[14] What we needed, he told a press conference in March, was not merely more laws but more enthusiasm in doing our everyday work. "I would rather see a few more parades in this country. I would rather have a few more bands playing. . . . Congress can't pass a law to make a man turn out more work in a given time. That is up to man and not the law."[15] Laws, of course, did have their place. In his Annual Budget Message in January he had urged an integrated anti-inflationary program, including price controls, flexible tax policies, rationing of scarce goods, and allocation and credit controls.[16] On April 27, the day before his Fireside Chat, FDR presented an "economic stabilization" program to Congress. Even as the message was being delivered on Capitol Hill, Hopkins, Rosenman, and Sherwood were working on incorporating its essence into the Fireside Chat the President was to deliver to the American people the next evening.[17]

He began his second Chat of 1942 by rapidly discussing recent war news, most of it still bad. He highlighted the "most important development" of the past year: "the crushing counter-offensive on the part of the great armies of Russia against the powerful German army. These Russian forces have destroyed and are destroying more armed power of our enemies — troops, planes, tanks and guns — than all the other United Nations put together." He pledged that the United States and its allies would not allow "the use of French territory in any part of the world for military purposes by the Axis powers," and vowed that "soon" American forces "will be fighting for the liberation of the darkened continent of Europe itself." He paid tribute to the Chinese and Filipino peoples and to American soldiers for their courageous resistance against Japanese aggression. He coyly referred to General James Doolittle's recent carrier-based air raid on Tokyo by observing: "It is even reported from Japan that somebody has dropped bombs on Tokyo. . . . If this be true, it is the first time in history that Japan has suffered such indignities."*

He then got down to business. Not everyone, he told his listeners, could have the privilege of serving in the armed forces or working in defense industries:

> But there is one front and one battle where everyone in the United States — every man, woman, and child — is in action, and will be privileged to remain in action throughout this war. That front is right here at home, in our daily lives, in our daily tasks. Here at home everyone will have the privilege of making whatever self-denial is necessary, not only to supply our fighting men, but to keep the economic structure of our country fortified and secure during the war and after the war.

We are now spending for war purposes alone, FDR announced, about a hundred million dollars every day in the week, and before the year is over "that almost unbelievable rate of expenditure will be doubled." The problem was that these expenditures went into the pocketbooks and bank accounts of the American people at the very same time as goods were being

---

*Although he had ordered the April 18 raid on Tokyo to boost American morale amid the otherwise dismal news from the Pacific, FDR spoke of it sparingly and always with an air of mystery. When reporters asked him where Doolittle's B-25 bombers had been based, he replied, "Shangri-La," borrowing the name of the imaginary Tibetan utopia James Hilton had described in his popular novel, *Lost Horizon*.

taken away from civilian use. "You do not have to be a professor of mathematics or economics to see that if people with plenty of cash start bidding against each other for scarce goods, the price of those goods goes up." He then summarized the anti-inflation program he had presented to Congress the day before:

> First. We must, through heavier taxes, keep personal and corporate profits at a low reasonable rate.
> Second. We must fix ceilings on prices and rents.
> Third. We must stabilize wages.
> Fourth. We must stabilize farm prices.
> Fifth. We must put more billions in War Bonds.
> Sixth. We must ration all essential commodities which are scarce.
> And seventh. We must discourage installment buying, and encourage paying off debts and mortgages.

He informed wholesalers, retailers, manufacturers, farmers, and landlords that ceilings would be placed on the prices they could charge for their goods or property. He informed wage workers that they would have to forgo higher wages for the duration of the war. He warned business owners and stockholders, "your profits are going to be cut down to a reasonably low level by taxation. Your income will be subject to higher taxes. Indeed in these days, when every available dollar should go to the war effort, I do not think that any American citizen should have a net income in excess of $25,000 per year after payment of taxes."*

As in his Fireside Chat on Pearl Harbor, FDR was reluctant to use the term "sacrifice" to describe what he was asking of the people:

> The price for civilization must be paid in hard work and sorrow and blood. The price is not too high. If you doubt it, ask those millions who live today under the tyranny of Hitlerism.

---

*This proposition that a ceiling be placed on incomes, which the *New York Herald Tribune* was quick to dub "a blatant piece of demagoguery," was never embodied in legislation because of opposition from many conservatives in Congress, who advocated a sales tax over progressive taxation as a means of raising money. Opposing a national sales tax as regressive, Roosevelt found other means of raising money. Nevertheless, the notion of limiting incomes proved greatly popular with many of those who responded to this and later Chats.

Ask the workers of France and Norway and the Netherlands, whipped to labor by the lash, whether the stabilization of wages is too great a "sacrifice."

Ask the farmers of Poland and Denmark, of Czechoslovakia and France, looted of their livestock, starving while their own crops are stolen from their land, ask them whether "parity" prices are too great a "sacrifice."

Ask the businessmen of Europe, whose enterprises have been stolen from their owners, whether the limitation of profits and personal incomes is too great a "sacrifice."

Ask the women and children whom Hitler is starving whether the rationing of tires and gasoline and sugar is too great a "sacrifice."

The war effort, he insisted, must not be impeded by the faint of heart, the selfish, the falsifiers of fact, the "bogus patriots who use the sacred freedom of the press to echo the sentiments of the propagandists in Tokyo and Berlin," or by "the handful of noisy traitors — betrayers of America, betrayers of Christianity itself — would-be dictators who . . . have yielded to Hitlerism and would have this Republic do likewise." He warned that he would use "all of the executive power that I have . . . to attain our objective of preventing a spiral in the cost of living." He was certain that the American farmer, worker, and businessman would "gladly embrace this economy and equality of sacrifice — satisfied that it is necessary for the most vital and compelling motive in all their lives — winning through to victory."

He ended with the detailed and dramatic stories of American war heroes: Lieutenant Commander Corydon Wassell, an American missionary doctor in China who served with the navy in the Java Seas and who with great personal bravery had rescued twelve wounded American servicemen and escorted them on a harrowing journey from Java to safety in Australia. The crew of the American submarine *Sailfish* who, sailing through thousands of miles of the Pacific, sunk a Japanese destroyer and cruiser and badly damaged an aircraft carrier. Captain Hewitt T. Wheless, pilot of an American Flying Fortress who had maneuvered his bomber through a successful attack on six Japanese transports landing troops in the Philippines and — although attacked by eighteen Japanese pursuit planes, seven of which his crew shot down in a battle in which his radio operator was killed, his engineer's right hand was shot off, and one of his gunners was badly wounded, and although one of his engines was shot out, one gas tank was hit, the radio and the oxygen system were entirely destroyed, seven of eleven control cables were shot away, the rear landing wheel was blown off entirely and the two front wheels were shot flat — managed to fly the plane to his home base, making an emergency landing in the dark.

These stories I have told you are not exceptional. They are typical examples of individual heroism and skill.

As we here at home contemplate our own duties, our own responsibilities, let us think and think hard of the example which is being set for us by our fighting men.

Our soldiers and sailors are members of well disciplined units. But they are still and forever individuals — free individuals. They are farmers, and workers, business men, professional men, artists, clerks.

They are the United States of America.

That is why they fight.

We too are the United States of America.

That is why we must work and sacrifice.

It is for them. It is for us. It is for victory.

APRIL 28, 1942

My dear Mr. President:

My heart is filled with joy to-night over the reference to the U.S.S. Sail-fish in your radio address.

The last information I had was that my husband, Lieut. Thomas H. Henry, was gunnery officer aboard the Sailfish. With word from him so infrequent, I was overjoyed that you should not only commend the ship on its successes but, and so important to me, by so doing tell me of his safety.

I am praying that every man aboard the Sailfish heard your voice to-night. It would be a tremendous incentive to them to know that these efforts had earned the appreciation of their Commander-in-Chief.

May God bless you and keep you,

Frances H. Henry
Birmingham, Alabama

APRIL [29], 1942

Dear President: —

In your speech last nite as you spoke of the Submarine U.S.S. Sail Fish we was very happy as we have a Grand Son on that Submarine, Fred E. Wheeler we had not heard from him sence Dec. 1 — and we feel like we have heard from him now and he is all right.

Yours Truly,

Mr. and Mrs. Fred Williams
Lone Grove, Okla.

* * *

Dear Sir. Pres Roosevelt

You would have liked to have seen us fellows lying around the barrack in the dark (it was after "lights out") listening to your voice coming from a little radio. We heard every sylable and though we didn't always understand (about the $25,000 a year incomes, etc) we did like the way you said every-thing. It made us feel that, there, away up on top was a fellow who knew and cared. You made the whole setup simpler and made us glad from the heart because its the complexity that's so hard to take. We liked those stories of war experiences and got a laugh when you told of the radio man on that bomber being killed first. You see we are radio men (students) and are aware of what usually happens to us. It's a favorite joke.

It's time for school now, but sir believe me we are doing and shall con-tinue to do all that we can to keep alive the "American Way" which you so greatly help us to perceive more clearly.

Sincerely

Pvt. Robert J. Metzger for the boys of barracks 723
Scott Field, Ill.

MAY 3, 1942

My dear Mr. President,

Your speech, heard Tuesday evening at the Cafe de Paris, brought you close to all of us, and anyone would have believed you were one of the guests. All the service stopped, the little place was crowded with wonder-ful faces — many gray heads and many white — with young faces as well as old. No one demanded service or made any complaints — all were listening to you, Mr. President. The only noise in the room was the clock on my desk. . . .

All eyes were shining, and I saw that they were filled with tears including my own. At the close of your speech when the national anthem was being played everyone rose including one crippled gentleman who found the strength for it. I felt in that beautiful little assembly of people that victory was on the way. . . .

I remain yours respectfully,

Henri Charpentier
Chicago, Illinois

APRIL 29, 1942

Dear Mr. President:

. . . We are an ordinary, average American family — just a very small cog in a very great machine, but we are trying ever so hard to do our bit. My husband is employed in the office of a steamship company handling Government transports — he does not mind the hard work or long hours sometimes involved as he feels that he is doing his bit to speed an urgently needed ship on its way to some far distant land. He is also an Air Raid Warden, and studied diligently in order to have the privilege of serving.

I am a housewife — my pledge is not to waste anything — food, clothes or any other necessity. We intend to do without luxuries and put this money in War Stamps and Bonds. I am completing a Red Cross course in Home Nursing today and am also attending a Nutrition class, after which it is my intention to take First Aid. Our only daughter, (13 years) is a member of the Junior Red Cross and is busy knitting soldier sweaters for the Red Cross.

As for being rationed on tires and sugar, we would gladly do without anything for VICTORY. When we are doing without desserts and foregoing that extra spoon of sugar in our morning coffee we have only to think of the heroic men of the Phillipines, Wake Island or the other countless outposts of American defense, and we are ashamed that we cannot do more; the extra sugar we might have used today may have gone into the making of a shell which might mean the difference between life and death to an American boy in some far corner of the world.

God bless you, Mr. President, and keep you!

Very respectfully,

(Mrs. Edw. W.) Bernadine Arledge
New Orleans, La.

APRIL 29, 1942

Dear Mr. President: — I was among the loyal Americans who felt it my patriotic duty to hear you last night, but, I was sadly disappointed for I expected to have you, tell me, as my official Leader where I could fit into the pattern to attain Victory I heard no suggestions; . . . I expected to hear what definite action is being taken in Administration to economizing as an example for me to follow I expected a vivid picture, sans frills, of what our men in Service are encountering every day in battle and to be brought to a keener realization that this is "my" war and that I must do something about it. I want to be recognized as an intelligent human being, capable of reasoning and having ability to understand, true hard cold facts; I want to use my God given powers, physically and mentally, to bring peace to my own land and to all nations upon earth without looking for any personal glory, in short I want to order my life as a Christian, knowing that no matter how much I may get away with here, that some day, perhaps today I shall have to stand before a Just God and account for the job He gave me to do. . . .

Respectfully yours,

(Mrs.) Augusta M. Garrison
Jersey City, N.J.

MAY 1, 1942

Honorable Sir:

After listening in to your most inspiring speech of Tuesday night I could not let another day go by without writing to let you know just how much I am wholly behind you in any and everything you plan to do.

Mr. President, I am just one of many "Works Progress Administration" clerks (1412-53497), trying to make a living for myself and little son who is a victim of Infantile Paralysis but I am willing & ready for any sacrifice you ask of me for I know that any sacrifice made will insure complete & permanent victory for you Mr. President, these United States Allied countries and oppressed nations.

I am an American Negro, proud of my heritage & proud of my country. What can I do to help?

Sincerely Yours,

Marion T. Adams
Chicago, Illinois

APRIL 28, 1942

STEPHEN EARLY [SECRETARY TO FDR]

THOUSANDS OF OUR SERVICE LADS ARE PASSING THROUGH HERE AND
WELL DEMEANOURED WITH A GLINT IN THEIR EYES AND SAYING NO
DAMNED YELLOW LEGGED JAP WILL TAKE ME PRISONER. MANY OF THEM
HEARD THE PRESIDENTS ADDRESS TONIGHT EULOGIZING A HUMBLE COW-
POUNCHER FROM TEXAS FLYING A FORTRESS AND MISTER YOU SHOULD
HAVE WITNESSED THE RESPONSE. TO REALIZE THAT THE PRESIDENT HAS
THE TIME AND TOOK IT TO RECOGNIZE SO HUMBLE A CITIZEN WHO LIKE
THOUSANDS OF OTHERS SERVE WITHOUT THOUGHT OF REWARD IS INSPIR-
ING. WITH CONTINUED BRACING LIKE THIS THERE CANNOT BE THE LEAST
DOUBT REGARDING THE OUTCOME OF OUR STRUGGLE. THOSE OUT HERE
WHO CANNOT ENTER THE SERVICE HAVE FORMED GUERILLA ORGANIZA-
TIONS SUPPLYING THEIR OWN GUNS AND AMMUNITION ALL SHARPSHOOT-
ERS TO TAKE A CRACK GOD WILLING AT THE SLANT EYES. PLEASE PARDON
THIS MESSAGE FROM AN OLDSTER WHO IS REFUSED THE DRAFT.

BERT CLARK
SAN DIEGO, CALIF.

MAY 8, 1942

Dear Sir Mr. President.

I heard your seven point program and I think it is a good idea. I think
the United States is lucky to have a President like you. I think your fifth
point about Bonds has been carried out before your words. WE have studied it in school and I think it is my duty to tell you it is a good and interesting program. Our class in one day bought one-hundred eighty-two stamps.
We also have organized a club and we go around the school and make
speeches to classes to help in the War Effort. I am proud to say that President Roosevelt leads us to VICTORY against the Axis.

Yours truly,

Melvin Moskowitz
Age 10¾
New York, N.Y.

APRIL 29, 1942

Very fine Fireside Chat. Mr. President, . . .

In regard to our women being drafted I can't see why not. They have the vote smoke and wear pants. So why should they not be drafted. The sooner the better.

Good health to you Mr. President

Yours,

Anna Van Blarcom
New York, N.Y.

APRIL 29, 1942

Sir:

I had the pleasure of listening to your speech to the nation last night. Believe me, Sir, when I say that it was not so much a speech as a personal conversation. I was made to feel that you were speaking directly to me — explaining, so simply, what my country expects of me in this hour of its greatest need. . . .

To my regret, age debars me from offering my services in the armed forces of my country; to my chagrin my color hampers me in giving service for which I am best fitted. Permit me, nevertheless, to assure you, Sir, that I shall continue to do whatever may be permitted me to make myself worthy of my country and of its Leader.

Believe me to be, Sir, in all obedience,

Respectfully yours

Faustino Gregoire
New York, N.Y.

MAY 16, 1942

Dear Sir;

I wish to express my endorsement of the seven point program. . . .

I would also urge, Mr. President, that you use your authority in reading real meaning into the words democracy, liberty and freedom by removing all discrimination against racial minorities and by removing the restrictions of Jim Crowism so that a large portion of the American people may join in the war effort to achieve victory and peace.

May you, dear President, enjoy a long and happy life in a world from which hate, intolerance, prejudice and war have been removed.

Respectfully yours,

Rose Gutman
[no address]

MAY 1, 1942

Dear Mr. President:

Your radio address this week was precisely what this country needed. We, the people, have been outraged by the rumors of tremendous war-profits. Defense workers could not see why they should accept limitations of wages and increase in working hours if their employers were raking in huge fortunes. Other people were angry at the schedule of defense wages and hours, all for the same reason. We wanted an assurance that we weren't the only people who were asked to sacrifice.

We know it took courage, and that it showed the greatness and sincerity of your leadership of the whole people, to demand that incomes be taxed on a basis of $25,000 as the maximum left anyone after taxes. Even the rich will at last have to share to some extent, and we feel that this is the assurance that profiteering will be prevented. We don't believe in equality of incomes, but we do believe there should be equality of sacrifice, nothing else you could have said would have so effectively assured the people that this is Their war. Because of that we can also believe that when the war is over we shall feel that the sacrifices were not really sacrifices, that they bought us the pearl of great price, the safety and liberty of our children. It would seem un-endurable that anyone should be permitted to make huge fortunes out of the anguish and deaths of our sons in the war.

That was a great and courageous speech.

Yours sincerely,

Robert Weston
Lexington, Massachusetts

APRIL 29, 1942

Mr. President,

Thank heaven at last I heard the good news, "A limit on incomes to 25,000 a year," it is my humble opinion that there is not a man in this great country of our's worth one cent more than 10,000, a year, You can't expect the poor and the middle class to be enthusiastic about buying bonds and making sacrifices, while the rich make the speaches, we don't need the rich in this country, in fact, we poor, hate them, what we need most of all is to make each pay for this war to the limit of his ability to pay, use the great fortunes to finance this war, using the pennys of the poor will never solve our problems.

Good luck.

Patrick J. McGee
Newark, N.J.

P.S I'm still blowing my bugle for you.

APRIL 29, 1942

NEGRO FRATERNAL COUNCIL OF CHURCHES IN SESSION AT CLEVELAND REPRESENTING SIX MILLION ORGANIZED NEGRO CHURCH MEMBERS STOPPED OUR PROGRAM LAST NIGHT TO HEAR YOUR MESSAGE TO THE NATION. WE ARE IN HEARTY ACCORD WITH YOUR DEMANDS THAT ALL AMERICANS BEAR THE BURDEN OF OUR WAR EFFORT THAT NONE BE ALLOWED TO ENRICH THEMSELVES WHILE OTHERS SACRIFICE THEIR LIVES. WE THEREFORE PLEDGE OURSELVES TO SUPPORT YOUR EFFORTS TO DESTROY HITLERISM BOTH HOME AND ABROAD.

W. H. JERNAGIN [PRESIDENT]
BISHOP R. R. WRIGHT JR. [EXECUTIVE SECRETARY]
CLEVELAND, OHIO

APRIL 29, 1942

Dear Mr. Early:

I think the President may enjoy the attached letter. He has such a delightful sense of humor. Will you please hand it to him during one of his rare moments of leisure.

The facts regarding my employer are true.

Sincerely yours,

(Miss) Belle C. Smith
New York, N.Y.

Dear Mr. President:

Last night's speech, like all previous speeches, was an inspiration. The greatest tribute I can pay to your public utterances is to say that I always forego all "brilliant" social functions (such as a secretary is accustomed to) when I know you are going to speak over the radio. I just like to sit back in my favorite easy chair and listen to what you have to say.

Please, Mr. President, hurry and put through that part of your program which has to do with freezing salaries at $25,000.00 per year. Not that I earn that much, but my employer does; at least almost that much, and all that money has ruined him. Within the past year his salary has been increased from $10,000.00 to $20,000.00 per year. Instead of buying War Savings Bonds he buys Scotch and soda and his view of the present world situation is blurred most of the time, to say nothing of how his work is affected! I have always appreciated the fact that you are a great man eager to help the little fellow, and you sure will be helping me when you put a ceiling on salaries, for the less money my boss has the less he will drink and the more he will be able to use his own mind, instead of my having to think for him.

Seriously, though, you are doing a GRAND job. You are not merely making history. You are shaping a pattern for all the world to follow in centuries to come!

Very truly yours,

(Miss) Belle C. Smith
New York, N.Y.

APRIL 29, 1942

Dear President

I heard you talk last evening and I heartily agree with all but one thing. I do not see how the barbers of the country are going to exist on only 25 thousand for a whole year. . . .

But to show you I will not hold up your whole program I will do my best to get along on twenty-five thousand

Yours To Command

F. M. Chapman
Indianola, Iowa

P.S. My net last year was 1,201.00

APRIL 30, 1942

Dear Mr. President:

I was bitterly disappointed in your speech. I am a life-long Democrat and a former supporter of your administration.

You spoke of enormous war expense and of curbing inflation; you urge us all to buy bonds to the limit, to work harder and to sacrifice, all of which is all right.

You entirely neglected to mention any curbing of the ever increasing wage of Union Labor. Union Labor is getting a large part of this bond money. Many of us in the mid-west cannot conceive of a war being won on a forty hour per week basis when the Japanese and Germans and their slaves are working seventy hours per week.

After Pearl Harbor, we were all united behind you; but you still encourage closed shop and wage increases to Union men. The rest of us work long hours and over-time without any additional pay at all.

Now, it is one thing to buy bonds freely and liberally and another to buy them from a sense of duty; and while I expect to buy my share of bonds I certainly do not get any pleasure out of thinking that Union labor is getting the larger and ever larger share of the money. This will not win the war and it will not stop inflation.

If you will put a curb on Union labor, you will find a much better feeling among the non-union classes and, more to the point, a decided increase in the sale of bonds.

You have done much for the country; but I, for one, will not back your present union labor policy or any part of it.

Yours truly,

A. B. Carter
Omaha, Nebraska

MAY 3, 1942

Dear Mr. President: —

. . . I am a member of American Federation of Labor and also employd by Norfolk & Western RY Co. . . .

I bought $5,000, in bonds January 4th of this year and paid for them in cash this is part of money that I have made and saved in your administration and will buy more bonds this fall.

Its bunch of business chislers in our country that we have got to watch in this War and also the United States Chamber of Commerce I must say they are swell eggs in time of crisis, I under stand that members of Chamber of Commerce were the principal ones that tried to change the 40 hour work week, they certainly did pick swell time to do it, almost in face of invasion of our country by enemy, they thought it was good time to jump on labors backs and push them out of existence for ever but as usual it did not work,

Mr President the working men and women of this country are behind you 100 percent in this great crisis that we are now in and ahead of us.

With kind personal regards I AM.

Yours very truly.

Z. D. Sisson
Northfolk, W.Va.

MAY 3, 1942

Dear President Roosevelt:

. . . I am a factory worker, and every day I give thanks to you for what you have done for the poor working man and woman. No longer can an employer take advantage of a worker and compel him to work for a dollar a day — and the employers certainly used to do so! When I started to work seven years ago, employees were protected by the NRA. Shortly afterwards the NRA was repealed, and we were left to the mercy of our employers. I shall never forget this period of hard and unfair treatment. Now that we have the wage-hour-law, we have decent working hours with fair wages.

As long as you are in the White House, I will feel safe and secure. I know that there will never be another man like you who thinks first of his people. You are the best president the United States has ever had or can hope to have. As far as I am concerned, I would like for you to stay in the White House forever. God bless you.

Yours truly,

Dorothea Girard
Cincinnati, Ohio

MAY 1, 1942

Dear Mr. President:

Everything you said in the late 'fireside chat' was fine and each of us should do his or her best to do what you say to help. I think the ordinary citizen is and will.

I have a small business in a small town. It has been frozen and I am practically put out of business by the freeze. I sell typewriters. If that will help win the war I am willing to go all the way. My income is less than $100.00 per month. Four of my own sons are now in the army and navy. All volunteers. My mother has 9 grand sons and two grand sons in law in the service. We are proud of that. One of my boys is now in Australia and we are not able to hear from him.

Your talk is, however, very notable on what you did not say about the labor situation. Both you and Mrs. Roosevelt seem to have the conviction that the labor union racket is alright and that the millions of us common citizens have no rights in that respect and every one is told to do his part but they. If your judgement in other matters is so bad as it is in this I am not so confident, tho I am for you all the way in prosecuting the war. Wages are good enough without time and a half. 48 hours is not too long to work in a week. Having to belong to any sort of union is unamerican and undemocratic. You, Mr. President, are protecting a criminal practice in allowing it. . . . All profit should be taken out of war whether it is capital or labor but you want it only from capital.

Sincerely yours,

J. W. Densford
Shawnee, Okla.

APRIL 28, 1942

Dear Frank:

And I use this salutation respectfully, warmly. For any man who could come so close to the people of the U.S. as you did tonight, certainly knows them well enough to be called by his first name.

This is from a 26½ year old chemical engineer, who would almost rather die than write a letter. . . .

Frank, tonight you made me proud of being an American and you made me want to write, made the urge to do so irresistible. . . .

Frank, there is one thrill, one sublime thrill that you will never know, or, rather, experience. And that is the thrill that comes to a person — who, having been brought up in a poor family, experienced and felt keenly many of the injustices in our system — when he hears one of our leaders, — — who has every justifiable right and reason, judging from his background, to be perfectly unaware of these inequalities — dedicate himself and rededicate the nation to the sublime principles of true democracy.

You see, Frank, there were times when my heart was heavy and filled, with doubts times such as the miserable shooting on the bonus army, or times, when as a relief investigator I visited hundreds of downtrodden and almost hopeless families, or events such as the Republic Steel massacre in

Chicago,* — and I wondered whether democracy would ever rise above such low levels.

Tonight, you reaffirmed my faith and reawakened in me, that which I thought was no longer there, namely, a feeling of being one of a large, united family, and a hope that this family, — Christian and Jew, White, Yellow, and Black — could and would live and work harmoniously together until victory is won — and forever after. — Tonight you gave me that thrill. And for that I am deeply grateful. . . .

Thank you fervently.

Your friend,

Joseph J. Hitov
New York, N.Y.

---

*During a strike against Republic Steel, ten workers were killed by police on Memorial Day 1937.

"THE FOLKS BACK HOME":
SEPTEMBER 7
AND OCTOBER 12, 1942

FROM HIS FIRESIDE CHAT on February 23, 1942 — his first after the United States became a full participant in World War Two — through his final Chat on January 6, 1945, a period of slightly less than three years, FDR delivered twelve Fireside Chats, more than during any other three-year period of his presidency. He gave four Chats in 1942, four in 1943, and four more in the twelve months from January 11, 1944, to his final Chat on January 6, 1945. Only once during the Great Depression — in the crisis year of 1933 — did he deliver as many as four Fireside Chats in a twelve-month period. Obviously, the urgencies of war prompted FDR to ease his fear of tiring the American people by speaking directly to them too often. While he certainly had the war situation on his mind during these wartime Chats and shared military news — bad and good — with his people, the situation at home was at least equally omnipresent.

We have already seen this demonstrated in his first two Chats of 1942; it remained equally true in his final two Chats of that year.[18] Roosevelt opened his Chat of September 7 by continuing the celebration of war heroes with which he had closed his April Chat. This time he focused on Lieutenant John James Powers, a navy flier in the Battle of the Coral Sea, which had taken place in early May. FDR described how, during the first two days of battle, Powers flew his dive bomber through withering anti-aircraft fire, demolishing one large enemy gunboat and putting another out of commission, severely damaging an aircraft tender and a twenty-thousand-ton transport, and scoring a direct hit on an aircraft carrier, which burst into flames and sunk soon afterward. The President went on to quote from the statement Powers made to his fellow fliers as they prepared to take off on the morning of the third day of battle: "Remember, the folks back home are counting on us. I am going to get a hit if I have to lay it on their flight deck." Powers, as Roosevelt depicted it for his tens of millions of listeners, "dived almost to the very deck of the enemy carrier, and did not release his bomb until he was sure of a direct hit. He was last seen attempting recovery from his dive at the extremely low altitude of two hundred feet, amid a terrific barrage of shell and bomb fragments, and smoke and flame and debris from the stricken vessel. He and his plane were destroyed by the explosion of his own bomb. But he had made good his promise to 'lay it on the flight deck.' "

"You and I," Roosevelt told his radio audience, "are 'the folks back home' for whose protection Lieutenant Powers fought and repeatedly risked his life. He said that we counted on him and his men. We did not count in vain. But have not those men a right to be counting on us? How are we playing our part 'back home' in winning this war?" The President gravely supplied the answer to his own question: "we are not doing enough."

For some time, the President had been anxious about Congress's failure to implement all of the requests he had made in his April congressional message and Fireside Chat, specifically those calling for stabilized farm prices and higher taxes. The problem, as the Administration envisioned it, was that with elections scheduled for November, many Congressmen hesitated to enact ceilings on farm prices or to raise taxes. A number of his advisers urged FDR to bypass Congress and use his war powers to put into effect the entire stabilization program he had recommended. "I joined in this recommendation," Sam Rosenman has revealed. "In fact, after consulting with the Solicitor General, I had drafted an executive order which would have this effect; and it was on the President's desk."[19] Roosevelt, however, decided to heed other advisers, who recommended that before taking this drastic step he appeal to Congress again in a second message and once more turn to the American people in a Fireside Chat. He did both of these on Labor Day, September 7.

For Roosevelt, a large part of what constituted "doing enough" was a serious assault on inflation. As we have seen, in both his message to Congress and his Fireside Chat at the end of April, FDR undertook to freeze the cost of living. Congress, however, insisted on exempting a large number of farm products used for food and clothing. Although the President had asked Congress to stabilize farm prices at no more than 100 percent of the established parity price, Congress decided to forbid setting the ceiling at below 110 percent of parity on some products and 116 percent on others. From January 1941 to May 1942, FDR told the people in his September 7 Chat, the cost of living had gone up about 15 percent. FDR denounced Congress's refusal to stabilize farm prices as an "act of favoritism for one particular group in the community" that increased the cost of food to everyone.

Since May, he asserted, "ceilings have been set on nearly all commodities, rents, services, except the exempted farm products. . . . Wages in certain key industries have been stabilized on the basis of the present cost of living. But it is obvious to all of us that if the cost of food continues to go up, as it is doing at present, the wage earner, particularly in the lower brackets, will have a right to an increase in his wages. I think that would be essential justice and a practical necessity." This potential series of increases posed a real and immediate threat:

> If the vicious spiral of inflation ever gets under way, the whole economic system will stagger. Prices and wages will go up so rapidly that the entire production program will be endangered. The cost of the war, paid by taxpayers, will jump beyond all present calculations. It will mean an uncontrollable rise in prices and wages, which can result in raising the over-all cost of living as high as another 20% soon. That would mean that the purchasing power of every dollar that you have in your pay envelope, or in the bank, or included in your insurance policy or your pension, would be reduced to about eighty cents worth. I need not tell you that this would have a demoralizing effect on our people, soldiers and civilians alike.

The remedy was for Congress to hold farm prices at parity or at recent levels, whichever was higher, as well as to keep wages at a level with the present cost of living. "Both must be regulated at the same time; and neither one of them can or should be regulated without the other." He had warned Congress in a message earlier that day that if it did not act according to what he called "plain justice — and plain common sense," by the first of October, he would have to fill the vacuum it created.[20] He repeated that warning in his Chat:

> In the event that the Congress should fail to act, and act adequately, I shall accept the responsibility, and I will act.
> The President has the powers, under the Constitution and under Congressional Acts, to take measures necessary to avert a disaster which would interfere with the winning of the war.
> . . . The responsibilities of the President in wartime to protect the Nation are very grave. This total war, with our fighting fronts all over the world, makes the use of the executive power far more essential than in any previous war.

> . . . I shall not hesitate to use every power vested in me to ac-
> complish the defeat of our enemies in any part of the world
> where our own safety demands such defeat.

There may be those, he added, who would argue that if the situation was as grave as he portrayed it, he should act immediately without waiting for Congress. "I can only say that I have approached this problem from every angle, and that I have decided that the course of conduct which I am follow-ing in this case is consistent with my sense of responsibility as President in time of war, and with my deep and unalterable devotion to the processes of democracy."

He asked Congress not only for a ceiling on farm prices but for a floor under farm prices and under wages to avoid catastrophic drops in either. He asked also for a tax bill to prevent "the incomes and profits of individu-als and corporations from getting too high." In his message to Congress, he had specifically requested "heavy taxes on everyone except persons with very low incomes." Personal incomes must be limited to twenty-five thou-sand dollars after taxes, and all "special privileges or loopholes in our tax law" must be eliminated so that "the sacrifices required by war are being equitably shared."[21] The nation, he told the people in his Chat, "must have more money to run the war. People must stop spending for luxuries. Our country needs a far greater share of our incomes." Battles, he insisted, "are not won by soldiers or sailors who think first of their own personal safety. And wars are not won by people who are concerned primarily with their own comfort, their own convenience, their own pocket-books."*

Five weeks later, in a Fireside Chat he delivered on Columbus Day, October 12, he continued to make wartime demands on his fellow citizens.

---

*On October 2, Congress passed a farm bill that did not go as far as FDR desired but did give him extensive powers over farm prices. Nineteen days later, Congress passed a tax bill that raised taxes on corporate income, excess profits, and luxuries. Though it fell substantially short of the progressive tax bill FDR had requested and placed more of a tax burden on lower-income groups than the Administra-tion thought fair, the President signed it as a step in the right direction. In October, Congress also passed the Price Control Act, which extended controls over prices and wages and, together with the farm and revenue bills, eased some of the Presi-dent's pressing anxieties concerning inflation. He centralized many of these func-tions in the Office of Economic Stabilization, which the following May became the Office of War Mobilization (OWM).

Between the two Chats, he had made a tour inspecting military training camps and war factories, which had taken him, as he informed his listeners, "out through the Middle West, to the Northwest, down the length of the Pacific Coast and back through the Southwest and the South." Traveling quietly without benefit of what he termed "a blare of trumpets . . . crowds on the sidewalks, . . . batteries of reporters and photographers . . . all of the politicians of the land," and "without having to give a single thought to politics," he had the opportunity "to talk to the people who are actually doing the work — management and labor alike — on their own home grounds. And it gave me a fine chance to do some thinking about the major problems of our war effort."

He was impressed by the large proportion of women employed at skilled jobs running machines. "As time goes on, and many more of our men enter the armed forces, this proportion of women will increase. Within less than a year from now, I think, there will probably be as many women as men working in our war production plants." He dealt with the stereotyped notions that women were not capable of efficient industrial work by making fun of the "old saying of us men that curiosity — inquisitiveness — is stronger among women." In fact, as FDR and his group drove down the middle aisle of a great war plant, it was more often the men who broke their concentration on their work to gawk: "It was chiefly the men who were arguing as to whether that fellow in the straw hat was really the President or not."

He praised Congress for helping to solve the cost-of-living problems of factory and farm workers through the legislation they had passed. "It was a splendid example of the operation of democratic processes in wartime." Problems, of course, remained, especially in mobilizing manpower. As new factories came into operation, it was crucial to find additional millions of workers. We had learned to ration materials, "we must now learn to ration manpower . . . we shall be compelled to stop workers from moving from one war job to another as a matter of personal preference; to stop employers from stealing labor from each other; to use older men, and handicapped people, and more women, and even grown boys and girls, wherever possible and reasonable, to replace men of military age and fitness; to train new personnel for essential war work; and to stop the wastage of labor in all nonessential activities." He urged school authorities to make it possible for high school students to take time off during the school year to work on farms and in war industries. He urged employers to put aside pettiness and bigotry: "In some communities, employers dislike to employ women. In others they are reluctant to hire Negroes. In still others, older men are not wanted. We can no longer afford to indulge such prejudices or practices." He urged workers to utilize the forty-five hundred United States Employment Service offices to find out where their skills were most needed and to be referred to employers with available jobs.

He dwelt on the problems farmers were having finding hands to harvest their crops. In the only reference he made in his Chats to the recent internment of more than a hundred thousand Japanese Americans, he spoke of a community of fruit growers where "the usual Japanese labor was not available; but when the fruit ripened, the banker, the butcher, the lawyer, the garage man, the druggist, the local editor, and in fact every able-bodied man and woman in town, left their occupations, went out, gathered the fruit, and sent it to market." If such voluntary efforts did not suffice, "we shall have to adopt new legislation. And if this is necessary, I do not believe that the American people will shrink from it." He pointed to the success of the selective service system in drafting soldiers and sailors and observed: "the same principle could be used to solve any manpower problem."

On the subject of the draft, he warned the nation: "I believe that it will be necessary to lower the present minimum age limit for Selective Service from twenty years down to eighteen. We have learned how inevitable that is — and how important to the speeding up of victory." He understood the feelings of parents who watched their children enter the armed forces; he had seen his own go. "I have an appreciation of that feeling — and so has my wife. I want every father and every mother who has a son in the service to know — again, from what I have seen with my own eyes — that the men in the Army, Navy and Marine Corps are receiving today the best possible training, equipment and medical care. And we will never fail to provide for the spiritual needs of our officers and men under the Chaplains of our armed services."

He hinted strongly that the second front was about to open and that American troops would soon be engaging Germany and Italy as well as Japan. He ended by speaking of the future. He assured his listeners that there were people who, once the tides of war changed, would announce that we were safe once more and should retreat to our former insularity. "But it is useless to win battles if the cause for which we fight these battles is lost. It is useless to win a war unless it stays won. . . . We are united in seeking the kind of victory that will guarantee that our grandchildren can grow and, under God, may live their lives, free from the constant threat of invasion, destruction, slavery and violent death."

These two Fireside Chats — which make clear the extent to which the wartime President was willing to enter directly into the everyday processes of his country and the lives of its citizens — help us contextualize the frequent insistence that it was World War Two and not the New Deal that finally ended the economic crisis that had held the United States in its grip for more than a decade. This charged observation is most often made in a manner that portrays the war as an impersonal phenomenon able to achieve what mere human liberal reformers could never have. Thus we have the war and not the President and his Administration to thank for the return of prosperity. But war is not an extrahuman force; it is forged and executed by human beings who make of it what they will or, at least, what they can. It is not an accident that even during peacetime reformers often adopt terms like "war" and "crusade" for their movements, understanding that actions are allowed in wartime that are beyond the bounds in peacetime. Thus in his First Inaugural Address, FDR likened the Depression to an invading army and warned that if Congress did not act appropriately, the Executive would act without Congress. And act they both did. But never did "Dr. New Deal" attempt remedies as deep or thoroughgoing as "Dr. Win-the-War." The language of war may have been a shrewd strategy in peacetime, but in the long run it was little more than a surrogate for the real thing.

War itself provided a new context, occasioned a shift in attitudes among both the people and their leaders, and permitted actions not contemplated in peacetime no matter how dire the crisis. In early 1942, six Cornell University professors gave a series of prescient lectures entitled "The Impact of the War on America," the first of which stated:

> There are no subject-matter limitations on the national war power. The federal government must step into any situation and manage and control anything necessary and helpful to the war effort. Prices, profits, wages, hours, rents, production, priorities, rationing, transportation, communication, disease, prostitution, and many other things are swept within the reach of federal power.[22]

And so it came to pass; the federal government did all of the things the professors invited it to. It became the nation's chief customer and its chief employer. It allocated resources, determined production, fixed wages, limited prices, rationed goods, drafted men, and set up a bureaucratic network that threatened to make the New Deal look simple. And it brought prosperity back to the nation, as it would have had it done these things five years earlier, when the enemy was not the fascists but the deadly and dangerous forces of economic poverty, dislocation, and hopelessness. Unemployment, which was at some eight million in 1940, virtually disappeared by early 1943. The reasons for the return of prosperity are easy enough to discern. What is more difficult to understand is why the American people and its leaders were willing and able to take actions in a foreign crisis they were unwilling and unable to take in the midst of a domestic crisis that, as FDR said again and again, threatened the viability and future of American democracy. Why, that is, it is discernibly easier for us as a people to act so much more decisively and effectively amid the threats of war than those of peacetime, though the latter may be no less inimical to our existence.

This was not a conundrum FDR raised or pondered seriously during these years. But when he did allow himself to think of the peacetime future, he understood how much unfinished business remained to be accomplished if the United States was to cure itself permanently of the ills that had become manifest throughout the prewar decade. More than a few of his correspondents had come to similar realizations.

OCTOBER 26, 1942

Dear Mr. President:

Any open-eyed traveling salesman could add "Amen" to your summation of your recent trip when you state "The American people are not complacent". You are absolutely right.

I am one of the species of traveling-men, and cover eight southern states, having been born and raised in Des Moines, Ia, for the past twelve years a resident of New York.

I have not seen the secret insides of our huge industrial plants or spoken to their captains, but — I have been far luckier. I have spoken to countless "little men"; farmers, mechanics, salesmen, grocers, clerks, porters, tradesmen, conductors, share-croppers and more. I've met them on busses, in trains, ferries, hotels, restaurants, stores, and along with them have been hundreds of Servicemen from every section of the country.

Their spirit is exemplary. They are willing to do anything they are asked to do. They may growl, a very few of them, but they are prepared to give to the limit if it means helping secure our freedom. The most remarkable thing of all is how little those who would sacrifice the most have. But, — that "little" is awfully important to them.

Walt Whitman saw Americans as I often see them. Tom Wolfe, had he lived longer, would have written reams about the kind of average-man I meet. I'm sure everyone would have your faith, which is my faith, if they could breathe the earthy sincerity and loyalty of these ordinary Americans.

One thing I would pass on to you, based upon my own personal experiences. All of these people yearn for just one thing — leadership — vigorous, honest, intelligent, faithful to them and the cause they are willing to sacrifice so much to win. They demand it of all leaders, civic, political, and military. Given divine leadership we can't miss. . . .

Good health, good luck to you.

Very sincerely yours

William H. Miller
New York, N.Y.

SEPTEMBER 15, 1942

Mr. President;

Let the senators rave — and our representatives rant, let them wonder and wait — for elections — the everyday man wants you to go ahead — even faster than you are!

Go ahead — tax us, take our cars for as long as they are needed, tax our payrolls, take bonds out of them, take the married men, or the eighteen year-old, or both! You wont hear any squawks, at least so few of them that no one will really listen. We're behind you in anything you see fit to do — We want to get it over with! We are willing, nay — eager to sacrifice for good things.

We hear the sore-heads rave about capitalistic wars, about Jews, about "the poor-man-gets-the-fighting-the-rich-man-gets richer! We know they are there, always whining!

They don't bother us. We know what we are doing — So do you — we are even surer of that fact.

I did not want to vote for you the first time, but I did, and now I am glad that I did.

Don't let us down by not cracking down. We can take it. Try us — and see!

Sincerely,

Dorothy Cameron Voelz
Chicago, Illinois

Just another American

SEPTEMBER 8, 1942

Dear President:

After hearing you last night, Sept. 7th. I felt, as once more, we, "the people" were stepping on to a firmer ground. I went to bed rested.

The mothers are in a queer state of mind, and we need to know our leader will hold the reins of our Country in a steady hand. My two sons are in this. I am doing all I can, defense, spotting, and R.C. surgical. I can do more and have applied for an F.B.I. job.

I believe I can speak for thousands and thousands. Gladly, we let our boys go. We are willing to give all we have. Just have our Government back of them. No time for petty quarrels.

And your message last night gave me this feeling "Now, one for all, all for one"....

Mrs. Johnny Gruelle
Norwalk, Ct.

OCTOBER 13, 1942

Most Honorable Sir:

I listened last night to your so-called "homey" fireside chat and I could hardly believe my ears at the statements that you made in that talk.

When you talk so glibly of drafting our eighteen and nineteen year old boys, it is absolute proof that you are war-mad. We now have in this country, whether you know it or not, several hundred thousand men who are unable to get into the armed forces and are waiting assignments to duty because you have managed the mobilization of our armed forces so miserably that we are unable either to train or get them to the point where they are needed and why you want to take these young men out of their homes and put them into ill-prepared camps in order to say that you are the commander and chief of the biggest army in the world. I suggest that you re-read several times the script of your speech and I believe that on mature reflection you will realize that it is the poorest speech that was ever made by any man....

Yours very truly,

Earl E. Wright
Santa Ana, California

OCTOBER 14, 1942

My dear Mr President: —

Hearing your talk last evening, Oct 12. it has impressed me so, being a Mother of a son in service, I am prompted to write you.

Mr President, let me say, it is an honor and a privilage for me and my boy to serve under you, our "Commander in Chief".

My son, was a volunteer, he left the states, to an Island in Hawaii, was there (8) months, when he was brought back to the States, to enter Officers Training School at Ft. Monmouth, N.J. where at the present time he is attending.

Where in God's world is there such golden opportunities for any American youth, but our dear old U.S.A.

I have an other son, just 18 years, waiting for his High school diploma, and then he will be in the Armed forces, as he is raring to go.

The treatment of our boys are second to none. . . .

I am ever grateful to you. You will never know how at ease of mind you make me & millions of Mother's feel giving our boys in such wonderful hands.

Ever thank full & grate full to you.

I am

Sincerely

Mrs. Marguerite M. Wolheim
New York, N.Y.

SEPTEMBER 9, 1942

Dear President Roosevelt

After listening to your fireside talk the night of the seventh I want to tell you how greatful I am to have a man like you at the head of this great nation. . . .

I am a widow my husban passed away two years ago he left me a little farm out here in West Texas.

I have eight children six boys and two girls. the girls have been living here with me. the oldest has joined the W.A.A.C and is to be trained at Des Moins Iowa.

two sons are already in the Army. MAC has been reported missing in action in the Philippines I have not heard from him since Nov. 11th 1941. needless to say that I am very anxious to hear from him. the two oldest boys a preacher, and a school Supt. are waiting the orders to go in to service one a chaplin, and the other as capt. they are world war I vets. the baby girl took a mans place in one of the Safeway stores so he could go in to the army.

so I think I will have to add another star to my service pin for her. she is a widow with a baby two years old.

Sincerely

Mrs. Tabitha Watson
Spur, Texas

OCTOBER 12, 1942

Dear Mr. President,

Your talk is just over, and with many others I cannot resist writing you a word of thanks. . . .

I'm an elderly country woman myself and live near the coast. Nineteen other women of similar circumstances have joined me in forming a Rifle Women's Association. We shoot every week, conserving our shells of course, and each of us is able to make good shots with rifles fair with pistols, and even an old-time shot gun has no terrors for us.

With the men away at business or on Defense Work often at night, we decided to take self-defense seriously, and just let parachutists try landing near us! Besides the feeling of confidence we have grown to know and like each other in the past two months — years of being neighbors had never made us as friendly. So the women are behind you. . . .

Sincerely

Madeleine Downing Knight
South Jacksonville, Florida

SEPTEMBER 7, 1942

Franklin D. Rosevelt

this is to let you no that we all no we are the luckeys people in all the World to have as Dear Leader as you are and we no that you pray for the nashion and we no that ever thing that you do is for us tho I no I cant do eny thing to help win this Blood War tho I work 20 hour a day and night to do what I can on the farm I planted 5 acres of peanuts for the Boys in uniforms and I am stacking them now and have 75 are 100 stacks 7 feet tall and I am not thro yet am hoping I will get thro this week pray for me that I can hold out it is all Right to give out But not give up

. . . it just gives one the Belly ace to here these peple say what can I do to stay out of the War I want to no what can I do to get in somthing that I can do a Big Job

I have just got little enoff sence to think I can do a little of eny thing eny Body else can do and I have a good mind I am 53 year old and do more work then eny one else around here all I want is to hold out untell their yellow Back Slides are all under 6 foot sement so I no they cant ever get out a gain

Them I Will set down and Rest. . . .

So long

Mary S. Dison
Cedar Cove, Ala.

OCTOBER 20, 1942

Dear Mr. President,

I am a boy of 10 in school P.S. 75. I did not hear your speech but my father told me it was very good. I am trying to do my best for my country. I buy war stamps weekly, and I give my money to different kinds of funds. My father works in a defense plant and my mother saves tin cans for me to bring to school. I think every american should understand what you are trying to do for us. My friend and I are helping Brooklyn win the scrap drive I brought in a box of tin cans. If every american will do what we do will surely win the war.

Thumbs Up.

An American Boy

Donald Katz
New York, N.Y.

SEPTEMBER 12, 1942

My dear Mr. Roosevelt,

. . . this home front is so difficult. The attackers of Democracy don't wear the Axis uniform, here, and there is so little one can do to refute their lies; they still control the bread and butter of so many of us even though they are so few. Please know your closing words in your speech on inflation gave new life to me, new strength to meet the dissenters and their lies of. . . .

"The industrialists haven't delayed the war program, the Government has;

"I'm not saying anything against the Jews, but — ;

"To be an Episcopalian is almost as bad as being a Catholic;

"The Jews sold the oil and scrap iron to Japan;

"The Russians are dirty and ugly;

"We'll never cooperate with any Orientals;

"Labor shouldn't receive decent wages; only intellectuals deserve such compensation;

"All Negroes are liars and wont work;

"If a cult preaches 'kill the Jew' and they use the Bible to prove their point, they can't be wrong;

"The people aren't supporting this war;

"My wealth and position result from the will of God. . . .

"I gave more than I could afford to help the 'poor Finns' you can't expect me to help the Russians now;

"If England would fight we wouldn't have to;

"Bring back prohibition, that'll save us;" and so forth & so on, they attack insidiously always opening the conversation so pleasantly, appear to have their speeches well planned with little or no pauses for a chance of refutation, with their closing remarks timed with their exits. I'm wondering how many are swayed into doubts about Democracy by these few. . . . These "spreaders" of dissension so obviously force their speeches upon one, they can't all be just innocently conversational. Maybe the innocent ones should go to classes to learn that America is the symbol, and intends to become the fact, of Democracy; that all races have contributed to build our Nation and today are contributing to keep alive and make real that Democracy; that each is important unto the other; that each shall receive honest remuneration for his strength and he contributes to the Cooperation of all. Just as all races gathered in our Nation have and believe in this common intent which holds us together, so do the peoples of all the world have this same common interest! . . .

Well we know how you will be harassed for championing freedom, be proud of it, this is the show-down, and you shall have the strength to meet it.

Sincerely,

Rita Queirolo
Berkeley, California

SEPTEMBER 7, 1942

Dear Mr. President:

. . . The people of this nation are not afraid of sacrifice, but that sacrifice must be borne by all. If this war produces a flock of millionaires, as the last one did, no legislative dam in the world can stem the flood of resentment, anger, and ill considered action that would inundate our land.

Have courage — look to the future — the verdict history will write across your record.

Respectfully yours,

R. N. McMaster
Margaret J. McMaster
Arcadia, California

SEPTEMBER 7, 1942

Esteemed Sir:

Kindly accept my heartiest congratulations for your courageous address and all that it involves.

It is altogether equitable that if men are drafted, money should be drafted too. God forbid that Americans should prosper by the blood of their brothers. . . .

Very truly yours,

F. R. Stoneburner
Dayton, Ohio

SEPTEMBER 8, 1942

Dear President Roosevelt:

Congratulations on your message to Congress and on your radio talk last night. — I am sure the overwhelming majority of the people are glad you have declared for action on the whole seven-point-program, to prevent inflation and that you will act if Congress fails to do so. More power to you in urging equality of sacrifice and taxing on ability to pay! A $25000 income is more than sufficient while millions of sharecroppers and underprivileged are free only to be undernourished. It is indeed time for us all to practice the democracy we so glibly talk about.

I am writing the N.J. Senators and the Congressman from my district, asking them to support you completely.

I trust you will use every means to bring victory as speedily as possible.

Sincerely yours,

Addie L. Weber
Trenton, New Jersey

SEPTEMBER 8, 1942

Dear Mr. President:

Your Fireside Chat of September 7 is one that brings renewed courage and determination to all of us. I am sure that the mass of Common people will give their unreserved support to you in the stand you have taken. Especially will we redouble our efforts in the election campaign to defeat those Congressmen who have so consistently sabotaged your Seven Point Program.

If Congress refuses to act on this program and you have to take new steps to guarantee the winning of the war, we know that certain elements of the press will scream "dictators" — but we also know that it is the only way to save our democracy from the terror of a real and fascist dictator, and we say more power to you.

I am sure that I speak for my husband too, who is keeping them sailing somewhere in the South Pacific.

Respectfully yours,

(Mrs) Clemmie S. Barry
San Francisco, California

SEPTEMBER 21, 1942

Dear Mr. Roosevelt:

This is to express our sincerest disagreement with the tenor of your Labor Day address in which you threatened Congress with executive action if it refuses to act by a certain deadline.

Whatever the merits of the different price control proposals, whatever the danger, and whoever deserves the blame for delay, it is antithetical to democratic principles for any executive to over-ride legislation which has been passed by the people's representatives.

Your threat is a threat to the democratic institutions of America and the world. Remember that Hitler and Mussolini also charged the democratic processes with inefficiency. We hope you will not undertake the action you have promised.

Sincerely yours

(Mr. and Mrs.) John and Irma Honigmann
New Haven, Conn.

SEPTEMBER 8, 1942

Dear Sir,

I wish to congratulate you on your Labor Day address; especially in regard to limiting prices on farm Products and wages. I am the sole support and wage earner of my wife & three children. I am employed in a so called War Defense Industry, my weekly salary is $32.00 and after deducting for Social Security and Defense Bonds I have about $29.00 to bring home for five persons to live on, for a week. This was bad enough before farm prices began to soar to where they are, but now it is almost impossible to exist on these wages, unless a limit is put on how high farm prices may go. . . . I think this farm bloc should be stopped before they ruin the Nation.

Sincerely Yours in faith,

Harold J. Leary
Richmond Hill, N.Y.

SEPTEMBER 11, 1942

Dear Mr. President,

I listened to your Fireside Chat of September 7, and wish to express my opinion of it. Knowing that you are a liberal person, I would not have expected you to attack the hardest-working group of people in our nation, the Farmers.

Farmers are not asking double pay for work they do "overtime". Instead, they have gotten in stride with the rest of the nation in our greatest undertaking in history, the defeat of the axis. In fact, they have far surpassed the efforts of any other class of people in these United States, for they work on an average of ninety hours per week, while factory laborers will not work more than forty hours without expecting a special bonus in the form of extra pay. . . . At least 50% of our nation's farms have no electricity, while 75% of them have no running water; and yet they remain the subject of constant attack by the "working" class. . . .

Respectfully yours,

Simmy Rothblatt
New York, N.Y.

SEPTEMBER 8, 1942

My dear Sir —

. . . The writer just returned from a swing thru the State of Texas and find a lot of people who are not supporting the war because of Congress and the way labor has been dictating affairs. . . . I visited a banker friend in Northeast Texas who told me he had sold $125.00 worth of bonds that day — that he had customers who should be buying defense bonds, but were not on account of labor — they did not feel like buying bonds so that labor could get an increase in wages. They did not want labor to fatten on thier money. These are facts and the real situation as I found it. . . .

Sincerely yours,

A. C. Robbins
Weslaco, Texas

SEPTEMBER 8, 1942

Dear Mr. President:

. . . as a member of organized labor, I was glad to note that wages, instead of being "frozen" will continue to be regulated according to the cost of living. Wage earners have already lost much because of the inflation that has set in. We are ready to buy bonds, and to sacrifice in any way necessary for the winning of the war. We do however believe in equality of sacrifice, and we are happy and proud that you have refused to crack down on labor as some reactionaries would like. An efficient working force for our factories is vital to victory. We commend you for refusing to cut our standard of living further. . . .

Very sincerely yours,

Agnes W. Spencer
Moorestown, N.J.

SEPTEMBER 11, 1942

Dear Sir:

... I want you to know how we feel about your leadership in these dark days. Around the radio, as our family sat & listened, my mother suddenly & spontaneously rose & said as your voice broke for a moment — said it in Yiddish which means more than translation can say it, that 'she would want to spare your every pain'. My mother is in her fifties. She came from Europe a generation ago. And she has seven children whom she has devoted her life to, & who she is ready to see serve her new country, America. And she can bear this pain because of the faith you have given her, & the millions of other mothers. ...

Respectfully yours,

David T. Weiss
New York, N.Y.

SEPTEMBER 7, 1942

Dear Mr. President. Thanks for your timely speech, — devotion and courage towards victory. If Congress knew the American People as well as you do and if each member had a son in the service I think they would act a little quicker sometimes and forget about party politics and selfish interest. ... Our Boy Harvey 17½ years old is serving in the Navy he is in the tropics as a Signal man fighting submarines and I am sure he will do his part for us all. ... when he said good by to his mother he said, well Mam, we are on our way I will be back soon dont worry about me you know I will be allright and if something should happen to me so I dont come back, allways think of this I fought for the finest and noblest cause in the world American Freedom.

Yours truly for Victory

Ydun Johansen and Chris Johansen
Los Angeles, Calif.

OCTOBER 12, 1942

I THANK YOU MOST GRATEFULLY FOR YOUR KIND AND DEMOCRATIC INCLU-
SION OF THE NEGRO IN YOUR INSPIRING FIRESIDE CHAT TONIGHT. I AM
SURE THAT I AM EXPRESSING THE THANKS AND APPRECIATION OF MIL-
LIONS OF NEGRO AMERICANS WHO ARE CLAMORING TO DO MORE THAN
THEIR SHARE IN EVERY ASPECT OF THE WAR EFFORT. YOUR EXPRESSION
CAN ONLY RESULT IN A LARGER MANIFESTATION OF NATIONAL UNITY. MAY
GOD BLESS YOU AND GUIDE YOU IN YOUR LEADERSHIP IN THIS GRAVE
HOUR.

JOHN H. SCOTT
CHICAGO, ILL.

OCTOBER 16, 1942

Dear Mr. President:

Just a word of appreciation for your fine talk of Monday night.

It took particular courage to mention the Negro prejudice, which very
few public officials dare to discuss. This letter comes from a member of the
Caucasian Race.

Very respectfully yours,

David Echil
Philadelphia

OCTOBER 12, 1942

Mr. President,

On Monday night Oct 12, I listened to your speech I was over whelmed
by it's greatness. I was pleased with the report of the trip and the unity of
the American people. As I pass thru the streets of Harlem and see the tiny
children gathering the scrap to-gether it gives a great satisfaction of a true
spirit of America. Mr. President I believe every one who dwells on our native land feels proud of you and your fine work you have done as President
of the United States. When you mentioned the employment of negros in
your speach I believe the spirit of Abranhan Lincoln stood be side you and
Kindled a new birth of freedom in the hearts of all people.

We are now engaged in a war and winning the war is very important. Next year the minds of our people will dwell on the election of a Presidint. We must have a man whose work and program we already Know. I would like to ask you if you will run as President of these United States. I am just a plain minded American I vote in all elections and I think I voice the approval of all Americans in asking you to be our President again. May God bless you and your family.

Anna Emmett
New York, N.Y.

SEPTEMBER 8, 1942

Sir:

May I, a Congregational minister congratulate you on your informing address of last night. It was informing AND DISILLUSIONING AS WELL. It was thought that a great democrat had been elected to the office of President; you made it abundantly clear that a DICTATOR was elected precisely as the republican party asserted.

And yet I know that we, the people are to blame. You never keep your word to the people. Do you recall your very solemn declaration to the mothers and fathers that their sons would never be asked to bear arms out side of the U.S.? Of course you did keep your word about bringing "booze" back, and I assume you are proud of that!

Then we should have known you cared nothing about American institutions or traditions. You have walked over them in ruthless fashion. You tried to pack the Supreme Court and failing in that you waited fore time to work and then appointed stool pigeons to do your bidding.

It would have been pathetic had it not been some thing else to hear you plead for us to make sacrifices. What sacrifices have you or yours made? Your patriotism at $75,000.00 per year appears to be, just plain shoddy.*

Respectfully,

David F. Bent
Columbus, Ohio

---

*As President of the United States, FDR earned an annual salary of $75,000, 15 percent of which he voluntarily returned to the U.S. Treasury in recognition of the nation's economic crisis.

OCTOBER 12, 1942

Dear President Roosevelt

I listened to you speak to us Monday night. I love to listen to you speak. I have been in Washington twice I would love to see you. I am glad that you can travel around in America to talk to them. It would be nice for you to come to Martinsbury W. Va. I would love to be one of the people to talk to you. I'd tell you how I am helping to win the war. I have a little pet mouse. My mother is teaching me the good way of life, and to learn to love people. I dont have fancies like other children or luxuries. I have two little sisters and one little brother. Mother and daddy works hard. But we are happy. And willing to help you all we can. In all the good things you do. We agree with you on your trip. I am glad you could take your trip. Thanks for your message tonight.

I am in the Fifth Grade. I am Velma Hess. My mother is Grace Hess. She sends her best wishes in my letter for your health and happiness. My mother is the one who writes to you. Mother is still remembering you in prayer. Also your wife Mrs. Roosevelt. Mother and I often wish we could shake hands with you and Mrs. Roosevelt. Some day we hope to.

With best wishes from my mother Grace Hess and I the daughter

Velma Hess, age 10½
Martinsbury W.Va.

This my daughters letter to you she recieved but little help from me writing it. She has often wished to send you a letter. I told her it would be alright to write one to you. She always after your messages has a long chat with me. She has big Ideas and can be trusted. Mrs. Grace Hess.

SEPTEMBER 7, 1942

My dear president Roosevelt

I have just listened to your speach, you are wonderful as ever. . . .

First of all, my dear President, is your health. You are taking every thing to heart, and that is bad for you. You used to smile but you don't any more you are (loosin) losing weight since this summer and that is not good.

I hope you will not think that I am to personal because your good health is an asset to us all good and those others. Since the war is on and you cannot go to sea to fish and get the fresh air you must use your swimming pool more often. Also find other ways to get fresh air.

. . . You must set 6 hours out of every 24 to do nothing but rest even if you are unable to sleep, drink some warm milk with puston every night don't take any medicine even if you have a head ache it is harmful don't eat any meat, or drink any coffee, or drink any strong wines, don't eat any rich foods or miss any meals if you want a drink of (watter) water drink milk instead read a Psalms every night and never be to busy to pray your good health depends on all of this. Remember that even a machine wears out with-out care so please take at least one day to relax out of each seven, refuse to think of anything. Make it a business to relax just as you make it a business of being President. Of course none of us grow younger in years but please don't grow older in spirit. Remember your a man of God you are here for a purpose.

Looking at your picture taken last week, and listening to your dear voice tonight my hearth bleeds for you, you are carring such a load and your voice is also tired. . . .

We little people are for you. We thank God for you, and there are alot of us. We haven't forgotten all that you have done and are still doing for us. . . .

God bless you, and keep you in good health but you have to help him too. . . .

Yours with the best

(Mrs) Caroline Nichols (Colored)
New York, N.Y.

THE COAL STRIKE: MAY 2, 1943

THE CONSTITUTIONAL PROVISION "The President shall be Commander in Chief of the Army and Navy of the United States" assumed full meaning for FDR in 1943. In that role he participated during 1943 in five strategy meetings with Allied leaders: in Casablanca, Washington, and Quebec with Winston Churchill, in Cairo with Churchill and Chiang Kai-shek, and in Teheran with Churchill and Stalin. Throughout the year, as the tides of war began to shift in America's favor, he held, as Sam Rosenman observed, "multitudinous meetings with his military leaders in Washington . . . when there were differences of opinion among the professionals, it was he who made the final decisions; and it was his leadership which dominated the major decisions which involved international diplomacy or politics."[23] "During the war years," Frances Perkins recalled, "his transcending preoccupation was with the war itself. He spent more time with Army and Navy officials, as was proper, than he did with the civilian officers of government. We saw him less."[24]

But as much as his roles as military and international leader occupied him, he was also, as this Fireside Chat reminds us, the domestic leader of the American people who could not ignore what was happening at home. He understood that the war would be won in the factories and farms of America as well as on the battlefields of Europe and the Pacific, and matters of production, economic stability, morale, unity, and domestic tranquility were never far from his mind. Indeed, when a reporter asked him during a July 27, 1943, press conference whether the focus of his Fireside Chat the next evening would be "abroad or at home," he gave a detailed and uncharacteristically testy reply:

> You know, I hoped you would ask that question just that way. . . . There are too many people in this country who go after a slogan, who simplify things down, who are not mature enough to realize that you can't take a piece of paper and draw a line down the middle of it and put the war abroad — or the war front — on one side of the line, and put the home front — so called — on another side of the line, because after all it all ties in together.

> When we send an expedition into Sicily, where does it be-
> gin? Well, it begins at two places, practically; it begins on the
> farms of this country, and in the mines of this country.

He pointed out that the raw materials were processed and converted into finished food and manufactured products in this country, transported to the seaboard in this country, put on transport vessels constructed in this country that were convoyed and protected by warships and planes made in this country, all of which were operated by sailors and airmen who learned their skills in this country and supported the troops that invaded Sicily af- ter having been trained in this country. We have to remember, he con- cluded, "that there is just one front, which includes home as well as abroad. It is all part of the picture of trying to win the war."[25] It was in this frame of mind that FDR approached problems between labor and industry during the war.

In the period after the United States entered the war, leaders of the major unions took no-strike pledges in the hope that their unions would be per- ceived not as adversaries but as partners worthy of sitting at the table with representatives of industry and government where the economic patterns of the wartime economy would be shaped. Labor leaders were wary of do- ing anything that would invite a repetition of the government's actions dur- ing the June 1941 strike at the North American Aviation plant in Inglewood, California, where some 25 percent of American fighter planes were built. In his Fireside Chat of May 27, 1941, proclaiming a national emergency, FDR had warned that "the machinery of defense must not be interrupted by dis- putes between capital and capital, labor and labor, or capital and labor. . . . this government is determined to use all of its power . . . to prevent interfer- ence with the production of materials essential to our Nation's security." Accordingly, the federal government took over the North American Avi- ation plant, brought in troops to disperse the picket lines and protect re- turning workers, and canceled the occupational draft deferments of the strikers who were threatened with immediate induction into the army. While John L. Lewis, the head of the United Mine Workers (UMW), called the second week of June "the blackest in American labor history," Secretary of the Navy Frank Knox wrote triumphantly that the takeover "has had a profound psychological effect and from now on I think our troubles from that source will grow less."[26] The government's actions not only crushed the strike but became the model Secretary of War Stimson urged upon

FDR in subsequent labor disputes. It was a model that union leaders worked diligently to render superfluous by their pledges of cooperation in the war effort.

In spite of such diligence, there were wartime strikes — almost four thousand in 1943 alone — the majority of them short, involving relatively few workers, and of the grassroots "wildcat" variety. This was precisely how the anthracite coal strike of late 1942 and early 1943 originated. John L. Lewis declared the strike unauthorized and in mid-January ordered the strikers back to work. When the union's wage agreement expired in early spring, however, Lewis, spurred on by the discontent of the miners he led, demanded a wage increase of two dollars a day for his six hundred thousand union members in both the anthracite and bituminous coal fields, arguing that the mine owners had been granted a substantial increase in the price of coal in the fall of 1942 and that the cost of living had risen some 20 percent since the workers' last pay raise. In the face of the intransigence of the mine operators and the government, on May 1, 1943, Lewis led the miners out in the first of a series of four strikes that stretched into the autumn and that finally won his workers substantial wage increases in spite of the government's five-month seizure of the mines during the struggle.

As Nelson Lichtenstein, the leading historian of wartime labor, has argued, Lewis originally agreed to the no-strike pledge on the assumption that the government would be even-handed in overseeing the relationship between prices and wages, between workers and employers. Lewis abandoned the pledge only when he became convinced that the government had unilaterally broken its part of the bargain and failed to keep labor's standard of living in line with increases in prices and profits. In this struggle Lewis had the aid of a key member of the Administration, Secretary of the Interior Harold Ickes, who, as the wartime Solid Fuels Administrator, operated the mines after the government took them over on May 1. Ickes viewed the coal operators as more responsible for the impasse than the miners. Proclaiming that "bayonets cannot mine coal," Ickes sought a solution to the conflict that would assure steady coal production throughout the duration of the war, and engineered the wage increase in November that helped accomplish that end.[27] The workers Lewis led also had the sympathy of Eleanor Roosevelt, who characteristically viewed the conflict from the perspective of the miners, almost sixty-five thousand of whom had been killed or injured on the job in 1941 alone. Referring to the practice of forcing miners into debt in company stores and then deducting the debt from paychecks, she told the *New York Times* eight days after her husband seized the mines, "I have seen pay envelopes containing three cents." The strike should be settled, she added, "in the light of what the miners and their families have lived through for the past ten years. I think they are entitled to some concessions."[28]

Lewis may ultimately have won his battle, but there were costs. In June Congress, over FDR's veto, passed the Smith-Connally War Labor Disputes Act, which broadened the President's power to seize plants, prohibited strikes at plants seized by the government, imposed fines or imprisonment for strike leaders, required a secret ballot and a thirty-day cooling off period before strikes could begin, and increased unions' financial liabilities in strikes.* Lewis also paid the price of becoming one of the most castigated men in America. There were of course more than a few union members who were unmoved by the argument that they had to suspend their rights for the duration. "If I had brothers at the front who needed 10 or 12 planes that were sacrificed," a striking aviation worker declared in 1943, "I'd let them die, if necessary, to preserve our way of life or rights or whatever you call it. . . . What's more, if I were in their place, I'd expect them to do the same thing. I'd expect them to let me die."[29] There were also those like Secretary of Labor Frances Perkins, who put the matter in perspective when she wrote: "Although there was a falling off in the production of coal, the industrial furnaces did not stop, the trains did not stop, and we got enough coal for war needs."[30] These, however, were not the prevailing views. Lewis was commonly depicted as a traitor whose selfish ambition crippled the war effort and imperiled America's fighting men. A Gallup poll in June found that 87 percent of those questioned had an unfavorable opinion of Lewis.[31] "John Lewis," the army newspaper *Stars and Stripes* thundered, "damn your coal-black soul."[32] "If I were on the front lines, and a Marine was scared or tired and refused to fight or advance, I would have to shoot him," John Jaqua wrote his father from overseas. "Unless my sense

---

*FDR's veto hinged on the fact that he already had many of the powers the act gave him, and he felt that the thirty-day cooling off period and the mandatory vote before a strike could begin would allow workers to break the no-strike pledge: "In wartime we cannot sanction strikes with or without notice. . . . Far from discouraging strikes these provisions would stimulate labor unrest and give Government sanction to strike agitations" ("The President Vetoes the Smith-Connally Bill, June 25, 1943," *Public Papers and Addresses of Franklin D. Roosevelt* [New York: Harper, 1950], 12:268–71).

of values is completely warped, he is doing no more than a laborer who strikes."[33]

There were those at home who agreed. At a White House dinner in 1943, FDR asked Madame Chiang Kai-shek, "What would you do in China with a labor leader like John Lewis?" Eleanor Roosevelt recorded Madame Chiang's response: "She never said a word, but the beautiful, small hand came up very quietly and slid across her throat — a most expressive gesture."[34] Harry Truman, who as Roosevelt's successor was to have his own troubles with John L. Lewis and the miners in 1946, wrote privately: "Lewis ought to have been shot . . . but Franklin didn't have the guts to do it."[35] These were hardly options open to Roosevelt, although when his secretary, William Hassett, told him of a friend who facetiously offered to shoot Lewis if given promise of "a reasonable immunity," FDR quipped: "No jury would convict."[36]

If beheading and shooting were not weapons available to the President, there were others he could utilize. The first of these, of course, was his seizure of the mines on May 1. The second was the radio, which he used to sway public opinion in a Fireside Chat the next day.[37] He addressed his Chat "in particular to those of our citizens who are coal miners." The war, he announced, "has reached a new critical phase . . . we have moved into active and continuing battle with our enemies. We are pouring into the world-wide conflict everything that we have — our young men, and the vast resources of our nation." He had just completed a two-week inspection tour of the nation and saw abundant crops ripening in the fields, unparalleled production of weapons pouring out of our factories, and hundreds of thousands of soldiers — "Young men who were green recruits last autumn have matured into self-assured and hardened fighting men. . . . The American people have accomplished a miracle." But the miracle could only be sustained by the "massed effort" of everyone: "it must not be hampered by any one individual or by the leaders of any one group back here at home."

Every striking coal miner, FDR declared, "no matter how sincere his motives, no matter how legitimate he may believe his grievances to be — every idle miner directly and individually is obstructing our war effort." Interfering with the coal supply involved "a gamble with the lives of American soldiers and sailors and the future security of our whole people . . . an unwarranted, unnecessary and terribly dangerous gamble with our chances for victory." He hurried through a brief history of the no-strike pledge — which every major labor union, including the UMW, had signed voluntarily — and the creation of the War Labor Board (WLB), which the same unions had agreed would adjudicate disputes not settled through collective bargaining. But the UMW, claiming that the WLB was prejudiced, had called a general strike throughout the industry that had begun on Friday night. "At ten o'clock, yesterday morning — Saturday — the Government took over the mines."

> You miners have sons . . . who at this very minute — this split second — may be fighting in New Guinea, or in the Aleutian Islands, or Guadalcanal, or Tunisia, or China, . . . and I only wish they could tell you what they think of the stoppage of work in the coal mines.
>
> Some of your own sons have come back from the fighting fronts, wounded. . . . I could tell you of one from Pennsylvania. He was a coal miner before his induction, and his father is a coal miner. He was seriously wounded by Nazi machine gun bullets while he was on a bombing mission over Europe in a Flying Fortress.
>
> . . . There is another, from Illinois. He was a coal miner — his father and two brothers are coal miners. He was seriously wounded in Tunisia while attempting to rescue two comrades whose jeep had been blown up by a Nazi mine.
>
> . . . You miners have ample reason to know that there are certain basic rights for which this country stands, and that those rights are worth fighting for and worth dying for. That is why you have sent your sons and brothers from every mining town in the nation to join in the great struggle overseas. . . .
>
> The toughness of your sons in our armed forces is not surprising. They come of fine, rugged stock. Men who work in the mines are not unaccustomed to hardship. It has been the objective of this Government to reduce that hardship, to obtain for miners and for all who do the nation's work a better standard of living.

FDR understood that the cost of living troubled miners as it did millions of other workers. The government had been doing what it could, but thus far prices had not been kept as low as they should have "not only in coal towns but in many, many other places. Wherever we find that prices of essentials have risen too high, they will be brought down. Wherever we find that price ceilings are being violated, the violators will be punished." He understood the devotion of the coal miners to their union. "I know of the sacrifices they have made to build it up. I believe now, as I have all my life, in the rights of workers to join unions and to protect their unions. I want to make it absolutely clear that this Government is not going to do anything now to weaken those rights in the coal fields. Every improvement in the conditions of the coal miners of this country has had my hearty support, and I do not mean to desert them now. But I also do not mean to desert my obligations and responsibilities as President of the United States and Commander in Chief of the Army and Navy." He promised that under the Secretary of the Interior the question of wages would be examined carefully and if adjustments were found necessary, they would be made retroactive to April 1.

Tonight, in the face of a crisis of serious proportions in the coal industry, I say again that the spirit of this nation is good. I know that the American people will not tolerate any threat offered to their Government by anyone. I believe the coal miners will not continue the strike against their Government. I believe that the coal miners as Americans will not fail to heed the clear call to duty. Like all other good Americans, they will march shoulder to shoulder with our armed forces to victory.

Tomorrow the Stars and Stripes will fly over the coal mines, and I hope that every miner will be at work under that flag.

MAY 4, 1943

Dear Mr. President:

I live in the West Virginia coal fields. My father is a coal miner. I am fifteen years and seven months old.

I heard your speech Sunday, May the second. It impressed me greatly. Mr. President, I want you to know that you are not alone in your efforts to maintain peace. All of my family, as well as every other citizen in the United States, I'm sure, approve fully of anything you do. It is my opinion as well as others, that you are the greatest and best loved president that our country has ever had.

Respectably yours

Mildred Wilburn
Omar, W.Va.

MAY 2, 1943

My Dear Mr. President,

I listened to your speech this evening and it was a very lovely speech in theory, but not in fact.

Up until the time when meat was frozen we were buying hamburger (that was all we could afford) at 20 cents per. The next day it disappeared from the market and in its place appeared ground steak at 42 cents per. We have been buying fish of late at 42 cents per; but Friday when we went to get some fish the price was 65 cents.

This is only a fair sample of what is going on, and what is being done about it; nothing, except we do get fed a lot of hot air over the radio and through the papers about what is going to be done, but that is about all.

When you accepted the promise of labor to not strike, you promised to stapleize incomes and prices. You have failed in both of these. I am not blameing you for this failure, but the fact remains, you failed to live up to part of the promise; why hold labor to their agreement. I am not a labor union man, never was, but I have a little sense of reason, I think. I, for one, have about lost confidence in our leadership. We are being lied to entirely too much; take for instance, the bombing of Japan. First report, it was highly successful; every bomber returned. A year later none returned.

It is strange how much the common people will stand in the way of being lied to by their leaders, but occasionally a few get fed up.

I know you are in a tough spot and I do not mean to be unjustly unfair in my remerks; I do remember, however, how labor was asked to bleed and die, in the first war, while big business piled up the millions. I hav'nt any figures to prove it but I understand that ten times the profits are being made, so far, in this war, as was made in the last one.

Very truly,

Perry A. Vaughn
Chico, California

MAY 3, 1943

Dear Boss,

Your speech last night was not angry enough. I thought that I could detect much more heat than my grape-vine reports. It is my belief that there is not an honest thinking man in the entire nation who does not feel and say that Lewis is the greatest traitor that this country has ever known. He should be hung! Benedict Arnold Lewis. Though it is a shame to couple Arnold's name with the personality of a skunk. At least Arnold thought that he was right in the moves that he made. I tell you these things not entirely out of my own head, but because I think it may be of some use to you to know how the common man and his wife are thinking. I hear the neighborhood talking. The men in the barracks growling. The man in the street cussing. The working men in the shops. All along the line I hear the same thing. It boils down to this. "Damn that Lewis, he ought to be shot." The enlisted force is I think really angry. They feel that Lewis should have been taken care of the minute Pearl Harbor was bombed. There has not been one dissenting voice in my lines as yet. (Grape-vine)

You cannot make a martyr of any man I know, but to kill a rattle-snake is as justifiable as killing a Jap. (Kill used locally for crush, smash, etc.) . . .

Devotedly,

George Durno
[no address]

MAY 2, 1943

Honorable Sir:

I have listened attentively to your speech this evening to the miners. It was with a sinking feeling in the pit of my stomach I heard you lay full responsibility for this strike at the door of the miners. What about the operators!

What is it we are fighting for in your own words if not "Freedom from want." Do not American miners have the right to this freedom?

You are ushering in a state of Fascism when you tell men to go back to work under the protection of the armed forces.

I only hope the miners are not misled by your words. Their only weapon is their united strength. Bayonets cannot mine coal.

Yours truly,

Alice J. Marsh
Long Island City, N.Y.

MAY 17, 1943

Dear Mr. President:

The Constitution defines treason as giving aid and comfort to an enemy of the United States. Under this basic law a little insignificant grocer in Detroit has been convicted of treason for harboring a saboteur and is to be hung.

John Lewis, with whom the President is wont to play a losing game of appeasement, is an infinitely greater traitor than Stephan, considering the aid and comfort he has already given Mr. Hitler. If the President allows Stephan to be hung (as he deserves to be under the law) and does not proceed to the hanging of Mr. Lewis, Americans will understand the reason lying behind such clemency and it will not be held to be loyalty to the Constitution and equal justice for all citizens. It will generally be held to be for quite a different reason and the President will be held to have abdicated in favor of the country's chief enemy and saboteur.

Respectfully,

George B. Kinkead
Poughkeepsie, N.Y.

[The preceding letter comes from Franklin D. Roosevelt, Papers as President, Official File, File 290, Box 2, United Mine Workers of America 1943–1945 (UMW)]

* * *

Dear President:

This may be an emotional fueling but it has caused me to write you my feeling's I have heard a lot of the dramatic play's on the radio but a real life play was broadcast on the radio Sunday evening a 9 o'clock thousand's of coal miners were on strike and it seemed according to the papers they would strike until hell froze over the whole world watched this movement and our enemie's were overjoyed about this coal strike Nothing would have pleased them more then to have the coal miner's stay out of the mines for ever the miners listened to their union boss with 1 ear and the President with the other. . . .

Mr. President you have showed the world that this is the United States of America Land of the Free. . . . We are not like in Germany shoot their people words speak louder than bullet's. . . . Mr. President in your radio address to the coal miner's you did not tell them what you would do to them if they did not return to their work You did not tell them what would happen to them if they did not return to work you just ask them to go back to work and they would recieve care and protection you did not denounce the union where by in Germany union's dont mean anything only a firing squad. . . . I have been a union member for 25 year's and if your word's affected the coal miners like it affected me they will all be to work in the morning I and my family are proud of you

Mr and Mrs. Walter Schoot
Chicago, Ill.

P.S. Appreciate a Reply

MAY 2, 1943

Dear Mr. President:

I listened with great interest to your speech tonight, and am sorry to say that I was extremely disappointed in your placing the entire responsibility of the miner's controversy upon the union leaders.

It is perfectly obvious to fair minded people that the miners are certainly entitled to a wage increase considering the work they perform and the high cost of living they have to meet.

It is also obvious that the coal operators have made no effort to grant any substantial wage increase despite the fact that their present profits would allow such an increase.

In your capacity as chief executive, why could you not order the coal operators to grant a wage increase just as you ask the miners to return to work.

Sincerely,

Josephine Palumbo
New York, N.Y.

MAY 2, 1943

My dear Mr. President:

My wife and I were greatly moved by your talk to the miners this evening. Believing that you will hear from many people throughout the country on this very important subject, we though that it might do some good if we added our own comment to the great body of opinion which this issue will bring forth.

Both of us feel that your handling of the miners' case is a fine demonstration to the world that we mean what we say when we speak of the four freedoms in stating our war aims. Only in a great free land such as ours could any body of working men expect to receive the patient and sympathetic handling of their grievances which you are extending to the miners.

We are aware that you may be incurring the enmity of certain people in this country as a result of your efforts in this crisis. We believe, however, that you will also win the undying love and admiration of a far greater number, and that, among these are the people who have always made America great and will continue to make her great when the little men of today have long been forgotten.

We note with a great deal of satisfaction that the handling of the present crisis is markedly different from the handling of similar situations in the administrations of other recent Presidents. The army has not had to march, there has not been one riot, not one miner lies dead at the hands of police or militia; yet the prestige of the Government of the United States, which was threatened, has not suffered. On the contrary, it stands with added strength and dignity as a result of your wise handling of this case. And best of all, the miners, even though their grievances are by no means settled, are going back to work. They are going back, not cowed and beaten, as the slave people of a fascist-minded regime, but proudly and freely, secure in the knowledge that they will get their grievances adjusted fairly and honorably. We hope that in some of the dark lands under the yoke of our enemies, the dictator nations, this news can be spread to lend courage to the people that they may endure until victory comes to rescue them.

My wife is a librarian and I am an engineer in a defense industry, where, for the past year and a half, I have worked fifty-seven hours a week without holidays or vacations. Neither of us know too much about miners at first hand. We have, however, tried to see their side in their controversy with the owners. It is too bad that the daily press has not been of better service to the country in this matter. As an example, three of our New York City papers differ widely on the average wages of the miners. The Sun says $46 a week; the Times says $41; PM says $37. We believe that, without the very great restraint exhibited by the Government, the press would have succeeded in fanning the flames of dissension into a first class conflagration, and there would have been very serious trouble. It would, of course, have been blamed on the miners. Yet, we have seen that the miners are decent, orderly, loyal Americans quite as much as the publishers of American newspapers are, but with an infinitely harder and dirtier job to do. You have given them full recognition for their great contribution to our war effort, and through you, the whole country has obtained a better view of their side than the press has been willing to give us.

We believe that the miners were ill-advised to strike at a time like this, but we are convinced that they did not do so with any malicious intent. Their grievances, we are convinced, are very real, and we are hopeful that they will now receive a full airing and be properly adjusted.

As we recall, it is not so long ago that the coal operators were granted an increase in the price of coal amounting to 23 cents a ton. This increase was granted expressly to enable the owners to pay the miners time and one half for over time work. The miners have not worked overtime to any great extent since this increase was granted, which means that the extra money has gone into the pockets of the owners. Yet the cost of living has risen in the mining regions as it has elsewhere in the country. And we are convinced that the miners are right when they say that they have produced more coal with less men during recent months than they did before Pearl Harbor.

It must be remembered, too, that the miners were receiving sub-standard wages before the outbreak of war. The depression hit them harder, perhaps, than it did any other section excepting, the farmers. Their job is a hard, dirty job. It is a hazardous job; not so hazardous, perhaps, as fighting Japs, but much more so than that of a carpenter, bank clerk or corporation executive. If it is unfair, as some people think, to deprive some individuals of the right to earn more than $25,000 a year during the war, it is equally unfair, we believe, to expect these miners to contribute so much to the war effort at a wage scale much lower than that obtaining in other jobs less hazardous and demanding less skill and endurance.

We hold no brief for Mr. Lewis, and prefer not to discuss his possible political objectives. We feel, however, that the mine owners deserve at least half the blame for this trouble, and feel that it is perhaps wisest that the government continue to run the mines for the duration of the war. If, after that, the mines are going to be allowed to return to the desperate condition in which they were before the war, it will, we believe, be time to think of nationalizing them for all time, in the interest both of the miners and the nation.

Yours very truly

Alexander H. Kuhnel
New York, N.Y.

THE GI BILL: JULY 28,
SEPTEMBER 8, AND
DECEMBER 24, 1943

THE PRESIDENT DELIVERED three more Fireside Chats in 1943.[38]
Of the three, the second one — the Chat of September 8 — was one of the
shortest he ever broadcast. Its primary purpose was to inaugurate and promote the Third War Loan Drive. The War Loan program was conceived
in 1942 by FDR and his Secretary of the Treasury, Henry Morgenthau, as
a voluntary program aimed not at significant investors but at everyday
Americans. This widespread sale of small-denomination war bonds and
war stamps* — which ultimately raised roughly one-sixth of the cost of the
war — had several objectives: to involve all Americans in freely offering to
help finance a war that cost over three hundred billion dollars; to direct the
greater incomes wartime Americans had at their disposal into noninfla-
tionary channels; and, through the massive bond drives conducted by the
popular culture icons of stage, screen, radio, and the print media, to increase the people's enthusiasm for and support of the war.

The war bond campaigns, Morgenthau was convinced, would "make
the country war-minded — there just isn't any other vehicle to do it."
There were millions of people, he told reporters off the record, "who say,
'What can we do to help?' . . . Right now, other than going in the Army and
Navy or working in a munitions plant, there isn't anything to do. . . . Sixty
per cent of the reason that I want to do this thing is . . . to give the people
an opportunity to do something." Morgenthau's most important decision,
the advertising executive Fred Smith declared, "was the decision to use
bonds to sell the *war,* rather than vice versa."[39]

FDR supported his Treasury Secretary in instituting this voluntary program in the face of the persistent pressure of such advisers as his Budget

---

*The most popular and accessible bonds were the E bonds, the cheapest of which
cost $18.75 and matured at $25 in fifteen years. War stamps, priced at as little as ten
cents, could be purchased, mounted in a booklet, and used to buy a bond when the
requisite amount was reached.

Director and the head of the Federal Reserve Board for the adoption of a compulsory 10 percent war savings tax. FDR felt that persuading Americans to buy bonds "willingly and enthusiastically" was the *democratic* way to get the people involved in supporting the war. "Henry," FDR told Morgenthau in early 1942, "you and I are the only people who understand it. Everybody else is against it, but we are going to do it." And do it they did. During the war bond drives of 1942, which elicited what Morgenthau called a "grand response by the people," the Treasury emphasized the device of voluntary monthly payroll deductions whereby employees contracted to purchase bonds on a regular basis. "I want a sign in everybody's window," FDR declared, "not just saying, 'I bought a war bond,' but that 'I buy a war bond every month.'"[40] By the end of 1942, twenty-four million workers had enrolled in the payroll deduction plan, which became embedded in American popular culture. "When I see all these [soldier] boys," the singer Frances Langford told Bob Hope on his radio show, "it just makes me want to do something for our country. . . . I'd like to help. . . . I think everyone has to pitch in." The show's announcer responded to her, and the radio audience, in what was a typical mass media appeal to the people to support the war: "That's right, Frances . . . this isn't only a job for the soldiers, marines and sailors. . . . Our job is to provide them with the stuff that will knock the stuffings out of the Axis. And we can do that by joining the '10% Club.'"[41]

It was as part of this campaign that FDR devoted most of his September 8 Chat to the Third War Loan Drive.* He began dramatically with a parable about a Midwestern city threatened by a great flood: "destruction and death stared them in the face." Its people — "business men, workers, farmers, and doctors, and preachers — people of all races" joined together in filling sand bags and keeping the levees above the flood's peak. Today, we are struggling to keep "the levees of civilization high enough to prevent the

---

*Morgenthau, who opened the drive by selling a $100 bond to Winston Churchill, who was then visiting the U. S., set $15 billion as the goal; the drive exceeded that amount. Treasury studies revealed that people bought bonds during the campaign for myriad reasons: "in order to help a member of the family in the armed service, to invest their money safely, to preserve 'the American way of life,' to combat inflation, to save for security against the chance of a postwar depression, or to save for some specific postwar use" (John Morton Blum, *From the Morgenthau Diaries: Years of War, 1941–1945* [Boston: Houghton Mifflin, 1967], 25).

floods of aggression and barbarism and wholesale murder from engulfing us all. . . . In this war bond campaign we are filling bags and placing them against the flood — bags which are essential if we are to stand off the ugly torrent which is trying to sweep us all away."

In the course of this brief Chat, FDR announced the signing of an armistice with Italy that put the Italian people on the side of the Allies and began their liberation "from their real enemies, the Nazis." But we still had to drive the Germans out of Italy and the other captive nations and then "strike them on their own soil from all directions." In spite of the good news, the war effort could not stop "for one single instant." The material costs of waging the war were "staggering." "It is not sufficient simply to put into War Bonds money which we would normally save. We must put into War Bonds money which we would not normally save. . . . So it is up to you — up to you, the Americans in the American homes — the very homes which our sons and daughters are working and fighting and dying to preserve." The President did not presume to tell his listeners how much to invest in war bonds. "No one can tell you. It is for you to decide under the guidance of your own conscience." But he did remind them: "Every dollar that you invest in the Third War Loan is your personal message of defiance to our common enemies — to the ruthless savages of Germany and Japan — and it is your personal message of faith and good cheer to our Allies and to all the men at the front. God bless them!"

This straightforward, pragmatic Chat was sandwiched between two that were more complex and significant, especially the first of the trio, that of July 28, which outlined a program that had some of the most far-reaching effects on the fabric of American life of any policy in FDR's tenure in the White House and which elicited a much greater written response than the other two.

The bulk of the July Chat was given to news of the war — especially his announcement of what he termed "the first crack in the Axis" — the fall of the Italian dictator, Benito Mussolini. He promised that Mussolini "and his Fascist gang will be brought to book, and punished for their crimes against humanity." In spite of Mussolini's resignation, FDR reminded the Italians that they could have peace only on the same terms as Germany and Japan: unconditional surrender. "We will have no truck with Fascism in any shape or manner. We will permit no vestige of Fascism to remain." As the Allied cause advanced, he promised that all the conquered peoples would be restored "to the dignity of human beings, masters of their own fate, entitled to freedom of speech, freedom of religion, freedom from want, and freedom from fear."

He repeated in this Chat his conviction that one could not separate the "fighting" front from the "home" front. He informed his audience that every Flying Fortress that bombed the Naples harbor from bases in North Africa "required 1,100 gallons of gasoline for each single mission, . . . the equal of about 375 'A' ration tickets — enough gas to drive your car five times across this continent. You will better understand your part in the war — and what gasoline rationing means — if you multiply this by the gasoline needs of thousands of planes and hundreds of thousands of jeeps, and trucks and tanks that are now serving overseas." He praised our allies in Britain, in China, and especially in Russia, which had withstood the worst Hitler could throw against them and hurled the German troops back: "The world has never seen greater devotion, determination and self-sacrifice than have been displayed by the Russian people and their armies," and he uttered as an assertion a sentiment that was in fact more of a fervent hope: "With a nation which in saving itself is thereby helping to save all the world from the Nazi menace, this country of ours should always be glad to be a good neighbor and a sincere friend in the world of the future." He praised the "superb skill and courage" of the young, raw American troops that swept across Sicily: "For many of our troops this was their first battle experience, but they've carried themselves like veterans."

He had good news militarily: our casualties in the conquest of Sicily "have been low — in fact, far below our estimate." And domestically: "to-night we are able to terminate the rationing of coffee. And we also expect within a short time we shall get greatly increased allowances of sugar." He also had sobering news: the war was far from over and "the driving, wartime conditions" under which Americans at home had to work and live would continue into the foreseeable future:

> The next time anyone says to you that this war is "in the bag," or says "it's all over but the shouting," you should ask him these questions:
> "Are you working full time on your job?"
> "Are you growing all the food you can?"
> "Are you buying your limit of war bonds?"

"Are you loyally and cheerfully cooperating with your Government in preventing inflation and profiteering, and in making rationing work with fairness to all?"

"Because — if your answer is 'No' — then the war is going to last a lot longer than you think."

The part of his Chat that made it memorable centered on his postwar plans for American military personnel. With painful memories of the discontented, alienated World War One veterans still fresh, he had assured American troops "that the American people would not let them down when the war is won," and he urged Congress to cooperate with him in transforming that assurance into reality. "The American people will insist on fulfilling this American obligation to the men and women in the armed forces who are winning this war for us," and "have been compelled to make greater economic sacrifice and every other kind of sacrifice than the rest of us." They must not, he insisted, "be demobilized into an environment of inflation and unemployment, to a place on the bread line, or on a corner selling apples. We must, this time, have plans ready — instead of waiting to do a hasty, inefficient, and ill-considered job at the last moment." He outlined "the least to which they are entitled":

First. Mustering-out pay to every member of the armed forces and merchant marine when he or she is honorably discharged, mustering-out pay large enough in each case to cover a reasonable period of time between his discharge and the finding of a new job.

Secondly. In case no job is found after diligent search, then unemployment insurance if the individual registers with the United States Employment Service.

Third. An opportunity for members of the armed services to get further education or trade training at the cost of their government.

Fourth. Allowance of credit to all members of the armed forces, under unemployment compensation and Federal old-age and survivors' insurance, for their period of service. . . . as if they had continued their employment in private industry.

Fifth. Improved and liberalized provisions for hospitalization, for rehabilitation, for medical care of disabled members of the armed forces and the merchant marine.

And finally, sufficient pensions for disabled members of the armed forces.

Roosevelt, of course, was making the initial announcement of what came to be known as the GI Bill, a plan that treated war veterans more generously and appropriately than at any previous time in U.S. history. But he was doing far more: he was articulating a social policy that permanently altered American higher education and profoundly influenced American culture and society.

"There is one great fear in the heart of any serviceman," Eleanor Roosevelt observed in her syndicated newspaper column in 1944, "and it is not that he will be killed or maimed but that when he is finally allowed to go home and piece together what he can of life, he will be made to feel he has been a sucker for the sacrifice he has made."[42] Her husband shared that fear. Less than a year after Pearl Harbor, the President appointed a committee of educators to formulate a program for veterans whose training and education, indeed, whose lives had been seriously interrupted by the war. "Nothing will be more conducive to the maintenance of high morale in our troops," he told Congress in October 1943, "than the knowledge that steps are being taken now to give them education and technical training when the fighting is over." But it wasn't merely a pragmatic move to bolster morale: It was a moral obligation and a crucial necessity. Our goal, he reminded Congress a month later, was "to rout the forces of insecurity and unemployment at home, as completely as we shall have defeated the forces of tyranny and oppression on the fields of battle."[43] The GI Bill was an integral weapon in the struggle to create a postwar society better than the one that had led to the Great Depression.

The Servicemen's Readjustment Act, popularly known as the GI Bill, which FDR signed on June 22, 1944, went further than Roosevelt initially intended thanks to the intense lobbying of the American Legion. The Legion, an organization of World War One veterans, became the first major veterans organization in our history to represent soldiers of more than one war by opening its doors to veterans of World War Two. It was determined that the new veterans would not suffer the fate of their predecessors, who during the Depression had been forced to march on Washington to demand the bonuses they had been promised and were fired upon and driven out of the nation's capital for their efforts. Thus the conservative Legion, which throughout the interwar years had opposed labor unions, leftist politics, and an expansive federal government, found itself in a unique political alliance with the New Deal, and in January 1944, it called for an omnibus "Bill of Rights for GI Joe and GI Jane."

The Legion embraced all of the points FDR had made in his Fireside Chat but expanded a number of them, most important, increasing the educational benefit from one year to four years, and added governmental loans to veterans to buy homes and farms. By appealing to its grassroots constituency, it was instrumental in helping to pass the bill over the objections of educators like Presidents James B. Conant of Harvard and Robert Maynard Hutchins of the University of Chicago, who were sure the influx of GIs would dilute higher education and turn universities into what Hutchins called "educational hobo jungles," and over the fears of congressional conservatives who worried about exposing GIs to radical professors who would destroy their values and transform them into overeducated loafers unable to function in the real world. "I would rather send my child to a red schoolhouse than to a red school teacher," declared Representative John E. Rankin of Mississippi, who also worried that providing unemployment insurance for returning veterans meant that "a vast majority" of the 50,000 Mississippi Blacks who were serving in the war "would remain unemployed for at least a year, and a great many white men would do the same thing."[44]

What the GI Bill did in fact do was to expand opportunity and mobility for the millions of young men and women who had served in the war. As significantly, it helped transform both American higher education and the popular conceptions of higher education, which after World War Two was no longer perceived as primarily the preserve of the privileged and the affluent. In the decade after the end of World War Two, while some 4 million veterans purchased homes with GI loans, almost twice as many — 7.8 million veterans, roughly half of all the war's veterans — took advantage of the educational provisions of the bill. In 1948, 11,000 of the 20,000 undergraduates at the University of Michigan were veterans. Nor was Michigan exceptional: from 1946 to 1948, veterans comprised the majority of male college students in the nation. Though, as we shall see, FDR had plans to reinvigorate the New Deal following the war, the GI Bill turned out to be the final great reform bill of his Administration.[45]

Roosevelt's sensitivity toward those serving in America's armed forces was not matched by a similar concern for racial justice, a cause that was to become an integral part of the progressive agenda only in the decades following the war. Although under the Black labor leader A. Philip Randolph's threat of a march on Washington the President on June 25, 1941, had issued Executive Order 8802 setting up the Committee on Fair Employment Practices to ban discrimination in defense industries, FDR said nothing about the rigid segregation that characterized an American military ostensibly fighting for freedom and had little to say concerning the blatant discrimination and racial injustice that marred the home front. Throughout the war, African American men and women moved in large numbers into cities offering wartime employment, just as the President urged all Americans to do. White workers in such industrial cities as Detroit greeted the hiring and promotion of Black workers with hostility — even instituting wildcat strikes to register their dismay — and opposed, often violently, renting African Americans decent housing in or adjacent to White neighborhoods. In 1943 alone, 242 racial battles took place in forty-seven American cities. "I would lie awake some nights," the civil rights lawyer and future Supreme Court Justice Thurgood Marshall remembered, "worrying that Detroit and other cities that had industries that were critical to the war effort were becoming tinderboxes because whites, from the Roosevelt brain trust to the unions, wanted to keep Negroes out of the mobilization jobs."[46]

Roosevelt was warned by his own Office of Facts and Figures that only his direct intervention "can prevent not only a violent race riot in Detroit but a steadily widening fissure that will create havoc in the working force of every Northern industrial city."[47] FDR was urged to use the radio to appeal to the conscience of the nation to uphold the constitutional guarantee of equal rights and seriously contemplated doing so, but once again his fear of losing the support of Southern Democrats for crucial legislation prevented any action. Little over a month before his July 28 Fireside Chat — on June 20, 1943 — Detroit exploded into one of the worst race riots of the century, resulting in the death of 25 Blacks and 9 Whites, injury to 675 people, the arrests of more than 1,000, property losses of two million dollars, and the loss of a million hours of wartime labor production.[48] "No lesser voice than yours can arouse public opinion," Walter White of the NAACP telegraphed the President and then predicted correctly: "Unless you act, these outbreaks will increase in number and violence."[49]

None of this, nor the anti–Mexican American riots in Los Angeles earlier in June, prompted Roosevelt to make the racial situation an essential part of his July Chat. Only days after that Chat, on August 1, Harlem erupted in bloody racial violence, which prompted the Black minister and New York City councilman Adam Clayton Powell, Jr., to speak of the United States as "a bastard democracy."[50] After reading a news story following the Harlem riot in which FDR expressed his "regrets" over "the recent outbreaks of violence in widely spread parts of the country," the Black writer Pauli Murray, who was then a college student, asked:

> What'd you get, black boy,
> When they knocked you down in the gutter,
> And they kicked your teeth out, . . .
> What'd you get when the police shot you in the back,
> And they chained you to the beds
> While they wiped the blood off?
> What'd you get when you cried out to the Top Man?
> When you called on the man next to God, so you thought,
> And you asked him to speak out to save you?
> What'd the Top Man say, black boy?
> "Mr. Roosevelt regrets . . ."[51]

The final Fireside Chat of 1943 was delivered on Christmas Eve. The President had returned a week earlier from an extensive and exhausting trip to Cairo, where he met with the Chinese and English, and then to Teheran, where he and Churchill held their first conference with Stalin, then back to Cairo, where he and Churchill had a final meeting together. FDR returned from his travels in an upbeat mood. He had achieved an agreement that Japan would lose the territories it had seized from China; that Korea would be a free and independent state at the close of the war; that in the spring of 1944 England and the United States would mount a cross-Channel invasion of France, which the Russians had been requesting since 1942 and which Churchill had been resisting; that the Russians would enter the war against Japan once Germany fell, which Roosevelt's military advisers assured him would save tens of thousands of American lives; and that the Allies would build the United Nations to preserve the peace.

In addition to these crucial agreements, FDR felt he had made important strides toward strengthening the ties between the United States, Great Britain, and the Soviet Union, and especially that he had reached a "meeting of the minds" with Stalin, a necessity if the mistakes that had led to World War Two were to be avoided in the future. "The ice," between himself and Stalin, he told Frances Perkins, "was broken and we talked like men and brothers." But he also reflected, perhaps more prophetically, "I wish I understood the Russians better. . . . I just don't know what makes them tick. I wish I could study them. . . . I like them and I want to understand them."[52] "He looked a little tired," Sam Rosenman remembered, "but there was none of the drawn and haggard expression that he brought back from Yalta a year later. He looked robust and healthy. He was indeed the 'champ' who had come back with the prize. I had seen that expression many times before; but, except for a few exhilarating moments during the election campaign of 1944 when the fighting got rough, I never saw that same expression again."[53]

Although FDR was convinced that what was achieved at these meetings safeguarded the prospects of peace and would bear fruit for decades to come, he could not be explicit about the details in his Christmas Eve Fireside Chat to the American people, which he delivered from his home in Hyde Park. He wanted to announce the selection of General Dwight D. Eisenhower to lead the invasion of France the following spring, for example, but was able to say only that Eisenhower would command a forthcoming attack on the Germans from what he vaguely called "other points of the compass." He was eager to share his optimism with the people, but he did so cautiously: "we still have much to face in the way of further suffering, and sacrifice, and personal tragedy. . . . many bigger and costlier battles are still to be fought. But — on Christmas Eve this year — I can say to you that at last we may look forward into the future with real, substantial confidence that, however great the cost, 'peace on earth, good will toward men' can be and will be realized and ensured. This year I *can* say that. Last year I could *not* do more than express a hope. Today I express a certainty — though the cost may be high and the time may be long. . . . At Cairo and Teheran we devoted ourselves not only to military matters, we devoted ourselves also to consideration of the future — to plans for the kind of world which alone can justify all the sacrifices of this war."

He spoke in general terms of the agreements that had been reached. He praised Chiang Kai-shek and Stalin, whom he had met and talked with face to face for the first time. He was particularly enthusiastic about the Russian leader, for whom he had much more respect and in whom he had considerably greater hope than the mercurial and undependable Chiang. "To use an

American and somewhat ungrammatical colloquialism, I may say that I 'got along fine' with Marshal Stalin. He is a man who combines a tremendous, relentless determination with a stalwart good humor. I believe he is truly representative of the heart and soul of Russia; and I believe that we are going to get along very well with him and the Russian people — very well indeed."

He spoke of the end of the war and assured his audience that the Allies had "no intention to enslave the German people," but did "intend to rid them once and for all of Nazism and Prussian militarism and the fantastic and disastrous notion that they constitute the 'Master Race.' " He was optimistic about the postwar world: "Britain, Russia, China and the United States and their Allies represent more than three-quarters of the total population of the earth. As long as these four nations with great military power stick together in determination to keep the peace there will be no possibility of an aggressor nation arising to start another world war." But such an alliance had to respect the rights of every nation large or small. "The doctrine that the strong shall dominate the weak is the doctrine of our enemies — and we reject it. But, at the same time, we are agreed that if force is necessary to keep international peace, international force will be applied." No longer would we be beguiled by the "pious hopes" that aggressor and warlike nations would turn to peaceful ways voluntarily without any threat of coercion. No longer would we heed those "cheerful idiots in this country" who believed that we could simply retreat within our own borders and lock our front doors behind us. "It is my intention to do all that I humanly can as President and Commander-in-Chief to see to it that these tragic mistakes shall not be made again."

Amid all of his optimism, he harbored one great fear, which he shared with his millions of listeners: "I think I see a tendency in some of our people here to assume a quick ending of the war . . . I think I discern an effort to resume or even encourage an outbreak of partisan thinking and talking." When he returned from Cairo and Teheran, he was so discouraged by the divisiveness he found in Congress and the nation that he grumbled to Harold Ickes, "It really would be a good thing for us if a few German bombs could be dropped over here."[54] Thus he tempered his Christmas cheer by alerting the people to what lay ahead: "The war is now reaching the stage where we shall all have to look forward to large casualty lists — dead, wounded and missing. War entails just that. There is no easy road to victory. And the end is not yet in sight. . . . The massive offensives which are in the making — both in Europe and the Far East — will require every ounce of energy and fortitude that we and our Allies can summon on the fighting fronts and in all the workshops at home."

He concluded his final Fireside Chat of 1943 with a series of holiday prayers culminating in these two blessings:

> God bless all of you who fight our battles on this Christmas Eve.
>
> God bless us all. Keep us strong in our faith that we fight for a better day for human kind — here and everywhere.

JULY 29, 1943

Dear Mr. President:

Possibly you would be interested in knowing how the public received your speech of last night.

Here at the Roxy Theatre, with a seating capacity of 6000, in a completely full theatre, at 9:29 the following announcement was made: "Ladies and gentlemen, we are interrupting our entertainment program to bring you a speech by the President of the United States." When this was heard by the audience, it sounded like 60,000 rather than 6,000 people in the theatre, they were so happy to hear from you. At the conclusion of the speech, warm enthusiasm was expressed. Good applause indicated their willingness to accept the thoughts you had been advancing. During the speech not a soul got up to leave. After it, there was a substantial exodus.

We are not commercial in doing this, but those of us charged with the executive management of the theatre feel that when the Commander-In-Chief has something to say to our citizenry we ought to make it possible for those in our theatre and not near radio sets, to receive the important words. We hope that in so doing we help to lighten the burden you are obliged to carry. . . .

I extend to you cordial and sincere good wishes.

Respectfully yours,

Irving Lesser
New York, N.Y.

JULY 28, 1943

Dear Mr. President,

My name is Howard Hill. I have just finished listening to youre speech over the radio. I know you are very, very busy & don't have time to listen to just a high school boy like me. But I thought I would write you & tell you how youre speech affected me just like it affects all the youths of America. I am 17 & am going into the Naval Air Corp as soon as I graduate from high school. After listening to you I would gladly give my life for my Country. I think you are the greatest man that ever lived & if it wasn't for you there would be lots of boy's like me who would think of there selves instead of their Country. You probably won't ever even read this but I thought I would write you & take a chance on your reading it. Every boy I have ever talked to respects, trusts, & believes in you as they would their own mother. You are the inspiration of every high school boy. Please forgive me for taking up your time.

Respectively,

Howard Hill
Fort Worth, Texas

JULY 29, 1943

Dear President Roosevelt:

I heard your talk on the radio last night and I was particularly impressed by the program you outlined which has for its purpose taking care of the men that are discharged from the Military Service.

I sincerely hope that Congress will adopt such a program. I was in the Service during the First World War and I remember very clearly all the talk that went on about what they proposed to do for the boys when they came back, and then I remember what actually did happen. I hope that it is not going to happen this time, and from the way you talked last night, I know you will do your part to see that the honorably discharged members of the Military get a better break than they did the last time.

Very truly yours,

J. Frank Traynor
Rochester, N.Y.

AUGUST 1, 1943

Dear Sir

Your speech the other night was excellent. . . .

My boy who was 19 years old 8th April is now in Camp Hale in the Ski troops — He was taking up Forestry and was in his Freshman Year at N.Y. State College of Forestry, Syracuse. He enlisted in the Reserves and was called up 8th March — He has never once complained but the day before your speech he wrote and told us of some plan to send the boys back to College to finish their education after the war He seemed very much pleased about it, and had read about it in the papers. I know it will be a happy day for me when I can see him off again and I think it will be wonderful for those boys to start where they left off at College.

. . . do take good care of your health sir, as our Country needs you — these dreadful days — we have never for one moment lost faith in you and never shall —

Respectfully yours

B. McNeill
Wood-Ridge, New Jersey

AUGUST 8, 1943

Dear Sir:

. . . I am impelled to register my disapproval of the proposals made in your last radio talk to the Nation. They amount to a knife in the back for democracy. Democracies which know no better solution of their economic problems than doles are on the skids. Government by doles is socialistic and the flowering of socialism is dictatorship. This has been the direction of your administration whether or not you recognize it. With three dictatorships before your eyes I do not see how you can fail to recognize it.

It is a tragedy that your leadership is not toward a just and equitable system, toward the abolition of special privileges. Men who can win through the jungles of the South Pacific, the ice and snow of Attu, the sands of North Africa and the heat of Sicily certainly do not need doles and it is insulting to offer them charity. Let government confine itself to its own business of seeing that all citizens have a "fair field and no favors". Paul does not want Peter's handouts, he will take care of himself when he is on an equal footing with all other citizens.

Unfortunately, you do not sponsor such a policy. But, either we adopt one such or this civilization will collapse and go the way of all previous ones. The writing is on the wall! It takes statesmanship — something far nobler than political acumen — to interpret it.

Very sincerely yours,

Olive Maguire
Berkeley, California

JULY 29, 1943

Dear Mr. President —

I heard your very excellent address last night and wish to acknowledge your sentiments with my whole-hearted support. Many of my buddies commented most favorably on the tentative program for soldiers rehabilitation, hospitalization, etc. . . . None of us here, and, I am certain, in the other Army Camps and foreign soil, wish to return to the chaotic conditions such as were prevalent in the aftermath of 1918. We want no pampering but we ask for a fair chance to once again integrate ourselves into civilian life after we return from the various fighting fronts. I hope Congress forgets Party lines and backs you on this program. . . .

With certainty of a speedy and decisive victory —

Sincerely,

Pvt Leon Rosenbloom
Camp Swift, Texas

JULY 28, 1943

Dear Mr. President:

Your fire-side chat delivered this evening was inspiring, stimulating, and challenging. Your words must have sounded like a Messianic message to the downtrodden and starving peoples of the Axis-dominated countries. To us in this country, your talk was equally comforting and assuring. Materially we are well off, but spiritually many of us are starved. May your vigor and far-sightedness lead and assist us in the difficult task of establishing a more humane world.

You spoke of the need for planning for a greater security and economic stability for the returning fighting men and women, as well as for those on the home front who are working to bring victory. I am confident that unless we have such overall security, we shall have a mass discontent and disillusionment which will surely lead to political and economic chaos. Is it asking too much of the popularly-elected legislators to cooperate with your plans, and pass legislation to facilitate such a program to insure social stability and full employment?

From past experience it can easily be gathered that the status quo of a "free enterprise" and shackling economy will be tenaciously held on to by certain individuals and groups. We must continue the fight here at home in order to overcome their opposition, and thus achieve an overall security for the masses of our people. To guarantee us the four freedoms will mean that we shall be called upon to help persistently and consistently in making them workable. You have envisaged such a world of freedom and security and with you we shall make it come true.

Please God that you may enjoy good health and strength for the arduous tasks that face you in the coming years.

Sincerely yours,

Sylvan J. Ginsburgh
San Francisco, California

JULY 31, 1943

Dear Mr. President:

I am one of those who believe in the system of free enterprise as opposed to bureaucratic government control. I am one of that group, which is increasing in numbers every day, who believe that your boondogling in our nation and in the world should be stopped immediately. Your political sounding promises, built around the four freedoms, can not possibly be attained. . . .

I do not believe that your New Deal can do for the people of America what free enterprise can do for them. The future welfare of America is going to be guided by the business men of America, who have received their training in the school of experience and not by the present inexperienced exponents of your New Deal.

Mr. President, we have taken as much regimentation as any sensible man can. Do not kill incentive, for without it a man loses energy, initiative and purpose. "We would be like a nation of contented cows grazing peacefully in an evergreen meadow." We do not intend to be lulled by promises of a false security, a security which will dull ambition, stifle initiative, and retard progress. Mr. President, an opiate never cures. . . .

Mr. President, my best wishes are extended to you when you return to private life at the end of 1944. Happiness will reign again when your New Deal is remembered as a nightmare.

Very sincerely yours,

W. Floyd Deacon
Grapevine, Texas

JULY 31, 1943

Dear President:

What a fine campaign speech you made the other night! . . .

If it wasn't a campaign speech you wouldn't have mentioned soldiers' pensions. You know that no political party would refuse the returning soldier these things. But you were very careful to make the point so that 10,000,000 service men and their families would be convinced that it was your idea when it comes election time.

And then you promised the rest of us more coffee and sugar. But you carefully avoided stating that we were getting another cut on milk, butter, eggs, etc.

And then that childish crack about the homefront and the warfront being one. You know what everybody means by the homefront and you know that you and your executive branch have it in one grand mess. And don't always blame it on Congress. You and not Congress is chiefly to blame for our mounting inflation. You and not Congress is chiefly to blame for our abominable labor situation. You and not Congress is chiefly to blame for the terrific mess the food situation finds itself in.

It would be fine if some other people would follow Mussolini's example and resign. Benito resigned when he saw he was falling down in his job. Some others I know about delude themselves into believing they are doing their job and doggedly hang on.

Yours for victory,

Wm. Buescher
Cleveland, Ohio

JULY 30, 1943

My Dear Mr. President,

I want to apologize for the outrageous attack on your last speech by some of the papers and narrow minded officials — I am sure a true America does not feel your speech, a campaign speech — I cried when I heard you, for I felt you spoke not only from your brain but also from your heart.

I do not know you personally, but would it be disrespectful to say I love you as I do my father? I trust my father and I feel he has my wellfare in mind in what he does — and that is the way I feel about you. We are your children, and you are trying to make this world better for us —

As a child, America to me was a beautiful story. American history was my bible. American people to me were, broad minded, liberal, kind people, who lived by their Constitution as well as the Golden Rule. As I grew up, my ideals were being smashed. I saw negro hatred, people trying to make money on other peoples sweat — Selfishness — Hatred of Jews as well as Christians. I was lost. I always dreamt of the day. My America would come back — And then you came along — You have done so much already, and you are trying to do more. You have not considered your health. But unselfishly have tried to restore Our America, have tried to make it greater than it already is. The country loves you as I do.

People who are against you, are the ones — who are satisfied to drive their fellow man for their own advantage, who are happy as long as they can get what they want and dont give a darn how they get it. But they are not true Americans. They dont really live in America. They live in a world of their own — and hate your interference

We've got to have a better America — We want it, and we want you to lead the way — To show us how to improve, not only ourselves, but the world — We want our ideals to live. We want to live with our neighbors and love them. No more hatred, because of color, race, or creed — It was not meant to be that way. This is America that so many people have lived and died for. This shall be the America that lives by its Constitution, the Bill of Rights and the Bible.

I love you Mr Roosevelt, for you are history, you are America —

Respectfully

Gloria Aronson
New York, N.Y.

JULY 29, 1943

Dear Mr. President:

I am sincerely overjoyed. Your recent address to the people was tremendously reassuring. I agree with you wholeheartedly that we are winning the war on both the battlefields and at home. I feel as I have never felt before that we shall be the victors on both fronts.

You could not have mentioned everything in your speech, but there was one thing which I hoped you would speak about. Because you neglected to, however, I was genuinely disappointed. I am referring to the recent race riots and the continued discrimination and assualts against Negro servicemen. As you know, we, like all other people, are sincerely helping in everyway we can to win the war. We are without doubt making a great contribution. We shall continue to do so despite any reverses. Because we believe so firmly in you, Mr. President, I believe that a positive statement from you regarding the Negro people in the present crisis would be the greatest stimulus we could receive at this time.

Sincerely yours,

Constance J. Baker
New York, N.Y.

JULY 30, 1943

Sir:

This is to express how much I enjoyed your fireside chat Wednesday evening, July 28, 1943.

It was quite informative and you seemed to be to your natural self. Your voice had a ring of sincerity . . . especially when you spoke of the four freedoms, yet, Mr. President, I must frankly admit that I was greatly disappointed when you did not speak out against mob violence, racial and religious intolerance, lynching, racial discrimination in the Armed Forces, poll tax; evacuation of American citizens from the Pacific coast, the Oriental Exclusion Act and the skyrocketing of food prices within our boarders.

Do you know, Mr. President, we have had more than one hundred sixteen lynchings within these United States since you first took office. This, together with race riots and the racial discrimination within our armed forces have become not only a national scandal but a globular shame.

Don't you think, Mr. President, that you should break down the four freedoms and fully explain just what you mean by the same, because it doesn't make sense to me. Here we are proclaiming that we are fighting for democracy, and not withstanding the fact, that you are the co-author of the four freedoms, still these things are happening within our boarders referred to herein, and you continue to remain silent and not do anything about it. . . .

Respectfully yours,

Frank C. Lyons
Cleveland, Ohio

JULY 29, 1943

Dear President Roosevelt: —

I, as a soldier's wife, want you to know how wonderful your speech was last night. . . .

My husband is overseas, and since listening to you, I feel that most men will come home & be provided for.

It makes a person feel good to know that we have a man in office who is for the people.

Sincerely,

Mrs. Selig Epstein
Vinton, N.J.

SEPTEMBER 11, 1943

Dear Mr. President,

I hope you wont think it presumptuous of me to be writing to such a busy man as yourself.

I'm going to make this short and too the point.

I'm on this 3rd War Bond Drive and have already sold as much as $1200 worth of Bonds in one day.

I would also like the "honor" of being able to sell a Bond to The President of My Country.

Of course I realize you are quite a distance out of my territory, but never the less to sell a Bond to as Great a Person as yourself would make me very proud and happy.

Am enclosing the necessary papers for your signature and a check enclosed, a small one would be perfectly satisfactory.

This Drive will be over shortly so will be hoping to hear from you in the not to distant future.

Thank you very kindly

I remain

Your Truly

Mrs Marie Weissburg
Santa Clara, California

SEPTEMBER 9, 1943

Dear President,

. . . I heard you speak last night and I liked it very much. I have two brothers in the service and am very proud to say that they are both serving the United States Army. I am a girl eleven years of age. I buy all the bonds I can to see my brothers once again. I buy bonds not only for my brothers but for your sons and all the other boys that are serving our country which is the United States of America. If you find my letter interesting please answer it. I'd like to have you write a letter to one of my brothers. . . .

Please tell him that his mother is very proud to have two sons in the service. Thank You.

Yours very truly

(Miss) Rose Boghosian
Lowell, Mass.

DECEMBER 24TH, 1943

Dear Mr. President,

I am writing this letter in tears and with a broken heart, after listening to your Christmas speech on December 24th, 1943. In reference to this program I have just this to say.

Not once did I hear you mention anything about our country's "Marines." The only two branches of services you spoke of were the Soldiers and Sailors. What is the matter with the Marines? Did you forget that there were such people? Who was it that fought the worlds widely known "bloody battle on 'Tarwara' "? The answer is just this; the Marines! I'm not trying to say anything against the Soldiers or Sailors. I realize they all have their part to do in winning this tragic war, but why show partiality? . . . The reason I took it so hard was because my boy-friend is in this branch of service, so called the Marine's. He is some place in Hawaii. I haven't seen him in ages and I'm lucky if I average at least one letter a week from him. This week I heard nothing from or about him, but I suppose this doesn't interest you.

Well, Mr. President, I have said just about all I should at this particular moment. I'm in hopes this letter reaches you saftly and that it will bring about a light to make you realize what you talked about in your speech. Must I say, "please", to ask you not to forget about our heroic Marines.

Sincerely,

Miss Ann Rockenstire
Albany, N.Y.

DECEMBER 24, 1943

Dearest Friend President Mr. Roosevelt & Famly,

I just got through listening to your nation wide greeting & talk to the nation & from the bottom of my heart I want to congratulate you & thank you. I thought it was a wonderful talk. I as the mother of one of our fighting men want to write you & say that this is our 3rd Christmas with out my only child he was in New Jersey at Fort Monmouth in the Signal Corps training camp, 2 years ago. Last Xmas he was in the Fiji Islands and this year as far as we can figure he is at Guadalcanal, he has been over seas exactly 18 month tomorrow. He has been in the Army since Oct 20th 1941 and he has only been home 1 week since that time and that is the only time we have been with him. it has been such a very long time seemingly. I never go to bed that I dont wonder if I will ever look in his face again, he is such a very fine young man & one to be proud of. his one outstanding habit is honesty I taught him from little boy-hood to never be afraid to speak the truth & he would never go wrong & time after time he has proven to have taken that teaching serious. I am writing & hoping to see him again & enjoy him being home again soon. today I went in his room and offered up a prayer for him & all of our fine boys & girls & may God be with them & hear them as they pray & yearn for home & thier loved ones, at this Christmas season especielly. . . .

I expect your time is to precious to take in reading my letter but I just felt I had to tell you how much I enjoyed your talk today. & feel so proud of you as our president & leader. You certainly have had a very heavy load to carry & done it mighty fine.

Now I must bring this to a close & hope you and your family a merry Xmas a very prosperous and a Happy New Year.

Yours Respectfully

Mrs. Mary L. Jester
Springport, Ind.

DECEMBER 24, 1943

Dear Mr. President: —

You have just finished speaking over the radio. Until you spoke I had been dreading Christmas eve a little. My husband Captain Allen Schauffler is with A.W.G. attached to the British Eighth Army in Italy, and my young son is in the Amphibious Command. But I want you to know that what you have just said so simply and honestly, has made everything seem right — and I am not dreading Christmas eve any longer. As you spoke it seemed as if Allen were sitting here beside me listening with me, as we have listened to you to-gether so many times.

Thank you, from the bottom of my heart.

Gratefully yours,

Helen Powell Schauffler
New Rochelle, N.Y.

DECEMBER 24, 1943

My dear President Roosevelt,

I've just got through listening to your broadcast to our servicemen abroad and here at home.

Your talk has given me the faith and inspiration that so many of us have been seeking for so long.

I for one won't be looking for a quick half settled peace but am going to fight and help with every ounce of strength in me during the hard struggle ahead for a wonderful lasting peace.

Your talk made me picture the remainder of the war as a terrific, horible, driving black thunderstorm and the peace, the wonderful freshness and cleaness that comes when the storm is over. When that day comes, it will always be like that forever and ever. . . .

Sincerely

From a proud Navy man's wife
Mrs. John L. Williams
New Haven, Conn.

AN ECONOMIC
BILL OF RIGHTS:
JANUARY 11, 1944

AS 1944 BEGAN, the United States found itself locked in a conflict more prolonged than any since the Civil War, and Roosevelt — like Lincoln before him — constantly worried about the home front and the problem of keeping the American people engaged in the war even as he was completing his most active year of international conferences. Following his return from Cairo and Teheran at the close of 1943, FDR felt "let down," as he phrased it on the evening of January 11 in his first Fireside Chat of 1944, because he found "many evidences of faulty perspectives here in Washington."* This was easily one of FDR's most caustic Fireside Chats; Sam Rosenman correctly termed it "unusually bellicose."[55] There were too many people, he told his radio audience, who seemed to be satisfied to fight a war whose only objective was survival, while he remained convinced that "out of this war we and our children will gain something better than mere survival." Then there were the "suspicious souls" who accused FDR of having made secret "commitments" for the future that would transform the United States into "a world Santa Claus," while he insisted that the only commitments he had made at the recent conferences were those necessary to win the war and create an international organization to preserve the peace.

Freedom from the "gangster rule" that had twice plunged the world into war could be created only on the bedrock of security. "And that means not only physical security which provides safety from attacks by aggressors. It means also economic security, social security, moral security — in a family of nations." There could be no enduring peace without "a decent standard

---

*At noon on January 11, FDR had delivered his Annual Message on the State of the Union to Congress. He had intended to address Congress personally, as had been his practice, but the flu prevented this: "my doctor simply would not let me leave the White House to go up to the Capitol," he explained. Because his Annual Message was delivered in written form and thus could not be broadcast to the nation, he decided to give it — with a number of alterations — as a Fireside Chat from the White House that evening at nine.

of living for all individual men and women and children in all nations. Freedom from fear is eternally linked with freedom from want." The President was furious at those who refused to understand this and instead "burrow through the nation like unseeing moles, and attempt to spread the suspicion that if other nations are encouraged to raise their standards of living, our own American standard of living must of necessity be depressed."*

FDR assured his listeners that the majority of the American people were meeting the demands of war with "magnificent courage and a great deal of understanding. They have accepted inconveniences; they have accepted hardships; they have accepted tragic sacrifices." His outrage was directed at that "noisy minority" demanding "special favors for special groups . . . pests who swarm through the lobbies of the Congress and the cocktail bars of Washington, . . . they have come to look upon the war primarily as a chance to make profits for themselves at the expense of their neighbors." Such "selfish agitation" was dangerous in wartime: "It creates confusion. It damages morale. It hampers our national effort, it prolongs the war." He condemned all forms of domestic disunity: "bickerings, self-seeking partisanship, stoppages of work, inflation, business as usual, politics as usual, luxury as usual."

Finally, he warned of the pitfalls of overconfidence and complacency as "the deadliest of all enemies" that "can lengthen this war. It can kill American boys." Those doing most of the complaining labored under the delusion "that the time is past when we must make prodigious sacrifices — that the war is already won and we can begin to slacken off." The "dangerous folly" of such views could be measured "by the distance that separates our troops from their ultimate objectives in Berlin and Tokyo — and by the sum of all the perils that lie along the way."

The situation created by these negative forces prompted Roosevelt to recommend the adoption of several laws by Congress. The first was "a realistic and simplified tax law — which will tax all unreasonable profits, both individual and corporate, and reduce the ultimate cost of the war to our sons and our daughters." The bill now being considered by Congress, he

---

*Roosevelt's original draft was even stronger, charging that "there are within our nation a group of people called moles who circulate constantly in the dirty darkness." "We persuaded him to soften that paragraph a little," Sam Rosenman has testified, "but it was a hard job" (*Working with Roosevelt* [New York: Harper and Brothers, 1952], 418).

insisted, "does not begin to meet this test."* His second recommendation was for a renegotiation of war contracts, "which will prevent exorbitant profits and assure fair prices to the government. For two long years I have pleaded with the Congress to take undue profits out of the war." The third law he sought would regulate the cost of food and "enable the government to place a reasonable floor under the prices the farmer may expect for his production; and to place a ceiling on the prices a consumer will have to pay for the necessary food he buys." His fourth request was for the reenactment of the anti-inflationary stabilization law of 1942 before it expired at the end of June.

Finally, and as it turned out, most controversially, he asked for a national service law, "which, for the duration of the war, will prevent strikes, and, with certain appropriate exceptions, will make available for war production or for any other essential services every able-bodied adult in this whole nation." Millions of Americans, FDR declared, "are not in this war at all." National service, which would be the civilian equivalent of the military draft, would oblige "each citizen to serve his nation, to his utmost, where he is best qualified." A few days earlier, several of Roosevelt's advisers wrote him that when "the very life of a nation is in peril . . . there can be no discrimination between the men and women who are assigned by the government to its defense at the battlefront and the men and women assigned to producing the vital materials that are essential to successful military operations." The President quoted these sentiments in his Chat and asserted: "I believe the country will agree that these statements are the solemn truth."

He was mistaken. From the beginning of the war until its end, national service was a recurrent issue dividing the Cabinet, the Congress, and the nation. Roosevelt, of course, was well aware of the divisions. When he was composing his Chat, he told Sam Rosenman and Robert Sherwood to keep the passage asking for national service "a complete and absolute secret — tell nobody about it." "I don't want to argue about it any more with anybody," he told his speechwriters, "I don't want to be talked out of it again. . . . I want you boys to go to work on it, and — remember — keep it

---

*That bill, which FDR was convinced would not only fail to raise sufficient money, but favored the wealthy and powerful, was enacted by Congress, vetoed by Roosevelt, and then passed over his veto in one of the many assertions of the independence on domestic issues Congress manifested during the war. Indeed, none of the bills the President outlined in this Chat passed, or at least passed in the form FDR desired.

quiet."[56] Though poll after poll showed large numbers, often a majority, in favor of some form of national service,[57] both organized labor and such powerful business organizations as the National Association of Manufacturers and the Chamber of Commerce were opposed to it, and for basically the same reason: the fear of a loss of autonomy. Union leaders denounced the scheme as "involuntary servitude" and "the high road to fascism." Business leaders feared it as a prelude to being forced to hire union workers and, worse still, to being subject to a civilian draft themselves.[58] What the President was asking for, the *Chicago Tribune* charged, was nothing less than a "universal slavery bill."[59]

The fact that the more than sixteen million Americans who served in the armed forces had already been deprived of their autonomy — and often more than that — too easily got lost in the argument, but consistency was not a hallmark of the wartime debates over the economy. Secretary of War Henry Stimson, for example, was the staunchest supporter of national service in FDR's Cabinet, testifying in its behalf before Congress by asserting that "the nation has no less right to require a man to make weapons than it has to require another man to fight with those weapons," urging Roosevelt to use the military to suppress wartime strikes, and advising the American Federation of Labor that there could be no "business as usual" while the nation was threatened by world strife. Yet this same man observed in his diary: "If you are going to try to go to war, or to prepare for war, in a capitalist country, you have got to let business make money out of the process or business won't work, and there are a great many people in Congress who think that they can tax business out of all proportion and still have businessmen work diligently and quickly. That is not human nature."[60] Robert Patterson, Stimson's Undersecretary of War, remarked similarly that "we had to take industrial America as we found it," but as the historian Richard Polenberg has observed, the relationship was not reciprocal: big business and the federal government did not leave industrial America as they found it in the period of mobilization for defense and then for war.[61]

These years witnessed the rapid concentration of economic power in fewer and fewer industrial hands, and there can be little doubt that the chief agent for this process was the federal government itself, as manifest in its wartime relationship with corporate America. Despite its official allegiance to an antimonopoly program, the way in which the New Deal awarded government contracts during the defense period beginning in 1938 and then throughout the years of war enormously enhanced the strength of a small number of industrial giants at the expense of smaller firms at the very moment when the federal government, as industry's biggest customer, had its greatest opportunity to alter the patterns of economic power in the nation. Although FDR in 1938 called the concentration of economic power an "inescapable problem" for a modern democracy, and although he understood very well the truth embodied in Walter Lippmann's wry comment that "competition is something of which producers have only as much as they cannot eliminate," by 1941 the government was giving fifty-six firms, which constituted less than half a percent of the manufacturing establishments of the country, 75 percent of all its contracts. Within this select group, concentration was even more marked: six of the fifty-six firms held 31 percent of the total. In spite of the prosperity of the war years, there was a decline in the number of businesses in the United States. In 1943 there were 17 percent fewer businesses than there had been in 1941. While businesses employing fewer than 125 workers saw an increase in the value of their product of some 16 percent, the value of the product of firms employing more than 125 workers increased by 96 percent. These larger firms experienced an increase in the number of workers they employed of 62 percent, compared to a growth of 1 percent for the smaller firms. Many comparable figures could be given, and they would all point to the same fact: that the war concentrated economic power in the hands of a very small group of American industries.[62]

This concentration was enhanced by the government's decision to run the mobilization program with what were called "dollar-a-year" men — businessmen who served the government but received their salaries from the firms they previously worked for and would serve again after the war — a decision that, according to Bruce Catton, "did nothing less than preserve the existing corporate control of American industry." Dollar-a-year men held hundreds of leading positions in the war economy and had a decisive voice in the distribution of raw and often scarce materials, the assigning of contracts to businesses, and the shaping of the industrial fabric of wartime America. When Senator Harry Truman, chair of the Senate Select Committee to Investigate the National Defense Program, asked Donald Nelson, the chair of the War Production Board, why these executives were not simply placed on the government payroll, Nelson answered that while he wished that were possible, it was not. "The reason is a very simple and practical one: these men have, in the main, been receiving larger salaries than those payable to government personnel, and they have, in many cases, incurred through the years extensive financial obligations, commensurate with their salaries, which make it extremely difficult for them abruptly to adjust to a much lower salary basis (life insurance, mortgages, etc.). This is unfortunate but it is a fact." Truman's response was obvious: he referred Nelson to those in the armed forces who had to adjust to a much greater disparity in income and lifestyle: "I just received a letter this morning from a young man who is getting $25,000 a year. He is a Reserve officer. He is going to get $140 a month, and he can't draw his $25,000 while he is gone." In reluctantly accepting Nelson's policy, Truman addressed what was perhaps the most troubling factor:

> The Committee does not like to have important procurement matters entrusted to men who have given such hostages to fortune. Those who cannot forego large incomes *temporarily* cannot reasonably be expected to take a chance of foregoing them *permanently* by taking positions on behalf of the government with which the controlling officials of their corporations are not in sympathy.[63]

Truman was not alone in his concerns. Secretary of the Interior Harold Ickes grumbled in his diary about "abandoning advanced New Deal ground with a vengeance" in allowing business to make large profits out of defense and war contracts. "We are supposed to be engaged in an earnest struggle to do away with the unjust disparities between the very rich and the very poor. The President has announced more than once that no new crop of war millionaires will spring up out of our war preparedness program." If private capital refused to supply munitions of war at a reasonable profit "then the Government ought to build its own plants and conscript the necessary managers to run them. What we are doing is what I have been protesting against at Cabinet meetings and elsewhere for some time; in effect, the Government is building these plants and equipping them at its own expense, while permitting private individuals and corporations to make excessive profits at practically no risk to themselves."[64]

As Ickes was discovering, the pressures of war could easily divert one's attention and rearrange one's priorities. That most devoted of reformers Harry Hopkins, now thoroughly absorbed by global matters, shocked Robert Sherwood on one occasion by fuming: "I'm getting sick and tired of having to listen to complaints from those goddam New Dealers."[65] FDR himself heightened the paradoxes of the government's domestic wartime policies by widely quoted statements he made at his press conference of December 28, 1943. Asked to explain his earlier remark to a reporter that the press ought to stop using the term "New Deal," Roosevelt launched into an elaborate and fanciful medical allegory. How, he asked, had the New Deal come into existence? "It was because there was an awfully sick patient called the United States of America, and it was suffering from a grave internal disorder — awfully sick. . . . And they sent for the doctor. And it was a long, long process — took several years before those ills, in that particular illness of ten years ago, were remedied. But after a while they were remedied." He went on to list some thirty of the remedies — from unemployment relief to conservation and flood control, abolishing child labor, eliminating monopolies, old age insurance, federal housing and slum clearance, protecting consumers, federal deposit insurance, rural electrification, drought relief and crop insurance — all of them central to the patient's cure. But, he continued, two years ago, on the seventh of December, the patient "was in a pretty bad smashup — broke his hip, broke his leg in two or three places, broke a wrist and an arm, and some ribs; and they didn't think he would live, for a while. . . . Old Dr. New Deal didn't know 'nothing' about legs and arms. He knew a great deal about internal medicine, but nothing about surgery. So he got his partner, who was an orthopedic surgeon, Dr. Win-the-War, to take care of this fellow. . . . And the result is that the patient is back on his feet. He has given up his crutches. He isn't wholly well yet, and he won't be until he wins the war." At the present time "the overwhelming first emphasis should be on winning the war. In other words, we are suffering from that bad accident, not from an internal disease." When victory came "the program of the past, of course, has got to be carried on. . . . We are not talking in terms of 1933's program. We have done nearly all of that, but that doesn't avoid or make impossible or unneedful another program, when the time comes. When the time comes."[66]

The time had obviously come just two weeks later in his Fireside Chat of January 11, 1944. If he sounded like Dr. Win-the-War in recommending national service, he concluded his Chat on a very different note; a note that has led one of his biographers to call this "the most radical speech of his life."[67] After pleading with Congress — futilely as it turned out — to pass legislation to ensure that the millions of Americans in the armed forces would have the right to vote in the national elections of 1944, since the military could not deal with forty-eight different state laws governing absentee ballots, FDR suddenly spoke once more in the voice of "Old Dr. New

Deal." "It is our duty now," he proclaimed, "to begin to lay the plans and determine the strategy for more than the winning of the war, it is time to begin the plans and determine the strategy for winning a lasting peace and the establishment of an American standard of living higher than ever known before." Our Republic, he reminded its citizens, began by ensuring certain inalienable political rights. "We have come to a clearer realization of the fact, however, that true individual freedom cannot exist without economic security and independence. 'Necessitous men are not free men.' People who are hungry, people who are out of a job are the stuff of which dictatorships are made." In our day, he insisted, "these economic truths have become accepted as self-evident. We have accepted, so to speak, a second Bill of Rights under which a new basis of security and prosperity can be established for all — regardless of station, or race or creed." Among these rights were:

> The right to a useful and remunerative job in the industries or shops or farms or mines of the nation;
>
> The right to earn enough to provide adequate food and clothing and recreation;
>
> The right of farmers to raise and sell their products at a return which will give them and their families a decent living;
>
> The right of every business man, large and small, to trade in an atmosphere of freedom from unfair competition and domination by monopolies at home or abroad;
>
> The right of every family to a decent home;
>
> The right to adequate medical care and the opportunity to achieve and enjoy good health;
>
> The right to adequate protection from the economic fears of old age, and sickness, and accident and unemployment;
>
> And finally, the right to a good education.

He ended by tying the war to this progressive agenda. "America's own rightful place in the world depends in large part upon how fully these and similar rights have been carried into practice for all our citizens. For unless there is security here at home there cannot be lasting peace in the world." He warned against a postwar "rightist reaction," arguing that "if history were to repeat itself and we were to return to the so-called 'normalcy' of the

1920s — then it is certain that even though we shall have conquered our enemies on the battlefields abroad, we shall have yielded to the spirit of Fascism here at home."

> I ask the Congress to explore the means for implementing this economic bill of rights. . . . Our fighting men abroad — and their families at home — expect such a program and have the right to insist on it. It is to their demands that this government should pay heed rather than to the whining demands of selfish pressure groups who seek to feather their nests while young Americans are dying. . . .
>
> Each and every one of us has a solemn obligation under God to serve this nation in its most critical hour — to keep this nation great — to make this nation greater in a better world.

The marked dissonance between Roosevelt's press conference of December 23 and his Annual Message and Fireside Chat of January 11 resulted from his frustration at the increasingly reactionary tone of the Congress elected in 1942, which rejected his requests for progressive domestic economic legislation, eliminated a number of New Deal programs — even one as popular as the Civilian Conservation Corps — and left him confused as how best to move politically, torn between his need for congressional support to wage the war effectively and his urge to protect and further his social and economic programs in the face of congressional recalcitrance.* On January 3, 1943, the day the new Congress convened, one of the Republican leaders, Representative Charles L. Gifford of Massachusetts, told the House that it was necessary to "win the war from the New Deal," while a leader of the Southern Democrats, Representative Eugene Cox of Georgia, told his colleagues that "Government by bureaucrats must be broken, and broken now."[68]

It is hardly surprising, then, that during the final year of his life FDR renewed his conviction that there had to be a new political alignment in the

---

*The 1942 elections created the most intractable Congress FDR had to deal with in his tenure of office. The Republicans gained more than forty seats in the House and seven in the Senate. The coalition of Southern Democrats and Old Guard Republicans, in this nominally Democratic Congress, was able to thwart FDR on issue after issue.

nation and that, having failed to liberalize the Democratic Party in the election of 1938, he had to throw his influence behind a new progressive political party composed of the liberal elements in the existing major parties. To this end, in the summer of 1944, he opened negotiations with his 1940 Republican opponent, Wendell Willkie, who had just been defeated by the conservatives in his party in the Wisconsin presidential primary and had withdrawn from the race for the Republican nomination. "I think the time has come," FDR told Sam Rosenman, whom he sent to begin talks with Willkie, "for the Democratic party to get rid of its reactionary elements in the South, and to attract to it the liberals in the Republican party. . . . We ought to have two real parties — one liberal and the other conservative. . . . Of course, I'm talking about long-range politics — something that we can't accomplish this year. But we can do it in 1948, and we can start building it up right after the election this fall. From the liberals of both parties Willkie and I together can form a new, really liberal party in America." Willkie seemed enthusiastic at the prospect. "Both parties are hybrids," he complained to Rosenman when they met on the fifth of July. "You tell the President that I'm ready to devote almost full time to this. A sound, liberal government in the United States is absolutely essential to continued cooperation with the other nations of the world." Like Roosevelt, however, Willkie spoke of reform in the future tense and was adamant that nothing could be done until after the 1944 elections.[69]

These efforts proved too little and too late — Willkie died a month before the election of 1944 and FDR survived it by only five months. If one of Roosevelt's greatest strengths was his ability to touch people through his articulation of such fundamental principles and goals as the Four Freedoms and Economic Bill of Rights, his greatest failure of vision and execution was his inability to create and leave behind him a political structure capable of bringing these principles to fruition.

JANUARY 12, 1944

Mr. President,

Two years ago I joined the Army to add my small share to the effort of destroying the international gangster. Tonight I listened to your annual speech to Congress. I don't believe that what we are fighting for, or what the Armed Forces desire could have been summed up in a more accurate manner.

We definitely want to vote — we are fighting to have a democracy not a dictatorship — they didn't vote in Germany. Neither will they vote this year. Is that whats in store for us? American soldiers?

We don't want strikes. Wouldn't the people back home pull their hair if we laid down our arms for a pay increase. The boys in the Pacific have just been given an advancement in pay of one step, from Pvt. at $60.00 per month to PFC at $64.00 per month and etc, is this enough to sleep(?) to eat(?), and to die in a fox-hole? I answer, Yes if we get what we are fighting for — a democracy.

We all knew that in 1918 there was not going to be anymore wars. But that was all that happened, they just talked — now we want action. We don't want our children in the next one, because at the rate we are killing now, in the next war with killing methods advanced it would spell finas for the entire human race.

By all means put into effect your Service Act. It is the only sensible way to wage war. In the prize ring, not only is the fighter in there pitching, but so are his trainer and manager. We want that 120 million in with us pitching — not just home cheering. Let them all pitch, with them doing their very best maybe I and my 10 million buddys in arms can be home by Christmas 1945.

The idea of ending it in 1944 is a real good one, for Germany. Between the RAF and us bombing the living hell out of her day and night and those wonderful Russians pushing them nearer to our bombs — it is possible — but we need help, and those at home have it to give. We must remember that we shall still have Tokio to visit.

If it is all over before 1945, my deepest thanks are herewith extended.

Sgt. Gerson I. Nadel

359th Bomb Squad
New York, N.Y.

JANUARY 12, 1944

Dear Sir:

I'm a Mother of two children, & the wife of a War Worker. Here In our Home everything is done for victory, with every available dollar going for War Bonds.

I'm In faver of the "National Service Idea," & I know I speak for the boy who writes from the jungles of New Guinea & says, I hope there Isn't any more strikes!! We look with contempt upon those who put personal greed ahead of the lives of our brothers & husbands.

"May God give you more strength for the Fight, & we will be Victors sooner."

Sincerely yours,

Mrs. Rufus Napier
Hamilton, Ohio

JANUARY 12, 1944

Dear Mr. President:

. . . Mr. President, the American people are with you. I doubt if you realize the extent of the trust and confidence the people have in you — even those who for party reasons do not go along with your programs. . . .

One of the unfortunate things in the present situation is that the men overseas are likely to attach undue blame to organized labor. Frankly, I believe that labor is doing as well or better than management in many fields. I felt it unfortunate at times — particularly in the mine and railroad situations — that the Labor Board did not recognize the truth that both of those groups were probably greatly underpaid in comparison with many other classes of labor and in both cases fix a pay scale where it ought to be in relation to other wage levels. . . . I find that view very common among people out here. They realize the great harm that was being done by the strikes or threats of strikes but felt that the basis of judgement of the Labor Relations Board was rather technical than statesmanlike. I am afraid the soldiers abroad do not see that quite so well as the people at home.

Much as I dislike increasing your mail by one single letter, I have not been able to refrain from saying "Amen" to your message of yesterday — even though I am not a Methodist.

Respectfully yours,

George F. Yantis
Olympia, Washington

JANUARY 30, 1944

Dear Mr.President,

I have noted with interest and approval your call for an Economic Bill of Rights for our nation. We greatly need something of this sort.

I welcome your recommendations for realistic taxes to prevent profiteering, for continuance of the renegotiation law to assure fair prices to the government, for a cost-of-food law to guarantee reasonable prices to farmers and fair prices to consumers, and for the extension of price control to hold off inflation. This is evidence of your continued concern for the common man and I warmly commend you for it. . . .

We have much house-cleaning to do here at home. I believe that we must give much concern for our economically underprivileged. I believe that the day of our freely competitive and comparatively unrestrained capitalistic system has gone. I find no justification for a system that permits concentration of wealth in the hands of a few while the many have little, and in some cases are destitute. Though the term may be in some disrepute I believe our national life must witness a greatly "socialized" emphasis.

Yours for a Speedy Victory and a Just and Durable Peace,

(Rev.) Valton V. Morse
Brewer, Maine

JANUARY 12, 1944

My dear President Roosevelt: —

Again we were thrilled by another of your great messages. Mr Hardison and I sat listening together. A usual rite on speech occasions. . . . I was lifted beyond myself with a deep and tremendous hope that at last something on an adequate scale was going to be done for so many needing a helping hand. Those handicapped by conditions and circumstances surrounding them.

. . . I've been attending our Mary Clifford Auxiliary of Calvary Episcopal Church. Periodically somebody chirps "We ought to do something about those children" referring to swarms of children from nearby mills.

On the first Monday of March 1943 I heard myself suggesting that I start a Children's Choir. Would that be any help? . . .

The next day I began my scouting in "Old Glory", the most forlorn mill section in our midst. . . .

Seventy-five children attend with a long waiting list — Ages from six to sixteen. A few a bit older — most of them younger.

We practice every afternoon. Many times after the evening meal. During the summer months we practiced in the morning and the evening. . . . They are singing Mozart, Handel, — selections from the Oratorio "Elijah" — and, believe it or not, the Bach-Gounod arrangement of Ave Marie in latin and loving it! Many barefoot and overalled!

In visiting amongst the families I have found clean homes — all are pitifully bare. A few chairs, a kitchen table. Double beds. Hard work in the mills and then home to a large family of children. . . .

Our very fine wellfare department has an almost impossible job of keeping some of the thirteen and fourteen year-olds in school. There is much of a tragic nature I could relate. . . .

One day two of my choristers came to see me after Choir Practice. They gave me two bill folds and said they were made ashamed by something I said. They had helped themselves to these articles in a store up town.

Upon talking it over with them I found they planned to sell the bill-folds in order to have money to buy lunch at the school cafeteria.

"What did you have for breakfast?" I asked.

"Nothing" both replied. One of the two hastened to add, "Sometimes now I gits a chance to slip a cup of milk out of the bottle that they gits for the new baby!"

Another child fainted in school several weeks ago. He had eaten nothing that day. . . .

Do you wonder that I was shaken by your words?

Similar conditions are prevalent all over the country. The whole thing is too gigantic for individuals to handle intelligently or adequately.

To hear you say such needs doing and furthermore will be done soon is indeed music to our ears! I felt you were talking directly to us! . . .

Cordially, and gratefully,

Susan M. Hardison
Wadesboro, N.C.

JANUARY 13, 1944

DEAR MR PRESIDENT . . . LET IT BE UNDERSTOOD THAT WE ARE OPPOSED TO A NATIONAL SERVICE ACT UNLESS YOUR PROGRAM IN ITS ENTIRETY IS ENACTED. . . . WE MAKE ONE DEMAND IN REGARD TO THE NATIONAL SER-VICE ACT AND THAT IS THAT OUR NEGRO BROTHERS AND MEMBERS OF OTHER MINORITY GROUPS BE FULLY UTILIZED AT THEIR HIGHEST SKILLS AND BE PERMITTED TO MAKE THEIR FULL CONTRIBUTION TO THE VICTORY EFFORTS OF OUR NATION. . . .

INTERNATIONAL LONGSHOREMEN'S & WAREHOUSEMEN'S UNION
CHARLES DAY, BUSINESS AGENT
SEATTLE, WASHINGTON

JANUARY 11, 1944

Dear Sir:

We listened to your radio broadcast tonight and thought it was wonderful I've never written to anyone like this before but I do want you to know how one small family feels. . . .

I am 34 my husband 39 our daughter 5.

But what I want to write is this. Please don't feel as though you have your hand on the heart of the people when you hear those "stuffed shirts" in your city talk, they don't really know how we little people feel. We have a lot of people like that out here too. To hear them talk one would think they were carring the whole load themselves, it disgusts us. . . .

My mother was an Army Nurse in the last war, served 18 months overseas you said tonight, "what can you tell your grand children you did to help win this war," I'm afraid I'll have to bow my head and say nothing.

And thats going to hurt like the devil, because I want to do something. I've wanted to join the W.A.C. so bad it was painful. I'm not a regestered nurse but I was just about raised in a hospital. I've worked in several and know my way around. I know there are a thousand places here and overseas where my hands would be needed and welcome — but what can I do?

My mother left me with her parents when she went over, but I have no one to leave my darling with even for an hour — for her welfare comes first always. I know you have tried to have nursery schools, you've done all you could — but the one I looked at in Oakland finnished me, a dark, damp cement basement, kids all huddled around in coats trying to keep warm, all with very bad colds, not for mine.

But will it be enough when all this is over for me to say "I was not active in World War II I stayed home so you could have a nice dry place to stay — warm balanced meals and a hug and a kiss when you bumped your head." Oh sure I walk blocks to do my shopping, saved paper, tin, fats, and anything else I can. But thats not enough — we want to do so much more, so ask it of us, we glory in it, we all love you and know you are trying so hard. God is surely with us to give you the strength to guide us through these times.

Sincerely

Mrs. Ellen A. Kyle
Sacramento, Calif.

*　　*　　*

Dear Mr. Roosevelt

This is the first letter I've ever written to you and I hope it will be the last.

I am listening to your fireside chat and <u>boiling</u>. I stood it as long as I could and now I can't take it any more.

What's the idea of a national service law. It isn't really half as necessary as you say it is — <u>and you know it</u>! The war plants have enough unskilled women as a whole — but what about men? Well, there's a shortage of man power everywhere and you certainly should know that!

Take the case of our family — My father has his own small business and is in his 50's. Under this service law, my mother who is also in her fifties — would have to go out and work — and what woman of that age is capable of taking a job & running a house. I am a high school senior and I shall be graduating on February 3rd. I had planned to get a job and work till fall — which I thought would help sufficiently. Then in fall, I <u>was</u> planning to go to school but if we have this <u>crazy</u> service law, I'd either have to enter school <u>right</u> after graduation and not work at all or else work till after the war is over and maybe not even get an education! I have read that in China <u>all</u> students are exempt — even from military service, so it seems to me that if China, invaded and hard pressed, cares enough about her future, we cer<u>tainly</u> ought not to have a service law cut down on the homes and the schools for which America has always been proud. . . .

Well, I am afraid this letter won't do much good because when the government gets an idea it's almost too difficult to influence it.

However, I'm hoping that if there is a national Service Law — another step toward far-reaching governmental control — some provisions will be made for students or would-be students.

Thank you for any attention you may have given to this letter.

Sincerely,

Barbara Randall
Wauwatosa, Wis.

JANUARY 13, 1944

Dear Mr. President:

Having voted for you three times and having watched your career during the past twelve years, often with admiration, it grieves me to be obliged to tell you that when I read your message in the press yesterday morning, I was shocked to think that the man I had admired could write such a wrong message, and I felt it my duty to write to you at once, as you have requested us to do, and tell you how I feel.

Conscription of labor means slavery for those conscripted. Free Americans must not enslave one another. While Congress still witholds from women equality under the law, as expressed in the Amendment to the Constitution before both Houses now, it is pathetic to find you planning to give to women the equality of enslavement with their brothers.

Permit me to beg you to immediately retreat from the disastrous position that you took yesterday in your message to Congress. It takes a brave man to be willing to acknowledge that he has been wrong. It is because I believe that you are brave, that I presume to send you this letter. I think you will find that you are facing an almost unanimous opinion of the American citizens of what I ask.

Very respectfully yours,

Katherine Devereux Blake
New York, N.Y.

JANUARY 12, 1944

Sir:

. . . I am writing to enter my objection to the proposal of a nationwide service draft. If democracy were equally applied to all citizens of this country and if economic opportunities were open alike to everyone, I would have no objection to any law which would demand service for the Government wherever the Government decided such service was needed; but I am wondering if you thought of what would happen to the minorities in this country if and when such a law is enacted.

It happens that I belong to the most kicked-around minority in the United States — the Negroes. What do you suppose will happen to colored people in the south when the administration of such a law is put into the hands of the average southern white official? Already in the Army, under selective service, Negroes are generally shunted to the least desirable jobs, and a work-draft would give anti-Negro whites of the South a golden opportunity to assign Negroes to low grade work. In the North, too, where prejudice against the Negro is as marked if not as openly admitted, white work-draft boards would certainly shift colored people into those jobs which they felt white men and women would not accept.

In lesser degree this same unjust administration of the law would apply to Jews, Mexicans, Indians, Chinese and Japanese citizens. And where the minority happened to be Catholic, that minority would likewise suffer from unfair application of the law's provisions.

In view of these prospects, I am hoping that the Congress will not grant the request you made in the speech yesterday.

I am sending a copy of this letter to Senators Burton and Taft and to Congressman John M. Vorys.

Very truly yours,

G. A. Steward
Columbus, Ohio

JANUARY 13, 1944

Dear President Roosevelt:

I heard part of your message to the Congress January 11th and I was much pleased with it. May God continually bless you in your work — may He also bless your beloved wife in her work.

That's right, all American citizens should have the right to vote. It's a matter which God would be pleased with — the right to vote. And the citizens of America should be paid equally for the same type of work. This would encourage them more to fight for their country.

And I suggest they be not segregated — the elimination of it (segregation) would make them more eager to serve our country.

I suggest also that full grown colored men be inducted into the U.S. Marine Corps to be powerful in God's name. . . .

Yours in Christ,

Rev. G. W. D. Danley, Prophet
Atlanta, Georgia

JANUARY 12, 1944

Hon Sir:

We want to take this opportunity to express to you our heartfelt thanks for your courageous and inspiring address to the nation. You still are the great leader you always were! Thank God, we still have a great Prophet leading us!

There is only one item which you left out and which we were hoping you would attack as you did attack the isolationists. We refer to racial and religious persecution and discrimination.

Nevertheless, we feel that you did a splendid job! May God watch over you and Protect you!

Very respectfully yours,

The Schwartzberg family
New York, N.Y.

P.S. We are writing to our Congressman to back your plans by voting for legislation!

JANUARY 11, 1944

Dear Sir:

This being my day off I had the great Pleasure of listening to your verry wonderful speach. It gave me hope for the future. I dout verry much if you will ever get to see this letter. As a citizen of this U.S.A. I have twice lent my youngest Son to this Cuntry for service in the U.S.A. and at the age of 64 I am serving as Military Police guarding the things esentual to war. I could not help but think what is in store for me after this Horable war is over. As social security is some help but the meager mite I and my wife would recieve would only be enough for us to sit in a chair and wait for the end to come. . . . your speech gave me hope for the future maby I will still be able to go to and fro without worring. . . .

yours for success

H. I. Zimmerman
Kent, Ohio

JANUARY 12, 1944

To whom it may concern:
Dear Secretary.

This letter to the President is of such a vital importance that I implore you to hand it to him.

~§ 534 §~

To withhold it from the President may judge you as a particeps criminis in the awful deluge of blood which is threatening our armed forces in Europe.

Very Respy

James L. Smiley

* * *

Dear Mr. President

In your eloquent address to Congress yesterday you persist in labelling the Axis powers as "gangsters." So be it. What shall we style ourselves?

The history of both Britain & the United States each is marked with most cruel imperialism. How can we stage ourselves as champions of Justice & Democracy? Not to go back earlier than the Civil War, our trail has been marked by the blood of innumerable innocents. All the 3 Presidents who plunged us into unnecessary wars came to a tragic end. Lincoln, Mc-Kinley, Wilson paid the penalty of their respective blunders.

President Roosevelt, in the sight of God and man, how can you sanction the proposed western invasion of Europe, predicted to be the worst sacrifice & effusion of blood which we have yet experienced.

How can you choose this monstrosity of fiendishness when God offers you the only reliable weapon — the Sword of the Spirit.

Truly yours

James L Smiley
Annapolis, Md.

JANUARY 11, 1944

Dear Mr. President,

I have just read & listened to your message to the Country. You should not be surprised at the apathy or callousness of the American people. In my opinion & that of many of my friends, your fundamental views on politics, how elections should be won, how Labor must be toadied to (right or wrong), waste of public funds, retention of incapable public servants (Francis Perkins as #1 exhibit) etc etc has removed much of this Nations moral fibre.

You find yourself in the position of indulgent, but unwise, parents who view with alarm & regret the actions of there grown children, who should have received spankings & not candy in their youths.

You have much to undo. I wish you luck in your reversal that we all hope has not come too late. If we win — & I hope & believe we will — it will be mainly because of our over-whelming production. You have not, during your Terms, done much to strengthen the character of the average American whose cry is "Gimme!"

Respectfully yours,

R. A. Gotuson
Oreland, Pa.

JANUARY 12, 1944

Your Honor

I was sitting by my radio the other night when you told our country what we would have to do. So i am writing you to tell you how i liked what you said. I think that was the best heart talk i have ever heard or know about in history. Any man who can talk to a nation & try to git it to do what he thinks it should do to live & be happy & free can't tell it from his brain he must tell it from his heart as you have been doing for near eleven years. Your Honor if the nation would pay more attention to what you say it would be better. But it cries when you say save this or that or give this or that when men are giving ther lives that we may live. Have Pease & Happiness Your Honor i love this country & love my President. I did not forget that he put bread in my mouth when i was hungry. But i can't think of words good enough for a man like you.

Your Honor you see i am a poor farm boy trying to get along. I am not smart i did not get much school. I am a father of three fine boys & good whife & willing to fight for them.

We have had a lot of sickness in our fambly but if i try hard i will (Win) as our nation should do.

Thats why i know what it means to have a man like you to lead our nation. Now Your Honor i hope you will forgive all my mistakes & beleave me when i say my say my heart is with you & your heart.

So i am yours
Willing

Oscar H. Bryan
Hagerstown, Maryland

* * *

Dearest President,

I am a colored girl fourteen years old, I go to Junior High School.

We are having a War bond drive, In this drive I have sold $400 worth of bonds. I sold the higest amount in any school. . . .

I am now listening to you over the radio. You are speaking your speach you spoke to the Congress.

I think you are a great president.

You are good to our people, We do thank you. . . .

Your speeches are so educational. You are now talking about the Bill of Rights We study about them in our civic.

God bless you president, and I do hope you will recover from the flue.

I'm sorry to stop you from your work, president, but I just wanted to let you know our race are doing our part, and we will continue until we whip the enemies.

Sincerely,

Gracie Mae Yancey
Austin, Texas

JANUARY 11, 1944

Sir:

May I, as an individual American, thank you, not only for your magnificent speech tonight, but for all the years of selfless devotion which you have offered for our beloved country.

My sweetheart gave his life in Italy sometime in October, one of my brothers is overseas, another is awaiting shipment. I have a war job.

For inarticulate working people, you voice our sentiments eloquently, and for those, who like myself, have lost some one dearly beloved, you stand as an enduring symbol of what we are fighting for.

Respectfully,

Katharine Donohue
Trenton, N.J.

PLANNING FOR PEACE:
JUNE 5, 1944; JUNE 12, 1944;
AND JANUARY 6, 1945

DURING THE LAST YEAR of his life, FDR delivered three Fireside Chats.[70] The first two of these were among the more perfunctory of his radio addresses and attracted a relatively sparse response.

When Roosevelt spoke to the nation on Monday, June 5, the Allied army on the English coast, in the words of its commander, Dwight Eisenhower, "was tense as a coiled spring . . . coiled for the moment when its energy should be released and it would vault the English Channel in the greatest amphibious assault ever attempted."[71] Troops had been aboard their ships since June 3 awaiting the scheduled June 5 landing on the French coast, but a fierce Atlantic storm delayed the Normandy invasion until June 6. FDR, of course, could not speak to the public of what he knew was about to take place and was forced to open his Fireside Chat with news that would soon be eclipsed:

> Yesterday, on June fourth, 1944, Rome fell to American and
> Allied troops. The first of the Axis capitals is now in our hands.
> One up and two to go!

The city of Rome, he reflected, was filled with monuments of the time when Rome "controlled the whole of the then known world." Thus its fall was symbolically significant, "for the United Nations are determined that in the future no one city and no one race will be able to control the whole of the world." Hinting at what was imminent, he declared that the victory in Rome occurred "while our Allied forces are poised for another strike at Western Europe — and while the armies of other Nazi soldiers nervously await our assault. And in the meantime our gallant Russian Allies continue to make their power felt more and more." Knowing the turbulent days about to unfold on the beaches of France, he did not exaggerate the importance of the victory in Italy: "It would be unwise to inflate in our own minds the military importance of the capture of Rome. We shall have to push through a long period of greater effort and fiercer fighting before we get into Germany itself. . . . Germany has not yet been driven to surrender. Germany has not yet been driven to the point where she will be unable to re-commence world conquest a generation hence. Therefore, the victory still lies some distance ahead . . . it will be tough and it will be costly, as I have told you many, many times."

In Italy, our troops had found "starvation, malnutrition, disease, a dete-riorating education, a lowered public health — all by-products of the Fas-cist misrule." It was now our task to "help local governments to reform on democratic lines . . . to give them bread to replace that which was stolen out of their mouth by the Germans . . . to make it possible for the Italians to raise and use their own local crops . . . to help them cleanse their schools of Fascist trappings." He was certain that the American people "approve the salvage of these human beings, who are only now learning to walk in a new atmosphere of freedom." He spoke generously of the Italian people, of "their virtues as a peace-loving nation," of their historic leadership "in the arts and sciences, enriching the lives of all mankind," of the millions of Italians who had made their way to the United States. "They have been welcomed, they have prospered, they have become good citizens, commu-nity and governmental leaders. They are not Italian-Americans. They are Americans — Americans of Italian descent."

One week later, after the nation had been able to absorb the news of D Day and the tumultuous days that followed, Roosevelt was back on the air to open the Fifth War Loan Drive. This time he spoke not of victory but of need; the need for funds to continue the struggle: "There is a direct con-nection between the bonds you have bought and the stream of men and equipment now rushing over the English Channel for the liberation of Eu-rope." He contrasted the present with the state of the world two years ear-lier, when Germany controlled almost all of Europe, North Africa, and the Mediterranean; when Japan stood triumphant in the Central and South Pacific and was threatening Australia, New Zealand, and India. "But today we are on the offensive all over the world — bringing the attack to our ene-mies. . . . The liberation forces now streaming across the Channel, and up the beaches and through the fields and the forests of France are using thou-sands and thousands of planes and ships and tanks and heavy guns. . . . There is a shortage of nothing — nothing! And this must continue." What the United States accomplished since the fall of France in 1940 "in raising and equipping and transporting our fighting forces, and in producing weapons and supplies for war, has been nothing short of a miracle. It was largely due to American teamwork — teamwork among capital and labor and agriculture, between the armed forces and the civilian economy — indeed among all of them." Every man, woman, and child who bought war bonds was a part of that teamwork and had to continue to be in order "to keep faith with those who have given, and are giving, their lives."

There was nothing restrained or subtle about FDR's approach or his willingness to use every form of societal and peer pressure available to push his fellow citizens into cooperating:

> There are still many people in the United States who have not bought War Bonds, or who have not bought as many as they can afford. Everyone knows for himself whether he falls into that category or not. In some cases his neighbors know too. To the consciences of these people, this appeal by the President of the United States is very much in order.

Almost seven months later, after he had been successfully reelected to a fourth term, he came before the American people again on Saturday, January 6, 1945, at ten in the evening Eastern Time. During the last year of his life, FDR became increasingly aware that he was a sick man, suffering not primarily from the sinus condition his doctor, Ross McIntire, had treated him for throughout his presidency, but from serious cardiovascular disease, which was finally diagnosed in March 1944, though he obviously had been afflicted with it for some time. The President's condition, consulting physician Howard Bruenn told Robert Ferrell many years later, was "God-awful." Roosevelt adjusted to his situation — taking digitalis, getting more rest, and losing weight — but he never fully regained his formidable energy.[72]

At no point did FDR allow the press or the people, or indeed, even his own closest associates, know his true condition. Less than five weeks before his death, when he addressed Congress on March 1, 1945, following his return from the Yalta Conference, he insisted that he had returned "refreshed and inspired. I was well the entire time. I was not ill for a second." Yet this was the first time he addressed Congress while seated and he apologized for it:* "I hope that you will pardon me for this unusual posture of sitting

*Robert Sherwood has written that FDR's Fourth Inaugural Address on January 20, 1945, was brief "due to the fact that the President was determined to stand up throughout it. (I don't think that he ever wore his braces and stood up again.)" See Robert Sherwood, *Roosevelt and Hopkins: An Intimate History* (New York: Harper and Brothers, 1948), 846.

down during the presentation of what I want to say, but I know that you will realize that it makes it a lot easier for me not to have to carry about ten pounds of steel around on the bottom of my legs; and also because of the fact that I have just completed a fourteen-thousand-mile trip."[73]

Though he knew he was not well, FDR had little notion of just how sick he was and certainly no suspicion that he would not live through his fourth term, which was to begin exactly two weeks after his January 6 Fireside Chat. Earlier that day, he had sent his Annual Message on the State of the Union to Congress and in the evening he summarized it for the radio audience. When Sherwood and Rosenman began to work on the Annual Message, the President told them he wanted it "to cover a very wide field: the status of the war, the international situation during and after the war, the formation of the peace and the United Nations Organization, and the future of America. He wanted it to synthesize everything he had said and promised during the campaign. He also wanted it to be a message from which all the freedom-loving peoples of the world could draw confidence and hope for the future." The result was his longest State of the Union message — twice as long as ususal — which made it especially difficult to cut down to Fireside Chat proportions. "I took a carbon copy of the original message and put brackets around the portions I thought should be omitted," Sam Rosenman has written. "The President approved or disapproved the cuts. Some entirely new paragraphs were written to make the radio speech a little more interesting." These origins made this Fireside Chat longer and more comprehensive than usual; appropriate qualities for what turned out to be his final Chat with his people.[74]

The President opened by discussing the devastating Battle of the Bulge in Belgium, which had begun on December 16 and saw the Germans surprise and repulse the Allied armies. The German counterattack had reached its high tide two days after Christmas. "Since then we have resumed the offensive, we have rescued the isolated garrison at Bastogne, and forced a German withdrawal. . . . Our men have fought with indescribable and unforgettable gallantry under most difficult conditions."

Even in its abbreviated Fireside Chat form, Roosevelt's address made it clear that he intended domestic liberalism and international involvement to be the bedrock of his Fourth Administration. He pleaded with people not to let the "power-politics" that had destroyed the peace after World War One to again dominate the postwar world. "We must not let that happen again, or we shall follow the same tragic road again — the road to a third world war." The future world must be governed by principles such as those embodied in the Atlantic Charter. It must not be torn apart by exploiting and exaggerating "the difference between us and our Allies." There were difficult situations, such as those in Greece and Poland, but he was confident they could be solved by "the establishment of permanent machinery for the maintenance of peace." The United Nations had won the war by acting together: "They must now join together to make secure the independence and freedom of all peace-loving states, so that never again shall tyranny be able to divide and conquer."

An enduring peace, he insisted, "cannot be achieved without a strong America — strong in the social sense, strong in the economic sense as well as in the military sense." Thus he reiterated his Economic Bill of Rights: the "right to a useful and remunerative job . . . to a decent home, to a good education, to good medical care, to social security, to reasonable farm income . . ." As part of future security, he briefly mentioned a proposal that, as the letters below demonstrate, constituted another of those relatively rare occasions when he seriously misread the public mood: "I am clear in my own mind that, as an essential factor in the maintenance of world peace in the future, we must have universal military training after this war, and I shall send a special message to the Congress on this subject."

Although concern for the future was an essential ingredient in his address, it was deeply touched by the exigencies of the present. He remained concerned that as the tide of war changed in the Allies' favor, the people would relax their vigilance in supporting the war. He brought his listeners good news — "We have no question of the ultimate victory." But it was coupled with bad — "We have no question of the cost. Our losses will be heavy." He reminded them, "We must never make the mistake of assuming that the Germans are beaten until the last Nazi has surrendered." Our attention had to remain fixed on the needs of the armed forces. Accordingly, he announced a critical shortage of nurses in the military. "Since volunteering has not produced the number of nurses required, I asked the Congress in my message, to amend the Selective Service Act to provide for the induction of registered nurses into the armed forces."

Although in his Fireside Chat of June 12, 1944, he had spoken of the "miracle" that the "teamwork among capital and labor and agriculture" had wrought "in producing weapons and supplies for war," he now suddenly declared that "the Lord hates a quitter," implying this was an appropriate term for American workers, and announced that the "only way to meet our increased needs for more weapons" was to pass a national service law "for the total mobilization of all our human resources — men and women — for the prosecution of the war." Those workers engaged in war production would not be allowed to leave their jobs and those not so engaged could be drafted into such jobs. Until such a law was passed, FDR asked Congress to grant him power to use "the services of the four million men now classified as 4-F in whatever capacity is best for the war effort."

It was a surprising announcement, coming as it did at the height of America's truly impressive war production and at a time when there was every indication that the country was making more war goods than needed. Obviously this was not sufficient to convince Roosevelt that the war had the undiluted support of the home front. It is hard to disagree with Bruce Catton that "this law was needed — not to make people work as they should, but to make them think and react emotionally as they should. This was psychological warfare, naked and undisguised, and it was psychological warfare directed at the American people themselves." FDR, Secretary of War Henry Stimson — who had informed a congressional committee that the home front was "on the point of going sour" and that "we have a situation of anarchy" — and their military advisers wanted such a law to prevent the American people from becoming complacent rather than because any documented complacency was threatening the needs of our armed forces.[75] In his Fireside Chat, FDR stressed symbolic reasons for a national service law, arguing that it "would provide supreme proof to all our fighting men that we are giving them what they are entitled to, which is nothing less than our total effort back home. And . . . would be the final, unequivocal answer to the hopes of the Nazis and the Japanese that we may become half-hearted about this war, and that they can get from us a negotiated peace."

This bleak note aside, FDR's final Fireside Chat was primarily an upbeat message. One of Franklin Roosevelt's enduring qualities was his deep belief in ultimate progress. "Out of every crisis, every tribulation, every disaster," he had told the Chicago convention in accepting the Democratic nomination for President in 1932, "mankind rises with some share of greater knowledge, of higher decency, of purer purpose."[76] This belief was at the root of FDR's supreme optimism, which had helped make him so popular and influential with the American people, and which he exuded from his First Inaugural Address ("The only thing we have to fear is fear itself") to an undelivered speech he was working on at the time of his death

("The only limit to our realization of tomorrow will be our doubts of today. Let us move forward with strong and active faith.").[77] It was in this spirit that he concluded the last Fireside Chat of his life with a litany of hope:

This new year of 1945 can be the greatest year of achievement in human history.

1945 can see the final ending of the Nazi-Fascist reign of terror in Europe.

1945 can see the closing in of the forces of retribution about the center of the malignant power of imperialistic Japan.

Most important of all, 1945 can, and must, see the substantial beginning of the organization of world peace — for we all know what such an organization means in terms of security, and human rights, and religious freedom.

We Americans of today, together with our Allies, are making history — and I hope it will be a better history than ever has been made before.

We pray that we may be worthy of the unlimited opportunities that God has given us.

* * *

Dear Mr. President

In the shuffle of mail that will be coming to your desk in the weeks to come, this letter will probably escape being brought to your attention. However, I could not withhold the expression of deepest admiration I felt for the perfect timing of your speech about the fall of Rome. It was the most perfect "Red Herring" ever devised to confuse and throw off guard a listening waiting enemy. How could D-day and H-hour be so close and you not drop even one hint of it nearness?

It must have called for the greatest effort in self control not to drop a hint of the dessert you held in your hand when you had to feed the people for weeks on the plain fare of, "be patient and trust your leaders, they will know when to strike and nothing can make them strike before everything is ready — stick to your jobs and redouble your efforts and your patience will be rewarded."

To go before the people last night with the certain knowledge that D-day was practically upon us and speak of an already accomplished victory of Rome, to throw the enemy off their guard, was one of the most wonderful pieces of perfect timing ever staged.

May God be beside you in all the decisions you will be called upon to make in the coming weeks. It must be the greatest comfort to all Americans to know that your ears are attuned to His voice in a crisis such as we are now facing.

In deepest admiration and respect and sympathy for one of the greatest Presidents this country has know I am

Most Sincerely,

(Mrs) Constance J. LaBelle
Stuyvesant Falls, New York

JUNE 7, 1944

My dear President:

What nerve you had to make a Political speach to get Italien votes, when at the same time you were sending our boys across the English channel to be murdered.

What insanity this war is, to drag our country in to save the British Empire.

The American people will never forgive you for the deaths, mained and insane boys you are directly responsible for.

What are our war aims and what are we fighting for? Our finish will come when we go bankrupt, total Chaos and Revolution all because a willful President planned it that way.

Got help you on Nov 7th hope you can take the humiliation without committing suicide.

Cordially,

Harriman H. R[illegible]
Braintree, Mass.

JUNE 5, 1944

My dear Mr. President,

I have just heard your talk on Rome, and feel impelled — for perhaps the hundredth time — to write a small word of thanks, encouragement, and congratulation to you. I am mother to five small Americans, and the tolerance and friendliness you show in your talks are the two things I try hardest to instill in them. My little ones begin about as high as my knee and stretch along to the oldest who taps my shoulder, and I, for one, approve of what you are trying to do to make this country the sort of place they can live — really live — in.

Please accept my heart felt loyalty — this seems a bit queer, but it is a free country and why I cant write to my President I dont know.

Very sincerely yours,

(Mrs. Peter van I. Burnett) Julia Penfield Burnett
Barrington, R.I.

JUNE 6, 1944

Dear Mr. President,

I liked your message on the conquest of Rome. Your words gave heart to Italians everywhere.

I wish you might have slipped in a phrase of praise for the Japanese-Americans who are fighting so well in Italy. Perhaps you can in a future address.

We need all the help you can give to building an America that is democratic, free from racial prejudice, and fair to all.

With a prayer for victory and lasting peace,

Sincerely,

James E. Walter
Newtonville, Mass.

JUNE 14, 1944

Dear Mr. Roosevelt:

. . . on June 12th you talked to all the people asking them to buy all the Bonds they can. on that same day. I bought some material. to make a dress. the material was four printed feed sacks. I bought four and the cost was 20 cents each, a total of 80 cents.

So I thought well tho Presedent asks us to by bond. so while I was listening to your speach I was sewing a dress. costing 80 cents. and had that day bought six hundred dollars worth of Bonds. wishe we could do the same every day. I will wear many feed sack dresses. So as to be able to put all the money we can in Bonds and to help in any way to win this war. May our dimes and dollars speed speed Victory. So our boys can come home. and the world be at peace once again. . . .

Respt.

Mrs. Rose L. Kimball
Wife of Master Sgt. Niles Lee Kimball, Army ret.
Atlanta, Ga.

JANUARY 7, 1945

Dear President Roosevelt: —

Thank you so much, for the wonderful address over the Radio. It is unfortunate that we nurses should be drafted. Each one of us should have offered her services to our Government right at the start of the war. We owe that loyalty to our country and to the young men who are giving their all. We do a lot of talking about freedom, don't we? But it is so nice to sit down, with a feeling of false security, and let others make the sacrifice. In fact, I believe that we have placed the wrong definition on the term "Freedom" and have suplanted it with soft living, and the line of least resistance. In fact, the public in general seems to believe that we are fighting Europe's war. We have failed to realize that if our Allies should lose, we wouldn't sit any more in complacent comfort. . . .

Please tell Congress that it is neither Unamerican nor harsh to draft nurses. If these nurses refuse to contribute their aid to the dying and wounded — they should be drafted. They were trained primarily to care for the sick. I am over fifty, have worked constantly at my profession, and will report for any kind of nursing in Government service.

God bless you, dear President Roosevelt.

I am

Yours respectfully,

(Mrs.) Martha Durnell R.N.
Los Angeles, California

JANUARY 9, 1945

Mr. President,

Your message to Congress on January 6th in which you recommended the drafting of nurses is responsible for this letter in which I wish to state my objections.

Draft nurses, indeed! That phrase bespeaks intellectual laziness or the inability to think a problem through from its causes to a logical conclusion.

Nurses, those with character and principles are tired of and refuse to be bruited about any longer. You'd get more volunteers than you need if you'd elevate the standards of wages and officer rank in the armed services. At least raise them as high as officers in other branches of women's services and permanently, not just for the duration of the war.

In your veterans' hospitals correct the wage scales. . . .

If you persist in being stupid I hope you have the moral courage to draft from the top downward. Induct A.N.A. officials, nurse hospital administrators, nurse registry and personnel directors, and members of Sisterhoods. They are those who have chanted that pious platitude "professional" — that proverbial carrot hung before the donkey's nose — in order to keep nurses' wages down to sub-starvation levels while buying new hospitals, paying off mortgages, and increasing their own salaries and bonuses by leaps and bounds. . . .

I absolutely refuse to be drafted until they first are made to go. . . .

Very sincerely,

Rosina Kathryn Kelling R.N.
Cadillac, Michigan

JANUARY 7, 1945

Dear President: —

I heard your message last night and reread it this morning. I am in agreement with every point, even to the drafting of nurses, of which I am one. I would ask you to go one step further — and draft all women; I do not feel that we should be discriminated against. . . . It doesn't take three years to learn to do the hard work that falls to the lot of a nurse — aides could be trained in a short time, just as our boys are trained to take over jobs that they have never done before. Nor do we have to wait until we find women who "like" or "can stand" seeing our boys mutilated and dying, none of us enjoy it — our boys do not enjoy the horrible things that they are being forced to do, either.

I do think that drafting is the answer — it is a difficult position to put ones self in — "Shall I enlist?" I have a twelve year old daughter, and cannot make up my mind where my duty lies — everyone can find a fairly reasonable alibi — but make this drafting just and fair to all; and we will do whatever is necessary to bring this war to a sucessful and speedy end.

Very sincerely yours,

Jessie Francis
Fenton, Michigan

JANUARY 8, 1945

Dear Sir:

Good for you for suggesting conscription of labor — and now will you push it thru! Why the best we have in 20 year olds should do all the paying in this as in all wars, I cant see. If they have not one word to say about what becomes of them, why should anyone else? Certainly, they are least to blame for the mistakes that have caused the war. As certainly, we can ill afford to lose them —

Clearly, the push on industry is essential in saving lives at this crucial time and there should be no nonsense about begging people to do this & that and no delays and less jockeying for profits.

Incidentally, the more everyone hates war, the better chance there is for peace. I am all for the lady who on hearing a bakery owner say that "the longer the war lasts, the better I like it, I make good profit" threw a lemon meringue pie in his face. Ordinarily it wouldn't indicate a lady to me but right now I count her a thoroughbred. There are plenty of us worried about one in the European invasion & another in the Pacific and we want 12 hours of work, a bread & milk diet and the boys home.

You dont hear much from us. That is why I am raising my voice, feeble as it is, against the cry of the ones who want profits, and are no doubt deafening your ears — Please hear the call of the "cream of the crop" from abroad and serve them.

Sincerely,

Jean Paton
New York, N.Y.

JANUARY 8, 1945

Dear Mr. Roosevelt:

Congratulations on your speech Saturday, January 6th!!

I was particularly impressed with your idea of drafting everyone. There are far too many people switching jobs because they seem to think they are out of the reaches of the draft.

Make them work or fight — after all were all in this war and the sooner we realize it the better.

Anything that will hasten back my husband (hes been in the army 42 months) and his three brothers (also in the army) has my full-hearted approval. . . .

Yours very truly

Mrs. Anthony Sams
Akron, Ohio

JANUARY 11, 1945

TAKE THE PROFIT OUT OF WAR. DRAFT CAPITAL. AND YOU WILL HAVE SIXTY MILLION WILLING MILITARY AND CIVILIAN WORKERS TO WIN THE WAR AND THE PEACE.

H. EARL HUMBERT
HOLLYWOOD, FLA.

JANUARY 8, 1945

Mr Roosevelt.

I have listened to your speech January 6. 1945. I was more then surprised that you still want unconditional surrender when you know that it means more lives. For what? well you told us that many sons and brothers will pay with their blood before we have peace, you can be sure your sons will not be one of those boys. If they are not home on furlough going to night clubs, they are home getting a divorce or getting married again. I am surprised to see the first family of America, including yourself, suppose to be good Christians, have broken everyone of the Ten Commandments. I don't see why you don't stope this war and bring our boys home. Mr Churchill and Marshal Stalin take good care of their people, they will get everything after this war. We Americans will be the suckers (as usuall) We will only have Gold Stars medals and heartaches. I don't see how you can sleep, if you have a conscience. To think how many poor boys are getting killed or crippled, just for your mistakes. Why don't Mrs Roosevelt get a defence job instead of useing up all the gas riding in planes, when all we hear is a shortage of this and that. Why not practise what the Roosevelts preach. Let us have one flag, and take care of one country, America.

May Gooszen
New York, N.Y.

JANUARY 21, 1945

Dear President Roosevelt: —

I am rather disappointed to learn of your stand on post war military conscription. If you actually mean what you said in your inaugural speech yesterday, "We can gain no lasting peace if we approach it with suspicion & mistrust — & with fear. We can gain it only if we proceed with the understanding & confidence & courage which flow from conviction", then what could we possibly do that would arouse more suspicion, mistrust & fear among our present allies than to change our historical policy & attitude on this matter of compulsory peacetime conscription? They would know that we need have no fear of our present enemies, who would be defeated at that time, & would conclude that we have designs on themselves — especially is this true of Russia — And as you suggest in your speech, mistrust & fear breeds like feelings in others.

To adopt conscription, especially now, would admit that we were convinced that the International Peace Organization will not work and that we had lost the peace before the finish of the war. For it is almost axiomatic that you get that for which you most heartily prepare. If we spent half the time, energy, to say nothing of money, on waging peace as we do on waging war, we might have that kind of world required to have a durable peace, about which we so glibly talk. But it is so much easier to destroy than it is to be creative.

Thank you for this opportunity of expressing my very deep & sincere convictions on this issue of monumental importance.

Yours for the building of a better world

Gwen Brockmiller
Detroit, Mich.

JANUARY 6, 1945

Dear Sir;

There has been much talk on the radio and in the newspaper as well as in many other places of compulsory military training for the boys. What I should like to know is what about the girls?

Perhaps it would help to straighten out some of the juvenile delinquents among the girls and also would be a healthy recreational venture.

Many girls would gladly join the Wacs, Waves or Spars if they were of age to do so. I believe that young girls when placed in a camp such as Girl Scouts or Camp Fire Girls are decidedly happy. These camps are the closest things that we have to these military things.

Would it be possible to have anything done about this? If this plan was taken up I believe that America's juvenile delinquency would go down, for in military training I think they would learn better citizenship and respect for authority.

Very truly yours,

(Miss) Charlotte Emerson Age 12
Portland, Oregon

* * *

Dear Mr. Presidident

It's a big problem trying to raise your family Then when you really need them, See them taken away from you. That's an awful bitter pill to take. I'm just a tenant farmer, hoping some day to farm for my self and my three boys give me a hand. But they won't have a chance neither will I. Therefore I'm very much opposed to compulsary training in peace time.

Herman Bruegge
Keota, Iowa

JANUARY 7, 1945

Dear Mr. President:

. . . On one hand we damn Hitler for everything he has ever done (and rightly so) yet on the other hand you and the War Department are in favor of adopting the most important feature of Hitlers entire program, for this democracy of ours. I cannot be so gullible as to believe that the Army is unanimous in wanting Compulsory training entirely and wholly for the purpose of filling a national need. I have no doubt at all that some of the proponents of compulsory military training are more concerned about retaining their wartime ranks and perogatives than they are about peacetime military requirements.

I have a son fifteen years of age. I have no desire to turn him over to the Army or Navy in peace time for experimental purposes. If the war is still going when he reaches the age of eighteen he will be in there fighting and with my blessing, but I shall do everything possible to defeat any proposition that would require involuntary servitude of my son in peace time. There is something quite sinister about the whole proposition — something that doesn't meet the eye.

Yours truly,

Freeman W. Daffer
St. Peter, Minnesota

JANUARY 7, 1945

Dear Mr. President: —

You have spoken for the people of this country as never before. Your Message to Congress and to the citizens expresses what so many of us wanted to see so finely and authoritatively spoken.

You shall have our support through these trying days when people become so confused, impatient, and demanding. . . . A strong government is essential to our cause. You did not ask for it, but we give what support we can. We intend to let our Congressmen and Senators and the leaders of both Houses know this resolution. I speak here for a family, and with two boys who have been in combat in Europe for months . . . we are absolutely for the National Service Act, for the drafting of women and of nurses. We shall tell our representatives in Congress so.

... private enterprise has to be subject to law and watched by government on behalf of the whole community. It runs to monopoly if left to itself, laissez faire, and it will do so internationally ... you can take it from us, we are not going to let this country be taken over by private enterprises of that sort. We want a government strong and vigilant, because we cannot watch these vast international operations ourselves.

There is a drive to get government out of everything. It cannot get out of international politics or international economics, and private business, finance or interests are not to have a free hand to go their own way without regard to the interests and comity of nations.

Our conscience is aroused over this matter as well as the question of the institutions for international peace. Count on our opinion and support both for what you have already proposed and for what must follow from your principles.

With gratitude for the "lift" of your Message and for the work you are engaged upon.

Yours faithfully,

Charles W. Hendel
New Haven, Conn.

JANUARY 6, 1945

Dear Sir:

I wish to express my extreme disfavor of your announcement to seek or even suggest peace time military conscription. . . .

You would do better to train American youth as teachers and help other nations help themselves to learn of the necessity of peace and the promotion of human good will, thru the educative process.

Sincerely,

Mrs. Helen Burson
Urbana, Illinois

JANUARY 7, 1945

My dear Mr. President:

. . . Peace can be won and held only by giving the world democratic governments which operate with the consent of the governed. The military must win the war but the peace can be lost, as it was before, by the statesmen. In the United States you and the State Department provide our leadership in international affairs. Only men with a true belief in democracy and the ability of the common man of all nations can put into practice our democratic principles for world cooperation and world peace. This requires men with vision and moral integrity who would be incapable of a "Munich". Through your choice of men in the key positions in the State Department you prepare for peace or another world war. . . .

If the United States State Department is staffed by men who fear and hate the Russian economic system through their ideals of property over human values, we will not affect the Russian economic system, but we will lose the peace and bring about our own destruction in a third and final world war. . . .

Respectfully yours,

Edith Gantt
Anne Hadden
Anna L. Williams
Alturas, California

EPILOGUE

I never realized the full scope of the devotion to him until after he died — until that night and after. Later, I couldn't go into a subway in New York or a cab without people stopping me to say they missed the way the President used to talk to them. They'd say, "He used to talk to me about my government."

Eleanor Roosevelt

I can remember the President ever since I was a little kid. America will seem a strange, empty place without his voice talking to the people whenever great events occur.

A soldier from Bowling Green, Ohio

FRANKLIN ROOSEVELT'S sudden death of a cerebral hemorrhage at his cottage in Warm Springs, Georgia, on April 12, 1945, generated the full panoply of responses common to the demise of a great leader: the funeral train wending its way slowly from Warm Springs to Washington, D.C.; the crowds of people, many crying openly and many more standing in mute silence, lining the tracks around the clock along the train's route through Georgia, the Carolinas, and Virginia; the slow procession from Washington's Union Station with tens of thousands of grieving, often sobbing, people on the sidewalks staring in disbelief at FDR's flag-draped casket resting on a caisson drawn by six white horses to the White House for a funeral service; the final train trip — once again with women, men, and children gathered along the tracks all through the night — to his ancestral home in Hyde Park, where he was buried in a simple ceremony; the myriad tributes, written and spoken, and even sung: "I sure feel bad, with tears runnin' down my face, / I lost a good friend, was credit to our race," the bluesman "Champion" Jack Dupree lamented:

> FDR was everybody's friend,
> Well, he helped everybody, right unto the end. . . .
> I know I can speak, for my friends if I choose,
> 'Cause he went away and left me, and I've got the FDR Blues.[1]

The national grief was profound enough to drive journalists to manifest their own version of the blues, as in this *New York Times* description of downtown Manhattan at the time of Roosevelt's funeral: "spattering raindrops slanted through the unwonted darkness in Times Square. They glistened like fresh tears on a woman's cheek. . . . The great heart of the city was still, just as his overburdened heart had been suddenly stilled."[2]

In his radio tribute to Roosevelt the day after his death, the actor and director Orson Welles expressed his sorrow by evoking the shared memory of how radio had eroded the distance between the President and his people:

> Our last president was a member of my family. He lived in our home as I know he lived in yours. My home seems empty now as yours does.[3]

In the privacy of their homes, millions of Americans reacted to the President's death in their own distinctive ways. On the day FDR's body arrived in Washington, D.C., just as she had on December 8, 1941, at the time FDR spoke to Congress following the Japanese attack on Pearl Harbor, John Idol's mother sat her boys down in front of the large Firestone console radio in the living room of her North Carolina farmhouse. Many years later her son still remembered what transpired:

> We listened as Arthur Godfrey and other correspondents narrated the event from their various observation posts. Born just days before FDR was elected, I had never known another President. . . . I was sorry to be giving up so fine a man, my sorrow being no doubt heightened by the solemnity I heard in the familiar voice of Godfrey. But what I recall most vividly was the clomp, clomp, clomp of the horses as they drew the draped coffin down Pennsylvania Avenue. They were no sound effects for "Let's Pretend" or "The Lone Ranger" but, instead, undeniable tokens that FDR was taking his last ride.[4]

It was fitting that John Idol's farewell to FDR was via radio, since it was through radio that Franklin Roosevelt had forged a surprisingly close relationship with the Idol family and with millions upon millions of other Americans, a relationship that would have been difficult to predict given the President's aristocratic background and demeanor and the fact that, for all his abundant charm, he was, as the historian Bernard Asbell has written, "a singularly private, *un*intimate man," possessing what his friend Felix

Frankfurter characterized as "that mystical touch of grace, a charismatic quality that stirs comfortable awe, that keeps a distance between men and a leader."[5] Frankfurter, and the many others who made similar observations, were undoubtedly correct. But so was the journalist Anne O'Hare McCormick, who wrote at the time of FDR's death: "The crowds in the streets felt close to the President. They felt they knew him intimately. He had that rare faculty of communicating himself to masses of people, so that millions who had never approached him knew he was approachable, and his relationship to these unknown friends was as personal as his ties with the friends he knew."[6]

Contemporaries who recognized the extent and depth of the President's hold on the people, especially through the medium of radio, were often unable to explain it. In 1942 Ruth Albert Cook, in the midst of her despairing verses depicting the wartime treatment of African Americans, puzzled over FDR's resonance with the nation's Black population:

> Last night a man with a Groton-Harvard accent
> Talked into the bedrooms, and parlors,
> And kitchens,
> And automobiles,
> Of fifteen million Americans who listened, . . .
> Last night, fifteen million Americans
> Were paled
> Into identity
> With one hundred fifteen million
> Other Americans.
> But today,
> The same fifteen million Americans,
> Became America's "tenth Americans,"
> Became America's largest minority
> Became Negroes again.[7]

We have seen this phenomenon repeatedly in the letters people wrote telling FDR how his radio talks had buoyed them even though, when his voice faded from the air, they remained poor, unemployed, undernourished, unfulfilled. They were, as Eleanor Roosevelt asserted, having a "dialogue" with their President, an act so novel to almost all of them that it assumed a significance in itself even though it might not rapidly bring material changes. "He's spoke very few words over the radio that I haven't

listened to," an unemployed cotton mill worker told an interviewer from the
Federal Writers' Project. "It's the first time in my ricollection that a president ever got up and said, 'I'm interested in and aim to do somethin' for the
workin' man.' Just knowin' that for once in the time of the country they was
a man to stand up and speak for him, a man that could make what he felt so
plain nobody could doubt he meant it, has made a lot of us feel a sight better
even when they wasn't much to eat in our homes."[8] Clarence Taylor of Baltimore, who described himself as "an unemployed carpenter, who hardly
knows where his next meal is coming from," wrote FDR on the day Germany invaded Poland that he was "investing the cost of the stamp" in order
to express his appreciation of the President's stand for peace in a world
riven by war.[9]

Frances Perkins opened her book *The Roosevelt I Knew* with the assertion: "Franklin Roosevelt was not a simple man. . . . He was the most complicated human being I ever knew." Many books, she predicted, "will be
written about Franklin Roosevelt, but no two will give the same picture.
For no two people saw the same thing in him."[10] The letters Roosevelt received from the people reveal the myriad images Americans had of him.
FDR's complexity, his lack of intimacy, allowed people to write to the President they imagined and molded to their own needs: FDR as father, brother,
neighbor, friend, fellow Christian, leader, protector, crusader, and to a considerably lesser extent, FDR as power-hungry traducer of America's sacred
political traditions, incompetent bureaucrat, relentless enemy of American business, reckless destroyer of sound economics, fomenter of war, dictator, Antichrist.

In whatever guise they pictured him, he was accessible and addressable.
The twist of a radio dial, a penny postcard, a three-cent stamp brought
Americans into close contact with their President, and whatever they
thought about him, they valued that contact. It was common for those who
heard his Fireside Chats to speak of a compulsion to write. "I don't know
exactly what impels me to write you but I must tell you the following or else
I know I'll never feel happy," Henry Fingerman, of Newark, New Jersey,
wrote.[11] "I havn't much knowlegd of letter writing," Mrs. Charles Boone
of Detroit confessed, "but I just had to write and tell you how your speech
made me feel."[12]

The Fireside Chats and the letters they generated created this two-way
"conversation" through which tens of millions of Americans felt empow-
ered and became, at least in their own eyes, participants in a process from

which they had hitherto felt distant. The interaction between radio personalities and their audience may seem totally removed from a personal two-
way colloquy in which what one says is determined or modified by what has
just been said or what one thinks will be said in return. But this type of dynamic reciprocal interplay is not confined to direct discussions. When the
singer and radio show host Kate Smith conducted her immensely successful 1943 marathon war bond drive over the radio, her listeners had no
difficulty imagining that she was speaking or singing to them personally,
which in a sense she was, since the reactions of her audience were never far
from her mind.[13] This was precisely the process that characterized FDR's
Fireside Chats and the written responses to them and explains why it is
valid to perceive them as an ongoing conversation between the people and
the President.

Following FDR's first Fireside Chat on the banking crisis, a visitor to
the White House asked him how he had managed to explain the banking
system in such clear and uncomplicated terms. Louis Howe recalled that
"Franklin swung around in his chair and pointed to a workman outside. . . . 'See that man?' he said. 'He was out there the day I started working on my speech about the banking crisis. I decided I'd try to make a
speech that the workman could understand. So you see,' he smiled, 'I really
made the speech to him.' "[14] "I often was at the White House when he
broadcast," Frances Perkins recalled, "and I realized how unconscious he
was of the twenty or thirty of us in that room and how clearly his mind was
focused on the people listening at the other end. As he talked his head
would nod and his hands would move in simple, natural, comfortable ges-
tures. His face would smile and light up as though he were actually sitting
on the front porch or in the parlor with them."[15]

In many letters, geography became both an example of and a metaphor
for how Roosevelt and radio had bridged the distance between the President and the people. "I am out here in western South Dakota, sixty miles
from the nearest railroad," L. M. Larson informed the President, "but the
radio puts us near to Washington, and your fireside chats are looked forward to."[16] "We are living up in the Mountains of Idaho, away from the
strife and tormoil of civalisation, you might say," Mrs. Sam Olson wrote.
"The only contact from the outside world we have, is our Radio. We have a
little four tube set on our table in the living room and as my husband and I
sat there last night listening, (I with my knitting) to the message coming to
us, It seemed as tho you were right there in the same room with us. Your

voice came in so clear and good. Some how you have a way of reaching the hearts of the people while you are speaking to them."[17]

This sense that FDR was a kindred spirit, an approachable being eager to hear from his fellow Americans was an omnipresent theme in a substantial number of the letters he received and certainly helps to explain why so many people felt both the need and the liberty to write to him. But communicating with the President was not invariably an easy act. "My impulse was to wire my congratulations; my purse made such indulgence impossible," Romance Koopman wrote from Madison, Wisconsin, after FDR's Chat on May 27, 1941. "Yet I glory in my privilege, as a free American citizen with a rickety typewriter, to write my president."[18] In Denver, John Sain complained to FDR: "We have no stenographers and have to quit our work to write to you — while the privileged few can have a Secretary write his disapproval while he plays Golf."[19]

Lack of money or time, of course, were not the sole or even the primary impediments. After mentioning that she hadn't written earlier because "there wasn't three cents for a stamp," Harriet D'Alessandro of Brockton, Massachusetts, was quick to add: "Then too, so many of us think: 'Oh what's the use to write and tell him how we feel, . . . who cares what we think.' We are so insignificant and powerless to make our individual voices heard. Those standing high, those having the rostrums, can speak and they are heard because of their influence and power and the high places where they stand. We are different."[20] Frank Quaife of San Diego wrote Roosevelt of his certainty that the bulk of the letters to Congress and the President "are not from the working people. . . . The large majority are from persons who have time and facilities for writing, persons who can be sure that their words will be correctly spelled, and persons who will not be embarrassed by the thought of addressing such important public personalities."[21]

These were sensitive delineations of the uncertainties and insecurities that doubtless inhibited numbers of Americans from writing their leaders. This had been the norm throughout U.S. history, and it is hardly surprising that it continued during the Depression and World War Two. What is more striking is how many Americans, from the beginning of Roosevelt's First Administration, overcame these inhibitions and did write. "I dont just know, possiably I shouldnt have written this letter, because my education is very much limited and I know that my English is not correct," William Kinzell wrote from Oregon, "but . . . I just had to express my true opinion."[22]

Some of his correspondents were insistent that FDR personally read their letters: "A devoted little friend" wrote, "I do hope you have read this letter yourself," while Edward McCann of Pittsburgh pleaded with the President's press secretary, Stephen Early, "Come on, Steve, pass it on — what if it was buried under 7,903,675 others!"[23] More often those who wrote understood the unlikelihood of their letters reaching the President, but they go on to say that what *counted* was the very act of writing itself: "I know you will never see this letter I am writing in my noon hour but I enjoy writing it just the same," Isabel Adlerholz wrote during the Supreme Court fight.[24] "The thought of having mailed this note to the greatest president of all time," A. A. Harrall of Tuskegee, Alabama, wrote in 1937, "will be sufficient."[25] Jim Vance of Memphis, who had just enlisted in the army in the spring of 1942, telegraphed: "JUST A THOUGHT OF KNOWING I'VE TALKED TO OUR CHIEF BY WAY OF WESTERN UNION IS RECOMPENSE ENOUGH."[26]

The impressive thing about this correspondence is how effectively it allowed his listeners to express the deep feelings — indeed even the love — they had for the President. An unemployed railroad worker from St. Louis confided: "After being in the claws of the Octupus (Depression) these last years I just can't express the feeling I have for you. I believe we all love you."[27] Charles L. Kimmel of Chicago summed up the sentiments of many radio listeners when he wrote: "Please pardon me for addressing you so familiar in some passages in this letter but your personality is such, and that kindly smiling face I see so much on paper and that kindly voice I hear on the air, how can any human being keep from it. We all feel (us common people) that you are our friend tho we may never meet face to face."[28] Gertrude Fagan concluded her 1942 letter "With respect, and may I say love," and a year later Thomas Bilyeu closed his "In Love."[29] A Republican from upstate New York was more diffident in expressing his affection: "I am a hundred per cent he man, both as to height, weight, and habits, but if I had been in easy reach of you last night when you finished your address, I believe that I would have been almost tempted to have given you a big bear hug."[30]

Even the simple use of the salutation "My Friends," with which FDR opened most of his Fireside Chats — a technique he had learned earlier in the century from an Irish American politician in upstate New York — particularly impressed his audiences.[31] As "friends" many felt free to write him with familiarity and ease, advising him to take care of himself, eat properly, get enough rest, not allow his many critics to depress him. "In the name of 'All that is Holy,'" wrote Virginia Miller of Sierra Madre, California, "please, Oh please give your body the rest and care it needs."[32] Mrs. Paul H. Russell of Haskell, Oklahoma, was one of the many who begged him to get more recreation "for Mr. Roosevelt you are too important, too necessary to your country. We cannot do without such a leader, such a friend."[33] "Now do not think me an alarmist," Edward Jewett wrote from Passaic, New Jersey, in 1933, "but we are Worried as to your Safety in Opening the World's fair in Chicago. . . . Be well gaarded."[34]

As "friends" they felt free to refer to FDR's polio, whose effects severely hampered his physical mobility and in their eyes helped to counter his privileged status and humanize him. In a sense, the heavy braces he was forced to wear on his legs were Franklin Roosevelt's log cabin: they functioned, as had Abraham Lincoln's humble birth, as a claim to kinship with those he led. "You hold a very tender spot in our hearts," Sue Hight of San Antonio wrote. "We had a brother that had your trouble at three & had to go thru his life on crutches. But like you he always had a smile, & was an inspiration to those who knew him."[35] Cloie Cain of Tacoma related to the President the plight of her nephew Willard, who suffered from debilitating arthritis: "I wrote him calling attention to your wonderful will power in overcoming your physical ill-health, and I said 'Just see to what heights are President rose, after that terriffic suffering, both physical and mental.' "[36] A resident of Long Island told FDR that he thought of him as "a man who understands suffering because he has suffered terribly and cruelly himself, who has faced personal catastrophe and lived to conqure it."[37]

As "friends" they wrote him about their own lives, told him about their families, revealed their hopes and worries and burdens. "Our Baby Boy was Born during this hard Struggle," James Manning of Bloomington, Illinois, wrote. "My wife did not have the care of a Doctor. Why Because I didin have the Money and they would not come with out the cold cash. I hade to Stand with my hands tied and See my wife . . . give birth to a Baby that was not healthy Because the Mother did not have the right Kind of food and care."[38]

Faith was the cornerstone of the relationship between FDR and the people. The term was used openly and implicitly in letter after letter. In 1937 William Froberg of New Buffalo, Michigan, referred to "the dark first days of 1933 when you gave us that new American feeling, Faith in our government."[39] "I back you," Frances Furnice of the Bronx assured him. "You are my sweepstake ticket to happiness, security and good health."[40] These feelings of faith and hope were based in no small part on the people's sense of FDR's greatness and leadership. "You are the Messia of our period," Ben Medofsky of Portland, Oregon, assured him.[41] There was a strong element of religiosity in a substantial number of the letters FDR received. Writing for himself and his wife, S. J. Flanders of Swainsboro, Georgia, declared: "We are as certain that God brought you to the world 'at such a time as this' as we are that He brought Queen Esther to Mordecai to free her people."[42] A woman from Philadelphia wrote as one of those "Americans to whom you are second only to their God," while another from Flint, Michigan, assured him that "Already you are 'God' to me."[43] They wrote asking for advice of all kinds, sent him copies of the letters they were writing members of Congress to make sure he approved, implored him to speak more often and give them what W. Edgar Bates of Philadelphia called "an authoritative word from you on the state of things here and abroad."[44]

But if part of this faith was built on deifying FDR, much of it was built on humanizing him. The letters are suffused with a depiction of the President as one of the folk. Gertrude Jablow of Jersey City apologized for writing so informally, "but you are one of the best and the plainest Presidents I ever remember."[45] Mrs. O. B. Bozeman of Albany, Georgia, had looked at FDR's picture on her wall and listened to his voice so much "I almost feel like I know you."[46] In West Hollywood, California, Pat Richmond sat down to write the President and assured him: "The fact that I use pencil & yellow pad paper is not intended as a mark of disrespect. Only my closest friends are written to on this paper."[47] After a wartime Chat, Flora Copple of Olympia, Washington, felt comfortable enough to engage the President in small talk: "You sounded like some friendly neighbor, come in to talk of neighborhood affairs — registering for the sugar ration next week — the hope that our tires will last another year or two — to bring us wood from the shingle mill where we used to work."[48]

The sense of identification was often so strong that it led his correspondents to propose visits. John Randolph contemplated a trip from Philadelphia to the capital so he could see FDR's stamp collection; Adella Cooper invited him to be a guest in her home while he was fishing in Texas; Don Taylor asked him to "please stop sometime when you are near Seattle," and sent succinct directions: "ask for Miss N. L. Taylor at Seattle Brass Mill."[49] In Colorado, Mrs. F. A. Warren allowed her imagination to take her even further: "I dreamt you, Mrs. Roosevelt, a son and wife were dining at my house. I could see you seated at the table. I had roast turkey & of course all the fixings. After dinner I was showing Mrs. Roosevelt my pieced quilts."[50]

The notion that FDR's relationship with his people was a reciprocal one — that he needed them just as they needed him — was common. The President received many offers of help from his correspondents. "I shall continue to advise you as to the public reactions as I find them. If there is anything else I can do, command me," a New Yorker wrote.[51] Harry Williams of Newport News, Virginia, informed the President that he had written his Congressman and Senators in support of reforming the Supreme Court. "My support will be very small," he concluded, "but I am glad to do this for you as you have done so much for me."[52] Berenice Harrison of Miami offered him "all I have in the way of ability, experience and my life . . . I know my services will be needed."[53] "I truly believe that you can lean on us, your fellow Americans, and regain from our hearts the greatest part of the courage you now give us," Dorothy Bates of New Hampshire assured him, as did many others.[54]

It's apparent from the Fireside Chats that Roosevelt used these closely tailored radio addresses to persuade his listeners, shape his program, and attain his ends both immediate and long range. What is often less clear — but no less true — is that the President was not the only one to use the Chats for his own purposes. They were also used by those who listened and responded to FDR by the millions. The letters to FDR that have become the most widely known and familiar are those from supplicants — people in dire straits — who wrote letters describing their difficulties in stark terms, most frequently followed by requests for help of various kinds, from obtaining a used coat Mrs. Roosevelt no longer needed so that the writer could go to church on Sunday to baby clothes for an expected child, help with an overdue mortgage, aid from government agencies, finding a job. These are the most dramatic and often heart-wrenching letters FDR received.[55] But as crucial as such letters are for a complete understanding of the American people during these difficult years, they are not sufficient.

Securing help was only one of the myriad reasons that impelled people to communicate with the President. Those who wrote after hearing the Fireside Chats not infrequently asked for help, of course. But more often they were responding to the specific information, messages, arguments, proposals the President had laid before them, and their purposes in writing were varied and not easily summed up. They saw the Fireside Chats not as mere speeches but as part of a dialogue and they treated them as such, which is precisely why there were so many letters. They took the occasion to pepper FDR with their views, their comments, their responses to the specifics of his Chats. They told him why and how he was important to them, what their vision of the future was, how they expected him to attain the ends they shared with him. They lauded and freely criticized him; deified and damned him; supported and challenged him. They introduced themselves and their loved ones to him and shared with him personal moments, memories, dilemmas, even secrets. They spoke to him with awe and familiarity, thought of him as an authority and a friend, a father and a buddy, a figure they imagined and constructed in a bewildering multiplicity of ways, a man they created and re-created over and over. They were parochial and independent in the views they expressed, traditional and innovative in the proposals they made, deeply religious and deeply political in their outlook, reserved and personal in their style. They were frequently hesitant but ultimately surprisingly open in what they wrote and shared and expressed.

When Anthony Rodrigues of Springfield, Massachusetts, wrote to FDR in 1937, "Our only means of expression is a ballot and a three cent stamp," he doubtless understood how profoundly his "means of expression" had expanded during these years.[56] Those three-cent-stamped letters, penny postcards, and telegrams that now reside so quietly and neatly boxed in the FDR Library were, in the 1930s and 1940s, dynamic instruments that gave voice to those who had been rendered inarticulate even in the ballot boxes, where the reasons for their votes, the hopes and expectations they attached to them, the future they imagined by casting them remained muted.

The radio expanded the ballot box. It enabled Roosevelt to come into the home, the workplace, the automobile; into the many sites of leisure activity; even into houses of worship. It helped FDR and his audiences transcend boundaries both spatial and social. It enabled large numbers of Americans to feel themselves part of the process, to imagine themselves in intimate contact with *their* President. It stimulated them to explore their sense of things, to think carefully and often deeply about the issues that confronted them and their nation. It stirred them to action, led them to pick up pens and pencils and fill sheets or even scraps of paper with their feelings and opinions for the edification of the President, their Representatives and Senators, their local newspapers. It brought them out on the street to talk with neighbors and friends, to sign petitions and send telegrams to officials of all kinds. It allowed them to create and, in the case of the letters they wrote to Franklin D. Roosevelt, to leave behind them a record of their voices that helps us envision and comprehend the world they inhabited.

APPENDIX

━◀◉▶━

A Note on the Fireside Chats

Although the American people and the press embraced the term "Fireside Chat" for a certain genre of FDR's radio addresses almost as soon as it was originated by Harry C. Butcher, of CBS's Washington, D.C., office, sometime between FDR's first radio Chat on March 12, 1933, and his second on May 7, and although the President accepted and used the term, it was never adopted officially. Robert Sherwood, one of FDR's speechwriters, thought Roosevelt always found it a bit "corny."[1] In a note to his Fireside Chat of March 12, 1933, in the 1938 edition of his *Public Papers and Addresses,* FDR referred to it as "the first so-called fireside chat."[2] In his Chat of June 24, 1938, he used the term ironically, telling his audience: "It is the warmest night I have ever seen in Washington and yet this talk will be referred to as a fireside talk."[3] Occasionally, some of his listeners recognized the irony as well. "The announcer graciously remarked that it was one of your 'fire-side addresses,' " wrote Blanche Poltrock in June 1934, "which sounded hospitable; even though the evening was warm, and we pictured you in a cool room, or on the porch."[4] Roosevelt continued his playful attitude when he referred to his address at the 1940 hundred-dollar-a-plate Jackson Day dinner as a "Plate-Side Chat."[5]

Whatever ambivalence FDR may have had about the term "Fireside Chat," it was eagerly taken up, both by his contemporaries and the generations that followed, and has become deeply lodged in our vocabulary and our imagination.* Stephen Early, Roosevelt's press secretary, and other members of FDR's staff, though they used the term, refused to supply definitions of what constituted a Fireside Chat, insisting that the term was not theirs but was created by the newspapers and broadcasting stations. Accordingly, the latter fell back on their own definitions, explaining in one

---

*The term is in wide use in contemporary America. An Internet search conducted with the help of the search engine www.google.com reveals the existence of thousands of "fireside chats" currently being held and sponsored throughout the United States by municipalities and religious, fraternal, and political organizations.

instance that a Fireside Chat was "one in which the President takes the people into his confidence or puts a proposal to them informally."[6]

Precisely because it was not an official term, there has been some imprecision in defining which of his radio talks were Fireside Chats and the number has varied. The Speech Index in the Franklin D. Roosevelt Library lists only twenty-one. Samuel Rosenman, who edited the thirteen volumes of *The Papers and Addresses of Franklin D. Roosevelt* and helped FDR write many of these addresses, identified twenty-seven radio addresses as Fireside Chats in the published papers and then added a twenty-eighth — the radio address of January 11, 1944 — in his 1952 autobiography. John Sharon, in his influential 1949 article on the Fireside Chats identified twenty-eight Chats by adding to Rosenman's original list the radio address of November 14, 1937, in which FDR asked the people's cooperation in the federal government's unemployment census. Sharon's list of twenty-eight became the generally accepted one until 1973, when the compilers of the edition of the taperecordings of the Fireside Chats issued by Mass Communications Inc. (MCI) expanded the list of Fireside Chats to thirty-one by adding the radio address of May 27, 1941, in which FDR declared a national emergency; the radio address of January 11, 1944 — which Rosenman had also decided belatedly was a Fireside Chat — in which FDR shared with the people the State of the Union Address he had sent to Congress earlier in the day; and the radio address of January 6, 1945, in which he summarized for a national audience his 1945 State of the Union Address. Steven Schoenherr, in his 1976 study of Stephen Early, using evidence in Early's papers, came up with the same list of thirty-one chats. This list was the basis for the first complete edition of the Fireside Chats, published in 1992. We have also accepted the list of thirty-one Fireside Chats for this volume.[7]

NOTES

PREFACE

1. James Thurber, "The 'Odyssey' of Disney," *Nation,* March 28, 1934.
2. The number of letters in the FDR Library is an estimate by its former director, Herman Kahn. See Leila A. Sussmann, *Dear FDR: A Study of Political Letter-Writing* (Totowa, N.J.: Bedminster Press, 1963), 87, 127 n. 1. It is our own estimate that FDR may have received up to twice that number since the White House sent millions of letters on to federal agencies and departments for relevant responses to specific queries and problems.
3. Quoted in Robert S. McElvaine, ed., *Down and Out in the Great Depression: Letters from the "Forgotten Man"* (Chapel Hill: University of North Carolina Press, 1983), 5.
4. Two previous volumes of letters to FDR and other officials have been published: McElvaine's 1983 volume, *Down and Out in the Great Depression,* which contains 173 letters to Herbert Hoover, Franklin and Eleanor Roosevelt, and a variety of government agencies and officials from 1930 to 1936, and Gerald Markowitz and David Rosner, eds., *"Slaves of the Depression": Workers' Letters about Life on the Job* (Ithaca: Cornell University Press, 1987), a collection of letters written by American workers during the 1930s and 1940s relating their work experiences and hardships to FDR, Secretary of Labor Frances Perkins, and other federal officials.
5. The percentage of households owning radios is given in Christopher H. Sterling and John M. Kittross, *Stay Tuned: A Concise History of American Broadcasting,* second edition (Belmont, Calif.: Wadsworth, 1990), appendix C, table 8; the percentage of households tuned in to the Fireside Chats is given in Betty Houchin Winfield, *FDR and the News Media* (Urbana: University of Illinois Press, 1990), 121; the percentage of adult Americans who heard or read his February 23, 1942, Chat is given in the unpublished report "The President's 'Map' Speech and Audience," conducted by the U.S. Office of Facts and Figures and the National Opinion Research Center (copy in the FDR Library).

INTRODUCTION

1. Margaret Atwood, *The Robber Bride* (New York: Doubleday, 1993), 4.
2. Hadley Cantril, *The Invasion from Mars: A Study in the Psychology of Panic* (1940; New York: Harper Torchbooks, 1966), xii.
3. Anne O'Hare McCormick, "Radio: A Great Unknown Force," *New York Times Magazine,* March 27, 1932; "Radio's Audience: Huge, Unprecedented," ibid., April 3, 1932; "The Mind Behind the Radio Broadcast," ibid., April 10, 1932.
4. Hadley Cantril and Gordon W. Allport, *The Psychology of Radio* (New York: Harper and Brothers, 1935), 14, 19.

5. Lew Sarett and William Trufant Foster, *Basic Principles of Speech* (Boston: Houghton Mifflin, 1936), 561.

6. Maxine Kumin, "Remembering Pearl Harbor at the Tutankhamen Exhibit," in *Our Ground Time Here Will Be Brief* (New York: Viking, 1982), 73–74.

7. Oral interviews in Ray Barfield, *Listening to Radio, 1920–1950* (Westport, Conn.: Praeger, 1996), 16–17.

8. Myra King Whitson, Houston, Texas, to FDR, March 13, 1933.

9. F. L. Brewer, Richland Center, Wisconsin, to FDR, March 13, 1933.

10. Nathan Weldon, Brooklyn, New York, to FDR, April 28, 1935.

11. Florence Gunnar Nelson, n. p., to FDR, May 26, 1940.

12. James W. Ceaser, Glen E. Thurlow, Jeffrey Tulis, and Joseph M. Bessette, "The Rise of the Rhetorical Presidency," *Presidential Studies Quarterly* 11 (spring 1981): 158–71.

13. McCormick, "Radio's Audience: Huge, Unprecedented."

14. Leila A. Sussmann, *Dear FDR: A Study of Political Letter-Writing* (Totowa, N.J.: Bedminster Press, 1963), 14.

15. Orrin E. Dunlap, Jr., *Radio in Advertising* (New York: Harper and Brothers, 1931), 67.

16. Orrin E. Dunlap, Jr., "Mail Reveals America's Reaction to Politics on the Air," *New York Times,* Sunday, July 17, 1932, 8:5.

17. Ira R. T. Smith, with Joe Alex Morris, *"Dear Mr. President . . .": The Story of Fifty Years in the White House Mail Room* (New York: Julian Messner, 1949), 156, 213–14.

18. Hugh Johnson, *The Blue Eagle from Egg to Earth* (Garden City, N.Y.: Doubleday, Doran and Company, 1935), 260.

19. *New York Times,* December 27, 1933, 1.

20. Smith, *"Dear Mr. President,"* 151.

21. Louis McHenry Howe, "The President's Mail Bag," *American Magazine,* June 1934, 23.

22. Ben Whitehurst, who was the chief of the Correspondence Division of the FERA and WPA during FDR's first administration, claimed that 60 to 70 percent of all White House mail was routed to and answered by his division (Ben Whitehurst, *"Dear Mr. President"* [New York: E. P. Dutton, 1937], 12).

23. Smith, *"Dear Mr. President,"* 189–91.

24. Howe, "The President's Mail Bag," 118. For FDR's treatment of the letters, see also the *New York Times,* May 1, 1938, 4:7.

25. Lela Stiles, a White House assistant who conducted many of these briefs, spoke about them in an interview with Leila A. Sussmann, on December 2, 1954, discussed in Sussmann, *Dear FDR,* 66–69, 84 n. 33.

26. Eleanor Roosevelt, *This I Remember* (New York: Harper and Brothers, 1949), 97–99; Bernard Asbell, *When F.D.R. Died* (New York: Holt, Rinehart and Winston, 1961), 161.

27. Quoted in Robert S. McElvaine, ed., *Down and Out in the Great Depression: Letters from the "Forgotten Man"* (Chapel Hill: University of North Carolina Press, 1983), 5.

28. Albert Moreau, Sr., North Adams, Massachusetts, to FDR, 1937.

29. Margie DeBett, St. Joseph, Michigan, to FDR, June 28, 1934.

30. C. V. Easterwood, Memphis, Tennessee, to FDR, May 28, 1941; Edwin M. Watson to C. V. Easterwood, June 3, 1941.

31. Charles Fisher, Chicago, Illinois, to FDR, December 29, 1940; Stephen Early to Charles Fisher, January 13, 1941.

32. Edwin M. Watson to Mrs. Mary L. Jester, Springport, Indiana, December 29, 1943.

33. Velma Hess, Martinsburg, West Virginia, to FDR, October 12, 1942; Grace G. Tully to Velma Hess, October 19, 1942.

34. Robert W. Woolley, Washington, D.C., to FDR, May 28, 1941; Stephen Early to Robert W. Woolley, June 4, 1941.

35. Jack McIntire, Jr., Detroit, Michigan, to Marvin McIntyre, October 24, 1933; Marvin H. McIntyre to Jack McIntire, October 27, 1933.

36. J. T. Cannon, Philadelphia, Pennsylvania, to FDR, September 16, 1941.

37. *One Third of a Nation: Lorena Hickock Reports on the Great Depression,* ed. Richard Lowitt and Maurine Beasley (Urbana: University of Illinois Press, 1981), 215.

38. *New York Times,* Sunday, January 21, 1934, 9:2.

39. *New York Times,* February 26, 1935, 1.

40. Stanley High, "Washington Hears the Voice of the People," *Literary Digest* 117 (February 24, 1934): 37.

41. Hal H. Smith, "A Deluge of Mail Falls on Congress," *New York Times,* Sunday, January 21, 1934, 9:2.

42. High, "Washington Hears the Voice of the People," 37–38.

43. L. H. Robbins, "The Country Writes to the President," *New York Times Magazine,* October 15, 1933, 3.

44. Smith, *"Dear Mr. President,"* 12.

45. Sussmann, *Dear FDR,* 11.

46. *New York Times,* Sunday, December 17, 1933, 1.

47. Howe, "The President's Mail Bag," 22.

48. James A. Farley, *Jim Farley's Story: The Roosevelt Years* (New York: McGraw-Hill, 1948), 79.

49. Quoted in W. Dale Nelson, *Who Speaks for the President? The White House Press Secretary from Cleveland to Clinton* (Syracuse: Syracuse University Press, 1998), 73.

50. Quoted in Asbell, *When F.D.R. Died,* 161.

51. FDR, Address at Chicago, October 5, 1937, *Public Papers,* 6:406–11; and Four Hundredth Press Conference, ibid., 414–25. The thirteen volumes of the *Public Papers and Addresses of Franklin D. Roosevelt* were compiled by Samuel Rosen-

man, with a special introduction and explanatory notes by the President. Volumes 1–5 were published by Random House in 1938, volumes 6–9 by Macmillan in 1941, and volumes 10–13 by Harper in 1950. Hereafter cited by volume and page number.

52. Samuel I. Rosenman, *Working with Roosevelt* (New York: Harper and Brothers, 1952), 165–68, 195–98.

53. Sussmann, *Dear FDR*, 67.

54. Ibid., 68–69.

55. Charles M. Flaig, Richmond, Indiana, to FDR, April 15, 1938.

56. FDR, Address to the Tammany Speakers' Bureau, January 18, 1929, quoted in Frank Freidel, *Franklin D. Roosevelt: The Triumph* (Boston: Little, Brown, 1956), 31.

57. Jeanette Sayre, *An Analysis of the Radiobroadcasting Activities of Federal Agencies* (Studies in the Control of Radio, June 1941, no. 3) is a detailed account of the New Deal's use of radio from which all the data in this paragraph has been drawn.

58. FDR to M. H. Aylesworth, December 15, 1932, quoted in Frank Freidel, *Franklin D. Roosevelt: Launching the New Deal* (Boston: Little, Brown, 1973), 230–31. For CBS's equally accommodating attitude after FDR's election, see Douglas B. Craig, *Fireside Politics: Radio and Political Culture in the United States, 1920–1940* (Baltimore: Johns Hopkins University Press, 2000), 79–80.

59. FDR to Russell C. Leffingwell, March 16, 1942, in *Franklin D. Roosevelt: Selected Speeches, Messages, Press Conferences, and Letters,* ed. Basil Rauch (New York: Rinehart, 1957), 310–11.

60. FDR to Mary T. Norton, March 24, 1942, in *F.D.R.: His Personal Letters, 1928–1945,* ed. Elliott Roosevelt (New York: Duell, Sloane and Pearce, 1950), 2:1300.

61. Belle Conwell, Birmingham, Alabama, to FDR, March 15, 1933.

62. B. J. Campbell, Memphis, Tennessee, to FDR, January 10, 1941.

63. *New York Times,* May 13, 1941, 1, 8; May 23, 1941, 1; May 24, 1941, 11; May 25, 1941, 1–2; May 27, 1941, 1, 4.

64. "World-Wide Radio Coverage Arranged for Roosevelt Fireside Chat on Tuesday," *New York Times,* May 24, 1941, 11.

65. We carefully checked three newspapers — the *New York Times, Chicago Tribune,* and *San Francisco Examiner* — for the editions published before, during, and after each of the thirty-one Chats to get a sense of newspaper coverage. The *Times* especially was a good source for the ways in which other newspapers across the nation treated the Chats.

66. Elizabeth Berg, New York City, to FDR, March 9, 1937.

67. Walter Edison, Oakland, California, to FDR, January 4, 1941.

68. Howe, "The President's Mail Bag," 118.

69. Paul Barrett, Philadelphia, Pennsylvania, to FDR, March 11, 1937; "Two Hundred of Us," n.p., to FDR, n.d.

70. A. M. Tebbetts, St. Louis, Missouri, to FDR, December 29, 1941.

71. William M. Ryerson, Little Falls, New Jersey, to FDR, March 10, 1937.

72. Donald Warren, *Radio Priest: Charles Coughlin, the Father of Hate Radio* (New York: Free Press, 1996), 26.

73. FDR, Introduction to *Public Papers and Addresses,* 1:8–9.

74. FDR, Announcement of First Radio "Fireside Chat," March 11, 1933, ibid., 2:59–60.

75. For the miles FDR traveled, see John Gunther, *Roosevelt in Retrospect: A Profile in History* (New York: Harper and Brothers, 1950), 139.

76. "Common Words Keynote of Roosevelt's Talks," *New York Times,* May 16, 1937, 10:10.

77. See FDR's note in *Public Papers and Addresses,* 2:60.

78. Audio recording of the March 12, 1933, Fireside Chat in the FDR Library, Hyde Park, New York. All quotes and summaries from the Fireside Chats in this volume are from the audio and stenographic records in the FDR Library. Except in the case of three Chats that were not taped, the stenographic records have been corrected to conform with the original recordings.

79. Halford R. Ryan, *FDR's Rhetorical Presidency* (Westport, Conn.: Greenwood Publishing, 1988); Earnest Brandenburg and Waldo W. Braden, "Franklin D. Roosevelt's Voice and Pronunciation," *Quarterly Journal of Speech,* February 1952, 23–30; Robert E. Sherwood, *Roosevelt and Hopkins: An Intimate History* (New York: Harper and Brothers, 1948), 217, 297; Grace Tully, *F.D.R. My Boss* (New York: Charles Scribner's Sons, 1949), 98; John H. Sharon, "The Fireside Chat," *Franklin D. Roosevelt Collector* 2 (1949): 17; Orrin E. Dunlap, Jr., "Roosevelt Keeps the Microphone Talking to the People," *New York Times,* March 19, 1933, 10:8.

80. *New York Times,* January 31, 1937, 11:6.

81. Felix A. Ury, Washington, D.C., to FDR, March 10, 1937.

82. W. M. Holmberg, Birmingham, Alabama, to FDR, October 12, 1942.

83. Quoted in Orrin E. Dunlap, Jr., "When Roosevelt Goes on the Air," *New York Times Magazine,* June 18, 1933.

84. "Roosevelt's Voice Held Radio's Best," *New York Times,* May 16, 1935.

85. "Mr. Roosevelt's Address," *New York Times,* April 30, 1935. For more newspaper focus on FDR's voice and radio style, see the *New York Times* for the following dates: February 9, March 1, September 6, November 8, 1936; January 24, 1937, 4:6; March 4, 1937, 11:12; November 7, 1937, 11:14; May 1, 1938, 8:3; August 28, 1938, 9:10; September 11, 1938, 10:10; January 4, 1942, 9:12; December 31, 1942.

86. *The Autobiography of Eleanor Roosevelt* (1961; New York: Da Capo Press, 1992), 162.

87. A. W. Lehman, the manager of the Cooperative Analysis of Broadcasting, wrote Stephen Early after the Fireside Chat of February 23, 1942, that that Chat, along with the one on December 9, 1941, set records for the size of radio audiences. Compared with the 83 percent of radio set-owners FDR drew on both occasions,

the three night-time commercial programs with the largest audiences drew less than 41 percent each (A. W. Lehman to Stephen Early, February 24, 1942, in FDR Papers, Hyde Park).

88. Harry Butcher to John H. Sharon, January 10, 1949, in Sharon, "The Fireside Chat," 6.

89. Richard Lee Strout in *The Making of the New Deal: The Insiders Speak,* ed. Katie Louchheim (Cambridge: Harvard University Press, 1983), 13.

90. Dunlap, "When Roosevelt Goes on the Air," 17.

91. Raymond Moley, *After Seven Years* (New York: Harper and Brothers, 1939), 155.

92. Eleanor Roosevelt, *This I Remember,* 72–73.

93. Sherwood, *Roosevelt and Hopkins,* 212.

94. FDR to Russell C. Leffingwell, March 16, 1942, in *Franklin D. Roosevelt: Selected Speeches, Messages, Press Conferences, and Letters,* 310–11.

95. FDR, *Public Papers and Addresses,* 5:391–92.

96. Charles Michelson, *The Ghost Talks* (New York: G. P. Putnam's Sons, 1944), 12–13.

97. Perkins, *The Roosevelt I Knew,* 113.

98. Tully, *F.D.R. My Boss,* 99; Rosenman, *Working with Roosevelt,* 11–12, 486.

99. E. D. Warren, Jackson, Michigan, to FDR, May 8, 1933.

100. Harry G. Nelson, Ithaca, Nebraska, to FDR, March 10, 1937.

101. Frank A. Mercato, San Francisco, to FDR, April 15, 1938.

102. "The Fortune Survey XX," *Fortune* 19, no. 2 (1939): 108.

103. Lawrence W. Levine, *The Unpredictable Past: Explorations in American Cultural History* (New York: Oxford University Press, 1993), 313, 316.

104. Charles E. Comer, Dayton, Ohio, to FDR, October 22, 1933.

105. C. E. Holiman, Canon City, Colorado, to FDR, October 1, 1934.

106. Bishop R. R. Wright, Jr., Cleveland, Ohio, to FDR, April 29, 1942.

107. Unsigned telegram from Philadelphia, Pennsylvania, to FDR, March 13, 1933.

108. James W. Henley, Chattanooga, Tennessee, to FDR, September 6, 1939.

109. Harry J. Myerson, Chicago, Illinois, to FDR, March 13, 1933.

110. Antonio Carneiro et al., New York City, to FDR, April 14, 1938.

111. Sidney Rothschild, Forest Hills, New York, to FDR, April 15, 1938.

112. Mrs. Cerena Cibolski, Manhattan, Kansas, to FDR, January 11, 1944.

113. Saul Bellow, "In the Days of Mr. Roosevelt," in *It All Adds Up: From the Dim Past to the Uncertain Future* (New York: Viking, 1994), 28–29.

114. Patrick H. O'Dea, Washington, D.C., to FDR, March 14, 1933.

115. Hal Warner, Director of Publicity, Affiliated Theatres Circuit, Philadelphia, Pennsylvania, to FDR, May 26, 1940.

116. Samuel B. Traum, Forest Hills, New York, to FDR, September 14, 1941.

117. Miss Ruth Lieberman, Brooklyn, New York, to FDR, March 14, 1933.

118. "Hutch," New York City, to FDR, March 13, 1933.

119. F. P. McMahon, Omaha, Nebraska, to FDR, March 10, 1937.

120. A. J. Hamilton, Atlanta, Georgia, to FDR, March 15, 1937.

121. W. A. Blees, Galesburg, Illinois, to FDR, March 10, 1937.

122. Paul F. Lazarsfeld, *Radio and the Printed Page* (New York: Duell, Sloane and Pearce, 1940), 204–5, 258–60; Harry Field and Paul F. Lazarsfeld, *The People Look at Radio* (Chapel Hill: University of North Carolina Press, 1946), 99.

123. "The Fortune Survey XXIV," *Fortune* 20, no. 2 (1939): 176. The 1945 poll was conducted by the National Association of Broadcasters and is reported in Field and Lazarsfeld, *The People Look at Radio,* 101.

124. Field and Lazarsfeld, *The People Look at Radio,* 96.

PART ONE: THE NADIR

1. All summaries of and quotations from the Fireside Chat of March 12, 1933, come directly from the audio recording of the Chat in the FDR Library, Hyde Park, New York.

2. FDR, Inaugural Address, March 4, 1933, *Public Papers and Addresses,* 2:11–16.

3. Frances Perkins, *The Roosevelt I Knew* (New York: Viking, 1946), 182–183; Lawrence W. Levine, *The Unpredictable Past: Explorations in American Cultural History* (New York: Oxford University Press, 1993), 262–66; Robert S. McElvaine, *The Great Depression: America, 1929–1941* (New York: Times Books, 1993), 75.

4. Levine, *The Unpredictable Past,* chap. 11.

5. Max Freedman, ed., *Roosevelt and Frankfurter: Their Correspondence, 1928–1945* (Boston: Little, Brown, 1967), 37.

6. FDR, Campaign Address at Fenway Park, Boston, Massachusetts, November 4, 1944, *Public Papers and Addresses,* 13:397–406.

7. FDR to Helen Wilkinson Reynolds, published in *Year Book Dutchess County Historical Society* 18 (1933): 35.

8. FDR, Note to Inaugural Address, March 4, 1933, *Public Papers and Addresses,* 2:16.

9. Will Rogers, *Sanity Is Where You Find It: An Affectionate History of the United States in the 20's and 30's,* ed. Donald Day (Boston: Houghton Mifflin, 1935), 167.

10. Raymond Moley, *After Seven Years* (New York: Harper and Brothers, 1939), 155.

11. Quoted in Arthur M. Schlesinger, Jr., *The Coming of the New Deal* (Boston: Houghton Mifflin, 1959), 5.

12. *The Autobiography of Will Rogers,* ed. Donald Day (Boston: Houghton Mifflin, 1949), 313.

13. Arthur A. Ballantine, "When All the Banks Closed," *Harvard Business Review* 26 (March 1948): 129–43.

14. *New York Times,* March 14, 1933.

15. The estimate was made by *Times* correspondent Charles Hurd. See his *When the New Deal was Young and Gay* (New York: Hawthorn Books, 1965), 247.

16. All summaries of and quotations from the Fireside Chat of May 7, 1933, come directly from the audio recording of the Chat in the FDR Library, Hyde Park, New York.

17. FDR, Inaugural Address, March 4, 1933, *Public Papers and Addresses,* 2:11–16.

18. Quoted in Schlesinger, *The Coming of the New Deal,* 1–2.

19. See the March 5, 1933, editions of the *New York Times,* the *New York Herald Tribune,* the *Washington Post,* the *Chicago Tribune,* and the *Los Angeles Times.*

20. Quoted in Schlesinger, *The Coming of the New Deal,* 3.

21. *Barron's,* February 13, 1933.

22. For a discussion of these comparisons with fascism, see Levine, *The Unpredictable Past,* chap. 12.

23. Rexford Guy Tugwell, *The Democratic Roosevelt: A Biography of Franklin D. Roosevelt* (Garden City, N.Y.: Doubleday, 1957), 11.

24. Perkins, *The Roosevelt I Knew,* 330.

25. Eleanor Roosevelt, *This I Remember* (New York: Harper and Brothers, 1949), 346.

26. Quoted in Bernard Bellush, *Franklin D. Roosevelt as Governor of New York* (1955; New York: AMS Press, 1968), 134, 147.

27. FDR's statement about being left of center is quoted in Perkins, *The Roosevelt I Knew,* 333.

28. Moley, *After Seven Years,* 281.

29. FDR, Address Delivered at Democratic State Convention, Syracuse, New York, September 29, 1936, *Public Papers and Addresses,* 5:389–90.

30. Eleanor Roosevelt, *This I Remember,* 347–48.

31. Moley, *After Seven Years,* 189.

32. Because no audio recordings were made of the Fireside Chats of July 24 and October 22, 1933, all summaries of and quotations from these Chats come directly from the stenographic copy in the FDR Library, Hyde Park, New York.

33. The lyrics are printed in Guido van Rijn, *Roosevelt's Blues: African-American Blues and Gospel Songs on FDR* (Jackson: University Press of Mississippi, 1997), 75.

34. Eric Barnouw, *The Golden Web: A History of Broadcasting in the United States* (New York: Oxford University Press, 1968), 8.

35. "President Explains Plan," *New York Times,* July 25, 1933, 1; "Roosevelt Gets 20,000 Messages," *New York Times,* July 28, 1933, 9.

36. Hugh S. Johnson, "The Nation Responds," *New York Times,* July 30, 1933, 4:4.

37. Rexford G. Tugwell, *Roosevelt's Revolution: The First Year — a Personal Perspective* (New York: Macmillan, 1977), 188.

38. For these complaints, see *New York Times,* October 24, 1933, 20; October 29, 1933, 4:4.

39. FDR to Edward M. House, May 7, 1934, in *F.D.R.: His Personal Letters, 1928–1945,* ed. Elliott Roosevelt (New York: Duell, Sloane and Pearce, 1950), 1:400–401.

40. Because no audio recording was made of the Fireside Chat of June 28, 1934, all summaries of and quotations from the Chat come directly from the stenographic copy in the FDR Library, Hyde Park, New York.

41. Quoted in James MacGregor Burns, *Roosevelt: The Lion and the Fox* (New York: Harcourt, Brace, 1956), 317, 203–204.

42. George Wolfskill, *The Revolt of the Conservatives: A History of the American Liberty League* (Cambridge: Houghton Mifflin, 1962), 35, 106, 108. For the League's campaign against FDR, see chap. 5.

43. Moley, *After Seven Years*, 291–92; FDR to Edward M. House, May 7, 1934, in *F.D.R.: His Personal Letters, 1928–1945*, 1:401.

44. Herbert Hoover, *The Challenge to Liberty* (New York: Charles Scribner's Sons, 1934), 85, 193, and passim.

45. Tugwell, *The Democratic Roosevelt*, 352–53.

46. All summaries of and quotations from the Fireside Chat of September 30, 1934, come directly from the audio recording of the Chat in the FDR Library, Hyde Park, New York.

47. Beard is quoted in Frank Freidel, *Franklin D. Roosevelt: A Rendezvous with Destiny* (Boston: Little, Brown, 1990), 141; the *Times* is quoted in McElvaine, *The Great Depression*, 229; FDR is quoted in Otis L. Graham, Jr., and Meghan Robinson Wander, eds., *Franklin D. Roosevelt: His Life and Times, An Encyclopedic View* (Boston: G. K. Hall, 1985), 117.

48. FDR's remark is in Schlesinger, *The Coming of the New Deal*, 504–5; Perkins's observation is in Perkins, *The Roosevelt I Knew*, 352.

49. Tugwell's comments are in Tugwell, "The Preparation of a President," *Western Political Quarterly* 1 (June 1948): 138–39; "The New Deal: The Rise of Business," part 2, ibid., 5 (September 1952): 503; *The Brains Trust* (New York: Viking, 1968), xxi–xxiv.

50. Quoted in Robert E. Sherwood, *Roosevelt and Hopkins: An Intimate History* (New York: Harper and Brothers, 1948), 64–65.

51. FDR to Ray Stannard Baker, March 20, 1935, in *F.D.R.: His Personal Letters, 1928–1945*, 1:466–67.

52. All summaries of and quotations from the Fireside Chat of April 28, 1935, come directly from the audio recording of the Chat in the FDR Library, Hyde Park, N.Y.

53. For the latter figure, see George McJimsey, *Harry Hopkins: Ally of the Poor and Defender of Democracy* (Cambridge: Harvard University Press, 1987), 110.

54. John Steinbeck, *The Grapes of Wrath* (New York: Viking Press, 1939), chap. 5.

55. All summaries of and quotations from the Fireside Chat of September 6, 1936, come directly from the audio recording of the Chat in the FDR Library, Hyde Park, New York.

PART TWO: THE CONTINUING CRISIS

1. *These Are Our Lives: As Told by the People and Written by Members of the Federal Writers' Project of the Works Progress Administration in North Carolina, Tennessee, and Georgia* (1939; New York: W. W. Norton, 1975), 210–11.

2. Quoted in Arthur M. Schlesinger, Jr., *The Politics of Upheaval* (Boston: Houghton Mifflin, 1960), 643.

3. FDR, *Public Papers and Addresses*, 2:14–15.

4. FDR, Two Hundred and Eighth Press Conference (Excerpts), May 29, 1935, ibid., 4:200–222.

5. *The Secret Diary of Harold L. Ickes: The First Thousand Days, 1933–1936* (New York: Simon and Schuster, 1954), 495.

6. Quoted in Schlesinger, *The Politics of Upheaval*, 453.

7. *The Secret Diary of Harold L. Ickes: The First Thousand Days*, 614.

8. FDR, Three Hundredth Press Conference (Excerpts), June 2, 1936, *Public Papers and Addresses*, 5:191–92.

9. *The Secret Diary of Harold L. Ickes: The First Thousand Days*, 705; FDR, Introduction, *Public Papers and Addresses*, 6:lxi–lxii.

10. Schlesinger, *The Politics of Upheaval*, 495.

11. FDR, Introduction, *Public Papers and Addresses*, 6:lix–lx.

12. FDR, Annual Message to the Congress, January 6, 1937, ibid., 5:634–42.

13. FDR, Plan for the Reorganization of the Judicial Branch of the Government, February 5, 1937, ibid., 6:51–66.

14. The letters Roosevelt received on the Court issue can be found in President's Secretary's File 165, Supreme Court, January 1937–July 1937, FDR Library, Hyde Park, New York.

15. George H. Gallup, *The Gallup Poll: Public Opinion, 1935–1971* (New York: Random House, 1972), 1:58–59, 70; Hadley Cantril, ed., *Public Opinion, 1935–1946* (Princeton: Princeton University Press, 1951), 148–51.

16. Samuel I. Rosenman, *Working with Roosevelt* (New York: Harper and Brothers, 1952), 161.

17. William E. Leuchtenburg, *The Supreme Court Reborn: The Constitutional Revolution in the Age of Roosevelt* (New York: Oxford University Press, 1995), chap. 5. See also chapter 4 for an excellent discussion of the origins of the Court plan.

18. Rosenman, *Working with Roosevelt*, 160.

19. FDR, Address at the Democratic Victory Dinner, Washington, D.C., March 4, 1937, *Public Papers and Addresses*, 6:113–21.

20. All summaries of and quotations from the Fireside Chat of March 9, 1937, come directly from the audio recording of the Chat in the FDR Library, Hyde Park, New York.

21. All summaries of and quotations from the Fireside Chats of October 12 and November 14, 1937, come directly from the audio recordings of the Chats in the FDR Library, Hyde Park, New York.

22. Rosenman, *Working with Roosevelt,* 170.

23. Arthur M. Schlesinger, Jr., *The Crisis of the Old Order, 1919–1933* (Boston: Houghton Mifflin, 1957), 241; Lawrence W. Levine, *The Unpredictable Past: Explorations in American Cultural History* (New York: Oxford University Press, 1993), 262–66; Irving Bernstein, *A Caring Society: The New Deal, the Worker, and the Great Depression* (Boston: Houghton Mifflin, 1985), 17–18, 276–78.

24. "Fortune Survey I," *Fortune* 12 (July 1935): 67; "Fortune Survey X," ibid., 16 (October 1937): 154–55, 174; Cantril, *Public Opinion, 1935–1946,* 893–95.

25. Rexford Guy Tugwell, "The New Deal: The Rise of Business," part 2, *Western Political Quarterly* 5 (September 1952): 503; "The Preparation of a President," ibid., 1 (June 1948): 142; Tugwell, *The Democratic Roosevelt: A Biography of Franklin D. Roosevelt* (New York: Doubleday, 1957), 15.

26. Roy W. Howard to FDR, August 26, 1935; FDR to Roy W. Howard, September 2, 1935, *Public Papers and Addresses,* 4:352–57.

27. FDR, Campaign Address at Chicago, Illinois, October 14, 1936, ibid., 5:487–88.

28. Quoted in Robert S. McElvaine, *The Great Depression: America, 1929–1941* (New York: Times Books, 1993), 297.

29. Roosevelt is quoted in *The Secret Diary of Harold L. Ickes: The Inside Struggle, 1936–1939* (New York: Simon and Schuster, 1954), 144.

30. Harry Hopkins, *Spending to Save: The Complete Story of Relief* (1936; Seattle: University of Washington Press, 1972), 180.

31. Cantril, *Public Opinion, 1935–1946,* 895.

32. FDR, Four Hundred and Seventh Press Conference (Excerpts), October 29, 1937, *Public Papers and Addresses,* 6:474–75.

33. *The Secret Diary of Harold L. Ickes: The First Thousand Days, 1933–1936,* 695.

34. John Morton Blum, *From the Morgenthau Diaries: Years of Crisis, 1928–1938* (Boston: Houghton Mifflin, 1959), 423–24; Rosenman, *Working with Roosevelt,* 172–74.

35. *New York Times,* April 15, 1938.

36. All summaries of and quotations from the Fireside Chat of April 14, 1938, come directly from the audio recording of the Chat in the FDR Library, Hyde Park, New York.

37. Rosenman, *Working with Roosevelt,* 175.

38. Harriette Ashbrook, New York City, to FDR, April 20, 1938; Charles M. Flaig, Richmond, Indiana, to FDR, April 15, 1938.

39. FDR, Annual Message to the Congress, January 3, 1934, *Public Papers and Addresses,* 3:12–13.

40. Walter White, *A Man Called White: The Autobiography of Walter White* (Bloomington: Indiana University Press, 1948), 168–70; Eleanor Roosevelt, *This I Remember* (New York: Harper and Brothers, 1949), 162.

41. Harvard Sitkoff, *A New Deal for Blacks: The Emergence of Civil Rights as a National Issue* (New York: Oxford University Press, 1978), chaps. 3, 4, 13; John B.

Kirby, *Black Americans in the Roosevelt Era* (Knoxville: University of Tennessee Press, 1980), chaps. 8, 9.

42. Sitkoff, *A New Deal for Blacks,* 93–94, 116.

43. Rexford Guy Tugwell, *In Search of Roosevelt* (Cambridge: Harvard University Press, 1972), 168 n; *The Secret Diary of Harold L. Ickes: The First Thousand Days,* 533.

44. FDR, Campaign Address at Madison Square Garden, New York City, November 5, 1932, *Public Papers and Addresses,* 1:860–65.

45. All summaries of and quotations from the Fireside Chat of June 24, 1938, come directly from the audio recording of the Chat in the FDR Library, Hyde Park, New York.

46. "The Old Roosevelt Magic," *New York Herald Tribune,* June 25, 1938, reprinted in "Editorial Comment on the President's 'Fireside Chat,'" *New York Times,* June 26, 1938.

47. Tugwell, *The Democratic Roosevelt,* 409–10, 461–69.

PART THREE: LOOKING ABROAD

1. Ben Fortin, Butler, Wisconsin, to FDR, May 8, 1933.

2. FDR, Acceptance of the Renomination for the Presidency, Philadelphia, Pennsylvania, June 27, 1936, *Public Papers and Addresses,* 5:230–36.

3. FDR, A Wireless to the London Conference, July 3, 1933, ibid., 2:264–66.

4. FDR, Address at San Diego Exposition, San Diego, California, October 2, 1935, ibid., 4:410.

5. Quoted in Robert Cohen, *When the Old Left Was Young: Student Radicals and America's First Mass Student Movement, 1929–1941* (New York: Oxford University Press, 1993), 73.

6. FDR, Presidential Statement on Approval of Neutrality Legislation, August 31, 1935, *Public Papers and Addresses,* 4:345–46.

7. FDR, Address at Chicago, October 5, 1937, ibid., 6:406–11.

8. *The Secret Diary of Harold L. Ickes: The Inside Struggle, 1936–1939* (New York: Simon and Schuster, 1954), 390, 474.

9. FDR, Annual Message to the Congress, January 4, 1939, *Public Papers and Addresses,* 8:1–4.

10. FDR to Mackenzie King, October 11, 1938, *F.D.R.: His Personal Letters, 1928–1945,* ed. Elliott Roosevelt (New York: Duell, Sloane and Pearce, 1950), 2:816–17.

11. FDR, Extemporaneous Remarks . . . Warm Springs, Georgia, April 9, 1939, *Public Papers and Addresses,* 8:192.

12. *The Secret Diary of Harold L. Ickes: The Inside Struggle,* 712–13.

13. All summaries of and quotations from the Fireside Chat of September 3, 1939, come directly from the audio recording of the Chat in the FDR Library, Hyde Park, New York.

14. FDR, Introduction to *Public Papers and Addresses*, 9:xxiii.

15. For these, and many other polls on these subjects for the years 1939 and 1940, see George H. Gallup, *The Gallup Poll: Public Opinion, 1935–1971* (New York: Random House, 1972), 133–256, and *Public Opinion, 1935–1946*, ed. Hadley Cantril (Princeton: Princeton University Press, 1951), 948–52.

16. Cantril, *Public Opinion, 1935–1946*, 949; *The Gallup Poll*, 184, 186, 193.

17. Cantril, *Public Opinion, 1935–1946*, 949; *The Gallup Poll*, 175, 182–83.

18. Raoul de Roussy de Sales, "America Looks at the War," *Atlantic Monthly* 165 (1940): 153, quoted in William E. Leuchtenburg, *Franklin D. Roosevelt and the New Deal, 1932–1940* (New York: Harper and Row, 1963), 293–94.

19. Rexford Guy Tugwell, *The Democratic Roosevelt* (Garden City, N.Y.: Doubleday, 1957), 560.

20. FDR, Introduction to *Public Papers and Addresses*, 9:xxiii.

21. *The Gallup Poll*, 225–26; Cantril, *Public Opinion, 1935–1946*, 973.

22. All summaries of and quotes from the Fireside Chat of May 26, 1940, come directly from the audio recording of the Chat in the FDR Library, Hyde Park, New York.

23. Samuel I. Rosenman, *Working with Roosevelt* (New York: Harper and Brothers, 1952), 195–96.

24. FDR, Message to the Congress, May 16, 1940, *Public Papers and Addresses*, 9:198–205.

25. Rosenman, *Working with Roosevelt*, 197.

26. FDR, Six Hundred and Forty-Seventh Press Conference, May 28, 1940, *Public Papers and Addresses*, 9:241.

27. FDR to William Allen White, December 14, 1939, *F.D.R.: His Personal Letters, 1928–1945*, ed. Elliott Roosevelt (New York: Duell, Sloane and Pearce, 1950), 2:967–68.

28. FDR, Campaign Address at Boston, Massachusetts, October 30, 1940, *Public Papers and Addresses*, 9:517.

29. FDR, Informal, Extemporaneous Remarks at Buffalo, New York, November 2, 1940, ibid., 543.

30. FDR, Address at University of Virginia, June 10, 1940, ibid., 259–64.

31. FDR, Note to the Annual Message to the Congress, January 6, 1941, ibid., 673–78.

32. Robert E. Sherwood, *Roosevelt and Hopkins: An Intimate History* (New York: Harper and Brothers, 1948), 221.

33. FDR, Seven Hundred and Second Press Conference, December 17, 1940, *Public Papers and Addresses*, 9:604–15.

34. All summaries of and quotes from the Fireside Chat of December 29, 1940, come directly from the audio recording of the Chat in the FDR Library, Hyde Park, New York.

35. Sherwood, *Roosevelt and Hopkins*, 227–28.

36. "President's Radio Audience in America Alone Is Estimated to Run as High as

80,000,000," *New York Times,* December 29, 1940; see also *San Francisco Examiner,* December 30, 1940.

37. These figures come from the Hooper ratings cited in Betty Houchin Winfield, *FDR and the News Media* (Urbana: University of Illinois Press, 1990), 121 n. 20.

38. Compton's opening and closing remarks are on the audio recording of the Chat in the FDR Library, Hyde Park, New York.

39. Sherwood, *Roosevelt and Hopkins,* 226.

40. Henry L. Stimson and McGeorge Bundy, *On Active Service in Peace and War* (New York: Harper and Brothers, 1948), 366.

41. Rosenman, *Working with Roosevelt,* 259–60.

42. Winston Churchill, *Their Finest Hour* (Boston: Houghton Mifflin, 1949), 404.

43. FDR, Annual Message to the Congress, January 6, 1941, *Public Papers and Addresses,* 9:663–72.

44. Cantril, *Public Opinion, 1935–1946,* 950, 954; Jerome S. Bruner, *Mandate from the People* (New York: Duell, Sloane and Pearce, 1944), 20–24; *The Gallup Poll,* 257.

45. *The Gallup Poll,* 262, 268.

46. Robert Dallek, *Franklin D. Roosevelt and American Foreign Policy, 1932–1945* (New York: Oxford University Press, 1979), 259–60; James MacGregor Burns, *Roosevelt: The Soldier of Freedom* (New York: Harcourt Brace Jovanovich, 1970), 43–46; Sherwood, *Roosevelt and Hopkins,* 264.

47. Rosenman, *Working with Roosevelt,* 271–72.

48. FDR, Note to the Annual Message of 1941, *Public Papers and Addresses,* 9:674.

49. John Morton Blum, *From the Morgenthau Diaries* (Boston: Houghton Mifflin, 1965), 2:251, 254; *The Secret Diary of Harold L. Ickes: The Lowering Clouds, 1939–1941* (New York: Simon and Schuster, 1955), 523.

50. *The Gallup Poll,* 280–82.

51. Blum, *Morgenthau Diaries,* 2:253–54.

52. *The Secret Diary of Harold L. Ickes: The Lowering Clouds,* 511.

53. Stimson and Bundy, *On Active Service,* 370–71.

54. Blum, *Morgenthau Diaries,* 2:254; *The Secret Diaries of Harold Ickes: The Lowering Clouds,* 523; *The Memoirs of Cordell Hull* (New York: Macmillan, 1948), 2:942.

55. All summaries of and quotations from the Fireside Chat of May 27, 1941, come directly from the audio recording of the Chat in the FDR Library, Hyde Park, New York.

56. Quoted in Dallek, *Franklin D. Roosevelt and American Foreign Policy,* 266.

57. Hooper ratings in Winfield, *FDR and the News Media,* 121 n. 20; "The President's Fireside Chat Encircled the Globe," *New York Times,* June 1, 1941.

58. "Speech Echoes in a Hushed City as Radios Go in Homes, on Streets," *New York Times,* May 28, 1941, 21.

59. *The Secret Diary of Harold L. Ickes: The Lowering Clouds,* 526.

60. Sherwood, *Roosevelt and Hopkins,* 298.

61. Ibid., 266.

62. Quoted in Sherwood, *Roosevelt and Hopkins*, 295.

63. Stimson and Bundy, *On Active Service*, 371–72.

64. Quoted in Dallek, *Franklin D. Roosevelt and American Foreign Policy*, 286.

65. Stimson quoted in ibid., 265.

66. Sherwood, *Roosevelt and Hopkins*, 299.

67. All summaries of and quotations from the Fireside Chat of September 11, 1941, come directly from the audio recording of the Chat in the FDR Library, Hyde Park, New York.

68. *New York Times*, September 12, 1941; Wayne S. Cole, *America First: The Battle against Intervention, 1940–1941* (Madison: University of Wisconsin Press, 1953), 141–54.

69. Rosenman, *Working with Roosevelt*, 292.

70. FDR spoke of his dream to Adolf Berle, who is quoted in Dallek, *Franklin D. Roosevelt and American Foreign Policy*, 265.

71. Oral interviews in Ray Barfield, *Listening to Radio, 1920–1950* (Westport, Conn.: Praeger, 1996), 71–72.

72. FDR, Address to the Congress Asking that a State of War Be Declared between the United States and Japan," *Public Papers and Addresses*, 10:514.

73. Oral interviews in Barfield, *Listening to Radio*, 72–73.

74. Sherwood, *Roosevelt and Hopkins*, 438. For the "good war" theme and its antidote, see Studs Terkel, *"The Good War": An Oral History of World War Two* (New York: New Press, 1984), and Paul Fussell, *Wartime: Understanding and Behavior in the Second World War* (New York: Oxford University Press, 1989). For a heavy dose of the nostalgia now surrounding that war, see Tom Brokaw, *The Greatest Generation* (New York: Random House, 1998).

75. Rosenman, *Working with Roosevelt*, 305.

76. For the charge, see Charles A. Beard, *President Roosevelt and the Coming of the War, 1941: A Study in Appearances and Realities* (New Haven: Yale University Press, 1948), and Charles C. Tansill, *Back Door to War: The Roosevelt Foreign Policy, 1933–1941* (Chicago: University of Chicago Press, 1952). For a convincing refutation, see Roberta Wohlstetter, *Pearl Harbor: Warning and Decision* (Stanford: Stanford University Press, 1962). See also David Kahn, "The United States Views Germany and Japan in 1941," in *Knowing One's Enemies: Intelligence Assessment before the Two World Wars*, ed. Ernest May (Princeton: Princeton University Press, 1984), for the argument that "disbelief in a Japanese attack was reinforced by belief in the superiority of the white race." John W. Dower, *War without Mercy: Race and Power in the Pacific War* (New York: Pantheon Books, 1986), develops in detail the stereotypes and racism that hampered both the Japanese and the Americans from comprehending each other realistically.

77. Stimson and Bundy, *On Active Service*, 393.

78. Winston S. Churchill, *The Grand Alliance* (Boston: Houghton Mifflin, 1950), 605–8.

79. Eleanor Roosevelt, *This I Remember* (New York: Harper and Brothers, 1949), 233.

80. Frances Perkins, *The Roosevelt I Knew* (New York: Viking, 1946), 379–80.

81. Sherwood, *Roosevelt and Hopkins,* 431.

82. Rosenman, *Working with Roosevelt,* 308.

83. All summaries of and quotations from the Fireside Chat of December 9, 1941, come directly from the audio recording of the Chat in the FDR Library, Hyde Park, New York. The estimate of FDR's audience comes from the Hooper rating cited in Winfield, *FDR and the News Media,* 121 n. 20.

84. For the President's style in delivering his Chat, see Halford R. Ryan, *Franklin D. Roosevelt's Rhetorical Presidency* (Westport, Conn.: Greenwood Press, 1988), 19–23.

85. *New York Times,* December 9, 1941; Rosenman, *Working with Roosevelt,* 309

86. Authors' interview with Louise Mozingo, June 6, 2001, Berkeley, California.

87. Rosenman, *Working with Roosevelt,* 312–13.

PART FOUR: AMERICA AT WAR

1. Quoted in Robert E. Sherwood, *Roosevelt and Hopkins: An Intimate History* (New York: Harper and Brothers, 1948), 437.

2. William D. Hassett, *Off the Record with F.D.R., 1942–1945* (New Brunswick: Rutgers University Press, 1958), 175.

3. Sherwood, *Roosevelt and Hopkins,* chap. 22; Samuel I. Rosenman, *Working with Roosevelt* (New York: Harper and Brothers, 1952), 328–29.

4. Henry L. Stimson and McGeorge Bundy, *On Active Service in Peace and War* (New York: Harper and Brothers, 1948), 394.

5. Oral interview in Studs Terkel, *"The Good War": An Oral History of World War Two* (New York: New Press, 1984), 35–36.

6. Richard Polenberg, *War and Society: The United States, 1941–1945* (Philadelphia: J. B. Lippincott, 1972), 60–72; Ronald Takaki, *Double Victory: A Multicultural History of America in World War II* (Boston: Little, Brown, 2000), chap. 7; Francis Biddle, *In Brief Authority* (Garden City, N.Y.: Doubleday, 1962), 212–26. For a thorough exploration of FDR's role in the internment, see Greg Robinson, *By Order of the President: FDR and the Internment of Japanese Americans* (Cambridge: Harvard University Press, 2001).

7. All summaries of and quotations from the Fireside Chat of February 23, 1942, come directly from the audio recording of the Chat in the FDR Library, Hyde Park, New York.

8. Rosenman, *Working with Roosevelt,* 329–33.

9. Preparations for this Fireside Chat are described in detail in ibid., 3–8.

10. Sherwood, *Roosevelt and Hopkins,* 504.

11. FDR, Eight Hundred and Seventh Press Conference (Excerpts), February 24, 1942, *Public Papers and Addresses,* 11:131.

12. *San Francisco Examiner,* February 24, 1942.

13. All summaries of and quotations from the Fireside Chat of April 28, 1942, come directly from the audio recording of the Chat in the FDR Library, Hyde Park, New York.

14. FDR, Address to the Congress on the State of the Union, January 6, 1942, *Public Papers and Addresses,* 11:38.

15. FDR, Eight-Hundred and Twelfth Press Conference (Excerpts), March 17, 1942, ibid., 173.

16. FDR, Annual Budget Message, January 5, 1942, ibid., 6–20.

17. FDR, Seven-Point Economic Stabilization Program, April 27, 1942, ibid., 216–27; Rosenman, *Working with Roosevelt,* 340–44.

18. All summaries of and quotations from the Fireside Chats of September 7 and October 12, 1942, come directly from the audio recordings of the Chats in the FDR Library, Hyde Park, New York.

19. Rosenman, *Working with Roosevelt,* 356.

20. FDR, Message to the Congress, September 7, 1942, *Public Papers and Addresses,* 11:356–67.

21. Ibid., 366–67.

22. *The Impact of War on America: Six Lectures by Members of the Faculty of Cornell University* (Ithaca: Cornell University Press, 1942), 3–4.

23. Samuel I. Rosenman, Introduction, *Public Papers and Addresses,* 12:vi.

24. Frances Perkins, *The Roosevelt I Knew* (New York: Viking, 1946), 380.

25. FDR, Nine Hundred and Eleventh Press Conference (Excerpts), July 27, 1943, *Public Papers and Addresses,* 12:324–26.

26. Knox and Lewis are quoted in Nelson Lichtenstein, *Labor's War at Home: The CIO in World War II* (New York: Cambridge University Press, 1982), 63, 262 n. 44.

27. See ibid., chap. 9; Ickes is quoted on 160.

28. Quoted in Doris Kearns Goodwin, *No Ordinary Time: Franklin and Eleanor Roosevelt, the Home Front in World War II* (New York: Simon and Schuster, 1994), 441.

29. Quoted in Alan Brinkley, *The End of Reform: New Deal Liberalism in Recession and War* (New York: Vintage Books, 1996), 214.

30. Perkins, *The Roosevelt I Knew,* 306.

31. George H. Gallup, *The Gallup Poll: Public Opinion 1935–1971* (New York: Random House, 1972), 389.

32. Quoted in William L. O'Neill, *A Democracy at War: America's Fight at Home and Abroad in World War II* (Cambridge: Harvard University Press, 1993), 210.

33. Quoted in Goodwin, *No Ordinary Time,* 440.

34. Eleanor Roosevelt, *This I Remember* (New York: Harper and Brothers, 1949), 284.

35. Quoted in O'Neill, *A Democracy at War,* 213.

36. William D. Hassett, *Off the Record with F.D.R., 1942–1945* (New Brunswick: Rutgers University Press, 1958), 194.

37. All summaries of and quotations from the Fireside Chat of May 2, 1943, come directly from the audio recording of the Chat in the FDR Library, Hyde Park, New York.

38. All summaries of and quotations from the Fireside Chats of July 28, September 8, and December 24, 1943, come directly from the audio recordings of the Chats in the FDR Library, Hyde Park, New York.

39. John Morton Blum, *From the Morgenthau Diaries: Years of War, 1941–1945* (Boston: Houghton Mifflin, 1967), 17–19.

40. Ibid., 17–18.

41. Gerd Horten, "Radio Goes to War: The Cultural Politics of Propaganda during World War II" (Ph.D. diss., University of California, Berkeley, 1994), 278, 311–12.

42. Eleanor Roosevelt, "My Day," June 25, 1944, quoted in Goodwin, *No Ordinary Time,* 512.

43. FDR, Statement on Signing the Bill Reducing the Draft Age, November 13, 1942, *Public Papers and Addresses,* 11:470; Message to the Congress on Education of War Veterans, October 27, 1943, ibid., 12:449–53; A Message to the Congress on Providing for the Return of Service Personnel to Civilian Life, November 23, 1943, ibid., 522–27.

44. Keith Olson, *The G.I. Bill, the Veterans, and the Colleges* (Lexington: University of Kentucky Press, 1974); David B. Ross, *Preparing for Ulysses: Politics and Veterans during World War II* (New York: Columbia University Press, 1969), chap. 4. Hutchins is quoted on 25 of Olson, and Rankin is quoted on 108 of Ross.

45. Helen Lefkowitz Horowitz, *Campus Life: Undergraduate Cultures from the End of the Eighteenth Century to the Present* (Chicago: University of Chicago Press, 1987), 184–87; Daniel A. Clark, " 'The Two Joes Meet — Joe College, Joe Veteran': The G.I. Bill, College Education, and Postwar American Culture," *History of Education Quarterly* 38 (summer 1998): 165–89; Theda Skocpol, "Delivering for Young Families: The Resonance of the GI Bill," *American Prospect* 28 (September/October 1996): 66–72.

46. Quoted in Takaki, *Double Victory,* 53.

47. Ibid, 53–54.

48. Gary Gerstle, "The Working Class Goes to War," in *The War in American Culture: Society and Consciousness during World War II,* ed. Lewis A. Erenberg and Susan E. Hirsch, (Chicago: University of Chicago Press, 1996), 118.

49. Quoted in John Morton Blum, *V Was for Victory: Politics and American Culture during World War II* (New York: Harcourt Brace Jovanovich, 1976), 204. See Walter White's account of the Detroit and New York race riots in *A Man Called White: The Autobiography of Walter White* (Bloomington: Indiana University Press, 1948), 224–41.

50. Quoted in Takaki, *Double Victory,* 56.

51. Pauli Murray, "Mr. Roosevelt Regrets," *Crisis*, August 1943, 252.

52. Perkins, *The Roosevelt I Knew*, 84–86.

53. Rosenman, *Working with Roosevelt*, 411.

54. Quoted in Dallek, *Franklin D. Roosevelt and American Foreign Policy*, 440.

55. Rosenman, *Working with Roosevelt*, 427. All summaries of and quotations from the Fireside Chat of January 11, 1944, come directly from the audio recording of the Chat in the FDR Library, Hyde Park, New York.

56. Ibid., 422–23.

57. Hadley Cantril, ed., *Public Opinion, 1935–1946* (Princeton: Princeton University Press, 1951), 1121–26; *The Gallup Poll*, 431, 486–87.

58. Richard Polenberg, *War and Society: The United States, 1941–1945* (Philadelphia: J. B. Lippincott, 1972), 176–83.

59. "And Now Slavery," *Chicago Tribune*, January 13, 1944.

60. Stimson and Bundy, *On Active Service*, 353, 483–84, 488.

61. Polenberg, *War and Society*, 219.

62. David Lynch, *The Concentration of Economic Power* (New York: Columbia University Press, 1946), 3–6. Lippmann is quoted on 109.

63. This entire episode is discussed by Donald Nelson in his *Arsenal of Democracy: The Story of American War Production* (New York: Harcourt, Brace, 1946), chap. 17. The Nelson and the second Truman quotes are on 333, 335. The Catton and the first Truman quotes are in Bruce Catton, *The War Lords of Washington* (New York: Harcourt, Brace, 1948), 118, 120.

64. *The Secret Diary of Harold L. Ickes: The Lowering Clouds, 1939–1941* (New York: Simon and Schuster, 1955), 295–96, 509.

65. Sherwood, *Roosevelt and Hopkins*, 280.

66. FDR, Nine Hundred and Twenty-Ninth Press Conference (Excerpts), December 28, 1943, *Public Papers and Addresses*, 12:569–75.

67. James MacGregor Burns, *Roosevelt: The Soldier of Freedom* (New York: Harcourt Brace Jovanovich, 1970), 424.

68. Roland Young, *Congressional Politics in the Second World War* (New York: Columbia University Press, 1956), 23.

69. Rosenman, *Working with Roosevelt*, chap. 24; FDR to Wendell L. Willkie, July 13 and August 21, 1944, *F.D.R.: His Personal Letters, 1928–1945*, ed. Elliott Roosevelt (New York: Duell, Sloane and Pearce, 1950), 2:1520, 1531–33.

70. All summaries of and quotations from the Fireside Chats of June 5, June 12, 1944, and January 6, 1945, come directly from the audio recordings of the Chats in the FDR Library, Hyde Park, New York.

71. Quoted in David M. Kennedy, *Freedom from Fear: The American People in Depression and War, 1929–1945* (New York: Oxford University Press, 1999), 716.

72. The President's health during his final year is discussed in considerable detail in Robert H. Ferrell, *The Dying President: Franklin D. Roosevelt, 1944–1945* (Columbia: University of Missouri Press, 1998). Dr. Bruenn's remark is quoted on 37.

73. FDR, Address to the Congress Reporting on the Yalta Conference, March 1, 1945, *Public Papers and Addresses,* 13:570.

74. Sherwood, *Roosevelt and Hopkins,* 845; Rosenman, *Working with Roosevelt,* 510–15.

75. Bruce Catton, *The War Lords of Washington,* 214–15; Stimson and Bundy, *On Active Service,* 480–88.

76. FDR, The Governor Accepts the Nomination for the Presidency, Chicago, Illinois, July 2, 1932, *Public Papers and Addresses,* 1:658.

77. FDR, Inaugural Address, March 4, 1933, ibid., 2:11; Undelivered Address Prepared for Jefferson Day, April 13, 1945, ibid., 13:616.

EPILOGUE

1. "Champion" Jack Dupree, *F.D.R. Blues.* The lyrics are printed in Guido van Rijn, *Roosevelt's Blues: African-American Blues and Gospel Songs on FDR* (Jackson: University Press of Mississippi, 1997), 195.

2. Alexander Feinberg, "Millions in City Ignore Rain to Pay Honor to Roosevelt," *New York Times,* April 15, 1945.

3. Quoted in David Thomson, *Rosebud: The Story of Orson Welles* (New York: Vintage Books, 1997), 262–63.

4. John Idol's oral reminiscences are in Ray Barfield, *Listening to Radio, 1920–1950* (Westport, Conn.: Praeger, 1996), 76.

5. Bernard Asbell, *The F.D.R. Memoirs* (Garden City, N.Y.: Doubleday, 1973), 52–53.

6. Anne O'Hare McCormick, "A Man of the World and the World's Man," *New York Times,* April 14, 1945.

7. Ruth Albert Cook, "Blackout," *Opportunity: Journal of Negro Life,* March 1942, 82.

8. *These Are Our Lives: As Told by the People and Written by Members of the Federal Writers' Project of the Works Progress Administration in North Carolina, Tennessee, and Georgia* (1939; New York: W. W. Norton, 1975), 210.

9. Clarence H. Taylor, Baltimore, Maryland, to FDR, September 1, 1939.

10. Frances Perkins, *The Roosevelt I Knew* (New York: Viking, 1946), 3–4.

11. Henry Fingerman, Newark, New Jersey, to FDR, March 16, 1933.

12. Mrs. Charles Boone, Detroit, Michigan, to FDR, May 26, 1940.

13. For a detailed examination of Kate Smith's 1943 war bond drive and the audience reaction, see Robert K. Merton, *Mass Persuasion: The Social Psychology of a War Bond Drive* (New York: Harper and Brothers, 1946), especially the discussion of two-way communication on 38–40.

14. Howe related this story to his assistant Lela Stiles, who later included it in her biography, *The Man Behind Roosevelt: The Story of Louis McHenry Howe* (Cleveland: World, 1954), 245.

15. Perkins, *The Roosevelt I Knew,* 71–73.

16. L. M. Larson, Zeona, South Dakota, to FDR, March 15, 1937.

17. Mr. and Mrs. Sam Olson, Idaho City, Idaho, to FDR, March 10, 1937.

18. Romance Koopman, Madison, Wisconsin, to FDR, n.d.

19. John M. Sain, Denver, Colorado, to FDR, March 20, 1937.

20. Harriet M. D'Alessandro, Brockton, Massachusetts, to FDR, March 10, 1937.

21. Frank M. Quaife, San Diego, California, to FDR, March 9, 1937.

22. William Kinzell, Portland, Oregon, to FDR, March 14, 1933.

23. "A devoted little friend," to FDR, May 8, 1933; Edward C. McCann, Pittsburgh, Pennsylvania, to FDR, October 23, 1933.

24. Isabel Adlerholz, n.p., to FDR, 1937.

25. A. A. Harrall, Tuskegee, Alabama, to FDR, October 16, 1937.

26. Jim Vance, Memphis, Tennessee, to FDR, April 28, 1942.

27. Railroad worker, St. Louis, Missouri, to FDR, March 13, 1933.

28. Charles L. Kimmel, Chicago, Illinois, to FDR, March 12, 1933.

29. Gertrude Fagan, New York City, to FDR, October 12, 1942; Thomas J. Bilyeu, Kansas City, Missouri, to FDR, August 3, 1943.

30. Geo. W. Showalld, Ogdensburg, New York, to FDR, March 10, 1937.

31. The politician was Richard Connell. See Alfred B. Rollins, Jr., *Roosevelt and Howe* (New York: Alfred A. Knopf, 1962), 17, 21.

32. Virginia Miller, Sierra Madre, California, to FDR, March 13, 1933.

33. Mrs. Paul H. Russell, Haskell, Oklahoma, to FDR, March 15, 1933.

34. Edward W. Jewett, Passaic, New Jersey, to FDR, March 9, 1933.

35. Sue E. Hight, San Antonio, Texas, to FDR, March 21, 1933.

36. Cloie Cain, Tacoma, Washington, to FDR, April 26, 1942.

37. J. Kwake, Woodside, Long Island, New York, to FDR, May 28, 1941.

38. James Manning, Bloomington, Illinois, to FDR, n.d.

39. William J. Froberg, New Buffalo, Michigan, to FDR, March 10, 1937.

40. Miss Frances Furnice, Bronx, New York, to FDR, April 27, 1938.

41. Ben Medofsky, Portland, Oregon, to FDR, December 30, 1940.

42. S. J. Flanders, Swainsboro, Georgia, to FDR, May 27, 1940.

43. Mrs. Millie Wimmers, Philadelphia, Pennsylvania, to FDR, April 8, 1937; Mrs. Ernest Bellows, Flint, Michigan, to FDR, March 10, 1937.

44. W. Edgar Bates, Philadelphia, Pennsylvania, to FDR, December 29, 1940.

45. Gertrude Jablow, Jersey City, New Jersey, to FDR, February 23, 1942.

46. Mrs. O. B. Bozeman, Albany, Georgia, to FDR, May 26, 1940.

47. Pat Richmond, West Hollywood, California, to FDR, July 28, 1943.

48. Flora I. Copple, Olympia, Washington, to FDR, April 29, 1942.

49. John H. Randolph, Philadelphia, Pennsylvania, to FDR, January 1, 1941; Mrs. Adella Cooper, Blum, Texas, to FDR, March 11, 1937; Don Taylor, Des Moines, Washington, to FDR, July 29, 1943.

50. Mrs. F. A. Warren, Haxtun, Colorado, to FDR, March 9, 1937.

51. "Hutch," New York City, to FDR, March 13, 1933.

52. Harry E. Williams, Newport News, Virginia, to FDR, March 12, 1937.

53. Mrs. Berenice M. Harrison, Miami, Florida, to FDR, May 28, 1941.

54. Dorothy S. Bates, Laconia, New Hampshire, to FDR, December 31, 1940.

55. Robert S. McElvaine's pioneering volume *Down and Out in the Great Depression: Letters from the "Forgotten Man"* (Chapel Hill: University of North Carolina Press, 1983) is filled with such letters.

56. Anthony N. Rodrigues, Springfield, Massachusetts, to FDR, March 9, 1937.

APPENDIX: A NOTE ON THE FIRESIDE CHATS

1. The word "corny" was used by Robert E. Sherwood in an interview with John H. Sharon on June 9, 1949, quoted in Sharon's article, "The Fireside Chat," *Franklin D. Roosevelt Collector* 2, no. 1 (November 1949): 7.

2. FDR, *Public Papers and Addresses,* 1:60.

3. Quotation from the audio recording of the June 24, 1938, Chat in the FDR Library, Hyde Park, New York.

4. Blanche E. Poltrock, Ottawa, Illinois, to FDR, June 29, 1934.

5. "Mr. Roosevelt Coins 'Plate-Side Chat' for Broadcasts from Dinner Table," *New York Times,* January 14, 1940, 12.

6. "When Is a Chat 'Fireside'?" *New York Times,* July 3, 1938, 9:10.

7. President's Personal File 1820, Speech File, FDR Library; Samuel I. Rosenman, *Working with Roosevelt* (New York: Harper and Brothers, 1952), 417; Sharon, "The Fireside Chat," 7–9; Steven E. Schoenherr, "Selling the New Deal: Stephen T. Early's Role as Press Secretary to Franklin D. Roosevelt" (Ph.D. diss., University of Delaware, 1976), 133–134; Russell D. Buhite and David W. Levy, eds., *FDR's Fireside Chats* (Norman: University of Oklahoma Press, 1992).

ACKNOWLEDGMENTS

The bulk of our research was done during several extended trips to the Franklin D. Roosevelt Library in Hyde Park, New York, where we were treated with courtesy by the knowledgeable and helpful staff. We especially want to thank Lynn Bassanese, Karen Burtis, Bob Clark, John Ferris, Robert Parks, Mark Renovitch, Nancy Snedeker, and Raymond Teichman. We also appreciate the help of the staffs at the National Archives II in College Park, Maryland, and the Division of Prints and Photographs at the Library of Congress. The Doe Library at the University of California, Berkeley, never failed to find the sources and materials we sought. Research funds from George Mason University and the Margaret Byrne Chair at the University of California, Berkeley, benefited our work substantially.

For helping to locate diverse printed materials relating to the Fireside Chats, we are indebted to Gerd Horten, who assisted us at the outset of this project, and Zoe Couacaud, who worked with us during its final stages. Zoe also provided critical aid in getting the letters ready for transcription and helping us proofread them. We thank Louise Mozingo for sharing her father's West Point story.

Robert McElvaine introduced us to the letters the American people wrote to FDR while he was a participant in the National Endowment for the Humanities summer seminar "The Folk in American History," led by Lawrence Levine at the University of California, Berkeley, in 1978. Bob's pioneering work with those letters during and after the seminar enhanced our understanding of the relationship between the American people and FDR and provoked us into asking questions that we have tried to answer in this volume. Our good friend Robert Dallek has taught us much over the years — both personally and in his published work — about FDR and American foreign policy; we trust we have used his lessons well.

Various versions of the materials in the introduction and epilogue were presented to an international gathering of scholars at the German Historical Institute in Washington, D.C.; to faculty and students at Arizona State University, Purdue University, The Johns Hopkins University, and Alfred University; to the school teachers participating in the UC Berkeley History–Social Science Project during the summer of 2001; to members of the Berkeley American Studies reading group; and — in what were largely informal, extended conversations — to colleagues and students in the Department of History and Art History and the Cultural Studies Program at George Mason University. The responses we received from these encounters were stimulating and extremely beneficial.

From the beginning of our labors our agent, Sandra Dijkstra, manifested a faith in and enthusiasm for this project that strengthened our own sense of confidence and resolve. Deb Chasman, our extraordinary editor at Beacon Press, provided indispensable criticism and advice that have improved our work in myriad ways. Deb, her assistant Julie Hassel, and the rest of the Beacon team were a haven of support, know-how, and diligence in helping us turn a complex manuscript into this book.

During our work on *The People and the President,* we have been nurtured and aided by so many people that we cannot begin to list each one here. Let us simply thank family, friends, and colleagues on both coasts who patiently heard us converse about the American people, FDR, and the Fireside Chats and who responded with a generosity and ingenuity that stimulated and informed us again and again. Any successful work of scholarship should involve a certain degree of reciprocity between the authors and their subjects. Ours certainly did. We have learned an enormous amount from the men, women, and children who wrote to Franklin Roosevelt. We recommend their company to everyone interested in the Great Depression and World War Two.

INDEX OF LETTER WRITERS

GENERAL INDEX

Adlerholz, Isabel, 565

African Americans, 195; and approach of war, 330, 355–57, 359, 371; discrimination against, 355–57, 359, 497–98; FDR's limited support for, 247–49, 456, 472, 497–98; prejudice against, expressed in letters, 196, 258; support of, for FDR, 113, 180–81, 229, 248–49, 258, 326, 386, 389, 472–73, 561; in wartime, 366, 440, 444, 472–73, 497–98, 532, 537

age discrimination, 116, 156–58, 192

Agricultural Adjustment Administration (AAA), 64, 120, 164, 192, 210, 253

agricultural programs. *See* farm programs

Albania, 273

alcohol, 51, 63

allegories, FDR's use of, 310–11, 521

Allies, 285, 343n, 417, 433, 476, 493, 498–50, 539–40. *See also* China; France; Great Britain; Soviet Union

Allport, Gordon, 1

America First Committee, 340, 364, 378, 389, 390

American Civil Liberties Union, 414

American Institute of Public Opinion (AIPO), 23, 206, 222, 286, 287, 342

American Legion, 495–96

American Liberty League, 108

anti-lynching bill (Wagner-Costigan), 247–48, 414

antisemitism, 261, 378, 382; expressed in letters, 95, 185, 196, 362, 381

antitrust laws, 203

Arnold, Benedict, 484

arts, support for, 88, 132, 242

Asbell, Bernard, 560

Atlantic Charter, 376, 419, 543

Atwood, Margaret, 1

Avery, Sewell L., 108

Axis, 273, 285, 396–97, 417, 418–19, 492, 539–40. *See also* Germany; Italy; Japan

Baker, Ray Stannard, 130

Banking Act of 1935, 133

banking crisis of 1933, 31, 74–75, 86, 138, 563; FDR response to, 16, 29, 31–35, 78, 238, 563; reassurance expressed about, 22, 34–35, 36–37, 38–42, 44–45, 53

banking system, 121, 133, 238. *See also* banking crisis of 1933

Barkley, Sen. Alben, 255

Barrett, Paul, 14

Barron's, 61

Bates, Dorothy, 568

Bates, W. Edgar, 567

Battle of the Bulge, 542

Battle of the Coral Sea, 451–52

Beard, Charles, 128

Beard, Mary Ritter, 196

Bellow, Saul, 21

Berg, Elizabeth, 13

Biddle, Francis, 414, 415

Bill of Rights, 94

Bilyeu, Thomas, 565

birth control, 244

Bismarck (German battleship), 374

Black, Rep. Loring, 61

"Black Monday," 164

bonds. *See* war bonds